NEW·ILLUSTRATED
ROCK
HANDBOOK

NEW·ILLUSTRATED
ROCK
HANDBOOK

BCA
LONDON · NEW YORK · SYDNEY · TORONTO

This edition published 1992
by BCA by arrangement with
SALAMANDER BOOKS LTD.

©Salamander Books Ltd., 1992

CN8464

All correspondence concerning the content of this volume should be addressed to
Salamander Books Ltd., 129-137 York Way, London N7 9LG

Credits

Editor: Lisa Dyer
Designer: Paul Johnson
Family Trees: Pete Frame
Chart/Discography Research: Heather Robinson
Filmset by The Old Mill, London
Colour Separation by Regent Publishing Services Limited, Hong Kong
Printed in Belgium by Proost International Book Production

Acknowledgements

The publishers would like to thank all the record companies and
publicity/management agencies who supplied and gave their permission to use
promotional photographs and record and CD sleeves for this edition.

With many special thanks to John Halsall of London Features International for use of
new pictures for this edition. All other photographs supplied by: Peter Anderson,
Brian Aris, Keith Bernstein, Adrian Boot, Fin Costello, DeMonde Advertising, Robert
Ellis, Simon Fowler, Jill Furmanovsky, Martin Godard, Phil Gorton, Terry Lott, MTV,
Duane Michaels, Chris Morphet, Pictorial Press, Barry Plummer, Michael Putland, Rex
Features, Scope Features, Tom Sheehan, Paul Slattery, Victor Skrebneski, John
Timbers, Trinifold and Eric Watson.

We would also like to thank Donna Clarke and Lee Cannon, for
researching new music groups. Thanks also go to contributors
Chris Welch, Chris Whyte and Johnny Waller.

US chart positions © 1955 through 1991 by Billboard Publications, Inc. Compiled by
the Billboard Research Department and reprinted with permission. UK chart positions
from 1956 through 1991 by kind permission of Music And Video Week/BBC/Gallup.
Also recognized are the contributions and assistance of the Schwann
Music Catalog and the Music Master Catalogue.

CONTENTS

Introduction 6
Performers 8
Appendix to Performers 198

AUTHORS

The Consultant

MIKE CLIFFORD played bass with 60s soul outfit The Errol Dixon Band. He has worked with Bad Company and Led Zeppelin and handled public relations for Aretha Franklin, James Brown, The Drifters, Richie Havens, and many other performers. Mike has written extensively on rock 'n' roll and was chief author and consultant of Salamander's Black Music and consultant co-author of their Illustrated Encyclopedia of Rock.

Contributors

JOHN BEECHER is a rock historian, rock music publisher, and owner of an oldies record shop. He compiled the comprehensive boxed set of Buddy Holly LPs.

GARY COOPER became editor of Beat Instrumental in the 70s and since then has been writing for musical instrument/musicians' magazines throughout the world, including Spotlight (West Germany), Music Maker (Holland) and Sonix (Australia), and UK publications Sounds, Music World and Sound International. In 1981 he co-founded and became editor of Music UK.

PETE FRAME is probably best known for his intricate Rock Family Trees, but he has also been a freelance rock journalist since 1969 when he founded Zig Zag magazine, which he edited for several years. Following work for Charisma and Stiff Records in the 70s, he specialized in group genealogies. Three volumes of his Rock Family Trees have been published to date.

ED HANEL plunged into rock journalism when he founded The Who fanzine Who's News. Still a fan himself and an avid record collector, Ed specializes in discographies. He has contributed to various US and UK rock publications, including Trouser Press, Zig Zag, and the History Of Rock series. He is the author of The Omnibus Rock Bibliography and The Who: The Illustrated Discography.

MARSHA HANLON has been a rock 'n' roll fan since she danced in the aisles of New York's Paramount in the 50s. In the 60s she co-founded a weekly entertainment newspaper in Boston. She has worked as a freelance publicist/journalist since.

CLIVE RICHARDSON was editor of Shout soul magazine from 1967 until its demise in 1976. He then became a regular contributor to Black Echoes and Blues Unlimited and has written sleeve notes for numerous soul and R&B albums. He was a contributor to Salamander's Black Music and Illustrated Encyclopedia of Rock publications.

ROGER ST. PIERRE has worked for nearly 20 years in the music industry, mostly as a publicist for such acts as The Drifters, Johnnie Ray, Frankie Laine, Marvin Gaye, The Temptations, Diana Ross and The Jacksons. He is also the author of several books, has contributed to Record Mirror, Blues And Soul, and New Musical Express, written several hundred sleeve notes, and was a co-author of Salamander's Black Music.

LINDA SANDAHL gained her early writing experience as assistant to James Robert Parish. Since then she has worked on Steven H. Scheuer's Movies On TV as an associate editor. Linda also researched and wrote for the collector's magazine Goldmine.

JOHN TOBLER has written for all the major music weeklies in the UK at one time or another, but concentrates on rock books, such as 25 Years Of Rock (co-written with Pete Frame), The Record Producers, and Guitar Greats, all of which have also been successful BBC Radio One series. He has written books on The Beach Boys, Buddy Holly, Cliff Richard and Elvis Presley, plus rock trivia books such as The Rock Lists Album.

CHRIS TRENGOVE played tenor sax with soul band Lester Square And The GTs and The John Dummer Blues in the 60s. In the 70s he worked as a publicist for Status Quo, Thin Lizzy and Bill Withers, among others. He has co-authored two novels and a biography of Keith Moon, and has contributed to Beat Instrumental, Album Tracking, Black Echoes, and Salamander's Black Music and Illustrated Encyclopedia of Rock.

INTRODUCTION

Welcome to the 1992 edition of The New Illustrated Rock Handbook. *This book has, in all editions, been around for approaching 20 years. We credit the longevity to an attractive design and unique format. Listing albums and hit singles gives the book a 'dip in and browse' factor, while the biographies provide the meat and drink for rock aficionados.*

This latest version of the Rock Handbook is, as usual, subject to a degree of heart-searching when deciding on acts to retain and others to include for the first time. We have made our decision based on the longevity, either real or projected, of individual performers and musical groups. Those unhappy at the exclusion of Archie Ripp And The Shoulderblades should ask themselves 'would I bet my house on this band being around in 12 months time?'.

At press time, Bill Wyman had failed to sign the Rolling Stones contract with Virgin Records, Paul Simon was subject to harrassment from political activists in South Africa, and, sadly, Freddie Mercury had succumbed to AIDS. These significant events are just a handful from the day-to-day headlines garnered from around the world which pertain to the mega-stars in the pop and rock business. Please bear with us if our deadline has excluded a monumental world event!

How To Read This Book:
1. Within the main text, individual artists are listed under their surnames, groups under group name. The name of an individual performer is followed by his or her country of origin and a description of talents (US vocalist, producer, composer) in order of renown. His or her date and place of birth and the real name (if known by a pseudonym) comes next. Group headings are followed by members and instruments played. In cases where a musician is particularly well known, his preference of instrument is listed, i.e. Guitar: Fender Stratocaster. (Where an artist has his or her own entry separate to group this instrument would be listed in their own entry.)
2. The biography beneath the heading outlines the career of the artist(s). The industry terms AOR, MOR, Gold Record and Platinum Record also appear frequently.

AOR stands for 'Adult Oriented Rock', meaning that which is easily digested by the record-buying public (The Eagles and Billy Joel, rather than Motorhead or Kiss, for example). MOR stands for 'Middle Of The Road', meaning easy-listening music which is not heavy metal, rock, blues or any other distinct sound.

Gold and Platinum albums are awarded by the RIAA (Recording Industry Association Of America) in the US and the BPI (British Phonographic Industries Association) in the UK, and the criteria required by each country differ slightly. In the US, a million singles sold earns a Gold Record, two million singles earns a Platinum. An LP which goes gold in the US has sold half a million copies. If it sells a further million copies, it becomes Platinum (12-inch singles are awarded in the same way).

In the UK, the singles version is based on sales figures, or 'pounds sterling', thus: £250,000=Silver; £500,000=Gold; and one million pounds=Platinum. For LPs, however, awards are based on units (as in the US) rather than sales: 60,000 copies sold=Silver; 100,000 copies sold=Gold; and 300,000 copies sold=Platinum. However, changes have been made to these figures over the years.

3. New Readers might need clarification of certain musical definitions. These are:

Ska/bluebeat — indigenous music of the West Indies, popularized by British audiences during the 'beat boom' of the 1960s, and the forerunner to reggae. This musical style is notable for its 'shuffle' sound, with the emphasis on the off-beat.

Heavy Metal — often abbreviated as HM, but also described as Thrash, Sonic, Trash, Glam, Nuclear, Garage, etc.

Skiffle — England's answer to American rockabilly, which featured a tea-chest bass (one string, mounted on a wooden tea chest via a broom handle!) and washboard (corrugated tin device used to wash clothes).

4. A discography follows the biography, beginning with Hit Singles. To be listed in this category, a single must have made the Top 20 in either the US or UK charts. If so, the position it reached in the corresponding chart, up to and including No. 60 (but not 61-100), would also be listed. Single positions were taken from the most respected chart compilers/publications in the trade: Billboard (US) and Music And Video Week/BBC/Gallup (UK). Billboard began a regular Hot 100 chart in November 1955, while Music And Video Week commenced their charts in January 1956 (figures were compiled by Record Mirror, now owned by Music And Video Week, at that time).

We are aware that some artists included in this book had million-selling records prior to the publication of charts; in such instances we have mentioned their biggest hits with their biographies. Our official cut-off date for charts was December 1991, though we have followed through the positions of any singles in the charts at that time.

5. Albums and CDs listed are currently available according to the trade catalogues, Schwann (US) and Music Master (UK) through December 1991. We have added on new LP releases through to press date whenever possible. In certain cases, re-released albums have the latter rather than the earlier date included. Due to lack of space, all album listings are selected, meaning recommended listening, rather than complete listings. This is especially true in the case of fringe artists, from country R&B, soul, etc, who have contributed a limited number of albums to the rock mainstream. Albums not readily available but which are essential to the understanding and appreciation of a performer and therefore merit a search through second-hand record shops, appear under the heading 'Worth Searching Out'.

Following the title of an album is the label on which the album is currently available. (Atlantic) would mean the album is available on Atlantic in both the US and the UK; (MCA/Polydor) means the album is available on MCA in the US and Polydor in the UK.

6. Ten of genealogy expert Pete Frame's Family Trees are included. These trees serve as a visual aid in explaining the relationships of several groups, and allow us to introduce some of the more obscure performers in rock.

Wishing you hours of reading enjoyment!

Mike Clifford
Lisa Dyer
March 1992

Abba

Swedish group formed 1971

Original line-up: Agnetha Fältskog, vocals; Anni-Frid Lyngstad-Fredriksson, vocals; Bjorn Ulvaeus, guitar, vocals; Benny Andersson, keyboards, synthesizer, vocals.

Career: Reputed to have earned more for the Swedish economy each year than the vast Volvo company, Abba leapt to international prominence when they won the 1974 Eurovision Song Contest. Before that, they had already put in long service as leading figures of Swedish pop scene.

Anni-Frid (born Norway, November 15, 1945; raised in Toshala, Sweden) moved to Stockholm in 1967 to start singing career. Agnetha (born Jonkopping, April 5, 1950) started recording at 17 and had several local hits. Bjorn (born Gothenburg, April 25, 1945) was the star of successful Hootenanny Singers in late 60s. Benny (born Stockholm, December 16, 1946) was leader of popular rock band The Hep Cats.

Pop industry entrepreneur Stikkan Andersson persuaded Bjorn, whom he already had under contract to his Polar Music company, and Benny to leave their groups and pool resources. Benny and Anni-Frid had been living together in Stockholm since 1970; Bjorn and Agnetha married in July 1971, a major event on Sweden's pop scene as both were already national figures. After Benny and Bjorn cut **Lycka** album as duo, Abba gradually came into being. The girls had been doing vocal back-ups on Benny and Bjorn recordings and as foursome had made some stage appearances.

Anni-Frid was unsuccessful solo entrant in 1971 Eurovision song contest; for next two years foursome worked hard on their act with view to using that event as springboard to stardom. Name Abba was chosen in 1973 and the group represented Sweden in that year's Eurovision with **Ring Ring** but failed to win. Next year, despite strongest ever competition, they came out on top with **Waterloo**. The event was televised from Brighton, England, to an audience of some 500 million. Eurovision triumph does not automatically spell big record sales but in Abba's case it did. **Waterloo** not only went to No. 1 in most European countries, but made No. 6 in the US where Eurovision was unknown.

However, it was 18 months before Abba could crack the true pop market. They did it with **S.O.S.**, which made charts all over Europe, precipitating them to superstardom. **Mama Mia, Fernando, Dancing Queen** and **Knowing Me, Knowing You** were all UK No. 1s, while **Money, Money, Money** went to No. 2. In 1977 **Dancing Queen** gave them their first American chart-topper. Every record was a perfectly crafted piece of pop commercialism, employing perfect harmonies, irresistible hooks, and impeccable production. Their accompanying promotional videos utilized equally flawless formula.

When they finally embarked on a world tour in 1977 it was done in the grandest manner with 14 musicians, elaborate sets and full-blown productions. Hits continued to flow, both albums and singles racking amazing sales. Personal problems, however, began to overshadow their artistic and commercial success.

Bjorn and Agnetha divorced in 1979. Agnetha reverted to maiden name Fältskog. Anni-Frid and Benny divorced in 1981. For some time they did not allow this to interfere with their career, but eventually they drifted apart, embarking on solo ventures.

Agnetha Fältskog enjoyed brief return to charts, when duet with former Chicago bassist Peter Cetera **I Wasn't The One (Who Said Goodbye)** sneaked into US Top 100 in 1989.

With Andersson and Ulvaeus filing litigation against former manager Stig Andersson, the Abba story unveiled new chapter when Australian band Bjorn Again, offered personal, affectionate tribute with UK tour in summer of 1991.

Hit Singles:

	US	UK
Waterloo, 1974	6	1
S.O.S., 1975	15	6
Mamma Mia, 1975	32	1
Fernando, 1976	13	1
I Do I Do I Do I Do, 1976	15	38
Dancing Queen, 1976	1	1
Money Money Money, 1976	56	3
Knowing Me Knowing You, 1977	14	1
The Name Of The Game, 1977	12	1
Take A Chance On Me, 1978	3	1
Summer Night City, 1978	—	15
Chiquitita, 1979	29	2
Does Your Mother Know, 1979	19	4
Angeleyes/Voulez-Vous, 1979	—	3
Gimme Gimme Gimme (A Man After Midnight), 1979	—	3
I Have A Dream, 1979	—	2
The Winner Takes It All, 1980	8	1
Super Trouper, 1980	45	1
Lay All Your Love On Me, 1981	—	7
One Of Us, 1981	—	3

Albums:
Waterloo (Atlantic/Epic), 1974
Abba (Atlantic/Epic), 1975
Arrival (Atlantic/Epic), 1976
Greatest Hits (Atlantic/Epic), 1976
The Album (Atlantic/Epic), 1978
Greatest Hits Volume II (Atlantic/Epic), 1979
Voulez-Vous (Atlantic/Epic), 1979
Super Trouper (Atlantic/Epic), 1980
The Visitors (Atlantic/Epic), 1981
Gracias Pour La Musica (—/Epic), 1981
The Singles (Atlantic/Epic), 1982
Thank You For The Music (—/Epic), 1983

Anni-Frid Solo:
Something's Going On (Atlantic/Epic), 1982
Shine (Epic), 1984

Agnetha Fältskog Solo:
Wrap Your Arms Around Me (Atlantic/Epic), 1983
Eyes Of A Woman (Epic), 1985

Benny And Bjorn (with Tim Rice):
Chess (RCA), 1984

ABC

UK group formed 1980

Original line-up: Martin Fry, vocals; Mark Lickley, bass; David Robinson, drums; Stephen Singleton, saxophone; Mark White, guitar.

Career: Martin Fry formed ABC out of demise of synth band Vice Versa. From experience gained as editor of fanzine (*Modern Drugs*) began creating an image of glamour and style for group. A year after signing with Phonogram, Fry had led ABC into UK pop charts with three hit singles and a gold album, **Lexicon Of Love**.

Band won widespread acceptance with American audience via MTV through strong, well-made videos. ABC's sound combined clever lyrics and good melody but relied heavily on Fry's excellent vocals, as well as

good production, and the sound tended to be a mite too polished.

ABC re-grouped as duo (Fry/White) in 1987, after Fry had recovered from debilitating illness. Tribute to Smokey Robinson, **When Smokey Sings**, returned group to charts in same year, and **Alphabet City** (with keyboardist David Clayton, bassist Brad Lang and drummer Graham Broad) was first album for nearly 30 months. However, this stylish and intelligent band's subsequent sporadic output has put them in the 'almost gone, but not forgotten' file.

Hit Singles:

	US	UK
Tears Are Not Enough, 1981	—	19
Poison Arrow, 1982	—	6
The Look Of Love, 1982	19	4
All Of My Heart, 1982	—	5
That Was Then But This Is Now, 1983	—	18
Be Near Me, 1985	9	—
Night You Murdered Love, 1987	—	31
When Smokey Sings, 1987	5	11

Albums:
The Lexicon Of Love (Mercury/Neutron), 1982
Beauty Stab (Phonogram/Neutron), 1983
How To Be A Zillionaire (Phonogram/Neutron), 1985
Alphabet City (Neutron), 1987
Up (Mercury/Neutron), 1989
Absolutely ABC Greatest Hits (Mercury/Neutron), 1990

Paula Abdul

US vocalist, choreographer
Born Los Angeles, California, June 19, 1963

Career: Highly rated choreographer, whose work with George Michael, Duran Duran, ZZ Top, Dolly Parton and Janet Jackson prompted Virgin America to invest in 1988 album **Forever Your Girl**.

This former member of the Los Angeles Lakers' Cheerleaders enjoyed four consecutive chart-topping hits from the LP, and in the years since it's release, reaped a host of prestigious awards for her vocal and dance achievements. 1991 set **Spellbound** followed same slick format, with the promise of similar success.

A theatrical veteran, who worked in summer-stock theatre and studied with Joseph Traime and his famed modern dance troupe The Bell Lewitzky Company, Abdul has sufficient savvy to overcome probable exhaustion of good material. Lucrative sponsorship deals with Reebok and Coca-Cola have certainly secured her financial future.

Hit Singles:

	US	UK
Straight, 1989	—	3
Forever Your Girl, 1989	1	24
The Way That You Love Me, 1989	3	—
Opposites Attract, 1990	1	2
Cold Hearted, 1990	1	46
Rush Rush, 1991	1	6
The Promise Of A New Day, 1991	1	—
Blowing Kisses In The Wind, 1991	6	—

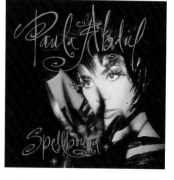

Spellbound, Paula Abdul. Courtesy Virgin Records.

Albums:
Forever Your Girl (Virgin), 1988
Shut Up And Dance (Virgin), 1990
Spellbound (Virgin), 1991

AC/DC

Australian group formed 1974

Original line-up: Malcolm Young, guitar; Angus Young, Gibson SG guitar; Phil Rudd, drums; Mark Evans, bass; Bon Scott, vocals.

Career: Malcolm and Angus Young formed band in Sydney, Australia, but moved to Melbourne where original line-up evolved. Malcolm and Angus are younger brothers of George Young of 60s pop outfit Easybeats. This connection proved invaluable to AC/DC in terms of experience and production. However, there is no trace of the Easybeats' pop melodies in the sonic, frontal assaults of AC/DC.

Now superstars on heavy-metal circuit, AC/DC were instrumental in breaking down prejudices against Australian rock. Strong home following was gained via release of two 1975 albums: **High Voltage** and **TNT**.

Below: AC/DC vocalist Brian Johnson grinds his larynx into the dust.

Then came low-budget, hard-working tour of UK which earned enough favourable response for UK album release. (Entitled **High Voltage**, UK LP is actually **TNT** minus two tracks, with two added from the Australian release **High Voltage**.)

Making every performance an athletic endurance contest for both band and audience, AC/DC gained notoriety in US. Clearly everyone else was back-up to Scott's rivet-driving vocals and Angus' head-bobbing gyrotechnics. (Change in bass players in 1977 from Mark Evans to Cliff Williams almost went unnoticed.) Bon Scott's death from alcohol abuse in April 1980 occurred when AC/DC was on fringe of super-group status. In a fortunate twist of fate, AC/DC hired Scott-soundalike Brian Johnson (from band Geordie).

Following classic **Back In Black** LP, band maintained set formula with little original spark. Rudd quit AC/DC in 1983, with Simon Wright taking drum chair. Period of relative inactivity ended in 1987, when **Heatseeker** single earned UK Top 20 placing. Further personnel upheavals occurred when an 'indisposed' Malcolm Young was replaced by cousin Stevie Young and former Gary Moore and Firm drummer Chris Slade stepped in for Wright.

1990 set **The Razor's Edge** returned group to both Top 10 UK/US album charts, and prompted major US tour that year, with Paul Gregg ousting Williams for bass spot. With notoriety never more than a whisper away, AC/DC suffered traumatic date at Salt Lake City (1991) when three fans were killed during frenetic crowd scenes at concert.

Hit Singles:

	US	UK
Rock 'n' Roll Ain't Noise Pollution, 1981	–	15
Let's Get It Up, 1982	44	13
For Those About To Rock, 1982	–	15
Who Made Who, 1986	–	16
Shake Your Foundations, 1986	–	24
Heatseeker, 1988	–	12
Blow Up Your Video, 1988	12	2
Thunderstruck, 1990	–	13

Albums:
High Voltage (Atco/Atlantic), 1976
Dirty Deeds Done Dirt Cheap (Atlantic), 1976

Right: Oleta Adams found fame with help from Tears For Fears.

Let There Be Rock (Atlantic), 1977
Powerage (Atlantic), 1978
If You Want Blood (Atlantic), 1978
Highway To Hell (Atlantic), 1979
Back In Black (Atlantic), 1980
For Those About To Rock (Atlantic), 1981
Flick Of The Switch (Atlantic), 1983
Fly On The Wall (Atlantic), 1985
Who Made Who (Atlantic), 1986
Blow Up Your Video (Atlantic), 1988
The Razor's Edge (Atco), 1990

Bryan Adams

Canadian singer/songwriter
Born Kingston, Ontario, November 1959

Career: Adams' 1985 European concert tour with Tina Turner finally focused the big-time limelight on an artist who had been building a steadily growing reputation over the decade since he started in club groups around Vancouver, British Columbia, at 16. Within a year of starting out, Adams was writing with Jim Vallance, their songs giving hits to Prism, Bachman-Turner Overdrive, Ian Lloyd, Bob Welch, Kiss, and others. Late 1979 recording deal with A&M led to four solid months touring USA.

Touring as opening act for Kinks, Loverboy and Foreigner in 1982 led to breakthrough album **Cuts Like A Knife** which went platinum and contained US hit single **Straight From The Heart**, covered successfully by Ian Lloyd and Bonnie Tyler.

Since then Adams has successfully pursued policy of touring almost continually throughout US and world, establishing reputation as consistent if hardly original performer. Policy has also paid off in terms of record sales, with platinum album **Into the Fire** prime example of Adams' across-the-board appeal. Subsequent absence from recording studios compensated for by occasional charity date, including Nelson Mandela's 70th Birthday Party and Roger Waters' The Wall.

All-around journeyman rocker, Adams takes craftsman-like approach to his profession, with occasional reward of mega-single or LP. Summer 1991 hit **Everything I Do (I Do It For You)** from *Robin Hood* movie created record for UK charts when it remained at No. 1 for 16 weeks.

Hit Singles:

	US	UK
Straight From The Heart, 1983	10	–
Cuts Like A Knife, 1983	15	–
Run To Him, 1985	6	11
Somebody, 1985	11	–
Heaven, 1985	1	–
Summer Of '69, 1985	5	–
One Night Love Affair, 1985	13	–
It's Only Love, 1985	19	29
Hearts On Fire, 1987	26	–
Heat Of The Night, 1987	6	–
Victim Of Love, 1987	32	–
Everything I Do (I Do It For You), 1991	1	1
Can't Stop This Thing We Started, 1991	2	12

Albums:
You Want It You Got It (A&M), 1982
Cuts Like A Knife (A&M), 1983
Reckless (A&M), 1985
One Good Reason (A&M), 1985
Into The Fire (A&M), 1987
Waking Up The Neighbours (A&M), 1991

Below: Bryan Adams broke UK and US chart records with Everything I Do in 1991.

Oleta Adams

US vocalist, composer, pianist
Born Yakima, Washington, 1961

Career: Destined for a lifetime sentence in clubs and cabaret before 'discovery' in Kansas City hotel lounge by Tears For Fears, who included artist on their **Seeds Of Love** album (1989). Adams provided vocals for their successful **Woman In Chains** single, and subsequently toured with duo.

Daughter of a Baptist minister, former gospel singer Adams first LP, **Circle Of One**, was released in 1990, with production by TFF's Roland Orzabel, with Dave Bascombe. Sleeper single **Rhythm Of Life** finally charted in UK in 1991, and **Get Here** was hugely successful follow-up.

A polished vocalist, Adams's fluid R&B styling was heard to great effect on 1991 single **Don't Let The Sun Go Down On Me**, the Elton John/Bernie Taupin classic.

Hit Singles:

	US	UK
Get Here, 1991	5	4

Albums:
Circle Of One (Fontana), 1990

Aerosmith

US group formed 1970

Original line-up: Steve Tyler, vocals; Joe Perry, guitar; Tom Hamilton, bass; Joey Kramer, drums; Brad Whitford, guitar.

Career: Legend has band forming in Sunapee, New Hampshire, during summer 1970. Lots of local gigging in Boston led to dates at Max's Kansas City where they were seen and signed by Clive Davis for CBS in late 1972. Despite emphasis on group participation, focal point was Jagger look-alike Tyler and guitarist Perry. Duo were main writers of original material and also took brunt of universal criticism as Rolling Stones/Yardbirds rip-offs.

Long-term liaison with producer Jack Douglas began with widely criticized second album **Get Your Wings**. By 1975 extensive touring finally paid off with success in American singles and album charts. **Toys In The Attic** went platinum within months of release and stayed in charts for two years. This sparked interest in first two albums which went platinum by the release of **Rocks**. 1976 saw re-issue of **Dream On**, which earned gold record three years after first appearance. Aerosmith seemed destined for long run as high-class Grand Funk Railroad, a people's band, working diligently for fans.

A well-deserved rest from touring may have caused **Draw The Line** to miss the fire of earlier albums. Original LP sleeve, which featured only a cartoon of band, also seemed ego trip which did not mesh with spirit of 1977 punk revolution.

1979 saw Perry quit, having devoted more time to solo projects than the band. His replacement was New Yorker Jimmy Crespo, former member of Flame.

Brad Whitford became the second original member to depart when he joined forces with former Ted Nugent guitarist Derek St Holmes. Rick Dufay took his place and this new aggregate cut just one album **Rock In A Hard Place**, release of which was delayed by Tyler's motorcycle injury.

Unhappy with new line-up, Tyler approached Perry, who had cut three LPs as Joe Perry Project and, later, Whitford, to rejoin Aerosmith. They agreed and reformed band quickly put a tour together and returned to the studios.

In 1986 Steven Tyler and Joe Perry forged an alliance between heavy metal and hip hop when they joined forces with Run DMC in remake of the Aerosmith hit **Walk This Way**. Featured on **Raising Hell** which went double platinum and the single was a big hit, boosted by a witty video.

In spring 1987 Aerosmith recorded new album **Permanent Vacation** in Vancouver, Canada, produced by Bruce Fairburn and

Below: Permanent Vacation, Aerosmith. Courtesy Geffen Records.

released in October. Earlier in June that year, the band played for 82,000 fans at the Texas Jam. The album sold out its first pressing and yielded a major hit single **Dude (Looks Like A Lady)**.

Pump album (1989) spawned UK Top 20/US Top 5 single **Love In An Elevator**, and led to first European tour for over a decade. Award-laden Aerosmith completed mammoth **Pump** tour, with the album on course for 4.5 million sales.

Twenty-plus year career shows no sign of slowing down, as witnessed by bands Grammy for **Janie's Got A Gun** and subsequent selection as Best Band in 1991 *Rolling Stone* awards.

Hit Singles:	US	UK
Dream On, 1976	6	—
Walk This Way, 1977	10	—
Dude (Looks Like A Lady), 1987	14	—
Love In An Elevator, 1989	5	13
Janie's Got A Gun, 1990	4	—
Dude (Looks Like A Lady) (re-issue), 1990	—	20
What It Takes, 1990	9	—

Albums:
Aerosmith (Columbia/CBS), 1973
Get Your Wings (Columbia/CBS), 1974
Toys In The Attic (Columbia/CBS), 1975
Rocks (Columbia/CBS), 1976
Draw The Line (Columbia/CBS), 1977
Live! Bootleg (Columbia/CBS), 1978
Night In The Ruts (Columbia/CBS), 1979
Greatest Hits (Columbia/CBS), 1980
Rock In A Hard Place (Columbia/CBS), 1982
Done With Mirrors (Geffen), 1985
Classics Live (CBS), 1986
Classics Live 2 (Columbia), 1987
Permanent Vacation (Geffen), 1987
Pump (Geffen), 1989

Allman Brothers Band

US group formed 1969

Original line-up: Duane Allman, Gibson Les Paul, Fender Stratocaster guitar; Gregg Allman, guitar, vocals, keyboards; Dickie Betts, Gibson Les Paul guitar; Berry Oakley, bass; Jai Johnny Johanson, drums; Butch Trucks, drums.

Career: Duane Allman (born Nashville, November 20, 1946) was raised in Daytona Beach, Florida; moved to Los Angeles in 60s. Formed Hour Glass with brother Gregg (born December 8, 1947) on keyboards, guitar, vocals; Paul Hornsby, keyboards, guitar, vocals; Jesse Willard Carr, bass, vocals; John Sandlin, drums, guitar. Debut Liberty album was cut at label's own LA studio. Band recorded follow-up at Rick Hall's Muscle Shoals Studio. Duane Allman had previously worked there as session guitarist (on Clarence Carter's 1967 **Road Of Love** sessions). Tapes for second album were rejected by Liberty and band broke up.

Allman worked on sessions with Percy Sledge, Aretha Franklin, Boz Scaggs, Wilson Pickett and others. Also cut material for projected but unreleased Atlantic solo album before signing to Phil Walden's Capricorn label (based in nearby Macon, Georgia).

Walden had previously managed the late Otis Redding and helped Allman put together what became Allman Brothers Band. The Brothers had been working informally with Butch Truck's band 31st February; when outfit jammed with Betts and Oakley's band

Second Coming in Jacksonville, foundations of Allman Brothers band were laid.

New band gigged around Southern States building big following. Debut album **The Allman Brothers Band**, 1969 (cut in New York), was potent mixture of progressive rock and R&B/blues roots. Interplay between Duane Allman's potent slide work and forceful technique of Dickie Betts was focal point of band's attractive new sound. From **Idlewild South** album (1970) single **Midnight Rider** was smash.

While band's reputation grew ever bigger, Duane Allman continued session work, both at Muscle Shoals and elsewhere. Allman's trading-off of licks with Clapton on the Derek And The Dominoes' **Layla** album was among his finest work.

Tragedy hit band when Duane Allman died in motorcycle crash on October 29, 1971; he was just 24 years old. Last testament was superlative **The Allman Brothers Band At Fillmore East** album, recorded shortly before. Contained superb versions of blues standards **Statesboro' Blues** and **Stormy Monday** plus a 22-minute 40-second workout on **Whipping Post**.

Three tracks for **Eat A Peach** had been laid down before Duane's death; it was decided to finish album without recruiting replacement. LP proved another massive seller.

Unbelievably, lightning struck twice: on November 11, 1972, Berry Oakley died in another motorcycle accident, also in Macon.

Band subsequently added Chuck Leavill, keyboards, and Lamar Williams, bass. Sound softened out into more melodic country-rock idiom for **Brothers And Sisters** album. From this, **Jessica** instrumental hit proved to be Betts' tour-de-force; revealed depth of talent which had previously been, to some degree, overshadowed by Duane Allman.

Following **Win, Lose Or Draw**, Betts and Gregg Allman embarked on solo projects. Gregg toured States under own name with new band. Allman Brothers Band LP **The Road Goes On Forever** was compilation rather than new material.

End seemed to have arrived when Allman testified against his personal road manager Scooter Herring who received a 75-year sentence on narcotics charges. 'There is no way we can ever work with Gregg again', aggrieved Betts told *Rolling Stone* magazine. Betts promptly departed to form own band, Great Southern, with debut album on Arista (1977). Jazz-rock group Sea Level was formed by Johnson, Williams and Leavill, plus guitarist Jimmy Nalls.

By now married to Cher Bono, Gregg Allman issued **Playin' Up A Storm** under own name in 1977. Rift was healed, however, when at a Great Southern concert

Left: Duane Allman, who died in a motorcycle crash at 24.

in Central Park, Betts was joined on stage for finale by Gregg and Butch Trucks. Soon after, at Capricorn Records' annual barbecue, core of Allman Brothers Band, plus David Goldflies, bass, and Dan Toler, drums, played 90-minute set; band was back in business with a vengeance.

Following 1980 move to Arista and **Reach For The Sky** album, band's internal problems resurfaced. Greg Allman eventually broke away to form Greg Allman Band which enjoyed US album success with **I'm No Angel**. Betts also formed own eponymous band, cutting **Pattern Disruptive** LP with marginal success. With a 20-plus year history, and the likelihood of their best days behind them, the Allman's reformed once more, recording **Seven Turns** for Epic (1990). The line-up included Allman, Betts, Trucks, Johanson, John Neal (keyboards), Warren Haynes (guitar) and Allen Woody (bass). A few months later, this new aggregation earned *Rolling Stone* magazine award for Comeback Of The Year.

Hit Singles:	US	UK
Ramblin' Man, 1973	2	—

Albums:
The Allman Brothers Band (Capricorn), 1969
Idlewild South (Capricorn), 1970
At Fillmore East (Capricorn), 1971
Eat A Peach (Capricorn), 1972
Beginnings (Capricorn), 1973
Brothers And Sisters (Capricorn), 1973
Win, Lose Or Draw (Capricorn), 1975
The Road Goes On Forever (Capricorn), 1975
Wipe The Windows, Check The Oil, Dollar Gas (Capricorn), 1976
Enlightened Rogues (Capricorn), 1979
Best Of (Capricorn), 1980
Reach For The Sky (Arista), 1980
Brothers Of The Road, (Arista), 1981
Dreams (six album set) (Polydor), 1989
Shades Of Two Worlds (Epic), 1991
Seven Turns (Epic), 1990

Duane Allman Solo:
Anthology (Polydor/Capricorn), 1972
Anthology Volume 2 (Polydor/Capricorn), 1974
Best Of (Polydor/Capricorn), 1979

Gregg Allman Solo:
Laid Back (Polydor/Capricorn), 1973
Playin' Up A Storm (Polydor/Capricorn), 1977
I'm No Angel (Epic), 1987

Dickie Betts Solo:
Dickie Betts And The Great Southern (Arista), 1977
Pattern Disruptive (Epic), 1989

Worth Searching Out:
The Hour Glass (Liberty), 1968
Duane And Gregg Allman (Bold/Polydor), 1972

Marc Almond

UK vocalist, composer
Born Southport, near Liverpool, 1957

Career: Studied design and fine art at college where he discovered performance art. Met multi-instrumentalist Dave Ball in 1978 and formed highly successful duo Soft Cell.

Also formed Marc And The Mambas as occasional off-shoot project to indulge in love of melodramatic ballads, covering songs by

Scott Walker, Lou Reed and Jacques Brel, and released **Untitled** in 1982.

Almond left Soft Cell in mid-83 to go solo and released second Mambas LP, flamenco-influenced **Torment And Torreros** before immediately announcing he was quitting the recording business. Changed his mind the next day, and later formed Marc Almond And The Willing Sinners to release **Vermine In Ermine** LP and played series of one-man shows in London theatres. Recorded **I Feel Love** hit single with label-mates Bronski Beat, fuelling (unfounded) rumours that he would replace Jimmy Somerville as Bronski Beat vocalist.

Left Phonogram and joined Virgin for **Stories Of Johnny** LP – his most commercial record since Soft Cell days, despite excellent title track failing to chart when released as single.

Follow-up album **Mother Fist And Her Five Daughters** explored darker side of Almond's songwriting, but once more proved his stunning interpretive talent on **A Woman's Story** single, which again failed to chart. In late 1987 he signed new deal with EMI, while EMI released compilation LP **Singles**.

Bizarre pairing with Gene Pitney produced UK chart-topper with Pitney's classic **Something's Gotten Hold Of My Heart**, while 1990 set **Jacques** was Almond's piquant tribute to Jacques Brel. Released by EMI in 1991 (with alleged high-figure debts to the company), artist signed with Warner Brothers for proposed **Tenement Symphony** LP.

Having established unique style, star embraces hopeless romanticism and sordid realism (his fanclub is called Gutter Hearts); he is an unrepentant modern recreation of tragic chanteuses like Judy Garland and Edith Piaf. Brilliant, disastrous, trashy, glamorous, over-emotional, Marc Almond is all of these and regrets nothing.

Hit Singles:

	US	UK
Something's Gotten Hold Of My Heart, 1989	–	1
Jacky, 1991	–	17

With Bronski Beat:
I Feel Love, 1985	–	3

Albums:
Vermine in Ermine (Some Bizarre), 1984
Stories of Johnny (Some Bizarre), 1985
Mother Fist And Her Five Daughters (Some Bizarre), 1985
Singles (EMI), 1987
The Stars We Are (Capitol/Parlophone), 1988
Enchanted (Capitol/Parlophone), 1990
Tenement Symphony (Warner Bros), 1991
Jacques (–/Parlophone), 1991

Marc And The Mambas:
Untitled (Some Bizarre), 1982
Torment And Torreros (Sire/Some Bizarre), 1983

The Animals
UK group formed 1960

Original line-up: Eric Burdon, vocals; Alan Price, keyboards; Hilton Valentine, guitar; Chas Chandler, bass; John Steel, drums.

Career: One of several important groups to emerge from vibrant British R&B scene of early 60s, the band started out with Saturday residency at Newcastle's Downbeat Club around 1960 before moving to city centre Club A Go-Go, changing name from Alan Price Combo to The Animals when Eric Burdon joined in 1962.

Cutting a demo disc, they sold 500 copies to local fans while their manager took a copy to London where it impressed producer Mickie Most enough to persuade him to travel North to see group. Most brought them to London to record cover of **Baby Let Me Take You Home** (from the first Bob Dylan album), and it charted in April 1964, winning the group a slot on that month's Chuck Berry tour. (As the Alan Price Combo they had backed Jerry Lee Lewis on tour.)

A semi-residency at London's Scene Club cemented their following and for their second release they lifted another song from same Dylan LP, the traditional New Orleans number **House Of The Rising Sun**. This plaintive blues ballad shot straight to No. 1 both sides of Atlantic, leading to debut US tour that summer.

1965 produced succession of hits kicking off with brilliant reading of Nina Simone masterpiece **Don't Let Me Be Misunderstood**, but despite the success he had brought them, band – and Burdon in particular – were unhappy with Most's choice of material. When their Columbia contract expired they refused to renew it, switching to Decca.

Never keen on air travel, Alan Price quit group to form the Alan Price Set, touring solely in UK, going on to work prodigiously with Georgie Fame while Dave Rowberry was drafted in from the Mike Cotton Sound to replace him. In February 1966 John Steel was replaced by Barry Jenkins.

After two more hits, **Inside – Looking Out** and **Don't Bring Me Down**, The Animals split in July, largely due to arguments over Eric Burdon's hard drinking and heavy flirtation with LSD.

Burdon moved to LA, then to San Francisco where he formed The New Animals

Left: The Animals in 1966, minus Alan Price, and with Burdon in centre.

with Jenkins and newcomers Mick Briggs (ex-Steampacket), guitar, and Danny McCullough, bass.

The New Animals made UK charts with **Help Me Girl** (1966), **Good Times** (1967) and **San Francisco Nights** (1967) before Burdon disbanded them to gig around LA rock scene with Jimi Hendrix (Andy Summers of Police was a member briefly in 1968). He met up with producers Jerry Goldstein and Steve Gold who teamed him with the rhythm section of black LA band Nite Shift to form new unit known as War featuring the brilliant Danish harmonica player Lee Oskar and Burdon's hoarse vocals. (Hilton Valentine worked as unit's roadie.)

War went on to become one of the most successful of new wave of black funk bands. The wild-natured Burdon once more went into limbo, drifting round the rock scene, recording with blues veteran Jimmy Witherspoon, touring UK in 1973 and 1976, retiring to France for a time, then returning to California.

Back in Britain, Alan Price had become TV regular while Chas Chandler had sold his bass guitars to launch Jimi Hendrix's solo career, then masterminded the campaign which took Slade to stardom.

During his 1976 UK visit, Burdon and the other original Animals got together to cut **Before We Were So Rudely Interrupted** album, released in 1977 on Jet in US.

Original Animals line-up reformed in 1983, and undertook six-week tour of America to promote **Ark** LP. Plans for a continuation of the group's activities were subsequently abandoned, with Burdon then revealing all in his autobiography *I Used To Be An Animal*, published in 1986.

Hit Singles:

	US	UK
House Of The Rising Sun, 1964	1	1
I'm Crying, 1964	19	8
Don't Let Me Be Misunderstood, 1965	15	5
Bring It On Home To Me, 1965	32	7
We Gotta Get Out Of This Place, 1965	13	2
It's My Life, 1965	23	7
Inside – Looking Out, 1966	34	12
Don't Bring Me Down, 1966	12	6
See See Rider, 1966	10	–
When I Was Young, 1967	15	–
San Francisco Nights, 1967	9	–
Monterey, 1968	15	–
Sky Pilot, 1968	14	–

Eric Burdon Solo:
San Francisco Nights, 1967	–	7

Albums:
The Animals (–/Starline), 1969
Most Of The Animals (–/MFP), 1971
Best Of (Abcko/–), 1975
Before We Were So Rudely Interrupted (Jet/Barn), 1977
Newcastle December 1963 (with Sonny Boy Williamson) (–/Charly), 1977
Ark (IRS), 1983
Greatest Hits (live) (–/IRS), 1984
Singles Plus (EMI), 1987
Animals With Sonny Boy Williamson (–/Charly), 1990

Erick Burdon Solo:
Survivor (Polydor), 1978
Black And White Blues (MCA), 1979
Winds Of Change (Polydor), 1985

Joan Armatrading
West Indian vocalist, guitarist, composer
Born St Kitts, December 9, 1950

Career: One of five children, Joan emigrated to Birmingham, UK, with her family in 1958. She starred in local production of rock musical *Hair* and formed songwriting partnership with fellow West Indian immigrant Pam Nester.

Moving to London in 1971, duo signed production and management deal with Cube Records but, when Gus Dudgeon-produced **Whatever's For Us** album appeared, Nester

Below: West Indian-born Armatrading has not quite achieved superstar status despite excellent albums.

received no label credit and resultant friction led to break-up of partnership and demise of Cube deal.

After two years in limbo, Joan was signed by A&M and, adding own lyrics to previous melody-writing, came up with praised **Back To The Night** album (1975). Lack of sales success led A&M to team her with legendary producer Glyn Johns (Rolling Stones, The Who, Eagles, Steve Miller, etc) whose work proved totally sympathetic to her mood-laden introverted style. **Joan Armatrading** (1976) yielded **Love and Affection** hit single, and her next album **Show Some Emotion** spent four months on US charts, breaking her into American market.

A third Glyn Johns-produced LP, **To The Limit** (1978), introduced harder cutting edge while in 1980 **Me, Myself, I** was successful single and album (produced by Richard Gottehrer of Blondie, Link Wray, and Robert Johnson fame).

1983 album **The Key** spawned major hit in **Drop The Pilot**, but decidedly low-key approach saw barren period from 1986 **Sleight Of Hand** set until self-produced return in 1990 with **Hearts And Flowers**. Diffident approach to music business has excluded continued mainstream success, but Armatrading has sufficient savvy and talent to remain in rock's second division.

Above: Joan Armatrading's 1976 album. Courtesy A&M Records.

Hit Singles:	US	UK
Love And Affection, 1976	–	10
Drop The Pilot, 1983	–	11

Albums:
Whatever's For Us (Hifly/Cube), 1974
Back To The Night (A&M), 1975
Joan Armatrading (A&M), 1976
Show Some Emotion (A&M), 1977
To The Limit (A&M), 1978
Steppin' Out (A&M), 1979
Me, Myself, I (A&M), 1980
Walk Under Ladders (A&M), 1981
The Key (A&M), 1983
Track Record (A&M), 1983
Secret Secrets (A&M), 1985
Sleight Of Hand (A&M), 1986
The Shouting Stage (A&M), 1988
Hearts And Flowers (A&M), 1990
Very Best Of (A&M), 1991

Rick Astley

UK vocalist, composer
Born Warrington, Cheshire, February 6, 1966

Career: Authentic blue-eyed soul stylist who enjoys public affection for 'boy next door' demeanor and heartfelt delivery.

Signed to Stock/Aitken/Waterman writing/production team in 1985, after brief tenure with FBI soul band; served apprenticeship in company studio as tape operator.

Uncredited debut as back-up singer on O'Chi Brown's **Learning To Live Without Your Love** encouraged management team to cut **Never Gonna Give You Up** (1987) with Astley, a UK and Stateside No. 1 and 1988 BRIT award winner.

Chart momentum maintained with **Whenever You Need Somebody** and pleasing cover of Nat King Cole's classic **When I Fall In Love**, which prompted Cole's record company to release original. Seminal album **Whenever You Need Somebody** topped UK listing selling almost 1.5 million copies. World tour (1988) encompassed UK, USA, Japan and Australasia, confirming Astley as serious force in pop market.

Following sequel LP **Hold Me In Your Arms** and 14-week US concert schedule, Astley retreated from business during sessions for projected third album, expressing concern at relationship with Stock/Aitken/Waterman. Bitter negotiations resulted in permanent split, allowing artist to resume recording for aptly-titled **Free** album, from which gospel-tinged **Cry For Help** (1991) returned Astley to charts.

Astley's collaborators on **Free** — Elton John, Mark King (Level 42) and Rob Fisher (Climie Fisher) — hinted at the respect this singer commands.

Hit Singles:	US	UK
Never Gonna Give You Up, 1987	1	1
Whenever You Need Somebody, 1987	–	3
When I Fall In Love/My Arms Keep Missing You, 1987	–	2
Together Forever, 1988	1	2
It Would Take A Strong Man, 1988	10	–
She Wants To Dance With Me, 1988	6	6
Take Me To Your Heart, 1988	–	8
Hold Me In Your Arms, 1989	19	10
Cry For Help, 1991	7	7

Albums:
Whenever You Need Somebody (RCA), 1987
Hold Me In Your Arms (RCA), 1989
Free (RCA), 1991

Aswad

UK group formed 1975

Original line-up: Brinsley Forde, vocals; Angus Zeb, drums; Courtney Hemmings, keyboards; George Levi, bass; Don Benjamin, guitar.

Career: Long-established UK reggae band whose melodic approach earned slew of UK hits in late 80s. Signed to Island Records in 1976, Aswad's first self-titled album topped British reggae chart. Regular club gigs, and tour with legendary Jamaican artist Burning Spear, placed band in forefront of burgeoning English black talent.

With Tony Gad replacing Hemmings, band was featured in 1980 movie *Babylon* (with former child actor Forde in a leading role), for which they also provided soundtrack. Although Aswad maintained busy road schedule, short-lived album deals thwarted opportunity to exploit success of *Babylon*. With a reduced line-up, band finally charted with lilting **Don't Turn Around** in 1988.

Aswad's commercial success saw more flexible musical approach, which was acknowledged when group supported

Right: UK band Aswad have impressed many with their mellow brand of reggae and disciplined touring.

Above: Aswad's first album. Courtesy Island Records.

English pop icon Cliff Richard at his 1989 Wembley Stadium concerts. First US tour (1991) followed release of cover of Eagles' AOR classic **Best Of My Love**, further shifting musical roots to the background.

Hit Singles:	US	UK
Don't Turn Around, 1988	–	1
Give A Little Love, 1988	–	11

Albums:
Aswad (Mango/Island), 1988
Distant Thunder (Mango/Island), 1988
Live And Direct (Mango/Island), 1989
New Chapter Of Dub (Mango/CBS), 1989

The B-52s

US group formed 1976

Original line-up: Kate Pierson, vocals; Cindy Wilson, vocals: Ricky Wilson, guitar; Fred Schneider, vocals, keyboard; Julian Strickland, drums, guitar.

Career: Eccentric good-time pop band formed in Athens, Georgia, who resurrected career with single-laden **Cosmic Thing** following death of Ricky Wilson in 1985.

Debut self-titled album followed interest in band's independent first single (1978), **Rock Lobster/B-52 Girls**. Signed to Warner Bros (US) and Island (UK), the B-52s charted in both territories. Group's quirky stage presence and ear for a good tune suggested a long-term future, contrary to their indifferent 'fun' approach to the rock business. Interest was maintained through a quartet of albums, including a mini-set **Mesopotamia**, produced by David Byrne.

After Wilson's death, B-52s dramatically curtailed their activities, although Schneider kept busy with his 'Shake Society' project. With augmented line-up, band resurfaced in 1989 with **Cosmic Thing** set, from which **Love Shack** and **Roam** were million-sellers.

Hugely successful 1990 tour schedule (USA, Japan, Australia) also saw B-52s at various benefit gigs, with animal rights and AIDS charities the principal benefactors. With ominous silence on the recording front, Schneider released solo self-titled set in the summer of 1991, very much in dance vein of **Cosmic Thing**.

Above: Cosmic Thing, The B52s. Courtesy Reprise Records.

Hit Singles:	US	UK
Wild Planet, 1980	18	18
Rock Lobster/Planet Claire, 1986	–	12
Love Shack, 1989	3	2
Roam, 1990	–	17

Albums:
The B-52s (Warner Bros/Island), 1979
Mesopotamia (Warner Bros/Island), 1982
Whammy (Warner Bros/Island), 1982
Bouncing Off The Satellites (Warner Bros/Island), 1986
Cosmic Thing (Reprise/WEA), 1989
Wild Planet (Warner Bros/Island), 1990
Fred Schneider (Reprise/—), 1991

Bad Company

UK group formed 1973

Original line-up: Paul Rodgers, guitar, vocals; Mick Ralphs, Guitar; Boz Burrell, bass; Simon Kirke, drums.

Career: Formed from the remnants of Free (Kirke and Rodgers), Bad Company — named after the Robert Benton western — carved no new ground in their lifetime but made one hell of a dent on the British and American markets during 70s.

The sparse, tight rhythm section of Burrell (ex-King Crimson), Kirke and Ralphs (ex-Mott The Hoople) was the perfect foil for Rodgers' explosive vocal talents, and on the right night they were among the very best of live bands.

After brief breaking-in period, Bad Company hit the road in March 1974, debuting at Rodger's home gig, Newcastle Town Hall (which remained group's favourite venue).

First album **Bad Company** went platinum in States, with debut single **Can't Get Enough** making US Top 10 and UK Top 20. All material released on manager Peter Grant's and Led Zeppelin's Swan Song label, breaking Company in States, and furthering Grant's managerial reputation.

Grant's policy of a world tour every two years kept audiences hungry, and explained original group's life-span of nearly ten years. Their later material was certainly not worthy of the adulation it received.

Apart from sax player Mel Collins' contribution to first album, Bad Company was a completely self-contained unit, working both studio and live with minimum of frills.

Although Rodgers was an aggressive powerhouse front-man (not unlike his personality) and centre of attention, Ralphs, Burrell and Kirke always turned in some memorable riffs and melodies.

1979 release **Desolation Angels** was surrounded by rumour of split, although this was not confirmed until summer 1982 (after successful **Rough Diamond** set), when Kirke and Burrell began putting together new bands. Paul Rodgers resurfaced with former Swan Song label sidekick Jimmy Page in The Firm (along with bassist Tony Franklin, and drummer Chris Slade), who enjoyed short-lived US success. Rodgers then co-opted former Who drummer Kenny Jones for The Law band and their eponymous album, recorded in 1991.

Bad Company re-formed with ex-Ted Nugent vocalist Brian Howe fronting, and enjoyed chart albums with **Fame And Fortune** (1986) and **Dangerous Age** (1988). With Kirke and Howe reluctant to let the past slip gracefully away, they added session guitarist Geoff Whitehorn and bass player Paul Cullen for 1990 album **Holy Water**, a US Top 40 entry.

Hit Singles:

	US	UK
Can't Get Enough, 1974	5	15
Movin' On, 1975	19	–
Feel Like Making Love, 1975	10	20
Young Blood, 1976	20	–
Rock 'n' Roll Fantasy, 1979	13	–
If You Need Somebody, 1991	16	–

Albums:
Bad Company (Swan Song/Island), 1974
Straight Shooter (Swan Song/Island), 1975
Run With The Pack (Swan Song/Island), 1976
Burning Sky (Swan Song/Island), 1977
Desolation Angels (Swan Song), 1979
Rough Diamonds (Swan Song), 1982
10 From 6 (Atlantic), 1986
Fame And Fortune (Atlantic), 1986
Dangerous Age (Atlantic), 1988
Holy Water (Atco), 1990

The Band

Canadian group formed late 50s

Original line-up: Jamie 'Robbie' Robertson, guitar; Garth Hudson, organ, saxophone; Richard Manuel, piano, vocals; Rick Danko, bass, vocals; Levon Helm, drums, vocals, mandolin.

Career: Levon Helm came from Arkansas, rest are Candians. Group started as backing band for Toronto-based rock 'n' roller Ronnie Hawkins, with whom they recorded covers of urban blues hits featuring Helm's vocals and Robertson's incisive guitar (classic example, Hawkins' **Who Do You Love**). Billed first as Canadian Squires then as Levon And The Hawks, they left Hawkins

Above: The Band's 1969 album. Courtesy Capitol Records.

and toured Canada and US. Recorded classic single **The Stones I Throw** while in New York, where they met white blues singer John Hammond Jr, whose father was A&R boss of Columbia.

Through the Hammond connection, the Band met Bob Dylan, who was then moving more heavily into electric music and saw their musical versatility (all play several instruments) as ideal backing. First collaboration was single **Can You Please Crawl Out Your Window** and some members played on **Blonde On Blonde** album. With Mickey Jones playing drums instead of Helm, The Band accompanied Dylan on 1965-66 US/European tour. A motorcycle accident in July 1966 put Dylan out of action and the band settled in Woodstock, New York. Rehearsed and recorded with him while he recovered, the results being heard on **The Basement Tapes**, a bootleg so successful that much of its material was officially released on LP of same name in 1975.

The crossflow influence between Dylan and The Band can be heard on Dylan's **John Wesley Harding** album and The Band's own **Music From Big Pink** (Capitol, 1968), from which **The Weight** remains true classic.

Robertson's songs for second LP, **The Band**, included **Up On Cripple Creek** and **The Night They Drove Old Dixie Down**, both subtle yet powerfully evocative traditional-style, truly American songs.

Undertaking lengthy tours on their own led to **Stage Fright** LP; title track told of perils of being on road. **Cahoots** (1971) reflected their weariness at then current American values, but seemed a trifle pretentious; it included track cut in collaboration with Van Morrison.

There followed four-year hiatus before Robertson came up with new material; after December 1971 concert at New York Academy Of Music (recorded live as **Rock Of Ages**), Band made no appearances until Watkins Glen Festival of July 1973. Their studio efforts, a planned thematic work by Robertson, was shelved and next record release was **Moondog Matinee**, a tribute to their rock 'n' roll roots.

Before The Flood encapsulated live work with Dylan on 1974 tour; they provided all back-up work on his **Planet Waves** album. In late 1975, own long-awaited album of new material hit stores, but **Northern Lights, Southern Cross** did not quite have stunning effect expected.

In late 1976 came shock announcement — their current tour was to be The Band's last and stage career was to climax with a special Thanksgiving Day concert at San Francisco's Winterland, to be dubbed, *The Last Waltz*. It was a triumphant occasion with such friends and collaborators as Bob Dylan, Ronnie Hawkins, Neil Young, Bobby Charles, Van Morrison, Joni Mitchell, Eric Clapton, Dr John, Neil Diamond and Muddy Waters turning out. (Robertson had produced two Neil Diamond albums, **Beautiful Noise** (1976) and **Love At The Greek** (1977), while Helm had produced **Muddy Waters In Woodstock** (1976).

Islands (1977), a very laid-back effort, completed group's contractual obligations to Capitol and they embarked on solo projects leaving the album and movie of *The Last Waltz* as their testament.

Individually, band members have aspired to a variety of projects. Robbie Robertson co-wrote, produced and starred in *Carney* with Gary Busey (Buddy Holly in *The Buddy Holly Story*) and Jodie Foster (1980).

Recorded critically acclaimed **Robbie Robertson** LP in (1987), followed three years later by **Storyville**, with contributions from Aaron Neville and the Rebirth Brass Band. Scored movies *Raging Bull*, *The King of Comedy* and *The Colour of Money* for director Martin Scorsese.

Levon Helm starred in *Coal Miner's Daughter* (1980), *The Right Stuff* (1983) and *The Dollmaker* (1984) with Jane Fonda. Toured with Rik Danko as country duo in mid-80s, following period with Levon Helm and RCO Allstars, featuring Steve Cropper (guitar), Dr John (keyboards), and the late Paul Butterfield (vocals, blues harp).

Rick Danko cut first solo LP **Danko** in 1978 before joining forces with Levon Helm. Featured on **Robbie Robertson** album in 1987, and returned to touring as part of Ringo Starr's American extravaganza in 1990. Richard Manuel commited suicide in March 1986 following re-formed Band concert in Florida.

Richard Hudson became part of the 'new' Band, which has had fitful career since reformation in 1986. With Danko, Helm, guitarist James Weider and keyboard player Stan Szelest, signed album deal with Columbia in 1990.

Hit Singles:

	US	UK
Rag Mama Rag, 1970	57	16

Albums:
Music From Big Pink (Capitol), 1968
The Band (Capitol), 1969
Stage Fright (Capitol), 1970
Cahoots (Capitol), 1971
Rock Of Ages (Capitol), 1972
Rock Of Ages Volume II (—/Capitol), 1972

Moondog Matinee (Capitol), 1973
Northern Lights, Southern Cross (Capitol), 1975
Best Of (Capitol/Fame), 1976
Islands (Capitol), 1977
The Last Waltz (Warner Bros), 1978
Anthology Volume I (Capitol), 1978
Anthology Volume II (Capitol), 1980
To Kingdom Come — 31 Songs! (Capitol), 1989

With Bob Dylan:
Before The Flood (Island), 1974
The Basement Tapes (Columbia), 1975

Rick Danko Solo:
Rick Danko (Arista), 1978

Levon Helm Solo:
American Son (MCA), 1978
The Legend Of Jesse James (with various artists), (A&M), 1980

The Bangles
US group formed 1980

Original line-up: Debbie Peterson, drums, vocals; Vicki Peterson, guitar, vocals; Susanna Hoffs, guitar, vocals; Annette Zilinskas, bass, vocals.

Career: Female quartet who successfully survived chauvinistic jibes about their talent before split in 1989.

The Peterson sisters and Hoffs featured in a myriad of bands before settling on quartet The Bangs with Zilinskas. First

single, **Getting Out Of Hand**, was cut for own Down Kiddie records (1982), for which mini-LP **The Bangles** was released a few weeks later. Group's name change was prompted by emergence of New York (male) band The Bangs.

Signed major deal with Columbia Records, who released **All Over The Place** in 1984. Interim personnel change had seen Michael Steele (ex-Runaways) replace Zilinskas, and this revised line-up embarked on first world tour in 1986

Single **Manic Monday** (a Prince song) began extended chart run for group, which included chart-topping singles **Walk Like An Egyptian** (December 1986) and **Eternal Flame** (April 1989). The Bangles maintained a further run of more moderate hits before Hoffs left to pursue solo career, signalling demise of the band.

Hit Singles:

	US	UK
Manic Monday, 1986	2	2
Walk Like An Egyptian, 1986	1	3
Walking Down Your Street, 1987	—	16
Hazy Shade Of Winter, 1988	—	11
In Your Room, 1988	5	—
Eternal Flame, 1989	1	1

Albums:
All Over The Place (Columbia), 1984
Different Light (Columbia), 1986
Everything (Columbia), 1989
Greatest Hits 1984-1988 (Columbia), 1990

The Beach Boys
US group formed 1950s

Original line-up: Brian Wilson, vocals; Dennis Wilson, vocals, drums; Carl Wilson, vocals, guitar; Mike Love, vocals; Al Jardine, vocals, guitar.

Career: Sons of California's 1960s surfing boom, The Beach Boys were based around the Wilson brothers. Songwriting genius Brian Wilson (born June 20, 1942), Dennis Wilson (born December 4, 1944), Carl Wilson (born December 21, 1946), cousin Mike Love (born March 15, 1941) and friend Al Jardine (born September 3, 1942) grew up in middle-class Los Angeles district of Hawthorne. Started out singing barber-shop/Four Freshman-styled harmonies at homes of friends and relatives. Then launched themselves as Carl And The Passions; name soon changed to Kenny And The Cadets (Brian being Kenny).

Dennis, already a surfing addict, suggested to Brian and Mike that they write a song about the cult sport. Result was **Surfin'**. The Wilson brothers' father Murray, himself an established songwriter, took them along to his music publisher. A cheapo production found Carl on guitar, Al on acoustic bass and Brian providing percussion courtesy of a garbage can. Record was issued on tiny local X label then switched to slightly bigger Candix label. It hung around low limits of US Hot 100 for six weeks.

Group worked for while as The Pendletones, a name taken from a make of heavy plaid shirt which was standard surfer wear and which they adopted as stage garb. Candix promotion man suggested The Beach Boys as better tag. First appearance under

new name was at Richie Valens' Memorial Concert, Long Beach Municipal Auditorium, December 31, 1961 (Mexicano rock singer Valens had perished in recent air-crash along with Buddy Holly and the Big Bopper).

Al Jardine left group to take up dental studies at college and he was temporarily replaced by neighbour David L. Marks (featured on sleeve pics of debut album).

Candix folded early 1962. Murray persuaded Capitol Records' producer Nik Venet to pick up group. With smooth harmonies, his own falsetto and a twangy guitar, Brian Wilson had created a whole new sound. What's more, his songs went beyond Tin Pan Alley-style romance and dealt with real teenage concerns — and fantasies — like surfing, hot rod cars and motorcycles.

First Capitol release, **Surfin' Safari**, went US Top 20. **Ten Little Indians** bombed, then **Surfin' USA** (a clever parody of Chuck Berry's **Sweet Little Sixteen**) went all the way to No. 3. **Surfin' USA** album (1963) brought the group first gold record. In same year Brian Wilson had further success when his composition **Surf City** gave his friends Jan and Dean, a million-seller.

Al Jardine rejoined the fold, Marks passing into rock history. Meanwhile, ballad **Surfer Girl**, **Fun Fun Fun**, **Little Honda** and chart-topping **I Get Around** continued run of hits. The Beach Boys' flawless harmonies impressed and influenced many artists, and group's success opened floodgates for profusion of imitators. When Wilson switched from songs about the wild surf to songs about drag strips, imitators also followed suit.

When I Grow Up To Be A Man, **Dance Dance Dance**, **Help Me Rhonda** (another chart-topper) kept things going but Brian, always something of an introvert, was feeling the strain. Suffering from working pressures, he had nervous breakdown in early 1965; also suffered loss of hearing in one ear. He decided to stop touring with band, though he continued to mastermind their records. Glen Campbell joined group as temporary replacement but left following argument over uneven split of income. He was replaced by Bruce Johnston who, as Bruce and Terry (with Terry Melcher), had been among Beach Boys imitators.

Increasingly influenced by Phil Spector's Wall Of Sound technique (Beach Boys eventually cut version of Spector song **Then I Kissed Her**), Brian Wilson's productions

Below: Brian Wilson when it all began — in the early 1960s.

Left: American female quartet The Bangles enjoyed a three year chart run before departure of Susanna Hoffs. US and UK No. 1 Eternal Flame was band's parting shot.

Left: The Beach Boys, circa 1980s. Despite personal tragedy and the quirks of Brian Wilson, this American surf band entered their fourth decade in the rock biz in 1990.

Hit Singles:	US	UK
Surfin' Safari, 1962	14	—
Surfin' USA, 1963	3	34
Surfer Girl, 1963	7	—
Little Deuce Coupe, 1963	15	—
Be True To Your School, 1963	6	—
Fun Fun Fun, 1964	5	—
I Get Around, 1964	1	7
When I Grow Up (To Be A Man), 1964	9	27
Dance Dance Dance, 1964	8	24
Do You Wanna Dance, 1965	12	—
Help Me Rhonda, 1965	1	27
California Girls, 1965	3	26
The Little Girl I Once Knew, 1965	20	—
Barbara Ann, 1966	2	3
Sloop John B, 1966	3	2
Wouldn't It Be Nice, 1966	8	—
God Only Knows, 1966	39	2
Good Vibrations, 1966	1	1
Then I Kissed Her, 1967	—	4
Heroes And Villains, 1967	12	8
Darlin', 1968	19	11
Do It Again, 1968	20	1
I Can Hear Music, 1969	24	10
Break Away, 1969	—	6
Cottonfields, 1970	—	5
Good Vibrations, 1976	—	8
Rock And Roll Music, 1976	5	36
Lady Lynda, 1979	—	6
Beach Boys Medley, 1981	12	47
Come Go With Me, 1981	18	—
Wipeout (with the Fat Boys)	12	—

became ever more inventive (with occasional relapses, like the beach party sing-along **Barbara Ann**). This sophistication helped band compete successfully with British invasion of US charts.

However, when Brian came up with his tour-de-force **Pet Sounds** (a monumental concept album on which he worked with lyricist Tony Asher), it was totally upstaged by the Beatles **Sergeant Pepper**, which came right on its heels. Brian was by now hanging out with Van Dyke Parks, who later wrote Beach Boys lyrics. Brian got into the drug scene, dropping acid, and drifted away from his brothers.(They had been on tour overseas at time of **Pet Sounds** release, of which they did not totally approve.)

Good Vibrations proved to be *the* classic Beach Boys' single but it took nine months to piece together. Complex though record was, this time-lag was due more to Brian's untogetherness than anything else.

Follow-up album project **Smile**, which eventually appeared as **Smiley Smile**, found Van Dyke Parks heavily involved with Brian, to disapproval of rest of group. Rather than being Brian's dreamed-of masterwork LP was eclipsed by emergent West Coast psychedelia movement; it seemed old hat.

With Brian more and more out of things The Beach Boys continued to churn out pleasant if time-warped singles — including **Wild Honey**, **Do It Again** and **I Can Hear Music**. Their albums also maintained totally distinctive sound. In 1967 formed own Brother Records label but ran into immediate legal problems. Their dispute with Capitol did not end until 1970 when label's distribution was switched to Warner Bros/Reprise. Brother was one of first artist-owned labels (preceding Beatles' Apple set-up but meeting similar problems).

New management by Jack Rieley, who also wrote lyrics for them, helped put group back on course. Rieley dug up some old, incomplete tapes for a song called **Surf's Up**, which had been intended as part of **Smile**. He got group to finish it off and make it title track of new album. Rieley also encouraged group to drop stage uniforms and come up with less structured stage show. Sets

now ran for as much as two hours and included newer, more obscure material alongside hits.

Bruce Johnston quit group after **Surf's Up**. In 1972 Rieley took band off to the Netherlands to cut critically applauded but commercially unspectacular **Holland** album. This led to his split from group. (Band had moved Brother studios to Holland — then Brian decided to return to California.)

At this time, a new rhythm section was formed, including black South Aricans Blondie Chaplin, guitar, and Rick Fataar, drums (both of SA Group Fire), making group more potent in concert, but the hits stopped.

Chaplin and Fataar quit in 1974. James Guercio, who had been associated with both Blood Sweat And Tears and Chicago, came in as manager. He also played bass on-stage in line-up which reverted to original.

Dennis and Carl Wilson were proving to be songwriters of some talent but magic spark of Brian Wilson was missing. Numerous attempts were made to tempt him out of his hermit-like existence at Bel-Air mansion. After nearly a decade of virtual inactivity, and following course of therapeutic songwriting prescribed by an analyst, 1976 album **15 Big Ones** (title referring both to number of tracks and the group's age) found Brian back with Beach Boys as singer, songwriter and 'director'. LP won plenty of publicity but did not really stand up. 1977's **The Beach Boys Love You** was more promising. Brian was now firmly back in command of his faculties, composing and producing all material; performed on US tour in summer 1977.

1978's **M.I.U.** album sold poorly and members of band seemed to be going off in own directions. Bruce Johnston came back to help with first Caribou/CBS album **The Beach Boys L.A. Light Album**; and also helped on **Keepin' The Summer Alive** project. Explained Carl: 'He was exactly what we needed. He helped us sort the good from the bad and get back to the basics — the vocals and harmonies — which have been our strength from the beginning'.

It was truly a joint effort: Carl Wilson and Randy Bachman of Guess Who and Bachman

Turner Overdrive fame wrote title cut; Brian Wilson/Al Jardine co-wrote five songs and did a new arrangement of Chuck Berry's **School Day**; and Bruce Johnston contributed **Endless Harmony** — an apt Beach Boys' theme.

Keeping The Summer Alive (1979) and **Ten Years Of Harmony** (1981) provided sufficient spark for group to maintain concert schedule through 80s, without quite resorting to self-parody. Although the death (by drowning) of Dennis Wilson in December 1983 temporarily clouded Beach Boys' future, they enjoyed fresh impetus with **Kokomo** hit single in 1988, part of *Cocktail* movie soundtrack.

The same year saw fragile Brian Wilson issue self-titled solo album from which **Love And Mercy** tickled the charts. Sadly, this effort did not enhance the Wilson legend. Furthermore, he was being sued by members of the group who claimed he was unfit to administer his part of set-up. However, his daughters Carnie and Wendy profited from dad's name when teamed with Chynna Phillips (daughter of Mamas And Papas' John Phillips) for successful Wilson Phillips trio, who enjoyed single success in 1990/91.

Now inducted into Rock 'n' Roll Hall Of Fame, The Beach Boys continue to ply their well-orchestrated trade, and, with regular release of compilation CDs, Beach Boys' legacy moves into the 90s.

Below: The Beach Boys album from 1981. Courtesy Caribou Records.

Albums:
Surfin' Safari (Capitol/Greenlight), 1962
Surfin' USA (Capitol), 1963
Surfer Girl (Capitol/Pickwick), 1963
Little Deuce Coupe (Capitol/Greenlight), 1963
All Summer Long (Capitol/MFB), 1964
Concert (live) (Capitol/—), 1964
Party (Capitol), 1965
Pet Sounds (Capitol/Greenlight), 1966
Best Of (Capitol), 1966
Smiley Smile (Capitol), 1967
Best Of Volume 2 (Capitol), 1967
Wild Honey (Capitol), 1967
Friends (Capitol), 1968
20/20 (Capitol), 1969
Sunflower (Reprise/Caribou), 1970
Surf's Up (Reprise/Caribou), 1971
Live In London (Capitol/MFP), 1972
Endless Summer (Capitol/MFP), 1974
Spirit Of America (Capitol), 1975
The Beach Boys Love You (Reprise), 1977
Fun Fun Fun (Capitol), 1978
California Girls (Capitol/—), 1978
Keepin' The Summer Alive (Caribou), 1979
L.A. (Light Album) (Caribou), 1979
Ten Years Of Harmony (Caribou), 1981
Beach Boys (Caribou), 1981
Sunshine Dream (Capitol/—), 1982
Very Best Of (Capitol), 1983
Beach Boys Rarities (Capitol), 1985
Made In The USA (Capitol), 1986
Summer Dreams (—/Capitol), 1990

Carl Wilson Solo:
Carl Wilson (Caribou), 1981

Dennis Wilson Solo:
Pacific Ocean Blue (Caribou), 1977
One Of Those People (Elektra), 1979

Worth Searching Out:
Surf's Up (Reprise/Stateside), 1971
Holland (Reprise), 1972

15

The Beatles

UK group formed 1959

Original line-up: John Lennon, vocals, guitar; Paul McCartney, guitar, vocals; George Harrison, guitar, vocals; Stuart Sutcliffe, bass; Pete Best, drums.

Career: Formed in Liverpool area: influenced strongly by American rock 'n' roll and R&B records brought to port by sailors. After becoming local success, began to work in Hamburg, West Germany, where bookings involved playing 8-10 hours per night for little money. However, this experience perfected crowd-pleasing ability (recordings from era are high on energy, short on polish). First studio records were in Germany 1961 as backing group for Tony Sheridan, legendary UK rocker. Sessions also provided first genuine Beatles tracks, notably **Ain't She Sweet**, although tracks not released until much later.

Discovered by Liverpool record shop manager Brian Epstein in late 1961, by which time Sutcliffe had left group, preferring to remain in Germany. McCartney then moved to bass, and group became quartet (Sutcliffe died of brain haemorrhage, 1962). Epstein tried to acquire recording contract for Beatles, but without success. Group cut demo tracks for Decca Records, but were rejected in favour of Brian Poole And Tremeloes. Finally, Epstein convinced then minor Parlophone label to provide audition. George Martin, head of label, signed group in late 1962, but suggested replacement of Pete Best — rest of band not unhappy, and recruited Ringo Starr from Rory Storme and The Hurricanes, fellow Merseyside group.

Prior to this, group had gone through several name changes — initially known as The Quarrymen (after school which Lennon attended), they became Silver Beatles, then simply The Beatles (name inspired by The Crickets, Buddy Holly's group). Sessions for Parlophone proved promising — first single **Love Me Do**, released October 1962, reached No. 17 in UK while follow-up, **Please Please Me**, released early 1962, became huge hit. Similarly titled debut LP topped UK charts. Three further chart-toppers, **From Me To You**, **She Loves You**, and **I Want To Hold Your Hand**, followed in 1963.

US success delayed until 1964 when **I Want To Hold Your Hand** (fifth UK hit) topped US singles chart, beginning deluge of releases in US, almost all becoming major hits. At one point in the first half of 1964, The Beatles held positions 1, 2, 3, 4 and 5 in US chart, with seven other singles in Top 100, and LPs at No. 1 and No. 2. While this success was never equalled, group enjoyed enormous worldwide success through mid-60s, with strings of chart-toppers in both US and UK. Almost all Beatles B-sides charted on their own in US.

Beatles' success opened floodgates for the 'British Invasion', when numerous British acts broke through in US charts, including Rolling Stones, Gerry And The Pacemakers, Dave Clark Five and many more. Beatles also starred in pair of ground-breaking rock films, *A Hard Day's Night* and *Help!*, which were enormously successful both artistically and commercially. Lennon and McCartney were recognized as most potent songwriting partnership of rock 'n' roll era; besides providing all Beatles' hits, they also wrote for Billy J. Kramer and Peter And Gordon.

Early beat group style, influenced by Chuck Berry, Everly Brothers, Carl Perkins, and Tamla-Motown, evolved by 1966 LP **Rubber Soul** into much more original sound and

approach, without affecting commercial success. By late 1966, as psychedelic album **Revolver** released, group gave up touring, mostly because hysterical fans made it too risky. This led to lengthy studio experimentation (and often, in retrospect, self-indulgence) culminating in arguably finest LP ever made.

Sergeant Pepper's Lonely Hearts Club Band was released in June 1967. Group also got involved with Indian guru Maharishi Mahesh Yogi; during their attendance at transcendental meditation course in August, Brian Epstein, who had directed group's career throughout hugely successful period, died (of alcohol/drug overdose).

Beatles plunged back into work, creating **Magical Mystery Tour** LP and TV film, an extension of **Sergeant Pepper**, and equally influenced by hallucinogenic drugs. It received critical roasting but latterly has been regarded as legendary. Although group by this time beginning to argue internally, they created remarkable double LP in 1968, known as **The White Album** because of completely white sleeve; it was preceded by **Lady Madonna** single, which heralded return to more basic rock 'n' roll, and by anthemic **Hey Jude**, single lasting seven minutes plus. Year also saw formation of Beatles' company, Apple Corps, with record label, shop, film company etc. *Yellow Submarine* cartoon movie was created around fictional characters suggested by Beatles' songs.

1969 was final year of Beatles' activities, including fated film project *Let It Be* which produced two chart-topping singles in title song and **Get Back**. Apple Records achieved great success with Mary Hopkin (recommended to Paul McCartney by Twiggy), but *Let It Be* film was virtually abandoned, as each Beatle wanted to work without the others. Having left producer and svengali George Martin for **Let It Be**, group returned

to him for final classic LP, **Abbey Road**, but opposing business interests, particularly of John Lennon and Paul McCartney, were becoming impossible.

Lennon and new wife, Japanese avant-garde artist Yoko Ono, formed splinter group, Plastic Ono Band, who scored with first single, **Give Peace A Chance**. Eventually, in 1970, new manager Allen Klein and famed record producer Phil Spector pulled together **Let It Be** project, but this further annoyed McCartney, who announced that he was leaving group. Subsequently, each Beatle enjoyed solo success to a greater or lesser extent. Compilations, re-issues and a few new recordings have kept group in charts ever since, although solo careers (see under individual entries) have in some cases tarnished reputation of undoubtedly most popular group of rock 'n' roll era, whose influence are unlikely ever to be equalled.

1987 saw 25th anniversary of release of **Love Me Do**, and 20th birthday of **Sergeant Pepper**. Memorial celebrations included release of plethora of tracks on compact disc, introducing music to new generation of high-tech buyers. Warts-and-all effect of CD technology was nevertheless welcomed by producer George Martin, who commented that the medium captured the raw vitality of original sessions.

The memorabilia explosion of the 80s saw anything and everything — from toast to Lennon's Rolls Royce — at auction, with Cynthia Lennon even clearing out her loft for a sale at Christies in the summer of 1991. 'The Beatles Revolution' exhibit at London's Trocadero shopping precinct features a myriad of artefacts connected with the

Above: Help! From the fab four film. Courtesy Capitol Records.

Above: The American issue, Beatles '65. Courtesy Capitol Records.

Below: US release, Meet The Beatles. Courtesy Capitol Records.

Below: Vastly underrated as a live band, The Beatles paid dues with gruelling schedule of German clubs in early days. Recordings from the time were raw but full of energy.

band; biography *The Beatles* (1991) included chapter on group's treasures. Hardly ever out of the news, The Beatles reached settlement in their long-standing court case with Apple Computers in October 1991, after costly litigation.

Hit Singles:

	US	UK
Love Me Do, 1962	1	17
Please Please Me, 1963	3	2
From Me To You, 1963	41	1
She Loves You, 1963	1	1
I Want To Hold Your Hand, 1963	1	1
Can't Buy Me Love, 1964	1	1
I Saw Her Standing There, 1964	14	–
Twist And Shout, 1964	2	–
Do You Want To Know A Secret, 1964	2	–
P.S. I Love You, 1964	10	–
A Hard Day's Night, 1964	1	1
Ain't She Sweet, 1964	19	29
And I Love Her, 1964	12	–
Matchbox, 1964	17	–
I Feel Fine, 1964	1	1
She's A Woman, 1964	4	–
Eight Days A Week, 1965	1	–
Ticket To Ride, 1965	1	1
Help, 1965	1	1
Yesterday, 1965	1	–
Day Tripper/We Can Work It Out, 1965	–	1
Day Tripper, 1966	5	–
We Can Work It Out, 1966	1	–
Nowhere Man, 1966	3	–
Paperback Writer, 1966	1	1
Yellow Submarine/Eleanor Rigby, 1966	–	1
Yellow Submarine, 1966	2	–
Eleanor Rigby, 1966	11	–
Penny Lane/Strawberry Fields Forever, 1967	–	2
Penny Lane, 1967	1	–
Strawberry Fields Forever, 1967	8	–
All You Need Is Love, 1967	1	1
Hello Goodbye, 1967	1	1
Magical Mystery Tour (EP), 1967	–	2
Lady Madonna, 1968	1	1
Hey Jude, 1968	1	1
Revolution, 1968	12	–
Get Back, 1969	1	1
Ballad Of John And Yoko, 1969	8	1
Something/Come Together, 1969	–	4
Come Together/Something, 1969	1	–
Let It Be, 1970	1	2
Long And Winding Road, 1970	1	–
Yesterday, 1976	–	8
Got To Get You Into My Life, 1976	7	–
Back In The U.S.S.R., 1976	–	19
Beatles Movie Medley, 1982	12	9
Love Me Do, 1982	–	4

Below: The Fab Four at the time they held the top five US chart positions.

Albums:

UK:
Please Please Me (Parlophone), 1963
With The Beatles (Parlophone), 1963
A Hard Day's Night (Parlophone), 1964
Beatles For Sale (Parlophone), 1964
Help (Parlophone), 1965
Rubber Soul (Parlophone), 1965
Revolver (Parlophone), 1966
A Collection of Beatles' Oldies (But Goldies) (Parlophone), 1966
Sergeant Pepper's Lonely Hearts Club Band (Parlophone), 1967
The Beatles (The White Album) (Parlophone), 1968
Yellow Submarine (Parlophone), 1969
Abbey Road (Parlophone), 1969
Let It Be (Parlophone), 1970
The Beatles 1962-1966 (Parlophone), 1973
The Beatles 1967-1970 (Parlophone), 1973
Rock 'n' Roll Music (Parlophone), 1976
Magical Mystery Tour (Parlophone), 1976
The Beatles At The Hollywood Bowl (Parlophone), 1977
Love Songs (Parlophone), 1977
Hey Jude (Parlophone), 1979
Rarities (Parlophone), 1979
The Beatles Ballads (Parlophone), 1980
Reel Music (Parlophone), 1982
20 Greatest Hits (Parlophone), 1982

Above: Sergeant Pepper's Lonely Hearts Club Band. Courtesy Parlophone Records.

US:
Introducing The Beatles (Capitol), 1963
Meet The Beatles (Capitol), 1964
The Bealtes' Second Album (Capitol), 1964
A Hard Day's Night (Capitol), 1964
Something New (Capitol), 1964
The Beatles Story (Capitol), 1964
Beatles '65 (Capitol), 1965
The Early Beatles (Capitol), 1965
Beatles VI (Capitol), 1965
Help (Capitol), 1965
Rubber Soul (Capitol), 1965
Yesterday And Today (Capitol), 1966
Revolver (Capitol), 1966
Sergeant Pepper's Lonely Hearts Club Band (Capitol), 1967
Magical Mystery Tour (Capitol), 1967
The White Album (Capitol), 1968
Yellow Submarine (Capitol), 1969

Abbey Road (Capitol), 1969
Hey Jude (Capitol), 1970
Let It Be (Capitol), 1970
The Beatles 1962-1966 (Capitol), 1973
The Beatles 1967-1970 (Capitol), 1973
Rock 'n' Roll Music (Capitol), 1976
The Beatles At The Hollywood Bowl (Capitol), 1977
Love Songs (Capitol), 1977
The Beatles Rarities (Capitol), 1980
Reel Music (Capitol), 1982
20 Greatest Hits (Capitol), 1982

Jeff Beck

UK guitarist, composer, vocalist
Born Surrey, June 24, 1944

Career: Studied at Wimbledon Art College. Played lead guitar for Tridents before being recommended to Yardbirds by Jimmy Page as replacement for Eric Clapton. Spent two years with group, contributing to new, more experimental, sound on singles like **Shapes Of Things To Come** and **Over Under Sideways Down**.

Left Yardbirds in December 1966 to sign solo deal on EMI's Columbia label. Scored with out-of-character sing-along **Hi Ho Silver Lining** (again hit on re-release via Rak in 1972 and still a UK disco/pub/juke-box/party standard). Also cut version of **Love Is Blue** and played guitar solo on Donovan's hit **Goo Goo Barabajagel** before forming Jeff Beck Group featuring: Rod Stewart, vocals; Ron Wood, bass; Ray Cook, drums. (Cook was replaced by Mickey Waller after group was thrown off Roy Orbison/Small Faces package tour in March 1967.)

Nicky Hopkins (keyboards) joined later, and group won big reputation in US with **Truth** and **Beck-Ola** LPs. Playing biting, R&B-edged heavy rock, group had exciting but tempestuous career, developing reputation for potent music and bawdy life-style. Wood and Stewart split to join Faces in 1969.

Beck planned new group with ex-Vanilla Fudge players Tim Bogert (bass) and Carmine Appice (drums) — friends met on early Yardbirds visit to New York — but when car

Above: Beck-Ola, Jeff Beck. Courtesy Columbia Records.

accident kept Beck out of action for 18 months the other two formed Cactus.

Beck re-appeared in late 1971 to form new Jeff Beck Group with Robert Tench, vocals, Max Middleton, piano, Clive Chapman, bass, and Cozy Powell, drums. After two albums he declared band wasn't what he wanted and, on break-up of Cactus, formed trio with Bogert and Appice. This new formation broke up after one album, **Beck Bogert Appice** (1973), and tour.

Beck retired again until, in 1975, George Martin produced **Blow By Blow** set, which found Beck experimenting heavily with jazz/rock fusion. Joining Jan Hammer Group

for co-billing tour (which produced joint album **Live** in 1977), Beck featured Hammer's synthesizer work on his 1976 album for Epic **Wired**.

Yet another inactive period ended in 1980 with appearance of **There And Back** album, again featuring Hammer, plus Tony Hymas, keyboards, Mo Foster, bass, and Simon Phillips, drums (Beck's first all-British band since Yardbirds).

In 1984, Beck joined with buddie Rod Stewart in aborted attempt to form new band, but had US success with Honeydrippers (plus Jimmy Page, Nile Rodgers and Robert Plant) a year later. Solo albums **Flash** (1985) and **Jeff Beck's Guitar Shop**(1989) both earned Grammys, but his exemplary guitar technique is now rarely seen on live dates (when joined by Hymas and Terry Bozzio, drums). Beck's fragmented career deserves more.

Hit Singles:

	US	UK
Hi Ho Silver Lining, 1967	–	14
Hi Ho Silver Lining, 1972	–	17

With The Honeydrippers:

Sea Of Love, 1985	3	–

Albums:
Truth (Epic/Columbia), 1968*
Beck-Ola (Epic/Columbia), 1969*
Rough And Ready (Epic), 1971
Jeff Beck Group (Epic), 1972
Beck, Bogert, Appice (Epic), 1973
Wired (Epic), 1976
Live (with Jan Hammer Group) (Epic), 1977
There And Back (Epic), 1980
Early Anthology (Accord/–), 1981
Best Of (1967-69) (Fame), 1985
Flash (Epic), 1985
Late 60s (with Rod Stewart) (–/EMI), 1988
Jeff Beck's Guitar Shop (with Terry Bazzio and Tony Hymas) (Epic), 1989
*Released as double LP (Epic/–), 1975

The Bee Gees

UK group formed 1950s

Original line-up: Barry Gibb, vocals, guitar; Robin Gibb, vocals; Maurice Gibb, vocals, guitar; Vince Melouney, guitar; Colin Petersen, drums.

Career: Formed in Manchester, England (Barry born September, 1946; non-identical twins Robin and Maurice born December 1949), Bee Gees performed on-stage in home city as pre-teens (father was bandleader). Emigrated to Australia with parents in 1958.

After winning radio talent contest, trio graduated to hosting own TV show. First single **Three Kisses Of Love** (1963) was mildly successful. Group's name was taken from Barry Gibb's initials. By 1966 they were top Antipodean group but market had limitations. Australian promoter/manager/entrepreneur Robert Stigwood decided to take band to UK in 1967 as challenge to Beatles. Former child actor Colin Petersen was recruited to go with them as drummer. On arrival in London, another Australian, Vince Melouney, was added on guitar. Their **Spicks And Specks** reached top of Australian charts after they arrived in UK.

This group scored almost immediately with **New York Mining Disaster 1941** in both Britain and America. Follow-ups **To Love Somebody** and **Holiday** were hits, while **Massachusetts** topped UK charts. **I've Got To Get A Message To You** confirmed brothers' songwriting talent. On one early Royal Albert Hall concert they had support from 60-piece orchestra, huge choir and Royal Air Force Brass Band.

Melouney left to form own short-lived band in 1969. Robin Gibb fell out with others and went solo; scored with **Robin's Reign** album and hit single **Saved By The Bell** but career soon floundered. His brothers remained relatively inactive (Maurice married Scottish singer Lulu; they subsequently divorced); Colin Petersen had departed amid much acrimony. Brothers reunited in late 1970.

Bee Gees had two million-selling American singles in 1971, with **Lonely Days** and **How Can You Mend A Broken Heart** but then languished. It was mid-70s disco explosion which not only revived their career but made them superstars.

Switching from somewhat self-pitying storyline-songs to an emasculated brand of soul/disco did trick. Robin's high-pitched lead matched to nasal falsetto harmonies gave unique sound. 1975 Arif Mardin-produced album **Main Course** went platinum. **Jive Talkin'** was the disco smash of 1975. Follow-up set **Children Of The World** was self-produced; contained **You Should Be Dancing** and **Love So Right** singles.

Their **Saturday Night Fever** soundtrack included three No. 1's for group. Two further chart-toppers from studio album **Spirits Having Flown** made it a remarkable six No. 1's in a row. Bee Gees-penned title song from *Grease* gave Frankie Valli No. 1 in 1978.

Their 1979 Music For Unicef charity project found them headlining worldwide televised New York spectacular. Also on bill were Abba, John Denver, Rod Stewart, Earth Wind And Fire, Elton John, and other major artists. Youngest Gibb brother Andy had four hit singles and became teeny-bopper heart-throb in late 70s, but sadly died of substance abuse in 1988. In 1980 Barry Gibb co-wrote, co-produced and contributed vocals to Barbra Streisand's smash album **Guilty**; went on to revive Dionne Warwick's career as her new producer. Robin Gibb produced LP for soul star Jimmy Ruffin, and wrote, performed and produced **Help Me** for movie *Times Square*. Group appeared in disastrous Stigwood movie production *Sgt Pepper*.

Based in Miami, where they have own recording studio, the brothers emerged from hitless period to score with **You Win Again** (1987). Occasional live concerts and charity shows have maintained career into fourth decade, with a remarkable resilience to pop's fads and fashions. Not bad for a group credited with inventing the disco boom! Authorised biography *The Illustrated Bee Gees* was published in 1979.

Hit Singles:	US	UK
New York Mining Disaster 1941, 1967	12	12
To Love Somebody, 1967	15	41
(The Lights Went Out In) Massachusetts, 1967	11	1
World, 1967	—	9
Holiday, 1967	16	—
Words, 1968	15	8
I've Gotta Get A Message To You, 1968	8	1
I Started A Joke, 1969	6	—
First Of May, 1969	37	6
Don't Forget To Remember, 1969	—	2
Lonely Days, 1971	3	33
How Can You Mend A Broken Heart, 1971	1	—
My World, 1972	16	16
Run To Me, 1972	16	9
Jive Talkin', 1975	1	5
Fanny (Be Tender With My Love), 1976	12	—
You Should Be Dancing, 1976	1	5
Love So Right, 1976	3	41
Boogie Child, 1977	12	—
How Deep Is Your Love, 1977	1	3
Staying Alive, 1978	1	4
Saturday Night Fever, 1978	1	1
Too Much Heaven, 1978	1	3
Tragedy, 1979	1	1
Love You Inside Out, 1979	1	13
Spirits Having Flown, 1980	—	16
You Win Again, 1987	—	1
Secret Love, 1991	—	5

Below (from left to right): Maurice, Robin and Barry Gibb, everyone's favourite whipping boys.

Robin Gibb Solo:

Saved By The Bell, 1969	—	2
Oh! Darling, 1978*	15	—

*From Sgt Pepper soundtrack featuring all Bee Gees

Albums:
Odessa (RSO/Polydor), 1969
Best Of (—/RSO), 1969
Best Of Volume 2 (RSO), 1973
Main Course (RSO), 1975
Children Of The World (RSO), 1976
Gold (RSO/—), 1976
Massachusetts) (—/Contour), 1976
Here At Last — Live (RSO), 1977
I've Gotta Get A Message To You (—/Contour), 1977
Bonanza — Early Days (—/Pickwick), 1978
Greatest Hits (RSO), 1979
Spirits Having Flown (RSO), 1979
The Bee Gees (—/Impact), 1979
Early Days Volume 1 (—/Pickwick), 1979
Early Days Volume 2 (—/Pickwick), 1979
Early Days Volume 3 (—/Pickwick), 1979
Living Eyes (RSO), 1981
Staying Alive (RSO), 1983
ESP (Warner Bros), 1987
One (Warner Bros), 1989
Tales From The Brothers Gibb (CD set) (Polydor), 1990
High Civilization (Warner Bros/—), 1991

Worth Searching Out:
Bee Gees First (Polydor), 1967

Pat Benatar

UK vocalist
Born Pat Andrejewski, Brooklyn, New York, 1953

Career: Possessed of undeniably unusual vocal ability, Pat Benatar trained in opera, but never actually attempted professional classical career. After short early marriage, she supported herself by singing in nightclubs, and quickly found her voice as the ultimate female hard-rocker.

Her musical and performing stance is original only in that she *is* female, however. Whether the power-chord clichés and humourless posturing of heavy metal are rendered any more interesting when performed by a tiny, spandex-clad redhead (even with natural talent) rather than by the usual macho howlers is questionable.

Still, Benatar's appearance on the rock scene in 1979 certainly filled in a niche. **In The Heat Of The Night** was surprisingly successful, and was followed by two hit singles in 1980 and 1981, **Heartbreaker** and **Hit Me With Your Best Shot**. Her second album, **Crimes Of Passion**, went straight to the top in 1981; quick follow-up LP **Precious Time** did just as well. She made acting debut in *Union City Blues* same year.

Handicapped to some extent by own material, with little inspiration from husband/guitarist/producer Neil Geraldo, Benatar has nonetheless shown good taste in choice of cover versions, which include John Mellancamp's **I Need A Lover**, Lennon/McCartney's **Helter Skelter** and Kate Bush's **Wuthering Heights**. Benatar returned to acting for ABC TV special in 1991, and cut R&B-oriented **True Love** album in the same year.

Hit Singles:	US	UK
Hit Me With Your Best Shot, 1981	9	—
Treat Me Right, 1981	13	—
Fire And Ice, 1981	5	—
Shadows In The Night, 1982	13	—
Little Too Late, 1983	20	—
We Belong, 1984	5	—
Love Is A Battlefield, 1985*	5	17
Invincible, 1985	10	—
All Fired Up, 1988	—	9

*1983 in US

Albums:
In The Heat Of The Night (Mobile/Chrysalis), 1979
Crimes Of Passion (Chrysalis), 1980
Precious Time (Chrysalis), 1981
Get Nervous, (Chrysalis), 1982
Live From Earth (Chrysalis), 1983
Tropico (Chrysalis), 1984
Seven The Hard Way (Chrysalis), 1985
Best Shots (Chrysalis), 1987
Wide Awake In Dreamland (Chrysalis), 1988
True Love (Chrysalis), 1991

Above: Seven The Hard Way, Pat Benatar. Courtesy Chrysalis Records.

George Benson

US guitarist, vocalist
Born Pittsburgh, Pennsylvania, March 22, 1943

Career: Began learning guitar at eight, and played and sang with several Pittsburgh R&B outfits during teens. However, models for guitar style were jazz men like Charlie Christian and Wes Montgomery rather than R&B practitioners.

Benson moved to New York in 1963 and joined band of organist Brother Jack McDuff; two years on road with McDuff's funky tenor- and organ-led outfit honed Benson's guitar style. In mid-60s recorded for Columbia with own group, before forming working relationship with Creed Taylor's CTI label in 1970, becoming 'house guitarist' and releasing albums under own name.

CTI period resulted in recognition of Benson's skills, and moderate success, including Grammy nomination for album **White Rabbit**. His vocal talents, however, were largely ignored.

Real success came when Benson joined Warner Bros in mid-70s, and was teamed with producer Tommy LiPuma. Result was **Breezin'**, a lightweight jazz-funk effort that struck lucrative chord with record-buying public. Eventually going double platinum, it yielded two hit singles in title track (an instrumental) and **This Masquerade**, on which Benson exhibited his attractive Stevie Wonder-influenced voice. Next album, **In Flight**, followed similar formula and also achieved double platinum sales.

Further hit singles and albums ensued, and Benson established himself as major concert draw throughout the world. Always accompanied by the very best musicians, Benson vocalizes to good effect, plays inventive guitar in effortless style, and occasionally combines both in unison scat-singing/guitar improvisations.

In 1980, partnership with renowned musician and producer Quincy Jones brought about renewed success with **Give Me The Night** LP and further hits through early 80s.

One of a handful of jazz musicians to achieve crossover success, Benson still delivers the goods in traditional vein, as witnessed by 1991 Grammy award for **Basie's Bag** album. However, as an inveterate concert performer, it is pop and soul that his large audiences demand.

Guitars: Ibanez G310, Gibson Super 400 CES.

Hit Singles:	US	UK
This Masquerade, 1976	10	–
On Broadway, 1978	7	–
Love Ballad, 1979	18	29
Give Me The Night, 1980	4	7
Love X Love, 1980	–	10
Turn Your Love Around, 1981	5	29
Never Give Up, 1982	52	14
Lady Love, 1983	30	11
In Your Eyes, 1983	–	7

Albums:
George Benson And Jack McDuff (Prestige/–), 1960s
It's Uptown (Columbia/–), 1965
Cookbook (Columbia/–), 1966
Shape Of Things To Come (A&M), 1968
White Rabbit (CTI), 1973
Breezin' (Warner Bros), 1977
Summertime: In Concert (CTI), 1977
In Flight (Warner Bros), 1977
Best Of (A&M/–), 1978
Stormy Weather (–/Embassy), 1978
Weekend In L.A. (Warner Bros), 1978
Livin' Inside Your Love (Warner Bros), 1979
Cast Your Fate To The Wind (CTI/–), 1979
Blue Benson (Polydor/–), 1980
New Boss Guitar (Prestige/–), 1980
Give Me The Night (Warner Bros), 1980
The George Benson Collection (Warner Bros), 1981
In Your Eyes (Warner Bros), 1983
Early Years (CTI), 1983
Body Talk (Musidisc, France), 1984

Best Of (CTI), 1984
20/20 (Warner Bros), 1985
The Love Songs (K-Tel), 1985
The Electrifying George Benson (Charly), 1985
The Silver Collection (Polydor), 1985
While The City Sleeps (Warner Bros), 1986
Collaboration (with Earl Klugh) (Warner Bros), 1987
Twice The Love (–/Warner Bros), 1988
Tenderly (Warner Bros), 1989
Big Boss Band (featuring Count Basie Orchestra) (–/Warner Bros), 1990
Basie's Bag (Warner Bros), 1991

Chuck Berry

US vocalist, guitarist, composer
Born Charles Edward Berry, San Jose, California, October 18, 1926

Career: Arguably the most influential guitarist and songwriter of the entire rock genre; a musically adequate vocalist, his highly articulate diction ensured maximum impact from inventive lyrics. Many of his songs became anthems of teenage life.

Family moved to St Louis, Missouri, in 1930s; young Berry gained musical experience in school glee-clubs and church choirs. Trained as a hairdresser, then worked in car factory; performed with small group evenings and weekends.

In 1955 recorded some songs for audition tape and travelled north to Chicago to look for successful bluesman Muddy Waters. Muddy suggested Berry take tape to Chess Records. Leonard Chess was interested in embryonic version of **Maybellene** and had the young hopeful record polished version for Chess debut; disc topped R&B chart and began prolific succession of hits like **Brown Eyed Handsome Man, Roll Over Beethoven, Sweet Little Sixteen, School Day.**

Berry's records are notable for their lyrical content and distinctive guitar style; most discs had guitar introductions and incisive

Left: Influential guitarist and songwriter Chuck Berry glides into his famous 'duckwalk' on stage.

solos midway. On stage, Berry played solo while hopping around in squatting posture; this came to be described as a 'duckwalk'.

Consistency of hit singles resulted in several movie parts; Chuck was committed to celluloid in *Go Johnny Go* and *Rock Rock Rock*; also featured in film of 1958 Newport Jazz Festival *Jazz On A Summers Day* singing **Sweet Little Sixteen**. His performance considered quite revolutionary in such context! Convicted for immorality offence (for taking underage girl across state lines) in 1959, Chess still issued Berry singles but with minimal sales.

Recorded fresh material upon release in 1964; scored hits with **Nadine, No Particular Place To Go** and **You Never Can Tell**. Made first overseas tour and played in England with Carl Perkins. Left Chess after financial temptation from Mercury but only decent Mercury disc was **Club Nitty Gritty** — others were mainly re-hashes of old hits; returned to Chess in 1969. During 1972 toured England and recorded 'live' and studio material; from live set, **My Ding-A-Ling** was issued as single. This version of old blues song with suggestive lyric topped US and UK charts (sadly Berry's only No. 1).

As Chess label faded, Chuck cut final **Bio** LP. Began to concentrate more on tours than recording; gained reputation for being hard to deal with financially. Has become regular attraction at cosmopolitan music festivals. Brief contract with Atlantic yielded solitary 1979 LP **Rock It**, patchy in quality, a commercial failure.

1988 saw interest in rock legend flare yet again with publication of *Chuck Berry: The Autobiography*, and movie *Hail! Hail! Rock And Roll*. However, notoriety was maintained with charges of child abuse, drug and firearm possession in the summer of 1990, the courts imposing a custodial sentence plus two years probation.

Hit Singles:	US	UK
Maybellene, 1955	5	–
School Day, 1957	3	24
Rock 'n' Roll Music, 1957	8	–
Sweet Little Sixteen, 1958	2	16
Johnny B Goode, 1958	8	–
Carol, 1958	18	–
Let It Rock/Memphis Tennessee, 1963	–	16
No Particular Place To Go, 1964	10	3
You Never Can Tell, 1964	14	23
My Ding-A-Ling, 1972	1	1
Reelin' And Rockin', 1972	27	18

Albums:
Golden Hits (Mercury/–), 1967
Greatest Hits (Archive Of Folk And Jazz Music/–), 1967
Bio (Chess), 1973
Chuck Berry Volume 1 (–/Impact), 1979
Chuck Berry Volume 2 (–/Impact), 1979
Rock It (Atlantic), 1979
Chess Masters (Chess/PRT), 1983
Best Of (Vogue, France), 1983
Reelin' And A Rockin' (The Collection), 1985
Greatest Hits (Charly), 1986
Two Dozen Berrys (Vogue, France), 1986
Rock 'n' Roll Rarities (Vogue, France), 1987
21 Greatest Hits (Bescol), 1987
The Chess Box (Chess), 1990

Worth Searching Out:
After School Session (Chess/–), 1958
One Dozen Berry's (Chess/–), 1958
Golden Decade Volumes 1-3 (–/Chess), 1973

Big Country

UK group formed 1983

Original line-up: Stuart Adamson, guitar, vocals; Bruce Watson, guitar; Tony Butler, bass; Mark Brzezicki, drums.

Career: Rhythm For Hire session team Butler and Brzezicki decided to throw in lot with Scots Adamson and Watson after working for them on demo session of **Harvest Home** at Phonogram Studios, London, at the end of 1983.

Catchy chorus and exciting guitar crescendos of debut record became group's hallmark but single **Chance** was a Springsteen-esque ballad revealing another side to group's talent. Debut album **The Crossing** produced, like singles, by Steve Lillywhite, established band.

Big Country's strident brand of rock is imbued with strong Celtic influence, reflecting Adamson's upbringing on diet of Scottish and Irish folk songs in his native Dunferline.

Adamson had earlier career with Skids for four years up to 1981 before going back home to write songs and germinate Big Country.

Big Country's songs have a strong element of social comment, as in **Steeltown**, but album failed to live up to promise of debut set. Matters were not helped by long recording hiatus which followed, although band maintained busy touring schedule.

Subsequent albums **The Seer** (1986) and **Peace In Our Time** (1988) kept band in time warp, although live gigs, including appearance at Soviet Peace Festival in Estonia (1988), were still commanding attention. Heavy financial losses sustained by Russian adventure temporarily curtailed band's career, but with new drummer Pat Ahern replacing Brzezicki (his debut was **No Place Like Home** LP, December 1991) and Greatest Hits package making UK Top 10, the 90s beckoned promisingly.

Hit Singles:	US	UK
Fields Of Fire (400 Miles), 1983	–	10
In A Big Country, 1983	17	17
Chance, 1983	–	9
Wonderland, 1984	–	8
East Of Eden, 1984	–	17
Where The Rose Is Sown, 1984	–	29
Just A Shadow, 1985	–	26
Look Away, 1986	–	7
The Teacher, 1986	–	28
One Great Thing, 1986	–	19
King Of Emotion, 1988	–	16

Below: Big Country's Adamson finds an A major on his Stratocaster.

Albums:

The Crossing (Mercury/Phonogram), 1983
Steeltown (Mecury/Phonogram), 1984
The Seer (Mercury), 1986
Peace In Our Time (Reprise/Mercury), 1988
Through A Big Country (greatest hits)
(—/Mercury), 1990
No Place Like Home (Mercury), 1991

Black Sabbath
UK group formed 1969

Original line-up: Ozzy Osbourne, vocals; Tony Iommi, Jay-dee guitar; Terry 'Geezer' Butler, bass; Bill Ward, drums.

Career: Started in Birmingham as blues band Earth; in late 1969 they changed name to Black Sabbath and recorded first album of same name, developing quasi occult, 'evil' image. Although album was largely ignored by radio and media, word of mouth eventually hoisted it into UK charts where it remained for 13 weeks.

International success followed quickly with release of 1970 album **Paranoid**; LP and single of same name hit on both sides of Atlantic. Band played first successful American tour in autumn 1970.

From that time until 1973, band toured regularly and recorded prolifically, establishing themselves as one of world's foremost heavy metal bands, though critical acclaim continued to elude them.

In 1973 managerial problems forced cessation of activities until 1975 release of album **Sabotage** re-established band as major force in heavy metal, a position they have maintained every since.

Since 1978 band has undergone several personnel changes. Ozzy Ozbourne left only to return a few months later, but in 1979 he departed for good to form own band, Ozzy Osbourne's Blizzard Of Oz, which has achieved considerable success. He was replaced by Ronnie James Dio, formerly singer with Ritchie Blackmore's Rainbow. At end of 1980 Bill Ward left for personal reasons, and Vinnie Appice, brother of the more famous Carmine, was recruited.

Fluctuating line-up saw Ian Gillan as new vocalist, until he left to rejoin Deep Purple, replaced by Dave Donato. Dio and Appice also split and Ward returned.

In July 1985 the original Sabbath with Ozzy reunited for an appearance at Live Aid in Philadelphia. Subsequently Sabbath suffered a series of personnel changes which led to dwindling audiences. Singer Dave

Donato did not record with Sabbath but his successor Glenn Hughes cut the **Seventh Star** album with them in 1986 and the band under the leadership of Tony Iommi toured the UK with Eric Singer (drums), Dave Spitz (bass), Geoff Nichols (keyboards) and Ray Gillen (vocals).

In November 1987 the Sabs released critically acclaimed **The Eternal Idol** with vocalist Tony Martin. However band criticized for visiting South Africa's Sun City to play. Then they cancelled a concert at London's Odeon Hammersmith at the last minute during Christmas, which upset even their most loyal fans.

Mind-boggling array of personnel changes continued, but line-up was reasonably settled for 1989 set **Headless Cross**, with Iommi; Cozy Powell, drums; Neil Murray, bass; and Tony Martin. Iommi's indefatigable spirit has sustained Black Sabbath beyond their sell-by date.

Hit Singles:	US	UK
Paranoid, 1970	—	4
Paranoid, 1980	—	14

Albums:

Black Sabbath (Nems/Warner Bros), 1970
Paranoid (Nems/Warner Bros), 1970
Master Of Reality (Nems/Warner Bros), 1971
Black Sabbath 4 (Nems/Warner Bros), 1972
Sabbath Bloody Sabbath (Nems/Warner Bros), 1973
Sabotage (Nems/Warner Bros), 1975
We Sold Our Souls For Rock 'n' Roll (Nems/Warner Bros), 1975
Technical Ecstasy (Nems/Warner Bros), 1976
Greatest Hits (Nems/Warner Bros), 1977
Never Say Die (Vertigo/Warner Bros), 1978
Heaven And Hell (Vertigo/Warner Bros), 1980
Mob Rules (Vertigo/Warner Bros), 1981
Live Evil (Vertigo/Warner Bros), 1983
Born Again (Vertigo), 1983
Seventh Star (Vertigo), 1986
The Eternal Idol (Vertigo), 1987
Headless Cross (IRS), 1989
Tyr (IRS), 1990

Ronnie James Dio Solo:
Holy Diver (Vertigo), 1983
The Last In Line (Vertigo), 1984
Trying To Burn The Sun (with ELF) (Safari), 1984
Sacred Heart (Vertigo), 1985
Dream Evil (Warner Bros/—), 1987
Lock Up The Wolves (Reprise/—), 1990

Below: Latter-day Sabbath line-up, with Tony Iommi still leading his troops.

Blondie
US group formed 1975

Original line-up: Debbie Harry, vocals; Chris Stein, guitar; Jimmy Destri, keyboards; Gary Valentine, bass; Clem Burke, drums.

Career: Band born out of mid-70s New York new wave, a splinter group of punk/sleaze outfit the Stilettoes. Lead singer was Debbie Harry, one-time front person of folk-rock band the Wind In The Willows, and well-known figure around New York music/art/night-life scene. Briefly calling themselves Angel And The Snake, band consisted of Harry, Chris Stein (guitar), Billy O'Connor (drums), Fred Smith (bass), and two back-up singers, Tish and Snooky. By 1975 the group had reached line-up (above) known as Blondie.

In 1976 band signed with producer Richard Gottehrer and released first single, **X Offender/In The Sun**. In October same year they contracted to Private Stock, and released first album, **Blondie**. Promotion concentrated on Monroesque good looks of Debbie Harry, as has much of publicity throughout life of band.

Lack of success with Private Stock prompted move to Chrysalis, who re-released first album and followed it with **Plastic Letters** in 1978. Gary Valentine had left, and was replaced by guitarist Frank Infante, who played bass on **Letters**. Album spawned international hits **Denis** and **(I'm Always Touched By Your) Presence Dear** and set band on road to success. Next album, **Parallel Lines**, with addition of bassist Nigel Harrison, established band as top international attraction and went on to eventually sell 20 million copies.

From 1978 to 1981 band was among most successful in world. Winning formula combined commercial material, clear, pop-style vocals, and rock backing with hint of punk aggression. Audiences were drawn from both pop and rock aficionados. Harry became much-photographed sex symbol of rock.

In 1982, however, it became apparent that runaway pace of success was slowing down. Album **The Hunter** was relatively unsuccessful (although it still made UK Top 10 and US Top 40), and British tour was cancelled because it failed to attract interest anticipated. Critics cited lack of regular live work for failure.

In meantime, Debbie Harry had some success with solo album **Koo Koo** (produced by Chic supremos Nile Rodgers and Bernard Edwards) and acting debut in *Union City Blues* and *Roadie* (1980). (Her career on Broadway lasted precisely one evening in 1983 New York play.) Other members of Blondie also branched out into production and projects with other musicians. In February 1983 band announced break-up. Burke went on to play with Eurythmics.

Accepting the inevitable, Debbie Harry admitted that her solo career had flopped, and announced plans for new band, tentatively called Tiger Bomb, featuring former beau Chris Stein, whom she had nursed through long illness.

Occasional acting spots — *Hairspray* movie, *Wiseguy* TV show — afforded Harry media spotlight, and she resumed recording, for Chrysalis, as 'Deborah' Harry in 1988 (Tiger Bomb having inexplicably disappeared) with **Def, Dumb And Blond** set. Unable to accept that Blondie and herself are permanently intertwined, Harry saw personal ambitions upstaged by release of **The Complete Picture**, a greatest hits package which made No. 3 in UK album listings.

Above: Harry grabbed the bleach when Blondie slid from prominence.

Hit Singles:	US	UK
Denis, 1978	—	2
(I'm Always Touched By Your), Presence Dear, 1978	—	10
Picture This, 1978	—	12
Hanging On The Telephone, 1978	—	5
Heart Of Glass, 1979	1	1
Sunday Girl, 1979	—	1
Dreaming, 1979	27	2
Union City Blues, 1979	—	13
Atomic, 1980	39	1
Call Me, 1980	1	1
The Tide Is High, 1980	1	1
Rapture, 1981	1	5
Island Of Lost Souls, 1982	37	11

Debbie Harry Solo:

	US	UK
French Kissin' In The USA, 1987	—	8

Albums:

Blondie (Private Stock), 1977
Plastic Letters (Chrysalis), 1978
Parallel Lines (Chrysalis), 1978
Eat To The Beat (Chrysalis), 1979
Autoamerican (Chrysalis), 1980
Best Of (Chrysalis), 1981
The Hunter (Chrysalis), 1982
Heart Of Glass (Old Gold), 1987
The Complete Picture (Chrysalis), 1991

Debbie Harry Solo:
Koo Koo (Chrysalis), 1981
Rockbird (Chrysalis), 1986
Def, Dumb And Blonde (Chrysalis), 1989

Blue Oyster Cult
US group formed 1970

Original line-up: Eric Bloom, vocals, guitar; Allen Lanier, keyboards, synthesizer; Donald 'Buck Dharma' Roeser, guitar, vocals; Joe Bouchard, bass, vocals; Albert Bouchard, drums, vocals.

Career: America's prime exponents of heavy-metal idiom started in New York as Stalk Forrest Group and Soft White Underbelly. Recorded two unreleased albums for Elektra before name change and Columbia contract, earned via mentor Sandy Pearlman, *Crawdaddy* magazine critic, in 1971. Released eponymous debut album.

Breakthrough came with third album **Secret Treaties** in 1974, which included

Patti Smith-penned **Career Of Evil**; 1975 live set **On Your Feet Or On Your Knees** captured their explosive stage presence — screaming vocals and savage guitar riffs overlaying a pounding rhythm section.

Patti Smith wrote two songs and guested on 1976 album **Agents Of Fortune** from which **(Don't Fear) The Reaper** was US hit. Since then, somewhat sinister mysticism of lyrics, album cover designs and image, and increasingly heavy playing has marked work. With Rick Downey replacing Albert Bouchard on drums, band have maintained reputation as premier cult HM band.

In 1985 band returned to Europe for concerts and released their 13th album **Club Ninja** produced by Sandy Pearlman, his first with the band since **Spectres** in 1977. Allen Lanier (keyboards), quit the band in protest at the material on album which he didn't like and was replaced by Tony Zvancheck. New drummer Jimmy Wilcox was recruited at the same time. Following 1988 set **Imaginos**, band returned to UK for tour, but have since gone into period of hibernation.

Hit Singles:

	US	UK
(Don't Fear) The Reaper, 1976	12	—
(Don't Fear) The Reaper, 1978	—	16

Albums:
Blue Oyster Cult (Columbia/CBS), 1972
Tyranny And Mutation (Columbia/CBS), 1974
Secret Treaties (Columbia/CBS), 1974
On Your Feet Or On Your Knees (Columbia/CBS), 1975
Agents Of Fortune (Columbia/CBS), 1976
Spectres (Columbia/CBS), 1977
Some Enchanted Evening (Columbia/CBS), 1978
Mirrors (Columbia/CBS), 1979
Cultasaurus Erectus (Columbia/CBS), 1980
Fire Of Unknown Origin (Columbia/CBS), 1981
Extraterrestrial (Columbia/CBS), 1982
Revolution By Night (Columbia/CBS), 1983
Club Ninja (Columbia/CBS), 1985
Imaginos (Columbia/CBS), 1988
Career Of Evil (Columbia/CBS), 1990

Buck Dharma Solo:
Flat Out (Columbia), 1982

Marc Bolan

UK vocalist, guitarist, composer
Born Mark Feld, London, July 30, 1947
Died September 16, 1977

Career: Always adept at self-promotion, in early 60s then 15-year-old Feld managed to win wide exposure in media as archetypal mod, which led to brief career as male model. Later dropped sharp besuited image for loose-fitting flower clothes, beads and espousal of 'flower power'. Changed name to Bolan for debut single **The Wizard** on Decca (1966). Briefly joined glam-rock band John's Children, scoring with **Desdemona**. Their **Go Go Girl** backing track was used for Bolan's **Mustang Ford**. On leaving group, Bolan cut sides for Track which did not surface until 1974, as **Beginning Of Doves** LP.

Joined by Steve Peregrine Took, Bolan attempted to form five-piece electronic band but hire-purchase company snatched back equipment. Bolan and Took consequently started working in 1968 as acoustic folksy-rock duo Tyrannosaurus Rex. Full of elves, fairies and flower-power mythology, Tyrannosaurus Rex albums (**My People Were Fair And Had Sky In Their Hair But Now They're Content To Wear Stars On Their**

Brows (1968), **Prophets, Seers And Sages** (1969), **The Angels Of The Ages** (1969) and **Unicorn** (1969)) may have been somewhat pretentious, but captured essence of the love-and-peace philosophy. Duo also benefited from support of influential BBC radio DJ John Peel (as did Bolan's book of poetry).

Overshadowed in duo by Bolan, Took quit in 1970, replaced by Mickey Finn (who met Bolan in a health food restaurant). On their **Beard Of Stars** album Bolan switched to electric guitar. Later that year, with name shortened to T.Rex, they notched surprise UK No. 2 with soft-rock but uptempo **Ride A White Swan**. Added drummer Bill Legend and bass player Steve Currie in time for next single **Hot Love**. Aimed direct at teeny-bop pop audience, it topped chart for six weeks in early 1971. **Get It On** was second No. 1 later same year; re-titled **Bang A Gong**, became group's biggest US success.

THE ULTIMATE COLLECTION
MARC BOLAN AND T-REX
CD INCLUDES FOUR BONUS TRACKS

Above: The Ultimate Collection, Marc Bolan & T-Rex. Courtesy Marc On Wax.

T.Rex had now fully undergone transition from esoteric folk-rock outfit to rocking pop band. Bolan had become pre-teen idol to rival earlier Beatles and Monkees.

Though **Jeepster** made UK No. 2, Fly Records had pulled it from **Electric Warrior** album without consulting Bolan. Angered, he split to start own T.Rex label, via EMI.

String of UK hits made 1972 big year. In 1973 ex-Beatle Ringo Starr directed movie, *Born To Boogie*, about T.Rex phenomenon but it flopped. By end of year Bolan's fickle young audiences were deserting him.

The glamour and glitter became tarnished. Bolan left wife June Child to live with black American soul singer Gloria Jones (who bore him a child). He put on weight alarmingly, churned out ever less satisfying material, split with Finn (in March 1975) and broke up T.Rex before slinking off to tax exile in Los Angeles.

Bolan undertook comeback tour with Jones early in 1976 and formed new T.Rex with veteran studio musicians Herbie Flowers, Miller Anderson and Tony Newman, and keyboard player Dino Dines.

Seeking rising star to hitch on to, Marc tried to become self-proclaimed guru of British new-wave movement and used the Damned as support on his spring 1977 tour. Hosted a rather unsatisfactory weekly TV music show and fought hard to rebuild career. Early one September morning in 1977, the mini car driven by Gloria Jones careered off road on dangerous bend and passenger Bolan was killed, aged 30. Totally shattered, Jones — who blamed tragedy on herself — had hard time until, with help of songwriter brother, she rebuilt career, wrote hit records for several artists, notably British soul act Gonzalez (worldwide disco smash **Haven't Stopped Dancing Yet**). Her composition **Tainted Love**, written back in 60s, became big 1981 hit for Soft Cell.

Above: Former HM belter Bolton found niche with blue-eyed soul.

Bolan's UK Appreciation Society are now responsible for collation of re-issued material, and have access to unreleased tracks for their own Marc On Wax label.

Hit Singles:

	US	UK
As Tyrannosaurus Rex:		
Deborah/One Inch Rock, 1972	—	7
As T.Rex:		
Ride A White Swan, 1970	—	2
Hot Love, 1971	—	1
Get It On, 1971	10	1
Jeepster, 1971	—	2
Telegram Sam, 1972	—	1
Metal Guru, 1972	—	1
Children Of The Revolution, 1972	—	2
Solid Gold Easy Action, 1972	—	2
20th Century Boy, 1973	—	3
The Groover, 1973	—	4
Truck On (Tyke), 1973	—	12
Teenage Dream, 1974	—	13
New York City, 1975	—	15
I Love To Boogie, 1976	—	13
20th Century Boy, 1991	—	13

Albums:
As Tyrannosaurus Rex:
Prophets.../My People...(—/Cube), 1972*
Beard Of Stars/Unicorn (—/Cube), 1972*
*Released as double albums two years after original release as singles

As T.Rex:
T.Rex (—/Cube), 1970
Electric Warrior (Reprise/Cube), 1971
Bolan Boogie (—/Cube), 1972
The Slider (Reprise/EMI), 1972
Greatest Hits Volume I (—/Hallmark), 1978
Collection (—/Hallmark), 1978
Solid Gold (—/Fame), 1979
Unobtainable (—/Nut), 1980
In Concert (—/Marc), 1981
Platinum Collection (—/Cube), 1981
Best Of 20th Century Boy (K-Tel), 1985
Zinc Alloy And The Hidden Riders Of Tomorrow (Marc On Wax), 1985
Bolan's Zip Gun (Marc On Wax), 1985
Dandy In The Underworld (Marc On Wax), 1985
Love And Death (Cherry Red), 1985
Marc Bolan And T.Rex (Marc On Wax), 1987

Michael Bolton

US vocalist, songwriter
Born Michael Bolotin, New Haven, Connecticut, February 26, 1953

Career: Authentic soul stylist, whose early work with bands Blackjack and Michael Bolton Band did not allow him full rein with R&B material.

Entrenched in AOR material, Bolton's self-titled debut album (1983) gave little indication of artist's true vocation, although single **Fools Game** made US Top 100.

Disenchanted, Bolton concentrated on writing with a variety of partners, and scored success with Laura Brannigan's version of **How Am I Supposed To Live Without You**. Acts including the Pointer Sisters, Kiss, Cher (**I Found Someone**) and Irene Cara have also recorded Bolton songs.

A second album, **Everybody's Crazy**, proved uninspiring, and Bolton had to wait until **The Hunger** set (1987) before attracting national attention.

The Hunger spawned successful **That's What Love Is All About** single, and decent cover version of Otis Redding's classic **(Sittin' On) The Dock Of The Bay**, both of which were included in Bolton's memorable spot on the *It's Showtime At The Apollo* US TV series (also seen in the UK).

Soul Provider LP (1989) confirmed Bolton's talents, and his version of **How Am I Supposed To Live Without You** secured No. 1 spot in USA, and a place in the British Top 10. Further single releases from the set included title track (with altoist Kenny G), the Ray Charles standard **Georgia On My Mind** and **How Can We Be Lovers**.

Bolton maintained chart success with upbeat **Love Is A Wonderful Thing** cut from 1991 **Time, Love And Tenderness** LP, which suggested a long tenure in the single and album charts if those bronze vocal chords hold out.

Hit Singles:

	US	UK
(Sittin' On) The Dock Of The Bay, 1988	11	—
Soul Provider, 1989	17	3
How Am I Supposed To Live Without You, 1990	1	3
How Can We Be Lovers, 1990	3	10
When I'm Back On My Feet Again, 1990	7	44

Love Is A Wonderful Thing, 1991	4	23
Time, Love And Tenderness, 1991	10	28
When A Man Loves A Woman, 1991	1	5

Albums:
Michael Bolton (Columbia), 1983
The Hunger (Columbia), 1987
Soul Provider (Columbia), 1989
The Early Years (RCA), 1991
Time, Love And Tenderness (Columbia), 1991

Bon Jovi
US group formed 1982

Original line-up: Jon Bon Jovi, vocals; David Bryan, keyboards; Richie Sambora, guitar; Tico Torres, drums; Alec Such, bass.

Career: Teen idols whose manicured locks and zippy stage outfits caused a torrent of tears at their sell-out stadium concerts during the 80s.

Formed by Jon Bon Jovi (real name Bongiovi), original single **Runaway** was cut with session musicians, and turntable action on several prominent radio stations persuaded singer to hire permanent group.

The original quintet subsequently survived four multi-platinum albums (**Slippery When Wet** topped 10 million sales), and steady diet of major gigs (having started as support act for ZZ Top and then Kiss). Monster world tour, which clocked nigh on 240 shows, saw band in Moscow for the Music For Peace concert, before exhausted members began hiatus in 1989.

Along with Elton John and guitarist Jeff Beck, Bon Jovi (singular) returned to record soundtrack album for *Young Guns II* movie, from which **Blaze Of Glory** earned the permed, teased and coiffured singer a US No. 1, while Sambora avoided unemployment with work for girlfriend Cher (band had supplied **We All Sleep Alone** hit) and 1991 collection **Stranger In This Town**.

Hit Singles:	US	UK
You Give Love A Bad Name, 1986	1	14
Livin' On A Prayer, 1986	1	4
Wanted Dead Or Alive, 1987	7	13
Bad Medicine, 1988	1	17
Born To Be My Baby, 1988	3	22
I'll Be There For You, 1989	1	18
Lay Your Hands On Me, 1989	7	18
Living In Sin, 1989	9	35

Below: Bon Jovi on stage following urgent hairdressing appointment.

Jon Bon Jovi Solo:		
Blaze Of Glory, 1990	1	13
Miracle, 1990	12	29

Albums:
Bon Jovi (Mercury/Vertigo), 1984
New Jersey (Mercury/Vertigo), 1988
7800 Degrees Fahrenheit (Mercury/Vertigo), 1985
Slippery When Wet (Mercury/Vertigo), 1986
Stranger In This Town (Mercury/Vertigo), 1991

Jon Bon Jovi Solo:
Blaze Of Glory (Mercury/—), 1990

Boomtown Rats/ Bob Geldof
UK group formed 1975

Original line-up: Bob Geldof, vocals; Garry Roberts, guitar; Gerry Cott, guitar; Johnny Fingers, keyboards; Pete Briquette, bass; Simon Crowe, drums; Albe Donnelly, saxophone.

Career: Band formed in a port town near Dublin in Ireland. In early stages Geldof was manager, Roberts lead singer. Once Geldof had taken over vocal duties, band started to attract attention from record companies, eventually signing with Ensign and making move to London.

Although offering more variety and coherence than run-of-the-mill punk outfits, Rats rose to fame on crest of new wave. Band had major hit with first single, **Looking After No. 1**, in 1977.

Several more Top 20 UK singles preceded first No. 1, **Rat Trap**, in 1978. This year also saw chart action with album **Tonic For The Troops**. Geldof became chief spokesperson for band; Donnelly and Cott left and were not replaced.

Finest hour came with next single, **I Don't Like Mondays**, a song based on true story of homicidal San Diego schoolgirl. **Mondays** broke band in foreign territories and extended touring ensued.

Productive period in early 80s saw easing of success, although **Mondo Bongo** LP made UK Top 10. In May 1984, aptly titled **Drag Me Down** 45 scraped into Top 50, marking end of Rats' chart reign. Moved by plight of Ethiopian refugees, Geldof shelved commitment to band to plan concerted relief effort. **Do They Know It's Christmas?** single, written by Geldof and Ultravox guitarist/vocalist Midge Ure was first tangible product of charity operation which consumed artist for two years.

In 1985, Geldof was among a myriad of talent to record **We Are The World** single in US, with simultaneous Band Aid and Live Aid concerts in London and Philadelphia.

Geldof signed to Mercury Records, and began long haul back into pop mainstream with Dave Stewart-produced **Deep In The Heart Of Nowhere** album (December 1986), although broad appeal also allowed publication of autobiography *Is That It?*.

After an absence of four years, Geldof returned to duty for **Vegetarians Of Love** LP in 1990, from which **The Great Song of Indifference** made UK Top 20.

Hit Singles:	US	UK
Looking After No. 1, 1977	—	11
Mary Of The Fourth Form, 1977	—	15
She's So Modern, 1978	—	12
Like Clockwork, 1978	—	6
Rat Trap, 1978	—	1
I Don't Like Mondays, 1979	—	1
Diamond Smiles, 1979	—	13
Someone's Looking At You, 1980	—	4
Banana Republic, 1980	—	3

Bob Geldof Solo:
The Great Song Of Indifference, 1990	—	15

Band Aid Single:
Do They Know It's Christmas?, 1984	13	1

Albums:
The Boomtown Rats (Mercury/Ensign), 1977
Tonic For The Troops (Columbia/Ensign), 1978
The Fine Art Of Surfacing (Columbia/Ensign), 1979
Mondo Bongo (Columbia/Mercury), 1981
Five Deep (Columbia/Mercury), 1982

Bob Geldof Solo:
Deep In The Heart Of Nowhere (Atlantic/Mercury), 1986
Vegetarian Of Love (Atlantic/Mercury), 1990

David Bowie
UK vocalist, composer, producer, actor
Born David Robert Jones, London, January 8, 1947

Career: Began musical career playing tenor sax in school group. Suffered eye injury following a fight; subsequent surgery left him with paralysed pupil. Leaving Bromley High School, secured job as commercial artist before forming succession of progressive R&B groups: Davie Jones And The King Bees, The Manish Boys, and The Lower Third. All recorded without success. Upsurge of Monkees forced name change from Jones to Bowie.

Subsequent contract with Pye and Decca as soloist produced series of pop/love songs, strongly influenced by Anthony Newley. Originally issued as **The World Of David Bowie**, these were re-released in 1973 as **Images 1966/67**. Included in set was embarrassing **The Laughing Gnome**, which actually reached Top 10 on re-release in 1973.

For brief period Bowie dropped out of music and flirted with Buddhism. Also joined Lindsay Kemp's mime company, a move that would greatly influence his later theatrical work. Re-emerged in 1969 and started an arts lab in Beckenham, recording **Space Oddity** for Mercury during same period. Song became surprise hit, followed

by average album of same title. Toured as support act, but returned, disillusioned, to one-man show in Beckenham. Failure to follow up novelty **Space Oddity** strongly indicated that he was little more than a one-hit-wonder.

By 1970, Bowie had consolidated resources, combining interest in mime, Buddhism, novelty and whatever else to produce epic **The Man Who Sold The World**.

Album was complete contrast to predecessor; acoustic strumming was replaced by heavy guitar work of Mick Ronson. Thematically, work was chilling: an Orwellian vision of a future riddled with sexual perversion, dominance by machines, loneliness and helplessness. Many of these themes would be extended to produce later albums, not least the Nietzschean vision of **The Supermen**.

Although initially a relatively poor seller, **The Man Who Sold The World** gave Bowie cult following and was hailed as excellent work by more perceptive buyers/critics of the period. An important and much-publicized US tour followed, with Bowie decked out as 1970s Garbo, complete with flowing dress. Switch to RCA proved timely, and with further publicity critics were well-primed for release of **Hunky Dory**. Work was more mellow than its predecessor but still haunting, original and commercially appealing in range of themes.

1972 was year of the breakthrough with most commercial work to date, **The Rise And Fall Of Ziggy Stardust And The Spiders From Mars**. Where he had used a number of different ideas/personae on

Below: Bowie as Ziggy in 1974. The eye-patch and henna hair were trademarks of his 'glam' period.

previous LPs, Bowie now created a single figure, Ziggy, the ultimate rock superstar destroyed by the fanaticism he creates. Negotiating ground between the heaviness of **The Man Who Sold The World** and the diverse quirkiness of **Hunky Dory**, an image of Ziggy was created that almost subsumed Bowie in later years. Artist and art, actor and part were inextricably linked. From this point on Bowie became the most important rock figure of 70s.

Activities broadened following hit single **Starman** and Bowie took on role as producer, literally saving the faltering career

Above: Young Americans, David Bowie. Courtesy RCA Records.

of Lou Reed (**Transformer**) and resurrecting the already dead Mott The Hoople (**All The Young Dudes**). 1972 US tour provided ideas for next conceptual work, **Aladdin Sane**. Album was not classic, though Ronson's work was exceptional and two hit singles were forthcoming via **Jean Genie** and **Drive In Saturday**. **Pin Ups** was a surprise *volte face* that brought suspicion from some critical quarters; a re-working of selected oldies from 1964-67 pop scene, it seemed rather too lightweight as concept. Period of uncertainty was punctuated by 'retirement' following Hammersmith Odeon concert in July 1973.

Later in year, recorded an NBC Midnight Special at London's Marquee Club titled 'The 1980 Floor Show'. Production inspired next album **Diamond Dogs** (1974), a return to Orwellian gloom of **Man Who Sold The World**, but minus fine guitar work of Ronson. Show was taken on road in US and performance at Philadelphia's Tower Theatre was used for double **David Live**. During tour, a new course was charted as Bowie picked up on soul/R&B style. Results were evident enough on Philly-influenced **Young Americans**, which included another couple of hit singles in title track and **Fame**. Latter, co-written by John Lennon, provided first US No. 1 single. Incredibly, 1975 UK re-release of first hit **Space Oddity** went to top in same year, the slowest No. 1 of all time (6 years 63 days!).

For remainder of 1975 Bowie involved himself in filming *The Man Who Fell To Earth*, released the following year. Long-awaited return to England in spring 1976 provided memorable gigs at Wembley Empire Pool. Having re-established himself commercially, Bowie felt free to record more adventurous material. **Station To Station**, consisting of six lengthy cuts, was return to top form, paving way for three albums recorded under supervision of Brian Eno. **Low**, originally titled **New Music: Night And Day**, was essentially a mood piece, consisting largely of instrumental music. (Nick Lowe 'retaliated' by calling his 1977 EP **Bowi**.) The experiment was continued on **Heroes**, but with enough conventional rock to attract larger listening audience. Trilogy was interrupted by **Stage**, an uninspired

double LP documenting 1978 tour. Final Bowie/Eno collaboration **Lodger** proved only partially successful in spite of strong tracks (**Boys Keep Swinging**', **Repetition**).

With **Scary Monsters (And Super Creeps)**, commitment and commerciality were neatly fused in old tradition. Album spawned several hit singles, including excellent **Ashes To Ashes**, which hit No. 1 in UK in August 1980. For his next album, Bowie promised some positive dance-orientated music as reaction against apocalyptic themes of yore. This was forthcoming in 1983 Nile Rodgers-produced album **Let's Dance**, a worldwide chart topper with its title track single. Soon after release, Bowie toured Europe and UK for first time in seven years.

Rightly acknowledged as rock's most important figure in the 70s, Bowie continued to wield enormous influence on 80s and 90s rock scene. Acting commitments and extra-curricular work may have appeared distracting, but his 1985 hit single duet with Mick Jagger, reworking Martha and The Vandellas' **Dancing In The Street**, indicated no sign of decline.

Bowie then formed Tin Machine in 1988 with Tony Sales, bass, Hunt Sales, drums, and Reeves Gabrels, guitar, following 1987 **Never Let Me Down** set with Peter Frampton. After 1990 'retrospective' Sound And Vision tour, when all the old hits were churned out to the adoring and faithful masses, Bowie vowed that Tin Machine would stand or fall on its own merits.

His parallel acting career has been generally pilloried, and a look at his credits would confirm imaginative, if unwise, choice of movies. Nervous debut was in first interna-

tional film *The Virgin Soldiers* (*Love You 'Til Tuesday* and three-reeler *The Image*, both late 60s, were destined for cine clubs). Bowie was featured in: *The Man Who Fell To Earth* (1976), *Just A Gigolo* (1979), *The Hunger* (1983), *Merry Christmas Mr Lawrence* (1983), *Into The Night* (1985) and the disastrous *Absolute Beginners* (1986). *Labyrinth* (1987) earned a few bucks for producer George Lucas, but Bowie looked distinctly uncomfortable in green paint.

On stage, Bowie played tragic John Merrick in Broadway re-telling of *The Elephant Man*, for which he received excellent reviews. For BBC Television, he starred in Bertolt Brecht's *Baal* (1981). Despite prolific acting career, rumours of David Bowie's move to new stage in music career circulated in early 90s.

Below: Bowie models a dress — androgynous?

Left: Showing extraordinarily good taste, David Bowie demonstrates his guitar technique on an estimable Takamine acoustic. Infant head-bangers please note.

Hit Singles:	US	UK
Space Oddity, 1969	–	5
Starman, 1972	–	10
John I'm Only Dancing, 1972	–	12
Jean Genie, 1972	–	2
Space Oddity, 1973	15	–
Drive In Saturday, 1973	–	3
Life On Mars, 1973	–	3
The Laughing Gnome, 1973	–	6
Sorrow, 1973	–	3
Rebel Rebel, 1974	–	5
Knock On Wood, 1974	–	10
Space Oddity, 1975	–	1
Young Americans, 1975	–	18
Fame, 1975	1	17
Golden Years, 1975	10	8
Sound And Vision, 1977	–	3
Boys Keep Swinging, 1979	–	7
John I'm Only Dancing (re-issue), 1979		12
Ashes To Ashes, 1980	–	1
Fashion, 1980	–	5
Scary Monsters, 1981	–	20
Let's Dance, 1983	1	1
China Girl, 1983	10	2
Modern Love, 1983	14	2
Blue Jean, 1984	8	6
This Is Not America, 1985	–	14
Loving The Alien, 1985	–	19
Day In Day Out, 1987	–	17
Never Let Me Down, 1987	27	34

With Bing Crosby:

Peace On Earth, 1982	–	3

With Mick Jagger:

Dancing In The Street, 1985	7	1

With Queen:

Under Pressure, 1981	29	1

Albums:
The World Of David Bowie (Decca), 1970
The Man Who Sold The World (Mercury/RSA), 1971
Hunky Dory (RCA), 1971
The Rise And Fall Of Ziggy Stardust And The Spiders From Mars (RCA), 1972
Space Oddity (RCA), 1972
Aladdin Sane (RCA), 1973
Pin Ups (RCA), 1973
Diamond Dogs (RCA), 1974
David Live (RCA), 1974
Young Americans (RCA), 1975
Images (Decca), 1975
Station To Station (RCA), 1976
Changesonebowie (RCA), 1976
Low (RCA), 1977
Starting Point (London/–), 1977
Heroes (RCA), 1977
Stage (RCA), 1978
Lodger (RCA), 1979
Scary Monsters (And Super Creeps) (RCA), 1980
Best Of (–/K-Tel), 1980
Another Face (Decca), 1981
Don't Be Fooled By The Name (tracks from 1966) (PRT), 1981
Changes (RCA), 1981
Christianne F (soundtrack) (RCA), 1981
Changestwobowie (RCA), 1981
The Manish Boys, Davy Jones And The Lower Third (Charly), 1981
Rare Bowie (RCA), 1982
Let's Dance (EMI), 1983
Tonight (EMI), 1984
Labyrinth (EMI), 1986
Never Let Me Down (EMI), 1987
Early On 1964-66 (Rhino/–), 1991

Billy Bragg

UK singer/songrwriter, guitarist
Born Barking, Essex, December 20, 1957

Career: Total expenditure of just £175 paid for two-track 'live' recording of **Life's A Riot With Spy Vs Spy** album, subsequently rejected by virtually every record label before Go! Disc decided to give it a shot. Fortunately Go! Disc was rewarded with more than 120,000 sales and a 12-week stint at No. 1 on the independent chart, turning Billy Bragg into instant cult hero.

Having previously worked in punk/R&B band Riff Raff, with an instantly deleted EP **I Wanna Be A Cosmonaut** on Chiswick, Bragg decided in 1982 to go solo, singing self-penned songs with strong political content but with international appeal, witness his growing success in America and Europe.

In many ways a latter-day Dylan, Bragg's protest songs made him a perfect candidate for the 1985 Labour Party 'Red Wedge' rock tour, part of a Jobs For Youth campaign.

Committed Socialist leanings tempered by romantic odes are unlikely to appeal to mass audience, although collaboration with Wet Wet Wet for **Sgt Pepper Knew My Father** was nice little earner for ChildLine charity. Bragg is an honest performer whose own label Utility maintains a 'low-price tag' policy. Damn those capitalists!

Hit Singles:

	US	UK
Between The Wars (EP), 1985	–	18
Levi Stubbs Tears, 1986	–	29
She's Leaving Home, 1988	–	1

Albums:
Life's A Riot With Spy Vs Spy (–/Go! Disc), 1983
Brewing Up With Billy Bragg (–/Go! Disc), 1984
Talking To The Taxman About Poetry (Elektra/Go! Disc), 1986
Back To Basics (Elektra/Go! Disc), 1987
Workers' Playtime (Elektra/Go! Disc), 1988
Help Save The Youth Of America (Elektra), 1988
Internationale (Elektra/Utility), 1990
Don't Try This At Home (Elektra/Go! Disc), 1992

James Brown

US vocalist, composer, also arranger, multi-instrumentalist
Born Macon, Georgia, May 3, 1933

Career: Born into rural poverty, Brown first came to music via gospel. He formed first version of Famous Flames, which included long-time colleague Bobby Byrd, in 1954. Group quickly gained local reputation, Brown already showing impassioned style that was to become trademark. Gospel material gradually shelved in favour of secular songs; **Please Please Please** came to attention of King Records, who signed Brown and Flames and released it as single. Record became major R&B chart success.

Successful follow-up was elusive, and group spent next few years touring small-time club circuit. In September 1958 they went to New York to record; result was gospel-flavoured **Try Me**, group's second hit. Brown consolidated success with string of hit records between 1959 and 1961.

By 1962 Famous Flames had metamorphosed into entire revue, consisting of back-up singers, sizeable band and even own support acts. Brown had developed dynamic

Above: The premier black superstar of the 60s, James Brown.

stage act and offered most exciting live performance of era. Exhilaration of Brown live in front of black audience is captured on seminal double album, **Live At The Apollo**. One of the first live recordings, it was also one of the most successful records by a black artist up to that point and marked beginning of acceptance by white American and international markets.

Hits continued throughout 60s, Brown achieving position as number one black super-star and figurehead for American black consciousness movement. He also acquired reputation as no-nonsense businessman and disciplinarian employer. He toured to capacity audiences all over world, and was especially successful in UK.

After disappearance of King Records in 1970, Brown signed to Polydor; hits continued unabated. During 70s his influence was discernible in work of many new soul/rock/funk bands. Sly And The Family Stone adapted Brown rhythmic patterns and combined them with rock sensibility; others such as Kool And The Gang, Ohio Players, Blackbyrds and Earth, Wind And Fire evolved directly out of Brown's musical approach, creating new funk/dance movement. Brown himself enjoyed massive success with **Body Heat** LP in 1976.

While late 70s were relatively fallow period for Brown, he came back in 1981 with **Rap Payback** his response to success of New York hip-hop cult.

By mid-80s, Brown's rehabilitation was in full swing, with release of Dan Hartman-produced **Gravity** set on Scotti Brothers label, and live set featuring notables like Wilson Pickett and Robert Palmer. Whilst no **Live At The Apollo**, this album nevertheless made most live offerings pale by comparison. With rapper/DJs using sampled Brown material (making our hero a trifle unhappy), the Godfather looked set to challenge a new generation before arrest for firearms offence in 1988. Brown was subsequently jailed for six years, earning release on parole in February 1991. He immediately resumed career, announcing world tour where the funk will be cranked out 'one mo' time'.

Hit Singles:

	US	UK
Prisoner Of Love, 1963	18	–
Papa's Got A Brand New Bag, Part 1, 1965	8	25
I Got You (I Feel Good), 1965	3	29
It's A Man's Man's World, 1966	8	13
Cold Sweat, Part 1, 1967	7	–
I Got The Feelin', 1968	6	–
Licking Stick, Part 1, 1968	14	–
Say It Loud — I'm Black And I'm Proud, 1968	10	–
Give It Up Or Turn It Loose, 1969	15	–
I Don't Want Nobody To Give Me Nothing (Open Up The Door, I'll Get It Myself), 1969	20	–
Mother Popcorn, Part 1, 1969	11	–
Get Up I Feel Like Being A Sex Machine, 1970	15	32
Super Bad (Parts I and II), 1970	13	–
Hot Pants (She Got To Use What She Got To Get What She Wants), Part 1, 1971	15	–
Get On The Good Foot, Part 1, 1972	18	–
Living In America, 1985	–	5
The Playback Mix, 1988	–	12

Albums:
Live At The Apollo (Polydor), 1962
Best Of (Polydor), 1975
Body Heat (Polydor), 1976
Solid Gold (Polydor), 1977
Soul Syndrome (RCA), 1980
Special (Polydor), 1981
Live In New York (SOPI Milan, France), 1981
Bring It On (Sonet), 1983
Greatest Hits (Polydor), 1985
The Compact Disc Of James Brown (Polydor), 1985
Gravity (Scotti Bros/–), 1986
In The Jungle Groove (Polydor), 1986
Sex Machine And Other Soul Classics (Polydor), 1987
Love Overdue (Scotti Bros/–), 1991
Sex Machine (Polydor), 1991
Startime (career set) (Polydor), 1991

Worth Searching Out:
It's A Man's Man's World (Polydor), 1966
Say It Loud I'm Black And I'm Proud (King/Polydor), 1968
Get On The Good Foot (Polydor), 1973
Sex Machine Today (Polydor), 1975

Jackson Browne

UK composer, vocalist, guitarist
Born Heidelberg, Germany, October 9, 1948

Career: Raised in Los Angeles, Browne moved to New York in 1967 and began playing guitar for Nico. She liked his original songs and used three on **Chelsea Girl** album. Soon Browne was placing songs with folk-rock artists such as Johnny Rivers, Nitty Gritty Dirt Band and Tom Rush. Although now largely forgotten or overlooked, Tom Rush was then important musician whose opinion carried great weight in folk community; if Rush was recording songs by somebody named Browne, then Browne must be good.

Browne's multi-talents could never be channelled into one area, so it's not surprising that he signed with Asylum in his own right. **Jackson Browne** LP (1971) contained mostly material already recorded by others. Sales not impressive, but critical reviews were strongly favourable. Browne worked closely with newly formed Eagles, co-writing first major hit, **Take It Easy**. His version is on his second LP, 1973's **For Everyman**. Again reviews bordered on ecstatic; again sales bordered on non-existent. Browne seemed doomed to cult status as excellent composer. His low-key stage performance also seemed antithetical to usual excess prevalent in rock.

But Browne's reputation for heartfelt emotion began spreading and with 1974 release **Late For The Sky** his back catalogue began selling well. Browne's careful approach is not conducive to dashing off albums. His next effort was delayed by suicide of his wife. **The Pretender** seemed to strip Browne to essentials and suddenly he was a star.

Below: Jackson Browne, the Democrats' answer to Arnold Schwarzenegger.

Refusing to cash in on success, he made extended tour of US and Europe, releasing **Running On Empty** in 1978. This album seemed radical departure from past work in that it had rough edges not normally associated with Browne. Critics did not know quite what to make of it, so emphasized risk Browne took in recording under adverse conditions while on tour. The public loved it and sales boomed.

1980 set **Hold Out** marked return of some order in personal life, and his commitment to **No Nukes** live triple album (from Madison Square Garden gig) with Bonnie Raitt, Linda Ronstadt, James Taylor, and others provided decent funds for 'Safe Energy' committee. Browne's determined anti-nuclear stance made him a regular at fund-raising concerts.

Lawyers In Love (1983) ended recording hiatus, but a further three years followed before **Lives In The Balance** surfaced. Both LPs made US Top 50.

With charity shows almost totally dominating Browne's career — he has appeared for American Indian benefits, at Nelson Mandela's 70th Birthday Party show and with Bruce Springsteen to generate funds for a lawsuit citing American Government involvement during Iran/Contra affair — the 1989 **World In Motion** album could conceivably herald another barren period.

Hit Singles:	US	UK
Doctor My Eyes, 1972	8	—
Running On Empty, 1978	11	—
Stay, 1978	20	12
Somebody's Baby, 1982	7	—
Lawyers In Love, 1983	13	—

Albums:
Jackson Browne, Saturate Before Using (Asylum), 1971
For Everyman, (Asylum), 1973
Late For The Sky (Asylum), 1974
The Pretender (Asylum), 1976
Running On Empty (Asylum), 1978
Hold Out (Asylum), 1980
Lawyers In Love (Asylum), 1983
Lives In The Balance (Elektra), 1986
World In Motion (Elektra), 1989

Above: London's own Kate Bush, just a well-kept secret in America.

Kate Bush
UK vocalist, composer
Born London, July 30, 1958

Career: Born into a musical family, Kate studied violin and piano. Leaving school at 16, she signed to EMI having recorded demo tape under aegis of Pink Floyd's Dave Gilmour. She then spent several years writing, making demos and studying dance.

Recorded first album, **The Kick Inside**, in 1978. Single from album, **Wuthering Heights**, shot to top of UK charts on release in early 1978. Instant impact of record was due partly to originality of subject matter and musical treatment, partly to unearthly

quality of Bush's voice. Critics were divided as to worth of artist, some decrying record as mere gimmickry.

However, **Heights** was first of string of hit singles for Bush, which established her as highly creative and innovative artist. Bush's writing style and vocal delivery are instantly recognizable, and her individuality is stamped on clutch of big-selling albums. She has also become renowned for her showmanship and idiosyncratic stage act, which involves elements of dance and mime.

Despite occasional silences, Kate Bush has gained sufficient reputation to intrigue audiences. Sporadic output through the 80s saw some chart action, with **Running Up That Hill** (1985) earning first US chart entry. Greatest hits package **The Whole Story** (1986) made No. 1 in UK album chart, and 1989 folk-styled **The Sensual World** peaked at No. 3, with title track making UK Top 20 singles list.

To commemorate her longevity with label, EMI issued boxed album/CD set **This Woman's Work** (October 1990), a career retrospective which prompted Bush to announce plans for new album and tour.

Hit Singles:	US	UK
Wuthering Heights, 1978	—	1
Man With The Child In His Eyes, 1978	—	6
Wow, 1979	—	14
On Stage (EP), 1979	—	10
Breathing, 1980	—	16
Babooshka, 1980	—	5
Army Dreamers, 1980	—	16
Sat In Your Lap, 1981	—	11
Running Up That Hill, 1985	21	3
Cloudbusting, 1985	—	20
Hounds Of Love, 1986	—	18
Experiment IV, 1986	—	23
Don't Give Up, 1987	—	9
The Sensual World, 1989	—	12
Rocket Man, 1991	—	8

Albums:
The Kick Inside (EMI), 1978
Lionheart (EMI), 1978
Never For Ever (—/EMI), 1980
The Dreaming (EMI), 1982
Hounds Of Love (EMI), 1985
Whole Story (EMI), 1986
The Sensual World (Columbia/EMI), 1989
This Woman's Work Anthology 1979-90 (CD set) (—/EMI), 1990

The Byrds
US group formed 1964

Original line-up: Roger McGuinn, lead guitar, vocals; David Crosby, rhythm guitar, vocals; Gene Clark, vocals, tambourine; Chris Hillman, bass; Michael Clarke, drums.

Career: Originally called the Jet Set before arrival of Hillman and Clarke; recorded series of demos for World Pacific, later released as **Preflyte**. As trio, cut one unsuccessful single for Elektra, **Please Let Me Love You**, then signed to Columbia as The Byrds. Acclaimed as America's answer to The Beatles, they successfully combined the lyrical genius of Dylan with The Beatles' melodic expertise to produce a distinctive style exemplified by million-selling **Mr Tambourine Man**, which topped US and UK charts during summer 1965.

Generally acknowledged as pioneers of 'folk rock', Byrds produced a string of consistently excellent singles during 1965-67, including **Turn! Turn! Turn!**, **Eight Miles High**, **So You Want To Be A Rock 'n' Roll Star** and **My Back Pages**. First two albums consisted mainly of Dylan covers and love songs from the prolific Gene Clark.

By early 1966, folk-rock repertoire was extended to include a number of jazz and hard-rock items. The seminal **Eight Miles High** rivalled the output of such contemporaries as The Beatles and The Stones, but Byrds suffered from radio bans; some numbers were unjustly labelled 'drug songs'.

In March, career development was further complicated by shock departure of Gene Clark. Continuing as quartet, they released **Fifth Dimension**, a neat amalgam of folk-rock orchestration, jazz and raga-tinged rock that fully demonstrated their ability to survive and thrive.

In late 1966, Byrds retired temporarily from live appearances amid speculation that they were breaking up.

1967 was most crucial year in their history, beginning with brilliant **Younger Than Yesterday** LP, which fully demonstrated David Crosby's growing importance as singer/songwriter. More surprisingly, album featured several country-flavoured songs from Chris Hillman, the fourth singer/songwriter to emerge from original line-up. Creative tensions in group led to several flare ups and a struggle for leadership between McGuinn and Crosby. Loss of management team, Jim Dickson and Eddie Tickner, only made matters worse.

Arguments over musical direction precipitated Crosby's sacking in October 1967. He was replaced by former Byrd Gene Clark, who lasted only three weeks before quitting due to ever-present fear of flying. Drummer Michael Clarke quit in disillusionment shortly afterwards, leaving McGuinn and Hillman to complete the excellent **Notorious Byrd Brothers** album, generally hailed as a creative peak in their illustrious careers.

Early in 1968, McGuinn and Hillman recruited Kevin Kelley (drums) and Gram Parsons (guitar/vocals) and plunged headlong into new musical direction. Although McGuinn was intent on recording an electronic-jazz album, it was Parsons and Hillman who proved strongest in determining group's subsequent musical policy. Country and western style **Sweetheart Of The Rodeo** was a perfectly timed reaction against the excesses of psychedelia,

Left: Mr Tambourine Man, The Byrds. Courtesy Columbia Records.

predating Dylan's **Nashville Skyline** by a year. The Byrds' interest in country music continued, even after Parsons decided to quit on eve of an abortive South African tour.

Late 1968 was another period of flux, culminating in departure of Hillman following a dispute with McGuinn. By end of year, group was almost totally restructured with introduction of bluegrass virtuoso Clarence White (guitar), John York (bass) Gene Parsons (drums).

From 1969 onwards, McGuinn assumed sole control of Byrds while ex-members went on to fame and fortune in offshoot groups, including Flying Burrito Brothers, Dillard And Clark, Crosby Stills Nash & Young, Manassas, the Souther-Hillman-Furay Band and Firefall.

Recruitment of bassist Skip Battin (replacing York) produced settled line-up during early 70s, but quality of group's work declined significantly. There were, however, occasional high points, particularly the double album (untitled) which included group's last hit single, **Chestnut Mare**.

By 1972, several members had drifted into various unproductive solo ventures and group shortly disbanded. Original quintet reformed for one album, but results were not encouraging enough to inspire follow-up. During same disastrous year, former members Clarence White and Gram Parsons died in tragic circumstances: White in hit and run accident, Parsons of drug overdose.

Following uneven set of solo albums, McGuinn, Hillman and Clark reunited during late 70s, but failed to revive group's career. Apart from Crosby, McGuinn has remained most prominent ex-Byrd, but his solo output has been almost non-existant, with just **Thunderbyrd** (1977) and **Back From Rio** (1991) to his name.

Following period with Souther-Hillman-Furay Band, Hillman formed The Desert Rose Band in 1984, and also joined Crosby and McGuinn for weekend gig at LA club in order to retain rights to Byrds name which had been used by Gene Clark (who died on May 21, 1991) and Michael Clark for their touring outfit. This trio also surfaced at Roy Orbison tribute night in LA (1990).

Following release of four CD boxed set **The Byrds** (1990), which McGuinn supervised, band was inducted into Rock 'n' Roll Hall Of Fame.

Hit Singles:

	US	UK
Mr Tambourine Man, 1965	1	1
All I Really Want To Do, 1965	40	4
Turn! Turn! Turn!, 1965	1	–
Eight Miles High, 1966	14	–
Chestnut Mare, 1971	–	19

Albums:
Preflyte (Together) (Columbia/CBS), 1969
Mr Tambourine Man (Columbia/CBS), 1965*
Turn! Turn! Turn! (Columbia/CBS), 1965*
Fifth Dimension (Columbia/CBS), 1966
Younger Than Yesterday (Columbia/CBS), 1967
Greatest Hits (Columbia/CBS), 1967
The Notorious Byrd Brothers (Columbia/CBS), 1968†
Sweetheart Of The Rodeo (Columbia/CBS), 1968†
Dr Byrd And Mr Hyde (Columbia/CBS), 1969
Ballad Of Easy Rider (Columbia/CBS), 1969
Greatest Hits Volume II (Columbia/CBS), 1971
History Of The Byrds (CBS), 1973
The Byrds Play Dylan (Columbia/CBS), 1979
The Original Singles Volume I (Columbia/CBS), 1980

Right: Mariah Carey, dance music's answer to the dog whistle.

The Original Singles Volume II (Columbia/CBS), 1982
The Byrds (four CD set) (Columbia), 1990
*Available as double LP set (Columbia), US only
†Available as double album, UK only, 1976

McGuinn Solo:
Back From Rio (Arista), 1991

Captain Beefheart
US composer, vocalist, multi-instrumentalist
Born Don Van Vliet, Glendale, California, January 15, 1941

Career: As young man in California Van Vliet tried playing straight with group called Blackouts. Assuming name Captain Beefheart (a name not so unusual now, but rather outrageous in 1964) he formed loose confederation of forever-changing musicians called the Magic Band. In what some called his last touch with reality, he released 'commercial' single **Diddy Wah Diddy** on A&M. Then he began changing record labels almost as fast as he changed band members.

Safe As Milk in spring 1967 was very avant-garde, very original, and very much an inside joke. Critics like to consider themselves insiders and Beefheart quickly became known as someone to like, not because you listened to his records, but to be 'cool'.

Above: Safe As Milk, Captain Beefheart. Courtesy Kama Sutra Records.

Beefheart recorded **Mirror Man** next but no one would release it until Buddah took a chance in 1973. With third line-up in 12 months, Beefheart recorded **Strictly Personal** which he got Blue Thumb to release in December 1968. Beefheart's excuse for this one was that it was mixed without his

supervision. Next record was definitely going to be *it*. He signed with old friend Frank Zappa's label, Straight.

Trout Mask Replica was made with no restraints, and no effort to be commercial. This was art. Critics fell over themselves praising it as one of rock's truly innovative moments; rock public fell over itself avoiding it. Zappa and Beefheart fell out over who was responsible. Straight released a second Beefheart album with one of rock's better titles, **Lick My Decals Off, Baby**.

Moving to Reprise, Captain released somewhat blues-based **The Spotlight Kid**, then **Clear Spot**. Both were departures in containing some identifiable tunes. Another record deal in 1974 (Mercury/Fame) launched Captain yet again. **Unconditionally Guaranteed** was commercial sell-out of his career. To avoid falling into rut, he quickly followed up with demented **Blue Jeans And Moonbeams**.

In 1975 he dissolved Magic Band (who resented dismissal and went on to fail on own as new group called Mallard). Beefheart collaborated with Zappa on **Bongo Fury** album and in 1976 recorded 'solo' effort. (Warner Bros eventually released **Shiny Beast Bat Chain Puller** in 1978.) With new Magic Band, Beefheart released **Doc At The Radar Station** (1980) and **Ice Cream For Crow** (1982), the latter a minor hit for the Captain.

Divided opinion for a man called either a 'visionary' or 'bonkers' has placed Beefheart in esoteric class. But his diffidence to the music business, and preference for painting, might eventually consign this eccentric to rock's scrap heap.

Albums:
Safe As Milk (Kama Sutra/Pye), 1967
Strictly Personal (Blue Thumb/Liberty), 1968
Trout Mask Replica (Straight), 1970
Lick My Decals Off, Baby (Straight), 1970*
The Spotlight Kid (Reprise), 1972*
Clear Spot (Reprise), 1972
Mirror Man (Buddah/Pye), 1973
Unconditionally Guaranteed (Mercury/Fame), 1974
The Captain Beefheart File (–/Pye), 1977
Shiny Beast Bat Chain Puller (Warner Bros/Virgin), 1978
Two Originals Of...(–/Reprise), 1979
Doc At The Radar Station (Virgin), 1980
Ice Cream For Crow (Virgin), 1982
Blue Jeans And Moonbeams (Virgin), 1984
*Released as double album set (–/Reprise), 1976

Mariah Carey
US vocalist
Born New York, March 22, 1970

Career: Genuine vocal talent, whose extraordinary range includes notes only bats can hear. Carey is the current queen of hip dance and soul crowd.

Born into a musical family (her mother was an opera singer), Carey was quickly signed by Columbia Records upon hearing demo tape. Lavish press launch preceded acclaimed rendition of national anthem before American national basketball championship finals in 1990.

With soul veteran Narada Michael Walden producing, first eponymous album provided single hit **Vision Of Love**, which earned artist a Grammy for Best Female Vocal Performance. *Rolling Stone* magazine and Soul Train TV show also honoured Carey with a collection of awards.

Second album **Emotions** (1991) provided US No. 1 hit with title track, but there was concern that there would be a paucity of good material beyond single cuts.

Hit Singles:

	US	UK
Vision Of Love, 1990	1	9
Love Takes Time, 1990	1	37
Someday, 1991	1	38
Emotions, 1991	1	16
I Don't Wanna Cry, 1991	1	–

Albums:
Mariah Carey (Columbia), 1990
Emotions (Columbia), 1991

Belinda Carlisle
US vocalist
Born Hollywood, California, August 16, 1958

Career: Former lead-singer of all-girl group Go Gos, whose termination in 1985 allowed Carlisle free-rein to develop glam image and pure pop approach.

First solo album **Belinda** (1986), co-produced by another ex-Go Go Charlotte Caffey, included chart single **Mad About You**. Having completed contractual obligations with IRS, Carlisle signed for MCA (1987), debuting with **Heaven On Earth** (released by Virgin UK in Britain). Title track topped both UK/US charts, while LP subsequently went platinum. A former 'chubby', Carlisle's revised figure and movie looks ensured a five-star rating for accompanying videos, sympathetically directed by Diane Keaton.

First major tour (1988) saw Carlisle appear in US, Canada, Japan and UK, where London media were all a 'go-go' upon her arrival. Alleged 'misdemeanours' while with band attracted tabloids in force, but artist's modest and considered temperament killed 'drug-crazed rock star' stories stone dead.

For 1989 set **Runaway Horses**, Carlisle recruited former members of Go-Gos for **Shades Of Michaelangelo** track and prompted rumours of possible reformation. Band did reunite for charity gigs in 1990, but permanent reconciliation looked ever more unlikely, despite success of greatest hits package in the same year.

Married to the late James Mason's son, Morgan, Carlisle is a vociferous campaigner for animal rights and the environment, and has lent her name to various charitable institutions.

Below: Belinda Carlisle forsook fame with the Go Gos to go solo.

Hit Singles:

	US	UK
Heaven Is A Place On Earth, 1987	1	1
I Get Weak, 1988	2	10
Circle In The Sand, 1988	7	4
Leave A Light On, 1989	11	4
(We Want) The Same Thing, 1990	—	6

Albums:

Belinda Carlisle (IRS/—), 1986
Heaven On Earth (MCA/Virgin), 1988
Runaway Horses (MCA/Virgin), 1989
Live Your Life Be Free (—/Offside), 1991

Kim Carnes
US vocalist, pianist, composer
Born Los Angeles, July 20, 1945

Career: Former member of New Christy Minstrels, Carnes' career was taking a distinctly MOR direction when **Bette Davis Eyes** cut loose in 1981.

One-time commercials writer/performer, Carnes first attracted attention with A&M albums **Kim Carnes** and **Sailin'**, produced by Mentor Williams and Jerry Wexler respectively. A prolific writer (with husband David Ellingson), her material has been recorded by such artists as Anne Murray, Frank Sinatra and Barbra Streisand.

Cut **Don't Fall In Love With A Dreamer** with Kenny Rogers, another ex-New Christy Ministrel, in 1979. Rogers subsequently recorded album of Carnes/Ellingson material, **Gideon** (1980).

Bette Davis Eyes (written by Jackie De Shannon, whose husky vocals Carnes successfully emulated) pushed the LA native into rock mainstream; though not quite emulating Grammy winning **Eyes**, a long-term deal with MCA resulted in promising **View From The House** set in 1988.

Hit Singles:

	US	UK
More Love, 1980	10	—
Bette Davis Eyes, 1981	1	10

With Kenny Rogers:

Don't Fall In Love With A Dreamer, 1980	4	—

Albums:

Kim Carnes (A&M), 1976
Sailin' (A&M), 1977
St Vincents Court (EMI), 1979
Romance Dance (EMI), 1980
Best Of (A&M), 1981
Mistaken Identity (EMI), 1981
Voyeur (EMI), 1982
Café Racers (EMI), 1983
Lighthouse (EMI), 1986
View From The House (MCA), 1988

The Carpenters
US duo formed 1969
Richard Carpenter, vocals, keyboards; born New Haven, Connecticut, October 15, 1945
Karen Carpenter, vocals, drums; born New Haven, Connecticut, March 2, 1950; died December, 1982

Career: Richard began playing piano at 12, while younger sister Karen developed interest in drums. When Carpenter family moved to Downey, California, in early 60s, brother and sister recruited bass player to form jazz outfit. Trio won Hollywood Battle Of The Bands contest, but was soon

Above: The late Karen Carpenter with brother Richard.

disbanded as Richard and Karen developed interest in vocal harmonies. Next band, Spectrum, comprised Richard and Karen plus four others, and was equally short-lived.

Duo decided to experiment on their own with vocal harmony effects, using overdubbing techniques. Demo tapes were eventually heard by Herb Alpert of A&M Records, who signed pair as The Carpenters. Success was almost immediate; 1970 Bacharach-David million-seller **Close To You** set pattern for string of hit singles lasting into mid-70s. At same time, duo notched up massive album sales worldwide (1974 album **The Singles 1969-73** became one of the all-time biggest-selling albums). Concert appearances were equally popular.

Appeal of act was based on Karen Carpenter's limpid voice, excellent material from writers such as Bacharach-David and Paul Williams, and unique vocal harmony blend. Richard Carpenter was mainly responsible for arranging and musical direction. Although often critically berated for blandness and wholesome, clean-cut image, The Carpenters were praised by musicians and industry insiders for musicianship, excellent choice of sidemen, such as virtuoso guitarist Tony Peluso and professionalism.

Debilitating illness suffered by Karen reduced duo's status during late 70s, although 1981 set **Made In America** enjoyed chart action. Sadly, The Carpenters' story ended in 1983 with the death of Karen due to heart failure exacerbated by anorexia. TV movie *The Karen Carpenter Story*, starring Cynthia Gibb (1989), and **Only Yesterday** greatest hits compilation saw renewed interest in family, with Richard also busy, re-mixing classic tracks for re-issue.

Hit Singles:

	US	UK
Close To You, 1970	1	6
We've Only Just Begun, 1970	2	28
For All We Know, 1971	3	—
Rainy Days And Mondays, 1971	2	—
Superstar/For All We Know, 1971	—	18
Superstar, 1971	2	—
Hurting Each Other, 1972	2	—
It's Going To Take Some Time, 1972	12	—
I Won't Last A Day Without You/ Goodbye To Love, 1972	—	9
Goodbye To Love, 1972	7	—
Sing, 1973	3	—
Yesterday Once More, 1973	2	2
Top Of The World, 1973	1	5
Jambalaya/Mr Guder, 1974	—	12
I Won't Last A Day Without You 1974	11	32
Please Mr Postman, 1975	1	2
Only Yesterday, 1975	4	7
Solitaire, 1975	17	32
There's A Kind Of Hush, 1976	12	22
Calling Occupants Of Interplanetary Craft, 1977	32	9
Touch Me When We're Dancing, 1981	16	—

Albums:

Close To You (A&M), 1971
The Carpenters (A&M), 1971
Ticket To Ride (A&M), 1972
A Song For You (A&M), 1972
Now And Then (A&M), 1973
The Singles 1969-73 (A&M), 1974
Greatest Hits (—/Hallmark), 1974
Horizon (A&M), 1975
Live In Japan (A&M), 1975
A Kind Of Hush (A&M), 1976
The Carpenters Collection (—/A&M), 1976
Live At The Palladium (A&M), 1977
Passage (A&M), 1977
The Singles 1974-78 (A&M), 1978
Made In America (A&M), 1981
An Old Fashioned Christmas (A&M), 1984
Yesterday Once More (EMI), 1985
Voice Of The Heart (A&M), 1987

The Cars
US group formed 1976

Original line-up: Ric Ocasek, guitar, vocals; Ben Orr, bass, vocals; Greg Hawkes, keyboards, vocals, sax, percussion; Elliot Easton, guitar; David Robinson, drums.

Career: Richard Otcasek was born and raised near Cleveland, Ohio. He went East to Boston and became Ric Ocasek. In early 70s he met and began working with Ben Orr in various small local bands. Mid-70s brought in Greg Hawkes. Ocasek was clearly focal point of this melting pot but he was also very much open to others' ideas and opinions. Trio did various demo tapes and kept in touch with each other while Ocasek came across Elliot Easton in another local band.

Meanwhile Bostonian David Robinson, who had been playing in Jonathan Richman's

Modern Lovers, moved to Los Angeles. After short time with highly underrated The Pop, he returned to Boston. There he joined Ocasek's group, was impressed by team spirit and offered up name he had been saving: The Cars.

In February 1977 Cars began playing at Boston's club The Rat where ability to mix enthusiasm with professional musicianship marked them as special. In 1978 they signed to Elektra who teamed them with Roy Thomas Baker as producer, and first album followed. As strong as album became after several plays, several tracks were masterpieces in own right as singles. Even new wave-orientated UK proved susceptible to Cars' music and made **My Best Friend's Girl** No. 3.

Candy-O (1979) could only prove anticlimatic, especially as recorded quickly between tours. But Cars proved their commitment to rock by refusing to do US TV's *Midnight Special* unless they got complete control of guests and presentation. They turned 1979 show into masterpiece of what rock *could* be on television.

Panorama (1980) seemed a reaction to the critics who complained Cars were too slick and too mechanical. 1981 saw release of **Shake It Up** which almost recaptured first album's balance. Despite public effort to present Cars in group image, Ocasek's personality was too strong not to emerge as head Car. 1982 proved this as no new Cars album appeared. However, US got **Beatitude**, a Ocasek solo album sounding a lot like . . . a new Cars album.

March 1984 saw release of fifth album, **Heartbeat City**, produced by Robert John 'Mutt' Lange of AC/DC and Foreigner renown, and major hit single **Drive** (latter entering UK charts in 1985 after its use during Live Aid concert). Following **Door To Door** set (1987) Ocasek announced break-up of band, allowing members to concentrate on solo projects, with Ocasek's **Emotion In Motion** single and 1991 LP **Fireball Zone**, with Nile Rodgers on guitar, proving, so far, the most successful releases.

Hit Singles:

	US	UK
My Best Friend's Girl, 1978	35	3
Just What I Needed, 1979	27	17
Let's Go, 1979	14	—
Shake It Up, 1982	4	—
You Might Think, 1984	7	—
Magic, 1984	12	—
Drive, 1984*	3	4
Hello Again, 1984	20	—
Tonight She Comes, 1986	9	—
You Are The Girl, 1987	17	—
*1985 in UK		

Right: Ex-Cars front-man Ric Ocasek, now working in the Fireball Zone.

Albums:
The Cars (Elektra), 1978
Candy-O (Elektra), 1979
Panorama (Elektra), 1980
Shake It Up (Elektra), 1981
Heartbeat City (Elektra), 1984
Greatest Hits (Elektra), 1985
Door To Door (Elektra), 1987

Elliott Easton Solo:
Change No Change (Elektra), 1985

Ric Ocasek Solo:
Beatitude (Elektra), 1982
This Side Of Paradise (Geffen), 1986
Fireball Zone (Reprise), 1991

Ben Orr Solo:
The Lace (Elektra), 1987

Tracy Chapman

US vocalist, composer, guitarist
Born Cleveland, Ohio, 1964

Career: Hypnotic performance at 1988
Nelson Mandela Birthday Party concert at
London's Wembley Stadium before a worldwide television audience and 80,000 sell-
out crowd thrust Chapman's self-titled debut
album to top of UK album chart less than
a month later.

A major in African Studies at Tufts University, Massachusetts, Chapman enjoyed
entertaining fellow pupils with her pointed
folk/blues style. Student Brian Koppelman
recommended Chapman to his father, president of publishing house SBK, whose connections with Elektra Records secured album
deal. With veteran folk producer David Ker-
shenbaum (Joan Baez, Richie Havens) in
charge, **Tracy Chapman** set was released
in 1988, from which **Fast Car** single made
both UK and US Top 10.

Chapman's politically motivated music
was ideally suited to aspirations of pro-
moters of Amnesty International global tour
in autumn 1988, which saw artist in exulted
company of Sting, Peter Gabriel and Bruce
Springsteen.

With reputation seemingly established, second LP **Crossroads** disappointed, although
achieved No. 1 status in UK. Following US
tour in 1990, Chapman felt critical and public
success might be better retained by a more
considered approach to career.

Hit Singles:	US	UK
Fast Car, 1988	20	5

Albums:
Tracy Chapman (Elektra), 1988
Crossroads (Elektra), 1989

The Charlatans

UK group formed 1986

Original line-up: Baz Kettley, vocals; Rob
Collins, keyboards; Jon Baker, guitar; Martin Blunt, bass; John Brookes, drums.

Career: Part of the Manchester 'baggy'
phenomenon (the 60s revisited) which also
sprouted Happy Mondays and Stone Roses
in the late 80s.

With their jangly guitars, moody organ and
Beatle haircuts, the post-hippy Charlatans
made immediate impact when debut album
Some Friendly debuted at No. 1 in UK album
chart, 1990. Managed by record shop pro-
prietor Steve Harrison, they had previously
cut indie single **Indian Rope** for own Dead
Good label and secured fan-base when supporting fellow Mancunians Stone Roses.

Some Friendly (with Tim Burgess as new
vocalist) provided chart cuts **The Only One
I Know** and **Then**, and band enjoyed
burgeoning following in France. Stand-alone
single **Over Rising** disappointed, and group
retreated after short English tour, with
bassist Blunt 'exhausted'.

With new guitarist Mark Collins (ex-
Waltones) replacing Baker, Charlatans
returned to studio in autumn 1991 to complete second LP, from which gloomy **Me In
Time** was projected single.

Hit Singles:	US	UK
The Only One I Know, 1990	–	9
Then, 1990	–	12
Over Rising, 1991	–	15

Albums:
Some Friendly (Beggar's Banquet/
Situation 2), 1990

Ray Charles

US vocalist, pianist, composer, arranger
Born Ray Charles Robinson, Albany, Georgia,
September 23, 1930

Career: Brought up in Greenville, Florida,
Charles was blinded by glaucoma at age six.
He showed early signs of musical talent, and
was sent to State School for Blind at seven.
He remained until 15, concentrating on
musical studies, and by early teens was
already playing piano semi-professionally.
On death of his mother in 1945 he became
full-time musician.

Early experience on road included stint as
part of blues singer Lowell Fulsom's band.
First band Charles led was called McSon Trio.
Recorded number of Nat Cole – influenced
sides for small local labels.

Big career break was signing with nascent black music label Atlantic; **It Should
Have Been Me**, a semi-humorous blues
number, was R&B hit in 1954.

During this period Charles began to move
away from Cole influence and developed idiosyncratic style based on mixture of seculariz-
ed gospel and blues. At same time he put
together band of top-echelon jazz musicians;
result was commercial and critical success.

Charles broke pop market in 1959 with
What'd I Say, a wildly exciting single that
synthesized blues, gospel, and rock 'n' roll
in one dynamic package. Made Top 10 of pop
charts and started Charles' career as performer of wide appeal.

**Left: Powerhouse singer-songwriter
Tracy Chapman was, literally, an overnight success in 1988.**

**Above: The five-piece Charlatans,
prominent members of the UK's
North-Eastern 'baggy' music scene.**

Following big money offer, Charles left
Atlantic for ABC-Paramount at end of 1959.
He continued to make excellent recordings,
particularly of blues-based material, and
notch up major hits. **Georgia On My Mind**,
a reading of Hoagy Carmichael standard
which set Charles' emotion-filled voice
against string backing, was Top 30 hit in
UK and established Charles internationally.

Further landmark was created in 1962
when Charles recorded album of country
songs, **Modern Sounds In Country And
Western**. Idea of black R&B star covering
country songs seemed outlandish at time,
but concept was successful both artistically
and commercially, and resulted in huge album
sales and hit singles like **I Can't Stop Loving You**. That year Charles sold then
phenomenal amount of eight million dollars
worth of records (he has had nearly 70 US
chart singles), and became major international star, in demand for TV and concert
dates all over world.

During 60s Charles' career assumed fairly consistent pattern; albums contained mixture of R&B and more pop-orientated
material, and live appearances became well-
oiled and disciplined runthroughs of hits.

The 70s saw changes in record company
arrangements. In 1973, he severed connections with ABC to form own label, Crossover,
and in 1977 Crossover became distributed
and marketed by his old company, Atlantic.

During 80s and early 90s, Charles took
advantage of 'legendary' status to feature
in movie *The Blues Brothers*, television roles
in *St. Elsewhere*, *Moonlighting* and *Who's
The Boss*, and promotional tie-in with Pepsi
Cola and Kentucky Fried Chicken. A prime-
mover behind **We Are The World** single,
Charles also appeared at John Lennon
Tribute Concert. Recipient of 1991 Grammy for **I'll Be Good To You** single (with
Chaka Khan), artist was also honoured by
NARAS with Lifetime Achievement award,
and, later, when classic **I've Got A Woman**
was selected for the Rock Hall Of Fame.

Still an energetic performer, Charles mixes
in the highest company for live dates, such
as BB King, Paul McCartney, and the New
York City Ballet, among others. He was inducted into Rock 'n' Roll Hall Of Fame in
1986, a fitting tribute for a true genius.

Hit Singles:	US	UK
What'd I Say, 1959	6	–
Georgia On My Mind, 1960	1	24
One Mint Julep, 1961	8	–
Hit The Road Jack, 1961	1	6
Unchain My Heart, 1961	9	–
Hide Nor Hair, 1962	20	–
I Can't Stop Loving You, 1962	1	1
You Don't Know Me, 1962	2	9
You Are My Sunshine, 1962	7	–
Your Cheating Heart, 1962	29	13
Don't Set Me Free, 1963	20	37
Take These Chains From My Heart, 1963	8	5
Busted, 1963	4	21
That Lucky Old Sun, 1964	20	–
Crying Time, 1966	6	50
Together Again, 1966	19	48
Here We Go Again, 1967	15	38

Albums:
Ray Charles At Newport (Atlantic), 1958
The Great Ray Charles (Atlantic/London),
1958
Genius Of Ray Charles (Atlantic/Boulevard),
1960
Ray Charles Live (Atlantic/–), 1965
25th Anniversary in Showbusiness (ABC/
Atlantic), 1971
Come Live With Me (Crossover/London),
1974
World Of (–/Decca), 1974
World Of Volume 2 (–/Decca), 1975
Focus On Ray Charles (London), 1975
My Kind Of Jazz Volume 3 (Crossover/–),
1975
Renaissance (Crossover/London), 1975
Porgy And Bess (with Cleo Laine)
(RCA/London), 1976
What Have I Done To Their Songs (London),
1977
True To Life (Atlantic/London), 1977
Love And Peace (Atco/London), 1978
Ray Charles Blues (–/Ember), 1978
20 Golden Pieces Of (–/Bulldog), 1979
Ain't It So (–/London), 1979
A Ray Of Hope (–/Manhattan), 1980
Brother Ray (London), 1980
Everything (–/Manhattan), 1980
I Can't Stop Loving You (–/Pickwick), 1980
Simply Ray (–/Manhattan), 1980
Great Hits (–/Phoenix), 1982
Standing On The Edge (Epic), 1985
The Right Time (Atlantic), 1987
Ray Charles (Entertainers), 1987
Just Between Us (Columbia/CBS), 1988

With Milt Jackson:
Soul Brothers (Atlantic/London), 1959
Soul Meeting (Atlantic), 1962

Worth Searching Out:
Yes Indeed (Atlantic/London), 1958
What'd I Say (Atlantic/London), 1959
Ray Charles And Betty Carter (ABC/HMV),
1960
Genius+Soul=Jazz (Atlantic/HMV), 1961
Modern Sounds In Country And Western
(ABC/HMV), 1962
Do I Ever Cross Your Mind (CBS), 1984
Tell The Truth (Charly), 1984
The Fantastic Ray Charles (Musidisc), 1985

Cher

US vocalist
Born Cherilyn Sarkasian LaPierre,
El Centro, California, May 20, 1946

Career: High priestess of glam rock, whose elegant and glossy persona hovers near the edge of good taste. Natural self-deprecating style saw her move effortlessly from pop arena to Hollywood in early 80s.

After unsuccessful early stint in LA, Cher was hired as session singer by Phil Spector, and featured on several classic Spectorama productions. Met Sonny Bono (born Salvatore Bono, Detroit, February 12, 1935) at Ronettes studio date, and he persuaded Spector to cut novelty single **I Love You Ringo** with Cher, released under Bonnie Joe Mason moniker in 1964; as Cherilyn, **Dream Baby** cut was issued by Imperial Records in same year.

Sonny Bono had extensive experience in music business, as writer and house producer for Specialty Records. Penned classic Searchers' million-seller **Needles And Pins** (with Jack Nitszche), **She Said Yeah** and **High School Dance**, an R&B hit for Larry Williams.

Anxious to obtain outlet for new material, Bono teamed with Cher (they were married in 1964), and cut singles for Reprise as Caesar And Cleo and for Vault as Sonny And Cher. After 1965 pact with Atco (subsidiary of Atlantic), debut 45 for label, **I Got You Babe**, earned No. 1 spot on both sides of the Atlantic. As the acceptable face of hippiedom, Sonny And Cher enjoyed crossover status, own television show and an almost permanent spot on charts during mid-60s.

After a nine year tenure, pair's personal and professional relationship was expunged, although duo reprised TV series in 1976. Bono subsequently eked out living on fringe

Below: Cher, resplendent in very little but her underwear.

of show biz, with an occasional movie role, before entering politics. Elected mayor of Palm Springs in 1988, and ran for Senate (as Republican) in autumn 1991.

Cher's solo career, precipitated while still with Sonny, flourished briefly before ill-advised period in mid-70s saw her flounder uncomfortably in heavy rock medium. Marriage to Gregg Allman, with whom she cut **Allman & Woman** (1977) and romance with Gene Simmonds of Kiss spelt unbridled joy for tabloid headline writers, but did not auger well with AOR audience. After barren period in charts, following a series of memorable hits including **Bang, Bang, Gypsies, Tramps & Thieves** and **Dark Lady**, Cher returned with disco fodder **Take Me Home** in 1979. Later featured with then current beau Les Dudek in his band, Black Rose, and was uncredited vocalist on Meat Loaf single **Dead Ringer For Love**.

Abrupt career move in 1982 saw Cher surprising member of Robert Altman's company for Broadway production of *Come Back To The Five And Dime, Jimmy Dean, Jimmy Dean*, and she later starred in Altman's movie interpretation. Disappointing performance of **I Paralyze** album in same year for new label CBS hastened Cher's decision to pursue possibilities in acting profession. In 1983, her prosaic manner in *Silkwood* earned Oscar nomination, and as unconventional mother of disabled Eric Stoltz in *Mask*, Cher unveiled formidable talent for gritty, down-to-earth characterization.

In 1987, Cher starred in *The Witches of Eastwick, Suspect*, and *Moonstruck*, the later earning her an Academy Award as Best Actress. For Geffen Records, singer returned to studios with **I Found Someone**, produced by Michael Bolton. Reunited with Sonny, pair sang **I Got You Babe** on David Letterman's NBC television show later in the same year.

Comfortable in dual role as singer/actress, Cher saw eponymously titled comeback album for Geffen label make both US and UK Top 40. Single **We All Sleep Alone**,

co-written and produced with Jon Bon Jovi, cracked US Top 20 in June 1988.

Taking advantage of resurgent music career, Cher cut **Heart Of Stone** album in 1989, from which **If I Could Turn Back Time** single made US/UK Top 10 listings. A return to live dates in 1990 (her back-up band included son Elija Allman) put film schedule temporarily on back-burner, although role as Bob Hoskins' moll in *Mermaids* film maintained celluloid connection. **Shoop Shoop Song** from the movie charted in US and UK in 1991.

A free-spirit and occasionally wayward angel, Cher has taken erotic image beyond what the Baptists would term 'decent'. Nonetheless, her unquestioned talent and doe-eyed innocence have united a wide band of supporters quite willing to forgive these minor indiscretions.

Hit Singles:	US	UK
All I Really Want To Do, 1965	–	9
Bang Bang, 1966	2	3
You Better Sit Down Kids, 1967	9	–
Gypsies, Tramps And Thieves, 1971	1	4
The Way Of Love, 1972	7	–
Half-Breed, 1973	1	–
Dark Lady, 1974	1	36
Take Me Home, 1979	8	–
I Found Someone, 1987	10	5
We All Sleep Alone, 1988	14	–
If I Could Turn Back Time, 1989	3	6
After All (with Peter Cetera), 1989	6	–
Just Like Jesse James, 1990	8	11
Shoop Shoop Song, 1991	33	1
Love And Understanding, 1991	17	10

Albums:
Cher (Geffen), 1982
I Paralyze (Columbia/CBS), 1982
Heart Of Stone (Geffen), 1989
Bang Bang: The Best Of (EMI), 1990
Gypsies, Tramps And Thieves (MCA), 1990
Love Hurts (Geffen), 1991

Chicago

US group formed 1968

Original line-up: Robert Lamm, keyboards, lead vocals; Terry Kath, guitar, lead vocals; Peter Cetera, bass, lead vocals; Lee Loughnana, trumpet, background vocals; James Pankow, trombone; Walter Parazaider, woodwinds, background vocals; Daniel Seraphine, drums.

Career: Formed as the Big Thin in 1968, name changed to Chicago Transit Authority. Made big reputation in Chicago (shortening name to simply 'Chicago' when sued by Mayor Daley) before moving to Los Angeles and linking with producer/manager James William Guercio. Debut album **Chicago Transit Authority** (1969) won immediate acclaim for its blend of black-influenced rhythm section and jazzy brass section – in similar mode to also emergent Blood Sweat And Tears. Album was massive seller, staying in chart for amazing six years.

Subsequent albums, called Chicago 1-11 etc., appeared at regular annual intervals and run of singles like **I'm A Man** (a punchy 1970 version of Spencer Davis Group oldie), **Make Me Smile, 25 Or 6 To 4** and romantic chart-topping ballad **If You Leave Me Now** have made them one of the highest-earning groups in rock. They are reputed to have generated more than $160 million in sales, their 14 albums selling 20 million copies.

Following death of guitarist Terry Kath (playing Russian roulette), band went into limbo for short time. He was eventually replaced by Donnie Dacus. Comeback 1980 world tour included concert before 150,000 audience at Chicago Festival.

Unceremoniously dumped by Columbia, who felt band had outlived their appeal, Chicago found welcome at Full Moon in 1982. Move revitalized stagnating recording career.

Loss of bass player and vocalist Peter Cetera, who enjoyed immediate single success in 1986 with **Glory Of Love** and duet with Amy Grant **The Next Time I Fall**, also failed to halt Chicago bandwagon. Cetera's replacement was Jason Scheff, son of former Elvis Presley sideman Jerry Scheff. Original member Seraphine also quit, in 1990, prior to **Twenty 1** album.

With regular output, and a solid touring schedule (band shared dates with Beach Boys in 1989), Chicago provide outstanding musicianship garnered in a 25-year career.

Hit Singles:	US	UK
I'm A Man, 1970	–	8
Make Me Smile, 1970	9	–
25 Or 6 To 4, 1970	4	7
Does Anybody Really Know What Time It Is? 1970	7	–
Free, 1971	20	–
Beginnings/Color My World, 1971	7	–
Saturday In The Park, 1972	3	–
Feelin' Stronger Every Day, 1973	10	–
Just You 'n' Me, 1973	4	–
(I've Been) Searchin' So Long, 1974	9	–
Call On Me, 1974	6	–
Wishing You Were Here, 1974	11	–
Harry Truman, 1975	13	–
Old Days, 1975	5	–
If You Leave Me Now, 1976	1	1
Baby What A Big Surprise, 1977	4	41
Live Again, 1978	14	–
No Tell Lover, 1979	14	–
Hard For Me To Say I'm Sorry, 1982	1	4
Stay The Night, 1984	16	–
Hard Habit To Break, 1984	3	8
You're The Inspiration, 1985	3	14
Long Comes A Woman, 1985	14	–
If She Would Have Been Faithful, 1987	12	–
Will You Still Love Me, 1987	2	–
I Don't Want To Live Without Your Love, 1988	3	–
One Good Woman, 1988	4	–
Look Away, 1988	1	–
You're Not Alone, 1989	10	–
What Kind Of Man Would I Be, 1991	5	–

Albums:
Chicago Transit Authority (Columbia/CBS), 1968
Chicago (Columbia/CBS), 1970
Chicago 3 (Columbia/CBS), 1971
Chicago 4 Live At Carnegie Hall (Columbia/CBS), 1971
Chicago 5 (Columbia/CBS), 1972
Chicago 6 (Columbia/CBS), 1973
Chicago 7 (Columbia/CBS), 1974
Chicago 8 (Columbia/CBS), 1975
Chicago 9 Greatest Hits (Columbia/CBS), 1975
Chicago 10 (Columbia/CBS), 1976
Chicago 11 (Columbia/CBS), 1977
Hot Streets (Columbia/CBS), 1978
Chicago 13 (Columbia/CBS), 1979
Chicago 14 (Columbia/CBS), 1980
Greatest Hits Volume 2 (Columbia/CBS), 1982
If You Leave Me Now (–/CBS), 1982
Love Songs (–/TV), 1982

Toronto Rock 'n' Roll Revival 1969, Volume 1
  (Accord/—), 1982
Chicago 16 (Full Moon), 1982
Chicago 17 (Full Moon), 1984
Chicago 18 (Warner Bros), 1986
Chicago 19 (Reprise/Warner Bros), 1988
Greatest Hits 1982-9 (Reprise), 1989
Liberation (Pair/—), 1990
Twenty 1 (Reprise/—), 1991

Clannad

Irish group formed 1976

Original line-up: Maire Ni Bhraonain; Pol O Braonain; Ciaran O Braonain; Noel O Dugain; Padraig O Dugain.

Career: Formed originally with the intention of entering local folk festivals, Clannad soon came to the forefront of Irish music. Early records were released in Ireland only but after writing the music for UK TV Series *Harry's Game*, Clannad's title song single reached No. 5 in UK and won them an Ivor Novello songwriting award.

Debut LP for RCA **Magical Ring** followed and went gold. After a lengthy European tour Clannad worked on songs for the UK TV series *Robin Of Sherwood*. Apart from the resulting album **Legend**, the group also wrote and performed all the atmospheric pieces for the 26 episodes. February 1985 Clannad received British Academy Award for best soundtrack of the year — the first Irish group to receive the award.

Third album for RCA , **Macalla**, recorded in Dublin, London and Switzerland, included single **In A Lifetime**. Featuring U2's Bono duetting with Maire, it charted as the group undertook a 23-date sell-out UK tour. **Sirius** set (1987) recorded in Wales and London, and mixed in LA by Greg Ladanyi and Russ Kunkel, prompted world tour, which included week of dates in Dublin to mark city's millenium.

Lilting, melodic approach belies strong political stance. Clannad, now without departed Pol O Braonain, entered 90s with secure reputation and new **Anam** album. Enya Ni Bhraonain, who enjoyed brief tenure

**Below: Sirius, Clannad.
Courtesy RCA Records.**

with group, re-surfaced as Enya for UK hit **Orinoco Flow** from multi-million-selling album **Watermark** in 1988 and No. 1 UK LP **Shepherd Moons** in 1991.

Hit Singles:	US	UK
Theme From Harry's Game, 1982	—	5
In A Lifetime, 1986	—	20
In A Lifetime (re-issue), 1989	—	17

Albums:
Clannad (Philips), 1973
Clannad 2 (Gael-Linn) (Ireland), 1974

Clannad In Concert (Ogham), 1978
Dulaman (Gael-Linn) (Ireland), 1979
Crannull (Philips), 1980
Fuaim (Tara) (Ireland), 1982
Magical Ring (RCA), 1983
The Legend (RCA), 1984
Macalla (RCA), 1985
Sirius (RCA), 1987
The Collection(K-Tel), 1987
Atlantic Realm (BBC), 1989
Pastpresent (RCA), 1989
Anam (RCA), 1990

Eric Clapton

UK guitarist, vocalist, composer
Born Ripley, Surrey, March 30, 1945

Career: Brought up by foster-parents. At 15 he started to listen to blues recordings by Muddy Waters, Chuck Berry, Big Bill Broonzy *et al*, and bought first guitar at 17. Taught himself to play while studying at Kingston Art College.

Formed first band in 1963, an R&B outfit called Roosters which also included at various times Paul Jones and Tom McGuinness, later of Manfred Mann, and Brian Jones, later of Rolling Stones. Band was short-lived, and in late 1963 Clapton spent two weeks with Casey Jones and The Engineers before replacing Anthony 'Top' Topham in the recently formed Yardbirds.

While with Yardbirds Clapton established reputation as blues stylist, and recorded **Five Live Yardbirds** and **Sonny Boy Williamson And The Yardbirds** albums. But when band took more commercial direction with 1965 single **For Your Love**, Clapton took off for more purist environment of John Mayall's Bluesbreakers.

Straight-down-the-line blues approach of Mayall's band provided perfect backdrop for Clapton, and the guitarist attracted even more fervent following. Shown to good effect on **Bluesbreakers** album, Clapton's playing began to influence other British players; he became widely regarded as *the* guitar hero.

Sitters-in with Bluesbreakers included Jack Bruce and Ginger Baker, bass player and drummer respectively, with Graham Bond Organization. Empathy with both musicians led to break from Mayall (Clapton replaced by Peter Green) and formation of Cream in 1967.

With Cream Clapton enjoyed first major commercial success and fully blown rock star status. Although band was important link in development of heavy rock — the first power trio — it was relatively short-lived, and folded in November 1968.

Period which followed saw Clapton involved with variety of projects, including ill-fated Blind Faith supergroup, touring and recording with Delaney And Bonnie, guesting on other artists' albums, and his first solo album in 1970. From this time onwards Clapton seemed to be trying to live down his axe hero past. He immersed himself in group as Derek And The Dominoes. December 1970 Dominoes album featured Duane Allman and is regarded by many as Clapton's best recorded effort. Single **Layla** — dedicated to then wife of George Harrison, Patti, whom Clapton was later to marry — has achieved classic status.

Nevertheless, Derek And The Dominoes were not huge commercial success, and this relative failure plus increasing drug problem took Clapton off music scene for several years. Eventually, with help of friends like Pete Townshend and course of electro-acupuncture, Clapton regained health.

Since 1974 Clapton has pursued fairly low-profile career, making relaxed, down-home albums, occasionally coming up with hit singles, and working live sporadically. He has continued to play down guitar hero persona, and has developed pleasing J.J. Cale-like voice to go with his simple but appealing compositions. Nowadays as often influenced by country and other forms of blues (he is for example fan of super-relaxed country artist Don Williams), Clapton appeals both to AOR audiences and diehard rock fans.

This crossover appeal has been seen to good effect on albums like blockbuster **August** (1986) and **Journeyman** (1989). Clapton also has no fear of unchartered territory, scoring TV series *Edge of Darkness* theme and *Lethal Weapon 1* and *2* movies with Michael Kamen.

Annual two-week plus residence at London's Royal Albert Hall enables devoted British audience to enjoy artist's variety.

Personal tragedy struck in 1990 when helicopter crash killed Colin Smythe, Bobby Brooks and Nigel Browne, following show in Wisconsin with Stevie Ray Vaughan, another victim. Clapton was further blighted by death of son Conor, who fell from skyscraper apartment in New York in 1991.

With a truckload of awards, including recent Grammy for **Bad Love** single, Clapton has the hardware and adoration to confirm status as superstar of superstars.

Guitars: Fender Stratocaster, Gibson Les Paul.

Hit Singles:	US	UK
After Midnight, 1970	18	—
I Shot The Sheriff, 1974	1	9
Swing Low Sweet Chariot, 1975	—	19
Lay Down Sally, 1978	3	39
Wonderful Tonight, 1978	16	—
Promises, 1979	9	37
I Can't Stand It, 1981	10	—
I've Got A Rock 'n' Roll Heart, 1983	18	—
Behind The Mask, 1987	—	15

Below: Clappers impresses at his annual Royal Albert Hall shindig.

Albums:
Eric Clapton (Polydor), 1970
History of Eric Clapton (Polydor), 1972
Eric Clapton At His Best (Polydor), 1973
Eric Clapton's Rainbow Concert (RSO), 1973
461 Ocean Boulevard* (RSO), 1974
There's One In Every Crowd (RSO), 1975
E.C. Was Here (RSO), 1975
The Blues World Of (—/Decca), 1975
No Reason To Cry (RSO), 1976
Slowhand* (RSO), 1977
Backless* (RSO), 1978
Just One Night (RSO), 1980
Another Ticket (RSO), 1981
Steppin' Out (—/Decca), 1981
Time Pieces (Best Of) (RSO), 1982
Money And Cigarettes (Warner Bros), 1983
Time Pieces, Volume II (RSO), 1983
Layla (RSO), 1983
Behind The Sun (Warner Bros), 1984
Too Much Monkey Business (Astan), 1984
Backtrackin' (RSO), 1985
Live 85 (Duck), 1985
August (Warner Bros), 1986
Cream Of Eric Clapton (Polydor), 1987
Rainbow Concert (Polydor), 1987
Crossroads (four CD set) (Polydor), 1988
Journeyman (Reprise/WEA), 1989
24 Nights (Duck/Warner), 1991
*Available as triple album set

The Dave Clark Five

UK group formed 1963

Original line-up: Dave Clark, drums, vocals; Lenny Davidson, guitar; Rick Huxley, guitar, banjo; Dennis Payton, saxophone, guitar, clarinet, harmonica; Mike Smith, keyboards, vibraphone, vocals.

Career: This 'British invasion' group followed The Beatles to US and found great, if temporary, fame and fortune there. Nowadays often considered pale imitation of Beatles, but in fact The Five had distinctive sound (called 'Tottenham Sound') of their own, based on Clark's steadily thudding

drums and chanting vocals. Smash hit single **Glad All Over** was amazingly considered rather risqué at the time. Group became involved in a ridiculous publicity war with The Beatles, The Five being touted as a neat, well-groomed London alternative. Then The Rolling Stones arrived. It was all a contrived tempest in a teapot, anyway, indicative of the innocent controversies that filled the pages of teen magazines at the time.

Band also starred in what turned out to be one of the best rock movies, *Having A Wild Weekend*, directed by then unknown John Boorsman in 1965. Despite title, it is a bitter-sweet story that looks at the price of sudden fame and at the hysteria that briefly surrounds popular young musicians. There's no great acting here, of course, but it is one of the few rock exploitation films that holds up.

Group had several hit singles in the States, including **Do You Love Me**, a cover of the 1962 dance hit by the Contours, and raucous stomper **Bits And Pieces**. After that, popularity faded; although The Five had an original and identifiable sound, it never varied. They weren't capable of the changes that more lasting bands were beginning to explore. They stayed together, a constant live attraction until 1973 when they finally broke up. Clark became successful in the business end of music by buying rights to near legendary *Ready Steady Go* TV series. Clark also staged musical *Time* starring Cliff Richard, Julian Lennon and Sir Laurence Olivier, and was awarded damages of £400,000 in 1990 against Rank Theatres, who were found to have operated inefficient box office for the musical.

Hit Singles:

	US	UK
Glad All Over, 1963	6	1
Bits And Pieces, 1964	4	2
Can't You See That She's Mine, 1964	4	10
Do You Love Me, 1964	11	30
Because, 1964	3	–
Everybody Knows (I Still Love You), 1964	15	37
Any Way You Want It, 1964	14	25
Come Home, 1965	14	16
I Like It Like That, 1965	7	–
Catch Us If You Can, 1965	4	5
Over And Over, 1965	1	45
At The Scene, 1966	18	–
Try Too Hard, 1966	12	–

Above: The Dave Clark Five with Ed Sullivan, who introduced many UK acts.

You Got What It Takes, 1967	7	28
Everybody Knows (I Still Love You), 1967	43	2
Red Balloon, 1968	–	7
Good Old Rock 'n' Roll, 1969	–	7
Everybody Get Together, 1970	–	8

Albums:
Best Of (–/Starline), 1979
Plays Good Old Rock 'n' Roll (–/MFP), 1975
25 Thumping Great Hits (–/Polydor), 1978

Worth Searching Out:
Greatest Hits (Epic/Columbia), 1966

The Clash
UK group formed 1976

Original line-up: Joe Strummer, vocals, guitar: Paul Simonon, bass; Mick Jones, guitar; Keith Levine, guitar; Terry Chimes, drums.

Career: Group formed in squat in London's Shepherd's Bush area in May 1976. Simonon and Jones were previously part of prototype punk outfit London SS and approached Strummer, then with 101ers. Keith Levine became group's second guitarist but was soon replaced. After several auditions, Terry Chimes (drums) completed line-up.

Moving headquarters to disused warehouse in Camden Town, group rehearsed under direction and guidance of manager Bernie Rhodes. An unpublicized appearance with The Sex Pistols was followed by their official unveiling in August 1976. The publicity afforded The Pistols and punk led to lucrative contract with CBS. Move regarded as treason by some hard-core punk fans. Nevertheless, The Clash quickly established themselves as one of the most forceful and committed spokesmen of the new wave; their impact was immediately felt.

First single **White Riot** reached No. 38 and was hailed as mini-classic of punk genre. Debut album **The Clash** entered LP chart at No. 12. During same period, drummer Terry

Chimes left, disillusioned with trappings of punk; antipathy felt by other members reflected on LP sleeve where Chimes is renamed Tory Crimes. An endless series of auditions followed before Nicky 'Topper' Headon was brought in as replacement.

Third single **Complete Control**, a riposte to CBS, was produced by Lee Perry and reached Top 30. Tour with Richard Hell and the Voidoids was followed by publicity in the form of group arrests on charges of petty vandalism and shooting racing pigeons. Another tour, appropriately titled The Clash Out On Parole, and new single, **White Man in Hammersmith Palais/The Prisoner**, maintained momentum.

Second LP **Give 'Em Enough Rope** hit No. 2 on album charts and provided first Top 20 hit single, **Tommy Gun**. Production by Sandy Pearlman caused further controversy amongst punk elite, who feared that Clash were being transformed into heavy-metal unit. Following split with manager Rhodes, group embarked on first US visit, dubbed the Pearl Harbour Tour. Positive response from US critics helped career prospects.

Returning to UK, began work on film *Rude Boy* (1980). On the day of Britain's General Election (May 11, 1979) **The Cost Of Living** (EP) was issued. Included a version of Bobby Fuller's **I Fought The Law**. Group's political credibility was promoted further by appearances at Rock Against Racism gigs. Another US tour saw group augmented by Blockheads' keyboardist Micky Gallagher.

Third LP, produced by Guy Stevens, was scheduled as **The New Testament**, a pretentious title finally dropped in favour of **London Calling**. Released in Christmas 1979 as a two for the price of one, the work was a strong seller. Follow up **Sandinista**, a triple album, followed same pattern, though less successfully.

Headon's increasingly idiosyncratic (drug related) behaviour resulted in his removal from group on eve of crucial US tour in May 1982. At short notice, Terry Chimes agreed to return to drummer's seat — a position he filled ably until December, when close-knit trio were once again diverted to search for a compatible cohort. Former Cold Fish Peter Howard was named in 1983.

Clash have continued to reach wider audience without greatly diverging from original punk stance. Purists, however, would contend this. US Top 10 breakthrough came with Glyn Johns-produced **Combat Rock** album in 1982. Band then played support on Who's 1982 farewell tour of US. New drummer Peter Howard joined in May 1983, but internal strife continued. Jones left to

Below: The late lamented Clash, a genuinely talented punk outfit.

form own successful band Big Audio Dynamite, and was replaced by two guitarists, Vince White and Nick Shepherd, at beginning of 1984.

Fallow period was broken by release of delightfully titled 1985 album **Cut The Crap**, but band disintegrated before going on road. Strummer (Latino Rockability War) and Simenon (Havana 3 AM) subsequently formed new bands, and Strummer also found an almost permanent spot with the Pogues. Clash enjoyed posthumous success with **Should I Stay Or Should I Go** which charted after exposure as jeans theme for TV advertisement.

Hit Singles:

	US	UK
Tommy Gun, 1978	–	19
London Calling, 1979	–	11
Bank Robber, 1980	–	12
Rock The Casbah, 1982	8	30
Should I Stay Or Should I Go/ Straight To Hell, 1982	–	17
Should I Stay Or Should I Go, 1991	–	1
Rock The Casbah, 1991	–	15

Albums:
The Clash (Columbia/CBS), 1977
Give 'Em Enough Rope (Columbia/CBS), 1978
London Calling (Columbia/CBS), 1979
Sandinista (Columbia/CBS), 1980
Combat Rock (Columbia/CBS), 1982
Cut The Crap (CBS), 1985
Story Of The Clash Volume 1 (Epic/Columbia), 1988

George Clinton
US vocalist, guitarist, producer, composer
Born Kannapolis, North Carolina, July 22, 1940

Career: Arguably the creator of funk, although James Brown might have claim to the rights. Extrovert personality whose excesses beyond the traditional boundaries of R&B have gained him 'legendary' status, if a limited commercial following.

Founded Parliament 'doo-wop' vocal group in 1955, who recorded unsuccessfully for ABC, New Records, Motown and Golden World before **(I Wanna) Testify** charted for Revilet Records in 1967. Clinton's admiration for the psychedelic movement of that time prompted formation of P. Funk troupe, whose wild regalia and repetitive rhythms intoxicated dance crowd.

Under P. Funk aegis, Clinton (with bass player William 'Bootsy' Collins) concocted a variety of groups, including Bootsy's

Rubber Band, Funkadelic (who cut **One Nation Under A Groove** set), Parlet and The Brides of Funkenstein, and founded own label; signed distribution deal with CBS.

Subsequent litigation with Atlantic (who had bought rights to Revilet Records) forced Clinton to curtail studio recordings, although solo deal with Capitol Records (1982) enabled artist to resume career.

Clinton's fanatical following has justified a succession of LPs of patchy quality, with just the occasional flash of inspiration. It seems doubtful if the performer, whose stage show seems stuck in a time warp, will again achieve the heights of the manic P. Funk offerings.

Hit Singles:

	US	UK
With Funkadelic:		
One Nation Under A Groove, 1978	28	9
With The Parliaments:		
(I Wanna) Testify, 1966	20	—
Flashlight, 1978	16	—

Albums:
Computer Games (Capitol), 1982
You Shouldn't Nuf Bit Fish (Capitol), 1984
Some Of My Best Friends Are Jokes (Casablanca), 1985
Best Of (Capitol), 1987
The Cinderella Theory (Paisley Park), 1989

With Bootsy's Rubber Band:
Ahh...The Name Is Bootsy, Baby! (Warner/—), 1977
Bootsy? Player Of The Year (Warner/—), 1978
Jungle Bass (4th & Broadway), 1990

With Funkadelic:
America Eats It Young (Westbound), 1972
Standing On The Verge Of Getting It On (Casablanca), 1974
Funkadelics Greatest Hits (Westbound), 1974
One Nation Under A Groove (Casablanca), 1978

With The Parliaments:
Osmium (Invictus/—), 1970
Up For The Downstroke (Casablanca), 1974
Chocolate City (Casablanca), 1975
The Clones Of Dr Funkenstein (Casablanca), 1976
Mothership Connection (Casablanca), 1976
P-Funk Earth Tour (Casablanca), 1977
Funkentelechy Vs The Placebo Syndrome (Casablanca), 1977
Motor Booty Affair (Casablanca), 1978
Brides Of Funkenstein (Casablanca), 1978
Gloryhallastoopid (Casablanca), 1979

The Coasters
US vocal group formed 1955

Original line-up: Carl Gardner; Bobby Nunn; Billy Guy; Leon Hughes.

Career: Legendary vocal quartet who added large dose of fun to classic age of rock 'n' roll. Group have such an involved history that it took whole book (*The Coasters* by Bill Millar) to explain. The legend began in 1949 with Los Angeles group the Robins; they had local R&B hits on Savoy and RCA. Moving to Spark Records, founded in 1954, scored big with R&B **Smokey Joe's Cafe.** Jerry Leiber and Mike Stoller's material became major factor in Coasters' success.

When Atlantic negotiated for acquisition of Spark, Robins' management didn't approve; Leiber and Stoller persuaded lead voice Carl Gardner and bassman Bobby Nunn to leave group. Joined Billy Guy and Leon Hughes to form Coasters; name derived from their west-coast origins. Debut **Down In Mexico** hit R&B Top 10. String of smash hits followed over next five years, with varying personnel; Nunn and Hughes left, replaced by Cornel Gunter and Wil 'Dub' Jones, first session yielding **Yakkety Yak**, The Coasters' first pop chart-topper in the summer of 1958.

Magical ingredients were Gardner's earthy, good-humoured tenor lead contrasted by Jones' rumbling bass; inventive Leiber/Stoller lyrics were punctuated by King Curtis raunchy tenor sax solos and embellished by Mickey Baker's catchy guitar phrases. Songs such as **Searching**, **Charlie Brown**, **Poison Ivy** and **Little Egypt** are rock 'n' roll classics.

Hits dwindled by late 1961; Cornel Gunter left, replaced by Earl Carroll from Cadillacs. Standards declined until 1964 when **'Tain't Nothin' To Me**, cut 'live' at the Apollo Theatre, was hit.

Connections with Leiber and Stoller were severed. Final Atco release revived Louis Jordan's jumping **Saturday Night Fish Fry**. In 1967 group signed with Columbia soul subsidiary Date; produced again by Leiber and Stoller in contemporary idiom. **Soul Pad** and **She Can** resulted, artistically excellent but commercial failures. Solitary single appeared on Lloyd Price's Turntable label in 1969.

In 1971 King Records bought all Date material, did doctoring in studio with overdubs, and hit with group's revival of Clovers' **Love Potion No. 9**. Coasters continue to tour with varying personnel; managed another disc outing in 1976 on Wilson Pickett's Wicked label. Fluctuating line-ups maintain Coasters name, but Atlantic re-union party in 1988 afforded opportunity for Gardner, Guy, Jones and Gunter to re-unite for a bit of Yakkety-Yakking.

Hit Singles:

	US	UK
Searchin'/Young Blood, 1957	3	30
Young Blood/Searchin', 1957	8	—
Yakkety Yak, 1958	1	12
Charlie Brown, 1959	2	6
Along Came Jones, 1959	9	—
Poison Ivy, 1959	7	15

Albums:
Greatest Hits (Atco/London), 1962
Greatest Recordings/The Early Years (Atco/Atlantic), 1978
20 Great Originals (—/Atlantic), 1978
Greatest Hits (Power/—), 1979
Juke Box Giants (—/Audio Fidelity), 1982
Thumbing A Ride (—/Edsel), 1985
The Ultimate (Warner Special/Super), 1988

Eddie Cochran
US vocalist, guitarist, composer
Born Oklahoma City, October 3, 1938
Died April 17, 1960

Career: Teamed with Hank Cochran (unrelated) as Cochran Brothers in 1954; recorded first single for Ekko label in hillbilly style. Met songwriter (later manager) Jerry Capehart in 1956 and signed to Crest Records in Los Angeles as solo. When first Crest single failed, Capehart negotiated contract with Liberty Records on strength of Cochran's successful audition for appearance in movie *The Girl Can't Help It*. First Liberty single **Sittin' In The Balcony** became hit, and album that followed revealed soft pop style. Returned, however, to rock 'n' roll with subsequent singles and biggest US hit **Summertime Blues**.

Two further cameo appearances in typical exploitive rock 'n' roll movies failed to capture dynamic stage performance, but nationwide tours soon established Cochran as teen idol. Made first British appearances early in 1960 with Gene Vincent and popularity in UK much increased by spots on *Boy Meets Girl* television show and tour of major UK theatres. During tour many British guitarists were influenced by Cochran's individual style and tuning of Gretsch semi-acoustic guitar with humbucker pickup.

Interrupted British tour in April 1960 intending to make brief visit to Los Angeles, died as result of injuries received in car crash when returning to London for flight. Biggest UK hit in May marked beginning of cult following and subsequent releases included material culled from demo sessions and studio jams. Cochran had recorded extensively as solo and as sideman and tapes of hitherto unheard of performances are still being discovered and released.

Cochran's involvement in studio production and arranging (he was first artist to make own demos, and innovated multi-tracking techniques) revealed talents which could hardly have failed to influence popular music had he lived. However, his death did not stop his influence through songs and style which found reflection in new wave records of 70s, notably The Sex Pistols covers of **Somethin' Else** and **C'mon Everybody**. The latter was re-released in 1988 to advertise jeans.

Guitar: Semi-acoustic Gretsch.

Hit Singles:

	US	UK
Sittin' In The Balcony, 1957	18	—
Summertime Blues, 1958	8	18
C'mon Everybody, 1959	35	6
Three Steps To Heaven, 1960	—	1
Weekend, 1961	—	15

Albums:
Memorial Album (Liberty), 1960
C'mon Everybody (—/Sunset), 1970
Legendary Masters (United Artists), 1971
Very Best Of (15th Anniversary), 1975
Many Sides Of (—/Rollercoaster), 1979
A Legend In Our Time (Union Pacific), 1979
The Eddie Cochran Singles Album (United Artists), 1979
20th Anniversary Album (—/United Artists), 1980
Gene Vincent And Eddie Cochran — Together Again (Capitol), 1980
Gene Vincent And Eddie Cochran — Rock 'n' Roll Heroes (Rockstar), 1981
Cherished Memories (Liberty/EMI), 1983
25th Anniversary Album (Liberty), 1985
Rock 'n' Roll Greats (EMI), 1986
Somethin' Else (Capehart), 1987
Best Of (EMI America), 1987
Rock 'n' Roll Legend (Rockstar), 1987

Joe Cocker
UK vocalist, composer
Born Sheffield, May 20, 1944

Career: 'Blue-eyed soul' exponent Cocker joined brother Victor's Cavaliers skiffle group at 12 as drummer/harmonica player. Became hooked on rock 'n' roll, blues and, especially, music of Ray Charles, on whom he based subsequent vocal style. First pro band was Big Blues, which evolved into Vance Arnold and The Avengers. Cocker was given six months' leave of absence by employers (the gas board), while he worked with band as support act for Rolling Stones, Manfred Mann, and Hollies. Group's debut single,

Below: 'Who nicked me guitar?' Wild-living vocalist Joe Cocker belts it out with the best.

Beatles' song **I'll Cry Instead**, on Decca (1964), flopped. Cocker went back to work as gas fitter then as packer for magazine distributor before co-writing **Marjorine** with fellow Sheffield musician Chris Stainton; they sent demo to Denny Cordell (producer of Move and Procol Harum), who secured release via Deram.

Cocker and bass player Stainton headed semi-pro Grease Band with Henry McCullough, guitar, Tommy Eyre, keyboards, and Kenny Slade, drums, playing Northern clubs and residency at Sheffield's King Mojo Club. Recorded limited issue live single for Sheffield University Rag Week. With **Marjorine**, issued under his name, hitting UK Top 50, Cocker moved to London. Follow-up single, a Ray Charles-styled cover of Lennon/McCartney's **With A Little Help From My Friends**, was massive European hit and title cut from debut album. It featured Grease Band plus a range of guest musicians, including Jimmy Page, Stevie Winwood, Albert Lee, and Procol Harum's drummer B.J. Wilson (who later became member of Cocker's touring band).

Success of record, plus appearance at Windsor Jazz And Blues Festival, made international reputation. During 1969 US tour Cocker appeared at Woodstock Festival and met Leon Russell, who co-produced (with Denny Cordell) his second album and hit single **Delta Lady**.

When Grease Band (except Stainton), went own way a year later, Bruce Rowland and Alan Spenner having replaced Eyre and Slade, Russell put together ambitious 40-strong musical entourage under title **Mad Dogs And Englishmen**. Tour yielded double album and movie of same title for Cocker. Excellent single **High Time We Went** made it to No. 22 in US.

Unfortunately, Cocker failed to follow-up on success; though it seemed he was used to handling cigarettes and booze, he couldn't cope with drugs. His hyper-energetic stage performances and emotion-laden recordings contributed to near mental and physical collapse. Became temporary recluse on West Coast at end of Mad Dogs tour, later slipping home to UK to live with parents. Made one fleeting live appearance when called up on-stage by Rita Coolidge in 1971.

With help of Stainton, Cocker formed new 12-piece band for 1972 comeback tour of US, Britain and Australia, where he was busted on drugs charge. When band split, Stainton helped his friend put together combination of concert tapes and studio material for **Something To Say** album.

Had 1974 US hit with Billy Preston's **You Are So Beautiful**. Regular album releases were counterbalanced by repeated on and off-stage traumas and a succession of abortive comeback attempts as major live act. Made guest vocal appearance on Crusaders' Top 100 single **I'm So Glad** (1981).

Cocker's 1982 Island album, **Sheffield Steel**, mixed soul, rock and ballads and following its success Cocker contributed to soundtrack of hit movie *An Officer And A Gentleman*, recording ballad **Up Where We Belong** with Jennifer Warnes for his first US chart-topper.

Subsequently contributed to movie soundtracks *9½ Weeks* (**You Can Keep Your Hat On**), *Harry And The Hendersons* (**Love Lives On**), and *Teachers* (**Edge Of Dreams**). Returned to USA Top 20 with **When The Night Comes** in 1990, and featured on John Lennon Tribute Concert bill in Liverpool in same year.

Intermingled with charity shows, Cocker still likes to grind it out coast to coast, as witnessed by marathon stint with Stevie Ray Vaughan in 1990.

Hit Singles:

	US	UK
With A Little Help From My		
Friends, 1968	–	1
Delta Lady, 1969	–	10
The Letter, 1970	7	39
Cry Me A River, 1970	11	–
You Are So Beautiful, 1974	5	–
When The Night Comes, 1990	11	–

With Jennifer Warnes:

	US	UK
Up Where We Belong, 1983	1	4

Albums:
With A Little Help From My Friends (A&M), 1969
Joe Cocker! (A&M), 1970
Mad Dogs And Englishmen (A&M), 1971
I Can Stand A Little Rain (A&M), 1974
Stingray (A&M), 1976
Luxury You Can Afford (Asylum), 1978
Platinum Collection (–/Cube), 1981
Sheffield Steel (Island), 1982
Space Captain (–/Cube), 1982
Civilised Man (Capitol), 1984
Cocker (Capitol), 1986
The Joe Cocker Collection (Castle Classics), 1986
Unchain My Heart (Capitol), 1987
One Night Of Sin (Capitol), 1989
Joe Cocker – Live (Capitol), 1990

Lloyd Cole And The Commotions
UK group formed 1983

Original line-up: Lloyd Cole, vocals guitar; Blair Cowan, vocals, keyboards; Neil Clark, guitar; Lawrence Donegan, bass; Steven Irvine, drums.

Career: One of Britain's brightest 80's bands, Lloyd Cole And The Commotions were conceived above infamous Tennant's Bar in Glasgow's West End by Cole, Cowan and Clark, and signed to management deal by Derek MacKellop who introduced Donegan and Irvine to complete line-up. With producer Paul Hardiman, band released debut single **Perfect Skin** in 1984, and quickly built strong reputation, enhanced by first album

Above: The moody Lloyd Cole went without The Commotions in 1990.

Rattlesnakes. Follow-up **Easy Pieces** spawned Top 20 singles and confirmed band's early promise.

Cole then invited Tears For Fears and Peter Gabriel engineer to produce **Mainstream** set, released 1987. With a successful European tour behind them, including sell-out date at Wembley Arena, band announced irrevocable split.

Cole's solo career was sparked by eponymous debut album which made UK Top 20, and June 1990 US tour, which included charity gig for homeless children in New York. Also cut **Downtown** for excellent *Bad Influence* movie starring James Spader and Rob Lowe (1991).

Hit Singles:

	US	UK
Brand New Friend, 1985	–	19
Lost Weekend, 1985	–	17
Jennifer She Said, 1987	–	31

Albums:
Rattlesnakes (Polydor), 1984
Easy Pieces (Polydor), 1985
Mainstream (Polydor), 1987
1984-89 Lloyd Cole And The Commotions (Capitol/Polydor), 1989

Lloyd Cole Solo:
Lloyd Cole (Capitol), 1990
Don't Get Weird On Me, Babe (Capitol/Polydor), 1991

Phil Collins
UK drummer, vocalist, keyboard player, composer
Born London, January 31, 1951

Career: Arguably the hardest working man in rock 'n' roll. Almost permanent fixture at charity events during the 80s, and was a prime mover in Band/Live Aid phenomenon, appearing in London and Philadelphia on the same day courtesy Concorde.

Former child actor and model who appeared in the stage version of *Oliver*, as an extra in the Beatles' movie *A Hard Day's Night*, and featured in mail-order knitwear

catalogue. Collins' first musical sortie was with Flaming Youth before earning the drum chair with Genesis, later becoming lead vocalist when Peter Gabriel quit in 1975.

In 1976 founded jazz/rock aggregation Brand X (with guitarist John Goodsall, bass player Percy Jones, and keyboard player Robin Lumley) and also found time to guest on albums by Robert Fripp, John Cale, Brian Eno, and Argent, among others.

First solo LP, **Face Value** (1981), confirmed Collins' expertise, with single **In The Air Tonight** making Top 20 in America and Great Britain. Album's melodious content and slick production, with Earth Wind And Fire brass section prominent, earned further chart success with **I Missed Again** and **If Leaving Me Is Easy**.

Low-key (sometimes non-existant) approach of Genesis allowed Collins' nomadic spirit to flit between a variety of production and session work with artists such as Eric Clapton (with whom he has acquired a seemingly permanent role as drummer), Adam Ant, Robert Plant, Frida (former Abba vocalist), John Martyn and Jethro Tull's Ian Anderson. Duets with Earth Wind And Fire front-man Phillip Bailey (**Easy Lover**) and Marilyn Martin (**Separate Lives**) were both million-plus sellers.

The advent of monster charity concerts brought Collins' pleasant demeanour to the fore, and secured TV and film roles in *Miami Vice*, *Buster* (as Buster Edwards, one of the great British train robbers), *Hook*, Steven Spielberg's movie adaptation of *Peter Pan*, and a project schedule for 1992, *Frauds*, to be shot in Australia.

Further solo albums, **Hello I Must Be Going** (1982), **No Jacket Required** (1985), **But Seriously** (1989), and culminating in 1990 **Serious Hits . . . Live!**, have been laden down with awards, including a quartet of prestigious Grammys, as well as supplying a stream of No. 1 singles to the States.

Collins has been subject to reticent critical acclaim, and appears uncomfortable with superstar status. But, as arguably *the* male performer of the 80s, he has bathed in commercial and public success with hardly a bat of those whispy eyebrows.

Hit Singles:

	US	UK
In The Air Tonight, 1981	19	2
I Missed Again, 1981	19	14
If Leaving Me Is Easy, 1981	–	17
You Can't Hurry Love, 1982	10	1
Against All Odds, 1984	1	2
Easy Lover (with Philip Bailey),		
1985	2	1
Sussudio, 1985	1	12
One More Night, 1985	1	4
Don't Lose My Number, 1985	4	–
Take Me Home, 1985	–	19
Separate Lives (with Marilyn		
Martin), 1985	1	4
In The Air Tonight (re-mix),		
1988	–	4
A Groovy Kind Of Love, 1988	1	1
Two Hearts, 1988	1	6
Another Day In Paradise, 1989	1	2
I Wish It Would Rain Down,		
1990	3	7
Something Happened On The		
Way To Heaven, 1990	4	15
Do You Remember, 1990	4	57

Albums:
Face Value (Atlantic/Virgin), 1981
Hello I Must Be Going (Atlantic/Virgin), 1982
No Jacket Required (Atlantic/Virgin), 1985
But Seriously (with Clapton, Crosby, Bishop and Winwood) (Atlantic/Virgin), 1989
Serious Hits Live (Atlantic/Virgin), 1990

Commodores

US group formed 1960s

Original line-up: Lionel Richie, vocals, tenor saxophone; William King, trumpet, Thomas McClary, guitar; Milan Williams, keyboards.

Career: Original four were school-friends in Tuskegee, Alabama; formed Commodores after merger of two other school groups, Mystics and Jays. With two additional musicians group played local gigs and gained strong reputation.

Eventually signed management deal with Benjamin Ashburn who secured band New York gigs. At one of these, Commodores were spotted by Suzanne DePasse, Motown vice-president; result was support spot on Jackson Five worldwide tour. In 1972, band signed contract with Motown; two latest recruits had by this time moved on and been replaced by drummer and vocalist Walter 'Clyde' Orange and bass player Ronald LaPread.

After three singles had made impact on soul market, simple but effective instrumental **Machine Gun** became hit on both sides of Atlantic. This and another single, **Do The Bump**, helped **Machine Gun** LP to eventual gold status. Following initial success of LP, band toured with Rolling Stones and Stevie Wonder.

From that time Commodores diversified material; **Sweet Love**, from 1975 album **Movin' On**, was melodic ballad, and showed direction in which writer Lionel Richie would lead group.

By late 70s group were a headlining international act, shipping platinum with every album. Band had also made impact with appearance in disco film *Thank God It's Friday* with Donna Summer, but high spot was 1978 single **Three Times A Lady**. Beautiful Richie-composed song went double platinum in US and became biggest-ever Motown single in UK, also gained numerous songwriting awards.

Following massive international hit with Diana Ross on movie theme *Endless Love*, Lionel Richie split to pursue highly successful solo career.

Black British singer J.D. Nicholas, formerly singer with Heatwave was brought in during 1984 to share lead vocals with Walter 'Clyde' Orange.

By group's 14th album, **Nightshift**, their total sales top 40-million unit mark. Band quit Motown, February 1986, signing with Polydor Records, for which **United** album was debut.

Hit Singles:

	US	UK
Machine Gun, 1974	22	20
Slippery When Wet, 1975	19	—
Sweet Love, 1976	5	—
Easy, 1977	4	9
Brickhouse/Sweet Love, 1977	5	32
Three Times A Lady, 1978	1	1
Just To Be Close To You, 1978	7	—
Sail On, 1979	4	8
Still, 1979	1	4
Old Fashioned Love, 1980	20	—
Lady (You Bring Me Up), 1981	8	56
Oh No, 1981	4	44
Nightshift, 1985	3	3
Goin' To The Bank, 1986	—	43
Easy (re-issue), 1988	—	15

Albums:
Machine Gun (Motown), 1974
Caught In The Act (Motown), 1975
Movin' On (Motown), 1975
Hot On The Tracks (Motown), 1976
Commodores* (Motown), 1977

Live (Motown), 1978
Natural High (Motown), 1978
Greatest Hits (Motown), 1978
Midnight Magic (Motown), 1979
Heroes (Motown), 1980
In The Pocket (Motown), 1981
All The Greatest Hits (Motown), 1982
All The Great Love Songs (Motown), 1982
13 (Motown), 1983
14 Greatest Hits (Motown), 1984
Nightshift (Motown), 1985
Best Of (Telstar), 1985
United (Polydor), 1986
Rise Up (Blue Moon), 1987
Rock Solid (Polydor), 1988
*Titled Zoom in U.K.

Above: Red, The Communards. Courtesy London Records.

The Communards

UK vocal/instrumental duo formed 1985

Original line-up: Jimmy Somerville, vocals; Richard Coles, keyboards.

Career: Formed when vocalist Somerville quit chart act Bronski Beat and teamed up with long-time friend (and occasional Bronski sidekick) Coles, originally as The Committee, then renamed The Communards after 19th Century French radicals.

First two singles, grandiose ballad **You Are My World** and electro-disco **Disenchanted**, both failed to chart. Concentrated instead on series of benefit concerts (especially Gay Switchboard and Red Wedge) featuring full backing band of eight females. This line-up

recorded debut LP **The Communards** which contained soul standard **Don't Leave Me This Way**.

Embracing sexual and social politics, Communards' musical mix of disco rhythms and soaring melodies found perfect match in lyrical combination of facts and frivolity on second LP **Red**. **Victims** and **If I Could Tell You** dealt with AIDS crisis, while another 70s classic, **Never Can Say Goodbye** was sheer exuberant dancefloor fun. Both this and **Tomorrow** became UK hits, maintaining impressive record for a duo determined to indulge in both pop and polemics.

Coles' classical training coupled with Somerville's effervescent presence seemed to ensure sparkling future, and announcement of group's demise in 1988 was genuine surprise.

Now LA-based, Somerville has subsequently enjoyed solo success with a succession of flighty covers. **The Singles Collection 1984-1990** (1991) was résumé of Somerville's three-pronged career to date.

Hit Singles:

	US	UK
Disenchanted, 1986	—	29
Don't Leave Me This Way, 1986	—	1
So Cold The Night, 1986	—	8
Tomorrow, 1987	—	23
Never Can Say Goodbye, 1987	—	4
There's More To Love, 1988	—	20

Albums:
The Communards (London), 1986
Red (London), 1987
The Singles Collection 1984-90 (London), 1991

Jimmy Somerville Solo:
Read My Lips (London), 1990

Ry Cooder

US guitarist, vocalist, producer, arranger
Born Los Angeles, March 15, 1947

Career: Former session player (predominantly slide guitar, also mandolin); one-time member of Taj Mahal and Captain Beefheart bands. After many years of fronting formidable R&B group, consisting of keyboard

Left: Richard Coles and Jimmy Somerville — The Communards.

Above: Borderline, Ry Cooder. Courtesy Warner Bros Records.

players Jim Dickenson and William D. Smith, bassist Tim Drummond, drummer Jim Keltner, percussionist Baboo and vocalists Bobby King, Willie Greene and Herman Johnson, Cooder now tours with fellow multi-instrumentalist David Lindley.

Ry Cooder worked on film scores *Candy* and *Performance* (which starred Mick Jagger) and made notable contribution to Rolling Stones' **Let It Bleed** album. Other sessions included work with Marc Benno, Crazy Horse, Randy Newman, John Sebastian and Maria Muldaur.

First solo LP **Ry Cooder** released by Reprise in 1970. Established Cooder's mean bottle-neck guitar style and strangled, authentic R&B vocalizing. Has run entire musical heritage of America with more than a smattering of cajun and country, 20s and 30s swing (**Jazz**), eclectic (**Chicken Skin Music**), down-home R&B (**Borderline**) and further soundtrack albums (**The Long Riders**, **Southern Comfort**, **The Border**, **Paris**, **Texas** and **Alamo Bay**).

Cooder's work has never fallen into rock mainstream, and this has prevented permanent niche in upper reaches of album charts. Concerts, however, are a different matter, with Cooder now established as major stage performer, particularly in Britain; on bi-annual pilgrimage to UK plays to capacity audiences.

True spirit of R&B is deeply implanted in this multi-talented veteran, and never better expounded than on Jimmy Reed's **How Can A Poor Man Stand Such Times And Live** and live **Show Time** album.

Guitars: Various Fenders, primarily 1968 Stratocaster, Washburn solid-body electric, Martin and Ovation acoustics; also Gibson F-style mandolin.

Albums:
Ry Cooder (Reprise), 1970
Into The Purple Valley (Reprise), 1971
Boomer's Story (Reprise), 1972

Below: The Man And His Music, Sam Cooke. Courtesy RCA Records.

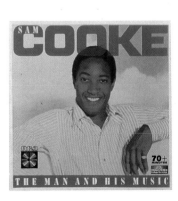

Paradise And Lunch (Reprise), 1974
Chicken Skin Music (Warner Bros), 1976
Show Time (live), (Warner Bros), 1977
Jazz (Warner Bros), 1978
Bop Till You Drop (Warner Bros), 1979
Borderline (Warner Bros), 1980
The Long Riders (soundtrack) (Warner Bros), 1980
Southern Comfort (soundtrack) (Warner Bros), 1981
The Border (soundtrack) (Warner Bros), 1982
The Slide Area (Warner Bros), 1982
Paris, Texas (soundtrack) (Warner Bros), 1985
Music From Alamo Bay (soundtrack) (Slash), 1985
Blue City (Warner Bros), 1986
Crossroads (Warner Bros), 1986
Why Don't You Try Me Tonight (Warner Bros), 1986
Get Rhythm (Warner Bros), 1987
Johnny Handsome (Warner Bros/WEA), 1989

Sam Cooke

US vocalist, composer
Born Chicago, Illinois, January 22, 1931
Died December 11, 1964

Career: Influential black performer/writer whose songs and vocal style have remained in vogue over three decades. Originally member of Soul Stirrers gospel group, Cooke turned to secular music in late 1950s.

First hit **You Send Me** (1957) was followed by classics **Only Sixteen, Wonderful World, Cupid, Bring It On Home To Me** and **A Change Is Gonna Come**. He started own label Sar in 1960, recording Sims Twins, Johnnie Taylor, and The Valentinos.

Under aegis of Hugo And Luigi (who later groomed The Stylistics), Cooke remained chart-bound until his untimely demise: he was shot by a woman in December 1964, after entering wrong motel room. The courts ruled the shooting 'justifiable homicide'.

Cooke is still considered the definitive soul vocalist some 20 years after his death. His phrasing and articulation may never be surpassed. His material has since been recorded by Aretha Franklin, Otis Redding, Dawn, Rod Stewart, and countless others.

Hit Singles:	US	UK
You Send Me/Summertime, 1957	1	29
(I Love You) For Sentimental Reasons, 1958	17	—
I'll Come Running Back To You, 1958	18	—
Only Sixteen, 1959	28	13
Wonderful World, 1960	12	27
Chain Gang, 1960	2	9
Cupid, 1961	17	7
Twistin' The Night Away, 1962	9	6
Having A Party, 1962	17	—
Bring It On Home To Me, 1963	10	23
Nothing Can Change This Love, 1962	12	—
Another Saturday Night, 1963	10	23
Frankie And Johnny, 1963	14	30
Send Me Some Lovin', 1963	13	—
Little Red Rooster, 1963	11	—
Good News, 1964	11	—
Good Times, 1964	11	—
Shake, 1965	7	—
Wonderful World, 1968	—	3

Albums:
Best Of (RCA/—), 1961
Golden Age Of (RCA/—), 1969
Two Sides Of (Speciality/Sonet), 1971
This Is Sam Cooke (RCA), 1971

When I Fall In Love (—/EMI), 1979
Mr Soul (—/RCA), 1980
When I Fall In Love (Arena), 1987
20 Greatest Hits, 1987
You Send Me, 1987

Alice Cooper

US vocalist, composer
Born Vincent Furnier, Detroit, Michigan, February 4, 1948

Career: Raised in Phoenix, Arizona. Formed first band at high school, which performed variously as Spiders, Earwigs, Nazz. Members included Glen Buxton (guitar), Michael Bruce (guitar, keyboards), Dennis Dunaway (bass), and Neal Smith (drums). Recorded locally with minor success.

After move to Los Angeles, group changed name to Alice Cooper. Signed to Frank Zappa's Straight label in 1969 by manager Shep Gordon. Debut LP **Pretties For You** released 1969.

After running up massive debts, outfit shifted to Detroit, working under aegis of Bob Ezrin. First album produced by Ezrin **Love It To Death** earned group instant credibility, and first chart single **I'm 18.**

Above: Imperial Bedroom, Elvis Costello. Courtesy F-Beat Records.

As a live act, Alice Cooper's bizarre antics disguised mediocrity of performance. Nevertheless, band was now on frontline of rock scene; scored further chart successes including million-selling **School's Out.**

1974 saw wholesale change of group personnel; Cooper recruited former Lou Reed sidemen Dick Wagner (guitar), Prakash John (bass), Steve Hunter (guitar), Whitney Panti Glan (drums), and Josef Chirowski (keyboards).

Last major tour undertaken in 1975 after release of **Welcome To My Nightmare**. Copper's long-term drink problem caused period of inactivity. Had re-think in face of developing punk scene (which made band's formerly outrageous tactics seem about as revolutionary as a Pat Boone concert).

During 80s Cooper has made persistent attempts at comeback, particulary in 1982 with new band and album **Special Forces**. Subsequent sporadic releases have filled in time for this golf fanatic, who occasionally returns to concert duty for a re-run of his horror show. At press time, Cooper was discussing role of Freddy 'Nightmare On Elm Street' Krueger's father for the final episode (we hope) of the movies series, and contemplating fate of **Hey Stoopid** album.

Hit Singles:	US	UK
School's Out, 1972	7	1
Only Women Bleed, 1975	12	—
I Never Cry, 1976	12	—
You And Me, 1977	9	—
How You Gonna See Me Now, 1978	12	—
Poison, 1989	7	2

Albums:
Love It To Death (Warner Bros), 1971
Killer (Warner Bros), 1971
School's Out (Warner Bros), 1972
Billion Dollar Babies (Warner Bros), 1973
Greatest Hits (Warner Bros), 1974
Welcome To My Nightmare (Atco/Anchor), 1974
Goes To Hell (Warner Bros), 1976
Lace And Whiskey (Warner Bros), 1977
Alice Cooper Show (Warner Bros), 1977
From The Inside (Warner Bros), 1978
Flush The Fashion (Warner Bros), 1980
Special Forces (Warner Bros), 1981
Zipper Catches Skin (Warner Bros), 1982
Da Da (Warner Bros), 1983
Constrictor (MCA), 1986
Freak Out Song (Showcase), 1986
Raise Your Fist And Yell (MCA), 1987
Trash (Epic), 1989
Hey Stoopid (Epic), 1991

Elvis Costello

UK composer, vocalist, guitarist
Born Declan McManus, London, August 25, 1954

Career: After unsuccessful early career in pub/country-rock band Flip City, Costello (son of erstwhile Joe Loss Band singer Ross McManus) took demo tapes in 1976 to then fledgling Stiff label. Jake Riviera was impressed enough not only to sign Declan, but also to manage him. With name change to Elvis Costello, first three singles built strong cult following, and debut LP reached UK Top 20, backing provided by San Francisco band Clover, performing under the name of the Shamrocks.

June 1977 saw formation of permanent backing group, The Attractions. Pete Thomas (drums, ex-Chilli Willi), Bruce Thomas (bass, ex-Quiver) and Steve Nieve (keyboards, ex-Royal Academy of Music). Elvis and band toured with first Stiff Records package along with Ian Dury, Nick Lowe (who had produced all Costello records up to this point), Dave Edmunds, and Wreckless Eric — concurrently scored first Top 20 hit with **Watching The Detectives**.

By early 1978 had made major US impact; moved with Riviera and Lowe to newly formed Radar label; three Top 30 hits followed in 1978, plus second acclaimed album; third LP released during first days of 1979. Biggest UK hit so far was **Oliver's Army**; 1979 also saw production of first LP by The Specials and collapse of Radar Records. Riviera subsequently set up new F-beat label, launched with UK Top 5 Costello single, **I Can't Stand Up For Falling Down** (cover of ancient Sam And Dave song). Made further hit singles (although smaller successes) during 1980, plus classic LP **Get Happy**.

1981 chiefly notable for release of Billy Sherrill-produced country LP **Almost Blue**, which polarized fans. Played concert at Royal Albert Hall with Royal Philarmonic Orchestra at start of 1982. Rest of year saw return to original abrasive style — thoughtful, meaningful, but often bitter songs — with **Imperial Bedroom** LP.

Below: Elvis Costello, a diverse talent, with The Attractions.

1984 album **Goodbye Cruel World** was also well received, and in that year Costello also performed theme tune of and acted in UK TV series *Scully*.

During 1984 and 1985 Costello toured extensively without regular backing band The Attractions, and also scored a personal success at the 1985 Live Aid concert. His acting career continued with a cameo role in the Liverpool-set black comedy movie *No Surrender*.

1986 album **King Of America**, featuring US West Coast session men, created new wave of approval for mercurial artist, acclaim which continued next year with **Blood And Chocolate** set.

Marriage to Cait O'Riordan from The Pogues (for whom he produced **Rum, Sodomy And The Lash**) hardly mellowed Costello, who harangued all and sundry in **Spike** and **Mighty Like A Rose** albums. Sunday Times critic Robert Sandall was prompted to describe the artist as 'the ill-tempered virtuoso'. Costello joined forces with that more passive rebel Paul McCartney for ex-Beatles' **Flowers In The Dirt** LP and Costello's **Veronica** single.

Toured US in 1989 with band featuring former Presley bass player Jerry Scheff and legendary session-keyboard player Larry Knechtel, accepting award from MTV for **Veronica** video in a break from schedule; he was named Best Songwriter in 1989 *Rolling Stone* poll.

Idiosyncratic, impetuous and thorny, Costello has aggravated two-thirds of the world's population. The remaining third are devoted to him.

Guitar: Fender Jaguar.

Hit Singles:

	US	UK
Watching The Detectives, 1977	—	15
(I Don't Want To Go To) Chelsea, 1977	—	16
Oliver's Army, 1979	—	2
I Can't Stand Up For Falling Down, 1980	—	4
Good Year For The Roses, 1981	—	6
Veronica, 1989	19	—

Albums:
My Aim Is True (Columbia/Stiff), 1977
This Year's Model (Columbia/F-Beat), 1978
Armed Forces (Columbia/Radar), 1979
Get Happy (Columbia/F-Beat), 1980
Trust (Columbia/F-Beat), 1981
Almost Blue (Columbia/F-Beat), 1981
Imperial Bedroom (Columbia/F-Beat), 1982
Goodbye Cruel World (Columbia/F-Beat), 1984
Punch The Clock (Columbia/F-Beat), 1984
10 Bloody Marys (Demon), 1984
Best Of (Telstar), 1985
King Of America (Columbia/F-Beat), 1986
Out Of Our Idiot (Demon), 1986
Blood And Chocolate (IMP), 1986
The Man (Demon), 1987
Spike (Warner Bros), 1989
Mighty Like A Rose (Warner Bros), 1991

Randy Crawford
US vocalist, composer
Born Macon, Georgia, 1952

Career: Prime claimant to title 'Queen of 80s Soul', Randy Crawford manages to mix deep-soul stylings of South with urban disco-slant.

Raised in Cincinnati, Ohio, grounded in gospel, she became regular night club performer from 15. During school holidays she had two-week gig in St Tropez, France, which was extended to three months and brought record deal offers, but she returned to US to complete education and take six-night-a-week stint at Cincinnati's Buccaneer Club.

On graduation, moved to New York where she sang with George Benson before signing with Cannonball Adderley's manager John Levy and guesting on Adderley's final album **Big Man**.

Shifting base to Los Angeles, Randy appeared before capacity 5,500 audience at Shrine Auditorium as part of World Jazz Association all-star package in tribute concert to Adderley who had just died. Show was taped and some of her set was used on her 1980 Warner Bros album, **Everything Must Change**, acceptance of which led to formation of own five-piece band.

First writer credit came with **I Got Myself A Happy Song** single on second album **Raw Silk** (1979).

Though uncredited on label, Randy was chosen to sing vocal on title track of

Below: Randy Crawford, a model of down-home Southern soul.

Crusaders' **Street Life** album, a transatlantic hit which established her reputation. Subsequently she undertook two successful European tours with Crusaders, who became involved with producing **Now We May Begin** set, star cut of which was haunting Joe Sample ballad **One Day I'll Fly Away**, Crawford's first major hit single (winning her Most Outstanding Performance award at 1980 Tokyo Music Festival).

Veteran West Coast producer Tommy LiPuma came in for **Secret Combination** LP from which **You Might Need Somebody** was perfect sample of her wistful and soul-searching style.

Though lacking raw power of Etta James or Aretha Franklin, or pure commercialism of Diana Ross, Randy Crawford has displayed rare penchant for understated performances which nevertheless wring last drop of emotion from a song.

Hit Singles:

	US	UK
Street Life (featured vocalist with Crusaders), 1979	36	5
One Day I'll Fly Away, 1980	—	2
You Might Need Somebody, 1981	—	11
Rainy Night In Georgia, 1981	—	18
Almaz, 1986	—	4

Albums:
Miss Randy Crawford (Warner Bros), 1977
Raw Silk (Warner Bros), 1979
Now We May Begin (Warner Bros), 1980
Everything Must Change (Warner Bros), 1980
Secret Combination (Warner Bros), 1981
Windsong (Warner Bros), 1982
Nightline (Warner Bros), 1983
Greatest Hits (K-Tel), 1984
Abstract Emotions (Warner Bros), 1986
Rich And Poor (Warner Bros), 1989

Robert Cray Band
US band formed 1983

Original line-up: Robert Cray, vocals, guitar; Richard Cousins, bass; Peter Boe, keyboards; David Olson, drums.

Career: Born in Georgia, and son of a serviceman, Cray spent his formative years moving from place to place. Robert Cray Band formed by Cray with bassist Richard Cousins and inspired by blues hero Albert Collins. Worked initially in the Eugene, Oregon area playing club and college dates.

First record deal with Tomato which produced album **Who's Been Talkin'** (released in UK on Charly). Four years later came a deal with Hightone Records and two albums **Bad Influence** and **False Accusations** (UK release on Demon). Albums and UK appearances helped increase UK profile of the band (both Demon LPs topped in the independent chart). In 1986 they signed a lucrative recording deal with Polygram (Mercury in UK) and recorded the **Strong Persuader** album.

Cray guested with Tina Turner on her *Break Every Rule* TV special, and toured in the US with Huey Lewis & The News and Eric Clapton. **Strong Persuader** climbed the US charts to become the most successful blues album in American chart history.

1988 saw release of **Don't Be Afraid Of The Dark** LP, a Grammy winner in 1989, a year which also saw guest appearance on John Lee Hooker's 'comeback' album **The Healer**. An inveterate performer, Cray has

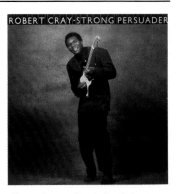

Above: Strong Persuader, Robert Cray. Courtesy Hightone Records.

hardly been off the road since band's inception, and enjoyed particularly good reviews when teamed with Eric Clapton for the guitar god's two-week-plus dates at Royal Albert Hall in 1990; also played on Clapton's **Journeyman** LP.

For Cray's sixth album, **Midnight Stroll** (1990), artist shuffled band line-up to include Cousins, James Pugh, keyboards; Timmy Kaihatsu, guitar, and Kevin Hayes, drums. The set also featured noted brasswork from legendary Memphis Horns.

Described as the heir apparent to BB King, Robert Cray has certainly lived up to those lofty accolades, and seems destined for career longevity.

Albums:
Who's Been Talkin' (Charly), 1985
Bad Influence (Demon/Hightone), 1986
False Accusation (Demon/Hightone), 1986
Strong Persuader (Mercury/Hightone), 1986
Don't Be Afraid Of The Dark (Mercury), 1988
Midnight Stroll (Mercury), 1990

Cream
UK group formed 1966

Original line-up: Eric Clapton, guitar; Jack Bruce, vocals, bass; Ginger Baker, drums.

Career: Clapton, previously with John Mayall's Bluesbreakers, joined forces with former Graham Bond Organization sidemen Bruce and Baker with object of forming blues supergroup. Immediate acclaim followed first gig at 1966 Windsor Festival.

First album, **Fresh Cream**, revealed winning format of blues-influenced songs plus extended improvised solos. Group also had ability to come up with hit singles, and during just over two years of existence scored with handful of unusual but effective cuts which, although showcasing Clapton's guitar work, were remarkably restrained and inventive by comparison with the products of later 'power trios'.

From 1967, however, band spent most of time in US where they had quickly gained huge reputation. Every Cream album exceeded sales of one million dollars, and gigs throughout country were standing room only. In 1968, however, members, decided that outfit had run its course, and in autumn played farewell concert at London's Royal Albert Hall. Shortly afterwards recorded last album, **Goodbye**.

Although somewhat given to overstatement, especially in live context — thunderous volume and seemingly endless solos being order of day — Cream were highly influential band; they set pattern for 'power trio' format, later endlessly copied by generally lesser talents. The group also acted as springboard to superstardom for Clapton, and to lesser extent for other members. Immediately following demise of band, Clapton and Baker, along with Rick Grech, became involved in short-lived Blind Faith while Bruce took up solo career.

Hit Singles:	US	UK
I Feel Free, 1966	–	11
Strange Brew, 1967	–	17
Sunshine Of Your Love, 1968	5	25
White Room, 1968	6	28
Badge, 1969	60	18

Albums:
Fresh Cream (RSO/Polydor), 1966*
Disraeli Gears (RSO/Polydor), 1967
Wheels Of Fire (RSO/Polydor), 1968
Goodbye (RSO/Polydor), 1969
Cream Live (RSO/Polydor), 1970
Cream Live 2 (RSO/Polydor), 1972
Off The Top (RSO/—), 1972
Heavy Cream (RSO/Polydor), 1973
Cream (—/Polydor), 1975
Cream Volume 2 (—/RSO), 1978
The Very Best Of Volumes I & II (Polydor), 1983
*Original version of Fresh Cream on Atco has more tracks.

Creedence Clearwater Revival

US group, formed 1967

Original line-up: Johny Fogerty, vocals, guitar; Tom Fogerty, rhythm guitar; Stu Cook, bass; Doug 'Cosmo' Clifford, drums.

Career: While attending junior high school in San Francisco Bay area of El Cerritto, foursome got together as Tommy Fogerty and the Blue Velvets. Locally based Fantasy Records offered recording deal on proviso that band changed name to the Golliwogs (in attempt to cash-in on then current British beat boom). Band reluctantly agreed and debut single was released in 1965. Further singles followed but none made impact except local hit Brown Eyed Girl. Group evolved new 'swamp rock' style of music based on mixture of R&B and cajun rhythms. They persuaded label's new boss Saul Zaentz to agree to change of name to Creedence Clearwater Revival.

New sound and image coincided with San Francisco rock music explosion. Band's eponymous debut album, a mix of rock 'n' roll/R&B standards and John Fogerty originals, made immediate impression. Two singles were lifted simultaneously. A version of Dale Hawkins' oldie Suzie Q, registered first in charts then classy reading of Screamin' Jay Hawkins' I Put A Spell On You also scored.

Group's albums were essentially collections of potential hits and CCR went against then current trend by remaining singles-orientated. John Fogerty-penned Proud Mary became instant rock/soul standard, eliciting superb cover versions by Solomon Burke, Arif Mardin, Ike and Tina Turner, and others. Checkmates Limited's version of song (masterminded by Phil Spector) was reputed to be most expensively produced single ever, several hundred musicians having been used on sessions.

Despite CCR's San Francisco origins, their spiritual home was deep in bayou country of the Southern states. Their songs like Bad Moon Rising, Lodi, Born On The Bayou and Green River were epics of the swamp rock music genre.

Above: One of CCR's greatest hits packages. Courtesy Fantasy Records.

Fifth CCR album Cosmo's Factory included three gold singles (Travelin' Band, Up Around The Bend and Lookin' Out My Back Door) plus incisive 11-minute version of Marvin Gaye/Gladys Knight And The Pips' Motown classic I Heard It Through The Grapevine.

Produced, arranged and largely written by John Fogerty, CCR's music was amazingly tight. It relied almost entirely on band's own integral musicianship rather than depending on studio over-dubs (aside from occasional addition of saxophone). Musical togetherness was not matched on personal front, however. Tom Fogerty (who died of respiratory failure while battling tuberculosis in 1990) quit following differences with others. They continued as trio for world tour which yielded Creedence — Live In Europe.

John Fogerty's increasing dominance caused further dissension. In what has come to be known as 'Fogerty's Revenge' he allowed Cook and Clifford equal creative participation in Mardi Gras album. Result was total disaster, lambasted by critics and leading to band's dissolution in October 1972.

Tom Fogerty went on to record moderately successful albums and his Joyful Resurrection single, cut with Cook and Clifford, was, he said, the story of CCR.

Clifford's solo outing was far less satisfactory. He continued working with Cook, however, as respected session rhythm team. They went on to join the Don Harrison Band.

Meanwhile, John Fogerty made low-key solo debut with Blue Ridge Rangers albums; he claimed it was made by group of that name but LP proved to be all his own work; he arranged, produced, played all instruments and sang. His re-make of Hank Williams' country oldie Jambalaya was US hit, as was version of Hearts Of Stone.

Protracted dispute with Fantasy Records caused three-year gap before he emerged with new Asylum deal, Top 30 hit single Rockin' All Over The World (covered in UK by Dave Edmunds) and applauded John Fogerty Album. Excellent Centerfield set caused further legal wrangles over Zanz Kant Danz track — a dig at Fantasy's bossman. Fogerty's boundless enthusiasm certainly revived memories of CCR, despite the fact that theirs was very much a 60s sound. The advent of electro-pop has been given short shrift by this purveyor of traditional rock 'n' roll.

Hit Singles:	US	UK
Suzie Q — Part 1, 1968	11	–
Proud Mary, 1969	2	8
Bad Moon Rising, 1969	2	1
Green River, 1969	2	19
Down On The Corner/Fortunate Son, 1969	3	31
Fortunate Son/Down On The Corner, 1969	14	–
Travelin' Band/Who'll Stop The Rain, 1970	2	8
Who'll Stop The Rain/Travelin' Band, 1970	13	–
Up Around The Bend, 1970	4	3
Lookin' Out My Back Door, 1970	2	–
Have You Ever Seen The Rain, 1971	8	36
Sweet Hitchhiker, 1971	6	36

Johny Fogerty Solo:
	US	UK
Old Man Down The Road, 1985	10	–
Rock And Roll Girls, 1985	20	–

Albums:
Creedence Clearwater Revival (Fantasy), 1968
Bayou Country (Fantasy), 1969
Green River (Fantasy), 1969
Willy And The Poor Boys (Fantasy), 1969
Cosmo's Factory (Fantasy), 1970
Pendulum (Fantasy), 1971
Mardi Gras (Fantasy), 1972
Gold (Fantasy), 1972
More Gold (Fantasy), 1973
Live In Europe (Fantasy), 1973
Golliwogs (Fantasy), 1975

John Fogerty Solo:
Blue Ridge Rangers (Fantasy), 1973
John Fogerty (Asylum), 1975
Centerfield (Warner Bros), 1985
The Collection (Impression), 1985

Worth Searching Out:
Tom Fogerty (Fantasy), 1972
Doug 'Cosmo' Clifford (Fantasy), 1972

Crosby, Stills, Nash & Young

US group formed 1968

Original line-up: David Crosby, guitar; Stephen Stills, vocals, guitar; Graham Nash, vocals, guitar.

Career: Band formed without Young, as Crosby, Stills And Nash; Crosby came from Byrds, Stills from Buffalo Springfield, and Nash from UK 'beat group' The Hollies. Debut album Crosby Stills And Nash released in 1969 to critical and commercial success. Semi-acoustic soft-rock with accent on vocal harmonies, music combined commercial appeal with 'sensitivity'; occasional banality camouflaged by slickness. Album went gold and single from it, Marrakesh Express, charted in US and UK.

Looking to fill out sound, band recruited another ex-Buffalo Springfield alumnus, Neil Young, then pursuing solo career. Young's chunky guitar and sombre vocals became major asset, and his songwriting ability gave authority to repertoire. Deja Vu, with added talents of bass-player Greg Reeves and drummer Dallas Taylor, also went gold. Critical plaudits tipped in favour of Young's contributions to album. Lyrical content was timely and in keeping with appearance at Woodstock festival.

Disappointing live set, Four Way Street, followed in 1971, but band members were already beginning to take individual directions and CSN & Y folded that year. Crosby and Nash continued to work as duo until late 70s; Stills took up threads of erratically successful solo career; and Young went onto become enigmatic rock superstar.

In 1977, Crosby, Stills And Nash cut reunion album CSN, before splitting and regrouping again in 1982.

Incarceration of Crosby should have sounded death knell for band. However, late 1987 saw yet another reformation. The trio have since cut American Dream LP, which made US Top 20 and 1990 offering Live It Up. Crosby also cut solo LP Oh Yes I Can in 1989, a year before nasty bike accident laid the veteran up for a few months.

Still playing for anyone who will have them, CS&N have proved that old hippies never die, they simply fade away . . . and reform . . . and fade away . . . and reform.

Hit Singles:	US	UK
Marrakesh Express (without Young), 1969	–	17
Woodstock, 1970	11	–
Teach Your Children, 1970	16	–
Ohio, 1970	14	–
Just A Song Before I Go (without Young), 1977	7	–

Albums:
Crosby, Stills And Nash (Atlantic), 1969
Deja Vu (Atlantic), 1970
Four Way Street (Atlantic), 1971
So Far (Atlantic), 1974
CSN (Atlantic), 1977
Replay (Atlantic), 1980
Daylight Again (Atlantic), 1982
Allies (Atlantic), 1983
American Dream (Atlantic), 1988
Live It Up (Atlantic), 1990

David Crosby Solo:
If I Could Only Remember My Name (Atlantic), 1971
Oh Yes I Can (A&M), 1989

Crosby And Nash:
Graham Nash And David Crosby (Atlantic), 1972
Wind On The Water (Polydor), 1975

Below (from left to right): Stills, Nash, Crosby and Young — CSN&Y.

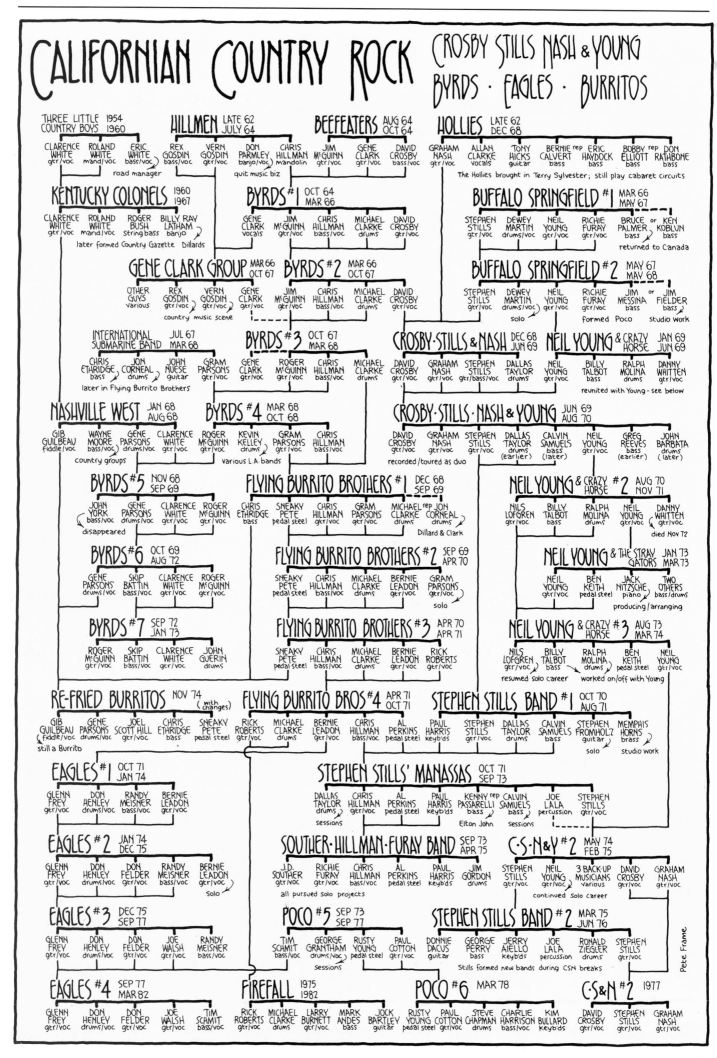

The Cure
UK group formed 1977

Original line-up: Robert Smith, vocals, guitar; Michael Dempsey, bass; Lol Tolhurst, drums.

Career: Signed originally to German label Hansa but dropped immediately, then released **Killing An Arab** single (based on *The Outsider* novel by Camus) on indie label Small Wonder. Linked up with producer Chris Parry who signed them to his newly formed Fiction Records, releasing **Three Imaginary Boys** debut LP and two sharp pop singles **Boys Don't Cry** and **Jumping Someone Else's Train**; both failed to chart.

Gained cult following for taut, angst-ridden, post-punk pop songs, but when Dempsey left, group expanded to four-piece (with Simon Gallup on bass and Matthieu Hartley on keyboards), gaining denser less concise sound. Second LP, **17 Seconds** was minor progression into complex arrangements but featured classic single of paranoia **A Forest**.

Subsequent LPs, **Faith** and **Pornography** found Smith dominating writing credits with dreary slabs of self-despairing dirges. First Harley, then Gallup, left and Tolhurst decided to abandon drums and learn keyboards. Smith, meanwhile, joined Siouxsie And Banshees as guitarist, helping write and record **Hyeana** LP, as well as collaborating with Banshee bassist Steve Severin on short-lived project The Glove. The Cure, it seemed, were dead.

But late 1982 saw Smith and Tolhurst reunited for hypnotic **Let's Go To Bed** single, followed by **The Walk**, which charted. Recruited Andy Anderson (drums) and **Pornography** producer Phil Thornalley (bass) for **Lovecats**, a jazz-tinged fantasy single which destroyed Cure's reputation for gloom and established Smith as sexy pin-up star with smudged lipstick. **The Top** LP followed and Smith quit the Banshees to concentrate on revitalized Cure.

Line-up stabilized as Gallup returned on bass, Boris Williams joined on drums and extra guitarist Porl Thomson was added. Playfully disturbed **Head On The Door** LP boasted UK hit singles **In Between Days** and **Close To Me** both showcased by delightfully zany videos.

Kiss Me, Kiss Me, Kiss Me double album (1987) and **Disintegration** (1989) contained dazzling array of styles and content crowning band's metamorphosis from pretentious pop philosophers to confident, teasing, beguiling, contemporary satirists, without sacrificing punk ideals. Despite further personnel changes — 12 month tenure of Roger O'Donnell (ex-Psychedelic Furs) on keyboards (Perry Bamonte later subbing), and the unceremonious dumping of Tolhurst, The Cure swept handsomely into rock elite following **The Prayer Tour** (1989); earned BRIT awards in 1990/91, the later as Best British Group.

A hundred-minute documentary, filmed for US cable television, contained scenes of band on tour and at work on proposed April 1992 album.

Hit Singles:	US	UK
The Walk, 1983	—	12
Lovecats, 1983	—	7
The Caterpillar, 1984	—	14
In Between Days, 1985	—	15
Close To Me, 1985	—	24
Boys Don't Cry, 1986	—	2
Just Like Heaven, 1987	40	29
Lullaby, 1989	—	5
Lovesong, 1989	2	18
Never Enough, 1990	—	13
Close To Me (re-mix), 1990	—	13

Albums:
Three Imaginary Boys (Fiction), 1979
17 Seconds (Fiction), 1980
Faith (Fiction), 1980
Japanese Whispers (Fiction/Sire), 1980
Pornography (Fiction/A&M), 1982
Boys Don't Cry (Fiction), 1983
The Cure Live (Fiction), 1984
The Top (Fiction/Sire), 1984
The Hanging Garden (Fiction), 1985
Head On The Door (Fiction), 1985
Standing On A Beach (Fiction/Elektra), 1986 — the singles
Kiss Me, Kiss Me, Kiss Me (double album) (Fiction), 1987
Disintegration (Elektra/Polydor), 1989
Mixed Up (Elektra/Polydor), 1990

Cutting Crew
US band formed 1982

Original line-up: Nick Van Eede, vocals, guitar; Kevin McMichael, guitar; Colin Farley, bass.

Career: First hit **(I Just) Died In Your Arms** on Siren elevated Cutting Crew to No. 4 in the UK charts followed by **I've Been In Love Before** the same year. Four major tours in one year found them working with The Bangles, Huey Lewis and Starship.

Cutting Crew rapidly built up a strong European following, from Finland to Italy, and played both San Remo and Montreux festivals before flying to Japan to pick up an award for the best new rock band at the Tokyo Music Festival. Their appeal has even extended to China where they are one of the few Western rock acts to play live, appearing before 10,000 at one single gig.

Debut album **Broadcast** notched up one million plus sales, while single success was achieved in all major territories, including US, where **I Just Died In Your Arms** earned Virgin their first American No. 1. With addition of keyboard player Tony Moore (ex-Iron Maiden), band cut 1988 single **I've Been In Love Before**, and then, with minimal communication, slipped swiftly away.

Above: Cutting Crew enjoyed two solid years before leaving the planet.

Hit Singles:	US	UK
I Just Died In Your Arms, 1986	1	4
I've Been In Love Before, 1986	9	24
One For The Mockingbird, 1987	38	—

Albums:
Broadcast (Siren/Virgin), 1986
The Scattering (Virgin/Siren), 1989

Roger Daltrey
UK vocalist, actor
Born London, March 1, 1944

Career: Daltrey grew up in non-musical family in working-class neighbourhood of London's Shepherd's Bush. Around 12 he began playing self-made guitars. Thrown out of school at 15, he formed his own band, The Detours, later to become The Who. After playing guitar in Detours for nearly two years, he became a singer and has remained so, generally as vocalist with The Who.

Daltrey's first solo project was singing part of 'Tommy' with Lou Reizner's London

Below: The Cure, with front-man Robert Smith (second from left).

Symphony Orchestra production of the Who opera. His single **I'm Free** from this version went to No. 13 in UK. First completely solo venture came in 1973 when he sang compositions of then unknown writers such as Leo Sayer on **Daltrey**, his best solo effort to date. Produced by Adam Faith, the album yielded a No. 5 hit in UK, **Giving It All Away**, a great boost to Sayer. Away from The Who, Daltrey was able to expand his vocal range, abandoning the screaming style he was best known for within band, and proving his ability to sing softer ballads. Daltrey was also interested in singing material written by other songwriters and artists, as he'd been the vehicle for Pete Townshend's compositions for ten years.

Above: Broadcast, Cutting Crew. Courtesy Virgin Records.

1975 was a big year for Daltrey: he starred in his first film, the highly successful *Tommy*, and millions again identified the golden-maned Daltrey as the central character. To erase this impression, Daltrey starred in second Ken Russel film, *Lisztomania*, portraying Franz Liszt as decadent 19th century pop star. Besides being heavily featured on the **Lisztomania** and **Tommy** soundtrack LPs, Daltrey also had another solo LP out that year, **Ride A Rock Horse**. Apart from award-winning cover, the LP broke no new ground, but was well-received. Daltrey again utilized unknown composers, giving them opportunities to expand. **One Of The Boys** (1977) was more of the same — a collection of songs sung quite well, but not surpassing The Who.

Daltrey's other film roles included a ghastly performance in the low-budget horror flick *The Legacy* in 1978 and the lead part in *McVicar* in 1980 opposite Adam Faith.

Prior to The Who's temporary re-formation in 1989 for money-spinning US venture, Daltrey saw two further solo LPs released, **Under A Raging Moon** (1985) and **Can't Wait To See The Movie** (1987). Also featured in a London production of *The Beggar's Banquet*, and then returned to movies with roles in *Threepenny Opera* and *Buddy*, the latter of which launched career of UK teen idol Chesney Hawkes — Daltrey played his father! An astute businessman, The Who's agreeable front-man has also enjoyed success outside of music business with trout farm and shrewd investments.

Hit Singles:

	US	UK
Giving It All Away, 1973	—	5
I'm Free (London Symphony Tommy), 1973	—	13
Without Your Love, 1980	20	—

Albums:
Daltrey (MCA/Track), 1973
Ride A Rock Horse (MCA/Polydor), 1975
Lisztomania (A&M Ode/A&M), 1975
One Of The Boys (MCA/Polydor), 1977
McVicar (soundtrack) (Polydor), 1980
Best Bits (greatest hits) (MCA/Polydor), 1983
Party Should Be Painless (Warner Bros), 1984
Under A Raging Moon (Ten), 1985
Can't Wait To See The Movie (Ten), 1987

The Damned
UK group formed 1976

Original line-up: Rat Scabies, drums; Captain Sensible, bass; Dave Vanian, vocals; Brian James, guitar.

Career: Close on heels of Sex Pistols, Damned were in forefront of mid-70s' assault on established rock. Line-up had settled down by May 1976 and signed to Stiff in September. **New Rose/Help** was

released in October and revolution was on. First 'punk' album was **Damned, Damned, Damned** released in February 1977.

In August 1977, Lu Edmunds joined as second guitarist. Pink Floyd's Nick Mason produced second album, **Music For Pleasure**. Then band seemed to sink into superstar trauma but without reaching super success. Rat Scabies left in October 1977. Dave Berk sat in on loan from Johnny Moped for tour in November. Jon Moss joined as permanent drummer in late 1977. Loss of street credibility and lack of sales resulted in Stiff dropping band in January 1978. Within month Captain Sensible and Brian James had usual musical differences and band folded. James eventually re-emerged with Deadboys' Stiv Bators as Lords Of The New Church.

Within six months of Rainbow farewell concert on April 8, 1978, Sensible and Vanian were back together. Sensible had talked Rat Scabies and Vanian into playing with him and Lemmy (from Motorhead) for one gig at Electric Ballroom. Damned alumni continued on with other musicians and appeared as the Damned while acquiring rights to old name.

In November 1978 re-vamped band appeared, with Sensible now on guitar, sharing vocals with Vanian. Rat Scabies on drums and Algy Ward from The Saints on bass completed line-up. Chiswick signed them and got a UK No. 20 with **Love Song** in April 1979. **Machine Gun Etiquette** LP did not appear until November. Ward left in early 1980 to enter heavy-metal sweepstakes with Tank. His place was taken by Eddie And The Hot Rods' bass player Paul Gray. This line-up released critically acclaimed **The Black Album** in November 1980. Arguably album is stronger as single LP in US version. Band seemed continually on road and new popularity prompted November 1981 release of **Best Of The Damned** which featured band's early work.

In early October 1982 Damned released excellent, but patchy, **Strawberries** album. Captain Sensible's vaudeville tendencies still sought other outlet. In July 1982 his cover of old Rodgers/Hammerstein tune **Happy Talk** was UK No. 1 and second single as well as album followed. This schizoid approach plagued Damned from earliest days. Captain's success and band's relative commercial failure caused new label, Bronze, to drop Damned in April 1983 but they found new deal with MCA. Revised line-up won applause for **Phantasmagoria** (1985) and **Anything** (1986) albums. Bizarre **Eloise** remake (a hit for Barry Ryan in 1968) earned band first Top 10 UK single in 1986 and opportunity to stretch career for a couple more years, before official confirmation of The Damned's demise at the end of 1988.

Hit Singles:

	US	UK
Love Song, 1979	—	20
Eloise, 1986	—	5

Captain Sensible Solo:

Happy Talk, 1982	—	1
Glad It's All Over, 1984	—	6

Albums:
Damned, Damned, Damned (—/Stiff), 1977
Music For Pleasure (—/Stiff), 1977
Machine Gun Etiquette (—/Chiswick), 1979
The Black Album (—/Chiswick), 1980
Best Of The Damned (—/Stiff), 1981
Strawberries (—/Bronze), 1982
Phantasmagoria (MCA), 1985

Left: Phantasmagoria, The Damned. Courtesy MCA Records.

Anything (MCA), 1986
Mindless Directionless Energy (ID), 1987
Best Of The Damned (Big Beat), 1987
The Light At The End Of The Tunnel (MCA), 1987
Live At Shepperton (Big Beat), 1988
Final Damnation (Reunion Concert June 1988) (Restless/Essential), 1989

Captain Sensible Solo:
Women And Captains First (A&M), 1982
The Power Of Love (A&M), 1983
Sensible Singles (A&M), 1984

Deacon Blue
UK group formed 1985

Original line-up: Ricky Ross, vocals; James Prime, keyboards; Graeme Kelling, guitar; Doug Vipond, drums; Ewan Vernal, bass.

Career: Scottish pop rock band who have struck happy medium of commercialism and street credibility, despite heavy-handed approach at concerts, and lukewarm reception from critics.

Signed by CBS Records in 1986, band spent several months writing and recording debut **Raintown**, with Lorraine McIntosh added on vocals. Almost one year after album's release, selected single **When Will You Make My Telephone Ring** charted in UK prompting heavy promotional burst by record company for LP. Album then made Top 20. Two new cuts, **Real Gone Kid** and **Wages Day** followed **Ring** into single listing, priming audiences for **When The World Knows Your Name** LP, which supplanted Madonna's **Like A Prayer** at No. 1.

Busy touring schedule, including promotional dates in America, and bill-topping appearance at Glasgow's Big Day concert (before 250,000 people) heightened Deacon Blue's profile; band then enjoyed second place in UK charts with Bacharach/David classic **I'll Never Fall In Love Again**, main cut on four-track EP.

Although the States have not yet been bitten by the Blue bug, signs are (as at December 1991) that **Hoodlums** album could burst the bubble.

Hit Singles:

	US	UK
Real Gone Kid, 1988	—	8
Wages Day, 1989	—	18
Fergus Sings The Blues, 1989	—	14

Above: Scottish band Deacon Blue look certain to attain success in the 1990s.

Burt Bacharach And David Songs EP, 1990	—	2
Twist And Shout, 1991	—	10

Albums:
Raintown (Columbia), 1987
When The World Knows Your Name (Columbia), 1989
Ooh Las Vegas (Columbia/CBS), 1990
Fellow Hoodlums (Columbia), 1991

Chris De Burgh
Irish vocalist, composer

Career: Despite low-key image, Chris De Burgh has built worldwide audience and sold huge numbers of records over more than a decade of increasing reputation.

Below: De Burgh hit the bigtime with The Lady In Red in 1986.

A student of Trinity College, Dublin, De Burgh (né Davison) was discovered by songwriter Doug Flett at a London party.

Flett and partner Guy Fletcher were working at A&M's publishing arm Rondor Music which led to publishing and recording deal for De Burgh in 1972. Flett and Fletcher hid De Burgh in a cupboard until A&M's director Dave Margereson came into the room at which De Burgh burst into song.

Strong record company commitment and tours with A&M acts Supertramp and Gallagher And Lyle led to growing following. First chart-topper came in Brazil with **Flying/Turning Round** double header while **Spanish Train And Other Stories** took him into North America via Canada.

When Sex Pistols spent four days of utter chaos signed at A&M it was Chris De Burgh who wrote the legendary 'There is life after the Sex Pistols' letter to label's UK boss, Derek Green.

De Burgh finally achieved major chart success with lilting **Lady In Red**, a tribute to his wife, and a song with which to build a career, however belated. Parent album **Into The Light** enjoyed Top 10 chart action, and was followed by UK No. 1 **Flying Colours**, which spawned **Missing You** single, and live **High On Emotion** set (1990).

De Burgh's easy and honest manner has made him a favourite of festival crowds and regular guest on prominent charity events; scored **The Simple Truth** single for Kurdish Refugee's aid programme.

Hit Singles:

	US	UK
The Lady In Red, 1986	8	1
Missing You, 1988	–	3

Albums:
Far Beyond These Walls (A&M), 1975
Spanish Train And Other Stories (A&M), 1975
At The End Of A Perfect Day (A&M), 1977
Crusader (A&M), 1979
Eastern Wind (A&M), 1980
Best Moves (A&M), 1981
The Getaway (A&M), 1982
Man On The Line (A&M), 1984
Very Best Of (Telstar), 1984
Into The Light (A&M), 1986
Flying Colours (A&M), 1988
High On Emotion Live From Dublin (–/A&M), 1990
The Lady In Red (Best Of) (A&M), 1991

Deep Purple
UK group formed 1968

Original line-up: Rod Evans, vocals; Ritchie Blackmore, guitar; Jon Lord, keyboards; Nick Simper, bass; Ian Paice, drums.

Career: Formed in Germany from remnants of UK band Roundabout (Blackmore; Lord; Dave Curtis, bass; Chris Curtis, vocals; Bobby Clark, drums) as pop-rock outfit. First single (with line-up above), **Hush**, made Top 5 in US as did next two singles. First albums also achieved American success. However, band did not gain credibility in homeland until 1970 when Ian Gillan and Roger Glover replaced Evans and Simper for ambitious **Concerto For Group And Orchestra** album, recorded at Albert Hall with Royal Philharmonic Orchestra. New line-up also gained single success with **Black Night** in August of that year.

Pursuing a heavier rock direction, Purple quickly became one of the most successful and influential bands of early 70s; joined Black Sabbath and Led Zeppelin in spreading

gospel of multi-decibel, piledriver British rock around the world. Main asset was Ritchie Blackmore, who, although somewhat derivative, established strong reputation as guitar hero.

However, by 1972 band was beset by various ego problems; a year later Gillan left (later to achieve considerable success with his own band), followed shortly by Glover (who went into production). Glenn Hughes, bassist with moderately successful band Trapeze, replaced Glover, while Gillan was replaced by complete unknown David Coverdale. In 1975 Ritchie Blackmore also quit to form Rainbow (where he was later joined by Glover), and American Tommy Bolin, formerly of James Gang, was recruited in his place.

By 1976, audience for Purple's music was beginning to diminish, and band died natural death that year. Coverdale, Lord and Paice eventually became three-fifths of Whitesnake. Glenn Hughes recorded a solo album and undertook session work. Tommy Bolin died suddenly in Miami in 1976.

Fans were delighted when the group reformed in April 1984 with the classic line up of Gillan, Lord, Paice, Blackmore and Glover. Their reunion LP **Perfect Strangers** released in November, was their first studio album in 11 years. It went platinum and their US tour was hailed as the second highest grossing of the year. They played to British fans at Knebworth in 1985, then began a world tour in 1987. With the highly successful **House of Blue Light** released the same year, it seemed the revived Purple might enjoy a prolonged lease of life.

Despite loss of Gillan, who went on to re-record **Walk On The Water** for HM Rock Aid, the band released confident **Slaves And Masters** album in 1990, with Joe Lynne Turner on vocals, fronting stalwarts Blackmore, Lord, Paice and Glover.

Hit Singles:

	US	UK
Hush, 1968	4	–
Black Night, 1970	–	2
Strange Kind Of Woman, 1971	–	8
Fireball, 1971	–	15
Smoke On The Water, 1973	4	21

Above: Heavy metal crew Def Leppard formed in the steel city of Sheffield.

Albums:
Shades Of Deep Purple (Tetragrammaton/Harvest), 1968
Book Of Taliesyn (Tetragrammaton/Harvest), 1969
Deep Purple (Tetragrammaton/Harvest), 1969
In Concert (Portrait/Harvest), 1970
Concerto For Group And Orchestra (Warner Bros/Harvest), 1970
In Rock (Warner Bros/Harvest), 1970
Fireball (Deep Purple/Harvest), 1971
Machine Head (Warner Bros/Purple), 1972
Made In Japan (Deep Purple/Purple), 1972
Who Do We Think We Are (Deep Purple/Purple), 1973
Burn (Deep Purple/Purple), 1974
Stormbringer (Deep Purple/Purple), 1974
Come Taste The Band (Deep Purple/Purple), 1975
24 Carat Purple (–/Purple), 1975
Purple Passages (Warner Bros), 1975
Made In Europe (Deep Purple/Purple), 1976
Powerhouse (–/Purple), 1977
Singles (–/Harvest), 1978
When We Rock We Rock (Warner Bros/–), 1978
Deepest Purple (Harvest), 1980
Live In London (–/Harvest), 1982

Below: House of Blue Light, Deep Purple. Courtesy Polydor Records.

Perfect Strangers (Mercury), 1984
Knocking On Your Back Door (Polydor), 1985
The Anthology (Harvest), 1985
House Of Blue Light (Polydor), 1987
Nobody's Perfect (Mercury/Polydor), 1988
Slaves And Masters (RCA), 1990

Def Leppard
UK group formed 1978

Original line-up: Steve Clark, guitar; Rick Savage, bass; Pete Willis, guitar; Rick Allen, drums; Joe Elliot, vocals.

Career: Sheffield lads, Def Leppard cut an impressive debut album **On Through The Night** with twin guitar leads which owed as much to Wishbone Ash as new wave of British heavy metal.

Immediate attention brought by 'overnight success' caused problems. 1981 set **High 'n' Dry** sounded rather sedated, just another heavy metal album, and Pete Willis developed personal problems which resulted in his being fired during recording of crucial third album. Band continued recording as foursome when Elliot heard that guitarist Phil Collen (ex-Girl) was available.

After 18 month delay, **Pyromania** LP (featuring Collen) released. Band then suffered cruel luck when drummer Rick Allen lost arm in car accident, although he remains with group.

Group spent four years perfecting their next album **Hysteria** released in 1987 and highly successful. It yielded a collection of hits including **Animal**, **Women**, **Hysteria**, **Pour Some Sugar On Me** and **Armageddon It**.

With augmentation by hired drummers and specially adapted drum kit, Alan still featured with band on 1988 world tour. Further tragedy struck when, in 1991, Steve Clark was found dead (from alcohol poisoning) at his home; remaining members of band confirmed Leppard's future, and planned a new album for early 1992 release.

Above: Hysteria, Def Leppard. Courtesy Vertigo Records.

Hit Singles:

	US	UK
Photograph, 1983	12	–
Rock Of Ages, 1983	16	–
Animal, 1987	19	6
Hysteria, 1988	10	26
Pour Some Sugar On Me, 1988	2	18
Armageddon It, 1988	3	20
Love Bites, 1988	1	8
Rocker, 1989	12	15

Albums:
On Through The Night (Mercury/Vertigo), 1980
High 'n' Dry (Mercury/Vertigo), 1981
Pyromania (Mercury/Vertigo), 1983
Hysteria (Vertigo), 1987

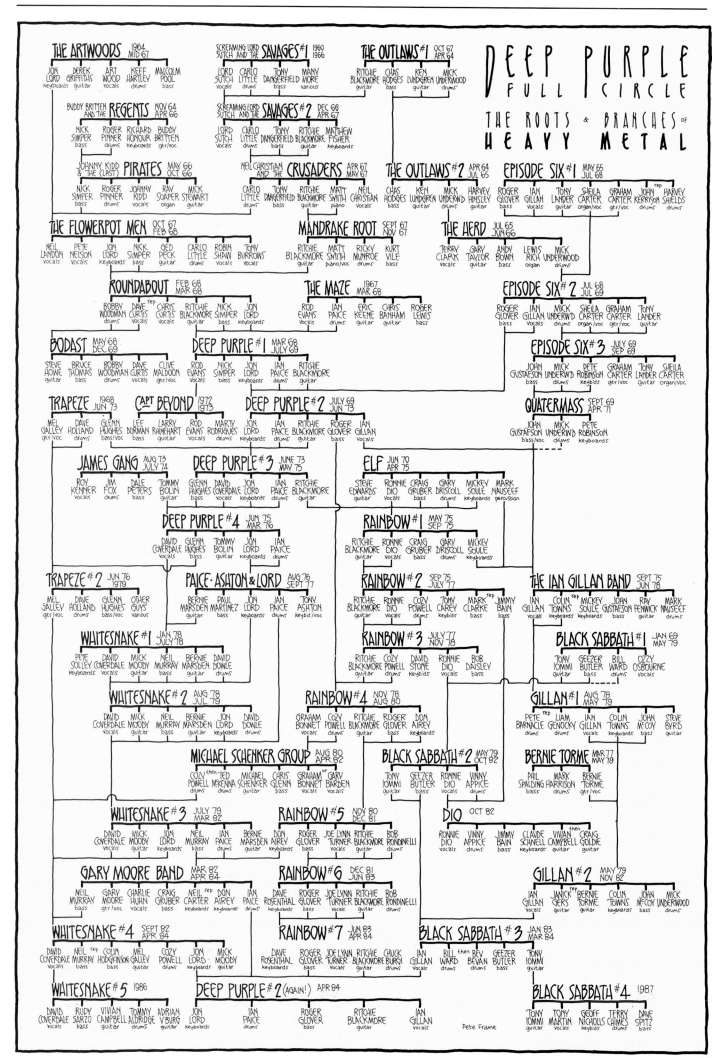

Del Amitri

Scottish group formed 1983

Original line-up: Justin Currie, bass, vocals; Iain Harvey, guitar; David Cummings, guitar; Brian McDermott, drums.

Career: Tuneful aggregation from Glasgow, Scotland, whose lengthy tenure (formed 1983) and recent high profile have still not convinced mainstream rock critics.

First single **Sense Of Sickness** was released on local indie label No Strings and determined self-promotion by band earned Del Amitri support berth on 1984 Smiths and The Fall tours. Debut self-titled album was cut shortly afterwards for Chrysalis' subsidiary Big Star.

Following successful club-date route of the States (1987), and saw Currie pursue relentless public relations activities, band signed to major A&M Records. **Waking Hours** set was released in the summer of 1989, having had a catalogue of production problems, and included chart cuts **Nothing Ever Happens, Move Away Jimmy Blue** and **Kiss This Thing Goodbye**, their first outing in the US single listings.

European tour, which commenced in the autumn of 1990 has sustained band's presence, particularly in Scotland, but another album would consolidate success. If Del Amitri remember that their clever mix of acoustic and electric music is pop, they should have a future.

Hit Singles:

	US	UK
Nothing Ever Happens, 1990	—	11

Albums:
Del Amitri (Chrysalis), 1985
Waking Hours (A&M), 1989

Depeche Mode

UK group formed 1980

Original line-up: Andy Fletcher, guitar, vocals; Martin Gore, guitar, vocals; Vince Clarke, synthesizers, vocals; Dave Gahan, vocals.

Career: Formed by Fletcher, Gore and Clarke in Basildon, Essex, under forgotten name. Acquired Depeche Mode tag from French fashion magazine. In 1981, dispensed with guitars to become all-electronic band. Early demo tapes met with zero response, until group began to play 'futurist'

nights at Bridge House pub in East London. Seen by group entrepreneur Stevo who included a track, **Photographic**, on semi-legendary Some Bizzare compilation LP; others on album included Soft Cell, Blancmange, The The and Naked Lunch. Group was also approached by Daniel Miller of Mute Records, who became group's Svengali and record producer.

First Mute single, **Dreaming Of Me**, was minor hit in early 1981. Since then, numerous singles and albums have reached UK Top 10, despite departure, after release of first LP, of Vince Clarke, who had been main songwriter to this point. Martin Gore assumed this role and success continued unabated, while Vince Clarke formed Yazoo (or Yaz in US) with Alison Moyet.

Early 1982 saw recruitment of ex-Hitmen synth operator Alan Wider, and resulting quartet maintained solid chart status despite loss of Clarke.

World tour in 1988 successfully tested audience response, and resulting footage from concerts was released as *Depeche Mode 101* movie and video.

Above: Music For The Masses, Depeche Mode. Courtesy Mute Records.

With no sign of Depeche Mode taking downward spiral, Gore excused himself for solo **Counterfeit** EP album, a minor hit in 1989, but found home is where the hits are when 1990 LP **Violator** became their biggest seller.

Hit Singles:

	US	UK
New Life, 1981	—	11
Just Can't Get Enough, 1981	—	8
See You, 1982	—	6
The Meaning Of Love, 1982	—	12
Leave In Silence, 1982	—	18
Get The Balance Right, 1983	—	13
Everything Counts, 1983	—	6
People Are People, 1984*	13	4
Master And Servant, 1984	—	9
Somebody, 1984	—	16
Shake The Disease, 1985	—	18
It's Called A Heart, 1985	—	18
Stripped, 1986	—	15
A Question Of Time, 1986	—	18
Strangelove, 1987	—	16
Never Let Me Down Again, 1987	—	22
Behind The Wheel, 1988	—	22
Personal Jesus, 1989	—	13
Enjoy The Silence, 1990	8	6
Policy Of Truth, 1990	15	16
World In My Eyes, 1990	—	17

*1985 in US

Albums:
Speak And Spell (Sire/Mute), 1981
A Broken Frame (Sire/Mute), 1982
Construction Time Again (Sire/Mute), 1983
Some Great Reward (Mute), 1984
The Singles 81-85 (Mute), 1985
Black Celebration (Sire/Mute), 1986
Music For The Masses (Mute), 1987
101 (live at Pasadena Rose Bowl), (Sire/Mute), 1988
Violator (Sire/Mute), 1990

Devo

US group formed 1976

Original line-up: Jerry Casale, bass; Mark Mothersbough, vocals, guitar, keyboards; Bob Casale, guitar; Bob Mothersbough, guitar; Alan Meyers, drums.

Career: Jerry and Mark met at Kent State in early 70s and began experimental non-musical approach to music, and mid-70s upheaval provided chance for hearing. Bob

Above: Are We Not Flowerpot Men? Devo, resplendent in The Searchers' old stage suits.

Casale (brother of Jerry) and Bob Mothersbough (brother of Mark), and fellow Akron friend Myers completed line-up.

In 1977 Iggy Pop, then with David Bowie, befriended band which won cult status. Self-released early singles (**Jocko Homo**, **Mongoloid**, and jerky, electronic cover of Stones' **Satisfaction**) with clinical, icy edge spread underground reputation. As befitting former Fine Art majors, Jerry and Mark marketed Devo with multi-media campaign incorporating masks, films, in-jokes about potatoes, philosophies of devolution, science and flower pots, as well as a self-developed language.

High Tech gloss was enhanced by Eno-produced first album. With Ken Scott-produced **Duty Now For The Future**, band took things more seriously, to its detriment, and **Freedom Of Choice** signified a shift to dance music with disco hit **Whip It**. Devo's electronic bop continued through quirky live mini LP and into precision beat of **New Traditionalists**.

Following **Oh No It's Devo**, another predictable pastiche, band found interest stagnating, although **Live: Devo** outing in 1987 was not without fire. The Enigma release **Total Devo** (1988) suggested time for a re-think for the radical technocrats, but **Smooth Noodle Maps** (1990) confirmed procrastination. Devo found the rest of the world catching up with them faster than they had imagined.

Hit Singles:

	US	UK
Whip It, 1980	14	51

Albums:
Q: Are We Not Men? A: We Are Devo (Warner Bros/Virgin), 1978
Duty Now For The Future (Warner Bros/Virgin), 1979
Freedom Of Choice (Warner Bros/Virgin), 1980
Live (mini-album) (Warner Bros/Virgin), 1981
New Traditionalists (Warner Bros/Virgin), 1981
Oh No! It's Devo (Warner Bros/Virgin), 1982
Shout (Warner Bros), 1984
Live: Devo (Virgin), 1987
Hardcore Volume 1, 1974-77 (Rykodisc/Essential), 1990
Smooth Noodle Maps (Enigma), 1990
Greatest Misses (Warner Bros), 1991
Greatest Hits (Warner Bros), 1991

Left: Depeche Mode, proving that as long as there is an electric socket on the wall, they can make music. Just can't get enough, or would you prefer to enjoy the silence?

Dexys Midnight Runners

UK group formed 1978

Original line-up: Kevin Rowland, vocals, guitar; Al Archer, guitar; Jimmy Paterson, trombone; Pete Saunders, organ; J.B., tenor saxophone; Steve 'Babyface' Spooner, alto saxophone; Pete Williams, bass; Andy Growcott, drums.

Career: Group's main-man Kevin Rowland (born Wolverhampton, August 17, 1953) started in Lucy and Lovers then joined the Killjoys. Made one record, **Johnny Won't Get To Heaven**. In July 1978 Birmingham-based Rowlands decided to form new band in 60s soul mould. Result was Dexys Midnight Runners. Image was based on New York 60s street gangs — inspired by movie *Mean Streets*.

Former Clash manager Bernie Rhodes was called in to help; got group onto Specials' tour as support. Via his own Oddball label, Rhodes secured an EMI/Parlophone recording contract leading to release of **Dance Stance** in October 1979. Brass-laden record, with lyrics about bigotry towards Irish, made UK Top 40. This capitalized on small but dedicated following built via controversial 44-date Straight From The Heart tour where Rowland's uncompromising attitude to audiences angered some, delighted others.

Having parted company with Rhodes, band issued second single. A-side **Geno** was tribute to 60s British soul club hero Geno Washington; flip-side was re-make of Johnny Johnson And The Bandwagon's soul oldie **Breaking Down The Walls Of Heartache**. On last day of recording debut LP, band snatched master-tapes from producer Pete Wingfield and refused to give them to EMI unless company came up with better contract; their nerve won out. Finally released in July 1980, **Searching For The Young Soul Rebels** stayed on charts for three months and was strong showcase for Rowland's stance — so strong that Rowland thought he would never be able to surpass it and made tentative plans to move into films. Third single **There There My Dear** was another hit.

Rowland continued to create controversy. Group took out full page adverts in which they slated music papers and rock writers as being 'dishonest and hippy'. They stated that in future they would communicate with fans by submitting their own essays to the press and by including written handouts with their records.

Band set off on aptly titled Midnight Runners Intense Emotion Revue Tour. Tired from exhaustive recording sessions and under-rehearsed for the road, group met hostile

Below: Too-Rye-Ay, Dexy's Midnight Runners. Courtesy Mercury Records.

reaction from audience. Rowland repaid compliment by abusing the crowd nightly.

Massive row broke out in group during European tour. Rowland had decided to release **Keep It Part 2** as next single. Rest of band disagreed and when Rowland insisted on having own way they quit, with exception of Paterson.

Rowland returned to Birmingham to put together new line-up. (Rowland; Paterson; Micky Billingham, keyboards; Paul Speare, tenor sax; Brian Maurice, alto sax; Billy Adams, guitar; Seb Shelton, drums). He asked that group's recent recordings should not be exploited but EMI decided to release **Plan**, a song which they rightly thought would prove Dexys ability to come up with the goods. In protest, Rowland decided to walk out on contract. New manager Paul Burton spent two days studying small print before he found loophole that enabled Rowland to get away with it.

When group returned to stage there was whole new look. Hooded anoraks, tracksuit trousers and boxing boots replaced previous gang image. In keeping with this 'keep fit' style, group banned consumption of alcohol at their gigs. Midnight Runners Projected Passion Revue climaxed with three nights at London's hallowed Old Vic theatre, the first rock band to play there.

New deal with Phonogram saw somewhat below par **Show Me** single make charts. Like image, the music was also changing direction. Rowland had been experimenting for some time with use of violins (playing riffs rather than as an orchestra). First result was **Liars A To E**, which was none too successful. Next time out, though, was the superb **The Celtic Soul Singers/Love Part Two**. On this, the fiddles of the Emerald Express — Helen O'Hara, Steve Brennan and Roger MacDuff — replaced familiar Dexys brass sound. Record only reached lower limits of chart but die was cast.

Yet another new image emerged: dungarees, neckerchiefs and leather jerkins

Above: Pictured at their peak are Dexy's Midnight Runners, with Kevin Rowland front row (sitting).

to fit almost folksy bent of much of the new music. **Come On Eileen** (first US hit) shot group back to top in early summer 1982. **Too-Rye-Ay** album featured neat blend of acoustic guitar and violins with soft brass and included brilliant brassy version of Van Morrison's **Jackie Wilson Said (I'm In Heaven When You Smile)**.

After 18-month hiatus, Rowland reappeared with **Don't Stand Me Down** set on Mercury, although self-proclaimed projects subsequently fizzled out and artist was compelled to file for bankruptcy. Billed as 'Kevin Rowland from Dexy's Midnight Runners', **The Wanderer** (1988) has been this artist's last sighting for three years, although TV-prompted **Greatest Hits** package (1991) spelled rumours of reformation of Runners.

Hit Singles:	US	UK
Geno, 1980	–	1
There There My Dear, 1980	–	7
Show Me, 1981	–	16
Come On Eileen, 1982	1	1
Because Of You, 1986	–	13

As Kevin Rowland and Dexys Midnight Runners:

	US	UK
Jackie Wilson Said, 1982	–	5
Let's Get This Straight (From The Start), 1982	–	17
The Celtic Soul Brothers (re-issue), 1983	–	20

Albums:
Searching For The Young Soul Rebels (EMI/ Fame), 1980
Too-Rye-Ay (Mercury), 1982
Geno (–/EMI), 1983
Don't Stand Me Down (Mercury), 1985

Kevin Rowland Solo:
The Wanderer (–/Mercury), 1988

Neil Diamond

US vocalist, composer, guitarist
Born Brooklyn, New York, January 24, 1941

Career: Became staff songwriter with Sunbeam Music in New York City's legendary Brill Building 'hit factory' in early 60s. Earned biggest successes with **I'm A Believer** and **A Little Bit Me, A Little Bit You** for The Monkees.

Fellow writers Ellie Greenwich and Jeff Barry recognized Diamond's potential as artist and took him to Bert Berns' new Bang label in late 1965. Debut single **Solitary Man** (1966) set off train of hits, including **Cherry Cherry**, **Sweet Caroline** and **Cracklin' Rosie**, all cut after switch to Uni label. Meanwhile, **Kentucky Woman** (Elvis Presley and Deep Purple) and **The Boat That I Row** (Lulu) gave Diamond further rewards as writer.

With **Tap Root Manuscript** album (1970), Diamond ventured beyond realms of pure pop for imaginative (if trifle pretentious) **African Trilogy** song cycle.

Earlier projected as a clean-cut 'all-American boy', Diamond grew hair longer and cultivated new image as introspective folk-poet; built ever wider audience. In 1973, earned record multi-million dollar advance on signing to Columbia for conceptual **Jonathan Livingston Seagull** soundtrack album. This was followed by **Serenade** (1974), then two years of silence before superb **Beautiful Noise** set, produced by The Band's Robbie Robertson, as was **Love At The Greek** live double album.

Teaming up with Barbra Streisand in late 1978, Diamond had huge hit with duet title track from **You Don't Bring Me Flowers** LP. (Diamond and Streisand had both recorded **Flowers** single; Colombia decided to record duet when they heard a DJ splice two versions together). Worked with Four Seasons' producer Bob Gaudio for follow-up set **September Morn** (1979).

The 1980 re-make of the classic Al Jolson movie *The Jazz Singer*, co-starring Sir Laurence Olivier, took Diamond to new heights and revealed his acting talents. Spine-tingling hit single **Love On The Rocks** from film showed his mastery of mood and innate soulfulness.

Perfunctory 'live' set preceded 1984 collection **Primitive**, although output has receded dramatically since prolific 70s decade. Often dismissed as a purveyor of somewhat trite efforts at artiness, Diamond has emerged as a distinctive songwriter.

Hit Singles:	US	UK
Cherry Cherry, 1966	6	–
I Got The Feelin' (Oh No No), 1966	16	–
You Got To Me, 1967	18	–
Girl, You'll Be A Woman Soon, 1967	10	–
I Thank The Lord For The Night Time, 1967	13	–
Sweet Caroline, 1969	4	–
Holly Holy, 1969	6	–
Cracklin' Rosie, 1970	1	3
He Ain't Heavy, He's My Brother, 1970	20	–
Sweet Caroline, 1971	–	8
I Am...I Said, 1971	4	4
Stones/Crunchy Granola Suite, 1971	14	–
Song Sung Blue, 1972	1	14
Play Me, 1972	11	–
Walk On Water, 1972	17	–
Longfellow Serenade, 1974	5	–
If You Know What I Mean, 1976	11	35

Beautiful Noise, 1976	–	13
Desiree, 1978	16	39
Forever In Blue Jeans, 1979	20	16
September Morn, 1979	17	–
Love On The Rocks, 1980	2	17
Hello Again, 1981	6	51
America, 1981	8	–
Yesterday's Song, 1981	11	–
Heartlight, 1982	5	47

With Barbra Streisand:

You Don't Bring Me Flowers, 1978	1	5

Albums:
The Feel Of Neil Diamond (Bang/–), 1966
Just For You (Bang/–), 1967
Greatest Hits (Bang/Joy), 1968
Velvet Gloves And Spit (MCA), 1968
Brother Love's Traveling Salvation Show (MCA), 1969
Touching You Touching Me (MCA), 1969
Gold (MCA), 1970
Shiloh/Solitary Man (Bang/–), 1970
Tap Root Manuscript (MCA), 1970
Do It (Bang/–), 1971
Moods (MCA), 1972
Hot August Night (MCA), 1972
Double Gold (Bang/–), 1973
Rainbow (MCA), 1973
Jonathan Livingston Seagull (soundtrack), 1973
Stones (MCA), 1974
12 Greatest Hits (Direct/MCA), 1974
Serenade (Columbia/CBS), 1974
Beautiful Noise (Columbia/CBS), 1976
And The Singer Sings His Song (MCA), 1976
Love At The Greek (Columbia/CBS), 1977
20 Golden Greats (MCA), 1978
September Morn (Columbia/CBS), 1980
The Jazz Singer (songs from the soundtrack) (Capitol), 1980
Love Songs (Columbia/CBS), 1981
On The Way To The Sky (Columbia/CBS), 1981
12 Greatest Hits, Volume II (Columbia/CBS), 1982
Heartlight (Columbia/CBS), 1982
Live Diamond (–/MCA), 1982
Classics (CBS), 1983
Primitive (CBS), 1984
Headed For The Future (CBS), 1986
Hot August Night II (CBS), 1987
I'm Glad You're Here With Me Tonight (CBS), 1987
Sweet Caroline (MCA), 1987
Sweet Caroline 2 (MCA), 1987
Lovescape (Columbia), 1991

With Barbra Streisand:
You Don't Bring Me Flowers (Columbia/CBS), 1978

Bo Diddley

US vocalist, guitarist, composer
Born Ellas McDaniel, McComb, Mississippi, December 30, 1928

Career: Raised by mother's cousin, Mrs Gussie McDaniel; taken to Chicago aged five. Studied classical violin for 12 years but also absorbed music of Baptist church services. Rhythm and blues influences were in complete contrast — balladry of Nat Cole, humour of Louis Jordan and guitar of John Lee Hooker. Streets of Chicago brought contact with Mississippi Delta blues style of Muddy Waters and Little Walter, who gigged in local clubs.

Right: Bo moves into turbo-speed on his Kellogg's Cornflake packet.

Given guitar by sister as teenager; taught himself to play and formed small group in early 1950s. Played on street corners: Diddley, vocals, guitar; Frank Kirkland, drums; Jerome Green, maraccas; Billy Boy Arnold, sometimes on harp.

Earned money as boxer, then construction worker, before realizing that music could also pay bills. Auditioned for Chess in 1954, cutting **I'm A Man** and **Bo Diddley**, a landmark with its throbbing jungle rhythm. Disc was released on Checker in spring 1955. A Top 10 R&B hit, it provided foundation for years of inimitable material. Regular band included half-sister 'The Duchess' on rhythm guitar. Diddley maintained phenomenal output of original, lyrically unorthodox material with strong humour content; **Cracking Up** provided Bo's first crossover pop hit in summer 1959; then **Say Man** became Top 20 smash.

In early 1960s Diddley's repertoire was used by many British beat groups, songs like **Road Runner**, **Pretty Thing**, **Mona**, **Who Do You Love**, **I Can Tell** and **You Can't Judge A Book By The Cover** clocking up good mileage. Diddley released prodigious quantity of LPs, mainly during 60s. Material was still mainly original, often predictable, but artist's humour and enthusiasm ooze from the grooves.

Distinctive pair of albums cut in 1967; **Super Blues**, with Bo, Muddy Waters and Little Walter, and **The Super Super Blues Band** with Bo, Muddy and Howlin' Wolf. Around 1970 Bo tried heavier musical context for LP **Another Dimension**, with uncomfortable results; similarly uninspiring was **Big Bad Bo** in 1974. In 1972 and 1973,

his stage performance was filmed for footage in movies *Let The Good Times Roll* and *Keep On Rockin'*.

Continued heavy schedule of live shows in US and Europe; disc career less active. With demise of Chess, signed with RCA; cut disappointing LP **20th Anniversary Of Rock 'n' Roll**, and **Not Fade Away**, a flop 45. As well as regular touring schedule with rock 'n' roll revival packages, Diddley enjoyed television prominence in early 90s with appearance in Nike TV commercial, where he was seen jamming with another Bo, US sports star Bo Jackson.

Guitars: Various custom-bodied Gibsons.

Hit Singles:	US	UK
Say Man, 1959	20	–

Albums:
Two Great Guitars (with Chuck Berry) (Pye), 1964
Golden Decade (–/Chess), 1973
Toronto Rock 'n' Roll Revival 1969 Volume 5 (Accord/–), 1981
Go Bo Diddley (recorded 1955-58) (Chess/–), 1987
The London Bo Diddley Sessions (with Roy Wood) (Chess), 1989
Breakin' Through The BS (Chess/–), 1989

Worth Searching Out:
Have Guitar Will Travel (Chess/–), 1962
Bo Diddley Is A Gunslinger (Chess/Pye), 1963
Black Gladiator (Checker/–), 1971
In The Spotlight (Chess), 1987
Bo Diddley (Vogue), 1987

Dion

US vocalist, songwriter
Born Dion Di Mucci, Bronx, New York, July 18, 1939

Career: First professional appearance was at 15 on Paul Whiteman's *Teen Club* TV show in Philadelphia. First group The Timberlanes formed in 1957; recorded one single for Mohawk label without success. During 1958 formed new group The Belmonts, named after Belmont Avenue in NY; recorded further single for Mohawk, which also failed. Moved to Laurie label where **I Wonder Why** (released as Dion And The Belmonts) quickly became hit, followed by two Top 50 entries. Then, in 1959, had first Top 10 hit, **A Teenager In Love**. All were in pure, if 'white', doo-wop style.

Dion And The Belmonts became most popular white vocal group of rock 'n' roll era, although chart successes were somewhat erratic. Biggest hit **Where Or When** preceded Dion's departure from Belmonts in 1960, and first solo hit in similar style, **Lonely Teenager**. Despite failure of immediate follow-ups, achieved even greater success when **Runaround Sue** reached No. 1 in 1961, consolidating popularity in both US and UK.

Moved to CBS Records in 1962. Continued to hit charts with singles still sounding like extension of Belmonts' style, until venture into MOR and, later, R&B, style failed to maintain popularity. Drugs problem forced semi-retirement during 1964 but returned in 1967 to reunite with Belmonts, recording minor hit **My Girl The Month of May** for ABC; failed to equal past glories.

By 1969 had re-signed with Laurie Records and regained magic touch, with **Abraham, Martin & John** reaching No. 4 and heralding turn to 'folk-protest' style for remainder of Laurie output. Signed to Warner Bros in 1970. Apart from further reunion with Belmonts, which resulted in fine live LP (1972), recorded in contemporary singer-songwriter style without commercial success.

Despite highly regarded recordings with Phil Spector in late 70s and several attempts at comeback singles and albums, Dion has never equalled his early successes.

A regular on 50s and 60s rock revival tours, Dion was inducted into the Rock 'n' Roll Hall Of Fame in 1990, a year which also saw him selected to compose theme for American comedy series *Lenny*. Other recorded work has included sessions for Christian label Dayspring.

Hit Singles:	US	UK
No One Knows,* 1958	19	–
A Teenager In Love,* 1959	5	–
Where Or When*, Dion 1960	3	–
Lonely Teenager, 1960	12	–
Runaround Sue, 1961	1	11
The Wanderer, 1961	2	10
Lovers Who Wander, 1962	3	–
Little Diane, 1962	8	–
Love Came To Me, 1962	10	–
Ruby Baby, 1963	2	–
Donna The Prima Donna, 1963	6	–
Drip Drop, 1963	6	–
Abraham, Martin And John, 1968	4	–
The Wanderer, 1976	–	16

*With The Belmonts

Albums:
Dion's Greatest Hits (Laurie), 1964
Greatest Hits (Columbia/–), 1978
Dion And The Belmonts Greatest Hits (Laurie), 1982

I Put Away My Idols (Dayspring), 1985
Kingdom In The Streets (Dayspring), 1985
Reunion Live At Madison Square (recorded 1972) (Rhino/—), 1987
Yo Frankie (Arista), 1989
The Return Of The Wanderer (DCC/Ace), 1990
Loves Who Wander (Ace), 1991

Dire Straits

UK group formed 1977

Original line-up: Mark Knopfler, Schecter, Fernandez guitars, vocals, producer; Dave Knopfler, guitar; John Illsley, bass; Pick Withers, drums.

Career: Thunderbirds are go! After a six-year hiatus, Dire Straits officially reformed in the summer of 1991 for worldwide tour and new studio album **On Every Street**. Revamped line-up (Knopfler, Guy Fletcher and Alan Clark on keyboards, a session drummer replacing Withers and original bass player John Illsley) featured on video for **Calling Elvis** directed by *Thunderbirds* TV series' director Gerry Anderson.

Knopfler's solo projects — The Notting Hillbillies, soundtrack music for *The Princess Bride*, studio work with Chet Atkins, Joan Armatrading, Randy Newman, charity shows, and a gig with Eric Clapton — had seriously threatened Dire Straits' future. To curtail speculation, Knopfler officially retired the band in 1988, ending an 11 year reign in the upper echelons of the rock-music stratosphere.

DS served brief apprenticeship after formation in Deptford, South London in 1977. Knopfler (from Glasgow, Scotland) set line-up with brother Dave (guitar), Illsley (bass) and Pick Withers (drums). First single **Sultans Of Swing** charted in both US/UK in 1979, and established Knopfler's mono-tone vocals and fluid guitar picking (but no pick, folks!).

After second LP, **Communique**, Hal Lindes replaced David Knopfler, and Withers was a further casualty when Terry Williams (ex-Man, Rockpile) took the drum seat after **Love Over Gold** album (1982). Session keyboard player Clark had been added permanently for this latter set.

The archetypal touring unit, DS nonetheless had difficult periods on the road, with Knopfler ever more uncomfortable with role as rock superstar. His independent projects, producing Bob Dylan's **Infidels**, scoring movies *Local Hero*, *Cal*, and *Comfort And Joy*, had observers speculating on the group's future. John Illsley also cut solo work **Never Told A Soul** for group's UK label Vertigo.

Two-year sabbatical ended by release of studio album **Brothers In Arms** (1985) which prompted 12-month world tour, and 13 keyboard augmentation of DS line-up which saw Guy Fletcher replace Clark. Self-deprecatory single **Money For Nothing** earned band first US No. 1 and permanent spot on MTV.

Despite a truckload of international awards and spiralling interest in his nomadic troup, Knopfler decided that the Nelson Mandela 70th Birthday Party concert at Wembley Stadium would mark the end of the Dire Straits.

Knopfler eventually returned to the road with low-key Notting Hillbillies, featuring Brendan Croker and Steve Phillips, and their album **Missing . . . Presumed Having . . .** surprised pundits (and Knopfler) by making UK album listings.

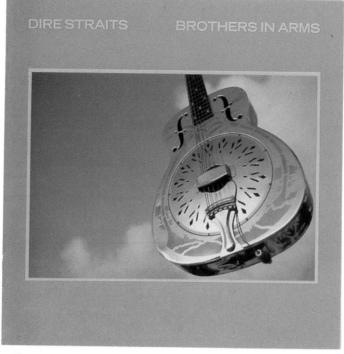

The continued clamour for a further chapter in the DS story, was appeased by staggering projected three-year continental tour, with 300 shows promised. Early signs (October 1991) indicate a return to DS mania, with ticket touts/scalpers claiming gigs will keep them in Mercedes Benz limos for years.

Hit Singles:

	US	UK
Sultans Of Swing, 1979	4	8
Romeo And Juliet, 1981	—	1
Private Investigations, 1982	—	2
Twisting By The Pool, 1983	—	14
So Far Away, 1985	—	20
Money For Nothing, 1985	1	4
Brothers In Arms, 1985	—	16
Walk Of Life, 1986	13	2
Your Latest Trick, 1986	—	26
Calling Elvis, 1991	—	21

Album:
Dire Straits (Warner Bros/Vertigo), 1978
Communique (Warner Bros/Vertigo), 1979
Making Moves (Warner Bros/Vertigo), 1980
Love Over Gold (Warner Bros/Vertigo), 1982
Alchemy Live (Warner Bros/Vertigo), 1984
Brothers In Arms (Warner Bros/Vertigo), 1985
On Every Street (Vertigo), 1991

John Illsley Solo:
Never Told A Soul (Vertigo), 1987
Glass (Warner Bros/Vertigo), 1988

Mark Knopfler Solo:
Local Hero (soundtrack) (Vertigo), 1983
Neck And Neck (with Chet Atkins), (Columbia/CBS), 1990

Notting Hillbillies:
Missing...Presumed Having A Good Time (Warner Bros/Vertigo), 1990

Fats Domino

US vocalist, pianist, composer
Born Antoine Domino, New Orleans, February 26, 1928

Career: One of nine children in family with little musical background. Became interested in piano at early age; taught to play by his brother-in-law Harrison Verrett.

Above: Brothers In Arms, Dire Straits. Courtesy Vertigo Records.

Quickly gained proficiency; played and sang in local clubs. At 17, was in Billy Diamond's band; leader tagged him 'Fats' and it stuck. Played nights in juke-joints and worked days in factory when spotted by trumpeter/ bandleader Dave Bartholomew.

Success began in 1949 with Imperial Records. December session yielded **The Fat Man**, a hit early in 1950. Fats had R&B hits for five years; style influenced by Albert Ammons, Meade Lux Lewis, Pleasant Joseph, Leon T. Gross (Archibald), Little Willie Littlefield.

Hit national charts in late 1955 with **Ain't That A Shame**; for next eight years was regular in US Top 50. Hits included **I'm In Love Again**, **Blueberry Hill**, **Blue Monday**, **Whole Lotta Loving**, **I'm Ready**, **Walking To New Orleans** and **Be My Guest**. Also had parts in rock movies *Shake Rattle & Roll*, *Disc Jockey Jamboree*, *The Big Beat*, *The Girl Can't Help It*.

1960s saw dilution of music with occasional strings; material less convincing in aesthetic content. At end of 1962 declining sales brought parting with Imperial. Signed to ABC Paramount, output tailored

Below: The veteran rocker from New Orleans, Fats Domino.

to contemporary needs; **Red Sails In The Sunset** was Top 50 hit, combining piano triplets with swirling strings. A dozen releases yielded one more hit, **Heartbreak Hill**; by late 1964 Fats and Paramount had parted. Artist joined Mercury in 1965, but brief association yielded only a couple of abysmal singles.

Company taped Domino in Las Vegas, producing excellent 'live' LP. Made British debut at the Saville Theatre, March 1967. Following two years of recording inactivity formed own label, Broadmoor. Cut two singles before being signed by Reprise in 1968.

Above: Donovan's Greatest Hits. Courtesy Epic Records.

Reprise album **Fats Is Back** was produced by Richard Perry; half-a-dozen singles had small sales, but single **Lady Madonna** made US charts.

Fats now seems content to live quietly at home with wife Rosemary and their eight children. Takes his pick of cabaret dates and occasional overseas tours; in 1978 went to Sea-Saint Studio to cut LP **Sleeping On The Job** for Sonet. In 1987, the Fatman was honoured with a NARAS Lifetime Achievement award, presented the Grammy awards that year.

After half decade away from recording, Domino cut live double album for New Orleans-based Tomato label, and featured on jazz revivalists The Dirty Dozen's Brass Band's first LP. His classic **My Blue Heaven** was theme of disappointing 1990 Steve Martin movie of same name, but prompted yet another greatest hits package.

Hit Singles:

	US	UK
Ain't That A Shame, 1955	10	23*
I'm In Love Again/My Blue Heaven, 1956	3	12
My Blue Heaven/I'm In Love Again, 1956	19	—
When My Dreamboat Comes Home, 1956	14	—

Blueberry Hill, 1956	2	6
Blue Monday, 1957	5	23
I'm Walkin', 1957	4	19
Valley Of Tears/It's You I Love, 1957	8	25
It's You I Love/Valley of Tears, 1957	8	25
The Big Beat, 1958	26	20
Whole Lotta Loving, 1959	6	–
Margie/I'm Ready, 1959	51	18
I'm Ready/Margie, 1959	16	–
I Want To Walk You Home/I'm Gonna Be A Wheel Someday, 1959	8	14
I'm Gonna Be A Wheel Someday/ I'm Gonna Walk You Home, 1959	17	–
Be My Guest, 1959	8	11
Country Boy, 1960	25	19
Walking To New Orleans, 1960	6	19
Three Nights A Week, 1960	15	45
My Girl Josephine, 1960	14	32
Let The Four Winds Blow, 1961	15	–

Albums:

Million Sellers (Liberty), 1962
Fats Domino (Archive Of Folk And Jazz Music/–), 1966
Fats Domino Volume 2 (Archive Of Folk And Jazz Music/–), 1967
Legendary Masters (United Artists), 1972
The Fats Domino Story Volumes 1-6 (–/United Artists), 1977
Sleeping On The Job (Polydor/Sonet), 1979
Best Of (Liberty), 1985
16 Grestest Hits (Bescol), 1987
My Blue Heaven – Best Of (EMI), 1990

Donovan

UK vocalist, guitarist
Born Donovan Leitch, Glasgow, Scotland, May 10, 1946

Career: Launched via UK's *Ready Steady Go* TV pop show (1965) as Britain's answer to Bob Dylan; Donovan projected diluted version of then fashionable 'protest singer' image. His imitation extended to denim dungarees, flat denim hat, harmonica harness and acoustic guitar bearing legend 'this machine kills' (which Dylan himself had borrowed from Woody Guthrie, who had included the important extra word 'fascists'). Switching to flower-power in 1966 he became very much his own man, with delightful results.

Signed to Pye Records, his first big hit, **Catch The Wind**, was still in Dylan mould, but by **Sunshine Superman** (1966) and **Mellow Yellow** (a US chart-topper in 1967) Donovan had evolved extremely catchy folk-pop sound, and consequent **Sunshine Superman** LP, produced by Mickie Most, was a gem, as was **A Gift From A Flower To a Garden** set. By this time Donovan had injected into his work a large measure of mysticism and colourful imagery.

After 1969 Jeff Beck collaboration on **Barabajagal** hit single, Donovan renounced drug culture, took up Eastern mysticism (following Beatles' lead) and retired to Ireland, emerging a year later to score movie *If It's Tuesday This Must Be Belgium*.

In 1972 he scored *The Pied Piper* (which he appeared in) and in *Brother Sun Sister Moon*. Also released was acclaimed **Cosmic Wheels** LP. However, most of Donovan's 70s LPs were poorly received in the US, where the flower-power image was 'out'.

Moving to US, he wrote stage show *7-Tease* in 1974 and cut concept album in Nashville before virtual retirement. Re-emerging at Edinburgh Festival, he toured

Germany and France, and appeared on London Palladium charity Christmas show with Ralph McTell and Billy Connolly which led to 1981 UK concert tour and new album.

After fitful decade, which saw just one studio album **Lady Of The Stars**, Donovan re-emerged courtesy British comedy duo The Singing Corner with new version of **Jennifer Juniper** in the winter of 1990. An unlikely teaming with popular Happy Mondays group for Wembley concert date and new album **Rising** paved way for serious career revival.

Hit Singles:	US	UK
Catch The Wind, 1965	23	4
Colours, 1965	–	4
Sunshine Superman, 1966	1	3
Mellow Yellow, 1966	2	8
Epistle To Dippy, 1967	19	–
There Is A Mountain, 1967	11	8
Jennifer Juniper, 1968	26	5
Hurdy Gurdy Man, 1968	5	4
Atlantis, 1969	7	23
Barabajagal, 1969	–	12

Albums:

Catch The Wind (Hickory/Hallmark), 1965
Sunshine Superman (Epic/Pye), 1966

Above: Stampede, The Doobie Brothers. Courtesy Warner Bros Records.

In Concert (Epic/Pye), 1968
Hurdy Gurdy Man (Epic/–), 1968
From A Flower To A Garden (Epic/Pye), 1968
Barabajagal (with Jeff Beck) (Epic/–), 1968
Greatest Hits (Epic/Pye), 1969
Colours (–/Hallmark), 1972
Cosmic Wheels (–/Epic), 1973
Donovan (–/Rak), 1977
The Donovan File (–/Pye), 1977
Greatest Hits (–/Embassy), 1979
Lady Of The Stars (RCA), 1984
The Classics Live (Great Northern Arts Ltd/–), 1991

Doobie Brothers

US group formed 1970

Original line-up: Tom Johnston, guitar, vocals; John Hartman, drums; Pat Simmons, guitar, vocals; Dave Shogren, bass.

Career: Founded in San Jose, California, from remnants of band Pud; first line-up included Johnston, Hartman and bassist Gregory Murphy. Shogren quickly replaced Murphy, and with acquisition of Simmons group cut self-titled debut album for Warner Bros in 1971.

Additional drummer Mike Hossack joined soon after release of **The Doobie Bros**; Tiran Porter recruited for departing Dave Shogren (who joined Dave Gardner group). Quintet soon earned reputation on West Coast, basing themselves in San Francisco, then San Anselmo.

Twin guitars of Simmons and Johnston courted comparison with Allman Bros. Doobies, however, were altogether lighter and less blues-influenced. Second album **Toulouse Street** introduced band to charts, both album and single (**Listen To The**

Below: The Doobie Brothers 'Takin' It To The Streets' in the late 1970s.

Above: Best Of The Doobies. Courtesy Warner Bros Records.

Music) confirming hard-driving, but commercial, approach.

Now prominent concert attraction, band debuted in UK using new drummer Keith Knudsen (ex-Lee Michaels); Hossack moved to short-lived Bonaroo in 1975. Reviews were mixed but audiences enthusiastic. This line-up cut **The Captain And Me** LP, which followed **Toulouse Street** as second gold record. Band's long-time favourite **Long Train Running** was major single success from album.

What Were Once Vices Are Now Habits included session work from Jeff 'Skunk' Baxter, former Steely Dan guitarist. Baxter joined Doobies permanently shortly after album's release. Two-million seller **Black Water** (another band anthem) was US No. 1 culled from **Vices** set.

Another former Steely Dan member, keyboard player/vocalist Michael McDonald, joined group in 1976; he had temporarily stood in for Johnston during 1975 US tour. McDonald's inclusion took band into new era, with emphasis on R&B-styled rhythms behind his high, impassioned voice — McDonald stands apart as one of the finest rock vocalist in the business (witness duet with Patti LaBelle, **On My Own**).

Never the rock critic's favourite outfit, Doobies reversed opinion with stunning **Minute By Minute** album. With group now trimmed to six-piece (Johnston having left permanently in 1978), and McDonald and Simmons splitting lead vocal role, **Minute** earned four Grammy awards. Title track and **What A Fool Believes** are now rock classics, having been covered by various prominent performers (Aretha Franklin had minor US hit with **Fool**).

Doobies' ever-evolving line-up saw further changes in 1979, when Baxter and Hartman quit. Baxter went on to produce (Nazareth, Terry Boylan) and doing session work after stint with Four On The Floor (with Al Kooper, Rich Schlosser, Neil Stubenhaus). Replacements were Cornelius Bumpus (ex-Moby Grape) keyboards and sax; John McFee (ex-Clover, sessions for Steve Miller and Bill Wyman) guitar; and drummer Chet McCracken (ex-Don Randi Band, Nick Gilder). Seven-piece Doobies recorded **One Step Closer** in 1980, with long-time producer Ted Templeman still at helm. Album included US hit **Real Love**.

Lack of studio recording since **Closer** (**Best Of Volume 2** released in interim) enabled McDonald to release debut solo album **If That's What It Takes** (1982) which featured leading session players Steve Gadd, drums; Willie Weeks, bass; Dean Parks, guitar; Louis Johnson, bass; and Edgar Winter and Jeff and Mike Porcaro (Toto). McDonald has also recorded with Gary Wright, Elton John, Jackie DeShannon, Christopher Cross and Kenny Loggins (with whom he wrote **What A Fool Believes**). Added keyboards to Tom Johnston's solo album **Everything You Feel Is True**.

Farewell Tour album (1983) marked end of road for band, with McDonald's solo work accelerating demise. Founder member Pat Simmons then enjoyed minor solo success before being persuaded to bring Doobies together for University benefit concert. Success of gig prompted permanent reformation, with Simmons, Johnston, Hartman, Porter and Hossack. Comeback album **Cycles** (1989) spawned US Top 10 **The Doctor**; coast-to-coast US tour included augmentation from latter-day member Cornelius Bumpus. Band then cut 1991 set **Brotherhood** to herald new decade.

Hit Singles:

	US	UK
Listen To The Music, 1972	11	29
Long Train Runnin', 1973	8	—
China Grove, 1973	15	—
Black Water, 1975	1	—
Take Me In Your Arms (Rock Me), 1975	11	29
Takin' It To The Streets, 1976	13	—
What A Fool Believes, 1979	1	31
Minute By Minute, 1979	14	47
Real Love, 1980	5	—
The Doctor, 1989	9	—

Albums:
Doobie Brothers (Warner Bros), 1971
Toulouse Street (Warner Bros), 1972
The Captain And Me (Warner Bros), 1973
What Were Once Vices (Warner Bros), 1974
Stampeded (Warner Bros), 1975
Takin' It To The Streets (Warner Bros), 1976
Best Of (Warner Bros), 1976
Livin' On The Fault Line (Warner Bros), 1977
Minute By Minute (Warner Bros), 1979
One Step Closer (Warner Bros), 1980
Best Of Volume 2 (Warner Bros), 1981
Farewell Tour (Warner Bros), 1983
Cycles (Capitol), 1989
Brotherhood (Capitol), 1991

Right: The late and unquestionably great Jim Morrison. Sadly missed.

Doors
US group formed 1965

Original line-up: Jim Morrison, vocals; Ray Manzarek, keyboards; Robby Krieger, bass; John Densmore, drums.

Career: Director Oliver Stone's 1991 movie *The Doors* provided a valuable visual testament to one of America's most notorious bands. Starring Val Kilmer as Jim Morrison, and featuring 'Twin Peaks' Kyle MacLachlan as Ray Manzarek, *The Doors* provided an accurate assessment of an era in history, but a sketchy and often fictitious account of the group.

The film's release prompted a plethora of associated merchandise and books, and revived sales of the most accurate telling of The Doors' story, *No One Here Get's Out Alive* (Danny Sugarman and Jerry Hopkins), first published in 1981.

Morrison was born James Douglas Morrison in Melbourne, Florida on December 8, 1943. Graduated from George Washington High School in 1961, then spent year at St Petersburg Junior College before moving to Los Angeles to major in film technique at UCLA. Met Chicago-born Manzarek, then running blues band Rick And The Ravens, with brothers Rick and Jim, and quartet recruited drummer and LAS native John Densmore from Psychedelic Rangers. Robbie Krieger, also from LA, and, like Densore, a student of meditation and former Psychedelic Ranger, was later added after Manzarek's brothers quit the group. With their line-up set, Doors opened career with gig at London Fog Club on Sunset Boulevard.

Early warning of subsequent tempestuous career came when they were banned from Los Angeles' prestigious rock club, Whiskey A Go-Go, for performance of **The End**, a half-spoken, half-improvised free-form epic song of apocalyptic imagery in which a young man murders his parents. A born rebel, Morrison claimed his own parents were dead and dropped one 's' from surname. His father was, in fact, a successful Rear Admiral from establishment family of long military standing.

The Doors' name was well chosen from William Blake: 'If the doors of perception were cleansed/All things would appear infinite'. Morrison's sense of theatrics aided him in acting out the fantasies, visions and fears of late 60s young America, from the innocuousness of flower power to the often frightening aspects of psychedelia and the self-destructiveness of drug culture. A charismatic figure on-stage, Morrison exuded animal sexuality with a mere glance.

Jack Holzman, who had been busy transforming his Elektra label from an esoteric folk outlet to major rock company, signed Doors; sensational debut album **Doors** included unedited version of **The End** as well as **Light My Fire**.

From sleeve art-work featuring various freaks, to bizarre lyrical content, second album, **Strange Days**, was archetypal Doors. Third set, **Waiting For The Sun**, yielded further No. 1 single **Hello I Love You** (only Doors recording which used a bass player — Doug Lubahn; Manzarek usually supplied bass lines through bass pedal of electric organ). Ray Davies of Kinks sued Doors, claiming **Hello** was rip-off of **All Day And All Of The Night**; UK royalties of **Hello I Love You** went to Davies instead of Doors. Featured on inner sleeve was full libretto of **The Celebration Of The Lizard King** but only small sampling, in form of **Not To Touch The Earth**, appeared on album, and plans for theatrical presentation were unfulfilled. Morrison did venture into movie world via *A Feast Of Friends* (in collaboration with two acquaintances from UCLA days) and two promotional films, *Break On Through* and *The Unknown Soldier*. He had also completed another screenplay (with novelist Michael McClure) shortly before his death.

Hippy generation felt Morrison's political and philosophical statements were diluted by an innate commercialism. Those in authority rated them anarchical heresies and when, on stage, he not only urged violent resistance to police repression but advocated blatant sexualism, he soon ran into trouble. He was arrested for using obscene language in New Haven, Connecticut in December 1967, and for indecent exposure on stage in Miami in March 1969.

Above: Live At The Hollywood Bowl, The Doors. Courtesy Elektra Records.

While court proceedings continued apace, rock critics alleged that Doors were merely pop outfit masquerading as leaders of youth revolution; this was confirmed in part when 1969 album **The Soft Parade** emerged with lightweight chart-style material and lack of direction. However, following album **Morrison Hotel** threw pretension to the wind, revealing hard and raw R&B. **Absolutely Live** set finally gave life to Morrison's reptilian fantasy (and alter-ego) via **The Celebration Of The Lizard**.

With **LA Woman** (1971), Doors reached creative zenith, blending brash rock 'n' roll with imagery of Morrison's lyrics in set which found them at most powerful and disturbing. From it came classic **Riders On The Storm**.

Four years of over-indulgence in sex, drugs, drink, philosophizing, soul-searching and rock 'n' roll were taking their toll. An angry, depressed and world-weary Morrison quit group to live in Paris and write poetry (published as two books *The Lords* and *The New Creatures* in 1971).

Fittingly, Morrison's death is shrouded in mystery and there are even rumours that he still lives. According to official records he died of a heart attack in his bath on July 3, 1971. He is buried in Père Lachaise cemetery in Paris, which also houses remains of many of France's most famous artists, musicians, statesmen and legendary eccentrics. Morrison's tomb has become a point of pilgrimage for latter-day hippies.

Though lacking Morrison's touch of demented genius, **Other Voices** album was commendable effort from the three surviving Doors. **Full Circle** was sub-standard and trio broke up (though Manzarek made aborted effort to re-form group later).

Manzarek continued career with solo albums for Mercury in 1975 — **The Golden Scarab** and **The Whole Thing Started With Rock 'N' Roll And Now It's Out Of Control**, a title that could well stand as most fitting epitaph for Jim Morrison.

Krieger and Densmore produced album for the Comfortable Chairs, then formed short-lived Butts Band, Krieger re-emerging in 1977 with jazz/rock outfit for **Bobby Krieger And Friends** album on Blue Note. Manzarek continues to work in California as producer/manager for bands.

Following **Greatest Hits** (1980), which went platinum in US, The Doors' fanatical following were temporarily appeased by new material from Krieger, now signed to Cafe Records. Stone's movie, considered likely to prompt thoughts of a reunion by the remaining trio, instead further fuelled fire of the Morrison legend.

Hit Singles:

	US	UK
Light My Fire, 1967	1	49
People Are Strange, 1967	12	—
Hello I Love You, 1968	1	15
Touch Me, 1969	3	—

Love Her Madly, 1971	11	–
Riders On The Storm, 1971	14	22
Light My Fire, 1991	–	7

Albums:
Doors (Elektra), 1967*
Strange Days (Elektra), 1967
Waiting For The Sun (Elektra), 1968
The Soft Parade (Elektra), 1969
Morrison Hotel/Hard Rock Café (Elektra), 1970
Absolutely Live (Elektra), 1970
13 (Elektra), 1971
LA Woman (Elektra), 1971
Weird Scenes Inside The Goldmine (Elektra), 1971
Best Of (Elektra), 1973
An American Prayer (Elektra), 1978
Greatest Hits (Elektra), 1980
Live At The Hollywood Bowl (Elektra), 1987
The Doors (soundtrack album) (Elektra), 1991
*Re-mastered version available under same title (Mobile/–), 1982

Robbie Krieger Solo:
Versions (–/Shanghai), 1984
No Habla (IRS), 1990

Ray Manzarek Solo:
The Golden Scarab (Mercury), 1975
Carmina Burana (A&M), 1983

Worth Searching Out:
Other Voices (Elektra), 1971

The Drifters
US vocal group formed 1953

Original line-up: Clyde McPhatter; Gerhardt Thrasher; Andrew Thrasher; Bill Pinkney.

Career: More like a football side than a group, The Drifters have featured constantly changing line-up. More than 50 individuals have worked with the official group over past three decades. Several breakaway groups have exploited name, notably Bill Pinkney's Original Drifters.

Masterminded by manager George Treadwell, then husband of Sarah Vaughan, group was launched to showcase lead singer Clyde McPhatter. First six releases, via Atlantic, were R&B hits.

In 1955, McPhatter left for military service, being replaced as lead singer briefly by David Baughn, then by Johnny Moore, who was in turn drafted. Bill Pinkney, Gerhardt Thrasher and Bobby Hendricks also sang lead at various times but most records flopped. The best was **Flip Flop**, led by Moore, and **Drop Drop**, led by Hendricks. Significantly, both songs were penned by Jerry Leiber and Mike Stoller. When Treadwell sacked his group in 1958 and set about finding a new set of Drifters he turned to Leiber and Stoller for material.

Group chosen – Ben E. King, Doc Green, Charlie Thomas, Elsbeary Hobbs – had been working with no real success as The Crowns. Moving King to lead singer and using Leiber/Stoller songs proved masterstroke and 1959 smash hit **There Goes My Baby** set in train whole gamut of big records.

King left for solo career, also with Atlantic, in 1960 and Rudy Lewis was brought in from Clara Ward Singers as new lead voice. Lewis held job for next three years. Rest of group was blended with female back-up quartet of Dionne and Dee Dee Warwick, Doris Troy and Cissy Houston. Arrangements by Phil Spector, Burt Bacharach, Bert Berns and Gary Sherman and songs from Gerry Goffin and Carole King, Burt Bacharach and Hal David, and Barry Mann and Cynthia Weil added to potent format, producing classic hits like **Up On The Roof, Sweets For My Sweet** and **Let The Music Play**.

Lewis died on eve of session for **Under The Boardwalk** and Johnnie Moore, who had returned to group, stepped into breach as new lead singer. Though no longer with Drifters, Moore can claim to have sung lead on more than 80 per cent of their records.

Group had capitalized on coming together of black and white teenage tastes in early 60s, but subsequent polarization of audiences saw their run of success subside. In 1972 UK Atlantic started to score on charts with re-issues of their classics.

Consequent recording deal with Bell, and link with British songwriters Roger Cook, Roger Greenaway and Tony Macauley, brought new run of hits, reviving the teen-ballad story-line themes of their Atlantic classics. **Saturday Night At The Movies** inspired **Kissin' In The Back Row Of The Movies**, and **Under The Boardwalk** and **Sand In My Shoes** provided theme for **Down On The Beach Tonight**.

With group now under management of Treadwell's second wife (and widow) Faye, a steady living was made playing cabaret venues around the world — helping people revive fond memories of their teens. Moore remained only constant factor in perpetually evolving line-up.

In 1980 Moore left for short-lived solo career. He rejoined for short spell then left again to form Slightly Adrift, with fellow Drifter Joe Blunt and former member Clyde Brown, when Faye Treadwell decided to sever 11-year business relationship with group's UK promoter Henry Sellers.

Treadwell brought Ben E. King back into Drifters as lead singer and he stayed on when Moore returned yet again in 1984.

In 1987, The Drifters were inducted into the Rock 'n' Roll Hall Of Fame, and Ben E. King returned to chart prominence with a re-issue of classic **Stand By Me**, which was used in television commercials for jeans.

Hit Singles:	US	UK
There Goes My Baby, 1959	2	–
Dance With Me, 1959	15	17
This Magic Moment, 1960	16	–
Save The Last Dance For Me, 1960	1	2
I Count The Years, 1961	17	28
Please Stay, 1961	14	–
Sweets For My Sweet, 1961	16	–
Up On The Roof, 1963	5	–
On Broadway, 1963	9	–
Under The Boardwalk, 1964	4	45
Saturday Night At The Movies, 1964	18	–
At The Club/Saturday Night At The Movies, 1972	–	3
Come On Over To My Place, 1972	–	9
Like Sister And Brother, 1973	–	7
Kissin' In The Back Row Of The Movies, 1974	–	2
Down On The Beach Tonight, 1974	–	7
There Goes My First Love, 1975	–	3
Can I Take You Home Little Girl, 1975	–	10
Hello Happiness, 1976	–	12
You're More Than A Number In My Little Red Book, 1976	–	5

Albums:
Golden Hits (Atlantic), 1966
Greatest Recordings—The Early Years (Atco/–), 1960
Love Games (–/Bell), 1975
24 Original Hits (Atlantic), 1975
Juke Box Giants (–/Audio Fidelity), 1982
Drifters With Ben E. King (Entertainers), 1987
Save The Last Dance For Me—The Definitive Collection (Atlantic), 1987
20 Greatest Hits (Spectrum), 1987
Let The Boogie Woogie Roll: 1953-58 (two CD set) (Atlantic/–), 1989

Duran Duran
UK group formed 1980

Original line-up: Simon Le Bon, vocals; Andy Taylor, guitar; Nick Rhodes, synthesizer; John Taylor, bass; Roger Taylor, drums.

Career: Nick Rhodes and John Taylor formed early version of band (name taken from villain in film *Barbarella*) with Steve Duffy (vocals) and Simon Colley (bass) — John played guitar at this point. Duffy and Colley left, replaced by Andy Wickett (vocals, ex-TV Eye) and Roger Taylor ex-Scent Organs. At this stage, band all from Birmingham area. Wickett left, John Taylor moved to bass, and Andy Taylor from Newcastle joined as a result of rock magazine *Melody Maker* advert. Simon (born 1958, Hertfordshire), then studying drama at Birmingham University, became final piece of jigsaw, assuming lyricist/vocal role.

In autumn 1980 band broke through to national attention touring as support to Hazel O'Connor, following up exposure with hit single **Planet Earth** in 1981. Album **Duran Duran** followed, spawning UK hit **Girls On Film**; hit also established Duran as video stars, status they would consolidate throughout their career.

From this point onwards band could do no wrong, garnering enormous commercial success both in UK and US. Somewhat mechanical formula made them less than favourites with critics, but teen buyers throughout world were convinced. Photogenic qualities of band members were no hindrance in conquest of pre- and post-pubescent females.

In mid-80s various dissatisfactions became apparent when Andy and John Taylor formed spin-off group Power Station with Robert Palmer, while remainder formed Duran-like outfit called Arcadia. Both aggregations enjoyed some success. Meanwhile, Simon Le Bon took up yacht racing and almost met a watery grave during transatlantic race.

Le Bon, Rhodes, and John Taylor re-formed for **Notorious** album (1986), with Andy Taylor (soon to cut solo **Thunder** and, in

Above: Duran Duran, teen favourites during the 1980s.

1990, **Dangerous** LPs) also featured. Album resumed band's chart career although trio were subject to continual gossip about long-term future.

With Warren Cuccurullo now added on guitar, Duran Duran cut **Big Thing** set for October 1988 release. Single **I Don't Want Your Love** made UK Top 20 and US Top 10. Although reticent to tour, Le Bon stated that quartet would resume live work when 'good and ready', although 1990 LP **Liberty** had come and gone before any sign of a return to the road.

Hit Singles:	US	UK
Planet Earth, 1981	–	12
Girls On Film, 1981	–	5
My Own Way, 1981	–	14
Hungry Like The Wolf, 1982	3	5
Save A Prayer, 1982*	16	2
Rio, 1982	14	9
Is There Something I Should Know, 1983	4	1
Union Of The Snake, 1983	3	3
New Moon On Monday, 1984	10	9
The Reflex, 1984	1	1
Wild Boys, 1984	2	1
A View To A Kill, 1985	1	2
Notorious, 1986	2	7
I Don't Want Your Love, 1988	4	14
All She Wants Is, 1989	22	9
Violence Of Summer (Love's Taking Over), 1990	–	20

*1985 in US

The Power Station:

Some Like It Hot, 1985	6	14
Get It On, 1985	9	22

Arcadia:

Election Day, 1985	8	7

Albums:
Duran Duran (Harvest/EMI), 1981
Rio (Capitol/EMI), 1982
Seven And The Ragged Tiger (EMI), 1983
Arena (EMI), 1984
Notorious (EMI), 1986
Big Thing (Capitol/EMI), 1988
Decade (–/EMI), 1989
Liberty (Capitol/Parlophone), 1990

The Power Station:
Power Station (Parlophone), 1985

Arcadia:
So Red The Rose (Parlophone), 1985

Andy Taylor Solo:
Thunder (MCA), 1987
Dangerous (MCA), 1990

Ian Dury

UK vocalist, composer
Born Billericay, Essex, 1942

Career: Crippled by polio at age seven, Dury spent early youth at institution for disabled until going to grammar school. At 17 he went to Walthamstow Art College, then on to Royal College of Art for postgraduate course.

While teaching he formed band Kilburn And The High Roads, which cut a couple of albums and achieved considerable cult following. After Kilburn folded, Dury signed with Stiff Records and released **New Boots And Panties** with Blockheads. Dury and co-writer/musical director Chas Jankel combined intriguing new blend of soul/disco with musical-hall lyrical approach.

Boots eventually sold almost half a million copies, mainly in UK, and spawned classic rock 'n' roll anthem **Sex And Drugs And Rock 'n' Roll.**

By now Blockheads had established reputation as hot live act, and were touring. First major single hit came in 1978 with **What A Waste**, which was followed by No. 1 **Hit Me With Your Rhythm Stick.**

1979 single **Reasons To Be Cheerful, Part 3** was band's swansong, although label deal with Polydor (1980) promised plenty. After fitful period, with Dury concentrating on solo projects, band reunited in 1985 after re-mix of **Rhythm Stick** charted briefly; rejoined in 1990 for benefit gigs to assist ailing drummer Charley Charles, which spawned live **Warts 'n' Audience** album.

With his enthusiasm for the music business seemingly waning, Dury threw himself in alternate acting career, and featured in movies *Pirates*, *Hearts Of Fire*, and *The Cook, The Thief, His Wife & Her Lover*, and on stage for Mary O'Malley's *Talk Of The Devil*. In television Dury appeared in *King Of The Ghetto* and in a host of television commercials.

Hit Singles:

	US	UK
What A Waste, 1978	—	9
Hit Me With Your Rhythm Stick, 1978	—	1
Reasons To Be Cheerful, Pt. 3, 1979	—	3

Albums:
New Boots And Panties (Stiff), 1977
Do It Yourself (—/Stiff), 1979
Laughter (—/Stiff), 1980
Lord Upminster (Polydor), 1981
Juke Box Dury (Stiff), 1981
4000 Weeks' Holiday (Polydor), 1984
Warts And Audience (Demon), 1991

Worth Searching Out:
Kilburn and the High Roads:
Handsome (—/Pye), 1975
Wot A Bunch (—/Warner Bros), 1978

Bob Dylan

US composer, vocalist, guitarist, harmonica player
Born Robert Allen Zimmerman, Duluth, Minnesota, May 24, 1941

Career: Quiet, serious Bobby Zimmerman got good grades, participated in school activities and graduated from Hibbing High in 1959. However, listened to blues and country music, and was more interested in becoming rock 'n' roll star. At University of Minnesota discovered remnants of beat era in nearby Dinkytown with its folk music coffee-houses. Seeing this as route to success, began playing at local folk clubs. Read Woody Guthrie's *Bound For Glory*, began calling himself Bob Dylan, and invented past as runaway with Okie roots.

With rambling boy image down pat, got blessing — and fare — from parents for December 1960 visit to Guthrie in hospital. Remained in New York, singing traditional songs in Greenwich Village clubs. *Village Voice* and *New York Times* predicted success, while others thought him Guthrie clone — but uncool, uncaring and mannered.

Played back-up harmonica on title track of Harry Belafonte's **Midnight Special** album, and for Carolyn Hester. Signed by Columbia Records' John Hammond in October 1961. First album **Bob Dylan**, including own compositions **Song To Woody** and **Talkin' New York**, plus traditional numbers, sold only 5,000 copies in first year.

Dylan predicted direction music was heading and took civil rights/anti-war stance, often using 'borrowed' tunes for self-righteous, moralizing topical songs filled with brilliant imagery and caustic irony. By March 1963 reputation was growing, and **The Freewheelin' Bob Dylan** was released (after power struggled between Hammond and Dylan's manager Albert Grossman led to Hammond's departure in mid-recording, replaced by Tom Wilson).

Album includes **Blowin' In The Wind**, highlight of Newport Folk Festival that summer when Dylan sang it with Peter, Paul And Mary. Trio's cover version became Top 10 hit,

Above: John Wesley Harding, Bob Dylan. Courtesy CBS Records.

Above: Knocked Out Loaded, Bob Dylan. Courtesy CBS Records.

switch from folk to rock, and from travelling to tripping. One side had four solo tracks, including **Mr Tambourine Man** and **It's All Over Now, Baby Blue**; other side with electric guitar and backup band featured **Subterranean Homesick Blues**. Released as single, this surreal, apocalyptic vision ultimately became Dylan's first gold record. The Byrds' two-minute version of **Mr Tambourine Man** went to No. 1 in US and UK, leading new folk-rock trend.

Although losing fans among protesters, Dylan gained wider audience of alienated young people who responded to funky music and sneering rejection of American Dream. May 1965 film *Don't Look Back* showed onstage and backstage dramas, including split with Baez, during Dylan's English tour. Returning to US, recorded **Like A Rolling Stone**, which gave him international stardom, with Mike Bloomfield on guitar and Al Kooper on organ. Single was released before rest of **Highway 61 Revisited**; album was produced by Bob Johnston.

Unveiling electric sound and Carnaby Street clothes at Newport and Forest Hills that summer, Dylan was booed by audience who saw prancing rock 'n' roller as sell-out. Next single **Positively 4th Street** was described as 'most vicious song ever to reach the Hit Parade'. Double album **Blonde On Blonde** was characterized by intense, poetic songs of drugs, dreams and nightmares about identity. Toured with The Hawks, later called The Band, and married Sara Lowndes.

selling 320,000 copies in first eight days of release. Personal relationship developed with Joan Baez and Dylan appeared at her concerts. Becoming hot property, he headlined Carnegie Hall concert; **The Times They Are A-Changin'** album made him hero of protest movement. Because of public pressure, by February 1964 Dylan became recluse, using bodyguards and drugs as protection from outside world.

With success as folk singer achieved, Dylan began changing image. During British visits, he heard English rock (and had small role in BBC-TV play). As usual, he had eye on barometer: though acoustic, 1964 LP **Another Side of Bob Dylan** was first step toward rock. Self-pitying and cruel, but vividly powerful, lyrics emphasized personal rather than political sentiments on songs like **All I Really Want To Do** and **It Ain't Me, Babe**. Folk fans and political protesters felt betrayed and album did not do as well as first two.

Spending much time in Woodstock, NY, Dylan wrote 18 new songs for 1965 **Bringing It All Back Home**, which completed

Dylan admitted to being a millionaire with over 10 million records sold.

In July 1966, shortly after his 25th birthday, motorcycle crash led to 18-month disappearance; while recuperating in Woodstock from broken neck, rumours of death, disfigurement and drug addiction abounded. During this period Dylan recorded **Basement Tapes** with The Band (not officially released until eight years later). Early 1968 saw his appearance at benefit concert for Woody Guthrie, the birth of his first child, and release of **John Wesley Harding**, recorded in Nashville with country instrumentation. Voice had mellowed, lyrics were more accessible and gave hint of compassion, and tunes were melodic. **Nashville Skyline** continued songs in praise of living and gave last Top 10 single with **Lay Lady Lay**. During summer 1969 he split with Grossman; performed for huge crowds at Isle of Wight and Woodstock Festivals.

Moving back to Greenwich Village, released two disappointing records in 1970, although **Self Portrait** became seventh gold album. Over next two years kept low

Above: Robert Allen Zimmerman, circa 1963, a 'freewheeling' folkie who dominated intellectual discourse in 60s.

Above left: Bob Dylan during the 70s, arguably his classic era, although we missed the strap-on harmonica.

profile, while books, fanzines and Dylanology clubs interpreted his words and scavengers searched his garbage for significance. Meanwhile, bootleg records proliferated, Dylan's book *Tarantula* was published, and he visited Israel. Performed at Madison Square Garden benefit for Bangladesh; recorded both electric and acoustic versions of **George Jackson** single, and did sessions for friends. **Greatest Hits II** was released.

Went to West Coast for small role in film *Pat Garrett And Billy The Kid*, and wrote score, including **Knocking On Heaven's Door**. When Columbia contract expired, recorded **Planet Waves** for Asylum; tour with The Band resulted in exciting live album **Before The Flood**. Re-signing with Columbia, recorded **Blood On The Tracks**. Filled with pain and bitterness (his marriage was breaking up), album was seen as return to form after recent simplistic good-time music. After recording new album **Desire**, toured with old friends and stars of 1960s in 1975-76 Rolling Thunder Revue. Dylan praised as charismatic entertainer; television special and live album **Hard Rain** released. During tour Dylan also created four-hour poetically rambling film *Renaldo And Clara*, screened in 1968.

At end of 1970s Dylan became born-again Christian. Somewhat self-righteously aimed moralizing at non-believers (including fellow rock 'n' rollers). First post-conversion album **Slow Train Coming** (1979) featured talented instrumentalists. Later albums added gospel flavour, but didn't create much commercial excitement.

Subsequent albums received patchy critical and commercial acceptance, but Dylan's live pulling power remained undiminished, as evidenced by 1986 tour with Tom Petty And The Heartbreakers, and 1987 outings with fellow 60s legends The Grateful Dead. Began annual pilgrimage to UK in 1989 (with sell-out dates in London and Birmingham) and for 1991 gigs introduced new band featuring Tony Garnier (bass), Cesar Diaz (guitar), John Jackson (guitar) and Ian Wallace (drums).

Some would say typecast, Dylan appeared as clapped-out middle-aged rock star in appalling *Heart Of Fire* movie, but has latterly enjoyed success as member of occasional Traveling Wilbury troupe, with George Harrison, Jeff Lynne, Tom Petty and, before his death, Roy Orbison.

Hit Singles:	US	UK
Times They Are A-Changin', 1965	–	9
Subterranean Homesick Blues, 1965	39	9
Maggie's Farm, 1965	–	22
Like A Rolling Stone, 1965	2	4
Positively 4th Street, 1965	7	8
Can You Please Crawl Out Your Window!, 1966	58	17
Rainy Day Women, No.s 12 & 35, 1966	2	7
I Want You, 1966	20	16
Lay Lady Lay, 1969	7	5
Knockin' On Heaven's Door, 1973	12	14
Baby Stop Crying, 1978	–	13

Albums:
Bob Dylan (Columbia/CBS), 1962
Freewheelin' Bob Dylan (Columbia/CBS), 1963
Times They Are A-Changin' (Columbia/CBS), 1964
Another Side Of Bob Dylan (Columbia/CBS), 1964
Bringing It All Back Home (Columbia/CBS), 1965
Highway 61 Revisited (Columbia/CBS), 1965

Blonde On Blonde (Columbia/CBS), 1966
Greatest Hits (Columbia/CBS), 1967
John Wesley Harding (Columbia/CBS), 1968
Nashville Skyline (Columbia/CBS), 1969
Self Portrait (Columbia/CBS), 1970
New Morning (Columbia/CBS), 1970
Greatest Hits Volume II (Columbia/CBS), 1971
Pat Garrett And Billy The Kid (soundtrack) (Columbia/CBS), 1973
Dylan (Columbia/CBS), 1973
Planet Waves (Columbia/CBS), 1974
Before The Flood (Asylum/Island), 1974
Blood On The Tracks (Columbia/CBS), 1974
Basement Tapes (Columbia/CBS), 1975
Desire (Columbia/CBS), 1975
Hard Rain (Columbia/CBS), 1976
Street Legal (Columbia/CBS), 1978
At Budokan (Columbia/CBS), 1978
Slow Train Coming (Columbia/CBS), 1979
Saved (Columbia/CBS), 1980
Shot Of Love (Columbia/CBS), 1981
Infidels (CBS), 1983
Empire Burlesque (CBS), 1985
Biograph (CBS), 1985
Down In The Groove (Columbia/CBS), 1988
Oh Mercy (Columbia/CBS), 1989
Dylan And The Dead (1987 tour recordings with Grateful Dead) (Columbia/CBS), 1989
Under The Red Sky (Columbia/CBS), 1990

Above: Bob Dylan on stage during the late 1970s.

Right: Dylan as he appeared in the Rolling Thunder Revue in 1976.

Above: The Times They Are A-Changin', Bob Dylan. Courtesy CBS Records.

Above: Self Portrait, Bob Dylan. Courtesy CBS Records.

Above: Street Legal, Bob Dylan. Courtesy CBS Records.

ELO (Electric Light Orchestra)
UK group formed 1971

Original line-up: Jeff Lynne, vocals, guitar; Roy Wood, vocals, guitar; Bev Bevan, drums, vocals.

Career: Band was formed out of remnants of Move; idea was to expand boundaries of orchestral rock. First album, **Electric Light Orchestra**, was recorded over considerable period of time with various string players; yielded hit single in **10538 Overture**.

Although Roy Wood split to form Wizzard, Lynne decided to rebuild group from scratch, hiring motley collection of musicians, some with rock and some with classical backgrounds. **ELO II** was released in 1973 to critical indifference, but it yielded another hit single, an updated and highly orchestrated version of Chuck Berry's warhorse **Roll Over Beethoven**.

Above: Balance Of Power, Electric Light Orchestra. Courtesy Epic Records.

By this time recognizable style was being set, and it was proving to be commercially acceptable. Pop-orientated but with thick, dense texture overlaid by characteristic strings, ELO sound became mid-70s winner. 1974 album **Eldorado** went gold in US, feat that most of following albums repeated or surpassed. At same time, band released almost unbroken string of Top 20 hit singles.

By end of decade it appeared that ELO could virtually do no wrong. Although involved in catastrophic movie *Xanadu*, band managed to walk away with massive hit single (with Olivia Newton-John) and retained most of their credibility. One-time member, violinist Mick Kaminski (1976), scored solo success in 1979 with **Violinski**.

After long period of inactivity, and temporary disbandment in 1983, Lynne resurrected group for excellent 1986 album **Balance Of Power**, with virtuoso violinist Kaminski back in the line-up.

Lynne's extensive extra-curricular recording commitments reduced ELO activities to zero in the late 80s, although Bev Bevan caused anguish when ELO II took to the road in 1991, without Lynne.

Meanwhile, Lynne took solace in production duties for Duane Eddy, Brian Wilson, Randy Newman, Del Shannon, Roy Wood, and, individually, George Harrison, Tom Petty and Roy Orbison, all members of the Traveling Wilburys, of which Lynne became part.

Hit Singles:	US	UK
10538 Overture, 1972	—	9
Roll Over Beethoven, 1973	42	6
Showdown, 1973	53	12
Can't Get It Out Of My Head, 1975	9	—
Evil Woman, 1976	10	10
Strange Magic, 1976	14	38
Livin' Thing, 1976	13	4
Rockaria, 1977	—	9
Telephone Line, 1977	7	8
Turn To Stone, 1977	13	18
Mister Blue Sky, 1978	35	6
Sweet Talkin' Woman, 1978	17	6
Wild West Hero, 1978	—	6
Shine A Little Love, 1979	8	6
The Diary Of Horace Wimp, 1979	—	8
Don't Bring Me Down, 1979	4	3
Confusion/Last Train To London, 1979	—	8
Confusion, 1979	37	—
Last Train To London, 1979	38	—
I'm Alive, 1980	16	20
All Over The World, 1980	13	11
Hold On Tight, 1981	10	4
Rock 'n' Roll Is King, 1983	19	13
Calling America, 1986	—	28

With Olivia Newton-John:

Xanadu, 1980	8	1

Albums:
Electric Light Orchestra (Jet/Harvest), 1971*
ELO (Jet/Fame), 1973
On The Third Day (Jet), 1973
Eldorado (Jet), 1974
Face The Music (Jet), 1975
Olé ELO (Jet), 1976
New World Record (Jet), 1976
Out Of The Blue (Jet), 1977
The Light Shines On (—/Harvest), 1977
The Light Shines On Volume 2 (—/Harvest), 1979
Discovery (Jet), 1979
Greatest Hits (Jet), 1979
A Box Of Their Best (Jet/—), 1980
Time (Jet), 1981
Secret Messages (Jet), 1983
Balance Of Power (Epic), 1986
First Movement (EMI), 1987
Afterglow (Epic Assoc), 1990
*Titled No Answer In US

Jeff Lynne Solo:
Armchair Theatre (Reprise), 1990

The Eagles
US band formed 1971

Original line-up: Glenn Frey, vocals, guitar; Randy Meisner, vocals, bass; Bernie Leadon, guitar, vocals; Don Henley, drums, vocals.

Career: Frey and Henley met as members of Linda Rondstadt's backing band. Following recruitment of former Poco member Meisner and former Flying Burrito Brother's Leadon, four flew to London to record first album as Eagles for Asylum.

Album **The Eagles** made major impact, as did single **Take It Easy**, co-written by Frey and stablemate Jackson Browne. **Desperado** consolidated success, and crystallized Eagles' image as laid-back California outlaws. By now band had become major live attraction, adding large orchestra for some concerts.

Having contributed to sessions for third album **On The Border**, guitarist Don Felder added as fifth member. Band went from strength to strength, breaking British market for first time in 1975 with single **One Of These Nights**. Same year saw first No. 1 single in US, **Best Of My Love**.

During mid-70s band could do no wrong, achieving status of mega-group with across-board appeal. Heaped with gold and platinum records, showered with awards, only problem was meeting demand for product and

Above: Desperado, The Eagles. Courtesy Asylum Records. This 1973 album put the band on the road to stardom.

live appearances. Strain proved too much for Bernie Leadon, who quit at end of 1975 to pursue unspectacular solo career. Slightly surprising choice of replacement was former James Gang guitarist Joe Walsh who had more recently been pursuing solo career. Walsh's songwriting/guitar work gave their 'laid-back' California sound a shot in the arm. In 1977 Randy Meisner also quit to go solo, and in came Timothy B. Schmidt, another former Poco stalwart.

By the end of the decade, by which time line-up had been further augmented by long-time friend Joe Vitale on keyboards, Eagles had become one of the most successful American recording acts of the 70s. Band sold 40 million albums worldwide since inception; **Hotel California** sold nine million in year of release, **Greatest Hits** seven million. All concerts during decade were immediate sell-outs.

1982 saw band in abeyance as both Glenn Frey and Don Henley had success with solo releases (Henley's **Dirty Laundry** (1982) in particular becoming major hit) but fans had consolation of **Greatest Hits Volume 2** album. The current split in ranks has lasted some years now, and band are unlikely to return as permanent unit.

Although criticized as epitome of unchallenging AOR, Eagles delivered impressively consistent body of work and showed that this particular genre doesn't have to be moronic. They combined solid songwriting abilities, musicianship and superb harmonies.

Hit Singles:	US	UK
Take It Easy, 1972	12	—
Witchy Woman, 1972	9	—
Best Of My Love, 1975	1	—
One Of These Nights, 1975	1	23
Lyin' Eyes, 1975	2	23
Take It To The Limit, 1976	4	12
New Kid In Town, 1977	1	20
Hotel California, 1977	1	8
Life In The Fast Lane, 1977	11	—
Please Come Home For Christmas, 1978	18	30
Heartache Tonight, 1979	1	40
The Long Run, 1979	8	—
I Can't Tell You Why, 1980	8	—

Don Henley Solo:

Leather And Lace (with Stevie Nicks), 1981	6	—
Dirty Laundry, 1982	3	—
The Boys Of Summer, 1985	5	12
All She Wants To Do Is Dance, 1985	10	2

Randy Meisner Solo:

Hearts On Fire, 1981	9	—

Albums:
The Eagles (Asylum), 1972
Desperado (Asylum), 1973
On The Border (Asylum), 1974
One Of These Nights (Asylum), 1975
Their Greatest Hits (Asylum), 1975
Hotel California (Asylum), 1976
The Long Run (Asylum), 1979
Eagles Live (Asylum), 1980
Greatest Hits Volume 2 (Asylum), 1982
Best Of (Asylum), 1985

Don Henley Solo:
I Can't Stand Still (Asylum/—), 1982
Building The Perfect Beast (Geffen), 1985

Randy Meisner Solo:
Randy Meisner (Asylum), 1978
One More Song (Epic), 1980
Randy Meisner (Epic), 1982

Sheena Easton
UK vocalist
Born Bellshill, Glasgow, April 27, 1959

Career: Chosen as subject for BBC television's *The Big Time* — a documentary tracing aspiring singer's struggle for stardom — Sheena Easton lived out the part to the full to establish herself as a major international artist.

While studying at Royal Scottish Academy Of Music And Drama, she spent evenings working local pub/club circuit before auditioning for *The Big Time*.

Signed to EMI, second single **9 To 5** became *the* summer hit of 1980 and screening of *The Big Time* in July focused attention on debut single **Modern Girl**, earlier a minor hit, which joined **9 To 5**, making her first British female singer to have two Top 10 hits at same time. In America she went

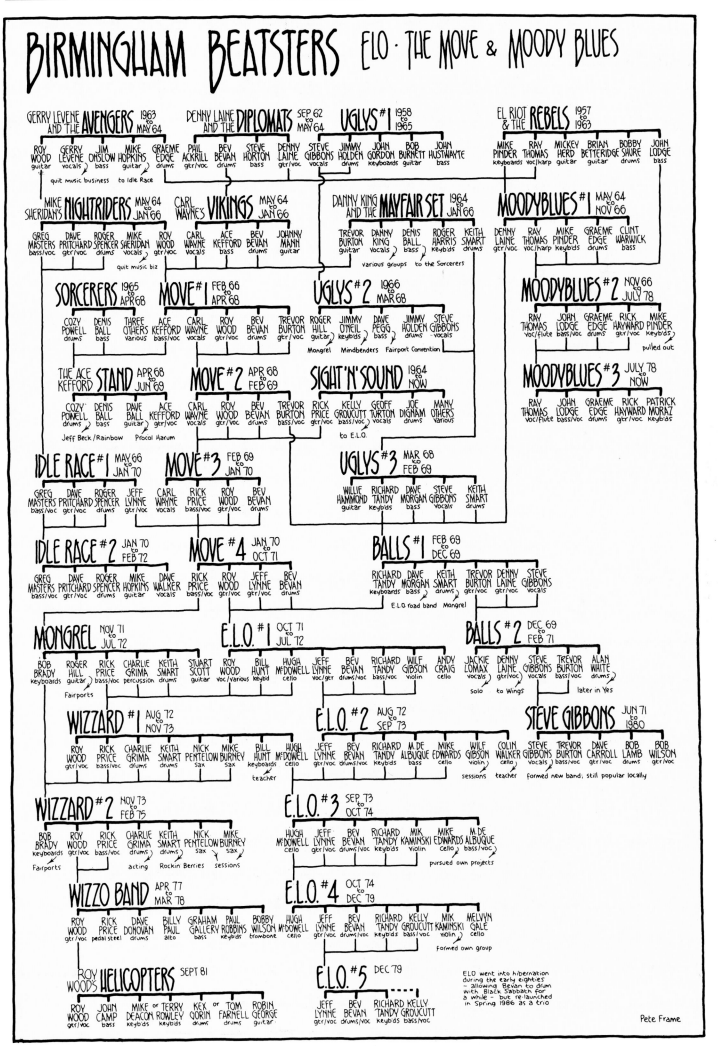

BIRMINGHAM BEATSTERS ELO · THE MOVE & MOODY BLUES

Pete Frame

one better: her first three singles all featured simultaneously in Top 50.

Easton's first year was topped off by Royal Variety Show appearance, while debut album quickly went gold in US and UK, and platinum in Japan and Canada, leading to awards as Best Female Singer of 1981 and Best Female Newcomer in US.

She not only sang theme to James Bond movie *For Your Eyes Only* but appeared in opening sequence, and later performed song at 1982 Oscar ceremony.

Now carefully groomed with keen eye for fashion, Easton took advantage of US success, moving to California where she flourished on night club circuit.

While chart success continued in US, including unlikely duets with Kenny Rogers and, most recently, Prince, Easton's UK appeal dwindled. However, latterly US audience has increased to point where she has become established showbusiness personality. Astute management must take lion's share of credit for this metamorphosis, as artist's abilities remain essentially modest.

Hit Singles:

	US	UK
Modern Girl, 1980	18	8
9 to 5, 1980*	1	3
One Man Woman, 1980	–	14
When He Shines, 1981	–	12
For Your Eyes Only, 1981	4	8
You Could Have Been With Me, 1981	15	54
Telephone (Long Distance Love Affair), 1983	9	–
Strut, 1984	7	–
Sugar Walls, 1985	9	–
The Lover In Me, 1989	2	15
What Comes Naturally, 1991	19	–
*Known as Morning Train in US		

Sheena Easton with Prince:

U Got The Look, 1987	2	11

Albums:
Take My Time (EMI), 1981
You Could Have Been With Me (EMI), 1981
Madness, Money And Music (EMI), 1982
Best Kept Secret (EMI), 1983
A Private Heaven (EMI), 1984
No Sound But A Heart (EMI), 1987
The Lover In Me (MCA), 1988
What Comes Naturally (MCA), 1991

Left: Sheena Easton, 'modern girl' of the 1980s.

Duane Eddy
US guitarist, composer
Born Corning, New York, April 28, 1938

Career: Raised in Phoenix, Arizona, Eddy began playing guitar at five and at 16 was working in local dance bands before coming under influence of ace guitarist Al Casey.

After tuition from jazz guitarist Jim Wybele, Eddy was signed by local DJ Lee Hazlewood — later a recording star/producer himself — and Lester Sill in 1957. He cut debut **Movin 'n' Groovin'** for Jamie with his backing band The Rebels (Larry Knechtel, Steve Douglas and Al Casey).

Above: Twangin' The Golden Hits, Duane Eddy. Courtesy RCA Records.

Eddy developed unique 'twangy' guitar sound by tuning normal six-string guitar down an octave and playing melody on bass rather than top strings. As much a part of his records' appeal were the raunchy saw solos of Steve Douglas and Jim Horn and the rebel yells of Ben De Moto. The overall effect was potent blend of rock 'n' roll, R&B and Southern states' influences.

Second release **Rebel Rouser** (1958) went gold and led to string of big sellers (12 million records sold by 1963, total sales having now topped 30 million from some 25 singles, 21 of which made UK charts). More than half his hits were self-penned.

Eddy acted in TV western series *Have Gun Will Travel*, and movies *Because They're Young* (his theme for which was 1960 million-seller), *A Thunder Of Drums* and *The Wild*

Westerner. He also composed the theme for 1961 movie *Ring of Fire*.

Eddy has continued to tour extensively, either solo or as part of 'revival packages', and enjoyed brief chart resurrection with re-recording of **Peter Gunn** (1987) in collaboration with Art Of Noise. The track won Best Instrumental Grammy in 1987, and prompted Capitol Records to sign artist for self-titled album, produced by Jeff Lynne and featuring Ry Cooder, Paul McCartney and George Harrison.

Hit Singles:

	US	UK
Rebel Rouser, 1958	6	19
Cannon Ball, 1958	15	22
Peter Gunn Theme, 1959	–	6
Yep!, 1959	30	17
40 Miles Of Bad Road, 1959	9	11
Some Kinda Earthquake, 1959	37	12
Bonnie Come Back, 1960	26	12
Shazam!, 1960	45	4
Because They're Young, 1960	4	2
Kommotion, 1960	–	13
Peter Gunn Theme, 1960	27	–
Pepe, 1961	18	2
Theme From Dixie, 1961	39	7
Ring Of Fire, 1961	–	17
Drivin' Home, 1961	–	18
Deep In The Heart Of Texas, 1962	–	19
Ballad Of Paladin, 1962	33	10
(Dance With The) Guitar Man, 1962	12	4
Play Me Like You Play Your Guitar, 1975	–	9
Peter Gunn (with Art Of Noise), 1986	–	8

Albums:
Movin' 'n' Groovin' (–/London), 1957
Have Twangy Guitar, Will Travel (Jamie/London), 1958
Especially For You (Jamie/London), 1958
Twang's The Thang (Jamie/London), 1959
Songs For Our Heritage (Jamie/London), 1960
$1,000,000 Worth Of Twang (Jamie/London), 1961
Girls, Girls, Girls (Jamie/London), 1961
$1,000,000 Worth Of Twang Volume 2 (Jamie/London), 1962
Twistin' (Jamie/–), 1962
In Person (Jamie/–), 1962
16 Greatest Hits (Jamie/–), 1962
Pure Gold (RCA), 1965
Best Of (RCA/Camden), 1965
Twangy Guitar (RCA), 1970
Duane Eddy Guitar Man (–/GTO), 1975
Legend Of Rock (–/Deram), 1975
Duane Eddy Collection (–/Pickwick), 1978
Greatest Hits Of (–/Ronco), 1979
20 Terrific Twangies (–/RCA), 1980
Duane Eddy (Capitol), 1987

Dave Edmunds
UK vocalist, guitarist, composer, producer
Born Cardiff, Wales, April 15, 1944

Career: Served eight-year musical apprenticeship in various local bands. Formed Love Sculpture with John Williams, bass, and Bob Jones, drums; their frenetic rock instrumental adaptation of Khachaturian's **Sabre Dance** on Parlophone skated to six on UK chart in 1968 and was band's only hit. Love Sculpture broke up following American tour.

Edmunds signed as solo to Gordon Mills' MAM agency before moving back to South Wales with Kingsley Ward to build own

Rockfield Studio in Monmouthshire. After months of experimentation, Rockfield developed unique sound, making it one of Britain's most active studios. Edmunds learned to exactly reproduce sounds of his favourite oldies. Re-make of Smiley Lewis's R&B classic **I Hear You Knocking** gave him three-million selling UK No. 1 in 1970. Debut album **Rockpile** (1972) featured John Williams and former Amen Corner leader Andy Fairweather-Low.

Besides own work, Edmunds produced Brinsley Schwarz, Ducks Deluxe, Flamin' Groovies, Shakin' Stevens And The Sunsets, and American legend Del Shannon. Recreating classic Phil Spector Wall Of Sound, had further hits of own with versions of Spector oldies **Baby I Love You** and **Born To Be With You.**

Former Brinsley Schwarz member Nick Lowe contributed to Edmunds' debut album with Swan Song label, **Get It** (1975). Lowe also became member of Rockpile road band formed by Edmunds, and featured heavily on 1980 LP **Seconds Of Pleasure**. Rockpile included Edmunds (vocals, guitar) and Billy Bremner (vocals, guitar).

Above: Subtle As A Flying Mallet, Dave Edmunds. Courtesy RCA Records.

1979 **Repeat When Necessary** album included chart singles **Girls Talk, Queen Of Hearts** and **Crawling From The Wreckage**. Edmunds enjoyed further UK Top 30 hit with version of Guy Mitchell's **Singing The Blues** in following year.

During latter part of 80s and into early 90s, Edmunds foresook personal ambition for production and session duties for a variety of performers, including kd lang, Stray Cats, Shakin' Stevens, Everly Bros, Dion and Status Quo; took time out for own **Closer To The Flame** set in 1989, and undertook selected gigs.

A rock all-rounder, Edmunds will undoubtedly remain a force to be reckoned with for many years, although influence may be largely as backroom boy as he eventually becomes an elder statesman of rock.

Guitars: Gibson 335, Gibson J200 acoustics, Fender Telecaster, Martin D45.

Hit Singles:

	US	UK
I Hear You Knocking, 1970	4	1
Baby I Love You, 1973	–	8
Born To Be With You, 1973	–	5
Girls Talk, 1979	–	4
Queen Of Hearts, 1979	–	11

Albums:
Subtle As A Flying Mallet (RCA), 1975
Get It (Swan Song), 1975
Tracks On Wax (Swan Song), 1978
Repeat When Necessary (Swan Song), 1979
Twangin' (Swan Song), 1981
Best Of (Swan Song), 1981
D.E. 7 (Columbia/Arista), 1982
Information (Swan Song), 1983
Live (Arista), 1987

I Hear You Rockin' (Arista), 1987
Closer To The Flame (Capitol), 1990

With Love Sculpture:
Classic Tracks 68-72 (—/One-Up), 1974
Singles, A's and B's (—/Harvest), 1980

With Rockpile:
Seconds Of Pleasure (Columbia/F-Beat), 1980
Original Rockpile, The Volume II (Harvest), 1987

Worth Searching Out:
Rockpile (NAM/Regal Zonophone), 1972

Emerson, Lake And Palmer
UK group formed 1969

Original line-up: Keith Emerson, keyboards; Greg Lake, bass, guitar, vocals; Carl Palmer, drums.

Career: Keith Emerson revealed classical background while with Nice and used that group to introduce knife-throwing, organ thrashing, musical mayhem act. Nice broke up in late 60s and Emerson began search for special talent to make up next venture.

He met Lake, then with the original King Crimson, and convinced him to join. They then tried to enlist Randy Bachman, late of Guess Who, and discussed union with Jimi Hendrix and Mitch Mitchell. Eventually Carl

Right: Keith Emerson (left) and Greg Lake run through their greatest hit, The Two Of Us (Where's The Drummer?).

Left: Rock's 'Jack of all trades' Dave Edmunds, who lends his talents to all and sundry, as well as maintaining a low-key solo career.

Friends, To The Show That Never Ends) for fans and then disappeared: no tours and no recordings.

In 1977, **Works Volume 1** appeared. Large sales, despite album's overly pretentious base, seemed to indicate ELP's fans were still there, but ELP was apparently stranded in 1969/1970 time zone and grand orchestral style clashed with musical revolution of late 70s. Wise enough to know when to quit, ELP planned extravaganza farewell tour. Naturally, live set was recorded and **In Concert** appeared for the memories.

In 1985 Lake and Emerson reformed band, minus Palmer who was playing with supergroup Asia. Replacing him with veteran session drummer and former Rainbow alumnus Cozy Powell, the new band released **Emerson, Lake And Powell** in 1986, supporting set with US tour. Further revival as trio, with Robert Berry replacing Powell, saw album **To The Power of Three** released in 1988, which sunk faster than the Titanic. But new LP for Victory label was projected for spring 1992.

Hit Singles:	US	UK
Fanfare For The Common Man, 1977	—	2

Albums:
Emerson, Lake And Palmer (Cotillion/Island), 1970
Tarkus (Cotillion/Island), 1971
Pictures At An Exhibition (Cotillion/Island), 1971
Trilogy (Cotillion/Island), 1972
Brain Salad Surgery (Manticore), 1973
Welcome Back, My Friends, To The Show That Never Ends (Manticore), 1974
Works Volume I (Atlantic/Manticore), 1977
Works Volume II (Atlantic), 1978
Love Beach (Atlantic), 1978
In Concert (Atlantic), 1979
Best Of Emerson Lake And Palmer (Manticore), 1980
Emerson Lake And Powell (Polydor), 1986

Emerson, Lake And Robert Berry:
To The Power Of Three (Geffen), 1988

Palmer, whose background (ex-Chris Farlowe, Atomic Rooster and Arthur Brown) prepared him for Emerson's dynamic stage show, was recruited.

Band's live debut was 1970 Isle Of Wight festival followed shortly by first album. Both recordings and stage shows became grandiose and flamboyant displays of technical skill. But after third album, **Pictures**, sameness crept in. ELP could still sell albums, but could they come up with anything new? They released live set (**Welcome Back, My**

Erasure
UK group formed 1985

Original line-up: Vince Clarke, keyboards; Andrew Bell, vocals.

Career: Electro-dance duo given distinction by ex-choirboy Bell's soaring vocals.

Old-stager Clarke (ex-Depeche Mode, Yazoo and The Assembly) secured services of Bell (ex-Void) after day-long audition at studio of Clarke's producer Eric Radcliffe, who soon cut debut single **Who Needs Love Like That** for Mute. Justifiable comparision of Bell's high tenor with baritone delivery of former Yazoo vocalist Alison Moyet prompted critics to question Clarke's break-up of partnership with Moyet.

Patchy **Wonderland** album (1986) struggled, and, following cancelled tour, Erasure's future was in question. However, European discos had latched on to upbeat **Sometimes** single, which finally cracked UK Top 10.

Concert-packed 1987, which included dates in US as support to Duran Duran and own 'The Circus' European tour to support album of same name, attracted leather-clad dance crowd who were mesmerized by Clarke's repetitive synth rhythms. Singles **It Doesn't Have To Be** and **Victim Of Love** completed successful UK chart sortie in same year.

American audiences, savaged by neanderthal HM outfits, finally saw the light when **Chains Of Love** single from **The Innocents** LP broke through. The album made No. 1 in its first week of release in UK in April 1988. For **Wild** set (1989), band logged a billion miles completing global dates, where UK section of tour featured Adamski, James, and Was (Not Was).

Workaholic Clarke maintained frenetic Erasure output, as band zoomed towards tenth successive UK hit with **Love To Hate You** (November 1991) from **Chorus** LP. Now firmly established in northern Europe and the States, duo embarked on joint PR operation in Poland for Sopot 1991 festival.

Erasure's high camp stage presentation is in contrast to their dignified commitment to Gay Rights and Animal Liberation Movement, the latter of which prompted the 1991 set **Tame Yourself**.

Hit Singles:	US	UK
Sometimes, 1986	—	2
It Doesn't Have To Be, 1987	—	12
Victim Of Love, 1987	—	7
The Circus, 1987	—	6
Ship Of Fools, 1988	—	6
Chains Of Love, 1988	—	11
A Little Respect, 1988	14	4
Crackers International, 1988	—	2
Drama!, 1989	—	4
You Surround Me, 1989	—	15
Blue Savannah, 1990	—	3
Star, 1990	—	11
Chorus, 1991	—	3
Love To Hate You, 1991	—	4
Am I Right?, 1991	—	16

Albums:
Wonderland (Sire/Mute), 1986
The Circus (Sire/Mute), 1987
Two Ring Circus (Sire/Mute), 1987
Crackers International (Sire/Mute), 1988
The Innocents (Sire/Mute), 1988
Wild (Sire/Mute), 1989
Chorus (Sire/Mute), 1991
Tame Yourself (Sire/Mute), 1991

Gloria Estefan

US vocalist
Born Gloria Fajardo, September 1, 1957, Havana, Cuba

Career: Latin-influenced Miami Sound Machine were major dance attraction of 80s, and Estefan's soulful vocals proved ideal focal point. In deference to her star status, group adopted her name for billing in 1987.

Estefan joined future husband and manager Emilio Estefan in his trio The Miami Latin Boys, interrupting education at University of Miami. Quartet cut first album in 1976, and, with addition of percussion and brass section, changed name of group to Miami Sound Machine.

With material sung almost exclusively in Spanish, the group established a loyal following in Florida which prompted self-financed second set, eventually distributed by CBS International, who signed band to a four-album deal.

First English language single **Dr Beat** (originally a B-side) made UK Top 10 and US success followed a year later with **Conga** track. MSM's dynamic visual presentation and virtuoso musicianship earned sell-out notices on band's frequent tours, and material from debut English-language album **Primitive Love** secured *Billboard* magazine award as Top Singles Act for 1986.

Increased attention given Estefan prompted name change for multi-million-selling set **Let It Loose**, which provided further single cuts. In 1989, Miami Sound Machine moniker was dropped, and all future recordings were as 'Gloria Estefan', with **Cuts Both Ways** her solo debut, although group was retained for recording and live shows.

With the Estefan bandwagon in full flight, activities were dramtically curtailed when serious road accident hospitalised artist with severe back injury. Slow rehabilitation process removed nine months from Estefan's career, although Spanish versions of her hits, released as **Exitos De Gloria Estefan**, were warmly received.

World tour, which commenced in March 1991 at the Miami Arena, prefaced return to Estefan fever, and instant resurrection of singer's productive career.

Right: Latin dance queen Gloria Estefan, now back in business after car crash.

Hit Singles:	US	UK
Can't Stay Away From You, 1989	6	7
Don't Wanna Lose You, 1989	1	6
Oye Mi Canto (Hear My Voice), 1989	48	16
Get On Your Feet, 1989	11	23
Here We Are, 1990	6	23
Coming Out Of The Dark, 1991	1	28

With Miami Sound Machine:

	US	UK
Dr Beat, 1984	—	6
Bad Boy, 1986	8	16
Conga, 1986	10	—
Words Get In The Way, 1986	5	—
Anything For You, 1988	1	10
1-2-3, 1988	—	9
Rhythm Is Gonna Get You, 1988	5	10

Albums:
Cuts Both Ways (Epic), 1989
Exitos De Gloria Estefan (—/Epic), 1990
Into The Light (Epic), 1991

Miami Sound Machine:
Primitive Love (Epic), 1986
Let It Loose (Epic), 1987
Anything For You (Epic), 1988
Eyes Of Innocence (Epic)

Eurythmics

UK duo formed 1981
David Stewart, guitar, keyboards, synthesizer, bass, composer; born Sunderland, 1952
Annie Lennox, vocals, composer, keyboards, flute, synthesizer; born Aberdeen, December 25, 1954

Career: Duo were both members of The Tourists, promising pop-styled band 1977-80 scoring five hit singles, including Top 10 items

I Only Want To Be With You (Dusty Springfield cover) and **So Good To Be Back Home Again**, plus three interesting LPs. Prior to forming Tourists, Stewart had worked in folk music, then had spell in Longdancer (early signing to Elton John's Rocket label). Lennox had studied at Royal Academy of Music (piano, flute) before working as part-time cabaret singer/waitress; met Stewart while working in restaurant.

When Tourists folded, duo started writing (which neither had previously done seriously) and recorded first Eurythmics LP, **In The Garden**, in Cologne, produced by Tourists' mentor Conny Plank. Instrumental help provided by Clem Burke (drums) of Blondie plus members of Can and D.A.F. Although LP not huge success, it effectively laid Tourists to rest. 1981-82 saw minor chart action but in 1983 duo came of age with two major hit singles, **Sweet Dreams Are Made Of This** (title track of second LP) and **Love Is A Stranger** (re-issued after success of **Sweet Dreams**). In fact, 1983 saw duo sell more than six million records worldwide, and world tour in following year increased status and pulling power.

Controversy followed with film score for movie *1984*. Eurythmics-composed soundtrack was used to replace work of original composer, causing furious protest. Situation was no fault of Stewart and Lennox, and upside was hit single **Sex Crime (Nineteen Eightyfour)**.

This most fashionable and enterprising duo maintained pop tour-de-force with **Sisters Are Doing It For Themselves** (with Aretha Franklin) chart cut and impressive **Revenge** album, which earned triple platinum recognition in UK and gold status in US. Lennox later teamed with veteran soulster Al Green for re-make of **Put A Little Love In Your Heart**, which hit the charts in 1988.

Recognition of Stewart's production abilities earned him employment with Bob Dylan, Bob Geldof, Tom Petty and Mick Jagger, among others, while maintaining heavy

Eurythmics workload; launched own label Anxious in 1987.

Signed to Arista in 1989, Lennox and Stewart recorded **We Two Are One** album, which topped UK listings, but provided little in the way of major chart single, and prompted Lennox' announcement of a break from group for unlimited period.

Stewart then formed The Spritual Cowboys, who toured States in 1990, following release of self-titled debut album. Enjoyed single hit (as David A. Stewart) with melodic instrumental **Lily Was Here**, featuring Scandinavian saxophonist Candy Dulfer; scored British television series **Jute City** in the autumn of 1991.

Although Eurythmics may now be part of pop history, interest in their endeavours remains constant, as witnessed by No. 1 placing in UK album charts of **Greatest Hits** set in 1991.

Hit Singles:	US	UK
Love Is A Stranger, 1982	23	6
Sweet Dreams Are Made Of This, 1983	1	2
Who's That Girl, 1983	21	3
Right By Your Side, 1983	29	10
Here Comes The Rain Again, 1984	4	8
Sexcrime (Nineteen Eightyfour), 1984	—	4
Would I Lie To You, 1985	5	17
There Must Be An Angel, 1985	22	1
Sisters Are Doing It For Themselves (with Aretha Franklin), 1985	18	9
It's Alright (Baby's Coming Back), 1986	—	12
Thorn In My Side, 1986	—	5
When Tomorrow Comes, 1986	—	30
Missionary Man, 1987	16	—
Beethoven (I Love To Listen To), 1987	—	25
You Have Placed A Chill In My Heart, 1988	—	16
Put A Little Love In Your Heart (Lennox with Al Green), 1988	8	28

Album:
In The Garden (—/RCA), 1981
Sweet Dreams (—/RCA), 1983
Touch (—/RCA), 1983
1984 For The Love Of Big Brother (Virgin), 1984
Be Yourself Tonight (—/RCA), 1985
Revenge (RCA), 1986
Savage (RCA), 1987
We Two Are One (Arista/RCA), 1989
Greatest Hits (Arista/RCA), 1991

The Everly Brothers

US vocal duo, guitarists, composers
Don Everly born Brownie, Kentucky, February 1, 1937
Phil Everly born Chicago, Illinois, January 19, 1939

Career: Both Don and Phil had early experience appearing on parents Ike and Margaret's radio show in Knoxville, 1955, singing hillbilly gospel material. First recordings for US Columbia label in 1956 came as result of encouragement from family friend Chet Atkins. First single **The Sun Keeps Shining** not successful but featured same harmonizing later to bring them to charts. In 1956, auditioned for publisher Wesley Rose and soon signed to Cadence Records. First release in 1957, Felice and

Boudleaux Bryant's **Bye Bye Love**, became major hit, followed by others in similar high-register harmony style. Rarely adventurous, material explored teen romance to limit with appropriately simple backing. Use of Gibson guitars prompted Gibson company to produce Jumbo-style Everly model in limited quantities.

Everlys signed to newly formed Warner Bros Records at peak of career in 1960, quickly expanding musical horizons with material and accompaniment. Continued to reach charts throughout 1960s with imaginative and well-produced singles and albums, surviving where other 1950s artists retired. Toured US and UK regularly even when singles failed to chart in late 60s.

Strain of touring contributed to growing friction which led to acrimonious split following on-stage row in 1973.

Both pursued solo careers and made fine records but these lacked commercial success of earlier efforts until Phil recorded with Cliff Richard, returning Everly name to charts with **She Means Nothing To Me**.

Differences settled, brothers reunited for triumphant world tour in 1985, and have continued to record and tour together. Inducted into Rock 'n' Roll Hall Of Fame in 1986, and subsequently honoured by hometown state of Kansas with unveiling of statue on Everly Brothers Boulevard.

Themselves influenced by notable country 'brothers' acts, such as the Louvin Bros, Jim and Jess McReynolds and Lilly Bros, Everly Brothers took close harmony style into the pop framework and inspired performers such as Beatles, Beach Boys, Hollies, Simon And Garfunkel and Eagles.

Hit Singles:

	US	UK
Bye Bye Love, 1957	2	6
Wake Up Little Susie, 1957	1	2
All I Have To Do Is Dream, 1957	1	1
Bird Dog/Devoted To You, 1958	—	10
Devoted To You/Bird Dog, 1958	10	—
Problems, 1958	2	6
Take A Message To Mary, 1959	16	29
('Til) I Kissed You, 1959	4	2
Let It Be Me, 1960	7	13
Cathy's Clown, 1960	1	1
When Will I Be Loved, 1960	8	4
So Sad/Lucille, 1960	7	4
Lucille/So Sad, 1960	21	4
Like Strangers, 1960	—	11
Walk Right Back/Ebony Eyes, 1961	7	1
Ebony Eyes/Walk Right Back, 1961	8	—
Temptation, 1961	27	1
Don't Blame Me/Muskrat, 1961	20	20
Cryin' In The Rain, 1962	6	6
That's Old Fashioned/How Can I Meet Her, 1962	9	12
No-One Can Make My Sunshine Smile, 1962	—	11
The Price Of Love, 1965	—	2
Love Is Strange, 1965	—	11

Phil Everly with Cliff Richard:

	US	UK
She Means Nothing To Me, 1983	—	9

Albums:

Very Best Of (Warner Bros), 1965
Golden Hits (Warner Bros), 1971
Walk Right Back With The Everlys (Warner Bros), 1975
Rock 'n' Roll Forever (Warner Bros), 1981
The Everly Brothers (Warner Bros), 1981
Rip It Up (Ace), 1983
Reunion Album (Impression), 1984
The Everly Brothers (Mercury), 1984
In The Studio (Ace), 1985
Born Yesterday (Mercury), 1985
Instant Party (Warner Bros), 1986
Rocking In Harmony (Ace), 1986
Roots (Warner Bros), 1986
Susie Q (Magnum Force), 1987
20 Golden Love Songs (Spectrum)
20 Greatest Hits (Spectrum)
Perfect Harmony (—/Knight), 1990
Rare Solo Classics (Curb/—), 1991

Extreme

US group formed 1987

Original line-up: Nuno Bettencourt, guitar; Gary Cherone, vocals; Pat Badger, bass; Paul Geary, drums.

Career: Boston-based quartet who signed with A&M Records in 1989. Mix of down-home heavy metal and dance rhythms has seen group enjoy success in both mediums, and they are current AOR favourites with US radio stations. In Portuguese-born Bettencourt, Extreme have a super-talented musician whose dexterity on acoustic guitar provides further string to bow.

Self-titled debut album was released in 1989, but band broke internationally when 1990 set **Pornograffiti** spawned hit singles **Get The Funk Out**, **More Than Words**, **Decadence Dance** and **Hole Hearted**.

Hit Singles:

	US	UK
More Than Words, 1991	1	2
Hole Hearted, 1991	—	13

Albums:

Extreme (A&M), 1989
Pornograffiti (A&M), 1990

The Faces

UK group formed 1968

Original line-up: Rod Stewart, vocals; Ron Wood, guitar; Ronnie Lane, bass; Kenny Jones, drums; Ian MacLagan, keyboards.

Career: When lead singer Steve Marriott left Small Faces to form Humble Pie with Peter Frampton in 1968, his erstwhile partners, Jones, MacLagan and Lane, brought in Rod Stewart and Ron Wood from the Jeff Beck Group and became simply The Faces (though first LP was released as Small Faces to keep old audience). Wood switched back to lead guitar, having played bass with Beck.

Signed by Warner Bros in early 1969, band spent two years establishing themselves via UK university and club circuits. They turned out high-energy, if inconsistent, albums. Reputation as a mischievous, free-

Below: The Very Best Of The Everly Brothers. Courtesy WEA Records.

boozing party band, plus growing success of Stewart's parallel solo career, made them one of the most popular on-stage outfits in UK/US during 1972-75.

Disappointing 1973 **Ooh La La** set was last album of fresh material Faces made together. Stewart's widely reported remarks that he didn't like it helped neither its commercial acceptability nor band's future as working unit.

Fed up with Stewart's dominance of band, Lane left (pursuing solo career) and was replaced by Japanese bass-player Tetsu Yamauchi (ex-Free); Stewart concentrated more on solo career. Wood released own solo effort **I've Got My Own Album To Do** (title meant as slap at Stewart's solo efforts) in 1974; guested on London dates with friends Keith Richard, Andy Newmark and Willie Weeks, and became increasingly involved with The Rolling Stones. All this pointed to imminent demise of Faces. In 1975, Wood toured States as guest replacement for departed Mick Taylor in Rolling Stones and then joined Faces for their tour there. He also recorded second solo album **Now Look**, on which Bobby Womack and other names guested. In 1976 Wood and Lane recorded **Mahoney's Last Stand** (originally to be a soundtrack) with Jones and MacLagan sessioning on LP.

Having degenerated into a drinking club rather than a working band, Faces finally broke up December 1975 when Stewart announced his expected and official departure for solo career.

Successful re-release of 1967 single **Itchycoo Park** led to temporary reunion in 1977. Members subsequently drifted away for variety of solo and band engagements.

Wood became member of Rolling Stones, and MacLagan (who married Keith Moon's

Above: Boston-based Extreme, whose Pornograffiti LP went platinum.

ex-wife Kim), along with occasional gigging with the Stones, enjoys 'keyboard for hire' status. Jones replaced Keith Moon as Who drummer in 1979. Lane, a victim of Multiple Sclerosis, cut albums with his Slim Chance band, and is active as fund-raiser for research into disease. Marriott, who recorded solo **30 Seconds To Midnight** (1989) and had returned to UK pub circuit, died in fire at home during the spring of 1991.

Hit Singles:

	US	UK
Stay With Me, 1971	17	6
Cindy Incidentally, 1973	48	2
Pool Hall Richard/I Wish It Would Rain, 1973	—	8
You Can Make Me Dance Or Sing Or Anything, 1974	—	12

Albums:

First Step/Long Player (Warner Bros), 1970
A Nod Is As Good As A Wink...To A Blind Horse (Warner Bros), 1971
Ooh La La (Warner Bros), 1973
Best Of (—/Riva), 1977
Faces (featuring Rod Stewart) (—/Pickwick), 1980
Faces (Edsel), 1987

Ronnie Lane Solo:
Rough Mix (with Pete Townshend) (MCA/Polydor), 1977

Ian McLagan Solo:
Troublemaker (Mercury/—), 1979
Bump In The Night (Mercury/—), 1981

Rod Stewart Solo:
See separate entry

Ron Wood Solo:
I've Got My Own Album To Do
   (Warner Bros), 1974
Now Look (—/Thunderbolt), 1975
Gimme Some Neck (Columbia/CBS), 1979
1 2 3 4 (CBS), 1981
Cancel Everything (—/Thunderbolt), 1987

Worth Searching Out:
Anymore For Anymore (GM), 1974
Slim Chance (A&M/Island), 1975
One For The Road (—/Island), 1976
Mahoney's Last Stand (Atco/Atlantic), 1976
See Me (—/GEM), 1979

Fairport Convention

UK group formed 1967

Original line-up: Simon Nichol, guitar, vocals; Richard Thompson, guitar, vocals; Ashley Hutchings, bass; Shaun Frater, drums; Judy Dyble, autoharp, vocals.

Career: 12-year career of Fairport involved 14 different line-ups and 20 members. Undoubtedly one of the most talented UK musical ensembles, their repertoire extends far beyond term 'folk-rock' to embrace rock 'n' roll, blues, country, cajun and bluegrass.

Original line-up (above) played debut gig in spring 1967. By November, Martin Lamble (drums) and lead singer Ian Matthews were recruited for first album, **Fairport Convention**, produced by manager Joe Boyd. Early repertoire consisted of contemporary American folk-rock and original material. Dyble was replaced by Strawbs' Sandy Denny in 1968, and group began eventual conversion to traditional British folk music. **What We Did On Our Holidays** revealed Thompson as major songwriting talent, while demonstrating healthy balance of original interpretations of traditional songs and excellent Joni Mitchell and Bob Dylan covers.

Disillusioned by musical policy, Matthews quit in January 1969, and was replaced by established folkie Dave Swarbrick (violin, vocals), who became Fairport's longest serving member. Traditionally based **Unhalfbricking** was succeeded by **Liege And Lief**, the definitive British folk-rock album, generally acknowledged as Fairport Convention's finest work.

In June 1969, following a Birmingham gig, the group's van skidded from motorway and Lamble was killed. By the end of the year, Sandy Denny had quit to form Fotheringay, while Ashley Hutchings left to start Steeleye Span. New members Dave Mattacks (drums) and Dave Pegg (bass) kept unit stable for a year during which **Full House** and **Live At The L.A. Troubadour** were recorded. The former, their first album without a female singer, revealed Swarbrick/Thompson partnership at its best. By January 1971, Richard Thompson had gone on to pursue highly acclaimed solo career, later duetting with wife Linda. Following two more British folk-rock albums, **Angel Delight** and **Babbacombe Lee**, the last of the original Fairports, guitarist Simon Nichol, left to form Albion Country Band with Ashley Hutchings.

From March to July 1972 group went through unprecedented period of flux with line-up changes involving Roger Hill (guitar), Tom Farnell (drums), and David Rea (guitar), before Trevor Lucas (guitar, vocals) and Jerry Donahue (guitar) settled long enough to complete two albums, **Rosie** and **Nine**.

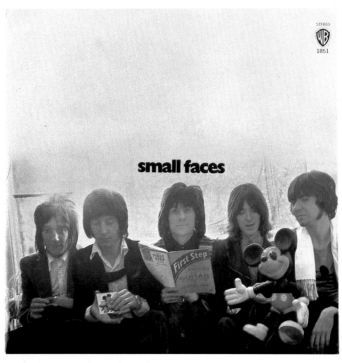

Above: First Step, (no longer Small) Faces. Courtesy Warner Bros Records.

Latter proved their best post-Thompson effort. Group's somewhat fading credibility was improved by dramatic return of Sandy Denny in March 1974. The disappointing **Live Convention** was followed by **Rising For The Moon**, a showcase for Denny insufficiently integrated into group context.

Mattacks left to join Etchingham Steam Band, and in January 1976 Denny returned to solo career. Lucas and Donahue also quit, precipitating Fairport's demise. New members were recruited, including Bruce Rowland (drums), Bob Brady (piano), Dan Ar Bras (guitar) and Roger Burridge (mandolin, fiddle). Final Island album, **Gottle O'Geer**, originally intended as Swarbrick solo, was recorded as contractual filler. A brief period with Vertigo in 1977 resulted in two average works, **The Bonny Bunch Of Roses** and **Tipplers Tales**, before anticlimactic **Farewell Farewell**. Former Fairports all succeeded at various levels with spin off/solo ventures. Sandy Denny died tragically of a brain haemorrhage on April 21, 1978, after falling downstairs at a friend's house.

Although Fairport's later work was decidedly patchy in comparison with earlier pioneering achievements, their influence on development of British electric folk music is inestimable, and annual reunions keep loyal supporters happy.

Albums:
Fairport Convention (A&M/Polydor), 1968
What We Did On Our Holidays
   (—/Island), 1969
Unhalfbricking (A&M/Island), 1969
Liege And Lief (A&M/Island), 1969
Live At The LA Troubadour (—/Island),
   1969
Full House (A&M/Island), 1970
Angel Delight (A&M/Island), 1971
Babbacombe Lee (A&M/Island), 1971
A History Of Fairport Convention
   (—/Island), 1972
Rosie (A&M/Island), 1973
Nine (A&M/Island), 1973
Fairport Live — A Moveable Beast
   (Island), 1974
Rising For The Moon (Island), 1974
Gottle O'Geer (Antilles/Island), 1976
Fairport Chronicles (A&M/—), 1976

The Bonny Bunch Of Roses (—/Vertigo),
   1977
Tipplers Tales (—/Vertigo), 1978
Farewell Farewell (—/Simons), 1979
Heyday (Hannibal), 1987
In Real Time (Island), 1987
Expletive Delighted (Varrick), 1987

Adam Faith

UK vocalist, actor, manager, producer
Born Terry Nelhams, London, June 23, 1940

Career: A messenger in UK film business, at Rank Screen Services he joined workmates in Worried Men skiffle group before TV pop producer Jack Good suggested he go solo as Adam Faith.

After two TV appearances, spell on road and flop HMV singles, he lost heart and returned to Rank as assistant film cutter before bandleader John Barry recommended him for TV series *Drumbeat*. Faith stayed for entire 22 week run and cut further flop single, for Top Rank, as well as appearing in *Beat Girl* teen movie.

Raindrops' member and songwriter John Worth offered Faith catchy song **What Do You Want?**. Exaggerating hiccupy style of Buddy Holly over unusual John Barry-arranged pizzicato string backing, Faith cut song in late 1959 and made it biggest selling British record of 1960. However, although one of biggest stars of 50s in UK, never had US success. Exploiting same vocal treatment and little-boy-lost lyrics, he had further chart-topper with **Poor Me**, then chartered **Someone Else's Baby**, **Lonely Pup** and **Who Am I?**.

Becoming increasingly interested in acting, he appeared in appalling *What A Whopper* before critically applauded dramatic role as condemned man in *Mix Me A Person*. In 1965, with recording career flagging, he turned full-time to the stage, touring for two years in relative obscurity of repertory, before regaining national limelight as loser/tarnished hero of *Budgie* TV series.

In 1973, produced Roger Daltrey's solo LP **Daltrey** featuring Leo Sayer compositions. He made recording comeback in 1974 with **I Survive** album (artistically far superior to earlier work). Returned to film in 1975 starring with David Essex in *Stardust*. 1977 saw Faith produce comeback album of erstwhile skiffle idol Lonnie Donegan and in 1979 he starred with Roger Daltry in *McVicar*, while mid-80s saw him appear in TV dramas.

Faith reprised *Budgie* role in unsuccessful stage musical presentation in 1988, despite score by Don Black and Mort Shuman. As a wheeler-dealer (typecast!), Faith featured in UK TV series *Love Hurts* in 1992. Latterly prime-mover in London's Stock Exchange, although alleged irregularities of associate Roger Levitt were causing heart murmurs during the autumn of 1991.

Below: Adam Faith, born Terry Nelhams, succeeded as singer, actor and manager.

Hit Singles:

	US	UK
What Do You Want?, 1959	–	1
Poor Me, 1960	–	1
Someone Else's Baby, 1960	–	2
When Johnny Comes Marching Home/Made You, 1960	–	5
How About That, 1960	–	4
Lonely Pup, 1960	–	4
This Is It/Who Am I, 1961	–	5
Easy Going Me, 1961	–	12
Don't You Know It?, 1961	–	12
The Time Has Come, 1961	–	4
Lonesome, 1962	–	12
As You Like It, 1962	–	5
Don't That Beat All, 1962	–	8
The First Time, 1963	–	5
We Are In Love, 1963	–	11
Message To Martha, 1964	–	12

Albums:
24 Golden Greats (–/Warwick), 1981
Not Just A Memory (C For Miles), 1983

Worth Searching Out:
I Survive (Warner Bros/WEA), 1974

The Fall
UK group formed 1977

Original line-up: Mark Smith, vocals; Tony Friel, bass; Una Baines, keyboards; Martin Bramah, guitar; Karl Burns, drums.

Career: Formed in Manchester, group were contemporaries of Joy Division, OMD and Human League, but with grittier approach and sound. Inspired and driven on by vocalist Mark Smith's blank verse rap/rant style, the music embraced punk, R&B and rockabilly in fierce rough 'n' ready amalgam to create growling hybrid. Debut single, **Bingo Master's Breakout**, was fast, direct and funny, while concerts were ramshackle and riveting — all preconceptions of rock 'n' roll tradition and professionalism were jettisoned in favour of brutal realism and haphazard spontaneity. Two live tracks on **Short Circuit** compilation album preceded the departure of bassist Tony Friel and keyboardist Una Baines, replaced by Marc Riley and Evonne Pawlett.

This line-up — still featuring original members Martin Bramah and Karl Burns — released ironic **It's The New Thing** single and ferocious **Live At The Witch Trials** debut album, which was recorded in a single day! Soon established as leading UK independent anti-rock cult group with European tours, second LP **Dragnet** and string of vitriolic but irresistible singles.

Bitter attack of both lyrics and music — especially after Pawlett left to be replaced by second guitarist — often masked scathing wit which bypassed critics and fans alike. But throughout following four years, continued to tour extensively with ever-changing line-up after Bramah left to form Blue Orchids with Baines.

Bassist Marc Riley took over on guitar and band released six further LPs before he too left, forming Marc Riley and The Creepers. Fall leader Smith met and married Californian blonde Brix, who then joined Fall as guitarist, adding both glamour and pop appeal. Joined Beggar's Banquet Records for **The Wonderful And Frightening World Of The Fall** and **This Nation's Saving Grace**. They continued to evolve and adapt throughout numerous line-up changes, but without losing sight of Northern roots. Eventually The Fall added a second female to the group, American Marcia

Schofield, on keyboards and vocals, and released surprise UK single with cover of **Ghost In My House**.

Teasing and adventurous, The Fall are an acquired taste, but have outlasted most of the sceptics, as espoused by 1990 release **Extricate**. New four-piece line-up, with Smith, Craig Scanlon, guitar, Steve Hanley, bass, and Simon Wolstencroft, drums, featured on **Shiftwork** (1991) and for Christmas 1991 dates in UK, suggesting a further period of impulsive musicology.

Albums:
Live At The Witch Trials (Step Forward/IRS/A&M), 1979
Dragnet (–/IRS), 1979
Grotesque (Rough Trade), 1980
The Fall Live (Rough Trade), 1980
Perverted By Language (Rough Trade), 1984
Total's Turns (Rough Trade), 1984
The Wonderful And Frightening World Of The Fall (Beggar's Banquet/PVC), 1984
Hip Priests And Kamerads (Situation), 1985
This Nation's Saving Grace (PVC), 1985
Bend Sinister (Beggar's Banquet), 1986

Above: This Nation's Saving Grace, The Fall. Courtesy Beggar's Banquet.

Frenz Experiment (Beggar's Banquet), 1988
45 84 89 (singles 1984-89) (Beggar's Banquet), 1990
Extricate (Mercury/Cog Sinister), 1990
Shiftwork (Mercury/Cog Sinister), 1991

Bryan Ferry
UK vocalist
Born Washington, County Durham, September 26, 1945

Career: Ferry had life-long interest in music groups. Upon graduation from Newcastle University, worked as teacher. By 1970 he had committed self to professional music with formation of Roxy Music.

Band held his full-time attention until solo release in 1973 of **These Foolish Things**, featuring Ferry singing covers of his favourite rock songs. His second solo album featured original material which appeared to be Roxy cast-offs.

Inability to balance both careers resulted in dissolution of Roxy Music in 1976. Instead of waiting to produce proper release, Ferry offered strange collection from his earlier solo singles as well as re-formed Roxy Music material. (The LP was really a compilation for US market.) Yet holding pattern of **Let's Stick Together** sounded interesting in comparison to next planned album, **In Your Mind**. Tours of UK/US failed to win any serious support for this new

Above: Bête Noir, Bryan Ferry. Courtesy EG Records.

material and made demise of Roxy Music all the more regrettable.

Just as public interest in Ferry reached low point, he produced superb **The Bride Stripped Bare** which reflected emotional trauma of break-up with girlfriend Jerry Hall. In August 1978 Ferry re-formed Roxy Music and began impressive return to public and critical favour.

Although Ferry and Roxy are inextricably linked, the gauche north-easterner retained a modicum of individuality with UK chart-topping **Boys And Girls** set (1985), a nice bonus after RM's **Flesh And Blood** and **Avalon** hit albums.

A further hiatus in career was resolved when Johnny Marr (The Smiths) produced **The Right Stuff** single hit from **Bête Noire** LP (1987), which also spawned **Kiss And Tell** 45 featured in *Bright Lights, Big City* movie. A reticent superstar, Bryan Ferry obliged fans with sell-out London concert dates at Wembley in 1989 before retreating once more.

Hit Singles:

	US	UK
A Hard Rain's Gonna Fall, 1973	–	10
The In Crowd, 1974	–	13
Smoke Gets In Your Eyes, 1974	–	17
Let's Stick Together, 1976	–	4
Extended Play (EP), 1976	–	7
This Is Tomorrow, 1977	–	9
Tokyo Joe, 1977	–	15
Slave To Love, 1985	–	10
Is Your Love Strong Enough, 1986	–	22
The Right Stuff, 1987	–	37
Let's Stick Together (re-mix), 1988	–	12

Albums:
These Foolish Things (Atlantic/Island), 1973
Another Time Another Place (Atlantic/Island), 1974
Let's Stick Together (Atlantic/Island), 1976
In Your Mind (Atlantic/Polydor), 1977
The Bride Stripped Bare (Polydor), 1978
Boys And Girls (EG), 1985
Bête Noir (EG), 1987
The Ultimate Collection (EG), 1988
Street Life — 20 Great Hits (EG), 1989

Fine Young Cannibals
UK group formed 1984

Original line-up: Andy Cox, guitar; David Steele, bass, keyboards; Roland Gift, vocals.

Career: Formed by Cox and Steele (both ex-members of highly successful group The Beat who disbanded in 1983), who recruited soul-influenced vocalist Gift from little-known group The Akrylix.

On strength of impressive tape of self-composed songs, they secured deal with London Records, celebrating with appearance on influential UK TV show *The Tube* and gig at London's Wag Club.

Released debut single **Johnny Come Back**, to universal acclaim worldwide. Debut LP **Fine Young Cannibals**, relied on concise songwriting, immaculate musicianship and Gift's insistent, rasping vocal style as highlighted on second single **Blue** which was only a minor hit due to politically sensitive lyrical message.

Updating of Elvis Presley's **Suspicious Minds** re-established commercial success,

Below: Roland Gift exercises his rasping vocal style on tour with FYC in 1987.

coinciding with sell-out European tour. Further cover of Buzzcocks' **Ever Fallen In Love?** (great choice of song, uninspired version) became minor hit before band disappeared from public view for a lengthy period of 18 months.

Prior to second album, Gift made acting debut in British film *Sammy And Rosie Get Laid*, while Cox and Steele combined for one-off disco project entitled Two Men, A Drum-Machine And A Trumpet, releasing the single **Tired Of Getting Pushed Around.**

The Raw And The Cooked album broke FYC in States in 1989, finally topping US chart almost one year after release; also made No. 1 in UK listings, but in first week. LP spawned hit singles **Good Thing** and **She Drives Me Crazy**, featured in movie *Scandal*, which also saw Gift take prominent role as murderer.

In 1990, FYC were presented with BRIT awards for Best British Group and Album, later returning trophies as protest against prominence of UK's governing Conservative party at event.

Hit Singles:

	US	UK
Johnnie Come Back, 1985	—	8
Suspicious Minds, 1986	—	8
Ever Fallen In Love, 1987	—	9
She Drives Me Crazy, 1989	1	5
Good Thing, 1989	1	7
Don't Look Back, 1989	11	34
I'm Not The Man I Used To Be, 1989	54	20

Albums:
Fine Young Cannibals (London), 1985
Candyman (IRS), 1986
The Raw And The Cooked (IRS/London), 1989
The Raw And The Re-Mixed (MCA/London), 1991

Fleetwood Mac

UK group formed 1967

Original line-up: Peter Green, Gibson Les Paul guitar, vocals; John McVie, bass; Mick Fleetwood, drums; Jeremy Spencer, guitar, vocals.

Career: Peter Green formed band when he, McVie and Fleetwood quit (or were fired from) Mayall's Bluesbreakers. For short period McVie considered re-joining Mayall and Fleetwood Mac's debut performance at Windsor Festival (August 1967) featured temporary bassist Bob Brunning (who also recorded B-side on band's first single).

First LP featured straight-ahead blues and became instant steady seller for over a year. Green then added third guitarist, Danny Kirwan, for third album. Many consider this classic line-up to be band's best.

In UK, band released **Then Play On**, **Pious Bird Of Good Omen** and **Blues Jam At Chess** before Green left in May 1970 to join religious sect. From this period came No. 1 UK single **Albatross**, **Man Of The World**, and concert favourite **Oh Well**.

Spencer and Kirwan assumed leadership roles and produced excellent set **Kiln House**. For all practical purposes, McVie's wife, Christine Perfect (ex-Chicken Shack), joined as full-time member.

Band was beginning to recover self-confidence by February 1971 when Jeremy Spencer jolted Mac with conversion to religious cult, Children of God. Like Green, he renounced his past and swore to leave rock business. Green stepped in to help band complete US tour. Permanent guitar duties

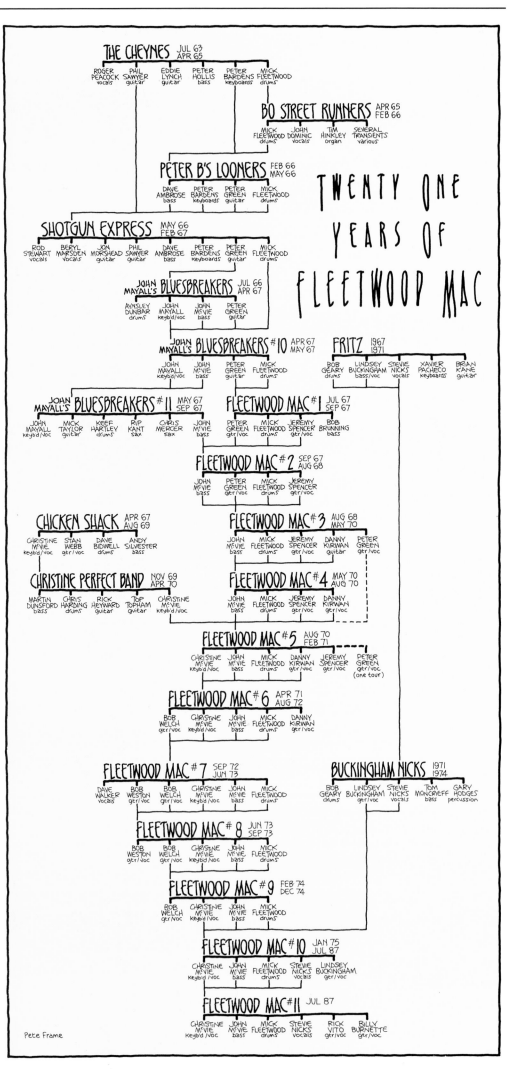

Pete Frame

were assumed in April 1971 by Bob Welch and with him Mac released spotty **Future Games** and highly underrated **Bare Trees**.

Next casualty was Kirwan who was fired in summer 1972 because of growing disenchantment with road life. Welch's influence took Mac from blues-based rock towards softer California sound. This trend was accelerated by Kirwan's replacements, Americans Bob Weston (guitar, vocals) and Dave Walker (vocals). Walker had been lead singer with Savoy Brown and his addition was experiment to reorganize traditional front-man vocalist lines. Mac released **Penguin** in 1973, indicating McVie's fascination for the Antarctic bird which became band's symbol.

By June 1973 Walker had left to work with Kirwan, and band floundered. **Mystery To Me** was critically disappointing and is of interest only because original pressing included **Good Things (Come To Those Who Wait)** which was immediately replaced by cover of Yardbirds hit, **For Your Love**. Weston left after recording this LP and resulting internal upheavals caused band to cancel US autumn 1973 tour. Their manager formed bogus group to tour in their place at start of 1974. Band seemed to disappear for good as litigation ensued over various claims to name Fleetwood Mac. They reappeared with **Heroes Are Hard To Find** but seemed doomed to perennial flux as Bob Welch left shortly after.

Legend has it that Mick Fleetwood was checking out LA studio to record Mac's next album when he was introduced to Lindsey Buckingham, who was working next door with Stevie Nicks on their second album **Buckingham Nicks**. Fleetwood asked then to join his group. Somewhat reluctantly, duo accepted. Result was smash hit LP, **Fleetwood Mac**. Album maintained sales as nearly every track proved to be strong single in own right. Any doubts about Mac's ability to sustain this success was dispelled by even better and bigger hit, **Rumours**.

Mac's capacity to survive is evidenced by **Rumours** since it followed break-up of John and Christine McVie's marriage, as well as Fleetwood's. Buckingham and Nicks also broke off long-term relationship. **Rumours'** strength is its ability to convey hurt and loss without resorting to sentimentalism.

New success of Mac pushed band into realm of superstars. Certain air of self-indulgence appeared in long-awaited follow up, **Tusk. Fleetwood Mac Live** broke no new ground and Mac seemed to lose

Below: Fleetwood Mac, circa late 1960s, with troubled figure of Peter Green (framed by Fleetwood and Mac) resplendent in red robe.

direction again as Nicks, Fleetwood and Buckingham all released solo offerings.

Demise of group looked permanent as individual careers took hold, particularly Nicks, but the lure of the dollar proved hard to resist, and 1987 saw release of brand new album **Tango In The Night**.

When Buckingham refused to tour to support **Tango**, Mac recruited guitarist Billy Burnette (son of late rock 'n' roll star Johnny) and West Coast session ace Rick Vito, a stalwart of albums by Jackson Browne, John Mayall, Bonnie Raitt, Roger McGuinn, John Prine, Todd Rundgren and Rita Coolidge. Ironically, Buckingham changed his mind and featured on US dates before embarking on solo career.

With Nicks and McVie enjoying individual successes, their joint decision to quit Fleetwood Mac following 1990 Mask world tour was hardly surprising. Reluctant to throw a veil over band's activities, particularly given group's ability to reap reward almost at will, Mick Fleetwood temporarily retired to ponder Mac's complex past, and probable indeterminate future.

Hit Singles:	US	UK
Albatross, 1968	–	1
Man Of The World, 1969	–	2
Oh Well, 1969	55	2
The Green Manalishi, 1970	–	10
Albatross, 1973	–	2
Rhiannon, 1976	11	46
Say You Love Me, 1976	11	40
Go Your Own Way, 1976	10	38
Don't Stop, 1977	3	32
Tusk, 1979	8	2
Sara, 1979	7	37
Think About Me, 1980	20	–
Hold Me, 1982	4	–
Gypsy, 1982	12	46
Oh Diane, 1982	–	9
Big Love, 1987	4	9
Little Lies, 1987	4	5
Seven Wonders, 1987	19	–
Everywhere, 1987	14	–

Christine McVie Solo:
Got A Hold On Me, 1984	10	–

Stevie Nicks Solo:
Edge Of Seventeen, 1982	11	–
Stand Back, 1983	5	–
If Anyone Falls, 1983	14	–
Talk To Me, 1986	11	–
Room On Fire, 1989	16	16

Stevie Nicks with Don Henley:
Leather And Lace, 1981	6	–

Stevie Nicks with Tom Petty:
Stop Draggin' My Heart Around, 1981	3	–

Albums:
London Live '68 (Thunderbolt), 1968
English Rose (Epic/–), 1969
Then Play On (Reprise), 1969
Fleetwood Mac In Chicago (compilation) (Sire/Blue Horizon), 1969
Kiln House (Reprise), 1970
The Original Fleetwood Mac (Sire/CBS), 1971
Black Magic Woman* (Columbia/CBS), 1971
Future Games (Reprise), 1971
Greatest Hits (Epic/CBS), 1971
Bare Trees (Reprise), 1972
Penguin (Reprise), 1973
Mystery To Me (Reprise), 1974
Heroes Are Hard To Find (Reprise), 1974
Fleetwood Mac (Reprise USA), 1975

Above: Rumours, Fleetwood Mac. Courtesy Warner Bros Records.

Vintage Years (Columbia/CBS), 1975
Albatross (–/Embassy), 1977
Rumours (Warner Bros), 1977
Tusk (Warner Bros), 1979
Live (compact collection) (Warner Bros), 1980
Mirage (Warner Bros), 1982
History Of Vintage Years (CBS), 1984
Tango In The Night (Warner Bros), 1987
Collection (Castle), 1987
Rattlesnake Shake (Shanghai), 1987
Tango In The Night (Warner Bros), 1987
Greatest Hits (Warner Bros), 1988
Behind The Mask (Warner Bros), 1990
*Titled Blues Jam At Chess In UK

Selected Solo Albums:
Lindsey Buckingham:
Law And Order (Asylum/Mercury), 1982
Go Insane (Mercury), 1984

Buckingham and Nicks:
Buckingham Nicks (Polydor), 1973

Mick Fleetwood:
The Visitor (RCA), 1981
I'm Not Me (RCA), 1983

Danny Kirwan:
Second Chapter (DJM), 1975
Midnight In San Juan (DJM), 1976
Hello There Big Boy (DJM), 1979

Christine McVie:
Christine Perfect (Sire/Blue Horizon), 1970
Christine McVie (Warner Bros), 1984

Stevie Nicks:
Bella Donna (Modern/WEA), 1981
The Wild Heart (WEA), 1983
Rock A Little (EMI), 1985
The Other Side Of The Mirror (Modern/–), 1989

Jeremy Spencer:
Jeremy Spencer (Reprise), 1970
Jeremy Spencer And The Children Of God (Columbia/CBS), 1972
Flee (–/Atlantic), 1979

Foreigner
US/UK group formed 1976

Original line-up: Mick Jones, guitar; Ian McDonald, guitar, keyboards; Dennis Elliot, drums; Lou Gramm, vocals; Al Greenwood, keyboards; Ed Gagliardi, bass.

Career: Formed in New York by two Englishmen — Jones (ex-Spooky Tooth, Leslie West Band) and McDonald (ex-King Crimson, McDonald & Giles). Adding English drummer Elliot (also ex-King Crimson) and three Americans — Gramm, Greenwood and Gagliardi — band recorded self-titled debut album in 1977.

Foreigner LP spawned hits **Feels Like The First Time** and **Cold As Ice**; established Gramm as premier rock vocalist and Jones as melodic composer in mêlée of heavy-metal outfits. After steady stream of sucessful chart singles and two further albums, Jones withdrew band from recording and touring in 1980.

With departure of McDonald, Greenwood and Gagliardi, Foreigner re-formed as four piece; Rick Wills (ex-Peter Frampton) took Gagliardi's bass spot. New line-up topped US album charts with **4** during winter 1981. Maintained single success, 1981 being most productive year since band's inception. Both **Urgent** (with stirring tenor solo by Junior Walker) and **Waiting For A Girl Like You** made US Top 5, the latter giving group first UK Top 20 chart entry.

Three years filled with sell-out concerts saw recording gap between **Best Of** in 1982 and massive selling **Agent Provocateur**. Tracks included Mick Jones' hit **I Want To Know What Love Is** which followed predecessors to platinum status.

1987 saw huge solo success for vocalist Lou Gramm, with US Top 10 single **Midnight Blue** and chart-topping album **Ready Or Not**. With rumours of Gramm's imminent departure rife, 1988 **Inside Information** release was genuine surprise, and vocalist hung on for nearly three years before being replaced by Johnny Edwards.

Edwards' debut was 1991 set **Unusual Heat**, with Jones still firmly at the helm. His own solo self-titled LP, featuring material from ill-fated **Metropolis** stage show, floundered badly, leaving guitarist in no doubt as to where his bread was buttered. Meanwhile, Gramm pursued individual stardom, scoring with 1989 set **Long Hard Look**, from which **Just Between You And Me** single made US Top 10.

Hit Singles:	US	UK
Feels Like The First Time, 1977	4	39
Cold As Ice, 1977	6	24
Long, Long Way From Home, 1978	20	–
Hot Blooded, 1978	3	42
Double Vision, 1978	2	–
Blue Morning, Blue Day, 1979	15	45
Dirty White Boy, 1979	12	–
Head Games, 1979	14	–
Urgent, 1981	3	–
Waiting For A Girl Like You, 1981	2	8
I Want To Know What Love Is, 1985	1	1
That Was Yesterday, 1985	8	–
Say You Will, 1987	6	–
I Don't Want To Live Without You, 1990	5	–

Lou Gramm Solo:
Just Between You And Me, 1990	6	–

Albums:
Foreigner (Atlantic), 1977
Double Vision (Atlantic), 1978
Head Games (Atlantic), 1979
4 (Atlantic), 1981
Best Of (Atlantic), 1982
Records (Atlantic), 1983
Agent Provocateur (Atlantic), 1985
Inside Information (Atlantic), 1988
Unusual Heat (Atlantic/—), 1991

Lou Gramm Solo:
Ready Or Not (WEA), 1987
Long Hard Look (WEA), 1989

Four Seasons
US group formed 1962

Original line-up: Frankie Valli, lead vocals; Bob Gaudio, vocals, keyboard; Nick Massi, vocals; Tommy De Vito, vocals.

Career: America's closest challengers to The Beatles (for short time both groups' records appeared on same US label, Vee-Jay). The Four Seasons' appeal hinged on unique falsetto-style lead vocals of Valli and song-writing talents of group member Bob Gaudio and producer Bob Crewe.

Record sales of more than 80 million copies, plus a career which outlasted that of their British rivals, make The Four Seasons arguably the greatest pop (as opposed to rock) group of all time.

Frankie Valli (born Francis Castelluccio, Newark, New Jersey, May 3, 1937) began career in 1953 joining local Variatone Trio (Nick and Tommy De Vito, Hank Magenski). Changing name to Four Lovers, group enjoyed minor hit in 1958 with **Apple Of My Eye** by black songwriter Otis Blackwell.

Dropped by RCA in 1959 after three lean years, they met New York/Philadelphia-based Bob Crewe. Four Lovers were initially used as back-up singers on sessions for Bob Crewe/Frank Slay-owned Swan label in Philly. Label had success with Freddy Cannon and launched careers of Mitch Ryder and The Toys.

Nick Massi replaced Magenski and Nick De Vito was replaced by Charles Callelo, who in turn gave way to Bob Gaudio. A protégé

Below: The Four Seasons, with the great Frankie Valli (centre).

of Crewe's, Gaudio (born Bronx, New York, November 17, 1942) had been member of the Royal Teens.

With new line-up and new name — The Four Seasons — group began to record, debut appearing on Gone. Signed to fast-rising Chicago-based independent Vee-Jay Records for second single **Sherry** (1962) for which Gaudio persuaded Valli to use his subsequent trademark falsetto sound.

Record shot to No. 1 in US, No. 8 in UK. **Big Girls Don't Cry** gave them second 1962 million-seller, followed in early 1963 by **Walk Like A Man**, making it three American chart-toppers in a row.

Four Seasons' emergence coincided with the 'Merseymania' explosion and they, plus the equally nascent Beach Boys, were the only groups able to challenge British domination of transatlantic charts.

Contractual arguments with Vee-Jay led to switch to Philips label in 1964. Vee-Jay, who also had US rights to Beatles material, issued double album set featuring both acts and billed as 'The International Battle Of The Century'.

Dawn (Go Away) made No. 3, and **Rag Doll** (1964) saw The Four Seasons back at top of charts. 1965's **Let's Hang On** was fifth chart-topping million-seller and marked move into a blue-eyed soul style which made subsequent **Workin' My Way Back To You** such a classic.

Parallel to group's continuing stardom, Valli issued solo record, scoring big with **The Proud One** and MOR-slanted **Can't Take My Eyes Off You**. Group also recorded anonymously as the Wonder Who with quirky version of Bob Dylan's **Don't Think Twice It's Alright** with view to proving that it was their music and not their image which gave them hits; record went to Top 20 in US.

With both The Beatles and The Beach Boys veering towards progressive pop/rock and issuing concept albums, The Four Seasons came up with ambitious **Genuine Imitation Life Gazette** (1969) project in answer to **Sergeant Pepper** and **Pet Sounds**. Lavishly produced — reputedly one of most expensive recordings ever — it lacked conviction. Album failed dismally in commercial as well as artistic terms, leading to split with both Bob Crewe and Philips.

The Four Seasons spent some years in recording retirement, contenting themselves with playing cabaret venues and cashing in on nostalgia market. They were then signed by Berry Gordy for Motown's new West

Coast label Mowest. **Chameleon** album and several singles passed relatively unnoticed at time though they have since become collectors' items.

Motown refused to release Valli's solo effort **My Eyes Adored You**, so he took it to Private Stock and was rewarded with massive transatlantic hit in late 1974. While Private Stock picked up Valli as solo artist and bought rights to all old Philips' material (re-packaged as hit album **The Four Seasons Story**), group itself signed new deal with Warner Bros. 1976 was good year for big comeback; cover versions of Four Seasons' oldies (**Bye Bye Baby** by the Bay City Rollers, **Sherry** by Adrian Baker, and Valli's **The Proud One** by The Osmonds) were peppering UK charts when their Motown oldie **The Night** was re-issued, reaching No. 3.

Classy Warner Bros album **Who Loves You** capitalized on both nostalgia of older audiences and emergent disco boom. The Four Seasons, albeit with much revised line-up, were right back on top. Follow-up single to **Who Loves You** was **December '63** on which new drummer Gerry Polci handled bulk of vocal; it became Four Seasons' first UK chart-topper. **Silver Star** also went Top 5 and resultant British tour was pure magic.

Though Bob Gaudio wrote all songs for **Who Loves You** album (with Judy Parker) he was no longer working member of group (except on record). Valli was still part-and-parcel of their greatness and the balance between his totally distinctive falsetto and the more gutsy voice of Polci added whole new dimension. Album's line-up comprised: Frankie Valli, vocals; Gerry Polci, drums, vocals; John Paiva, guitar; Lee Shapiro, keyboards; Don Ciccone, bass.

Spring 1976 saw same team, with more Gaudio songs, involved in **Hellicon** album. However, it lacked sparkle of its predecessor. In September 1977 Valli announced he was ending his long stint as leader of The Four Seasons to concentrate on solo projects. Had US No. 1, UK No. 3 in 1978 with theme from movie *Grease*.

Despite serious ear problem, Valli succumbed to pleas for group's return when teamed with Beach Boys for lacklustre **East Meets West** single, and, a year later, for MCA **Streetfighter** set, with Gaudio at the helm once again. Surprise return to charts of re-mixed **Oh What A Night** and **Big Girls Don't Cry** (from *Dirty Dancing II* movie) in 1988 saw renewed interest for tours.

Like their erstwhile rivals The Beatles, Four Seasons' appeal has remained strong through the years. They have consistently attracted new audiences. The group's shows have always been crowd-pullers even when they have had no chart success.

Hit Singles:	US	UK
Sherry, 1962	1	8
Big Girls Don't Cry, 1962	1	13
Walk Like A Man, 1963	1	12
Candy Girl, 1963	3	—
Dawn (Go Away), 1964	3	—
Stay, 1964	16	—
Ronnie, 1964	6	—
Rag Doll, 1964	1	2
Save It For Me, 1964	10	—
Big Man In Town, 1964	20	—
Bye Bye Baby, 1965	12	—
Let's Hang On, 1965	1	4
Workin' My Way Back To You, 1966	9	50
Opus 17 (Don't Worry 'Bout Me), 1966	13	20
I've Got You Under My Skin, 1966	9	12
Tell It To The Rain, 1967	10	37
Beggin', 1967	16	—
Come On Marianne, 1967	9	—
The Night, 1975	—	7
Who Loves You, 1975	3	6
December '63 (Oh What A Night), 1976	1	1
Silver Star, 1976	38	3

As The Wonder Who:
	US	UK
Don't Think Twice It's Alright, 1965	12	—

Frankie Valli Solo:
	US	UK
Can't Take My Eyes Off You, 1967	2	—
I Make A Fool Of Myself, 1967	18	—
You're Ready Now, 1970	—	11
My Eyes Adored You, 1975	1	5
Swearin' To God, 1975	6	31
Our Day Will Come, 1975	11	—
Fallen Angel, 1976	36	11
Grease, 1978	1	3

Albums:
Chameleon (Mowest), 1972
Who Loves You (Warner Bros), 1975
Greatest Hits (—/K-Tel), 1976
Story (Private Stock), 1976
Helicon (Warner Bros), 1977
Reunited Live (Warner Bros), 1981
Frankie Valli And The Four Seasons (K-Tel), 1982

Frankie Valli Solo:
Heaven Above Me (MCA), 1980
The Very Best Of (MCA), 1980

Worth Searching Out:
Sherry (Vee-Jay/Atlantic), 1963
Gold Vault (Philips), 1965
Working My Way Back To You (Philips), 1965

The Four Tops
US vocal group formed 1954

Original line-up: Levi Stubbs, lead vocals; Renaldo Benson, vocals; Abdul 'Duke' Fakir, vocals; Lawrence Payton, vocals.

Career: Formed as The Four Aims in Detroit, during period 1954-64, group signed to Chess, Singular, Riverside and Columbia without significant success. Eventually joined Motown in 1964, and changed name to Four Tops. Famed Motown team Holland/ Dozier/Holland were assigned to writing and production duties; first release, **Baby I Need Your Loving**, was hit.

Success was consolidated in 1965 with **I Can't Help Myself**, US No. 1, international hit and million-seller. Next few releases established Four Tops as major headlining act, much of the spotlight falling on Levi Stubbs as a particularly powerful and distinctive lead singer.

Group was forging style as fairly conventional Motown act, and thus surprised public and critics in 1966 with landmark record **Reach Out I'll Be There**. Superb production, with innovative rhythmic pattern and searing vocal by Stubbs, blasted record to No. 1 spot on both sides of Atlantic. It established Motown as force in contemporary music as well as highly successful commercial company.

Further hits followed, continuing even after Tops lost Holland/Dozier/Holland when team split to form Invictus Records. By 1969 Tops began to feel overlooked among large number of acts now signed to Motown, particularly as musical supremo Norman Whitfield was concentrating on following rock-influenced directions with Temptations. Tops split from Motown, apparently relatively amicably.

Group eventually signed with ABC/Dunhill in 1972, and achieved minor hits in early 70s. Their recorded output was not up to quality of Motown releases, but they continued to record throughout 70s with varying degrees of success. Meanwhile, they continued to tour steadily, being particularly popular in UK.

By the end of the decade it seemed group were headed towards gold-plated semi-retirement on lucrative cabaret circuit, but events turned out differently. Having signed to Casablanca in 1981, they released **Tonight**, a classy collection of relaxed pop-soul songs that recaptured great deal of magic of Tops' great days. Album yielded hit singles which re-established act as credible force. 1988's **Loco In Acapulco** hit (from *Buster* movie starring Phil Collins) and **Indestructable** set reinforced opinion of their staying power; inducted into Rock 'n' Roll Hall Of Fame in 1989.

Seems likely that Tops will go on forever as perennial mainstays of good black pop music. Although not overly innovative or sociologically significant, The Four Tops have in their time produced some superb and memorable music, much of which has achieved classic status.

Hit Singles:

	US	UK
Baby I Need Your Loving, 1964	11	—
I Can't Help Myself, 1965	1	23
It's The Same Old Song, 1965	5	—
Something About You, 1965	19	—
Shake Me Wake Me (When It's Over), 1966	18	—
Reach Out I'll Be There, 1966	1	1
Standing In The Shadows Of Love, 1966	6	6
Bernadette, 1967	4	8
Seven Rooms Of Gloom, 1967	14	12
You Keep Running Away, 1967	19	26
Walk Away Renee, 1967	14	3
If I Were A Carpenter, 1968	20	7
Yesterday's Dreams, 1968	49	20
What Is A Man, 1969	53	16
Do What You Gotta Do, 1969	—	20
I Can't Help Myself (re-issue) 1970	—	10
It's All In The Game, 1970	24	5
Still Water (Love), 1970	11	10
Simple Game, 1971	—	3
Keeper Of The Castle, 1972	10	18
Ain't No Woman (Like The One I've Got), 1973	4	—
Are You Man Enough, 1973	15	—
When She Was My Girl, 1981	12	3
Don't Walk Away, 1982	—	16
Reach Out I'll Be There (re-mix), 1988	—	11
Loco In Acapulco, 1988	—	7

With Supremes:

River Deep Mountain High, 1970	14	11

Albums:

Four Tops Second Album (Tamla Motown), 1966
Reach Out (Tamla Motown), 1967
Greatest Hits (Tamla Motown), 1968
Still Waters Run Deep (Tamla Motown), 1970
Greatest Hits Volume 2 (Tamla Motown), 1971
The Magnificent Seven (with Supremes) (Tamla Motown), 1971
Keeper Of The Castle (Dunhill/MFP), 1972
Four Tops Story (—/Tamla Motown), 1973
Main Street People (Dunhill/Probe), 1973
Shaft In Africa (Probe/Anchor), 1974
Live In Concert (Dunhill/Anchor), 1974
Night Lights Harmony (ABC/Anchor), 1974
Super Hits (—/Tamla Motown), 1976
Anthology (Tamla Motown), 1976
Catfish (ABC), 1976
The Show Must Go On (ABC/Anchor), 1977
Motown Special (—/Tamla Motown), 1977
At The Top (ABC), 1978
It's All In The Game (—/MFP), 1979
20 Golden Greats (—/Tamla Motown), 1980
Tonight (Casablanca), 1981
Greatest Hits (ABC), 1982
Hits Of Gold (—/Pickwick), 1982
One More Mountain (Casablanca), 1982
Best Of (K-Tel), 1982
The Fabulous Four Tops (—/Pickwick), 1982
Main Street People (Charly), 1986
Hot Nights (Motown), 1986
Indestructible (Arista), 1988

Peter Frampton
UK vocalist, guitarist, composer
Born Beckenham, England, April 22, 1950

Career: British pop music press traditionally seized cute faces to pump up, and cherubic-faced Peter Frampton was their choice for 'Face of 68' teen idol. He was then leader of The Herd who hit with **From The Underworld** (1967), **Paradise Lost** (1968) and **I Don't Want Our Loving To Die** (1968). But Frampton had other ideas, seeking recognition as talented musician rather than mere pin-up. He quit Herd to form highly rated Humble Pie with Steve Marriott, Greg Ridley (bass) and Jerry Shirley (drums), with hard-driving R&B-influenced style.

In 1971 Frampton left to pursue more melodic and romantic direction with increasing emphasis on tasteful guitar work and songs with potent hooklines. He also guested on George Harrison's **All Things Must Pass**, Harry Nilsson's **Son Of Schmilsson** and other projects.

First solo album, **Frampton**, featured Ringo Starr, Billy Preston, Klaus Voorman, former Herd cohort Andy Bown, ex-Spooky Tooth member Mike Kellie and Rick Wills from Cochise. Kellie and Wills were drafted into Frampton's new band Camel with Mick Gallagher, ex-Bell 'n' Arc. Kellie soon moved back to re-formed Spooky Tooth, being replaced by American drummer John Siomos (ex-Mitch Ryder).

Camel toured US and concentrated on American market until break-up in 1974. Frampton continued to record solo albums and tour with various back-up bands, scoring best-selling live album (10 million) with 1975 **Frampton Comes Alive!** LP, which included hit singles **Show Me The Way**,

Baby I Love Your Way and **Do You Feel**. Mick Jagger, Stevie Wonder and other names helped on 1977 success **I'm In You**. Frampton's role in poorly received film *Sgt Pepper's Lonely Hearts Club Band*, put him back to pre-**Comes Alive!** status.

A near-fatal car crash took him off road in 1978, and by mid-80s it seemed as though his solo career had gone into headspin. However, he returned to limelight with old chum David Bowie in 1987, as member of megastar's touring band, and cut **When All The Pieces Fit** album in 1989.

Hit Singles:

	US	UK
Show Me The Way, 1976	6	10
Baby I Love Your Way, 1976	12	43
Do You Feel Like We Do, 1976	10	39
I'm In You, 1977	2	41
Signed, Sealed, Delivered (I'm Yours), 1977	18	—
Will To Power, 1988	1	—

Albums:

Wind Of Change (A&M), 1972
Frampton's Camel (A&M), 1973
Frampton (A&M), 1975
Frampton Comes Alive! (A&M), 1975
I'm In You (A&M), 1977
Where I Should Be (A&M), 1979
Super Disc Of Peter Frampton (—/A&M), 1979
Breaking All The Rules (A&M), 1981
The Art Of Control (A&M), 1982
Premonition (A&M), 1986
When All The Pieces Fit (Atlantic/—), 1989

Above: FGTH's Welcome To The Pleasuredome. Courtesy ZTT Records.

Frankie Goes To Hollywood
UK Band formed 1981

Original line-up: Holly Johnson, vocals; Paul Rutherford, vocals; Peter Gill, drums; Mark O'Toole, bass; Gerard O'Toole, guitar.

Career: Named (so they say) after seeing poster announcing Frank Sinatra concert, Frankie and the lads formed in Liverpool towards the end of 1981.

First gig was at Liverpool pub 'Pickwicks'. This was an early highlight, as band was booked into an assortment of strip joints and gay haunts.

Despite raw ability and poorly received 1982 concert in Liverpool's Sefton Park, hometown following was established.

Band's first studio venture was demos of **Relax** and **Two Tribes** for Arista Records, but company did not exercise option and group was also rejected by Phonogram. Brian Nash then replaced guitarist Gerard O'Toole.

Left: The Four Tops, one of Motown's most consistent acts of the 1960s.

British TV appearance on pop programme *The Tube* (January 1983), prompted producer. Trevor Horn to sign them to his ZTT label. Horn persuaded Chris Blackwell of Island Records and distributor of ZTT that, despite bizarre image, group would deliver the goods. Blackwell agreed and Horn went to work in studio.

First single **Relax**, released October 1983, quickly attracted notoriety, with lyrics expounding gay sex, although Holly Johnson denied this. Record banned by powerful BBC, after DJ Mike Read refused to air record. Unavailability bred interest and single became No. 1 in UK, having sold a million copies by March 1984.

Frankie compounded success with second single **Two Tribes**, an instant No. 1. With **Relax** at No. 2, Frankie enjoy feat only previously accomplished by Presley, The Beatles and Lennon.

Debut album **Welcome To The Pleasuredome** went straight to the top of UK LP chart in October 1984, while third single **The Power Of Love** gave Frankie third consecutive No. 1 single (emulating other Liverpool group Gerry And The Pacemakers).

Brief visit to Hollywood in late 1984 paved way for FGTH's US success in following year, although dissension in ranks was already apparent. Internal ranklings did not, however, prevent reprise of success in autumn 1986 with **Rage Hard** although single did not achieve heights attained by **Relax** and **Tribes**.

Band eventually went critical, erupting into legal meltdown which involved ZTT seeking court injunction to stop Holly Johnson going solo. During long and messy court case it was revealed that none of band (except Johnson) had played on first two hit singles, impact of records being almost entirely result of Trevor Horn's production expertise.

In February 1988, Johnson and lads won damages against ZTT, a decision which marked their final triumph together. Various solo projects fizzled and died, although Johnson enjoyed single success with **Love Train**, **Americanos** and **Atomic City** in 1989, all taken from **Blast** album. Rutherford formed The Pressure Zone in 1991, removing a little of the limelight from Johnson's second solo bonanza **Dreams That Money Can't Buy**.

Hit Singles:	US	UK
Relax, 1983	10	1
Two Tribes, 1984	–	1
The Power Of Love, 1984	–	1
Welcome To The Pleasuredome, 1985	–	2
Warriors (Of The Wasteland), 1986	–	19

Albums:
Welcome To The Pleasuredome (ZTT), 1984
Liverpool (ZTT), 1986
Welcome To The Hippodrome (ZTT), 1987

Aretha Franklin
US vocalist, pianist, composer
Born Memphis, Tennessee, March 25, 1942

Career: 'Lady Soul' is daughter of Rev. C.L. Franklin, who has had more than 80 albums of sermons released in US. Along with sisters Erma and Carolyn — both subsequently successful soul artists — Aretha sang in choir at father's New Bethel Church in Detroit.

Her aunt was renowned gospel singer Clara Ward; legendary black singer Sam Cooke was family friend. With their encouragement she began recording career

with local JVP label and Checker; then cut demos with Major Holly, bass player with jazz pianist Teddy Wilson. These brought her to attention of Columbia Records' A&R man John Hammond, who pronounced her 'best natural singer since Billie Holiday'.

Debut Columbia album was mix of jazz, R&B and show-business standards. Entire six-year period of her stay with Columbia showed lack of direction, though every album contained its share of gems.

When then husband/manager Ted White signed her to Atlantic in early 1967, Aretha's career took off. Atlantic vice president Jerry Wexler took personal charge of project. Debut album **I Never Loved A Man (The Way I Love You)**, hinged around single of same title, was masterpiece. Wexler had taken Aretha to Muscle Shoals, Alabama, for recordings, and classy studio team there were at best. By end of 1967, further gold had been mined with **Respect**, **Baby I Love You** and **Chain Of Fools**. Second album also sold over a million copies as did third LP **Lady Soul**, which used Atlantic's own New York session crew and featured masterful Eric Clapton guitar solo on **Good To Me As I Am To You**. LP helped earn Aretha accolade as R&B Singer Of The Year in Grammy Awards.

1968 European tour — which yielded **Aretha In Paris** live album — helped **Think**, co-penned with her husband, to international hit status, but marriage was heading for rocks. After **Soul '69** album, Aretha was out of studios for more than a year before recording patchy **This Girl's In Love With You** LP in Miami and New York. Her stage shows too were less than satisfying as she reverted to mixing show-biz standards with solid soul.

Re-marriage and scrapping of large orchestra in favour of small, all-star combo

Below: 'Lady Soul' Aretha Franklin, the extremely talented preacher's daughter raised in Detroit.

led by King Curtis seemed to put fire back into the lady. By late 1970 Aretha was back on top, thanks to some great records and exciting stage performances (one of which was captured on **Live At Fillmore West** album).

In 1972, Aretha returned to gospel roots for **Amazing Grace** album. This was recorded live at Temple Missionary Baptist Church in Los Angeles with gospel superstar James Cleveland and Southern California Community Choir.

Subsequent work saw gradual diminution in her magic. At her best when fronting a small Southern-soul flavoured combo, Franklin was recorded in increasingly sophisticated settings. While following general trend in soul music of the era, these were not the best frame for talent. Despite working with such formidable producers as Quincy Jones, Van McCoy, Lamont Dozier and Curtis Mayfield, vast majority of her mid-to-late 70s output was below par.

Switch of labels to Arista in 1980 began steady revival of fortunes. From first Arista album **Aretha** came frenetic version of Otis Redding's oldie **I Can't Turn You Loose**. This recalled feel of her 1960s triumphs. Re-work of Sam and Dave's **Hold On, I'm Coming** from next album was even more potent. Also scored in duet with George Benson on **Love All The Hurt Away**, the album's title cut. Appeared in *Blues Brothers* film in 1980 (and on LP).

Although most critics would rate late 60s as classic period, Aretha has achieved greatest record sales in 80s. Pop-soul outings like **Freeway Of Love** and **Who's Zoomin' Who** have re-established chart potential, and she has regained pop credibility by recording with current luminaries like Annie Lennox and George Michael. Franklin/Lennox collaboration led to smash **Sisters Are Doin' It For Themselves**, while effort with Michael produced UK No. 1, **I Knew You Were Waiting**, in 1987.

Although Aretha has revamped image and approach to fit in with slick 80s, she did not forget gospel roots. 1987 saw her returning to New Bethel Baptist Church in Detroit to cut first religious album in more than 15 years. Straight gospel outing complete with homilies **One Lord, One Faith, One Baptism** was dramatic testament to swirling power of her voice, and ebullient tribute to her father, who had died after two years in coma following shooting accident. The album was subsequently awarded Best Gospel Performance at 1989 Grammy presentations.

Further duets, with Whitney Houston, Elton John, James Brown and Four Tops on **Through The Storm** LP, kept Franklin in pop charts, although her reclusive personality was out of step with machismo rap era of the late 80s and early 90s.

This Rock 'n' Roll Hall Of Fame inductee (1987) is worthy of any accolade, having endured personal strife, an occasionally blighted career, and period when deemed 'unfashionable'. Irrefutably the greatest female soul-stirrer of them all.

Hit Singles:	US	UK
I Never Loved A Man (The Way I Love You), 1967	9	–
Respect, 1967	1	10
Baby I Love You, 1967	4	39
A Natural Woman, 1967	8	–
Chain Of Fools, 1968	2	43
(Sweet Sweet Baby) Since You've Been Gone/ Ain't No Way, 1968	5	47
Ain't No Way/(Sweet Sweet Baby) Since You've Been Gone, 1968	16	–
Think, 1968	7	26
I Say A Little Prayer/The House That Jack Built, 1968	10	4
The House That Jack Built/ I Say A Little Prayer, 1968	6	–
See Saw, 1968	14	–
The Weight, 1969	19	–
Share Your Love With Me, 1969	13	–
Eleanor Rigby, 1969	17	–
Call Me, 1970	13	–
Don't Play That Song, 1970	11	13
You're All I Need To Get By, 1971	19	–
Bridge Over Troubled Water, 1971	6	–
Spanish Harlem, 1971	2	14
Rock Steady, 1971	9	–
Day Dreaming, 1972	5	–
Until You Come Back To Me (That's What I'm Gonna Do), 1974	3	26
I'm In Love, 1974	19	–
Freeway Of Love, 1985	3	–
Sisters Are Doing It For Themselves (with Annie Lennox), 1985	18	9
Who's Zoomin' Who, 1985	–	7
I Knew You Were Waiting (For Me) (with George Michael), 1987	1	1
Through the Storm (with Elton John), 1989	16	41

Albums:
I Never Loved A Man (Atlantic), 1967
Aretha's Gold (Atlantic), 1969
Greatest Hits (Atlantic), 1971
Amazing Grace (Atlantic), 1972
Ten Years Of Gold (Atlantic), 1976
Aretha (Arista), 1980
Sweet Bitter Love (Columbia/–), 1981
Love All The Hurt Away (Arista), 1981
Jump To It (Arista), 1982
The Legendary Queen Of Soul (Columbia/ CBS), 1983

Get It Right (Arista), 1983
Best Of (Atlantic), 1984
Who's Zoomin' Who (Arista), 1985
Soul Survivor (Blue Moon), 1986
The Aretha Franklin Collection (Castle
    Collectors), 1987
Never Grow Old Chess with Reverend
    Franklin, 1987
One Lord, One Faith, One Baptism (Arista),
    1987
The Aretha Franklin Collection (Castle)
20 Greatest Hits (WEA),
Through The Storm (with Elton John, James
    Brown and Whitney Houston) (Arista)
    1989
I Dreamed A Dream, (Arista/—), 1991

Worth Searching Out:
Aretha Arrives (Atlantic), 1967
Lady Soul (Atlantic), 1968
Soul '69 (Atlantic), 1969
Spirit In The Dark (Atlantic), 1970*
Live At Fillmore West (Atlantic), 1971
*Issued as Don't Play That Song in UK

Free

UK group formed 1968

Original line-up: Paul Kossoff, Gibson Les
Paul guitar; Simon Kirke, drums; Andy
Fraser, bass; Paul Rodgers, vocals.

Career: Kossoff and Kirke were in second
division band Black Cat Bones. They saw
Rodgers perform with Brown Sugar and
asked him to join. Andy Fraser (then only
15) was in Mayall's Bluesbreakers but
dissatisfied with jazz direction. Mutual
friend contacted him and the four got
together for jamming session; first evening produced four songs and group decided
to make unit permanent.

Alexis Korner supported group and provided name from band he called Free At Last,
while with Ginger Baker and Graham Bond
UK gigs impressed Island Records who signed band. First LP made substantial UK impact but second, **Free**, won massive US
support; **All Right Now** single went Top
10 everywhere. Sudden success seemed to
bring out friction as members strove for
limelight. After **Highway** album, band split.
Rodgers' solo effort flopped as did Fraser's.
Kirke and Kossoff recorded **Kossoff, Kirke,
Tetsu And Rabbit** LP with Texan keyboards
player Rabbit Bundrick and bassist Tetsu
Yamauchi.

**Above: Free Live!, Free.
Courtesy Island Records.**

In 1972 original band re-formed for **Free
At Last** album. During tour Kossoff's drug
habit and Rodgers/Fraser fights split group
again. Kossoff and Fraser left, Tetsu and
Rabbit replacing them. This line-up recorded **Heartbreaker** (Kossoff helped with
guitar work). Single from LP, **Wishing Well**,

prompted tour. Kossoff started but again
collapsed and Wendell Richardson (ex-
Osibisa) stepped in. At end of US tour, Free
folded for good.

Fraser failed to follow up success with
either Andy Fraser Band or Sharks. Kossoff
died in 1976 of drug-induced heart failure
shortly after setting up Back Street Crawler.
Tetsu joined Rod Stewart's Faces, and Rabbit did session work and two solo LPs before
joining Who as tour 'member', from 1978-82.
Rodgers and Kirke set up Bad Company.

Certainly one of UK's finer bands, with
understated, sparse arrangements and high
energy spirit, Free had far-ranging influence.
Unfortunately, it is yet another story of
talent which failed to reach its potential;
drugs and egos doomed Free from the start.
But, by way of a more pleasant footnote,
the 1991 re-release of **All Right Now**,
featured in sexy chewing gum ad, returned
Free to the UK charts, with hastily compiled **Best Of** package also making UK Top 10.

Hit Singles:

	US	UK
All Right Now, 1970	4	2
My Brother Jake, 1971	—	4
Little Bit Of Love, 1972	—	13
Wishing Well, 1973	—	7
All Right Now, 1973	—	15
Free (EP), 1978	—	11
All Right Now, 1991	—	8

Albums:
Tons Of Sobs (A&M/Island), 1969
Free (A&M/Island), 1969
Fire And Water (A&M/Island), 1970
Highway (A&M/Island), 1970
Live (A&M/Island), 1971
Free At Last (A&M/Island), 1972
Heartbreaker (A&M/Island), 1973
Best Of (A&M/—), 1975
Completely Free (compilation) (A&M/Island),
    1983
Best Of Free—All Right Now (Island), 1991

Glen Frey

US vocalist, guitarist
Born Detroit, Michigan

Career: One-time member of Linda
Ronstadt's backing band, Frey was founding member of hugely successful Eagles,
penning many of their hits including classic
Hotel California. On group's break-up he
found niche as writer and performer of TV
and movie themes, scoring with **The Heat
Is On** from film *Beverley Hills Cop* and
Smuggler's Blues which was used in US
TV's *Miami Vice* series, in which Frey also
made acting debut.

An ardent charity worker, Frey was
presented with Reebok From The Heart
award in 1990, and his live gigs have included charity benefits for both AIDS and
cancer research.

Following **Soul Searching** album in 1988,
Frey took time out before **Part Of Me, Part
Of You** looked chart-bound following inclusion in Oscar-nominated 1991 cult road
movie *Thelma And Louise*.

Hit Singles:

	US	UK
The One You Love, 1982	15	—
Sexy Girl, 1984	20	—
The Heat Is On, 1985	2	12
Smuggler's Blues, 1985	12	22
You Belong To The City, 1985	2	—

Albums:
No Fun Aloud (Asylum), 1982
The Allnighter (MCA), 1984
Soul Searching (MCA), 1988

Peter Gabriel

UK vocalist, composer, producer
Born London, May 13, 1950

Career: Musical career began at
Charterhouse Public School in Garden Wall,
a short-lived unit featuring Tony Banks
(piano) and Chris Stewart (drums). Group
was formed primarily as vehicle for Gabriel's
songwriting; dressed in kaftan, beads and
flowers he already revealed theatrical bent.
Love of soul music, particularly Otis Redding, James Brown and Nina Simone, was
major musical influence.

Garden Wall gradually evolved into
Genesis, and Gabriel systematically steered
group's musical direction in early 70s; contributed much to their visual/theatrical appeal, as well as penning their best work. From
1970's **Trespass** through to 1974's **The
Lamb Lies Down On Broadway**, Genesis
emerged as one of UK's most popular groups.
An elaborate tour to promote **Lamb Lies
Down On Broadway**, featuring Gabriel
playing album's leading character, proved
enormously successful in both UK and US.

In May 1975, Gabriel shocked rock world
by announcing his departure from band to
pursue solo career. Debut **Peter Gabriel**,
an intelligent and adventurous work, was
well received and spawned hit single
Solsbury Hill. For second album, replaced
producer Bob Ezrin with Robert Fripp. A less
accessible work, album showed collaboration to best effect on **Exposure**.

Third and fourth albums, also titled **Peter
Gabriel**, showed growing confidence, with
artist taking control of production. Two
evocative hits from third album established
reputation in singles charts. **Games
Without Frontiers**, a scathing anti-
jingoistic comment inspired by BBC television programme *It's A Knockout*, was followed by 33 RPM single **Biko**, about the
controversial death of South African activist
Stephen Biko.

Following **Live** set in 1985, Gabriel hired
Daniel Lanois to co-produce future work.
They cut **Birdy** soundtrack in 1985, then
fifth studio album **So** a year later, which
included mega-hit **Sledgehammer**. Award-

**Above: Since departing Genesis in
1975, Peter Gabriel has found a home
with world music.**

ed Grammy for score from Martin Scorsese's
The Last Temptation Of Christ (1988).

Diligent charity worker, Gabriel has
featured in concerts for Amnesty International (Conspiracy Of Hope and Human
Rights Now! tours), at Nelson Mandela's
70th Birthday Party tribute, and in The Simple Truth performance for Kurdish refugees.

Founded own label Real World in 1988,
with associated studio, to provide opportunity for new acts otherwise stifled by commercial requirements. With no sign of a new
album, a greatest hits package **Shaking The
Tree** was released in 1990; title taken from
duet with Youssou N'Dour, which featured
on N'Dour's **Set** LP.

Sometimes criticized for lack of spontaneity, Gabriel's work still shows greater adventure and experimentation than Genesis days.
Freed from commercial restraints, he has frequently worked on rock/avant-garde fringe;
allied himself closely with such contemporaries as Robert Fripp and Brian Eno. In
recent years, Gabriel has successfully
broadened his musical and lyrical frames of
reference encompassing a variety of contrasting ethnic sounds deriving from the
Californian Indians, Central Africa and in-
dustrial Europe. Ever inventive, he has
simultaneously incorporated unusual
rhythms and sounds from factories,
scrapyards, and even smashing television
screens to complement his studio experimentation. Acclaimed for his role in organizing
WOMAD (World Of Music, Arts and Dance
Festival) in 1982, which has since provided
significant gathering of artists from all corners of the globe.

Hit Singles:

	US	UK
Solsbury Hill, 1977	—	13
Games Without Frontiers, 1980	—	4
Sledgehammer, 1986	—	4
Big Time, 1987	3	13
In Your Eyes, 1987	—	19

With Kate Bush:

	US	UK
Don't Give Up, 1986	—	9

Albums:
Peter Gabriel (Atco/Charisma), 1977
Peter Gabriel (Mercury/Charisma), 1978
Peter Gabriel (Charisma), 1980
Peter Gabriel (Charisma), 1982
Security (Geffen/—), 1982
Peter Gabriel Plays Live (Charisma), 1983
Birdy (soundtrack) (Charisma), 1985
Plays Live (Charisma), 1985
So (Virgin), 1986
Music For The Last Temptation Of Christ
   (soundtrack) (Geffen/Virgin), 1989
Shaking The Tree (Geffen/Virgin), 1990

Rory Gallagher

UK guitarist, vocalist, composer
Born Ballyshannon, County Donegal, Ireland,
March 2, 1948

Career: One of rock's true grafters. Raised
in Cork; played in local bands until 15. Joined the Fontana Showband, an amalgam of
brass and guitars which played pop hits to
enthusiastic dance-hall crowds.

With Charlie McCracken, bass, and John
Wilson, drums, formed Taste, high-energy
blues/rock trio. Band learned trade in Hamburg and home country before moving to UK
in 1969.

Polydor recording contract produced
several spirited albums. As live act, band
headlined throughout Britain and Europe.
Earned ecstatic reviews for Gallagher's
dominant acrobatic stage presence and
dazzling guitar technique; McCracken and
Wilson provided energetic rhythm section.

With Gallagher taking central role, dissension in group grew to extreme proportions,
a situation aggravated by unsympathetic
management. Wilson often refused to take
stage for group encores, leaving Gallagher
and McCracken to appease audience. Trio
split in 1971, Wilson and McCracken forming short-lived Stud with Jim Cregan.

Gallagher took to road with Wilgar Campbell, drums, and Gerry McAvoy, bass, using
own name as band title. Line-up completed
three successful albums before Campbell
was replaced by Rod De'Ath. Lou Martin was
added on keyboards.

Pursuing a hectic touring schedule, Rory
Gallagher Band secured reputation in Europe
and America. Steady album sales meant considerable output, with several memorable
highlights. Live album **Irish Tour 74** captured gregarious Gallagher at his best. Director Tony Palmer filmed gigs for his movie *Rory
Gallagher — Irish Tour '74* which premiered
at prestigious Cork Film Festival that year.

After 1976 set **Calling Card**, De'Ath and
Martin quit. Drummer Ted McKenna (ex-Alex
Harvey band) joined for **Photo Finish** (1978).
1980 world tour provided live cuts for **Stage
Struck**. Album showed Gallagher still loved the road. 1982 **Jinx** collection maintained enthusiastic studio approach, although
barren period followed before **Fresh
Evidence** LP appeared in 1990.

Complete absence from both UK/US
singles charts during recording career belies
Gallagher's popular appeal. Steadfastly
refusing to 'commercialize' his work and rejecting 'pop' format TV shows, which he feels
could not do his work justice, Gallagher is
secure in knowledge that he is playing
authentic rock-based blues to undiminished ecstatic audiences.

Guitars: Fender Stratocaster, Martin
acoustic, mandolin.

Albums:
Rory Gallagher (—/Polydor), 1971

Deuce (—/Chrysalis), 1971
Live In Europe (live) (Chrysalis), 1973
Blueprint (Chrysalis), 1973
Tattoo (Chrysalis), 1973
Irish Tour '74 (live) (Chrysalis), 1974
In The Beginning (—/Emerald Gem), 1974
Against The Grain (Chrysalis), 1975
Calling Card (Chrysalis), 1976
Photo Finish (Chrysalis), 1978
Top Priority (Chrysalis), 1979
Stage Struck (live) (Chrysalis), 1980
Jinx (Chrysalis), 1982
Defender (Demon Solo), 1987
Fresh Evidence (IRS/Castle), 1990

With Taste:
Taste (Atco/Polydor), 1969
On The Boards (Atco/Polydor), 1970
Live Taste (—/Polydor), 1971
Live At The Isle Of Wight (—/Polydor),
   1972
Taste (—/Polydor), 1977

Art Garfunkel

US vocalist, actor
Born Forest Hills, New York, November 5,
1941

Career: Although responsible for arranging
highly-praised two-part vocal harmonies as
well as being half of singing duo, Garfunkel
felt like junior partner of Simon And Garfunkel, as Simon wrote both words and
music and played guitar. Having acted in one
film, *Catch-22*, Art began moving in independent direction. In light of Simon's desire to
attempt solo career split in 1970, seemed
logical decision for duo.

After some time on Scottish farm, Garfunkel returned to US West Coast to pursue both acting and recording career. His
performance in films *Carnal Knowledge*
(1971) and *Bad Timing* (1979) were critically well received.

Solo recording career began with 1973
Angel Clare, produced by Simon And Garfunkel's Roy Halee, which went gold.

**Above: Angel Clare, Art Garfunkel.
Courtesy Columbia Records.**

Breakaway in 1975, under influence of new
producer Richard Perry, surpassed it and
resulted in UK No. 1 with **I Only Have Eyes
For You**. Album included one-off reunion
with Paul Simon on **My Little Town** (also
released on Simon's LP **Still Crazy After
All These Years**).

Self-produced **Watermark** in 1977
featured James Taylor (for whom Garfunkel
had done session in 1976) and Paul Simon
on **(What A) Wonderful World**, one of few

*Left: Rory Gallagher, the blues star who
refuses to compromise.*

tracks not by Jimmy Webb. **Fate For
Breakfast**, partly recorded in London,
featured Cliff Richard hit **Miss You Nights**.
Single **Bright Eyes** from movie *Watership
Down* gave him second UK No. 1 in 1979,
and **Since I Don't Have You** made charts
same year. **Scissors Cut** album was ignored.

Fragmented career following reunion concert with Simon at New York's Central Park
in 1981 included few highlights. Starred in
forgettable *Good To Go* movie in 1986, and
was co-opted for Disney TV series *Mother
Goose Rock 'n' Rhyme*. UK compilation **The
Art Garfunkel Album** made Top 20, but
later work, including 1988 set **Lefty**, disappeared without trace. Garfunkel was inducted into the Rock 'n' Roll Hall Of Fame
with Paul Simon in 1990.

Hit Singles:	US	UK
All I Know, 1973	9	–
I Only Have Eyes For You, 1975	18	1
(What A) Wonderful World (with James Taylor and Paul Simon), 1978	17	–
Bright Eyes, 1979	–	1

Albums:
Angel Clare (Columbia/CBS), 1973
Breakaway (CBS), 1975
Watermark (Columbia/CBS), 1977
Fate For Breakfast (Columbia/CBS), 1979
Scissors Cut (Columbia/CBS), 1981
The Art Garfunkel Album (CBS), 1984
The Animal Christmas (CBS), 1986
Lefty (Columbia/CBS), 1988

Marvin Gaye

US vocalist, composer, keyboard player,
drummer
Born Marvin Pentz Gaye Jr, Washington DC,
April 2, 1939

Career: Son of a minister, Gaye began singing in church choir and learned organ. After
spell in US Air Force sang in various doo-
wop bands before joining seminal black vocal
group Rainbows. (Membership has also included soul legends Don Covay and Billy 'Fat
Boy' Stewart.) Formed Marquis in 1957 with
two other former Rainbows. With help from
Bo Diddley, cut album for Okeh. In 1959,
Harvey Fuqua — later major figure at
Motown Records — invited Marquis to
become his backing group, The Moonglows.

**Below: Art Garfunkel, owner of one of
the most pure voices in rock music.**

This new line-up made two singles for Chess (some years earlier, Gaye had won a Fuqua-judged talent contest singing Moonglows' classic **Ten Commandments Of Love**).

When Fuqua moved from Chicago to Detroit in 1960, to set up his Tri-Phi and Harvey labels, Gaye joined him. The labels were soon to come into fledgling Motown Records' fold. Fuqua married Gwen Gordy, sister of Motown founder Berry Gordy Jr; soon after Gaye married another Gordy sister, Anna.

In 1961, Gaye's contract with Gwen Gordy's label, Anna, was taken over by brother Berry. While waiting for recording career to flower, Gaye filled in time as drummer for Motown sessions and for stage appearances of Smokey Robinson and The Miracles (for two years). He also sang back-up, notably on Marvelettes' recordings, and displayed talent as multi-instumentalist.

Above: What's Going On, Marvin Gaye. Courtesy Motown Records.

Gaye's fourth single in own right, the mid-tempo **Stubborn Kind Of Fellow** (1962), was breakthrough — first of nearly 30 Top 50 hits over next decade. First hit's producer, Mickey Stevenson, was also involved in **Hitch Hike** and **Pride And Joy** successes before Berry Gordy, then the Holland/Dozier/ Holland team, took over reins.

Can I Get A Witness (covered by Rolling Stones) and **You're A Wonderful One** were classics of Motown's Detroit Sound idiom. In 1964, Gaye was teamed with Mary Wells for duet album from which both sides of single scored. This was first of several successful partnerships with Motown ladies — Kim Weston, Tammi Terrell, Diana Ross.

Gaye/Terrell partnership was longest lasting (from 1967-70) and most fruitful. Terminated tragically when Tammi died following several operations for brain tumour. The then 24-year-old Gaye was deeply affected and became something of a hermit, dropping out of touring scene and rarely appearing in studio. In 1971, he returned with introspective **What's Going On** album, a landmark in development of black music and, particulary, of the Motown Sound, being a conceptual LP rather than a collection of singles. Moreover Gaye produced/wrote album himself. Songs were covered by such major black artists as Diana Ross (**Save The Children**), Quincy Jones (**What's Going On**), Aretha Franklin (**Wholly Holy**) and Gil Scott-Heron (**Inner City Blues**).

1972 movie soundtrack **Trouble Man** continued vein as did sensual concept album **Let's Get It On**, before release of duo album with Diana Ross, **Diana And Marvin**.

By 1974, Gaye was established as leading solo vocalist in black music. Fronted 34-piece orchestra at Oakland Coliseum, California, for first stage appearance in four years.

Personal problems over break-up of his second marriage led to further stage/recording hiatus; and eventualy to the self-pitying concept album **Here My Dear**.

Wife's affair with Teddy Pendergrass (one of Gaye's closest friends), troubles over alimony, tax arrears (which led to seizure of his recording studio) and disagreements with Motown resulted in inner turmoil and an increasingly unpredictable personality. Gaye even disappeared to Hawaii for time to live in a converted bread van.

Visit to UK for 1980 tour saw contrast between sensationally exciting performances and series of blown TV dates and late appearances. Virtually unmanageable, Gaye was released by Motown; moved base to Belgium and lapsed into obscurity.

New deal with CBS was fruit of two years of careful reassessment; resultant 1982 album **Midnight Love** showed all his old mastery. Single (**Sexual**) **Healing** brought him back into charts with vengeance.

Despite resurgence of career, Gaye's mental state remained parlous, and he threatened suicide several times. Following violent family argument, Gaye was shot dead by his father during April 1984, ending the turbulent life of this wayward genius.

Previously unreleased material kept Motown's marketing machine busy during late 80s, with issue of **Dream Of A Lifetime**, **Romantically Yours** and **Motown Remembers . . .** albums.

Above: The late legendary soulster, Marvin Gaye.

	US	UK
Inner City Blues (Make Me Wanna Holler), 1971	9	–
Trouble Man, 1972	7	–
Let's Get It On, 1973	1	31
Got To Give It Up, Part 1, 1977	1	7
(Sexual) Healing, 1982	3	4

With Diana Ross:
	US	UK
You're A Special Part Of Me, 1973	12	–
You Are Everything, 1974	–	5
My Mistake (Was To Love You), 1974	19	–

With Tammi Terrell:
	US	UK
Ain't No Mountain High Enough, 1967	19	–
Your Precious Love, 1967	5	–
If I Could Build My Whole World Around You, 1968	10	41
Ain't Nothing Like The Real Thing, 1968	8	34
You're All I Need To Get By, 1968	7	19

With Mary Wells:
	US	UK
What's The Matter With You Baby, 1964	17	–
One Upon A Time, 1964	19	50

With Kim Weston:
	US	UK
It Takes Two, 1967	14	16

Albums:
M.P.G. Greatest Hits (Tamla Motown), 1970
What's Going On (Tamla Motown), 1971
Trouble Man (Motown), 1972
Let's Get It On (Tamla Motown), 1973
Anthology (Tamla Motown), 1974
Best Of (Tamla Motown), 1976
I Want You (Tamla Motown), 1976
I Heard It Through The Grapevine/I Want You (Motown), 1976
Live At The London Palladium (Motown)
Marvin Gaye And His Women (Motown)
Here My Dear (Tamla Motown), 1979

Hit Singles:
	US	UK
Pride And Joy, 1983	10	–
You're A Wonderful One, 1964	15	–
Try It Baby, 1964	15	–
How Sweet It Is (To Be Loved By You), 1964	6	49
I'll Be Doggone, 1965	8	–
Ain't That Peculiar, 1965	8	–
I Heard It Through The Grapevine, 1968	1	1
Too Busy Thinking About My Baby, 1969	4	5
That's The Way Love Is, 1969	7	–
Abraham Martin And John, 1970	–	9
What's Going On, 1971	2	–
Mercy Mercy Me (The Ecology), 1971	4	–

Early Years (Tamla Motown), 1980
Motown Superstar Series Volume 15 (Motown), 1981
In Our Lifetime (Tamla Motown), 1981
Magic Of (–/Pickwick), 1982
Midnight Love (Columbia/CBS), 1982
Romantically Yours (Columbia/CBS), 1986
Compact Command Performances Volume 2 (Motown), 1987

With Diana Ross:
Diana And Marvin (Motown), 1974

With Tammi Terrell:
United (Tamla Motown), 1966
Greatest Hits (Tamla Motown), 1969
Motown Superstar Series, Volume 2 (Motown/–), 1970

Worth Searching Out:
How Sweet It Is (Tamla/MFP), 1964
Greatest Hits (Telstar), 1983
Dream Of A Lifetime (CBS), 1985

Genesis
UK group formed 1967

Original line-up: Anthony Phillips, guitar, vocals; Michael Rutherford, bass, guitar, vocals; Tony Banks, keyboards, vocals; Peter Gabriel, vocals; Chris Stewart, drums.

Career: Original members were attending Charterhouse public school when they met in mid-60s. Passing demo tapes to Charterhouse alumnus Jonathan King led to first contract, with Decca. King suggested name Genesis. Two early singles did little and Stewart was replaced with John Silver. King produced first album and when told to change group's name (because of American group of same name) he refused and worked up LP title **From Genesis To Revelations**. King's production muddled Genesis sound and as LP was poorly received, King and Decca lost interest.

Band almost broke up. Instead *Melody Maker* magazine ad found John Mayhew to take over drums and ex-school mate Richard MacPhail took over as road manager. Besides providing transportation, he rented cottage in October 1969 where band lived, wrote and rehearsed **Trespass** LP. Charisma boss Tony Stratton-Smith became interested in their live work and signed them in spring 1970; **Trespass** appeared in October.

Below: Nursery Cryme, the album that defined the Genesis sound. Courtesy Charisma Records.

Both Phillips and Mayhew quit soon after and another MM ad came up with Phil Collins, who was added as drummer. It was not until December 1970 that band settled on Steve Hackett as guitarist. Band was still very 'art-rock' orientated, but 1971

Nursery Cryme showed sense of adventure and began to define mature Genesis sound. Gabriel had started wearing stage costumes, which were becoming more and more outrageous, but won favour with audiences. 1972 **Foxtrot** finally pushed them into major league and band started drawing larger crowds. 1973 **Genesis Live** is excellent account of band development at this point. Same year saw release of **Selling England By The Pound** and UK single **I Know What I Like**.

Band was clearly at forefront of progressive rock upon release of double LP, **Lamb Lies Down On Broadway**, with American interest sparked by elaborate stage show in which Gabriel acted out story-line. Rumours of Gabriel's loss of interest were confusing considering band's success, but were eventually confirmed by his shock announcement in 1975 that he had quit.

Remaining members held many auditions to locate replacement. Eventual announcement puzzle fans and critics alike: Gabriel's replacement would be Phil Collins. Many backing vocals since 1971 had been by Collins, but at time it seemed unlikely Collins could replace Gabriel with any self-assurance. Even release of excellent **Trick Of The Tail** LP and two-month US tour (assisted by Bill Bruford on drums) could not put down rumour band would completely fold. But within 11 months **Wind And Wuthering** was released and Genesis seemed permanently on road, this time with Chester Thompson (ex-Zappa, Weather Report) assisting on drums. Paris dates were recorded and produced double live set **Seconds Out**.

Mid-1977 brought more adjustments when Hackett left after 45-city US tour and three sell-out London gigs, again raising speculation that band's days were over. But **And Then There Were Three . . .** became band's biggest seller and produced UK Top 10 hit, **Follow Me Follow You**. Supergroups seemed out of touch with musical upheavals of late 70s, and band wisely took recording break. Banks' 1979 solo LP **A Curious Feeling** and Rutherford's **Smallcreep's Day** (1980) filled void. **Duke**, when released in 1980, proved Genesis could maintain energy levels, and if anything, become more accessible with rhythmic melodies. 1970s pretensions disappeared as band successfully moved back into smaller venues on UK 1980 and 1982 tours (including surprise London Marquee gig).

Phil Collins' personal problems and ultimate divorce made up the content of highly successful solo LP, **Face Value**. 1981 also saw group release **Abacab** which continued healthy trend toward group compositions. Collins, resident workaholic, managed to record another solo LP, **Hello I Must Be Going**, which yielded No. 1 hit with old standard **You Can't Hurry Love**.

Below: We Can't Dance, Genesis. Courtesy Virgin Records.

Rutherford's **Acting Very Strange** was also solid but failed to attract as much attention. However, with alter-ego Mike And The Mechanics, featuring ex-Ace vocalist Paul Carrack, Rutherford enjoyed single success with **Silent Running, All I Need Is A Miracle** and the poignant **The Living Years**, the latter from hugely successful LP of same name.

Despite solo projects, trio reunited in 1986 for **Invisible Touch** LP, which spawned several hit singles, including *Mona Lisa* movie theme **In Too Deep**. Genesis then embarked on world tour, giving fans an opportunity to hail their heroes before planned lengthy hiatus.

In November 1991, Rutherford, Collins and Banks re-emerged with **We Can't Dance**, their first album for five years, and recorded at their own Farmyard Studio. **Dance** was co-produced by Nick Davis, who worked with Rutherford on **Living Years** and aided Tony Banks on his 1990 LP **Still**. An abbreviated US/UK tour was (as of autumn 1991) being co-ordinated.

The power of Genesis, both musically and commercially, has bemused and disappointed many critics, who suggest that the trio now play safe, and are drifting into cosy middle-age. Collins' soulful vocals and the undeniable technical expertise demonstrated by Rutherford and Banks suggests otherwise, and their well-crafted music has hardly offended their legion of fans.

Hit Singles:

	US	UK
Spot The Pigeon (EP), 1977	—	14
Follow You Follow Me, 1978	23	7
Misunderstanding, 1980	14	42
Turn It On Again, 1980	58	8
Abacab, 1981	—	19
Paperlate (EP), 1982	32	10
Mama, 1983	—	4
That's All, 1983	6	16
In Too Deep, 1986	3	19
Invisible Touch, 1986	11	15
Land Of Confusion, 1986	11	14
Tonight Tonight Tonight, 1987	3	18
Throwing It All Away, 1987	1	—
No Son Of Mine, 1991	—	5

Mike Rutherford Solo:

The Living Years, 1989	1	2
Word Of Mouth, 1991	—	13

Albums:
Trespass (ABC/Charisma), 1970
Nursery Cryme (Charisma), 1971
Foxtrot (Charisma), 1972
Genesis Live (Charisma), 1973
Selling England By The Pound (Charisma), 1973
In The Beginning (1st LP retitled) (London/Decca), 1974
The Lamb Lies Down On Broadway (double album) (Atco/Charisma), 1974
A Trick Of The Tail (Atco/Charisma), 1976
Wind And Wuthering (Atco/Charisma), 1976
Seconds Out (double live) (Atco/Charisma), 1977
...And Then There Were Three...(Atco/Charisma), 1978
Duke (Atco/Charisma), 1980
Abacab (Atco/Charisma), 1981
Three Sides Live (Atco/Charisma), 1982
Genesis (Atco/Charisma), 1983
Invisible Touch (Charisma), 1986
When The Sour Turns To Sweet (mini LP) (Razor), 1986
We Can't Dance (Virgin), 1991

Tony Banks Solo:
A Curious Feeling (—/Charisma), 1979
Deaf Fugitive (—/Charisma), 1983
Still (—/Virgin), 1990

Mike Rutherford Solo:
Smallcreep's Day (—/Charisma), 1980
Acting Very Strange (—/WEA), 1982
Mike And The Mechanics (WEA), 1985
The Living Years (WEA), 1988
Word Of Mouth (Virgin), 1991

Boy George
UK vocalist, composer, producer
Born George Alan O'Dowd, London, June 14, 1961

Career: Pop's answer to Judy Garland, the foppish George is a genuine talent seemingly unable to focus his energy, although Culture Club had seemed a perfect vehicle.

With drummer Jon Moss (ex-Clash, Damned, Adam And The Ants), George formed Culture Club in 1981 after stint with Malcolm McLaren vehicle Bow Wow Wow. Adding guitarist Roy Hay and bass player Mickey Craig, quartet cut debut album **Kissing To Be Clever** for Virgin in 1982. LP spawned cute reggae-styled **Do You Really Want To Hurt Me** single, a UK No. 1.

Succession of well-crafted pop songs plundered pop charts until 1984, with **Time (Clock Of The Heart)**, **Church Of The Poisoned Mind** (which featured soul-belter Helen Terry on vocals) and **Victims**, typical of the brilliant lyrical content and subtle melodic variations.

Hounded by the tabloid press, Boy George adopted reclusive pose but could not shake stories concerning drug abuse; death of US musician Michael Rudetski in 1986 at George's home exacerbated the situation, despite subsequent exoneration of the Boy's involvement. Seeking personal restitution, Rudetski's family pursued George through the court without success. Following revelations by his brother, George finally admitted heroin addiction, which sealed Culture Club's fate and caused great consternation as to his future well-being.

George's return to the studio in 1987 saw successful (UK No. 1) re-working of Ken Boothe's reggae classic **Everything I Own**, originally recorded by pop quartet Bread. Solo album, **Sold**, was released in May of that year, and the title track provided another chart single for the artist.

Content with new low-profile image and proper haircut, George took time to form own label More Protein in 1989, which saw his studio band Jesus Loves You debut with **After The Love**.

A supporter (but not member) of the Hare Krishna sect, George moved to India to study and record with Indian musician Asha Bhosel in 1990, and returned for **Martyr Mantras** LP in February 1991, which espoused Krishna lifestyle, although single **Bow Down Mister** was a secular, and rather timid, love song.

An unlikely survivor, Boy George could have succumbed to the notoriously fickle 80s which saw every conceivable musical fashion come and go, some in a matter of days. The airy-fairy Culture Club might have been just a stepping stone for the flighty but ever-more resilient Londoner.

Hit Singles:

	US	UK
Sold, 1987	—	24
To Be Reborn, 1987	—	13
Everything I Own, 1987	—	1

With Culture Club:

	US	UK
Do Your Really Want To Hurt Me, 1982	3	1
Time (Clock Of The Heart), 1982	2	1
I'll Tumble 4 U, 1983	9	—
Church Of The Poison Mind, 1983	10	2
Karma Chameleon, 1983	1	1
Victims, 1983	—	3
Miss Me Blind, 1984	5	—
It's A Miracle, 1984	13	4
The War Song, 1984	17	2
Move Away, 1986	12	7

Albums:
Sold (Virgin), 1987
High Hat (Virgin), 1989
The Martyr Mantras (Virgin), 1991
Tense Nervous Headache (Virgin), 1991

With Culture Club:
Kissing To Be Clever (Epic/Virgin), 1982
Colour By Numbers (Epic/Virgin), 1983
Waking Up With The House On Fire (Virgin), 1984
From Luxury To Heartache (Virgin), 1986

Above: Gerry And The Pacemakers compilation. Courtesy EMI Records.

Gerry And The Pacemakers
UK group formed 1961

Original line-up: Gerry Marsden, vocals, guitar; Freddie Marsden, drums; Leslie Maguire, piano; Les Chadwick, bass.

Career: After stints, often with brother Freddie, in various skiffle and rock 'n' roll bands, Gerry Marsden formed Mars-Bars in hometown of Liverpool, playing local clubs for six months before break-up. Following split, the Marsdens were joined by Les Chadwick to form Pacemakers trio.

After two months at Top Ten Club in Hamburg they returned to Merseyside, added Leslie Maguire and were signed by Beatles' manager Brian Epstein in June 1962.

Beatles' producer and Parlophone A&R chief George Martin saw performance at Birkenhead and chose to record Mitch Murray song **How Do You Do It?** which he had earlier tried to record with The Beatles (but they preferred to cut own material). Song climbed quickly to No. 1, as did another Mitch Murray song, **I Like It**, and their reading of Rodgers and Hammerstein ballad standard, **You'll Never Walk Alone**, making them only group ever to top charts with each of their first three records.

Belated Merseymania movie *Ferry Cross The Mersey* (1965) gave group final Top 10 single with Marsden-penned theme.

Band was equally popular in US (after first US single success **Don't Let The Sun Catch You Crying**, their earlier singles were released there), but quickly faded from limelight and broke up in 1968. Marsden embarked on solo career which yielded no hits but five-year starring role opposite Anna Neagle in West End musical production *Charlie Girl*.

In 1975 Gerry And The Pacemakers re-formed for triumphant Mersey Beat revival tour of US and again for similar Sounds Of The Sixties tour of UK in 1979.

Marsden has remained active in variety, pantomine and cabaret, and was prime-mover behind fund-raising for victims of UK Bradford Football Club fire with 1985 re-make of **You'll Never Walk Alone**, a UK No. 1. Reprised **Ferry 'Cross The Mersey** in 1989, with Paul McCartney, Holly Johnson and The Christians, to benefit the Hillsborough soccer ground disaster fund. Marsden's efforts saw the track top the UK singles chart.

Hit Singles:

	US	UK
How Do You Do It? 1963	9	1
I Like It, 1963	17	1
You'll Never Walk Alone, 1963	48	1
I'm The One, 1964	—	2
Don't Let The Sun Catch You Crying, 1964	4	6
Ferry Cross The Mersey, 1964	6	8
I'll Be There, 1965	14	12

Albums:
Best Of (Capitol/Nut), 1977
Very Best Of (MFP), 1984
Hit Singles Album (EMI), 1986
The Singles Plus (EMI), 1987
The Collection (—/Connoisseur), 1989

Gillan

UK group formed 1975

Original line-up: Ian Gillan, vocals; Ray Fenwick, guitar; John Gustafson, bass; Mark Nauseef, drums.

Career: Ian Gillan was originally lead singer with Deep Purple; he left in 1973 and two years later formed Ian Gillan Band with above line-up and released **Child In Time** album. Band released two more albums under same name. Major personnel shake-up and shortening of name to Gillan heralded 1979 Top 20 album in the UK, **Mr Universe**. Line-up on this album was: Gillan; Steve Bird, guitar; John McCoy, bass; Pete Barnacle, drums; Colin Towns, keyboards.

Success was consolidated by 1980 signing to Virgin Records, although by this time personnel had changed again: Bernie Torme replaced Steve Bird on guitar and Mick Underwood took over drums. 1981 was successful year with two Top 20 LPs and Top 20 single, a version of Gary US Bonds' classic **New Orleans**. In the summer of the same year, Torme quit and was replaced by Janick Gers.

By this time Gillan had established reputation as hard-working live act, undertaking gruelling tours in UK and abroad. 1982 saw consolidation of UK success with album **Magic**, but in 1983 Gillan disbanded; Ian Gillan joined Black Sabbath and, later, the re-formed Deep Purple.

Ian enjoyed greater success and fulfilment with the new Purple than he had with his own band or Sabbath. He later revealed that while recording with Sabbath, he spent most of the time living in a tent outside the studio!

After recording **Perfect Strangers** and **The House Of Blue Light** with Purple, Gillan returned to solo work for 1986 album **What I Did On My Vacation**, although fitful period followed before 90s saw **Naked Thunder** and **Toolbox** albums, the latter prompting a series of live dates, starting October 1991.

Hit Singles:

	US	UK
Trouble, 1989	—	14
New Orleans, 1981	—	17

Albums:
Clear Air Turbulence (Virgin), 1977
Scarabus (Virgin), 1977
Live (—/Island), 1978
Mr Universe (—/Acrobat), 1979
Gillan (—/Flyover), 1979
Glory Road (—/Virgin), 1980
Future Shock (Virgin), 1981
Double Trouble (Virgin), 1981
Magic (Virgin), 1982
What I Did On My Vacation (Ten), 1986

Ian Gillan Solo:
Naked Thunder (East West), 1990
Toolbox (East West), 1991

Gillan and Glover:
Accidentally On Purpose (Virgin), 1988

Gary Glitter

UK vocalist
Born Paul Gadd, Banbury, Oxfordshire, May 8, 1940

Career: As Paul Raven, he pursued undistinguished early career with string of unsuccessful solo singles for Decca and then Parlophone. In 1965 he joined TV pop show *Ready Steady Go* as programme assistant and met writer/producer Mike Leander, later to become his mentor.

In 1967, again as Paul Raven, he signed with MCA and released yet more flop singles. Total lack of success continued until 1971 when he signed with teenybop specialists Bell Records and met up with Leander again.

Leander and Gadd set out to capitalize on then-current glitter-rock fad. Gadd created character 'Gary Glitter' and came up with sound to go with persona. First single, **Rock & Roll (Parts 1 & 2)**, was a spare, atmospheric opus, heavily reliant on bass and drums; public response was slow but eventually record made British charts, reaching No. 2 in June 1972. (It also became a No. 1 in US but remained his only major transatlantic success.)

Between June 1972 and June 1975 Glitter turned in 11 UK Top 10 hits, including three No. 1s. All followed basic style set by **Rock & Roll**, and seemed to touch lucrative chord among pubescent Britons. Stranger perhaps than Glitter's long-awaited record success was his elevation to sex symbol. Apart from the fact that his birthdate was rumoured to be considerably earlier than that given on his biography, he had something of a weight problem; stuffed into his shimmering jumpsuits and platform heels he often seemed more comic than sexy.

In 1976 Glitter announced retirement, but returned to performing in December that year, and switched labels to Arista in 1977 for a couple more minor hits. During years of stardom he was a big spender, and profligacy took its toll when he was declared bankrupt. A circus tent tour with Gerry Cottle brought him back to the public but was a financial failure. Latterly he has been making strenuous efforts to re-establish himself as major attraction, and has become something of a father figure to post-punk musicians. (Joan Jett And The Blackhearts had a US hit with **Do You Wanna Touch Me** in 1982).

Glitter's light-hearted and self-deprecating style served him well into the late 80s and early 90s. Featured as 'talking head' of TV show *Night Network* in 1988, and annual Christmas *Gary Glitter Gang Show* ensures a dusting off for those spangled flared trousers and high-rise platform-soled boots. 1991 LP **Leader II** introduced a new generation of Glitter, with singer's son, Paul Gadd Junior, producing.

Hit Singles:

	US	UK
Rock & Roll (Parts 1 & 2), 1972	1	2
I Didn't Know I Love You (Till I Saw You Rock 'n' Roll), 1972	35	4

Above: The Go Gos, one of few all-girl bands and launching pad for Carlisle.

	US	UK
Do You Wanna Touch Me (Oh Yeah), 1973	—	2
Hello Hello I'm Back Again, 1973	—	2
I'm The Leader Of The Gang (I Am), 1973	—	1
I Love You Love Me Love, 1973	—	1
Remember Me This Way, 1974	—	3
Always Yours, 1974	—	1
Oh Yes! You're Beautiful, 1974	—	2
Love Like You And Me, 1975	—	10
Doing Alright With The Boys, 1975	—	6
Another Rock 'n' Roll Xmas, 1984	—	7

Albums:
Remember Me This Way (Bell), 1974
G.G. (Bell), 1975
Greatest Hits (Bell), 1976
Gary Glitter's Golden Greats (—/GTO), 1977
I Love You Love Me Love (—/Hallmark), 1977
The Leader (—/GTO), 1980
Boys Will Be Boys (Arista), 1984
Alive And Kicking (APK), 1985
Gary Glitter (The Collection), 1987
The Leader II (—/Attitude), 1991

Go Gos

US group formed 1978

Original line-up: Belinda Carlisle, vocals; Charlotte Caffey, lead guitar; Jane Wiedlin, rhythm guitar; Elissa Bello, drums; Margot Olavera, bass.

Career: Formed to open for The Dickies, May 1978, in Los Angeles. Struggled around LA club scene under original name of The Misfits, before changing to Go Gos. Prior to this, Belinda invited to join The Germs (prevented from doing so by illness); performed with Black Randy and the Metro Squad. Charlotte played with both The Eyes and Manual and The Gardeners.

During 1980, signed one-off singles deal with Stiff for **We Got The Beat**, but expected major record deal failed to transpire. Shortly before single, Elissa was replaced by Gina Shock; and shortly afterwards, Margot replaced by Kathy Valentine.

By 1981, group signed with I.R.S. label and recorded **Beauty And The Beast** LP, from which came first hit single **Our Lips Are Sealed**, co-written by Jane and Terry Hall (then of Specials, and with whom Go Gos toured UK).

1982 was band's zenith, with two Top 10 US singles, and album **Beauty And The Beast** topping American chart. Follow-up **Vacation** enjoyed similar success, although recognition out of their home country remained a problem.

Internal turmoil accounted for break-up of band in 1984, following illness of Caffey and heart surgery to Shock. Both Wiedlin and Carlisle pursued solo careers, before band's reunion for Californian Environmental Protection Initiative in 1990. A permanent reconciliation was then planned, although Carlisle (see separate entry) was continuing to enjoy burgeoning career, with Wiedlin finding favour in movies, most notably *Star Trek IV (The Voyage Home)*.

Hit Singles:

	US	UK
Our Lips Are Sealed, 1981	20	47
We Got The Beat, 1982	2	—
Vacation, 1982	8	—

Albums:
Beauty And The Beast (IRS), 1981
Vacation (IRS), 1982
Talk Show (IRS), 1984

Grand Funk
US group formed 1968

Original line-up: Mark Farner, vocals, guitar; Mel Schacher, bass; Don Brewer, drums.

Career: Probably the most critically savaged successful band in rock history, Grand Funk began as Grand Funk Railroad. Members played with various local bands around Michigan until late 1968. Crucial move was appointment of Terry Knight as manager (Knight was lead singer of Brewer's former band The Pack).

Knight secured band a spot at Atlanta Pop Festival in 1969, where their brand of sledge-hammer rock went down a storm. Contract with Capitol followed, and first album **On Time** was released same year. Although ignored by radio stations and reviled by press, album reached top of American charts and achieved gold status. Two singles, **Time Machine** and **Mr Limousine Driver**, were also smash hits.

Above: Good Singin', Good Playin', Grand Funk Railroad. Courtesy EMI Records.

Two years of astounding success followed. Albums notched up mega-sales, and singles were equally popular. As live act, Funk became huge attraction nationwide, selling out massive venues such as New York's Shea Stadium.

In late 1971, however, band decided they could manage without Terry Knight and fired him. He counteracted with legal proceedings, but eventually lost. Once removed from Knight's Midas-like commercial influence, band sought 'artistic' respectability. Craig Frost (keyboards) joined at time of self-produced **Phoenix** album.

Of remainder of output, **We're An American Band** (1973) is notable in that it was produced by Todd Rundgren and yielded half-way decent hard-rock single in title track. **Good Singin' Good Playin'** featured production talents of Frank Zappa, but even he was unable to make much out of the unpromising material.

Grand Funk eventually folded in 1976 after the Zappa album. The theory 'right place, right time' goes some way towards explaining phenomenal success of this

Above: Back of Europe 72, The Grateful Dead. Courtesy Warner Bros Records.

mediocre head-banging outfit. As a home-grown American band at time of invasion by British heavy rock outfits like Zeppelin and Black Sabbath, they filled a lucrative if temporary gap. Re-formed in 1981, with Farner, Brewer and Dennis Bellinger, bass. Cut **Grand Funk Lives** LP (1981) and **What's Funk?** (1983) before irrevocable split. Brewer and Frost teamed up with Bob Seger in his Silver Bullet Band, while born-again Christian Farner cut **Just Another Injustice** album for gospel Frontline label (1988).

Hit Singles:

	US	UK
We're An American Band, 1973	1	—
Walk Like A Man, 1974	19	—
Locomotion, 1974	1	—
Shinin' On, 1974	11	—
Some Kind Of Wonderful, 1975	3	—
Bad Time, 1975	4	—

Albums:
On Time (Capitol/—), 1969
Grand Funk (Capitol), 1970
Closer To Home (Capitol), 1970
Live Album (Capitol), 1970
Survival (Capitol), 1971
E Pluribus Funk (Capitol), 1972
Mark, Don And Mel 1969-71 (Capitol), 1972
Phoenix (Capitol), 1973
We're An American Band (Capitol), 1973
Shinin' On (Capitol), 1974
Masters Of Rock (—/EMI), 1975
Caught In The Act (Capitol), 1975
Good Singin' Good Playin' (MCA/EMI), 1976
Hits (Capitol), 1977
Grand Funk Lives (Full Moon), 1981
What's Funk (WEA), 1983
Grand Funk Railroad (Capitol), 1991
More Of The Best (Rhino/—), 1991

Grateful Dead
US group formed 1966

Original line-up: Jerry Garcia, guitar; Phil Lesh, bass; Ron 'Pigpen' McKernan, keyboards; Bob Weir, guitar; Bill Kreutzmann (aka Bill Sommers), drums; Robert Hunter, lyrics.

Career: Grateful Dead burst forth from San Francisco's hippy scene as amalgamation of several bands. Garcia joined up with Hunter at San Mateo Junior College in early 60s. While playing blues in local spots, they came across Weir and Pigpen McKernan. Garcia met Kreutzmann when working in a record store.

Kreutzmann and Pigpen formed rock bank Zodiacs, while Garcia and Hunter joined David Nelson (later New Riders Of The Purple Sage) and Pete Albin (later Big Brother & The Holding Co.). This collection played bluegrass as Wildwood Boys and later as Hart Valley Drifters.

Garcia then formed Mother McCree's Uptown Jug Champions with Pigpen, Weir and John Dawson. Pigpen convinced band to change from ethnic music to electric blues and came up with name Warlocks. Dawson was replaced by Kreutzmann and after several gigs Phil Lesh joined on bass.

Warlocks were befriended by Tom Wolfe who documented the social milieu and cultural influences on band in his book *The Electric Kool-Aid Acid Test*. In 1966 band chose name Grateful Dead and began the long, loose concert format so closely associated with group.

Garcia refused to commit himself to standard recording contract and band remained unsigned while other Bay area bands 'sold out' to commercial world. Finally signing with Warner Bros in 1967 and recording first LP in three days, Grateful Dead became known as band who did things their own way.

Unsatisfied with sound on first album, Garcia took six months to record follow-up, **Anthem Of The Sun**. Mickey Hart joined as second drummer for recording and soon after Tom Constanten added keyboards to band's sound. Third LP **Aoxomoxoa** put band even deeper into debt as Warner Bros had yet to recover studio costs for second release. Problem was inability to capture atmosphere of band on stage. Next effort attempted to correct that by presenting double live set, **Live Dead**.

Band now entered what many consider to be classic period. Constanten dropped out. Remaining line-up switched studio work from drawn-out jams to short, structured songs. **Workingman's Dead** and **American Beauty** reflect this care and remain among Dead's best efforts.

Unfortunate incident involving embezzlement charges against manager (Hart's father), caused Hart to leave band. Drug charges after bust in New Orleans raised question of band's future. But Dead played in Europe and continued to perform from three to five hours per set. Fans of the band became known as 'Dead Heads' and were famous for their incredible devotion and loyalty — they would travel anywhere the band was playing.

Growing reputation ensured success of **The Grateful Dead**, band's second live album; it marked peak which in many ways Dead has not regained. **Europe '72** was triple live set featuring some of Pigpen's last days with Dead and introduced Keith Godchaux (keyboards) and wife Donna Godchaux (vocals) who began filling in for

Pigpen. Pigpen had liver disease which became serious and was shortly to force his retirement. He died in May 1973. Although outsiders might not appreciate his influence, this loss marked start of rough period for Dead.

Warners released **History Of The Grateful Dead, Volume I (Bear's Choice)** from February 1970 Fillmore East shows. It hardly seemed up to quality demanded when band had been with label. Yet band's own effort, **Wake Of The Flood**, did nothing to dispel concern about Dead's falling standards.

Continuing outside activities took attention away from group. However, excellent **Blues For Allah** LP proved Dead could still try for new sounds. It also marked Mickey Hart's return to fold.

In March 1976 Dead and Who were paired by Bill Graham for massive 100,000-strong two-day outdoor concert in Oakland, California. Although critically in same class, difference in styles seemed to make this a strange coupling, but it worked (and was repeated for 1981 gig in Essen, Germany).

Band continued to record and was willing to take new approaches; **Terrapin Station** was first Dead LP to use outside producer (Keith Olsen) and **Shakedown Street** was recorded at band's private studio, using producer Lowell George, in effort to get 'live' feel. This period also saw Warners release nostalgic retrospective, **What A Long Strange Trip It's Been**.

In 1978 Dead set up special night concert in front of Great Pyramid, Cairo, Egypt. **Go To Heaven** was last appearance of the late Keith Godchaux and wife Donna. Most artists who've been associated with Dead cannot be ruled out from future work. **Heaven** also featured keyboards by Brent Mydland who subsequently toured and recorded with band. **Reckoning** was interesting side aspect of Dead which presents all-acoustic live work.

Despite Garcia's fragile health, the Dead maintained status through 80s and early 90s, earning platinum album for 1987 **In The Dark** set and Top 30 placing with **Built To Last** LP (1989). Despite death (in 1990) of Mydland (Vince Welnick was added on keyboards), the Dead soldier on, with their legion of fans — the 'Dead Heads' — either oblivious to, or unconcerned about America post-Woodstock.

Above: Let's Stay Together, Al Green. Courtesy London Records.

Hit Singles:

	US	UK
Touch Of Grey, 1987	9	—

Albums:
Grateful Dead (Warner Bros), 1967
Anthem Of The Sun (Warner Bros), 1968
Aoxomoxoa (Warner Bros), 1969
Live Dead (Warner Bros), 1970
Workingman's Dead (Warner Bros), 1970
American Beauty (Warner Bros), 1970

The Grateful Dead (Warner Bros), 1971
Europe '72 (Warner Bros), 1972
History Of The Grateful Dead, Volume 1—
  Bear's Choice (Warner Bros), 1973
Wake Of The Flood (Grateful Dead), 1973
Live From The Mars Hotel (Grateful Dead),
  1974
Blues For Allah (Grateful Dead), 1975
Steal Your Face (Grateful Dead), 1976
Terrapin Station (Arista), 1977
What A Long Strange Trip It's Been (Warner
  Bros), 1977
Shakedown Street (Arista), 1978
Go To Heaven (Arista), 1980
Reckoning (Arista), 1981
Dead Set (Arista), 1981
Skeletons In The Closet (Thunderbolt), 1986
In The Dark (Arista), 1987
Dylan And The Dead (CBS), 1988
Built To Last (Arista), 1989
Without A Net (live) (Arista), 1990

Al Green

US vocalist
Born Forrest City, Arkansas, April 13, 1946

Career: Musical grounding came singing in family gospel group the Greene Brothers from age nine; family moved north to Grand Rapids, Michigan, in 1959. There Al made initial foray into secular musical styles, joining local group Creations (aged 17), recording some sides for Zodiac.

Progress was slow, until early 1967 when two group members, Palmer Jones and Curtis Rodgers, persuaded Al to sing a song of theirs so they could produce disc for Hot Line Music Journal lable; thus emerged **Back Up Train**, a gently haunting love song, credited to Al Greene (with third 'e') and the Soul Mates, which climbed into R&B Top 10 early in 1968, crossing over to Top 50 in pop charts. Two subsequent singles in similar style, **Don't Hurt Me No More** and **Lover's Hideaway**, sold well enough locally, but failed to break nationally.

Group became unsettled at failure to maintain initial impact; Soul Mates split, leaving Al high and dry. Continued as solo performer, and Green was soon noticed at Texas gig by Willie Mitchell, renowned R&B musician/ writer/producer scouting for Hi Records in Memphis.

Initial product dabbled in variety of styles from impassioned deep soul balladry **One Woman** and crisp funky **You Say It** to thumping power of **Right Now Right Now**. Also evident was blues influence (he cut version of Roosevelt Syke's vintage **Driving Wheel**); it was an interesting combination of blues and funk which yielded first major hit on Hi — Al Green's (now minus third 'e') powerful, ponderous treatment of **I Can't Get Next To You**, reviving Temptation's 1969 chart-topper.

In summer 1971, Al was back in upper reaches of charts with yet another change of musical direction; **Tired Of Being Alone** returned to Green's gospel roots — his tenor delivery, partly restrained, almost tearful, drawing on soaring emotional falsetto and crooning soulful melismatic sound lifted from Baptist choir heritage. Top 10 R&B, Top 20 pop was the result. Formula generated lengthy succession of smash hits over the next half-dozen years. **Let's Stay Together** topped R&B and pop charts in February 1972. Sound began to stagnate, slipping into predictable groove; main relief came with occasional burst of down-home gospel like **Have A Good Time**.

Al's vocals began to suffer from overkill of wistful introversion; became almost parody of himself. On stage he purveyed image of eternal romeo, playing heavily to female element in audience. Love-man image was to be his Waterloo however; a jealous female fan broke into Al's apartment while he was taking bath and tipped basin of boiling grits down his back; Al suffered severe skin burns, was unable to record or perform for some time. During lay-off, he 'found' religion again, and took to preaching around Memphis.

In 1977, Green cut highly-rated **Belle Album**; title track single, an intense soulful ballad, charted. 1978 brought fresh approach with LP **Truth 'n' Time**. Ballad **To Sir With Love** had some chart action, while funky flip **Wait Here** had crisp, punchy beat; Al produced himself with more vigour than even Willie Mitchell had ever generated.

By 1980, Green had moved away from secular music and back into gospel. He starred in off-Broadway production of *Your Arms Too Short To Box With God* (with Patti LaBelle) in 1982. Although successful in the spiritual field, artist had avoided rock mainstream until duet with Annie Lennox on **Put A Little Love In Your Heart** (1988) returned the emotional Green to pop charts. A further collaboration, this time with Arthur Baker and his Backbeat Disciples, saw single **The Message Is Love** make UK Top 40 in 1989. Al Green went on to earn Grammy for superb **As Long As We're Together** album in 1990.

Hit Singles:

	US	UK
Tired Of Being Alone, 1971	11	4
Let's Stay Together, 1972	1	7
Look What You Done For Me, 1972	4	44
I'm Still In Love With You, 1972	3	35
You Ought To Be With Me, 1972	3	—
Call Me (Come Back Home), 1973	10	—
Here I Am (Come And Take Me), 1973	10	—
Livin' For You, 1974	19	—
Sha La La (Make Me Happy), 1974	7	20
L.O.V.E., 1975	13	24
Put A Little Love In Your Heart, (with Annie Lennox), 1988	8	28

Albums:
Let's Stay Together (Hi), 1972
Greatest Hits Volume 1 (Hi/—), 1976
The Belle Album (Motown), 1977
Truth 'n' Time (Motown), 1978
Greatest Hits Volume 2 (Hi/—), 1978
Cream Of (Hi-Cream), 1980
Tokyo/Live (Hi-Cream), 1981
The Lord Will Make A Way (Myrrh/—), 1982
Precious Lord (Hi-Cream), 1982
Higher Plane (Hi-Cream), 1982
Explores Your Mind (Demon)
Trust In God (Hi), 1985
Love Ritual (previously unreleased material 1968-76) (MCA/Hi), 1989

Peter Green

UK guitarist, vocalist, composer
Born Peter Greenbaum, London, October 29, 1946

Career: In February 1966 Peter Bardens (later of Camel) finished short stint with Them and returned to London to form new band. He contacted Mick Fleetwood who had drummed for him in previous local group and got young Peter Green to fill in on bass. The Peter Bees folded within months, but

Green and Fleetwood stayed on to join Bardens and unknown Rod Stewart in Shotgun Express.

By now Green was playing guitar and playing well enough to gain the attention of John Mayall. Green was given unenviable task of assuming Eric Clapton's place in Mayall's Bluesbreakers. He appeared on **A Hard Road** and put a halt to the cries 'bring back Eric'.

Above: Sammy Hagar from Blow Up film. Courtesy Capitol Records.

Fleetwood sat in with Mayall's band and shortly after, in rather unclear circumstances, Green, McVie and Fleetwood began forming what was to become Fleetwood Mac. After brilliant run in that group, Green's history becomes difficult to pin down. He left Mac to join US fundamentalist religious group. His sincerity was beyond doubt as he began donating royalties to charity. **The End Of The Game** LP appeared in late 1970, but showed none of the ability expected of Green. He filled in awhile for Mac in 1971 after Jeremy Spencer left and did some one-off gigs around London.

Amid various rumoured activities, Green appeared in court in February 1977 following incident in which he belligerently renounced continued royalties from Fleetwood Mac. Following commitment to mental institution, he began recording again for first time in nearly a decade. Unfortunately nothing has matched grace and style of his early years.

Guitar: Gibson Les Paul.

Albums:
The End Of The Game (Reprise), 1970
In The Skies (Sail/PVK), 1979
Little Dreamer (Sail/PVK), 1980
Whatcha Gonna Do? (Sail/PVK), 1981
Blue Skies (Sail/PVK), 1981
Kolors (Creole), 1983
A Case For The Blues (Compact Collection), 1986
In The Skies (Creole), 1986
A Case For The Blues (Nightflite), 1987
Legend (Creole), 1988

Guns N' Roses

US group formed 1985

Original line-up: Axl Rose, vocals; Rob Gardner, drums; Michael McKagan, bass; Izzy Stradlin, guitar; Tracii Guns, guitar.

Career: The 90s answer to The Sex Pistols, heavy metal purveyors Guns N' Roses are a modern day horror story whose off-stage antics have generated greater interest than their music.

Founded in LA by Indiana natives Rose (born William Bailey) and Stradlin (born Jeffrey Isabelle), band swiftly re-generated

with Saul Hudson and Steve Adler replacing Guns and Gardner. Debut album on Geffen Records, the aptly titled **Appetite For Destruction**, was instant success, and has now sold in excess of 16 million copies.

Gruelling tenure on road, originally as support act for HM outfits including Mötley Crüe and Iron Maiden, maintained interest in band, whose recorded output remained scarce. Privately produced EP **Live ?!* @ Like A Suicide** (later released by Geffen with additional tracks) bridged gap between first set and 1991 simultaneous album releases of **Use Your Illusion I** and **II**.

New drummer Matt Sorum (ex-Cult), who replaced Adler in 1990, was featured on **Illusion** LPs, prompting Adler (who formed Road Crew in the autumn of 1991) to sue band, citing induction to heroin. Late in 1991, Stradlin was fired from the group and replaced by Gilbey Clarke (ex-Kills For Thrills).

Guns N' Roses frightening persona and trail of disaster — arrests, divorce, law suits, drugs and drink — have masked a satisfactory degree of ability, albeit undisciplined, which might yet replace 'tanks and naked models' in the headlines.

Hit Singles:

	US	UK
Sweet Child O' Mine, 1988	1	24
Welcome To The Jungle/ Nightrain, 1988	7	24
Paradise City, 1989	5	6
Sweet Child O' Mine (re-mix), 1989	—	6
Patience, 1989	4	10
Nightrain (re-issue), 1989	—	17
You Could Be Mine, 1991	29	3
Don't Cry, 1991	10	8

Albums:
Appetite For Destruction (Geffen), 1987
Lies (Geffen), 1988
Use Your Illusion I (Geffen), 1990
Use Your Illusion II (Geffen), 1991

Sammy Hagar

US guitarist, vocalist, composer
Born October 13, 1947

Career: Son of a prizefighter, Hagar first came to prominence as guitarist in Montrose. Left in 1975 to pursue solo career as heavy metal guitarist. Debut **Nine On A Ten Scale** showed promise with some interesting echobox phrasing, particularly on **Urban Gorilla**. 1977's eponymous album, recorded at Abbey Road, was less impressive and led to predictable mundane material on subsequent **Musical Chairs**. Within seven months **All Night Long** appeared, a rushed work seemingly bereft of new ideas.

His popularity having declined considerably, Hagar waited a year before releasing next work; **Street Machine** was distinct improvement, with Hagar taking control of production. Set included his paean to fast cars, **Trans-Am** which became a great audience favourite. Fortunes continued to improve in 1979 and he enjoyed hugely successful appearances on Boston's US tour. A brief UK visit gained him some commendation, and with resurgence of interest in heavy metal he was pushed into limelight. Christmas single, **This Planet's On Fire/Space Station No. 5**, provided minor hit, and two months later **I've Done Everything For You** climbed in UK Top 50, paving the way for a sell-out tour in April 1980.

Release of live **Loud And Clear** (March 1980) was an inspired move, indicating that faulty earlier work could still sound impressive in live setting. Set included nine Hagar numbers, seven of which had originally appeared on swiftly deleted **All Night Long**; a version of Montrose's driving **Bad Motor Scooter** was another clever addition.

Completed Capitol contract with excellent **Danger Zone**, arguably his best album. Switched to Geffen label for 1982 set **Standing Hampton**, and subsequently enjoyed US top single **I Can't Drive 55** from **Voa** set (1984). With career on up-and-up, Hagar's sudden decision to link with Eddie Van Halen (as replacement for David Lee Roth) in 1985 came as major shock, although singer maintained solo output with **Looking Back** album in 1987. Debuted (in 1986) for Van Halen on **5101** LP.

Hit Singles:

	US	UK
Your Love Is Driving Me Crazy, 1982	13	–
I Can't Drive 55, 1984	6	–
Give To Love, 1987	23	–

Albums:
Nine On A Ten Scale (Capitol), 1976
Sammy Hagar (Capitol), 1977
Musical Chairs (Capitol), 1978
All Night Long (live) (Capitol), 1978
Street Machine (Capitol), 1979
Danger Zone (Capitol), 1979
Loud And Clear (Capitol), 1980
Standing Hampton (Geffen), 1982
Three Lock Box (Geffen), 1982
Voa (Geffen), 1984
Looking Back (Geffen), 1987
Best Of (Warner Bros), 1989

Hagar, Schon, Aaronson and Shrieve:
Through The Fire (Geffen), 1984

Bill Haley

US vocalist, guitarist, composer
Born William John Clifton Haley Jr., Detroit, July 6, 1927
Died February 9, 1981

Career: Bill Haley's career lived up to name of his backing group, The Comets. It was his classic single **Rock Around The Clock** (arguably the all-time anthem of rock music — and its biggest and most consistent selling single with total sales of more than 20 million copies) which really triggered off rock 'n' roll revolution when featured in 1955 movie *The Blackboard Jungle*.

Moving to Booth-Winn, Pennsylvania, at four and raised on parents' farm, Haley played hillbilly music at local country fairs as teenager and spent two years in early 1940s as guitarist in cousin Lee's band. Cut first solo record, **Candy Kisses**, in 1945 when 18.

After four years with various country and western bands, in 1949 Haley became DJ at Radio WPWA in Chester, Pennsylvania. Formed own group, the Four Aces Of Western Swing, to broadcast for station. Recorded for various labels (including one single on Atlantic) before signing to Dave Miller's Essex label in Philadelphia.

Jackie Brenton's 1951 R&B single **Rocket 88** has often been cited as first rock 'n' roll hit and Haley covered it for white audiences in rockabilly style, selling 10,000 copies. He then notched 75,000 sales for follow-up single, **Rock The Joint**, another R&B cover.

Sensing innate commercial potential of R&B/C&W hybrid, Haley stopped recording hillbilly material, changed band's name to Comets and made national charts in 1953

with **Crazy Man Crazy**, a pulsating record which formulated his successful and instantly recognizable style.

Already long past teens, his moon-shaped face crowned by a soon-to-be-famous kiss curl, Haley fronted band of seasoned musicians: John Grande, Al Reed, Francis Beecher, Billy Williamson, Don Raymond and Rudy Pompelli. Although belonging to different age group, they touched chord of rising youth cult and suddenly became hottest property in music business.

Rock Around The Clock, recorded in April 1954 after move from Essex Records to Decca, was cut as favour to Haley's manager Dave Myers, who had written song 18 months earlier for Sunny Dae. Released late 1954, record reached No. 17 in UK in January 1955, then quickly dropped from chart. After follow-up **Shake Rattle And Roll** (re-make of Joe Turner R&B hit) scored on both sides of Atlantic, it was re-issued to top charts in June (US) and October (UK). It has subsequently been re-released several times, most recent chart revival being 1974 when it reached No. 12 in UK.

1955 saw no fewer than six Haley records scorch up charts. 1956 produced a further five hits with two final hits in 1957.

Haley's American success was surpassed in UK, where in February 1957 he was mobbed by many thousands of fans on arrival in a train specially chartered by the *Daily Mirror* newspaper at London's Waterloo Station. Cinema audience had rioted at showings of the two exploitation movies *Rock Around The Clock* and *Don't Knock The Rock* in which Haley starred. Concert tour produced similar scenes with theatre seats being ripped out and fans going into hysterics.

However, despite sometimes wild live act which saw Pompelli cavorting all over stage, playing saxophone flat on his back and the like, group couldn't hide fact that they were essentially middle-aged musicians pandering to kids. With arrival of Presley, Haley's comet burned out, since these kids now had a hero of their generation. Haley's fate was sealed. A chubby-faced, rather sedate, happily married man, he could offer the excitement of his music but not the sex appeal of his younger rival. His music also soon lost its edge, later recordings lapsing into lightweight MOR genre.

Moving to Rio Grande Valley, Haley contented himself with occasional nostalgia-appeal tours with Comets. He was set for one such in autumn 1980 but it was called off due to illness and in November he was admitted to an LA hospital with suspected brain tumour. Three months later the first hero of rock 'n' roll — a man who sold nearly 70 million records — was dead at early age of 54.

Hit Singles:

	US	UK
Crazy Man Crazy, 1953	12	–
Shake, Rattle And Roll, 1954	7	4
Rock Around The Clock, 1955	1	1
Dim, Dim The Lights, 1955	11	–
Birth Of The Boogie, Mambo Rock, 1955	17	–
Mambo Rock, 1955	18	14
Razzle-Dazzle, 1955	15	–
Rock-A-Beatin' Boogie, 1955	23	4
Burn The Candle, 1955	9	–
See You Later Alligator, 1956	6	7
R-O-C-K/The Saints Rock 'n' Roll, 1956	16	–
The Saints Rock 'n' Roll, 1956	18	5
Rockin' Thru The Rye, 1956	–	3
Razzle-Dazzle, 1956	–	13
Rock Around The Clock, 1956	–	5
Rip It Up, 1956	25	4
Rockin' Thru The Rye, 1957	–	19

	US	UK
Rock The Joint, 1957	–	20
Don't Knock The Rock, 1957	–	7
Rock Around The Clock, 1968	–	20
Rock Around The Clock, 1974	39	12
Shake, Rattle And Roll, 1974	–	12

Albums:
Rock Around The Clock (Decca/MCA Coral), 1955
Twistin' Knights At The Round Table (Roulette/PRT), 1961
Rock The Joint (London/Roller Coaster), 1963
Greatest Hits (MCA), 1968
Rock 'n' Roll (GNP/–), 1970
On Stage (–/Hallmark), 1970
Rock Around The Country (GNP/Sonet), 1971
Golden King Of Rock (–/Hallmark), 1972
Just Rock 'n' Roll Music (–/Sonet), 1973
Mister Rock 'n' Roll (–/Ember), 1974
Golden Hits (MCA), 1974
Bill Haley Collection (–/Pickwick), 1976
R.O.C.K. (–/Sonet), 1976
Armchair Rock 'n Roll (MCA), 1978
Everyone Can Rock 'n' Roll (–/Sonet), 1979
Golden Country Origins (–/Roller Coaster), 1979
20 Golden Pieces (–/Bulldog), 1979
Rockin' And Rollin' (Accord/Bear Family), 1981
Greatest Hits (Piccadilly/–), 1981
Tribute (–/MCA), 1981
The King Of Rock 'n' Roll (Bellaphon), 1986
The 16 Greatest Hits (Bescol), 1987
Bill Haley Rarities (Ambassador), 1987

Hall And Oates

US vocal/instrumental duo
Daryl Hall, vocals, keyboards; born Philadelphia, October 11, 1948
John Oates, vocals, guitar; born New York, April 7, 1949

Career: Hall doubled working with Philadelphia Orchestra and singing back-up for soul artists recording in the city. Made first record with The Romeos, a group led by Kenny Gamble. When Gamble and The Romeos' keyboard player Leon Huff started producing records, firstly for Jimmy Bishop's Arctic label then for their own Neptune and Philadelphia International labels, they used Hall as a regular back-up musician. As habitué of Sigma Sound Studios, Hall also worked on records by The Stylistics, The Temptations, and others.

Hall and Oates first met at teenage dance; later they sang together in various doo-wop outfits. While Oates went to college to get a degree in journalism, Hall teamed with

singer/songwriter Tim Moore and producer Tim Sellers to record an album for Elektra as Gulliver. Oates occasionally played with band; he started to play regularly with Hall when it broke up. Duo landed contract with Atlantic in 1972, cutting folksy debut album in New York and Arif Mardin producing. 1973 saw them on US charts with soulful **She's Gone** from more R&B-flavoured **Abandoned Luncheonette** album. Third Atlantic LP, the Todd Rundgren-produced **War Babies** was in heavy-rock mould.

A more precise sense of direction came with move to RCA in 1975 for **Hall And Oates** set which yielded **Sara Smile** hit. Charted on both sides of Atlantic with **Bigger Than Both Of Us** LP (1976) from which came 1977 US chart-topper **Rich Girl**. 1980 found duo producing themselves, and next two albums, **Voices** and **Private Eyes**, contained eight hit singles of which **I Can't Go For That (No Can Do)** was a crossover phenomenon, topping US pop, adult contemporary, R&B and dance charts.

In 1980 Hall had success with Robert Fripp-produced solo album **Sacred Songs**, while Oates wrote soundtrack for film *Outlaw Blues*. Moving ever closer to soul music — like a latter-day Righteous Brothers — Hall And Oates have been prolific songwriters, often in collaboration with Sara and Janna Allen who penned Diana Ross's hit single **Swept Away** for which the band laid down the backing tracks.

Hall And Oates have also worked apart, Hall staying on in London at end of tour to record a duet with Elvis Costello, **The Only Flame In Town**.

In 1985 the pair was involved in one-off re-opening New York concert at Harlem's legendary Apollo Theatre, shrine of black music for 50 years. They sang on-stage with Eddie Kendricks and David Ruffin of The Temptations.

1988 marked end of two-year split for duo who signed for Arista Records and **Ooh Yeah!** album. Live work was restricted to occasional charity gig, although pair did return for US/UK all-acoustic tour in 1991 following release of **Change Of Seasons** LP in October 1990.

Hit Singles:

	US	UK
Sarah Smile, 1976	4	–
She's Gone, 1976	7	42
Rich Girl, 1977	1	–
It's A Laugh, 1978	20	–
Wait For Me, 1979	18	–
You've Lost That Lovin' Feeling, 1980	12	55
Kiss On My List, 1981	1	33

Below: Daryl Hall (left) and John Oates (right) now reconciled.

	US	UK
You Make My Dreams, 1981	5	—
Private Eyes, 1981	1	32
I Can't Go For That (No Can Do), 1981	1	8
Did It In A Minute, 1982	9	—
Maneater, 1982	1	6
One On One, 1983	7	—
Family Man, 1983	6	15
Say It Isn't So, 1983	2	—
Adult Education, 1984	8	—
Out Of Touch, 1984	1	—
Method Of Modern Love, 1985	5	—
Some Things Are Better, 1985	19	—
A Nite At The Apollo, 1985	20	—
So Close, 1990	11	—

Albums:
Whole Oates (Atlantic), 1972
Abandoned Luncheonette (Atlantic), 1973
War Babies (Atlantic), 1974
Hall And Oates (Atlantic), 1975
Bigger Than Both Of Us (RCA), 1976
Beauty On A Backstreet (RCA), 1977
Past Times Behind (Chelsea), 1977
Live Time (RCA), 1978
Along The Red Ledge (RCA), 1978
X-Static (RCA), 1979
Voices (RCA), 1980
Private Eyes (RCA), 1981
H₂O (RCA), 1982
Greatest Hits, Rock 'n' Soul Part 1 (RCA), 1984
Big Bam Boom (RCA), 1984
Live At The Apollo (with Eddie Kendricks and David Ruffin) (RCA), 1985
Hall And Oates Intertape
20 Classic Tracks (Meteor)
Ooh Yeah! (Arista), 1988
Change Of Seasons (Arista), 1990
Best Of (RCA), 1991
Looking Back (Arista), 1991

Hammer

US vocalist, composer, producer
Born Stanley Kirk Burrell, Oakland, California, March 30, 1962

Career: Presenting the acceptable face of rap, the Hammer nonetheless delivers a punchy message, and is actively involved in teenage anti-drug drive.

Former batboy for Oakland A's baseball club (where he earned nickname, MC Hammer), Hammer began career with loan from team player's Dwayne Murphy and Mike Davis after short-lived college term and stint in US Navy. Murphy and Davis later filled lawsuit to recover profits allegedly owed from their deal with Hammer.

First single **Ring 'Em** prompted Hammer to recruit backing group titled Oakland 3-5-7, and outfit signed for Capitol Records. Debut album **Let's Get It Started** (summer of 1988) was instant success, and electrifying and athletic stage presence ensured growing support.

Hammer's future was sealed when **U Can't Touch This** single (from **Please Hammer Don't Hurt 'Em** LP) became dance sensation of 1990, and international corporations Pepsi and Nike signed him to promotional contracts.

Grammy and BRIT award winner (1991), the Hammer was further honoured when Fremont, California declared January 22 'MC Hammer Day', citing his positive image and unrelenting charity work.

1991 world tour (which included spot on The Simple Truth concert at London's Wembley Stadium) and formation of own label (Bust It) maintained the Hammer work ethic, as the artist looked to consolidate reputation beyond rap boundaries.

Above: Now known as just 'Hammer', Stanley is a jive jumper extraordinaire.

Hit Singles:	US	UK
U Can't Touch This, 1990	8	3
Have You Seen Her, 1990	4	8
Pray, 1990	2	8
Here Comes The Hammer, 1991	54	15
Yo!! Sweetness, 1991	—	16
(Hammer, Hammer) They Put Me In The Mix, 1991	—	20
Addams Family Groove, 1992	—	3

Albums:
Feel My Power (Capitol), 1988
Let's Get It Started (Capitol), 1988
Please Hammer Don't Hurt 'Em (Capitol), 1990
2 Legit 2 Quit (Capitol), 1991

Happy Mondays

UK group formed 1983

Original line-up: Shaun Ryder, vocals; Paul Davis, keyboards; Mark Day, guitar; Paul Ryder, bass; Gary Whelan, drums.

Career: Shaun Ryder's loose collection of mates was finally formulated into a 'proper band' after a three-year period gigging in pubs and clubs around Manchester.

Early singles on Factory Records did not disturb indie chart until **Tart Tart** (1987), by which time percussionist Mark Berry had been added to the line-up. The sextet cut debut album **Squirrel And G-Man** with former Velvet Underground member John Cale as producer.

Second LP **Bummed** received good reviews, and dented independent album chart; undercurrent of enthusiasm in States saw band make US tour debut in 1989. Faddish mix of dance and acid house earned Happy Mondays immediate plaudits. Following productive period in UK, with sell-out appearance at Wembley Arena, group returned to America for six-concert fling and recording date (in Los Angeles).

To support release of third album **Pills 'n' Thrills And Bellyaches**, Happy Mondays undertook first major UK tour, temporarily abandoned when Shaun Ryder was booked into detox clinic near Manchester. Ryder had previously been found in possession of cocaine, and his self-confessed abuse of narcotics found the scurrilous UK tabloids digging for further dirt at every opportunity. Unhappy Mondays?

Hit Singles:	US	UK
Manchester Rave On, 1989	—	19
Step On, 1990	57	5
Kinky Afro, 1990	—	5
Loose Fit, 1991	—	17

Albums:
Squirrel And G-Man (—/Factory), 1987
Bummed (Elektra/Factory), 1988
Pills 'n' Thrills And Bellyaches (Elektra/Factory), 1990
Up All Night (—/Baktabak), 1991

George Harrison

UK vocalist, guitarist, composer
Born Liverpool, February 25, 1943

Career: As youngest member of Beatles, spent several years in shadow of Lennon and McCartney, and in early days was rarely allowed to demonstrate not inconsiderable songwriting talent on Beatle records. In fact, achieved first single A-side for Beatles (**Something**) on last Beatle LP, **Abbey Road**. Even before that, Harrison had released solo Beatle record in shape of rather tedious soundtrack for film *Wonderwall*, first LP to be released on Apple label, in 1968. Also released experimental and similarly unlistenable LP, **Electronic Sounds**, before Beatles split up.

In late 1969, became involved with US white soulsters Delaney And Bonnie, touring and recording with them. Perhaps curiously, Harrison was last of four Beatles to release genuinely musical album, triple set **All Things Must Pass**, in 1970. Set was immediate success, particularly **My Sweet Lord**, which was released as single, and topped charts around world. However, this song was to become notorious in view of court case over its similarity to **He's So Fine**, hit for the Chiffons. Harrison lost case and in late 70s had to pay damages of more than half a million dollars to publishers of **He's So Fine**.

During later Beatle years, Harrison became besotted by India, leading to interest in transcendental meditation and the sitar. This aspect of his work was thankfully mostly absent from **All Things Must Pass**, but when leading Indian sitar player

Ravi Shankar asked for help for starving people of Bangladesh in form of charity concert, Harrison was delighted to oblige. With star-studded line-up, including Bob Dylan, Eric Clapton, Billy Preston, Leon Russell and Ringo Starr, Harrison organized two concerts at Madison Square Garden, New York, which were recorded and filmed, with all proceeds theoretically going to assist Bangladesh victims. In reality, prevarication on part of record companies to which other stars were contracted meant long delays, although eventually substantial sum was donated to effort.

By next LP, Harrison's interest in Eastern religion had largely changed musical direction, resulting in very poor LP. His marriage to 60s model Patti Boyd also fell apart; Patti moved in with Eric Clapton. 1974 LP, **Dark Horse**, was still overly religious and thus not popular; next LP was no improvement.

In 1976, launched own Dark Horse label with A&M Records. By end of year, disagreements with A&M meant that Dark Horse (and George) moved to Warner Bros amid heavy lawsuits, although first Dark Horse LP by Harrison, **33⅓** was best thing since Bangladesh days. After long hiatus, next LP, **George Harrison** (1979), appeared to little success. Harrison was rarely seen in public, and only emerged following John Lennon's murder with tribute single **All Those Years Ago**, on which Paul McCartney and Ringo also guested. Follow-up LP, **Somewhere In England**, failed to improve much on previous few years' output, and releases **Gone Troppo** LP and **Wake Up My Love** single were released almost secretly in late 1982.

Surprising return to charts in 1987 with single **Got My Mind Set On You** from **Cloud Nine** LP prefaced formation of Traveling Wilburys outfit with Bob Dylan, Jeff Lynne, Tom Petty and, before his death, Roy Orbison. Also featured on Petty's **Full Moon Fever** and Eric Clapton album **Journeyman** during same period.

Attending ceremony in New York (with Ringo Starr and Yoko Ono) when Beatles were inaugurated into Rock 'n' Roll Hall Of Fame in 1988, and was subjected to media

Below: The occasionally Happy Mondays, who have been beset by vocalist Shaun Ryder's (third from left) unusual personal habits.

blitz upon CD release of **Sgt Pepper** master-piece. Harrison acknowledges that his career is inextricably linked with the Fab Four, and is now a gracious spokesman for The Beatles.

Hit Singles:

	US	UK
My Sweet Lord, 1970	1	1
What Is Life, 1971	10	—
Bangladesh, 1971	23	10
Give Me Love (Give Me Peace On Earth), 1973	1	8
Dark Horse, 1974	15	—
You, 1975	20	38
Crackerbox Palace, 1977	19	—
Blow Away, 1979	16	51
All Those Years Ago, 1981	3	13
Got My Mind Set On You, 1987	1	2

Above: Cloud Nine, George Harrison. Courtesy Dark Horse Records.

Albums:
Wonderwall (Apple), 1968
Electronic Sounds (Apple), 1969
All Things Must Pass (Apple), 1970
Concert For Bangladesh (Apple), 1972
Living In The Material World (Apple), 1973
Dark Horse (Pathe), 1974
Extra Texture (Apple), 1975
33⅓ (Dark Horse), 1976
Best Of (Capitol/Parlophone), 1977
George Harrison (Dark Horse), 1979
Somewhere In England (Dark Horse), 1981
Gone Troppo (Dark Horse), 1982
Cloud Nine (Dark Horse), 1987
Best Of 1976-89 (Dark Horse), 1989

With Traveling Wilburys:
Volume 1 (Wilbury), 1988
Volume 3 (Wilbury), 1990

Hawkwind
UK group formed 1969

Original line-up: David Brock, guitar, vocals; Huw Lloyd Langton, guitar; Terry Ollis, drums; Nik Turner, saxophone; John Harrison, bass; Dik Mik, electronics.

Career: Founded by Brock and Turner, unit emerged from Ladbroke Grove area of London as Group X, then Hawkwind Zoo and, finally, Hawkwind. Quickly established themselves as darlings of Notting Hill long-hair set. Manager Doug Smith negotiated recording contract with United Artists.
First album **Hawkwind** (1970) proved in-auspicious, but strong live following boosted sales. Group's improvisational style was widely known after numerous festivals, including 1970 Isle Of Wight, where they played free for fans outside the site's fence.
Group soon emerged as heroes of under-ground, playing community gigs and benefit concerts at every opportunity. Reputation and notoriety was further increased after reports about their apparent drug habits.

In June 1971, played at Glastonbury Fayre Festival, aided by poet/painter/vocalist Bob Calvert, whose presence attracted interest from sci-fi writer Michael Moorcock. This performance also introduced dancer Stacia, later to become regular feature at live gigs. Group's cosmic/space rock phase was in-dicated on 1971's **In Search Of Space**.
By early 1972, 'resident poet' Calvert join-ed as full-time member. In February, played London's Roundhouse alternative music spectacle, later double album featured one side of Hawkwind performing **Masters Of The Universe** and **Born To Go**. Also played on triple album set **Glastonbury Fayre** with a host of celebrated rock heroes. Their highest single placing occurred during same period with No. 3 hit **Silver Machine**. Flush-ed with success, they financed their own Space Ritual Road Show which spawned **Space Ritual Live**.
As youthful following increased, Langton, Harrison and Ollis drifted away, replaced by Simon King (drums), Del Detmar (elec-tronics) and a series of bassists: Thomas Crimble, Dave Anderson and, finally, Ian 'Lemmy' Kilminster. Dik Mik left as did Calvert. Detmar was replaced by Simon House who joined for spring 1974 US tour.
During Stateside jaunt, Lemmy was caught in possession of amphetamines. Resulting fracas led to his dismissal and he flew back to England to form Motorhead. Pink Fairies' Paul Rudolph was replacement. When King suffered an accident following soccer match, Alan Powell was granted per-manent membership.
In 1976, signed deal with Charisma Records, and **Astounding Sounds Amaz-ing Music** was released shortly afterwards. Further changes followed: Nik Turner left and Rudolph and Powell were fired.
Adrian Shaw (bass, vocals) was recruited in time for **Quark, Strangeness And Charm**. Next album, **PXR5**, was not releas-ed until May 1979, by which time Hawk-wind had effectively split. Some remaining members became Hawklords, recording album under that title.
By September 1979, Hawklords had been replaced by revamped Hawkwind, compris-ing Dave Brock, Harvey Bainbridge, Simon King, Huw Lloyd Langton and Tim Blake.
In 1980, signed to Bronze, releasing **Live '79**, which restored them to album charts. Ginger Baker replaced King on drums. Next album, **Levitation**, hit Top 20. Further line-up changes followed with departure of Blake (replaced by Keith Hale) and Baker (replaced by Martin Griffin).
In 1981, band pacted with RCA before switch to Flicknife label and solid **Zones** LP. Live work was depleted until 1988 UK tour saw new line-up take to road. Members were: Langton, Brock, Bainbridge, Alan Davis, bass guitar, and Daniel Thompson, drums. During same year, Calvert died following heart attack at his Kent retreat.
As celebration of 20th anniversary of release of first album, Hawkwind rounded up sufficient walking frames to ease them into studios for **Space Bandits**.

Hit Singles:

	US	UK
Silver Machine, 1972	—	3

Albums:
Hawkwind (Liberty/UA), 1970
In Search Of Space (Fame), 1971
Greasy Trucker's Party (Liberty/UA), 1972
Doremi Fasol Latido (Liberty/UA), 1972
Space Ritual Live (Liberty/UA), 1973
Hall Of The Mountain Grill (Liberty/UA), 1974
Warrior On The Edge Of Time (Liberty/UA), 1975

Roadhawks (Liberty/UA), 1976
Astounding Sounds Amazing Music (—/Charisma), 1976
Masters Of The Universe (—/UA), 1977
Quark, Strangeness And Charm (Sire/Charisma), 1977
Hawklords (—/Charisma), 1978
PXR 5 (—/Charisma), 1979
Repeat Performance (—/Charisma), 1980
Hawkwind Live 1979 (—/Bronze), 1980
Levitation (Castle), 1980
Sonic Attack (—/RCA), 1981
Church Of Hawkwind (—/RCA), 1982
Choose Your Masques (—/RCA), 1982
Zones (—/Flicknife), 1983
Bring Me The Head Of Yuri Gagarin (Demi-Monde), 1985
Space Ritual 2 (Magnum Force), 1985
Out And Intakes (Flicknife), 1987
Chronicle Of The Black Sword (Flicknife), 1987
Anthology Volumes 1 and 2 (Samurai), 1986
Anthology Volumes 1, 2 and 3 (Samurai), 1986
The Hawkwind Collection Parts 1 and 2 (Castle), 1986
Live 70/73 (Dojo), 1986
Angels Of Death (RCA), 1987
British Tribal Music (State Of The Art), 1987
The Xenon Codex (—/GWR), 1988
Space Bandits (—/GWR), 1990

Heart
US group formed 1973

Original line-up: Ann Wilson, guitar, key-boards, vocals; Nancy Wilson, vocals, guitar; Michael Derosier, drums; Howard Leese, guitar, keyboards; Steve Fossen, bass; Roger Fisher, guitar.

Career: Wilson sisters grew up on British-influenced rock of 60s. Began playing Seat-tle bars when women's role in rock was strictly limited to vocals. They knocked this concept on the head by playing Led Zep-pelin covers with flair and gusto. Despite growing popularity, band pulled up roots and moved to British Columbia, primarily to avoid draft problems of Roger Fisher. While in Canada, Heart signed with small new Mushroom label. **Dreamboat Annie** became word of mouth hit and Heart found it was picking up national radio play. Debut LP was unusual in that it ranged from easy, quiet ballads to heavy metal without soun-ding unfocused or without direction.
With new, larger audience, band return-ed to US and found that Mushroom's distribution system couldn't handle demand for first LP, so signed to Portrait Records. Mushroom promptly sued for breach of con-tract. Heart counter-sued over rights to recording for second LP, alleging Mushroom was about to release rough, unfinished demo work. While case was being settled

Below: Sonic Attack, Hawkwind. Courtesy RCA Records.

in Seattle's Federal District Court, Portrait released excellent **Little Queen** LP.
Bootleg copies of second Mushroom LP began fetching ridiculous amounts and Mushroom released **Magazine** with its original mix outside US. With wisdom of Solomon, Seattle Federal judge settled suit out of court by suggesting Heart had over-stepped bounds in signing to Portrait but that Heart had the right to mix second Mushroom LP as they deemed artistically suitable; Mushroom finally released this new version of **Magazine** in US during 1978. Whether aesthetic differences between two versions make any sense outside of legal flail is questionable, but principle sets im-portant precedent for other artists.
Next official LP, **Dog And Butterfly**, began with classic live cut, then seemed to fall apart. This time switch between hard rock and ballads didn't work as well and resulting confusion stalled band's career. **Bebe Le Strange** acknowledged break-up of Wilson/Fisher romance with Fisher's departure from band. His guitar work was missed and Heart's studio work seemed to continue downward. **Greatest And Live** compounded confusion by including a few new tracks, re-issuing some old selections, and adding nearly an entire LP's worth of live stage work; LP was cut down to single album a year later and released in the UK as **Heart**.
Taking time to reorganize their thoughts and ideas, Wilson sisters took two-year break before releasing **Private Audition**. This marked a return to spirit of early band as well as making Top 30 in US LP charts. In 1982, both Fossen and Derosier quit, citing, ho hum, 'musical differences'. Replacements were Gunne bassist Mark Andes, and drummer Denny Carmassi. New line-up supported Queen on 1982 British tour, before cutting 1983 **Passion Works**.
Self-titled debut (1985) for Capitol Records (produced by Ron Nevison) even-tually spawned UK breakthrough single **These Dreams**, a majestic ballad with poig-nant lyrics by Bernie Taupin. From 1987 LP **Bad Animals**, Heart enjoyed first US No. 1 single, when **Alone** peaked in July. **Track**, written by composers Tom Kelly and Bill Steinberg, also broke UK Top 5.
For 1990 **Brigade** album, Heart embark-ed on extensive US tour as word that original band members Fisher, Derosier and Fossen had formed new outfit Atlas.

Hit Singles:

	US	UK
Magic Man, 1976	9	—
Barracuda, 1977	11	—
Straight On, 1978	15	—
Tell It Like It Is, 1980	8	—
What About Love, 1985	10	—
Never, 1985	4	—
Alone, 1987	1	3
There's The Girl, 1987	12	—
Who Will You Run To, 1987	7	30
Never/These Dreams (re-issue), 1988	—	8
What About Love, 1988	10	14
Surrender To Me, (with R. Zander), 1989	6	—
All I Wanna Do Is Make Love To You, 1990	2	8
Stranded, 1990	13	60

Albums:
Dreamboat Annie (Mushroom/Arista), 1975
Little Queen (Portrait), 1977
Dog And Butterfly (Portrait), 1979
Bebe Le Strange (Epic), 1980
Greatest And Live (Epic/—), 1980
Private Audition (Epic), 1982
Passion Works (Epic), 1983

Heart (−/Epic), 1985
Bad Animals (Capitol), 1987
With Love From Heart (−/Capitol), 1988
Brigade (Capitol), 1990

Worth Searching Out:
Magazine (Capitol), 1978

Jimi Hendrix

US guitarist, vocalist
Born Johnny Allen Hendrix (name changed to James Marshall Hendrix in 1946), Seattle, Washington, November 27, 1942
Died September 18, 1970

Career: The most legendary guitarist in rock music, Jimi Hendrix spent early years, following military service, as back-up musician for such R&B luminaries as B. B. King, Ike and Tina Turner, Solomon Burke, Jackie Wilson, Tommy Tucker, Sam Cooke, Little Richard, Wilson Pickett, The Isley Brothers and King Curtis.

Settling in New York, Hendrix was heard playing in club by then girlfriend of Rolling Stones' Keith Richards who persuaded former Animals' bass player turned manager, Chas Chandler, to check him out. Chandler decided to forgo own playing career and sold his bass guitars to buy equipment for Hendrix. He took the young black musician to London and embarked on major publicity campaign, bringing The Beatles, Pete Townshend and Eric Clapton to 'in' clubs to see Hendrix's outrageously flashy performances.

A master showman, Hendrix exploited tricks learned from watching T. Bone Walker, Johnny Guitar Watson and other relatively unknown black American musicians, playing the guitar behind his neck or with his teeth, and experimenting with a whole new range of sound effects on his Fender Stratocaster. Polydor Records rushed to sign him and debut single **Hey Joe** stormed UK charts. In 1967 Hendrix debuted in his own country at the Monterey Pop Festival. His guitar-burning act (preserved in film *Monterey Pop*) left the audience stunned.

Switching to associated Track label, Hendrix had further single success before becoming major album artist, reaching zenith of commercial success and artistic creativity in 1968 with classic **Axis Bold As Love** and **Electric Ladyland** LPs. (In the studio, session man Alan Douglas added to Hendrix's basic tracks and was later responsible for **Crash Landing**, **Midnight Lightning** and **9 To The Universe**, released, like the vast majority of Hendrix LPs, after his death.)

After masterful appearance at Woodstock in August 1969, the Jimi Hendrix Experience (British musicians Noel Redding, bass, Mitch Mitchell, drums) broke up amid welter of personal and business problems, as well as drug-linked difficulties with the authorities. Mostly, however, Hendrix felt cornered by the style of music.

Under some pressure from Black Power movement in US, Hendrix decided to form Band Of Gypsys (Billy Cox, bass; Buddy Miles, drums) but, despite phenomenal powers as a concert-draw, band was short-lived; Hendrix walking out on 19,000 fans in middle of second number at Madison Square Garden gig in January 1970. That summer Hendrix played to nearly a quarter of a million people at the Isle Of Wight Festival, his last major concert and one which met with poor response from critics.

Three years of incredibly hard touring, recording, and drink and drug abuse took

their toll and on September 18, 1970, Hendrix was pronounced DOA at a Kensington Hospital, suffocated by his own vomit.

For 20th anniversary of his death in 1990, both Hendrix' sidemen Mitch Mitchell (*The Hendrix Experience*) and Noel Redding (*Are You Experienced?*) had biographies published, two of several volumes issued during period casting a critical eye over the wayward genius.

At times verging on the totally self-indulgent, Hendrix's guitar work nevertheless showed touch of sheer genius, opening up new musical horizons for a generation of rock musicians, while his vocals, despite their limited scope, oozed raw power. With-

out a doubt Hendrix remains one of the most influential and popular artists in rock, as evidenced by the vast catalogue of his work still available.

Guitar: Fender Stratocaster.

Hit Singles:	US	UK
Hey Joe, 1967	−	6
Purple Haze, 1967	−	3
The Wind Cries Mary, 1967	−	6
Burning Of The Midnight Lamp, 1967	−	18
All Along The Watchtower, 1968	20	5
Voodoo Chile, 1970	−	1

Left; The unique and supremely innovative Jimi Hendrix with Noel Redding (left) and Mitch Mitchell (right) − the Jimi Hendrix Experience.

Albums:
Are You Experienced (Polydor), 1967
Axis−Bold As Love (Reprise/Polydor), 1967
Smash Hits (Reprise/Polydor), 1968
Electric Ladyland (Polydor), 1968
Electric Ladyland 2 (−/Polydor), 1968
Band Of Gypsys (Capitol/Polydor), 1970
Monterey (one side only; other side featured Otis Redding) (Reprise), 1970
Cry Of Love (Reprise/Polydor), 1971
Rainbow Bridge (Reprise), 1971
Isle Of Wight (−/Polydor), 1971
Eternal Fire Of (−/Hallmark), 1971
Experience (soundtrack) (Mode/Bulldog), 1971
Friends From The Beginning (with Little Richard) (−/Bulldog), 1971
In The West (Reprise/Polydor), 1972
Jimi Hendrix (−/Polydor), 1973
Loose Ends (−/Polydor), 1973
Jimi Hendrix Volume 1 (−/Pan), 1973
Jimi Hendrix Volume 2 (−/Pan), 1973
Jimi Hendrix Volume 3 (−/Pan), 1973
War Heroes (Reprise/Polydor), 1973
The Wild One (with Curtis Knight) (−/Hallmark) 1973
Crash Landing (Reprise/Polydor), 1975
Rare Hendrix (Explosive/Enterprise), 1975
Jimi Hendrix 2 (−/Polydor), 1975
Midnight Lightning (Reprise/Polydor), 1976
For Real (−/DJM), 1976
The Essential (Reprise/Polydor), 1978
The Essential Volume 2 (Reprise/Polydor), 1978
More Experience (−/Bulldog), 1979
Recording From Jimi (−/Reprise), 1979
20 Pieces Of (−/Bulldog) 1979
10th Annniversary Box (−/Polydor), 1980
9 To The Universe (Warner Bros/Polydor), 1980
Woke Up This Morning And Found Myself Dead (Red Lightnin'), 1980
Hendrix '66 (−/President), 1980
Free Spirit (Accord/Phoenix), 1981
Cosmic Turnaround (−/AFE), 1981
Cosmic Feeling (Accord/−), 1982
The Jimi Hendrix Concerts (Reprise/CBS), 1982
Moods (−/Phoenix) 1982
Roots Of (−/Phoenix), 1982
Voodoo Chile (−/Polydor), 1982

Above: Rainbow Bridge soundtrack, Jimi Hendrix. Courtesy Reprise Records.

20 Golden Pieces Of, Volume 2 (−/Bulldog), 1982
The Singles Album (Polydor), 1983
Kiss The Sky (Polydor), 1984
Jimi Plays Monterey (Polydor), 1986
Live At Winterland (Polydor), 1987
Best Of (EMI), 1987
Cornerstones 1967-70 (Polydor), 1990

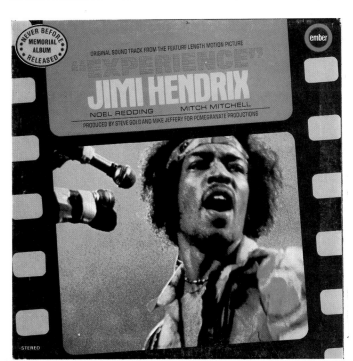

Left: Experience, Jimi Hendrix soundtrack album. Courtesy Ember Records.

Herman's Hermits

UK group formed 1963

Original line-up: Peter Noone, vocals; Keith Hopwood, guitar; Derek Leckenby, guitar; Karl Green, bass; Barry Whitwarm, drums.

Career: With his little-boy looks, wide grin and big shiny teeth, Peter Noone (born November 5, 1947) was prototype for Donny Osmond, David Cassidy and other teenybopper pin-ups to come. Producer Mickie Most saw Noone's appearance as actor in massively popular *Coronation Street* TV soap opera series and decided Noone's was to be the face of 1964.

Group had been formed a year earlier as The Heartbeats; Most changed Noone's name to Herman and effectively projected him as front-man. Indeed, The Hermits didn't even play on most of their records (**Mrs Brown You've Got A Lovely Daughter**, **I'm Into Something Good** and **I'm Henry The VIII I Am** being exceptions). Instead he used such luminaries as Big Jim Sullivan and, later, Led Zeppelin founders Jimmy Page and John Paul Jones (Jones also did all the arranging).

Debut single **I'm Into Something Good** (1964) went to UK No. 1 and made low-key breakthrough in US where they eventually became far more popular than in home market.

Despite 10 entries in UK Top 20 in just three years, Herman's Hermits had unobtrusive image there, and records made more impact than group. In America, however, Herman's return to clean-cut, polite, boy-next-door image of early Beatles' days (while most British acts of era were into brash rebellious R&B mould of Stones and The Who), was a relief to parents, and just what American media were looking for. **Mrs Brown** and **I'm Henry The VIII** both sailed to No. 1 while Herman became TV and magazine personality of first order.

Below: Successful British export Peter Noone, vocalist for hugely successful Herman's Hermits, who enjoyed six-year chart status in the 60s.

By 1967 American bubble had burst and title of US Top 20 entry **There's A Kind Of Hush** proved prophetic. However, UK hits continued before Noone went solo in 1970 (using real name).

He rejoined group briefly in 1973 for Richard Nader's English Invasion Revival tour while Hermits remained in America purveying their lightweight, happy style of innocuous pop. In 1979 Noone formed band The Tremblers (Noone, vocals, guitar, piano, bass; Gregg Inhofer, keyboards, guitar, vocals; Robert Williams, drums; George Williams, drums; George Connor, guitar, vocals; Mark Browne, bass) and in 1980 they recorded **Twice Nightly** LP. In 1983, Noone starred in new hit musical version of *The Pirates of Penzance*, and later presenter for US television show *My Generation*. Noone's recording of **I'm Into Something Good** was featured in Leslie Neilsen/Priscilla Presley movie *The Naked Gun* in 1988.

Hit Singles:	US	UK
I'm Into Something Good, 1964	13	1
Show Me Girl, 1964	—	19
Can't You Hear My Heart Beat, 1965	—	2
Silhouettes, 1965	5	3
Mrs Brown You've Got A Lovely Daughter, 1965	1	—
Wonderful World, 1965	4	7
I'm Henry The VIII I Am, 1965	1	—
Just A Little Bit Better, 1965	7	15
A Must To Avoid, 1965	8	6
Listen People, 1966	3	—
You Won't Be Leaving, 1966	—	20
Leaning On The Lamp Post, 1966	9	—
This Door Swings Both Ways, 1966	12	18
No Milk Today, 1966	35	7
Dandy, 1966	5	—
There's A Kind Of Hush, 1967	4	7
Don't Go Out Into The Rain (You're Going To Melt), 1967	18	—
I Can Take Or Leave Your Loving, 1968	22	11
Sleepy Joe, 1968	—	12
Sunshine Girl, 1968	—	8
Something's Happening, 1968	—	6
My Sentimental Friend, 1969	—	2
Years May Come, Years May Go, 1970	—	7
Lady Barbara, 1970	—	13

Peter Noone solo:

	US	UK
Oh You Pretty Thing, 1971		12

Albums:
Greatest Hits (Abcko/—), 1973
20 Greatest Hits (—/K-Tel), 1977

The Hollies

UK group formed 1962

Original line-up: Allan Clarke, vocals; Tony Hicks, vocals, guitar; Graham Nash, vocals, guitar; Eric Haydock, bass; Don Rathbone, drums.

Career: Formed from members of two other Manchester groups, Deltas and Dolphins (Rathbone was almost immediately replaced by Bobby Elliot). Like many British beat groups they took early material from US R&B catalogue. First two singles were covers of Coasters' hits, second of which, **Searchin'**, started run of UK Top 20 hits.

Lacking positive image, band's appeal was based on Clarke's strong lead vocals, distinc-

tive harmonies and excellent choice of single material. Most early material came from outside band, from top writers like Graham Gouldman, but by 1966 they were writing own songs with considerable success. **Bus Stop** reached American Top 5, and established group as regular US hitmakers.

In 1966 Haydock left to be replaced by former Dolphins' bass player Bernie Calvert. As 'psychedelic' era dawned, problems over musical direction arose. While band were still massive singles sellers, they were unable to break LP market despite making several interesting albums at this time.

Disillusioned by band's failure to compete with newer, critically rated album bands, Graham Nash left in 1968 to join forces with David Crosby and Stephen Stills to form Crosby, Still And Nash. Former Swinging Blue Jeans Terry Sylvester replaced Nash.

By 1971, band had reached something of a plateau; single releases were only moderately successful. Clarke left to pursue solo career. Replacement was Swedish singer Michael Rickfors. In 1972, however, single recorded with Clarke as lead singer, **Long Cool Woman In A Black Dress**, made No. 1 spot in America (although strangely only 32 in UK). Rickfors was ousted and Clarke rejoined band, which signed new contract with Polydor. Last big hit was **The Air That I Breathe**.

Band continued to record throughout 70s however, and found lucrative niche in cabaret and 'revival' circuit. 1981 re-mix **Holliedaze**, a medley of classic hits, prefaced Nash/Clarke reconciliation and **What Goes Around** LP also featuring Hicks and Elliot. The temporary reunion failed to ignite public, and remaining trio signed with Columbia Records, for which **Too Many Hearts** single was debut (1985).

Seemingly destined for life on low-level music circuit, timely re-release of **He Ain't Heavy** earned Hollies No. 1 spot on UK charts in 1988, following inclusion in novel beer advertisement.

The Hollies' hard-edged pop style and choice of quality material allowed career longevity without resorting to parody. They have, ironically, outlasted most of the more pretentious groups they strove to emulate in late 60s.

Hit Singles:	US	UK
Searchin', 1963	—	12
Stay, 1963	—	8
Just One Look, 1964	—	2
Here I Go Again, 1964	—	4
We're Through, 1964	—	7
Yes I Will, 1965	—	9
I'm Alive, 1965	—	1

Above: The resurrected John Lee Hooker, veteran bluesman who mixes with rock's superstars.

	US	UK
Look Through Any Window, 1965	32	4
If I Needed Someone, 1965	—	20
I Can't Let Go, 1966	42	2
Bus Stop, 1966	5	5
Stop Stop Stop, 1966	7	2
On A Carousel, 1967	11	4
Carrie-Anne, 1967	9	3
King Midas In Reverse, 1967	51	18
Jennifer Eccles, 1968	40	7
Listen To Me, 1968	—	11
Sorry Suzanne, 1969	56	3
He Ain't Heavy He's My Brother, 1969	7	3
I Can't Tell The Bottom From The Top, 1970	—	7
Gasoline Alley Bred, 1970	—	14
The Air That I Breathe, 1974	6	2
He Ain't Heavy, He's My Brother (re-issue), 1988	—	1

Albums:
Hollies' Greatest (Capitol/Parlophone), 1968
Sing Dylan (Epic/Parlophone), 1969
Stop Stop Stop (Imperial/Starline), 1971
Greatest Hits (Epic/Polydor), 1974
I Can't Let Go (—/MFP), 1974
Another Night (Epic/Polydor), 1975
Best Of EPs (—/Nut), 1975
Russian Roulette (—/Polydor), 1976
Live Hits (—/Polydor), 1977
A Crazy Steal (—/Polydor), 1978
Sing Buddy Holly (—/Polydor), 1980
Long Cool Woman In A Black Dress (—/MFP), 1979
Five Three One-Double Seven O Four (—/Polydor), 1979
20 Golden Greats (EMI), 1979
All The Hits And More — The Definitive Collection (EMI), 1988

Buddy Holly

US vocalist, guitarist, composer
Born Charles Hardin Holley, Lubbock, Texas, September 7, 1936
Died February 3, 1959

Career: During 1954-55 appeared on hometown radio station KDA, with partner Bob Montgomery. Played on package shows visiting towns who used local talent as warm-up acts to major artists. Spotted by Nashville talent scout on show headlined by Bill Haley and signed to Decca.

Dissatisfaction with company and producers encouraged Holly to record independently at Norman Petty's Clovis, New Mexico, studio. Master of **That'll Be The Day** made there subsequently sold to New York subsidiaries of Decca where group recordings as The Crickets (Joe B. Mauldin, bass; Niki Sullivan, guitar, replaced by Tommy Allsop in 1959; Jerry Allison, drums) were released on Brunswick; Holly's solo efforts appeared on Coral. Resulting hits gave Holly dual career strengthened by own writing talents and those of Crickets, notably Allison.

Several US package tours and short visit to Australia preceded tour of UK in March 1958. Many UK musicians were impressed with his guitar style and the then unknown Fender Stratocaster guitar which, together with horn-rimmed glasses, became Holly's trademark.

Management problems and move to New York following marriage to Maria Elena Santiago in 1958 forced split with Crickets (who went on to record many more LPs without Holly). Recorded trendsetting session with Dick Jacobs Orchestra in New York and planned to record with Ray Charles Band.

Royalty disputes and lack of funds forced Holly into uncomfortable ballroom tour through frozen Mid-West states during early 1959. Halfway through tour, Holly chartered small plane with Ritchie Valens and Big Bopper to escape discomfort of tour buses. All three were killed when plane crashed into snow-covered field.

Single coupling **It Doesn't Matter Anymore** and **Raining In My Heart** from orchestral session subsequently became biggest solo hit. Although Holly then disappeared from US chart, his popularity in England ensured continuation of hits for several years.

The Holly legend was surprisingly well-served by movie industry, when Gary Busey's uncanny interpretation of artist in *The Buddy Holly Story* (1978) was outstanding critical success. The actor later purchased Holly's horn-rimmed specs and acoustic guitar at a New York auction of Holly memorabilia.

In London's West End, the musical *Buddy* has had them jiving in the aisles, and the show transferred to the States for tour in 1990. The Crickets have been occasional tourists to UK, but infrequent visitors to recording studio, although 1988 deal with CBS had promised new material.

Hit Singles:

	US	UK
That'll Be The Day* 1957	1	1
Peggy Sue, 1957	3	6
Listen To Me, 1958	–	16
Oh Boy*, 1958	10	3
Maybe Baby*, 1958	17	4
Rave On, 1958	37	5
Think It Over*, 1958	27	11
Early In The Morning, 1958	32	17
It Doesn't Matter Anymore, 1959	13	1
Peggy Sue Got Married, 1959	–	13
Baby I Don't Care, 1961	–	12
Reminiscing, 1962	–	17
Brown Eyed Handsome Man, 1963	–	3
Bo Diddley, 1963	–	4
Wishing, 1963	–	10
*With Crickets		

Crickets:

Don't Ever Change, 1962	–	5
My Little Girl, 1963	–	17

Albums:
Buddy Holly (MCA), 1958
The Chirping Crickets (MCA), 1958
Legend (MCA), 1974
Greatest Hits (MCA), 1974
The Nashville Sessions (MCA), 1975
20 Golden Greats (MCA), 1978
The Complete Buddy Holly (6 LP box set) (MCA), 1979
Love Songs (MCA), 1981
For The First Time Anywhere (MCA), 1983
Best Of (Grand Prix), 1986
Buddy Holly—Historical Recordings Undubbed And Unreleased Versions (Nor-Va-Jak), 1987

John Lee Hooker

US vocalist, guitarist, composer
Born Clarkesdale, Mississippi, August 22, 1917

Career: Proving the old adage 'it's never too late to become a pop star', Hooker's extraordinary metamorphosis in the 90s might be the rock story of the decade.

The blues pioneer moved to Detroit in 1943, cutting the million-selling single **Boogie Chillun** for Modern in 1948. Unusually, Hooker maintained a solid output for a variety of labels (including Stateside, Chess, ABC and Vee-Jay) for two decades before gaining attention during British 'beat boom' of early 60s. His classic tracks **Dimples** and **Boom Boom** launched a thousand UK R&B bands, and the artist enjoyed a resurgence of popularity which seemed unlikely to be repeated.

With career seemingly winding down, Hooker still recorded throughout the 70s and 80s, with sets for Atlantic and Tomato Records; re-issues also appeared in stores. During this period, Hooker also popped up in a cameo role in *Blues Brothers* movie, which was followed by soundtrack contribution to Spielberg's *The Colour Purple*.

His work with Bonnie Raitt, Carlos Santana and Robert Cray, among others, propelled the septuagenarian back into prominence in 1989 with **The Healer** set, from which **I'm In The Mood** duet with Raitt won a Grammy award. Hooker then found himself the unlikely star of a couple of international television advertisements, and a favourite with MTV producers. Hooker was recipient of 'John Lee Hooker Night' at 1990 Benson & Hedges Blues Festival, held at Madison Square Gardens, and inducted into Rock 'n' Roll Hall Of Fame In January 1991.

Below: Hothouse Flowers, who hit charts with Don't Go single, and who invaded millions of homes in UK when featured in Lovejoy TV series.

Albums:
House Of The Blues (rec. 1951-54) (Chess/ Charly), 1960
Tupelo Blues (Riverside), 1962
Folklore Of (Stateside), 1962
Preachin' The Blues (Stateside), 1964
Big Soul Of (Veejay/Joy), 1964
Boogie Chillun (rec. 1962) (Fantasy/Official), 1971
Best Of (Veejay/Joy), 1974
Black Snake (Fantasy); 40th Anniversary Album 1948-1961 (with S. Cotton, Andrew Dunham, E. Burns) (Compact Classics), 1978
Mad Man Blues, (Vogue)
Goin' Down Highway 51 (Speciality)
Live At Sugarhill Volumes 1 and 2 (–/Ace)
Sad And Lonesome (Muse)
That's Where It's At (Stax)
Travelin' (Veejay)
Detroit Blues With Eddie Burns 1950-51 (Collectables)
Live At The Fox Venice Theatre (Rhino)
The Detroit Lion (Denon)
This Is Hip (Charly), 1980
Sittin' Here Thinkin' (rec. late 1950s) (Muse), 1980
Tantalizing With The Blues (MCA), 1982
Solid Sender (Charly), 1984
Black Rhythm 'n' Blues (Festival), 1984
Infinite Boogie (rec. 1970) (Rhino), 1987
The Real Folks Blues (rec. 1966) (Chess), 1988
Plays And Sings The Blues (rec. Detroit 1951-52) (Chess), 1989
The Healer (with R. Cray, C. Santana, B. Raitt and Los Lobos) (Capitol/Silverstone), 1989
Never Get Out Of These Blues Alive (MCA/See For Miles), 1990
Mr Lucky (Silverstone), 1991

Hothouse Flowers

Irish group formed 1985

Original line-up: Liam O'Maonlai, vocals, piano; Fiachna O'Broainain, guitar; Maria Doyle, vocals.

Career: Former street buskers, who went legit when U2 label Mother Records signed group to one single (**Love Don't Work This Way**) deal.

O'Maonlai and O'Broainain (both students in Dublin) found expectance of Flowers (named after Wynton Marsalis album) high when *Rolling Stone* magazine suggested they were the best unsigned outfit in Europe. With U2 dominating the album and single charts, interest in fellow-Irish groups was

frenzied. London Records won the bidding war, and album **People** was released in May 1988, with revised line-up including Leo Barnes, Peter O'Toole and Jerry Fehily, with Doyle departing. **Don't Go** track was selected as promotional single.

The heavy influence of blues, rock and traditional Irish music earned astonishing plaudits, and when second album **Home** appeared, group had established critical and personal reputation.

Hit Singles:

	US	UK
Don't Go, 1988	–	11

Albums:
People (London), 1988
Home (London), 1990

The Housemartins

UK group formed 1984

Original line-up: Paul (P.D.) Heaton, vocals; Stan Cullimore, guitar, vocals; Norman Cook, bass, vocals; Hugh Whittaker, drums, vocals.

Career: Formed in Hull, first as duo of Heaton And Cullimore, then expanding by stealing Whittaker and bassist Ted Key from local rivals The Gargoyles. Won Viking Radio talent contest, leading to recording sessions for Radio One and support slot on tour with Billy Bragg who then recommended band to his label, Go! Discs.

Breezy style of English pop owing much to Buzzcocks, Squeeze and The Smiths, they emerged as hybrid of 60s beat/skiffle influences with genuine love for gospel and soul. Early shows featured rousing version of Hollies' **He Ain't Heavy, He's My Brother**. Released debut single **Flag Day** before Key quit, replaced by Cook; then released singles **Sheep** and **Happy Hour**. Debut album, **London 0 Hull 4** blended simple musical enthusiasm with clever lyrical subtleties, tackling social and political themes with surprising vehemence. Reinforced Christian stance with cover of Isleys' **Caravan Of Love**, topping UK chart at Christmas 1986.

Continued to maintain down-to-earth image and devoted concert following before releasing second album, **The People Who Grinned Themselves To Death**.

In January 1988, band shocked the rock world by announcing their dissolution when they seemed just about to conquer America. Formal statement maintained they had achieved all they set out to do and there was nothing else left! Whittaker then rejoined Key in reformed Gargoyles; Heaton launched new band The Beautiful South with drummer Dave Hemmingway (a Housemartin for **Grinned** album), vocalists David Rotheray and Brian Corrigan, bassist Sean Welch and percussionist Dave Stead. Debut album **Welcome To The Beautiful South** made No. 2 on UK LP listings in 1989. Cook enjoyed success as DJ, joining Billy Bragg as Beats International in 1989.

Hit Singles:

	US	UK
Caravan Of Love, 1986	–	1
Happy Hour, 1986	–	3
Think For A Minute, 1986	–	18
Five Get Over Excited, 1987	–	11
Me And The Farmer, 1987	–	15
Build, 1987	–	15

Albums:
London 0 Hull 4 (Go! Discs/Elektra), 1986
The People Who Grinned Themselves To Death (Go! Discs), 1987

Left: The Housemartins. Paul Heaton (right) later formed The Beautiful South.

Above: Dare, The Human League. Courtesy Virgin Records.

Whitney Houston
US vocalist
Born New Jersey, 1963

Career: If anyone was born for stardom, it was Whitney Houston. Blessed with startling combination of good looks, bubbly personality and major-league vocal talent, she spent only a few years in the wings before breaking through as international megastar in 1986-87. Daughter of near-legendary session singer Cissy Houston who, as member of Sweet Inspirations, sang back-up on record and on stage for Elvis Presley and Aretha Franklin. Whitney started out as a top-ranking fashion model, earning description 'the woman every girl would like to be and every man would like to go out with'.

Showing talent as well as beauty, Whitney served musical apprenticeship singing backings on albums by Lou Rawls, Chaka Khan, Neville Brothers and others before being asked to duet with Teddy Pendergrass on US hit **Hold Me**. A further duet hit with Jermaine Jackson on **Take Good Care Of My Heart** led to solo contract with Arista and chart-topping single **Saving All My Love For You**.

Below: Whitney, from 1987. Courtesy Arista Records.

However, 1987 was the year of Whitney Houston, when second album **Whitney** went multi-platinum, with over 8 million copies sold in US alone. Surefire combination of uptown soul and emotive Las Vegas-style ballads **Whitney** catapulted singer into international bigtime. Single **I Wanna Dance With Somebody** was *the* single of summer 1987, with bouncy video showing singer's talents off to irresistible effect.

Despite lukewarm verdict from purist critics, Whitney may well transcend superstar status; a Diana Ross for the Reagan/Bush generation. Her fluid vocal styling has earned host of music-biz treasures, including Grammys and 1990 Hitmaker Award; artist's rendition of **Star Spangled Banner** prior to US football's Super Bowl XXV even sold middle America on her abilities.

Hit Singles:	US	UK
Saving All My Love For You, 1985	1	1
How Will I Know, 1986	1	5
Greatest Love of All, 1986	2	8
I Wanna Dance With Somebody, 1987	1	1
Didn't We Almost Have It All, 1987	1	14
So Emotional, 1987	1	1
Where Do Broken Hearts Go, 1988	1	14
Love Will Save The Day, 1988	9	10
One Moment In Time, 1988	5	1
I'm Your Baby Tonight, 1990	1	5
All The Man That I Need, 1990	1	13
Miracle, 1991	9	—
My Name Is Not Susan, 1991	20	—

Albums:
Whitney Houston (Arista), 1985
Whitney (Arista), 1987
I'm Your Baby Tonight (Arista), 1990

Human League
UK group formed 1977

Original line-up: Philip Oakey, vocals; Ian Craig Marsh, synthesizers; Martyn Ware, synthesizers; Adrian Wright, visual director, synthesizers.

Career: Computer operators Marsh and Ware, and hospital porter Oakey, made up original nucleus of band, formed in Sheffield to explore possibilities of electronic music. Wright joined slightly later.

Almost immediately band began to gain reputation for innovation; first single **Electronically Yours** was released in June 1978 on independent Fast label. Following exposure on Siouxsie And Banshees tour, band was signed to Virgin in April 1979. First album **Reproduction** released in late 1979.

1980 saw beginnings of chart success with low placings for **Holiday '80** and **Empire State Human**, but in autumn of that year band broke up; Ware and Marsh left to establish Heaven 17 and British Electric Foundation. Oakey and Wright took new direction, recruiting old friend (actually bass player) Ian Burden to play synthesizers, and adding two girl dancers, Joanne Catherall and Susanne Sulley.

The girls quickly became vocalists; new sound was featured on first Top 50 single **Boys And Girls** at beginning of 1981. That year saw band go from strength to strength, with addition of guitarist Jo Callis (ex-Rezillos). Huge breakthrough came with single **Don't You Want Me** and album **Dare**. Both topped UK charts, and at beginning of 1982 repeated feat in territories all around world, most notably in US.

Human League had established themselves as stylish electronic pop outfit which combined irresistibly catchy tunes with lyrics of above-average intelligence. In recent years Oakey has undertaken solo projects (film music, solo hit **Electric Dreams**) while maintaining band's position in public eye, although prolonged absence after **Crash** (1986) tested fans patience.

In 1990, revamped League, with Oakey, Catherall, Sulley, Russ Dennett, guitar, and Neil Sutton, keyboards, appeared with **Romantic?** set, a short-lived success in UK, although **Heart Like A Wheel** single from LP made noises on US chart.

Hit Singles:	US	UK
The Sound Of The Crowd, 1981	—	12
Love Action (I Believe In Love), 1981	—	3
Open Your Heart, 1981	—	6
Don't You Want Me, 1981	1	1

Left: Whitney Houston, whose musical upbringing almost guaranteed success.

	US	UK
Being Boiled, 1982	—	6
Mirror Man, 1982	—	2
Fascination, 1983	8	2
The Lebanon, 1984	—	11
Life On Your Own, 1984	—	16
Louise, 1984	—	13
Human, 1986	2	8

Phil Oakey and Georgio Moroder:
Together In Electric Dreams, 1984 — 3

Albums:
Reproduction (–/Virgin), 1979
Travelogue (–/Virgin), 1980
Dare (A&M/Virgin), 1981
Crash (Virgin), 1986
Greatest Hits (A&M/Virgin), 1988
Romantic? (A&M/Virgin), 1990

Phil Oakey and Georgio Moroder:
Hysteria (Virgin), 1987

Humble Pie
UK group formed 1969

Original line-up: Peter Frampton, guitar, vocals; Steve Marriott, guitar, vocals; Greg Ridley, bass, vocals; Jerry Shirley, drums.

Career: Began in blaze of publicity as late 60s supergroup with Frampton 'the face of 68', from The Herd, and Marriott from the fashionable Small Faces. Greg Ridley (ex-Spooky Tooth) provided underground musical credibility to offset hype.

Arduous rehearsals at Marriott's house preceded release of first album, **As Safe As Yesterday**, on Small Faces' former label, Immediate. In spite of early Top 5 hit, **Natural Born Bugie**, Humble Pie were plagued by 'supergroup' publicity and LPs failed to fulfil critics' expectations. Much hoped-for early US success did not materialize and, following liquidation of Immediate, group almost folded, but resurfaced on A&M.

Through extensive gigging, group gradually enlarged following in States, and record sales increased. Marriott slowly achieved greater control of unit, moving away from Frampton's somewhat lightweight material towards heavy-metal sound. Policy proved sound, with **Performance — Rockin' At The Fillmore** selling in vast quantities. Inevitably, Frampton quit to pursue solo career, replaced by more compatible Dave 'Clem' Clempson from Colosseum.

Early 70s album **Smokin'** and live double **Eat It** revealed increasing move towards heavy rock. Group briefly experimented with soul during 1973, employing vocal trio The Blackbirds for live revue.

With no new musical direction forthcoming, group gradually stagnated. Clempson quit to form Strange Brew, tolling death knell for Humble Pie, who finally broke up in July 1975. Marriott went on to form Steve Marriott All Stars, before involving himself in Small Faces reunion in 1978. Marriott then got involved in Humble Pie reunion with Bob Tench (guitar, vocals), Anthony Jones (bass, vocals) and Jerry Shirley (drums).

Further attempts at re-formation foundered, and Marriott retreated from mainstream, surfacing occasionally for pub gigs with Packet Of Three before tragic death in April 1991, when family home in Essex burned down.

Right: The godfather of punk, Iggy Pop, is one of life's survivors.

Hit Singles:	US	UK
Natural Born Bugie, 1969	—	4

Albums:
As Safe As Yesterday (Immediate), 1969
Humble Pie (A&M), 1970
Rock On (A&M), 1971
Performance—Rockin' At The Fillmore (A&M), 1971
Smokin' (A&M), 1972
Eat It (live double) (A&M), 1973
Thunderbox (A&M), 1974
Lost And Found (A&M/—), 1976
Back Home Again (—/Immediate), 1976
On To Victory (A&M), 1980

Ice-T
US rap artist
Born Tracy Marrow, Los Angeles, California

Career: Articulate rapper whose career fork into movies was instantly successful.

Street-wise former gang member in famous 'killing fields' of south-central Los Angeles, Ice-T (named after legendary black thriller writer Iceberg Slim) escaped destitution with slick political poems.

Pacted to Sire Records in 1987, debut album **Rhyme Pays** covered full rap resume from drugs to sex. Furthermore, his public rap protestations about gangland killings earned respect from wary music-biz executives, still uncomfortable with his new form of black expression.

After move to Warner brothers in 1988, the Iceman delivered powerful trio of LPs, culminating (to date) in the autumn 1991 release **Original Gangsta**. Fears that his delivery was being 'toned-down' were not evident on October 1991 single release **New Jack Hustler**; vocal tour-de-force revived memories of Ice-T's distinguished film debut in the acclaimed *New Jack City*, in which he featured as, ironically, a cop based in the Bronx. Ice-T signed to star in *The Looters* with fellow rapper Ice Cube.

Albums:
Rhyme Pays (Sire), 1987
Power (Sire/Warner Bros), 1988
The Iceberg/Freedom Of Speech (Sire/Warner Bros), 1989
O.G. Original Gangsta (Sire/Warner Bros), 1991

Billy Idol
UK vocalist, guitarist, composer
Born Edgware, London, November 30, 1955

Career: Young, angry, aggressive and strikingly good-looking, Billy Idol was a major figure on UK punk rock scene during heady days of 1977. One of the notorious 'Bromley Contingent' of punks, from which emerged The Clash, Sex Pistols, Siouxsie, and others, Idol joined Generation X as lead singer in time for their historic gig on opening night of seminal club The Roxy in London's Covent Garden.

Above: Whiplash Smile, Billy Idol. Courtesy Chrysalis Records.

Generation X was first punk band to appear on *Top Of The Pops* and logged several hits, with punk rock wane, before Idol left group in 1981. He rode into New York on wave of Gen. X's final hit **Dancing With Myself** which was featured on his debut solo EP **Don't Stop**.

Working with producer Keith Forsey and guitarist Steve Stevens, the expatriate Idol completed album **Billy Idol** which met with mixed response, but single **Hot In The City** hit US Top 50 leading to album recovering from slow start to spend more than 80 weeks on chart. This success was emulated by the re-released **Don't Stop** single which was in *Billboard* listings in America for over 50 weeks.

The Idol/Stevens collaboration continued with **Rebel Yell** for which they co-wrote eight of the nine singles. Album went on to sell a couple of million copies, in process establishing Idol as bona fide teen icon.

1986 album **Whiplash Smile** spawned **To Be A Lover** and **Don't Need A Gun** hit singles, although revival of Tommy James And Shondells' classic **Mony Mony** was first US No. 1.

Following starring role in charitable performance of *Tommy* musical in Los Angeles in August 1989, Idol's career was put on hold following motorbike accident. Resurfaced in June 1990 with aptly titled **Charmed Life** album; tour of same name saw singer needed support of walking stick, and then dates in northern Europe were cancelled due to eye trouble.

However, with those lips in good working order, Idol's threat to pursue movie career was paying dividends, with several offers of Arnie Schwarzenegger-type roles for the early 1990s.

Hit Singles:	US	UK
White Wedding, 1983*	36	6
Eyes Without A Face, 1984	4	18
Rebel Yell, 1985	—	6
To Be A Lover, 1986	5	22
Sweet Sixteen, 1987	—	17
Hot In The City, 1987	48	13
Mony, Mony, 1987	1	7
Cradle Of Love, 1990	2	34
*1985 in UK		

Albums:
Billy Idol (Chrysalis), 1982
Rebel Yell (Chrysalis), 1984
Vital Idol (Chrysalis), 1985
Whiplash Smile (Chrysalis), 1986
Interview By Kris Needs (Lip Service), 1986
Idol Songs—11 Of The Best (Chrysalis), 1988
Charmed Life (Chrysalis), 1990

Iggy Pop
US vocalist, composer
Born James Jewel Osterberg, Ann Arbor, Michigan, April 21, 1947

Career: Iggy Pop is a rock icon of sorts; can justifiably be called 'grandfather' of punk. Fans and critics alike are polarized by Pop; one either loves him or hates him. His personality can only be truly appreciated on stage, where he routinely rants, screams, falls down, knocks into the musicians and invites — or commands — the audience to perform unnatural acts. Has been known to flail about so desperately that he ends show dripping with blood. Audiences often respond by hurling not just abuse, but beer bottles and anything else that is at-hand.

Osterberg named himself Iggy in early days in Detroit, when he performed with band called the Prime Movers. When he joined the infamous pre-punk band The Stooges (Ron Asheton, guitar; Dave Alexander, bass; Scott Asheton, drums; Steve McKay, sax) became Iggy Stooge. Iggy And The Stooges were a band (and a philosophy) whose time had not yet come. Had moderate cult success, but eventually fizzled out, leaving the albums **The Stooges** (1968), **Funhouse** (1969), and **Raw Power** (1973).

Iggy was rediscovered as an 'artist' by David Bowie in 1977. He changed his name symbolically to Iggy Pop, and toured with new mentor. This led to contract with RCA, for whom he recorded three albums in 1978. **The Idiot** and **Lust For Life** met with critical approval, but limited sales; switched to Arista in 1979, cutting two albums.

A further label-hopping ensued, while singer's reputation was enhanced by Bowie's 1983 hit cover version of Pop song **China Girl**. In 1986, after apparently winning protracted battle against toxic abuse,

Pop emerged with new label (A&M) and successful album **Blah Blah Blah**. Album spawned UK single **Real Wild Child**, and Pop's career looked set to finally enter mainstream.

However, singer's general unpredictability of career and history of drug problems mean that he is unlikely to become elder statesman of rock.

Albums:
The Idiot (RCA), 1978
TV Eye (RCA), 1978
Lust For Life (RCA), 1978
New Values (Arista), 1979
Soldier (Arista), 1979
No Fun (Elektra), 1980
Party (Arista), 1981
Zombie Birdhouse (Animal), 1982
Choice Cuts (RCA), 1984
Blah Blah Blah (A&M), 1986
Instinct (A&M), 1988
Brick By Brick (Virgin), 1990

With Stooges:
The Stooges (Elektra), 1968
Funhouse (Elektra), 1969
Raw Power (Columbia/CBS), 1973
Metallic KO (Sky Dog/—), 1976

Worth Searching Out:
Killer City (with James Williamson) (Radar), 1977

INXS
Australian group formed 1979

Original line-up: Michael Hutchence, vocals; Andrew Farriss, keyboards, guitar; John Farriss, drums; Tim Farriss, lead guitar; Kirk Pengilly, guitar; Garry Beer, bass.

Career: Formed in Sydney 1977 by Andrew, John and Tim under name of The Farriss Brothers, expanding to six-piece immediately with line-up unchanged to this day.

Renamed group INXS in 1979; one year later they released debut album **INXS** on Deluxe Records and scored Australian hit single **Just Keep Walking**.

Second LP, **Underneath The Colours**, released via RCA, yielded two more Australian hits **Stay Young** and **Loved One**. INXS secured worldwide deal with WEA and released third album **Shabooh, Shoobah**, then toured US with Kinks and Adam Ant. Debut UK single **Don't Change** was accepted favourably.

Having built up loyal following for their brand of muscular yet melodic rock (comparisons include Simple Minds, Bowie and Psychedelic Furs), they turned to Nile Rodgers to produce **Original Sin** single, hoping for US hit.

Eventually **Listen Like Thieves** LP broke band in America. Released in UK 1986 and promoted by UK tour, LP led to prestigious sell-out concert at London's Royal Albert Hall and two appearances supporting Queen at Wembley Arena. **Kick** album and **Need You Tonight** single firmly established band as rising stars.

Solo projects temporarily halted INXS bandwagon in 1988-89, with Hutchence featuring in cult-director Roger Corman's *Frankenstein Unbound*, and forming Ma Q band. Sextet returned to studio in 1990 for **X** album, from which **Suicide Blonde** was chart single on both sides of Atlantic (and in Australia). Awarded Best International Group at 1991 BRIT presentations, with Hutchence additionally taking International Artist honour. Same year saw **Live Baby**

Live album, a 16-track collection from live dates in 1990-91, plus one studio cut.

With Antipodean rock an infrequent visitor to UK/US charts, INXS's achievements are remarkable, and should charismatic Hutchence stick around, band should have bright future.

Hit Singles:	US	UK
What You Need, 1986	5	—
Need You Tonight, 1987	1	—
New Sensation, 1987	—	25
Never Tear Us Apart, 1988	7	24
Need You Tonight (re-issue), 1988	—	2
Mystify, 1989	—	14
Suicide Blonde, 1990	9	11
Disappear, 1990	8	21

Albums:
Underneath The Colours (Atco/Vertigo), 1984
The Swing (Mercury/Atco), 1984
Shabooh Shoobah (WEA), 1982
Kick (Mercury), 1987
X (Atlantic/Mercury), 1990
Live Baby Live (Mercury), 1991

Iron Maiden
UK group formed 1977

Original line-up: Steve Harris, bass, vocals; Paul Di'anno, vocals; Dave Murray, guitar; Doug Sampson, drums.

Career: Steve Harris formed Iron Maiden amid new wave/punk breeding ground of London's East End. Harris went for deliberate high-energy, power-driven sound, while taking name from medieval torture cage. Iron Maiden went through numerous personnel changes; settled down to line-up above by mid-1979.

Harris refused lucrative offer for gigs and record contract that required him to remould Maiden into fashionable new wave band. Instead, band released **Soundhouse Tapes** EP on own label which sold quite well via mail order. Sampson left to be replaced by Clive Burr, drums, and Dennis Stratton on guitar, joined, adding even stronger drive to band.

EMI signed group in December 1979 amid growing signs that new wave wasn't as all-pervasive as it had first seemed. **Running Free** made UK Top 30 which led to Maiden's historic live appearance on BBC TV's *Top Of The Pops* — the first live gig since The Who in 1973. March 1980 found Maiden on road supporting Judas Priest. Their impact was soon seen: debut album entered UK charts at No. 4. Album success led to headlining UK tour and European tour opening for Kiss. Stratton left at this point and Dave Murray brought in old friend Adrian Smith, to keep twin guitar sound.

Killers LP, released in January 1981, broke band internationally; extensive world tour took most of year. Band now seemed ready for superstardom when departure of vocalist Di'anno was announced. What could have been devastating blow turned into even stronger line-up as Bruce Dickinson (ex-Samson) took over vocals. March 1982 saw release of excellent **Number Of The Beast** and another massive world tour.

Burr was replaced on drums by Nicko McBrain (ex-Pat Travers, Trust) for **Piece Of Mind** in 1983. A year later, group embarked on mammoth World Slavery tour — 200 performances spread over 322 days in 26 countries. This led to big-selling live album, live single **Running Free**, and hit

video which captured their brand of sonic assault with added merit of interesting lyrics and, oftimes, strong melody.

The band progressed further with the **Somewhere In Time** album released in 1986 when they played concerts in Yugoslavia as part of their world tour. The album was recorded in the Bahamas, Amsterdam and New York, resulting in different 'feel' to the various tracks. In April 1988 they came up with a concept album **Seventh Son Of A Seventh Son** which ignored the trend towards thrash and resembled more 70s progressive rock. The songs were linked and told the story of a boy endowed with occult powers. The playing was excellent; Murray and Smith outstanding, and the album yielded a UK Top 10 hit.

After a 15-month hiatus, which saw Smith quit to form ASAP (replaced by Dutch guitarist Jan Gers) and Dickinson issue solo **Tattooed Millionaire** set, Maiden resurfaced with **No Prayer For The Dying** album (1990), from which **Bring Your Daughter To The Slaughter** single made UK No. 1. In January 1991, band embarked on No Prayer On The Road world tour, which commenced in USA.

While Iron Maiden offer usual ear-booming audio attack, their creative juices flow a little more than most HM crews, as testified by horde of gold and platinum albums.

Hit Singles:	US	UK
Run To The Hills, 1982	—	7
The Number Of The Beast, 1982	—	18
The Flight Of Icarus, 1983	—	11
The Trooper, 1983	—	12
2 Minutes To Midnight, 1984	—	11
Aces High, 1984	—	20
Running Free, 1985	—	19
Wasted Years, 1986	—	18
Stranger In A Strange Land, 1986	—	22
Can I Play With Madness, 1988	—	3
The Evil That Men Do, 1988	—	5
The Clairvoyant, 1988	—	6
Infinite Dreams, 1989	—	6
Holy Smoke, 1990	—	3
Bring Your Daughter To The Slaughter, 1991	—	2

Dickinson Solo:
	US	UK
Tattooed Millionaire, 1990	—	18

Albums:
Iron Maiden (Harvest/EMI), 1980
Killers (Harvest/EMI), 1981
The Number Of The Beast (Capitol/EMI), 1982
Piece Of Mind (Capitol/EMI), 1983
Powerslave (EMI), 1984

Above: Iron Maiden, mega HM stars ready to rock into the 90s.

Live After Death (EMI), 1985
Somewhere In Time (EMI), 1986
Seventh Son Of A Seventh Son (Capitol/EMI), 1988
No Prayer For The Dying (Epic/EMI), 1990
Maiden Japan (Capitol/—), 1991

Chris Isaak
US vocalist, guitarist, composer
Born Stockton, California, June 26, 1956

Career: Formed rockabilly quartet Silvertone (Rowland Salley, bass, Kenny Johnson, drums, and James Wilsey, guitar) in 1984, and group signed Warner Bros record deal a year later. Debut album **Silvertone** was warmly received by critics.

Follow-up **Chris Isaak** (1987) notable for inclusion of **Blue Hotel** (a major hit four years later) while third LP, **Heart Shaped World**, prompted film director David Lynch, an Isaak fan (he had used the artist's material for *Blue Velvet*), to request an instrumental version of **Wicked Game** cut. **Game** featured prominently in Lynch's controversial *Wild At Heart*, and Isaak's original vocal version was subsequently released, making UK Top 10 in 1989.

Parallel movie career also gathered strength, with roles in *Married To The Mob* and *The Silence Of The Lambs*, and Isaak also provided incidental music for TV shows and feature films.

With re-issued **Blue Hotel** finally cracking UK charts, Isaak saw home country take a serious interest when **Wicked Game** reached No. 6 in March 1991. Artist's confident and witty delivery (his backing group is original Silvertone trio) endeared him to variety of television audiences during extensive promotional tour in 1991.

Isaak's homely personality and sharp style has created a niche for a musical and showbiz performer whose greatest achievement is likely to be on celluloid.

Hit Singles:	US	UK
Wicked Game, 1990	6	10
Blue Hotel, 1991	—	17

Albums:
Chris Isaak (Warner Bros), 1987
Silvertone (Warner Bros/WEA), 1987
Heart Shaped World (Reprise/WEA), 1989
Wicked Game (Reprise), 1991

Right: Chris Isaak, who owes his success to David 'Twin Peaks' Lynch.

Isley Brothers

US group formed 1957

Original line-up: Ronald Isley, vocals; Rudolph Isley, vocals; O'Kelly Isley, vocals.

Career: Began performing gospel around hometown of Cincinnati. Moved to New York in 1957, changed to more secular style and recorded for several small labels. Eventually signed with RCA in 1959, and released **Shout**, wild gospel-flavoured stomper that made Top 50 and spawned several later cover versions.

Although group continued to build up reputation as hot live act, no more hits were forthcoming until 1962 release of **Twist And Shout** on Wand. Record made US Top 20 and was later covered by Beatles (who were great Isley fans).

Slump again followed, during which time Isleys formed own label, T-Neck. This period also saw group employing Jimi Hendrix as session guitarist. Continued success only came after signing to Motown in 1965. First release, **This Old Heart Of Mine**, became US hit (and major hit in Britain two years later). Over course of four-year period, band notched up variety of single successes on both sides of Atlantic, with greater consistency in UK charts.

Nevertheless, group eventually felt constricted by Motown formula and split from company in 1969. Simultaneously they

Below: 3 Plus 3, The Isley Brothers' 1973 album for T-Neck label. Courtesy Epic Records.

revived dormant T-Neck operation and signed distribution deal with Buddah. New business arrangements were matched by new approach to music, influenced by West Coast psychedelic bands, Hendrix and Sly And Family Stone.

Ronald, Rudolph and O'Kelly recruited brothers Ernie, on guitar and drums, and Marvin, on bass, plus cousin Chris Jasper on keyboards. Revitalized outfit exploded into new era of creativity and impact. Final barrier to international pop success was crossed with records which carried them into mid-80s.

In 1985, Ernie, Marvin and Jasper cut acclaimed **Isley Jasper Isley** album, while original brothers reverted to trio format

before O'Kelly's untimely death (aged 48) in 1986. Ronald and Rudolph cut **Smooth Sailin'** LP in 1987, while Isley/Jasper/Isley aggregation forged on with **Different Drummer** collection.

The complex innerworking of family names was resolved when Ronald and Rudolph adopted 'The Isley Bros featuring Ronald Isley' moniker in 1989, although record stores were kept on their toes by solo sets from both Jasper (**Superbad**) and Ernie (**High Wire**).

The original brothers' frantic R&B styling survived over three generations, and, while hardly innovative, was surely the way soul music was meant to be sung.

Hit Singles:

	US	UK
Twist And Shout, 1962	17	—
This Old Heart Of Mine, (Is Weak For You), 1966	12	47
This Old Heart Of Mine, (Is Weak For You), 1968	—	3
I Guess I'll Always Love You, 1969	—	11
Behind A Painted Smile, 1969	—	5
It's Your Thing, 1969	2	30
Put Yourself In My Place, 1969	—	13
Love The One You're With, 1971	18	—
That Lady, 1973	6	14
Summer Breeze, 1974	60	16
Fight The Power, 1975	4	—
Harvest For The World, 1976	—	10
It's A Disco Night (Rock Don't Stop), 1979	—	14

Albums:
Twist And Shout (Wand/DJM), 1962
This Old Heart Of Mine (Tamla Motown), 1966
3+3 (T-Neck/Epic), 1973
Live It Up (T-Neck/Epic), 1974
The Heat Is On (T-Neck/Epic), 1975
Harvest For The World (T-Neck/Epic), 1976
Super Hits (Tamla Motown), 1976
Go For Your Guns (T-Neck/Epic), 1977
Forever Gold (T-Neck/Epic), 1977
Showroom (T-Neck/Epic), 1978
Winner Takes All (T-Neck/Epic), 1979
Go All The Way (T-Neck/Epic), 1980
Grand Slam (T-Neck/Epic), 1981
Inside You (T-Neck/Epic), 1981
Motown Superstar Series Volume 6 (Motown/—), 1982
The Real Deal (T-Neck/Epic), 1982
Between The Sheets (Epic), 1983
Forever Gold (Epic), 1984
Smoother Sailin' (Warner Bros), 1987
Spend The Night (Warner Bros), 1989
Complete VA Sessions (EMI), 1991
Complete Victor Sessions (RCA), 1991

Isley/Jasper/Isley:
Broadway's Closer To Sunset Boulevard (T-Neck/Epic), 1985
Caravan Of Love (Columbia/Epic), 1985
Different Drummer (CBS), 1987

The Jacksons

US group formed 1966

Original line-up: Michael Jackson, lead vocals; Jackie Jackson, vocals, guitar; Tito Jackson, vocals, guitar; Marlon Jackson, vocals; Jermaine Jackson, vocals, bass.

Career: Black America's answer to The Osmonds, The Jackson Five proved to have international, multi-racial appeal. Sons of Joe Jackson, once guitarist with Falcons soul group, and clarinettist Kathy, family

grew up in Gary, Indiana, where they were all born (Jackie, May 4, 1951; Tito, October 15, 1953; Jermaine, December 11, 1954; Marlon, March 12, 1957; Michael, August 29, 1958; Randy, October 29, 1962). Boys have three sisters of whom two youngest, LaToya and Janet, have logged hits.

Tito had intense interest in music and persuaded others to form family group. Gigged in nearby Chicago and won several talent competitions, culminating in campaign benefit show for Gary's Mayor, Richard Hatcher. Diana Ross was in attendance and brought group to attention of Motown boss Berry Gordy. They had already recorded unsuccessfully for small local label, but Gordy saw them as major talent, especially with then nine-year-old Michael.

Debut single, **I Want You Back**, was immediate smash, Michael earning comparison with former child prodigy Stevie Wonder. **Diana Ross Presents The Jackson 5** album and group's inclusion in her 90-minute TV spectacular *Diana* in 1971 helped build immediate fame. Following singles poured out at rapid rate giving them hits nearly every three months. Early material was all written and produced by The Corporation, that is, Motown's multi-talented songwriting, arranging and production team.

Rivalry with Osmonds and resultant fan mania helped both groups; so did electric stage presence featuring colourful outfits and dazzling dance routines. The Jacksons were even made into a cartoon series.

Parallel — and ever more important — solo career for Michael began at 13 with 1972 hit **I'll Be There**. Tito and Jermaine also had solo releases but made less impact.

Steady flow of albums and singles led to multi-million dollar contract offer from Epic in 1976, which took group from Motown fold. Having married Hazel, daughter of Motown boss Berry Gordy Jr, Jermaine opted to stay and left group. Name was changed to simply The Jacksons, and addition of youngest brother Randy kept the number at five.

First Epic album **The Jacksons** went gold; hit singles continued. In 1978 hit highest spot yet with superb **Destiny** album; smash singles **Blame It On The Boogie** and **Shake Your Body (Down To The Ground)** set world's discos alight. Album was self-produced, using cream of West Coast session musicians. During sellout UK tour, band played in front of the Queen at Silver Jubilee celebrations in Glasgow.

Although individual projects — particularly Michael's — were threatening The Jacksons' future, both **Triumph** (1981) and **Victory** (1984) albums saw family on road, the latter with Jermaine back in the fold. However, December 1984 saw group's final live gig with Michael.

The 1989 album **2300 Jackson Street**, featuring Jermaine, Tito, Randy and Jackie, did not significantly damage LP charts, despite well-publicized guest appearance on title track by Michael.

Jermaine's parallel solo career included 1979 smash **Let's Get Serious** before move to Epic Records, where **Dynamite** was debut album. LP included **Take Good Care Of My Heart** duet with Whitney Houston, for whom Jermaine produced trio of tracks for her eponymous debut. Unhappy at perceived double-standards of brother Michael, Jermaine aired bitterness in public with **World To The Badd** single, which appeared in November 1991.

Marlon Jackson recorded LP **Baby Tonight** for Captiol Records (1987) and also produced material for Betty Wright. Randy Jackson was sent to prison in November

1991 after assaulting his wife and baby daughter. Father Joe Jackson announced plans for the Jackson Entertainment Corporation to go 'public' in 1991, with associated record and film deals, and also planned a mini-series about the family's life, which prompted heavy bidding by American TV companies.

Hit Singles:

As Jackson Five:

	US	UK
I Want You Back, 1970	1	2
ABC, 1970	1	8
The Love You Save, 1970	1	7

Above: Greatest Hits, The Jackson Five. Courtesy Motown Records.

I'll Be There, 1970	1	4
Mama's Pearl, 1971	2	25
Never Can Say Goodbye, 1971	2	33
Maybe Tomorrow, 1971	2	—
Sugar Daddy, 1972	10	—
Little Bitty Pretty One, 1972	13	—
Lookin' Through The Windows, 1972	16	9
Corner Of The Sky, 1972	18	—
Doctor My Eyes, 1973	—	9
Hallelujah Day, 1973	28	20
Dancing Machine, 1974	2	—
I Am Love (Parts 1 and 2), 1975	15	—

As The Jacksons:

Enjoy Yourself, 1977	6	42
Show You The Way To Go, 1977	28	1
Blame It On The Boogie, 1978	54	8
Shake Your Body (Down To The Ground), 1979	7	4
Lovely One, 1980	12	29
Can You Feel It, 1981	—	6
Walk Right Now, 1981	—	7
State Of Shock, 1984	3	14
Torture, 1984	17	26
I Want You Back (re-mix), 1988	—	8

Jermaine Jackson Solo:

Daddy's Home, 1973	9	—
Let's Get Serious, 1980	9	8
Dynamite, 1984	15	—
Do What You Do, 1985	13	6

Albums:

As Jackson Five:
ABC (Tamla Motown), 1970
Lookin' Through The Windows (Tamla Motown), 1972
Greatest Hits (Tamla Motown), 1972
Anthology (Tamla Motown), 1977
20 Golden Greats (—/Motown), 1979
Motown Superstar Series Volume 12 (Tamla/—), 1981

As The Jacksons:
The Jacksons (Epic), 1976
Goin' Places (Epic), 1977
Destiny (Epic), 1978
Triumph (Epic), 1981
Live (Epic), 1982
Victory (Epic), 1984
Maybe Tomorrow (Motown), 1989
Third Album (Motown), 1989

Jermaine Jackson Solo:
Jermaine (Tamla Motown), 1980
Let's Get Serious (Tamla Motown), 1980
I Like Your Style (Tamla Motown), 1981
Let Me Tickle Your Fancy (Tamla Motown), 1982
Dynamite (Arista), 1984
Precious Moments (Arista), 1988
Don't Take It Personal (Arista), 1989

Marlon Jackson Solo:
Baby Tonight (Capitol), 1987

Randy Jackson Solo:
Randy And The Gypsies (A&M/—), 1989

Janet Jackson

US vocalist
Born Gary, Indiana, May 16, 1966

Career: Sister of Michael, and fleeting member of The Jackson Five, Janet Jackson is epitome of 90s soul erotica since breaking free of family constraints.

Debuted with her brothers in 1973 (aged seven) before roles in *Good Times*, *Different Strokes* and *Fame* US TV shows. Signed to A&M Records in 1982; self-titled debut LP had limited success, but follow-up **Dream**

Below: The Jacksons with Michael in the centre, wearing the green shirt.

Street was notable for **Two To The Power** duet with British pop icon Cliff Richard. In 1986, Jackson cut explosive **Control** album, produced by Jimmy Harris/Terry Lewis combo (SOS Band, Alexander O'Neal, Patti Austin) which spawned floor-filler **What Have You Done For Me Lately?** and four other US Top 5 hits. Paula Abdul-choreographed videos provided sexy and exciting complement to singer's efforts.

1989 set **Rhythm Nation 1814** maintained impetus, heading US chart and providing vocalist with six Top 5 US singles, of which **Miss You Much**, **Escapade** and **Black Cat** topped listings; swept all before her at Billboard presentations during same year, winning separate categories, including Top Album and Hot 100 Singles Artist.

In 1991, Jackson signed with Virgin Records for a multi-million dollar figure, the third highest deal in recording history, following brother Michael and Madonna.

A tireless performer onstage — her Rhythm Nation tour proved exhausting — Jackson is also a spokesperson for anti-drug lobby, having seen former husband James DeBarge suffer from cocaine addiction.

Hit Singles:

	US	UK
What Have You Done For Me Lately?, 1986	4	3
Nasty, 1986	3	19
When I Think Of You, 1986	1	10
Control, 1986	5	42
Let's Wait Awhile, 1987	2	3
Miss You Much, 1989	1	25
Rhythm Nation, 1989	2	23

Escapade, 1989	1	—
Alright, 1989	4	20
Come Back To Me, 1989	2	20
Black Cat, 1990	1	15
Love Will Never Do, 1990	4	34

Albums:
Janet Jackson (A&M), 1983
Dream Street (A&M), 1984
Control (A&M), 1986
Rhythm Nation 1814 (A&M), 1989

Michael Jackson

US vocalist, composer
Born Gary, Indiana, August 29, 1958

Career: Dominant brother of The Jacksons, Michael was youngest in original line-up (before Randy joined) and was heralded as infant genius by his Motown mentors. Just as Little Stevie Wonder's early promise reached potential so Michael Jackson's talent has stood test of time. Besides singing lead on The Jacksons' amazing run of hits, Michael has achieved enormous success in own right.

First solo hit was **Got To Be There** (1971). Other successes included movie theme-song **Ben**, a ballad which contrasted with usual uptempo style of Jackson Five. Between 1971-76 enjoyed six best-selling albums with

Below: The increasingly pallid Michael Jackson. Just a child at heart.

Motown. His last collaboration with the company was starring as the scarecrow, opposite Diana Ross, in *The Wiz* black re-make of *The Wizard Of Oz*. The film was heavily criticized but Jackson won applause for his role. His duet with Diana Ross, **Ease On Down The Road**, was hit single.

Moving with his family to Epic label, Michael continued to front The Jacksons. He was also teamed up with producer Quincy Jones (whom he had met while both worked on *The Wiz*) for the appropriately epic **Off The Wall** solo album. This included superb material by Paul McCartney, British writer Rod Temperton (ex-Heatwave) and Jackson himself. Claimed as biggest selling album by a black artist of all time, the Los Angeles-recorded album had no weak spots. In US a number of tracks were lifted as singles. In one week three singles from the LP were in US Top 10, a unique achievement. Cashing in on this phenomenal success, Motown re-issued old track **One Day In Your Life** for 1981 UK chart-topper. In 1982 Michael scored US/UK duet hit with Paul McCartney on McCartney's composition **The Girl Is Mine**.

Follow-up album **Thriller** (1982), also produced by Jones, eclipsed success of **Off The Wall**, with a raft of mega-singles including **Billie Jean** and **Beat It** (which featured HM guitar god Eddie Van Halen). Crucial feature of LP's marketing campaign was video, exploited to the full by ace director John Landis in ground-breaking mini-feature that showed Jackson's fluid dance style to stunning effect.

With sales of **Thriller** approaching 40 million, relatively disappointing numbers for **Bad** prompted flurry of finger-pointing when album hit the streets in 1987. Despite a

Above: Bad, Michael Jackson. Courtesy Epic Records.

plethora of hit singles, the backing of the mighty Pepsi Cola, who promoted the parallel world tour, and a mammoth advertising campaign courtesy of Epic Records, the LP stalled in the sales stakes.

Having re-signed with CBS, Jackson formed own Nation label, and secured alleged 500 million dollar advance from Sony Records, new owners of the CBS conglomerate. For 1991 LP **Dangerous**, Jackson used John Landis to oversee controversial supporting video for **Black Or White** single, which was later edited after criticism of Jackson's erotic posturing. With Quincy Jones ousted in favour of Teddy Riley (who produced The Jacksons' **2300**, The Winans and Keith Sweat), **Dangerous** did not set the critics' hearts-a-pumping. In fact, the palpitations were felt by Japanese executives, wary of the unprecedented multi-media business Jackson must generate in order to justify his extravagant fees.

Whether your perception of Jackson is of a hapless loonie-tune or enigmatic genius, there can be no doubt about his musical talent. Rumours about plastic surgery and

Above: The Jam, pictured before they split at the end of 1982.

skin toning abound, while his reclusive life-style was ripped asunder after hosting Liz Taylor's autumn 1991 marriage, when Jackson's California ranch was used to host the event.

Hit Singles:

	US	UK
Got To Be There, 1971	4	5
Rockin' Robin, 1972	2	3
I Wanna Be Where You Are, 1972	16	—
Ain't No Sunshine, 1972	—	8
Ben, 1972	1	7
Don't Stop 'Til You Get Enough, 1979	1	3
Off The Wall, 1979	10	7
Rock With You, 1979	1	7
She's Out Of My Life, 1980	10	3
One Day In Your Life, 1981	55	1
Billie Jean, 1983	1	1
Beat It, 1983	1	3
Want To Be Startin' Somethin', 1983	5	8
Human Nature, 1983	7	—
PYT (Pretty Young Thing), 1983	10	11
Thriller, 1984	4	10
Farewell My Summer Love, 1984	—	7
The Way You Make Me Feel, 1987	1	3
Bad, 1987	1	3
Man In The Mirror, 1988	1	21
Dirty Diana, 1988	1	4
Another Part of Me, 1988	11	15
Smooth Criminal, 1988	7	8
Leave Me Alone, 1989	2	2
Liberian Girl, 1989	—	13
Black Or White, 1991	1	1

With Siedah Garrett:

	US	UK
I Just Can't Stop Loving You, 1986	1	1

With Paul McCartney:

	US	UK
The Girl Is Mine, 1982	2	8
Say Say Say, 1983	1	2

Albums:
Ben (Tamla Motown), 1972
Got To Be There (Tamla Motown), 1972
Best Of (—/Motown), 1975
Off The Wall (Epic), 1979
One Day In Your Life (—/Motown), 1981
Thriller (Epic), 1982
Ain't No Sunshine (—/Pickwick), 1982
Bad (Epic), 1987
Got To Be There/Ben (Motown), 1987
Dangerous (Epic), 1991

The Jam
UK group formed 1976

Original line-up: Paul Weller, vocals, bass; Steve Brookes, guitar; Bruce Foxton, guitar; Rick Buckler, drums.

Career: Above quartet got together while at school in Woking, Surrey, to play rock 'n' roll and R&B. Youth and social club gigs followed; after Steve Brookes left, Weller switched to guitar, Foxton to bass.

Line-up in this form made London debut in summer 1976, displaying image based

Above: In The City, The Jam's first album. Courtesy Polydor Records.

on early 60s 'mod' look and playing sharp, well-crafted rock songs that showed songwriter Weller's debt to Pete Townshend. Although band had little in common with most of new wave outfits, Jam won contract as part of mass record company signings that followed 'summer of punk'.

First single **In The City** hovered around bottom of UK chart, but follow-up **All Around The World** made No. 13. In meantime, debut album, also called **In The City**, made No. 20 in album chart. During next three years band became chart regulars with both singles and albums, establishing themselves as one of most interesting new outfits of late 70s. Weller (born May 25, 1958) set direction of band, and showed himself to be perceptive writer and spokesman.

1980 saw further triumphs for band, with first No. 1 single **Going Underground/The Dreams Of Children** and title of Best Group in the *New Musical Express* Readers' Poll. Next single, **Start**, also made No. 1.

Despite massive success during 1982 — they swept board in all British polls and toured Britain and abroad to universal acclaim — Jam announced that band would

fold at end of year. Apparently Weller found format too constricting and wished to move on to other things. During December, band undertook farewell tour to usual ecstatic crowds, and retired from scene. 1982 LP, **The Gift**, entered UK charts at No. 1. Jam singles/sleeves are such collectors' items that Polydor re-issued entire catalogue for third time.

Weller has already found further success with new band, The Style Council, and other acts such as Tracie on his own Respond label. Other members are involved with their own solo projects.

Although they never achieved more than cult status in US, Jam, always an intense live act, became one of most important bands in UK in 80s. Success was largely due to Paul Weller; his current projects and any future ones should be worth watching.

Hit Singles:

	US	UK
All Around The World, 1977	—	13
Down In The Tube Station At Midnight, 1978	—	15
Strange Town, 1979	—	15
When You're Young, 1979	—	17
The Eton Rifles, 1979	—	3
Going Underground/The Dreams Of Children, 1980	—	1
Start, 1980	—	1
Funeral Pyre, 1981	—	4
Absolute Beginners, 1981	—	4
Town Called Malice/ Precious, 1982	—	1
Just Who Is The 5 O'Clock Hero, 1982*	—	8
The Bitterest Pill (I Ever Had To Swallow), 1982	—	2
Beat Surrender, 1982	—	1
*German import		

Albums:
In The City (Polydor), 1977
This Is The Modern World (Polydor), 1977*
All Mod Cons (Polydor), 1978*
Setting Sons (Polydor), 1979
Sound Affects (Polydor), 1980
The Gift (Polydor), 1982
Dig The New Breed (live) (Polydor), 1982
Snap (Polydor), 1983
Compact Snap (Polydor), 1983
*One track different on US/UK versions.

Jan And Dean
US vocal duo formed 1958
Jan Berry, born Los Angeles, April 3, 1941
Dean Torrence, born Los Angeles, March 10, 1940

Career: Major figures of California surf-music scene, Jan And Dean's career was abruptly terminated when a horrific car smash in 1966 left Jan with serious brain damage and considerable loss of mobility.

Below: Golden Hits, Jan And Dean. Courtesy Liberty Records.

By no means originators, Jan And Dean were as much reliant on talents of their songwriters and producers as on own vocal abilities, but records like **Surf City**, **Little Old Lady From Pasadena** and **Dead Man's Curve** remain classics of their idiom — the totally unpretentious, fun-music, West Coast sound of the early 60s.

They started singing together in shower room after football practice at Emerson Junior High School in Los Angeles, and recorded on a twin-track machine in garage with help from friend Bruce Johnston, later to become a Beach Boy.

In 1958, Berry managed to place **Jenny Lee** (which featured Berry, Torrence and Arnie Ginsburg as trio but appeared as Jan and Arnie on label because Torrence was in Army and unavailable to sign contract), a song about a burlesque stripper, with Arwin, and it became US Top 10 hit. A year later Berry was back with Dean Torrence as Jan and Dean, with **Baby Talk**, produced by Lou Adler and Herb Alpert. Concurrently, they attended college, Berry studying medicine, Torrence design.

Music soon took over, however, and after Top 30 hit on Challenge with **Heart And Soul** in 1961 they signed to Liberty the following year and started singing about their big passion — surfing.

After a show with The Beach Boys, Brian Wilson played them demo of his composition **Surf City**. Their rendition went to No. 1 and was quickly followed by string of surf and hot-rod flavoured high-school epics, many of them written or produced by Brian Wilson. They repaid the favour, Jan Berry singing lead on The Beach Boys' live recording of **Barbara Ann**.

While filming *Easy Come Easy Go* in spring 1966, Berry crashed his car into a parked truck. Despite some sides recorded for A&M and occasional stage appearances with erstwhile partner (where they were somewhat cruelly accused of going for sympathy market), Jan Berry's contribution to rock music remains rooted in his brief spell of 60s stardom. Dean Torrence was involved with the Legendary Masked Surfers and now runs a design studio which specializes in pop posters. 1978 movie *Dead Man's Curve* chronicled duo's career.

Hit Singles:	US	UK
Jenny Lee (As Jan and Arnie), 1958	8	—
Baby Talk, 1959	10	—
Surf City, 1963	1	26
Honolulu Lulu, 1963	11	—
Drag City, 1964	10	—
Dead Man's Curve, 1964	8	—
Little Old Lady From Pasadena, 1964	3	—
Ride The Wild Surf, 1964	16	—

Album:
Dead Man's Curve (Liberty/—), 1964
Ride The Wild Surf (Liberty/Greenlight-Liberty), 1964
Little Old Lady From Pasadena (Liberty/—), 1964
Legendary Masters (Liberty/—), 1971
Very Best Of (—/Sunset), 1974
Greatest Hits (MCS), 1987
Silver Summer (Showcase), 1987

Jefferson Airplane/Starship

US group formed 1965

Original line-up: Marty Balin, vocals; Paul Kantner, guitar; Signe Anderson, vocals; Jorma Kaukonen, guitar; Jack Casady, bass; Skip Spence, drums.

Career: Balin and Kantner met on San Francisco's folk coffee-house circuit in early 1965. Balin felt it was time to return to his roots and explore rock 'n' roll of Elvis, Jerry Lee Lewis and Little Richard. Anderson joined, then Kaukonen. Balin called Washington, D.C., and asked long-time friend Casady to join on bass. Spencer was recruited in mid-65 and Airplane began building local reputation as band who played folk lyrics to rock beat. Bill Graham helped foster exciting, vibrant image for band by providing priority booking at new Fillmore Hall. This lead to RCA contract, the first for the Bay area band.

Spencer Dryden replaced Spence (later to form Moby Grape) while band recorded **Jefferson Airplane Takes Off**. National promotion helped 'folk-rock' sound achieve gold LP status and aroused industry interest in West Coast bands. Anderson left due to pregnancy and Kantner recruited Grace Slick (ex-Great Society) from band who used to open for Airplane.

This classic line-up scored big US hit with **Somebody To Love**. This song and **White Rabbit** were old Great Society songs. Slick's vocals made them, and whole of **Surrealistic Pillow** LP, a haunting, emotive experience. To band's delight, critics and fans fell in love with album and it is marked as essential listening for understanding the 1960s era.

Sudden success meant band could live in communal bliss, but community living also brought problems. **After Bathing At Baxter's** reflected this by reducing Balin's songwriting contributions and by trying new sounds and formats. Unlike previous LP, **Baxter's** experiments no longer hold interest upon re-hearing today.

Slick and Kantner had become lovers; when they began assuming full leadership roles, Balin backed off. **Crown of Creation** reduced Balin's role even further by including weak Slick song, **Lather**, and non-rock David Crosby song, **Triad**. Daring at time of release, and containing some good harmony, this LP is high point of early Airplane.

Bless Its Pointed Little Head was average live set. Next album, **Volunteers**, pushed band into forefront of counter-culture's political stance. Considering shallow, preachy tone, LP has remained surprisingly interesting. Balin felt band was becoming too big and too smooth and left. Several US tours followed (including playing at Stones' Altamont concert), then band seemed to lose all sense of direction. Balin's loss, Slick's pregnancy with Kantner's child and Dryden's departure left Airplane grounded. Kaukonen and Casady began electric blues country band, Hot Tuna. At first a part-time affair, project eventually removed duo from Airplane altogether. In telling omen for the future, Slick and Kantner used several famous 'session' players (Jerry Garcia, David Crosby, Graham Nash) to record LP **Blows Against The Empire**, which they credited to 'Paul Kantner and the Jefferson Starship'.

Airplane returned with Joey Covington (drums) on **Bark** LP. State of Airplane is reflected by superior Slick-Kantner solo, **Sunfighter**, released at same time. With one more sub-par set, **Long John Silver**, Airplane finally crashed. David Frieberg, ex-Quicksilver Messenger Service, added vocals on live but uninspired **Thirty Seconds Over Winterland**. Then with no formal announcement, Airplane disappeared. Casady and Kaukonen worked full time turning Hot Tuna into early heavy-metal band. Slick, Kantner and Frieberg produced weak solo effort, and Slick released unsatisfactory **Manhole** LP.

Below: Jefferson Airplane before they developed booster rockets. Grace Slick is pictured second from left.

Two years later in 1974, Slick and Kantner decided to re-form band. Using Frieberg, 'Papa' John Creach (fiddler Hot Tuna had introduced to Airplane on **Bark**), ex-Turtles' John Barbata (drums), Peter Sears (bass) and Craig Chaquico (guitar), new formation took name Jefferson Starship.

US tour, using early Airplane and solo material, convinced Slick and Kantner that band was viable proposition. **Dragon Fly** wasn't overly brilliant but sold well. More importantly, it had one Balin credit and indicated reunion with his creative influence; Balin began appearing with Starship and contributing efforts to recording sessions. However, he refused to sign with group or formally commit self to Starship. His **Miracles** became mammoth US hit in summer 1975 and pushed LP **Red Octopus** to US No. 1 (Airplane/Starship's first after 10 years of work).

The success of **Octopus** obviously influenced sales of next LP, **Spitfire**, but album was inferior and seemed a sell-out/cash-in. **Earth** reflected growing personal problems and confusion over what to do next. Slick, Balin and Barbata all left and there seemed no reason to continue.

Kantner recruited Aynsley Dunbar, drums, and Mickey Thomas, vocals, **Freedom At Point Zero** was first line-up not to feature female lead vocals. Critically dismissed, Kantner pushed on to **Modern Times**; Slick provided some backing vocals. Having resolved bout with alcohol and various personal problems, she rejoined full time on **Winds Of Change** (after release of two solos LPs).

Break-up of Kantner/Slick's personal relationship led to Kantner leaving group June 1984 amid much acrimony; resultant law suits forced band to abbreviate name in March 1985 to simply Starship for **Knee Deep In The Hoopla** album.

With a line-up now missing Kantner (who formed KBC band), Frieberg, Slick and Company enjoyed a US No. 1 single in 1985 with **We Built This City** from the **Knee Deep** LP. Further success was attained with **Nothing's Gonna Stop Us Now** (1987), a rip-roaring pop anthem.

In 1989, Jefferson Airplane was relaunched when Slick reunited with Kantner, Casady, Balin and Kaukonen for self-titled album. Meanwhile, Starship (Thomas, Sears, Baldwin, Chaquico, Brett Bloomfield, bass, and Mark Morgan, keyboards) soldiered on, and enjoyed modest success with **Love Among The Cannibals** set (August 1989). But, notepads at the ready folks, Sears was another casualty in ongoing cast change, while Thomas took time out when hospitalized after bust-up in San Franciscan bar.

With the Airplane/Starship variety show emulating that other sci-fi fantasy *Star Trek*, news of the reborn band prompted readers of *Rolling Stone* to vote event Most Unwelcome Comeback in 1990.

Hit Singles:	US	UK
As Airplane:		
Somebody to Love, 1967	5	—
White Rabbit, 1967	8	—
As Starship:		
Miracles, 1975	3	—
With Your Love, 1976	12	—
Runaway, 1978	12	—
Count On Me, 1978	8	—
Jane, 1979	14	—
We Built This City, 1985	1	12
Nothing's Gonna Stop Us Now, 1987	1	1
It's Not Over, 1987	9	—
It's Not Enough, 1989	12	—

Above: They built this city on regular personnel changes. Starship grounded.

Albums:

As Airplane:
Jefferson Airplane Takes Off (RCA), 1966
Surrealistic Pillow (RCA), 1967
After Bathing At Baxter's (RCA), 1968
Crown Of Creation (RCA), 1968
Bless Its Pointed Little Head (RCA), 1969
Volunteers (RCA), 1969
Worst Of (RCA), 1970
Bark (Grunt), 1971
Thirty Seconds Over Winterland — Live (Grunt), 1973
2400 Fulton Street—The CD Collection (RCA), 1987

As Starship:
Dragon Fly (Grunt), 1974
Red Octopus (RCA), 1975
Spitfire (Grunt), 1976
Earth (Grunt), 1978
Gold (Grunt), 1979
Freedom At Ground Zero (Grunt), 1980
Modern Times (Grunt), 1981
Winds Of Change (Grunt USA), 1982
Nuclear Furniture (Grunt USA), 1984
Knee Deep In The Hoopla (RCA), 1985
Love Among The Cannibals, 1989

Kantner-Slick:
Blows Against The Empire (RCA), 1970
Sunfighter (Grunt), 1971

Grace Slick Solo:
Dreams (RCA), 1980
Welcome To The Wrecking Ball (RCA), 1981

Slick and the Society:
Collectors Item (Columbia), 1990

The Jesus And Mary Chain

UK group formed 1982

Original line-up: Jim Reid, vocals; William Reid, guitars; Douglas Hart, bass; Murray Dalgleish, drums.

Career: Formed in 1982 in East Kilbride, near Glasgow in Scotland (which also spawned Aztec Camera), group played mere handful of local gigs — being banned from one venue and rejected by Glasgow rock cognoscenti as being brash and tuneless — before releasing seminal debut single, **Upside Down**, on Creation Records.

Early reputation based on low-key shambolic gigs highlighted by guitar feedback on stage and crowd trouble off. Series of singles via Blanco Y Negro licensing deal — **Never Understand**, **You Trip Me Up** and **Just Like Honey** — showed band moving into sweet melodies with harsh arrangements, like Velvet Underground reinterpreting Beach Boys songbook. Debut LP, **Psycho Candy**, featured temporary drummer Bobby Gillespie and received critical acclaim before **Some Candy Talking** became a UK hit single.

Band then split from would-be Svengali manager Alan McGee and disappeared for year, experimenting with drum-machine and extra guitarist before re-emerging with **April Skies** and second LP **Darklands** which proved their talent for brooding ballads and atmospheric rock in vein of The Cure.

With Reid Brothers now working outside of band framework (although drummers John Moore and Richard Thomas were temporarily recruited), fourth album **Automatic** (1989) was introverted and moody. For supporting UK tour, the Reids hired guitarist Ben Laurie.

Following controversial North American concerts in 1987, J&MC's return to the continent in 1990 was unexpected, and, in Canada, unwelcome (Jim Reid had previously been arrested for assault in Canada).

1991 saw release of John Peel radio show recordings (1985-86) for **The Peel Sessions** LP in November 1991, and outfit were planning new studio album for projected release in March 1992.

Hit Singles:	US	UK
Some Candy Talking, 1986	—	13
April Skies, 1987	—	8
Happy When It Rains, 1987	—	25
Darklands, 1987	—	33

Below: The Peel Sessions, Jesus And Mary Chain. Courtesy Strange Fruit Records.

THE JESUS & MARY CHAIN
the peel sessions

Albums:
Psycho Candy (Blanco Y Negro), 1985
Darklands (Blanco Y Negro), 1987
Barbed Wire Kisses (Warner Bros/Blanco Y Negro), 1988
Automatic (Warner Bros/Blanco Y Negro), 1989
The Peel Sessions (—/Strange Fruit), 1991

Jethro Tull

UK group formed 1968

Original line-up: Ian Anderson, vocals, flute; Glenn Cornick, bass; Mick Abrahams, guitar; Clive Bunker, drums.

Career: Ian Anderson joined John Evan Band in native Blackpool in early 1966. Rapidly changing personnel brought him in contact with various musicians who would later work for him in Tull.

John Evan Band moved to London in winter 1967 and tried to break into club scene. Lack of success caused band's break-up, leaving Anderson and Cornick on their own. Abrahams and Bunker joined them in early 1968 and Anderson named band after 18th Century author/agriculturist Jethro Tull. Anderson's eccentric vocals and image caught attention of MGM records. Single **Aeroplane/Sunshine Day** was fortunate flop in that band's name was misprinted as Jethro Toe. Island Records released next single, **Song For Jeffery**, which gathered bigger following and put band on road to success. Tull's albums began selling well as 'art-rock' in US and provided large, loyal following there.

Abrahams left in late 1968 (forming Blodwyn Pig). Tony Iommi (later Black Sabbath) filled in for few weeks until Martin Barre was picked from auditions as permanent guitarist. This line-up recorded excellent **Stand Up** LP which was first indication of Anderson's true talent as songwriter. Adding old mate John Evan as session keyboard player, band recorded equally strong **Benefit** LP.

With flamboyant dress (usually like that of a mad jester) and leg-hopping antics, Anderson was now critical and popular success. Extended himself with rock opera **Aqualung** which took on typical early 70s targets (organized religion, society in general), but offered no substitute. Despite overblown tone, LP **Aqualung** became huge US success and continues to sell well today. For this album John Evan became full member, but co-founder Cornick was replaced by yet another Blackpool mate, Jeffery Hammond-Hammond. Cornick formed Wild Turkey; later he co-founded Paris with ex-Fleetwood Mac, Bob Welch. By late 1971 Bunker had left and his place was taken by last ex-John Evan Band recruit, Barriemore Barlow.

Concept album ideas were extended in live show through use of stage props and pre-recorded films. After **Thick As A Brick**, Anderson threw caution to wind and presented **A Passion Play**. Rather than playing old hits or catering to any audience desire, Jethro Tull played new opera to astonished crowds.

Move proved to be rock 'n' roll suicide as both fans and critics turned off. In retaliation, Anderson announced break-up of group. He quickly realized his mistake explaining he really only meant group would take break from touring. Using same basic line-up from **A Passion Play**, Anderson recorded 'comeback' LP **War Child**, as part of film project. Finally realizing rock opera and concept albums were passé, film was abandoned and LP was released by itself.

Despite this background, **War Child** recaptured early Tull flavour and seemed excellent indication for band's future. More surprising was LP's single, **Bungle In The Jungle**, which became big US hit, an event rare for Tull even when band played huge stadium concerts.

Anderson's concept LP **Too Old To Rock 'n' Roll, Too Young to Die** was prophetic, and Tull began winding down as front-line attraction. A trio of folk-styled albums, of which **Songs From The Wood** was outstanding, heralded the end of the 70s which had seen further personnel upheaval for the band, with Dave Palmer, keyboards, and John Glasscock, bass, joining the group, although Glasscock succumbed to a heart attack in 1979.

With Anderson also enjoying new-found 'country squire' status (and managing salmon farm on his Isle Of Skye retreat) he maintained Tull output throughout the 80s. He also found time to cut solo LP **Walk Into Light** (1983), although **A** set two years previously (with Barre, Pegg, Mark Craney, drums, and former Roxy Music keyboardist Eddie Jobson) was also planned as solo effort before ending up in Tull catalogue.

With a fluctuating line-up, which had seen drummer Gerry Conway and keyboardist Peter Vettesse join for **Broadsword And The Beast** (1982), Tull continued to gig and were still able to fill 20,000-seat stadiums in US. 1987 Grammy for Best HM Album **Crest Of A Knave** ensured crossover audience, and a certain irony for Britain's premier purveyors of folk-rock.

As part of 20th anniversary festivities in 1988, JT embarked on month-long American tour, with Anderson, Barre, Pegg, Duane Perry, drums, and Martin Allcock, keyboards, and also played London's Wembley Arena. Chrysalis' contribution to the anniversary was **20 Years Of Jethro Tull**, a 65-track multi-format package.

In autumn 1991, Jethro Tull released their 25th album **Catfish Rising** and took to the road one more time.

Hit Singles:	US	UK
Living In The Past, 1969	11	3
Sweet Dream, 1969	—	9
The Witch's Promise/Teacher, 1970	—	4
Life Is A Long Song/Up The Pool, 1971	—	11
Bungle In The Jungle, 1974	12	—

Albums:
This Was (Reprise/Island), 1968

JETHRO TULL · SAVOY BROWN · TEN YEARS AFTER

JAYBIRDS #1 1961 to AUG 65
DAVE QUICKMIRE (drums), ALVIN LEE (gtr/voc), LEO LYONS (bass)
quit music biz

MANSFIELDS 1962 to AUG 65
RIC LEE (drums), STUART LANE (guitar), MICK HODKINSON (bass/voc), KEITH WILLIAMS (gtr/voc)
current whereabouts unknown

SAVOY BROWN #1 1966 to 1967
BRICE PORTIUS (vocals), BOB HALL (piano), KIM SIMMONDS (guitar), RIVERS JOBE (bass), rep RAY CHAPPELL (bass), LEO MANNINGS (drums), MARTIN STONE (guitar)
Latimer Road Blues Band / Mighty Baby

McGREGOR'S ENGINE JAN 67 to NOV 67
PETE FENSOME (vocals), ANDY PYLE (bass), MICK ABRAHAMS (gtr/voc), CLIVE BUNKER (drums)

JOHN EVAN'S SMASH 1966 to NOV 67
GLENN CORNICK (bass), IAN ANDERSON (vocals), TONY WILKINSON (sax), CHICK MURRAY (guitar), JOHN EVAN (keyb'ds), BARRIE BARLOW (drums)
both quit rock biz

JAYBIRDS #2 AUG 65 to NOV 66
ALVIN LEE (gtr/voc), LEO LYONS (bass), RIC LEE (drums)

SOUNDS OF BLUE MAR 64 to MAR 65
DAVE YEATS (vocals), CHRISTINE PERFECT (piano/voc), STAN WEBB (gtr/voc), ANDY SILVESTER (bass), CHRIS WOOD (sax), ROB ELCOCK (drums)
record co exec / Traffic / Montanas

SAVOY BROWN #2 1967 to 1969
KIM SIMMONDS (guitar), DAVE PEVERETT (gtr/voc), ROGER EARL (drums), TONE STEVENS (bass), CHRIS YOULDEN (vocals), BOB HALL (piano)
various bluesers

JETHRO TULL #1 NOV 67 to NOV 68
MICK ABRAHAMS (gtr/voc), CLIVE BUNKER (drums), GLENN CORNICK (bass), IAN ANDERSON (voc/flute)

TEN YEARS AFTER NOV 66 to MAR 74
ALVIN LEE (gtr/voc), LEO LYONS (bass), RIC LEE (drums), CHICK CHURCHILL (keyboards)
producing manager publishing

CHICKEN SHACK #1 APR 65 to APR 67
STAN WEBB (gtr/voc), ANDY SILVESTER (bass), DAVE BIDWELL (drums) rep AL SYKES (drums)
ex B.B.King

SAVOY BROWN #3 DEC 69 to MAY 70
KIM SIMMONDS (guitar), DAVE PEVERETT (gtr/voc), ROGER EARL (drums), TONE STEVENS (bass), CHRIS YOULDEN (vocals)
solo

BLODWYN PIG #1 NOV 68 to SEP 70
ANDY PYLE (bass), RON BERG (drums), JACK LANCASTER (sax), MICK ABRAHAMS (gtr/voc)

JETHRO TULL #2 DEC 68 to APR 70
GLENN CORNICK (bass), CLIVE BUNKER (drums), IAN ANDERSON (voc/flute), MARTIN BARRE (guitar)

CHICKEN SHACK #2 APR 67 to AUG 69
CHRISTINE PERFECT (piano/voc), STAN WEBB (gtr/voc), ANDY SILVESTER (bass), DAVE BIDWELL (drums)
Fleetwood Mac

SAVOY BROWN #4 MAY 70 to DEC 70
KIM SIMMONDS (guitar), DAVE PEVERETT (gtr/voc), ROGER EARL (drums), TONE STEVENS (bass)

BLODWYN PIG #2 SEP 70 to DEC 70
PETE BANKS (bass), ANDY PYLE (bass), RON BERG (drums), JACK LANCASTER (sax)
ex Yes / see below

JETHRO TULL #3 APR 70 to DEC 70
GLENN CORNICK (bass), CLIVE BUNKER (drums), IAN ANDERSON (voc/flute), MARTIN BARRE (guitar), JOHN EVAN (keyboards)
Wild Turkey

ALVIN LEE & CO #1 SEPT 74 to APR 75
ALVIN LEE (gtr/voc), MEL COLLINS (sax), IAN WALLACE (drums), STEVE THOMPSON (bass), RONNIE LEAHY (keyboards)

CHICKEN SHACK #3 AUG 69 to DEC 70
STAN WEBB (gtr/voc), ANDY SILVESTER (bass), DAVE BIDWELL (drums), PAUL RAYMOND (keyb'd/voc)

FOGHAT DEC 70 to 1977
DAVE PEVERETT (gtr/voc), ROGER EARL (drums), TONE STEVENS (bass), ROD PRICE (gtr/voc)

MICK ABRAHAMS OCT 70 to JUL 72
BOB SARGEANT (keyb/voc), WALT MONAGHAN (bass), MICK ABRAHAMS (gtr/voc), RITCHIE DHARMA (drums)
hot shot producer

JETHRO TULL #4 JAN 71 to MAY 71
CLIVE BUNKER (drums), IAN ANDERSON (voc/flute), MARTIN BARRE (guitar), JOHN EVAN (keyb'ds), JEFFREY HAMMOND (bass)

CHICKEN SHACK #4 JAN 71 to JUL 73
STAN WEBB (gtr/voc), PAUL HANCOX (drums), BOB DAISLEY (bass) rep JOHN GLASCOCK (bass)
computers Rainbow Jethro Tull

SAVOY BROWN #5 JAN 71 to APR 71
DAVE BIDWELL (drums), DAVE WALKER (vocals), KIM SIMMONDS (guitar), PAUL RAYMOND (keyb'ds), ANDY PYLE (bass)

JUICY LUCY #2 JUN 70 to JUL 71
MICK MOODY (guitar), JEAN ROUSSEL (keyb'ds), PAUL WILLIAMS (vocals), ROD COOMBES (drums), JIMMY LEVERTON (bass)
Stealers Wheel Hemlock

JETHRO TULL #5 MAY 71 to DEC 75
BARRIEMORE BARLOW (drums), IAN ANDERSON (voc/flute), MARTIN BARRE (guitar), JOHN EVAN (keyb'ds), JEFFREY HAMMOND (bass)
quit music

CHICKEN SHACK #5 JUL 73 to DEC 73
DAVE WILKINSON (keyb'ds), ROB HULL (bass), ALAN POWELL (drums), STAN WEBB (gtr/voc)
Stretch Mungo Jerry Hawkwind

SAVOY BROWN #6 MAY 71 to SEP 72
ANDY SILVESTER (bass), DAVE BIDWELL (drums), DAVE WALKER (vocals), KIM SIMMONDS (guitar), PAUL RAYMOND (keyb'ds), RON BERG (drums)
session work Fleetwood Mac

JUICY LUCY #3 JUL 71 to SEP 72
ANDY PYLE (bass) rep by CHRIS STEWART (bass), MICK MOODY (guitar), JEAN ROUSSEL (keyboards), PAUL WILLIAMS (vocals)
Spooky Tooth Whitesnake Cat Stevens Tempest

JETHRO TULL #6 DEC 75 to OCT 76
BARRIEMORE BARLOW (drums), IAN ANDERSON (voc/flute), MARTIN BARRE (guitar), JOHN EVAN (keyb'ds), JOHN GLASCOCK (bass)

ALVIN LEE & CO #2 MAR 76 to JUL 76
ALVIN LEE (gtr/voc), BRYSON GRAHAM (drums), TIM HINKLEY (keyb'ds), ANDY PYLE (bass)
session/studio work Kinks

HEMLOCK JAN 73 to JAN 74
MICK WEAVER (keyboards), MILLER ANDERSON (gtr/voc), ERIC DILLON (drums), JIMMY LEVERTON (bass)

SAVOY BROWN #7 SEP 72 to JAN 74
KIM SIMMONDS (guitar), PAUL RAYMOND (keyb'ds), RON BERG (drums), ANDY PYLE (bass), JACKIE LYNTON (vocals)
UFO Network solo

JETHRO TULL #7 OCT 76 to AUG 79
DAVID PALMER (keyb'ds), BARRIE BARLOW (drums), IAN ANDERSON (voc/flute), MARTIN BARRE (guitar), JOHN EVAN (keyb'ds), JOHN GLASCOCK (bass)
died after heart surgery

TEN YEARS LATER FEB 78 to MAY 80
ALVIN LEE (gtr/voc), TOM COMPTON (drums), MICK HAWKSWORTH (bass)
sessions

SAVOY BROWN #8 JAN 74 to DEC 74
KIM SIMMONDS (guitar), MILLER ANDERSON (gtr/voc), ERIC DILLON (drums), JIMMY LEVERTON (bass), STAN WEBB (gtr/voc)
to Dog Soldier Leo Sayer

BLODWYN PIG #3 FEB 74 to JUL 74
MICK ABRAHAMS (gtr/voc), ANDY PYLE (bass), CLIVE BUNKER (drums), JACK LANCASTER (sax)
new bands

JETHRO TULL #8 AUG 79 to JUN 80
DAVID PALMER (keyb'ds), BARRIE BARLOW (drums), IAN ANDERSON (voc/flute), MARTIN BARRE (guitar), DAVE PEGG (bass), JOHN EVAN (keyb'ds)
Tallis Tandoori Cassette building firm

ALVIN LEE #1 JUN 80 to OCT 81
ALVIN LEE (gtr/voc), TOM COMPTON (drums), MICKY FEAT (bass/voc), STEVE GOULD (gtr/voc)
session work

SAVOY BROWN 9 1975 to 1977
KIM SIMMONDS (guitar), IAN ELLIS (bass/voc), TOM FARNELL (drums)
last known line-up

CHICKEN SHACK 6 1975 to 1979 plus many more musicians
STAN WEBB (gtr/voc), ED SPEVOCK (drums), STEVE YORK (bass), ROBBIE BLUNT (guitar)

AVIATOR 1978 to 1979
CLIVE BUNKER (drums), JACK LANCASTER (sax), JOHN PERRY (bass/voc), MICK ROGERS (gtr/voc)
Poor Mouth

JETHRO TULL #9 JUN 80 to MAY 81
IAN ANDERSON (voc/flute), MARTIN BARRE (guitar), DAVE PEGG (bass), EDDIE JOBSON (keyb'ds), MARK CRANEY (drums)
Yes / jingles sessions

ALVIN LEE #2 NOV 81 to FEB 82
ALVIN LEE (gtr/voc), TOM COMPTON (drums), MICK TAYLOR (guitar), FUZZY SAMUELS (bass)

Ten Years After re-formed for US tour in 1988

Chicken Shack are still going strong... Stan Webb is the only constant factor

CHICKEN SHACK #7 MAY 80 to MAY 82
STAN WEBB (gtr/voc), RIC LEE (drums), PAUL BUTLER (gtr/voc), ALAN SCOTT (bass) rep by ANDY PYLE (bass)

Pete Frame

Jethro Tull hire keyboard players when and as necessary

JETHRO TULL #10 JUN 81
IAN ANDERSON (voc/flute), MARTIN BARRE (guitar), DAVE PEGG (bass), DOANE PERRY (drums) or GERRY CONWAY (drums)

Above: Benefit, Jethro Tull. Courtesy Island Records.

Stand Up (Reprise/Island), 1969
Benefit (Reprise/Island), 1970
Aqualung (Chrysalis), 1971
Thick As A Brick (Chrysalis), 1972
Living In The Past (Chrysalis), 1972
A Passion Play (Chrysalis), 1973
War Child (Chrysalis), 1974
M.U. Best Of Jethro Tull (Chrysalis), 1975
Minstrel In The Gallery (Chrysalis), 1975
Too Old To Rock 'n' Roll, Too Young To Die (Chrysalis), 1976
Songs From The Wood (Chrysalis), 1977
Repeat: Best Of Jethro Tull Volume II (Chrysalis), 1976
Heavy Horses (Chrysalis), 1978
Live: Bursting Out (Chrysalis), 1978
Stormwatch (Chrysalis), 1979
A (Chrysalis), 1980
Broadsword And The Beast (Chrysalis), 1982
Under Wraps (Chrysalis), 1984
Original Masters (Chrysalis), 1986
Crest of A Knave (Chrysalis), 1987
20 Years Of (3 CD set) (Chrysalis), 1988
Rock Island (Chrysalis), 1989
Catfish Rising (Chrysalis), 1991

Joan Jett And The Blackhearts

US group formed 1979

Original line-up: Joan Jett, guitar, vocals; Eric Amble, guitar; Lee Crystal, drums; Gary Ryan, bass.

Career: Jett came under spell of heavy metal when in early teens; she later cited T. Rex and Black Sabbath as major influences; was inspired to take up guitar after catching Suzi Quatro gig in 1975. Linked with legendary West Coast impressario Kim Fowley to form Runaways in 1975, who enjoyed success in Far East, but who attracted scorn from rock mainstream. Band folded in 1979, and Jett auditioned musicians for new outfit, having decided to front own group.

Signed to indie Blackheart label for eponymous debut (1980), but major companies were indifferent to product. Deal was finally struck when Boardwalk president Neil Bogart pacted Jett to his company. Album was re-mixed and re-released (as **Bad Reputation**) in 1982.

Heavy workload saw Jett establish street credibility and prompt further promotion of first LP. Radio station picked up on **I Love Rock 'n' Roll**, one of three tracks recorded with former Sex Pistols' Steve Jones and Paul Cook. Single made US No. 1 and also cracked UK Top 5 in 1982. Consolidated chart status in same year with re-makes of

Tommy James's **Crimson And Clover** and Gary Glitter's **Do You Wanna Touch Me**. In 1983 both **Fake Friends** and **Everyday People** made US Top 50.

While never regaining heights of early 80s success, Jett and troupe became sought after live attraction, and enjoyed solid sales from album releases, particularly 1988 set **Up Your Alley** (London). In 1990, they signed with Chrysalis for **The Hit List**, an uncomfortable set of cover versions of popular rock anthems. The Blackhearts line-up at this time was Crystal, Ryan, and Ricky Byrd, guitar.

Jett also fulfilled movie ambitions when co-opted for 1987 flick *Light Of Day*, which saw singer team with Michael J. Fox in on-screen rock outfit.

Hit Singles:	US	UK
I Love Rock 'n' Roll, 1982	1	4

Albums:
With The Runaways:
The Runaways (Mercury), 1976
Queens Of Noise (Mercury), 1977
Live In Japan (Mercury), 1977
Waitin' For The Night (Mercury), 1977
And Now The Runaways (Mercury), 1979
Flamin' Schoolgirls (Mercury), 1980
I Love Playing With Fire (—/Cherry Red), 1982
Little Lost Girls (Rhino), 1987

With The Blackhearts:
Bad Reputation (Epic), 1982
I Love Rock 'n' Roll (Epic), 1982
Joan Jett (Epic), 1983
Glorious Results Of A Misspent Youth (Epic), 1984
Up Your Alley (CBS Assoc/London), 1988
The Hit List (Blackheart/Chrysalis), 1990

Billy Joel

US vocalist, pianist, composer
Born Long Island, New York, May 9, 1949

Career: Encouraged by German-born father, Joel learned piano from age four. In 1964, joined first group, The Echoes, which later became Lost Souls. Further early aggregations included The Hassles, who recorded two albums for United Artists, and Attila,

a duo which made one album for Epic.

In 1971, demo tape of own songs gained Joel contract with Family Productions, and year later first solo album, **Cold Spring Harbour**, was released. Record created some interest despite appalling production, but business problems led to Joel's exodus to California. During this time he performed in bars and hotels under name Bill Martin.

However, song called **Captain Jack** had come to attention of Columbia records, and company traced Joel to California and signed him. Album **Piano Man** was released in 1973, providing Top 30 single in title track. Album eventually went platinum.

Strangely, next album, **Street Life Serenade**, did not do as well, and Joel decided to return to familiar environment of New York. 1976 album **Turnstiles** reflected home town lifestyle and furthered Joel's reputation as writer of memorable melodies and often perceptive lyrics.

Massive breakthrough came with release of next album, **The Stranger**. It eventually became Columbia's biggest-selling album in US, surpassing even **Bridge Over Troubled Water**. LP also yielded instant standard in **Just The Way You Are** single, covered by every artist from Englebert Humperdinck to Barry White.

While recording **The Nylon Curtain** album, Joel had serious motorcycle accident on Long Island, resulting in fractures which needed extensive surgery. LP struck raw nerve in American consciousness, title song being hailed as first to express the experience of soldiers in Vietnam War. **Allentown** did same for steel workers and led 16,000 of its citizens to petition singer to include their town in his 1982 tour.

For **Innocent Man**, Joel turned back to the music he loved as a teenager — the soul, R&B and rock of late 1950s early 1960s. He recaptured the mood while avoided being derivative, except in the case of the catchy hit **Tell Her About It** which came close to Frankie Valli and The Four Seasons' sound without inciting a 'passing off' action.

Now married to top model Christie Brinkley (the **Uptown Girl**), Joel spread his net as far as Russia, where live set **Kohuept** (1988) was recorded. For powerful **Storm Front** LP (1989), Joel hired Foreigner-mentor Mick Jones to co-produce. Single from album **We Didn't Start The Fire** was acidic political statement.

Recovered from surgery, and with a protracted lawsuit filed against former manager Frank Weber behind him, Joel looked set to maintain dominance of AOR market, with grudging approval from new wave and heavy rock crowd.

Hit Singles:	US	UK
Just The Way You Are, 1978	3	19
Movin' Out (Anthony's Song), 1978	17	35
She's Always A Woman, 1978	17	—
My Life, 1978	3	12

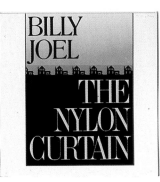

Above: The Nylon Curtain, Billy Joel. Courtesy Columbia Records.

	US	UK
Big Shot, 1979	14	—
You May Be Right, 1980	7	—
It's Still Rock And Roll To Me, 1980	1	14
Say Goodbye To Hollywood, 1981	17	—
Pressure, 1982	20	—
Allentown, 1983	17	—
Tell Her About It, 1983	1	4
Uptown Girl, 1983	3	1
An Innocent Man, 1984	10	8
The Longest Time, 1984	14	25
Keeping The Faith, 1985	18	—
You're Only Human, 1985	9	—
A Matter Of Trust, 1987	16	—
This Is The Time, 1987	18	—
We Didn't Start The Fire, 1989	1	7
I Go To Extremes, 1990	6	—

Albums:
Cold Spring Harbor (Columbia/CBS), 1972
Piano Man (Columbia/CBS), 1973
Street Life Serenade (Columbia/CBS), 1975
Turnstiles (Columbia/CBS), 1976
The Stranger (Columbia/CBS), 1977
52nd Street (Columbia/CBS), 1978
Glass Houses (Columbia/CBS), 1980
Songs In The Attic (Columbia/CBS), 1981
The Nylon Curtain (Columbia/CBS), 1982
An Innocent Man (Columbia/CBS), 1983
Greatest Hits Volumes I and II (Columbia/CBS), 1985
The Bridge (CBS), 1986
Kohuept (CBS), 1987
Storm Front (Columbia/CBS), 1989

Below: Kohuept, Billy Joel. Courtesy CBS Records.

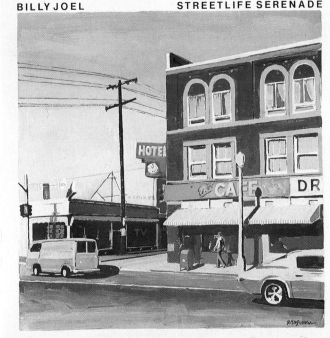

Right: Streetlife Serenade, Billy Joel. Courtesy Columbia Records.

Elton John

UK vocalist, composer, pianist
Born Reginald Kenneth Dwight, Pinner,
Middlesex, March 25, 1947

Career: Took piano lessons at early age. After leaving school in 1964, combined day job as messenger for music publisher with evening gig playing piano in pub. Following year joined local band Bluesology, which specialized in providing backing for visiting US soul stars like Bill Stewart, Patti LaBelle and Major Lance. Band eventually became permanent backing outfit for Long John Baldry; this situation lasted until Baldry achieved pop stardom (albeit fleetingly) with **Let The Heartaches Begin** in late 1967.

By now John was collaborating as songwriter with lyricist Bernie Taupin, both having answered advertisement for talent placed by Liberty Records. Although Liberty lost interest, pair were signed by music publisher Dick James. After two years of attempting to write MOR material for other artists, John and Taupin concentrated on songs suitable for John's own voice. First single, **Lady Samantha**, was released in 1969 by Phillips.

Although it failed to chart, single created enough interest to boost first album, **Empty Sky**. Produced by DJM staffer Steve Brown on four-track machine, this in turn furthered John's growing reputation. But real breakthrough came with **Elton John**, more elaborately produced by Gus Dudgeon and featuring sensitive **Your Song**. Released as single, this became smash in both the UK and US.

A few months later, **Tumbleweed Connection** was released to almost universal acclaim. Atmospheric, evocative, filled with images of old American West, album made UK Top 20 and was soon joined in chart by earlier **Elton John**.

Below: A relatively restrained Elton John, a genuine rock mega-star.

In meantime, John had formed Elton Band with bass player Dee Murray and drummer Nigel Olsson. Outfit played Troubadour Club in Los Angeles to ecstatic audiences in August 1970; around same time **Elton John** and **Tumbleweed Connection** made US charts, and Elton John had made first steps towards huge American success.

Live album **17-10-70**, and **Friends**, soundtrack for obscure movie, were next two issues, but **Madman Across The Water**, released in October 1971, was regarded as next 'official' release. Top 10 album on both sides of Atlantic, it initiated period lasting until 1976, during which artist could virtually do no wrong. John became one of world's most famous and highest-paid solo rock performers, breaking records for sales and live performance audiences. Singles and albums met with equal success. He established reputation for elaborate stage shows and over-the-top costumes, becoming in many ways the 'Liberace' of rock.

During 1973 John set up own record company Rocket Records (although artist himself did not start releasing product on label until 1976 when contract with DJM ran out). When Elton asked Lennon for permission to record 1974 cover hit **Lucy In The Sky With Diamonds**, Lennon agreed to appear on stage with Elton if it reached No. 1; when it did Lennon joined Elton in NYC concert — this proved to be Lennon's last public performance.

In 1975 Elton participated in Ken Russell's movie *Tommy* as Pinball Wizard and in 1976 topped UK singles chart for first time, via duet with Rocket artist Kiki Dee, **Don't Go Breaking My Heart**.

Elton reached a peak in mid-70s; by the end of the decade began to keep a lower profile. In 1977, after years of punishing schedules and massive stage shows, played series of concerts accompanied only by percussionist Ray Cooper, an exercise he repeated in 1979 for tour of USSR.

In 1978 partnership with Bernie Taupin terminated, and John began new collaboration with lyricist Gary Osborne. Although

Above: Elton John ponders the value of his old albums.

many critics predicted that departure of Taupin would have significant effect on John's career, in fact he continued to turn out hits, albeit less spectacularly. 1982 saw Top 20 album in UK and US with **Jump Up**, as well as a handful of hit singles and reunion with Taupin.

His earlier visit to Russia inspired 1985 hit single **Nikita** and his music continued to develop, so too did his bank balance, thoughts of which led to huge court case against the late Dick James which ended in split decision. This enabled John and Taupin to regain control of their songs and squeeze some extra money but did not produce the asked-for damages.

An honest and open personality, Elton is soft target for tabloid press, who had a field

Below: Sleeping With The Past, Elton John. Courtesy Rocket Records.

day with short-lived marriage (to Renata Blauel in 1984), 'rent-boy' (gay prostitution) scandal in 1988, when John was subsequently awarded million-pound damages by *Sun* newspaper, and his on-off-on-again affair with Watford Football Club. His receding hairline, increased waistline and career-threatening throat surgery (1987) were also considered fair game for the press. However, his personal standing (into the 90s) has never been higher.

Elton enjoyed first solo UK chart-topper with **Sacrifice** in 1990, and was awarded BRIT as Best Male Artist in 1991 — same year which saw chart-topping duet with George Michael on **Don't Let The Sun Go Down On Me** 'live' single.

Hit Singles:	US	UK
Your Song, 1970	8	7
Rocket Man, 1972	6	2
Honky Cat, 1972	8	31
Crocodile Rock, 1972	1	5
Daniel, 1973	2	4

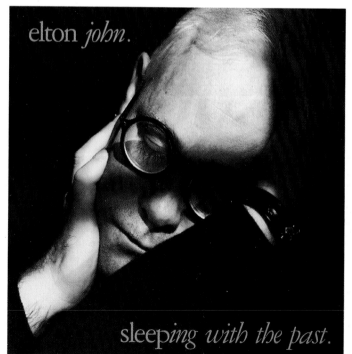

elton *john.*

sleep*ing with the past.*

Above: Captain Fantastic, survivor of the tabloid press and various hair treatments and transplants.

Right: Resplendent in silly hat (one of two million in collection), 'our Elt' belts out another classic.

Saturday Night's Alright For Fighting, 1973	12	7
Goodbye Yellow Brick Road, 1973	2	6
Candle In The Wind, 1974	–	11
Bennie And The Jets, 1974	1	37
Don't Let The Sun Go Down On Me, 1974	2	16
The Bitch Is Back, 1974	4	15
Lucy In The Sky With Diamonds, 1974	1	10
Philadelphia Freedom, 1975	1	12
Someone Saved My Life Tonight, 1975	4	22
Island Girl, 1975	1	14
Grow Some Funk Of Your Own/ I Feel Like A Bullet (In The Gun Of Robert Ford), 1976	14	–
I Feel Like A Bullet (In The Gun Of Robert Ford)/Grow Some Funk Of Your Own, 1976	18	–
Pinball Wizard, 1976	–	7
Sorry Seems To Be The Hardest Word, 1976	6	11
Part Time Love, 1978	22	15
Song For Guy, 1978	–	4
Mama Can't Buy You Love, 1979	9	–
Little Jeannie, 1980	3	33
Empty Garden, 1982	13	51
Blue Eyes, 1982	12	8
I Guess That's Why They Call It The Blues, 1983	4	5
I'm Still Standing, 1983	–	12
Kiss The Bride, 1983	25	20
Sad Songs (Say So Much), 1984	5	7
Passengers, 1984	–	5
Who Wears These Shoes, 1984	16	–
Nikita, 1985	–	3
Wrap Her Up, 1985	19	23
Candle In The Wind, 1988	–	5
I Don't Wanna Go On With You Like That, 1988	2	30
A Word In Spanish, 1988	19	–
Sacrifice/Healing Hands, 1990	13	1

Right: A new hat change for Elton John (this time a Homburg) as he smiles for the camera.

With Kiki Dee:

Don't Go Breaking My Heart, 1976	1	1

With Aretha Franklin:

Through The Storm, 1989	16	41

With George Michael:

Don't Let The Sun Go Down On Me, 1991	–	1

Albums:

Empty Sky (MCA/DJM), 1969
Elton John (MCA/DJM), 1970
Tumbleweed Connection (MCA/DJM), 1970
17-11-70 (MCA/DJM), 1971
Madman Across The Water (MCA/DJM), 1971
Honky Chateau (MCA/DJM), 1972
Don't Shoot Me, I'm Only the Piano Player (MCA/DJM), 1973
Goodbye Yellow Brick Road (MCA/DJM), 1973
Caribou (MCA/DJM), 1974
Captain Fantastic And The Brown Dirt Cowboy (MCA/DJM), 1974
Rock Of The Westies (MCA/DJM), 1975
Here And There (MCA/DJM), 1976
Blue Moves (MCA/Rocket), 1976
Greatest Hits (MCA/DJM), 1977
Single Man (MCA/Rocket) 1978
Greatest Hits Volume 2 (MCA/DJM), 1979
Victim Of Love (Rocket), 1979
Live Collection (–/Pickwick), 1979
21 at 33 (Rocket), 1980
Very Best Of (–/K-Tel), 1980
The Fox (Geffen/Rocket), 1981
Jump Up (Geffen/Rocket), 1982
Love Songs (–/TV), 1982
Too Low For Zero (MCA/Rocket), 1983
Superior (Rocket), 1983
Superior Sound Of Elton John (DJM), 1984
Breaking Hearts (MCA/Rocket), 1984
Ice On Fire (Rocket), 1985
Leather Jackets (Rocket), 1986
Live In Australia (Rocket), 1987
Reg Strikes Back (MCA/Rocket), 1988
Sleeping With The Past (MCA/Rocket), 1989
The Thom Bell Sessions (MCA/–), 1989
To Be Continued (CD set), MCA/–), 1990

Grace Jones

West Indian vocalist, composer
Born Jamaica, May 17, 1952

Career: Epitomizing new genre of assertive sexually dominant women, Grace Jones embodies the bi-sexual, unisex concept.

Raised in Syracuse, New York, from age 12. Studied acting before becoming model for prestigious Manhattan agency and appearing in movie *Gordon's War*. Followed twin brother to Paris and became top model, appearing on covers of *Vogue, Elle* and *Der Stern*. Earned worldwide assignments before turning to singing with a French label.

Switching to Island Records, Grace capitalized on disco boom. Became darling of New York's jet set and first artist to perform live at Studio 54.

Bizarre conceptual stage act, with undertones of sado-masochistic fantasy, masterminded by French artist Jean-Paul Goude, outrageous outfits (though best known for sleek men's trousers and suit jacket look) and decadent sensuality made her cult figure. Records became increasingly more commercially successful. Her recordings, which incorporate semi-reggae rhythms, feature vocals often half-spoken or whispered, are provocative. In UK her infamous appearance on Russell Harty's TV show, when she attacked her interviewer, brought her nation-wide notoriety.

Jones' masterly theatrics have more than compensated for limited singing voice, although **Inside Story** LP (1989), produced by Nile Rodgers, suggested maturity. Her menacing image has been seen to good effect in movies *Conan The Destroyer, A View To A Kill* and *Vamp*.

Below: Fresh from Madam Tussaud's wax museum, the menacing West Indian pop diva and actress Grace Jones sizes up a likely victim.

Above: The Inside Story, Grace Jones. Courtesy Island Records.

Hit Singles:

	US	UK
Private Life, 1980	—	17
Slave To The Rhythm, 1985	—	12
Pull Up To The Bumper, 1986	—	12
Love Is The Drug, 1986	—	35

Albums:
Portfolio (Island), 1977
Fame (Island), 1978
Warm Leatherette (Island), 1980
Nightclubbin' (Island), 1981
Living My Life (Island), 1982
Slave To The Rhythm (Island), 1985
Island Life (Island), 1985
The Inside Story (EMI), 1989
Bullet Proof Heart (Capitol), 1989

Howard Jones

UK vocalist
Born Southampton, February 23, 1955

Career: Jones was 28 before signing first recording contract but in following year had five hit singles and topped UK charts with debut album **Human's Lib**.

Above: Southampton-born Howard Jones, who came to prominence with excellent 1983 hits New Song and What Is Love. Currently missing in action.

Previously employed as fruit and veg salesman, Jones gigged around pubs in native High Wycombe, using borrowed synthesizer, before compensation money from wife's injuries in a car smash enabled him to invest in proper equipment and take up music full-time.

Jones' single, danceable but not quite disco, thought-provoking without being pretentious, brought a raft of US and UK hits throughout 80s, of which **Things Can Only Get Better** made both US and UK Top 10. However, following 1986 album **One To One** (produced by Atlantic label veteran Arif Mardin), Jones retreated from studios to promote his vegetarian lifestyle, but he periodically re-emerged to feature in the occasional charity concert.

In April 1989, Jones cut **Across That Line** LP, from which **Everlasting Love** single made US Top 20. His technical expertise, reflecting early classical training, should ensure continued output, but his commitment is questionable.

Hit Singles:

	US	UK
New Song, 1983	27	3
What Is Love, 1983	33	2
Hide And Seek, 1984	—	12
Pearl In Shell, 1984	—	7
Like To Get To Know You Well, 1984	—	4
Things Can Only Get Better, 1985	5	6
Look Mama, 1985	—	10
Life In One Day, 1985	19	14
All I Want, 1986	—	35
No One Is To Blame, 1986	—	16
You Know I Love You, 1987	8	—
Everlasting Love, 1989	12	—

Albums:
Human's Lib (WEA), 1984
The 12'' Album (WEA), 1984
Dream Into Action (WEA), 1985
One To One (WEA), 1986
Across That Line (Elektra), 1989

Quincy Jones

US conductor, composer, arranger, producer
Born Chicago, 1934

Career: When Ray Charles moved to Seattle in 1948 at age 16 he was befriended by local resident Quincy Jones. Jones was destined to play major role in the emergent soul star's future career but their paths diverged for a while as Jones chose to enrol in Berkley School of Music in Boston rather than go out with Charles on black club-touring circuit.

Regular visits to New York furthered Jones' enthusiasm for jazz. Before graduation he landed job as trumpeter with the Lionel Hampton Big Band, which took him around world. Following visit to France he decided to settle in Paris to further his studies in writing and arranging, working under teacher Nadia Boulanger, who also counted classical genius Stravinsky among her pupils.

Jones worked for Discques Barclay and won numerous European awards for work as composer, arranger and conductor during six-year sojourn in Paris. Attempts to run 18-piece big band, however, brought him close to bankruptcy in 1961. On his return to US, Mercury Records employed him as musical director, and he became first black to hold job as Mercury's vice president in charge of A&R.

Lesley Gore's **It's My Party** in May 1963 gave Jones his first pop chart-topper as producer; his own album **Big Band Bossa Nova** charted at same time. Further success at Mercury came with productions for Brook Benton, Billy Eckstine, Sarah Vaughan and others, as well as run of own albums. Jones also undertook freelance work for such artists as Frank Sinatra, Johnny Mathis, Tony Bennett and Ray Charles (including his **Genius + Soul = Jazz** album, an R&B masterpiece).

The mid-60s found Jones branching successfully into sphere of movie score writing, which was to take up most of his time for some seven years. Starting with music for *The Pawnbroker* work included

Bob And Carol And Ted And Alice, *The Anderson Tapes*, *Cactus Flower*, *In the Heat Of The Night* (a particularly inventive effort which featured elements of country, pop, soul, jazz and electronic free-form, again working with Ray Charles), *They Call Me Mr Tibbs*, *Mirage*, *Walk, Don't Run*, *Dollars* and *The New Centurions*. Also scored television series *Ironside*, *I Spy* and *Roots* (1977).

Moving back into popular music mainstream in 1969, Jones signed recording deal with A&M and began series of jazz-funk albums. Charted for first time since 1962 with **Walking In Space** LP, which won Grammy Award.

In early 70s, Jones was largely responsible for creating jazz-funk explosion, producing artists like fellow A&M act The Brothers Johnson and Chaka Khan-led group, Rufus.

But it was in the 80s that Jones came to the fore, courtesy Michael Jackson and the trio of Jones-produced albums **Off The Wall**, **Thriller** and **Bad**. Reputation as rock and soul's premier backroom boy was also consolidated by organization and production of African aid single **We Are The World** in 1985 and work with George Benson and Donna Summer. Worked with Stephen Speilberg on acclaimed *The Colour Purple* movie for which he co-opted his pal Oprah Winfrey.

Formed own Qwest label in 1982, which saw outstanding work from gospel family The Winans, and Keith Washington, and later inaugurated Quincy Jones Entertainment Company to produce television shows. Cut **Back On The Block** set in 1989, which topped three million sales.

In 1991, Jones was subject of full-length feature documentary *Listen Up! The Many Lives Of Quincy Jones*, shot during the making of his 1989 multi-million-selling **Back On The Block** album.

Hit Singles:

	US	UK
Ai No Corrida, 1981	—	14
Razzamatazz, 1981	—	11
Just Once (featuring James Ingram), 1981	17	—
One Hundred Ways (featuring James Ingram), 1981	14	—

Albums:
Smackwater Jack (A&M), 1974
Mellow Madness (A&M), 1975
I Heard That! (A&M), 1976
Quintessential Charts (Impulse/—), 1976
Sounds...And Stuff Like That (A&M), 1978
Body Heat (A&M), 1979
Great Wide World Of (Emarcy USA), 1981
The Dude (A&M), 1981
The Best (A&M), 1982
Birth Of A Band (Emercy), 1984
The Quintessence (MCA), 1985
Back On The Block (Qwest), 1989

Rickie Lee Jones
US vocalist, guitarist, composer
Born Chicago, November 8, 1954

Career: Ethereal jazz-styled troubadour who failed to fully capitalize on stylish self-titled debut album. Fitful career appears to be the stuff movies are made of.

Raised in Phoenix, Arizona, Jones suffered a troubled education before moving to Los Angeles in 1973. Waitressing jobs subsidized occasional club dates, which were beginning to secure a growing reputation. Signed with Nick Mathe after recommendation from Tom Waits.

Jones signed with Warner Bros in 1978 after successful 'audition' at Troubadour Club, where the company's executives were poised, contract in collective hand.

Single **Chuck E's In Love** from premier LP made both US and UK charts, and Jones embarked on US tour, receiving plaudits for her well-structured material and easy delivery. Received Grammy award as Best New Artist in 1979.

Second album, **Pirates**, took two years to deliver, during which time her delivery had become less fashionable. Difficult personal period saw artist move to the East Coast, then to Paris, and then disappear from music world altogether.

Jones' return with **Girl At Her Volcano** LP (1983) received scant attention, while 1984 set **The Magazine** ensured she remain only a favourite of the few. Successful 1985 UK tour preceded further enforced hiatus, when artist became pregnant, although found time to record **Flying Cowboys** set, produced by ex-Steely Dan bassist Walter Becker.

Jones' partial resurrection was completed when **Makin' Whoopee** cut from **Cowboys** album earned Grammy in February 1990, and summer tour that year with Lyle Lovett raised public profile.

Hit Singles:

	US	UK
Chuck E's In Love, 1979	4	18

Albums:
Rickie Lee Jones (Warner Bros/WEA), 1979
Pirates (Warner Bros/WEA), 1981
Girl At Her Volcano (Warner Bros), 1983
The Magazine (Warner Bros), 1984
Flying Cowboys (Geffen), 1989
Pop Pop (Geffen), 1991

Janis Joplin
US vocalist
Born Port Arthur, Texas, January 19, 1943
Died Los Angeles, October 4, 1970

Career: An early fan of old Bessie Smith and Leadbelly blues records, Joplin started out in early 60s singing country and blues

Above: The tragic figure of Janis Joplin, whose excesses proved fatal.

with bluegrass band in Texas. In 1966 she settled in hippy mecca of San Francisco and became lead vocalist of Big Brother And The Holding Company which featured: James Gurley, guitar; Sam Andrew, guitar; Pete Albin, bass; and David Getz, drums.

Raucous, ill-disciplined, and, in some areas, musically inept, band nonetheless had rare brand of raw energy which showcased Janis to good effect, especially on her classic reading of Erma Franklin's soul opus **Piece Of My Heart**. This set, from the 1968 Columbia album **Cheap Thrills**, confirmed the promise shown on the band's earlier LP for Mainstream (which Columbia re-released in 1970). **Cheap Thrills** sold more than a million copies and the management talents of Albert Grossman made them Stateside superstars, though neither band nor Janis ever made it big in UK.

Janis Joplin's stature rapidly outgrew that of Big Brother (but band carried on for several years, Nick 'The Greek' Gravenites joining as vocalist in 1972) and in 1969 she went solo, earning immediate plaudits for **I Got Dem Ol' Kozmic Blues Again** set.

Her career was meteoric in its rapid rise, heights of adulation, and tragic fall. Seemingly trying to live up to her image, she became increasingly outrageous, drinking heavily, indulging in drug abuse and, in March 1970, being fined for using profane language on-stage. Seven months later she was found dead in a Hollywood hotel room of a heroin overdose. The album she had been working on with new backing outfit, the Full Tilt Boogie Band (comprising: Richard Bell, piano; Ken Pearson, organ; John Till, guitar; Brad Campbell, bass; and Clark Pierson, drums), was issued under title **Pearl** (Janis's nickname) and included her memorable interpretation of Kris Kristofferson's **Me And Bobby McGee** which featured her vocals at their most spine-tinglingly soulful and became posthumous US No. 1.

Right: Steve Perry, Journey's charismatic lead vocalist who was added to the line-up in 1977.

The 11-track album included two tracks for which she had not yet recorded vocals. Nick Gravenites was invited to sing them but declined so they appeared as instrumentals.

On her death, an immediate legend was created. A documentary titled *Janis* was released in 1974, along with double-album soundtrack and biographies *Buried Alive* by Myra Friedman and *Going Down With Janis* by Peggy Caserta were widely read. Her tumultuous career and lonely private life were the inspiration for the film, *The Rose*, starring Bette Midler as Joplin. Both a product and a victim of the drug culture, Janis remains female personification of psychedelic/acid, rock/hippie era.

Hit Singles:

	US	UK
Me And Bobby McGee, 1971	1	—

With Big Brother And The Holding Company:

	US	UK
Piece Of My Heart, 1968	12	—

Albums:
Cheap Thrills (originally released as by Big Brother And The Holding Company) (Columbia/CBS), 1968
I Got Dem Ol' Kozmic Blues Again (Columbia/CBS), 1969
Pearl (Columbia/CBS), 1971
In Concert (Columbia/CBS), 1972
Janis (Columbia/CBS), 1974
Anthology (Columbia/CBS), 1982
Farewell Song (Columbia/CBS), 1982
Janis Joplin In Concert (CBS), 1987

Journey
US group formed 1973

Original line-up: Gregg Rolie, vocals, keyboards, guitar; Neal Schon, guitar; George Tickner, guitar; Ross Valory, bass; Aynsley Dunbar, drums.

Career: Rolie and Schon were together in Santana when jazz influence created musical conflict of interest. They ran across Walter 'Herbie' Herbert who was attempting to assemble supergroup to play San Francisco area. Valory had played with Steve Miller and Dunbar with nearly every rock band with a drum kit — John Mayall, Jeff Beck, and Zappa, among others. Tickner was excellent session man.

For first gig, Journey played San Francisco's Winterland on last day of 1973. Interest from Columbia Records followed extensive touring, and first LP, **Journey**, appeared in spring 1975. Lack of response was discouraging and Tickner and Valory left band. Valory soon returned, however, and band continued year-round touring.

Next two albums (**Look Into The Future** and **Next**) were released in 1975 and 1976 with little notice. Manager Herbert suggested addition of lead vocalist Steve Perry, leaving Rolie free to fill out band's sound. **Infinity** can be considered Journey's first real album with powerful vocals and synthesizer riffs. Perry also earned band US Top 20 hit, **Lovin' Touchin' Squeezin'**.

Live shows shifted from interminable solos to tight format. Such restraint never fitted Dunbar's style and he quit. Steve Smith (who had played with Ronnie Montrose, who opened **Infinity** tour) took Dunbar's place. Subsequent albums increased band's popularity, although not with critics, who dismissed Journey as 'commercial'.

Renewed interest in band's history resulted in compilation LP, **In The Beginning**. **Captured** is strong live set and **Escape** introduced keyboard player Johnathan Cain. He is also songwriter, and co-wrote hit single **Who's Crying Now**.

Escape achieved multi-platinum status, and, with band's reputation secure, Schon ventured into extra-curricular projects, most notably with Jan Hammer and Sammy Hagar. Vocalist Perry also took time out, scoring with Kenny Loggins on **Don't Fight It** single and solo LP **Street Talk**, from which **Oh Sherrie** cut made No. 3 in US.

Band re-grouped for **Only The Young** album in 1985, but **Raised On The Radio Set** in 1986 featured only Schon, Perry and Cain on the credits. Although album spawned four chart singles, including **I'll Be Alright Without You** in 1987, Journey's career stuttered, and, with Perry actively focusing on solo pursuits, group's future was put on permanent hold.

Hit Singles:

	US	UK
Lovin' Touchin' Squeezin', 1979	16	—
Who's Crying Now, 1981	4	—
Don't Stop Believin', 1981	9	—
Open Arms, 1982	2	—
Still They Ride, 1982	14	—
Separate Ways' (Worlds Apart), 1983	8	—
Faithfully, 1983	12	—
Only The Young, 1985	9	—
I'll Be Alright Without You, 1987	11	—
Girl Can't Help It	11	—

Steve Perry with Kenny Loggins:

Don't Fight It, 1982	17	—

Steve Perry Solo:

Oh Sherrie, 1984	3	—
Foolish Heart, 1985	18	—

Albums:
Journey (Columbia/CBS), 1975
Look Into The Future (Columbia/CBS), 1975
Next (Columbia/CBS), 1976
Infinity (Columbia/CBS), 1978
Evolution (CBS), 1979
In The Beginning (Columbia/CBS), 1979
Departure (Columbia/CBS), 1980
Captured (CBS), 1980
Escape (CBS), 1981
Frontiers (Columbia/CBS), 1983
Raised On The Radio (CBS), 1986
Greatest Hits/Best Of (Columbia), 1989

Steve Perry Solo:
Street Talk (CBS), 1984

Joy Division/New Order

UK group formed 1977

Original line-up: Ian Curtis, vocals; Bernard Albrecht (né Dicken), guitar; Stephen Morris, drums; Peter Hook, bass.

Career: In 1977 Curtis, Albrecht and Morris came together and called themselves Warsaw. Early career consisted of nondescript playing throughout Manchester. They changed name to Joy Division, though there was never anything joyful about their sound, Curtis's flat voice being backed by depressing dirge-like instrumentals. Indications of things to come appear on live 10-inch compilation album **Short Circuit**. (**At A Later Date** is track by band while still Warsaw).

Joy Division released four-track EP **An Ideal For Living** on own label Enigma. (Also released as 12-inch with vast improvements in sound quality on Anonymous Records.) Band's real potential for stark, sheer realism appeared first on new Factory label. **A Factory Sample** was EP to show off label's new talent. Two Joy Division tracks **Glass** and **Digital** were EP's high point.

National interest stirred by Martin Hannett-produced **Unknown Pleasures**, a bleak, troublesome, yet powerful debut album. Two out-takes given to Fast Records (Edinburgh) were released on **Earcom Two** compilation. Another two releases, **Atmosphere** and **Dead Souls**, appeared in 1,000 copy editions on the small French Sordid Sentimentale label.

Joy Division's 1979 UK tour with Buzzcocks earned ecstatic response from critics and audience alike but the suicide of Curtis (in May 1980) curtailed planned US tour. Single **Love Will Tear Us Apart** and second album appeared after his death. Another out-take, **Komankino/Incubation**, appeared for awhile as free flexi-disc from Factory. Excellent **Still** release (1981) included live/studio material, covering the band's entire career.

Joy Division had agreed to 'kill' the name should any member leave the group, and remaining line-up thus became New Order.

By early 80s ethos of band had begun to change, with more dance-orientated sound coming to fore. New appeal was reflected in success of Top 30 UK entry **Temptation**. Further commercial progress was made in 1983 when band scored with **Blue Monday**, single which went on to sell more than a million worldwide.

Signed to Quincy Jones' Qwest label in the States, New Order debuted with **The Perfect Kiss** in 1984, although had to wait a further three years before US chart success with **True Faith** single.

Having moved from constraints as 'dance band', New Order developed cult status with **Low Life** LP, and double set **Substance**, a compilation of re-mixed singles. **Technique** album (1989) saw band debut at No. 1 in UK charts. Now well into the party spirit, band conspired with English soccer team to score with UK No. 1 single **World In Motion** (1990), a clever rap/dance mix released to coincide with World Cup finals. Although happy to indulge in solo projects — Hook formed Revenge for one-off album **One True Passion** (1989) and Barney Sumner, latter-day member of JD, featured in Electronic with Johnny Marr and Neil Tennant — New Order's collective talent is a thing to wonder at. **Palatine**, Factory Records' retrospective boxed set (December 1991) included band with label mates Happy Mondays and James.

Hit Singles:

	US	UK
Love Will Tear Us Apart, 1980	—	13

As New Order:

Blue Monday, 1983	—	9
Confusion, 1983	—	12
Thieves Like Us, 1984	—	18
World In Motion, 1990	—	1

Albums:
Unknown Pleasures (—/Factory), 1979
Closer (—/Factory), 1980
Still (—/Factory), 1981

As New Order:
Movement (Factory), 1981
Power, Corruption And Lies (Factory), 1983
Low Life (Factory), 1985
Brotherhood (Factory), 1986
Substance (Factory), 1987
Technique (Warner Bros/Factory), 1989

Peter Hook with Revenge:
One True Passion (Capitol), 1989

Worth Searching Out:
An Ideal For Living (12-inch EP) (Anonymous), 1977
The Ideal Beginning (EP; released 1981 as Warsaw), (Enigma)

Judas Priest

UK group formed 1973

Original line-up: Rob Halford, vocals; Ken 'KK' Downing, Gibson Flying 'V' guitar; Ian Hill, bass; John Hinch, drums.

Career: One of Birmingham's local bands, Judas Priest always had extra spark setting them apart from usual heavy-rock treadmill. First album wears quickly but gained enough attention at the time to put group on first rung of ladder.

Initial change in drummers came as Alan Moore replaced Hinch; this line-up released second LP which got UK support but left band unknown in US. Simon Phillips played drums on band's debut CBS album **Sin After Sin**. Band spent 1978 in frenzied counter-attack on growing influence of new wave. **Stained Glass**, then **Killing Machine**, sounded the bombardment (Les Binks was now on drums).

Critics tended to dismiss band as outdated, but younger audience began picking up on TNWOBHM (The New Wave Of British Heavy Metal). This became apparent with single success of **Take On The World** in January 1979. Live recording from Japanese tour, **Unleashed In The East**, was 1979 LP and indicated band was rethinking direction. **British Steel** proved this to be true by providing balance of melody and vocal ballistics (with yet another new drummer, Dave Holland). Critics realized band was serious, and sales finally improved in US. Appropriately titled album **Screaming For Vengeance** dispelled any doubt regarding band's commitment to heavy metal. It also became band's first platinum success in US which led to release of **Rocka Rolla**, nine years after UK release.

In May 1988 Judas Priest released their 11th studio album **Ram It Down** recorded at Puk Studios in Denmark, marking a determined effort to return to roots. A new version of Chuck Berry's **Johnny B. Goode** was also released on Atlantic as part of a soundtrack for movie of same name.

1988 saw band cause a stir by recording Stock, Aitken and Waterman songs at a session in Paris, but Halford explained it was done as an experiment, 'to see what would happen'. But none of the songs made it on the album.

Below: UK group Judas Priest hits audiences with heavy metal energy.

Aware of the need to experiment, and to challenge audience, Judas Priest have proven long-lasting talent. Even accusations in US law courts that band included 'satanic messages' on their albums (later thrown out of court) failed to halt their single-minded approach. For new decade, band released **Painkiller** set and embarked on mega US and UK tours, featuring their new drummer Scott Travis.

Hit Singles:

	US	UK
Take On The World, 1979	—	14
Living After Midnight, 1980	—	12
Breaking The Law, 1980	—	12

Albums:
Rocka Rolla (—/Gull), 1974
Sad Wings Of Destiny (Janus/Gull), 1976
Sin After Sin (Columbia/CBS), 1977
Best Of (Gull), 1978
Stained Glass (Columbia/CBS), 1978
Killing Machine (Columbia/CBS), 1978
Unleashed In The East (Columbia/CBS), 1979
Hell Bent For Leather* (Columbia/CBS), 1979
British Steel (Columbia/CBS), 1980
Point Of Entry (Columbia/CBS), 1981
Screaming For Vengeance (Columbia/CBS), 1982
Defenders Of The Faith (CBS), 1984
Turbo (CBS), 1986
Priest Live (CBS), 1987
Ram It Down (Columbia/CBS), 1988
Painkiller (Columbia/CBS), 1990
*US version of Killing Machine with extra track

Chaka Khan

US vocalist
Born Chicago, March 23, 1953

Career: Consistently successful in field of black music, notably with 1978 mega-hits **I'm Every Woman** and **We Got The Love** (the latter a duet with guitarist/singer George Benson), Chaka Khan started out fronting multi-racial band which played mixture of soul, rock and pop.

Under name Rufus, band won major recording deal and made heavy impact as much for electric stage presence as for atmospherically classy, funk-slanted records like **Tell Me Something Good**, **You Got The Love** and **Once You Get Started**, which kept them in the US charts from 1972-77.

With her often bizarre stage outfits, belting vocals and stage charisma, the petite and curvaceous Chaka became focal point of Rufus and in 1978 group's then label, Warner Bros, offered her solo deal under production aegis of talented Turkish emigré Arif Mardin.

A succession of acclaimed albums and singles, and her participation in Lenny White's ambitious 1982 project **Echoes Of An Era** which recreated 50s jazz classics using contemporary artists, has kept Khan in musical forefront. She has also worked with Rick Wakeman, Ry Cooder and jazz legend Dizzy Gillespie on different projects, while her 1983 world tour took her to Carnegie Hall and similar prestigious venues.

Her 1984 US No. 3 **I Feel For You** (taken from early Prince album), which earned Grammy, should have established artist in upper stratosphere of soul performers, but severe throat problem and idiosyncratic approach saw career subsequently falter.

Khan featured on Robert Palmer's funky **Addicted To Love** (1986), duetted with David Bowie on **Underground** track from *Labyrinth* movie and provided backing vocals for Steve Winwood's classic **Higher Love**. Although 1987 **Destiny** set (with Mardin still at helm) provided a further UK/US Top 100 entry, subsequent work failed to impress public. Only re-mix of **I'm Every Woman** (1989) and Quincy Jones' **I'll Be Good To You** (1990), with Khan and Ray Charles on vocals, saw significant chart placing for artist, who might be content to follow 'and featuring . . .' on the billboards.

Hit Singles:

	US	UK
I'm Every Woman, 1978	21	11
I Feel For You, 1984	3	1
This Is My Night, 1985	—	14
Eye To Eye, 1985	—	16
I'm Every Woman (re-mix), 1989	—	8
I'll Be Good To You (with Ray Charles), 1990	18	—

With Rufus:

Tell Me Something Good, 1974	3	—
You Got The Love, 1974	11	—
Once You Get Started, 1975	10	—
Sweet Thing, 1976	5	—

Albums:
Chaka (Warner Bros), 1979
Naughty (Warner Bros), 1980
Whatcha' Gonna Do For Me (Warner Bros), 1981
Chaka Khan (Warner Bros/—), 1982
I Feel For You (Warner Bros), 1984
Life Is A Dance (Warner Bros/WEA), 1989

With Rufus:
Rags to Rufus (MCA), 1974
Rufus Featuring Chaka Khan (MCA), 1975

B. B. King

US vocalist, guitarist, composer
Born Itta Bena, Indianola, Mississippi, September 16, 1925

Career: Truly living up to his name, Riley B. 'Blues Boy' King has majestically dominated the blues scene for over 35 years. Astute management and an ear for the modern has maintained enthusiastic concert crowds and undiminished reverence.

King has matched talents with finest of musicians, from black American greats The Crusaders to rock stars like Leon Russell, Carole King, Ringo Starr and Nicky Hopkins. He has recorded hits in a hotel room, in a garage, and in the world's foremost studios. His material has ranged from pure blues (both urban and rural), to country songs (his cousin is country blues legend Bukka White), rock numbers, pop songs and even Broadway material, though in every case transferred to the blues idiom.

His emergent style was heavily influenced by both T. Bone Walker and the jazz of Charlie Christian. Joining radio WGRM in Greenwood, Mississippi, in late 50s, he was spotted by Sonny Boy Williamson (Rice Miller) who took him to the far more important Memphis station WDIA. King became resident DJ and was dubbed 'The Beale Street Blues Boy', later shortened to 'B.B.', by station manager Don Kearn.

King's recording debut came with **Miss Martha King** (1949). Then talent scout Ike Turner signed him to Modern Records' RPM subsidiary where he enjoyed 11-year stint, soaring to No. 1 on R&B charts in 1950 with **Three O'Clock Blues** which featured Turner on piano, Hank Crawford on saxophone and Willie Mitchell on trumpet.

Quickly becoming most in-demand artist on blues circuit, King quit WDIA. (His show was taken over by Rufus Thomas who went on to fame as a soul singer.)

King's flashy guitar lines with their torrent of notes were matched to the response of his highly emotive vocals, a mix of falsetto wailing and rich gospel-flavoured tenor. Despite a couple of quirks (he can neither play particularly good rhythm nor sing while playing) King has clearly been maestro of his chosen music, influencing countless other players, notably Buddy Guy, Otis Rush and Eric Clapton.

In 1961 he switched to major ABC Paramount label who sought to broaden his appeal with a more sophisticated flavour.

Commanding an increasingly broad-based audience throughout 70s, his concerts drawing both black and white, young and old,

Above: Blues legend B.B. King pictured with his pride and joy 'Lucille'.

King's recorded output became somewhat inconsistent. Often ill-matched with material and musicians as he tried to please wider following by diversity of music, at times he seemed in danger of sinking into MOR mire. Duets with Bobby Bland — an old friend adding a more sophisticated flavour to his music through lush arrangements by Johnny Pate (The Impressions' producer) and Quincy Jones (who was concurrently working with Charles), and even adding string sections on several recordings.

In 1969, strings were used in stunning fashion for epic smash **The Thrill Is Gone**, and the **Completely Well** album, which included single, was arguably his best ever.

In 1985, he figured heavily on soundtrack of movie *Into The Night* and celebrated 50th album (there have actually been many more if compilations and re-workings of old material are included).

King's continually majestic stage performances now tend to surpass his recorded work and he remains king among the blues' Kings (neither Albert King nor the late Freddie King managed to reach his heights despite their undoubted class). In 1987, King was deservedly awarded a Lifetime Grammy for achievements in music.

Hit Singles:

	US	UK
The Thrill Is Gone, 1970	15	—
When Love Comes To Town (with U2), 1989	—	6

Albums:
Live At The Regal (MCA/HMV), 1965
His Best: The Electric B. B. King (MCA/ABC), 1969
Live And Well (MCA/ABC), 1970
Completely Well (MCA/ABC), 1970
Live At Cook County Jail (MCA/Probe), 1971
Back In The Alley (MCA/ABC), 1973
The Best Of B. B. King (—/Ace Cadet), 1981
Love Me Tender (MCA), 1982
Alive in London (with the Crusaders) (MCA), 1982
Midnight Believer (MCA), 1984

Spotlight On Lucille (Ace), 1986
The Best Of B.B. King (MCA), 1987
Completely Well (MCA), 1987
One Nighter Blues (Ace), 1987
Rarest B.B. King (Blues Boy), 1987
Across The Tracks (Ace), 1987
King of The Blues (MCA), 1988
Live At San Quentin (MCA), 1990
There's Always One More Time (MCA),
   1991

*With Pat Metheny, Dave Brubeck, Heath
   Bros:*
Live 1987 (Kingdom Jazz), 1987

With Bobby Bland:
Together For The First Time (MCA), 1974
Together Again (MCA), 1976

Worth Searching Out:
Indianola Mississippi (MCA/ABC), 1970

**Above: Live At The Regal, B.B. King.
Courtesy ABC Records.**

Carole King

US composer, vocalist, pianist
Born Carole Klein, Brooklyn, New York,
February 9, 1942

Career: Played piano from age four; smitten by rock 'n' roll in early teens; started hanging out at rock 'n' roll shows. Formed own group in high school. After school, attended Queen's College, where she met aspirant songwriter (later her husband) Gerry Goffin. Personal and musical collaboration followed, resulting in first hit **Will You Still Love Me Tomorrow**; recorded by Shirelles, song made No. 1 in US and No. 3 in UK.

Goffin and King then became part of 'Brill Building' stable of writers under aegis of entrepreneur/publisher Don Kirshner. During this period pair wrote seemingly endless series of classic hits, including **Up On The Roof** and **When My Little Girl Is Smiling** for Drifters, **Take Good Care Of My Baby** for Bobby Vee, **One Fine Day** for Chiffons, **Halfway To Paradise** for Tony Orlando and Billy Fury, **Every Breath I Take** for Gene Pitney, and **The Locomotion** for Little Eva (actually pair's babysitter, Eva Boyd).

Don Kirshner launched King as solo recording artist in 1962 with **It Might As Well Rain Until September**. Despite this international hit, follow-ups were not successful and King was not to make serious attempt to become artist as well as writer until end of decade. Having moved to West Coast, in 1970 King recorded first solo album, **Writer**.

Although not huge success, it paved way for next offering, **Tapestry**, which was to become one of most successful albums ever. Released in 1971, **Tapestry** struck chord with post-psychedelic generation with its

**Right: Carole King acquired fame as a
top-notch singer/songwriter with
Tapestry album.**

emphasis on simple life and values. Spawning clutch of hit singles, it went on to around 13 million sales over course of next decade.

After **Tapestry**, King never quite achieved same heights. Despite recording and working live with varying success, she only had two further major hits as artist (**Jazzman** in 1974, **Nightingale** in 1975). She cut **City Streets** LP in 1989, her first studio album for several years, and was inducted (with Gerry Goffin) into Rock 'n' Roll Hall Of Fame.

Tapestry and equally valid body of work from early 60s ensure continued veneration among fans of good pop songs. Not one of the great singers, King is nevertheless convincing interpreter of own material.

Hit Singles:	US	UK
It Might As Well Rain Until		
September, 1962	22	3
It's Too Late, 1971	1	6
So Far Away, 1971	14	—
Sweet Seasons, 1972	9	—
Jazzman, 1974	2	—
Nightingale, 1975	9	—
One Fine Day, 1980	12	—

Albums:
Writer (Ode), 1970
Tapestry (Ode), 1972
Music (Ode), 1972
Rhymes And Reasons (Ode), 1972
Fantasy (Ode), 1973
Wrap Around Joy (Ode), 1974
Thoroughbred (Ode), 1976
Simple Things (Capitol), 1977
Welcome Home (Capitol), 1978
Greatest Hits (Ode), 1978
Touch The Sky (Capitol), 1979
Pearls — Songs Of Goffin And King
   (Capitol), 1980
One To One (Atlantic), 1982
Speeding Time (Atlantic), 1983
City Streets (Capitol), 1989

King Crimson

UK group formed 1969

Original line-up: Robert Fripp, guitar, mellotron; Ian McDonald, reeds, keyboards; Greg Lake, bass, vocals; Peter Sinfield, lyricist; Mike Giles, drums.

Career: Evolved from Giles, Giles And Fripp, a pop-influenced trio from Dorset that recorded two singles and one barely noticed album, **The Cheerful Insanity Of Giles Giles And Fripp**. Group split in November 1968, Peter Giles temporarily quitting business; brother Mike and Fripp founded King Crimson. With new members McDonald and Lake (aided by lyricist Sinfield) rehearsals were completed below café in London's Fulham Road. Debut gig at Speakeasy (April 1969) established

small cult following, dramatically increased following appearance at Rolling Stones' celebrated Hyde Park concert in July. First album **In The Court Of The Crimson King** received ecstatic response and established unit as one of most progressive of era. From this point on, group were dogged by series of personnel changes and upheavals.

An 11-day US tour in November/December 1969 took its toll; on return to London both Giles and McDonald quit. While seeking permanent line-up, Fripp employed a number of session men/friends to complete second LP **In The Wake Of Poseidon**. Giles returned as bassist, jazzer Keith Tippett played piano, Mel Collins added saxophone and Gordon Haskell contributed vocals. Sinfield was by this time credited as lyricist, light show operator and synthesizer player. Prior to album's release Fripp had declined invitations to join Yes and Aynsley Dunbar's Blue Whale. Lukewarm response afforded **Poseidon** meant that only Collins and Haskell were retained for third album, aided by drummer Andy McCullough. **Lizard** was noticeable improvement, but following recording sessions Haskell and McCullough quit.

Fripp and Sinfield again restructured group, with Mel Collins, Ian Wallace (drums) and Boz Burrell, a singer whom Fripp taught to play bass. Following release of **Islands**, Sinfield left to reappear as Roxy Music's producer. Less than successful US tour killed off remaining members, leaving live **Earthbound** as final comment.

The ever-eccentric Fripp returned to England and, following period of hibernation, introduced another unit, comprising Bill Bruford (former Yes drummer), bassist John Wetton (ex-Family), percussionist James Muir and David Cross (violin, mellotron). The power and promise of line-up was fully revealed on excellent **Lark's Tongue In Aspic** and vindicated in concert. Unfortunately, Muir quit, leaving four-piece Crimson to record acceptable **Starless And Bible Black**.

In July 1974, Crimson closed tour with concert at New York's Central Park, captured for posterity on second live album, **USA**. In September, Fripp officially announced that Crimson no longer existed. A posthumous album, **Red**, was released in 1974 and saw return of original member Ian McDonald.

Few would disagree that Crimson split at the right time; they would have been in danger of losing credibility had they continued. Unlike their contemporaries, group managed to avoid worst excesses of self-indulgent 70s art rock. Their reputation as one of truly innovative progressive rock groups was aided by Fripp's forays into avant garde and ambient music. Between 1974-80, Fripp worked with number of artists, most notably Eno (collaborated on **No Pussyfooting** and **Evening Star**). Work with Peter Gabriel and David Bowie also attracted great interest, leading to new-found respect.

In 1981, Fripp took unusual step of reforming King Crimson with Adrian Belew (guitar, lead vocal), Robert Fripp (guitar, devices!), Tony Levin (bass, vocals) and Bill Bruford (drums). Album **Discipline** was released in September 1981 amid critical arguments about whether Crimson were an anachronism, a seminal progressive rock band, or both. **Beat**, released following year, was first Crimson studio album to have same personnel on two consecutive releases. Since then, group have laid to rest any misconceptions about a possible 'cash in' on the King Crimson name.

Fripp further developed outside ventures with self-produced albums including **I Advanced Masked** with Andy Summers and production work with Daryl Hall project **Sacred Songs** and two LPs for US band The Roches.

Albums:
In The Court Of The Crimson King
   (Island), 1969
In The Wake Of Poseidon (Island), 1970
Lizard (Island), 1970
Islands (Island), 1971
Earthbound (Island), 1972
Lark's Tongue In Aspic (Island), 1973
Starless And Bible Black (Island), 1974
Red (Island), 1974
USA (Island), 1975
A Young Person's Guide To King Crimson
   (Island), 1976
Discipline (EG/Polydor), 1981
Beat (EG/Polydor), 1982
Three Of A Perfect Pair (Polydor), 1984
The Compact King Crimson (EG), 1986

Robert Fripp Solo:
Exposure (EG), 1987
Let The Power Fall (EG), 1987

Robert Fripp with Brian Eno:
No Pussyfooting (EG), 1973
Evening Star (EG), 1975

*Robert Fripp with League Of
   Crafty Guitarists:*
Live (EG), 1986
Show Of Hands (EG), 1991

Robert Fripp with Andy Summers:
I Advance Masked (A&M), 1982
Bewitched (A&M), 1984

The Kinks

UK group formed 1964

Original line-up: Ray Davies, vocals, guitar; Dave Davies, guitar, vocals; Peter Quaife, bass; Mick Avory, drums.

Career: Dressed in red huntsman's jackets and sporting mod haircuts, The Kinks were launched on British public as an image-heavy beat band. Debut Pye single **Long Tall Sally** was straight copy of Beatles' cover of Little Richard's classic; it bombed, as did follow-up **You Do Something To Me**, which only sold 127 copies. The rough, propulsive **You Really Got Me** was something quite different. Close in form to The Kingsmen's **Louie, Louie**, it had an R&B edge which British audiences were looking for at time and shot to No. 1.

Producer Shel Talmy had found a golden vein and exploited it well over next 18 months with string of charters, mostly written by Ray Davies. From straightforward pop songs, Davies started composing ever more pictorial lyrics, strongly British in inspiration yet with a wide appeal. The humourous **Dedicated**

Follower Of Fashion (taking off 60s fashion fanatics) the atmospheric Waterloo Sunset (which proved songs didn't have to have American locations to be effective), Autumn Almanac and others showed depth of his writing talent, which some rated on par with Lennon/McCartney.

As band began touring less, Ray Davies involved himself in solo projects, including score for The Virgin Soldiers. Brother Dave had solo UK hit (backed by Kinks and issued as Kinks single in US) in 1967 with Death Of A Clown. This was included along with Waterloo Sunset and the funny yet perceptive David Watts on brilliant Something Else By The Kinks album, marking end of group's partnership with Shel Talmy.

With Ray Davies now producing, the Kinks followed Beatles and others into realms of concept albums, notably with The Kinks Are The Village Green Preservation Society and Arthur (Or The Decline And Fall Of The British Empire); latter was originally commissioned as TV soundtrack. By then Peter Quaife had been replaced by John Dalton. In 1970 group returned to singles charts with controversial but

excellent Lola, a song about transvestism and a hit on both sides of Atlantic. Kinks Part 1: Lola Versus Powerman And The Moneygoround had biting lyrics about rampant manipulation in pop music scene. Meanwhile, Ray Davies completed soundtrack of Percy and had main role in television play The Long Distance Piano Player.

Getting out of current management deal and Pye record contract, group pacted with RCA. Opening RCA album, Muswell Hillbillies, introduced John Gosling on keyboards plus brass section from the Mike Cotton Sound. Laurie Brown, Alan Holmes and John Beecham subsequently became regular members of The Kinks. Despite including Alcohol and Skin And Bone, two of the most atypical Kinks' classics, album sold poorly.

Ironically, their following in America was burgeoning. Increasingly theatrical in concept, with strong roots in music-hall traditions, The Kinks' subsequent albums were often somewhat grandiose projects. Sleepwalker (1977) found group switching to Arista Records and album was another in string of Stateside successes.

In 1974 The Kinks had formed own Konk label, signing Claire Hamill. Ray Davies produced her Stage Door Johnnies album, and debut set by Café Society, also on Konk. 1977 label moved to Arista saw departure of John Dalton; Davies then dropped horn-section. Andy Pyle (ex-Savoy Brown) took up bass for a while but left by May 1978. Jim Rodford has filled spot since. John Gosling also left and was replaced on keyboards by Gordon Edwards, then Ian Gibbons. In 1979 group recorded Low Budget, their first venture in an American studio, and the following year issued One For The Road, a live double LP of their best-known material, recorded while on tour in US; a live version of Lola made US Hot 100 in 1980.

By 1983 and Give The People What They Want album, Ray Davies' writing abilities seemed in decline, despite unexpected Come Dancing single hit and later Think Visual and UK Jive LPs. Unable to give up life of the road, band continued gigging; US tour in 1989 featured new drummer Bob Henrit (ex-Argent) and, on keyboard, Mark Haley.

Although The Kinks' finest days are almost certainly behind them, their material is consistently rehashed. Notable covers include The Pretenders' Stop Your Sobbing and I Go To Sleep, while The Fall, Kirsty Mac-Coll, The Jam, David Bowie and Van Halen have all dug into the vaults. And, in 1986, The Stranglers enjoyed chart success with a note-for-note version of All Day And All Of The The Night.

Now inducted into Rock 'n' Roll Hall Of Fame, band deserve honoured place in pantheon of UK rock, not least because of Ray Davies' idiosyncratic songs and entirely 'British' approach.

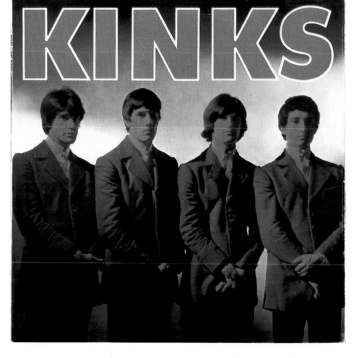

Above: Kinks' first LP in 1964. Courtesy Pye Records.

Below: The Kinks perform for British TV show Ready Steady Go.

Hit Singles:	US	UK
You Really Got Me, 1964	7	1
All Day And All Of The Night, 1964	7	2
Tired Of Waiting For You, 1965	6	1
Everybody's Gonna Be Happy, 1965	–	17
Set Me Free, 1965	23	9
See My Friend, 1965	–	10
A Well Respected Man, 1965	13	–
Till The End Of The Day, 1965	50	8
Dedicated Follower of Fashion, 1966	36	4
Sunny Afternoon, 1966	14	1
Dead End Street, 1966	–	5
Waterloo Sunset, 1967	–	2
Autumn Almanac, 1967	–	3
Days, 1968	–	12
Lola, 1970	9	2
Apeman, 1970	45	5
Supersonic Rocket Ship, 1972	–	16
Come Dancing, 1983	6	12

Dave Davies Solo:
Death Of A Clown, 1967	–	3
Susannah's Still Alive, 1967	–	20

Albums:
The Kinks (–/Hallmark), 1964
You Really Got Me (Reprise/Pye), 1965
Live At The Kelvin Hall (Reprise/Pye), 1967
Something Else By The Kinks (Reprise/Pye), 1967
Village Green Preservation Society (Reprise/Pye), 1968
Arthur (Or The Decline And Fall Of The British Empire) (Reprise/Pye), 1969
Kinks Part 1: Lola Versus Powerman And The Moneygoround (Reprise/Pye), 1970
Lola (–/Hallmark), 1971
Everybody's In Showbiz (RCA), 1972
Kink Kronikles (Reprise/–), 1972
Soap Opera (RCA), 1975
Schoolboys In Disgrace (RCA), 1975
Celluloid Heroes – The Kinks' Greatest (RCA), 1976
The Kinks File (–/Pye), 1977
Sleepwalker (Arista/Fame), 1977
Misfits (Arista), 1978
20 Golden Greats (–/Ronco), 1978
Low Budget (Arista), 1979
Second Time Around (RCA/–), 1979
One For The Road (live double) (Arista), 1980
Collection (–/Pickwick), 1980
Give The People What They Want (Arista), 1982
State Of Confusion (Arista), 1983
Dead End Street, Greatest Hits (PRT), 1983
Word Of Mouth (Arista), 1984
Greatest Hits, 1984
Face To Face, 1986
Kinks Kontroversy, 1986
Percy (soundtrack), 1986
Think Visual, 1986
Well Respected Men (PRT), 1987
Hit Singles (PRT), 1987
UK Jive (MCA/London), 1989

Worth Searching Out:
Kinks-size (Reprise/–), 1965
Kinda Kinks (Reprise/Pye), 1965
Muswell Hillbillies (RCA), 1971
The Great Lost Kinks Album (Reprise/–), 1973
Preservation Act I (RCA), 1973

Kiss

US group formed 1973

Original line-up: Ace Frehley, guitar; Paul Stanley, guitar; Gene Simmons, bass; Peter Criss, drums.

Career: Kiss began by taking Lou Reed/ David Bowie glitter rock and pushing it to extreme. Band obliterated members' past by hiding behind comic-book costumes and greasepaint. With first concerts, Kiss managed to alienate rock press, offend parents and win undying loyalty of New York's younger rock fans.

Albums emphasized gothic, bigger-than-life aspects of rock music. Live shows had massive drum kits rising 40 feet into air and explosives flashing everywhere, while Simmons spat fire (real) and blood (fake) or just rolled out his foot-long tongue. Critics wondered what this had to do with the music while kids made Kiss hottest-selling band of decade.

Japan in particular took to Kiss early on and band showed appreciation by putting Japanese credits on second album in late 1974. **Alive** LP had giant **Rock And Roll All Nite** single and showed band was not all flash. Next LP, **Destroyer**, proved even more of surprise by including excellent ballad, **Beth**. Super hero/hidden identity ploy enhanced by band's refusal to be photographed or interviewed without make-up, finally went over top by actually including comic-book history of band in **The Originals** (special re-issue of first three LPs). Next two album covers, **Rock And Roll Over** (1976) and **Love Gun** (1977), also had colourful comic-style covers instead of usual pictures.

By 1977, Kiss management had organized fans into Kiss Army and provided them with range of Kiss memorabilia and products. Disdain of other bands and managers had suspicion of jealousy. First sign that Kiss fans were possibly outgrowing their heroes came in 1978. Amid much publicity, four solo LPs, one from each member of Kiss, went platinum before day of release. All four began appearing in cut-out tracks shortly after. **Dynasty** (1979) and **Unmasked** (1980) lacked outrageousness of early Kiss. Peter Criss quit, claiming face could no longer cope with make-up; band had first photos taken without it.

Surprisingly, Criss's replacement, Eric Carr, not only filled position well, but band produced excellent **The Elder**. It seemed to be rock-opera soundtrack for non-existent movie. Such a concept would drag down any album in 1981 and **The Elder** flopped. **Creatures Of The Night** returned to old Kiss style; problem was finding audience for it. One puzzling aspect is why this most visual of bands hasn't translated well into video age, though **Creatures Of The Night** video is superb.

Personnel changes marked uncertain period for band. Frehley left, and Vince Cusano took permanent guitar spot. Cusano then quit after world tour, with Mark Norton added. But Norton, who works under stage name Mark St. John, suffered debilitating illness and ex-Blackjack guitarist Bruce Kulick took most temporary guitar job in town.

In mid-80s, band abandoned garish stage make-up, deciding that their musical ability should stand on it's own merits. **Lick It Up** was first 'naked' album, while 1984 set **Animalize** made US and UK Top 10.

Following **Crazy Nights** LP, Kiss embarked upon North American tour (1988) with

Above: Gladys Knight And The Pips before split in 1990 when Knight announced plans for a solo career.

veterans Cheap Trick in support; also visited UK in same year. With Frehley's band Frehley's Comet enjoying US success, Kiss faltered for a couple of years before regaining Top 10 status with **Forever** single (composed by Paul Stanley with Michael Bolton) in 1990.

The band's risky image transplant paid dividends, although latter part of career has faltered. Nonetheless, band has weathered many stylistic storms to attain place near top of commercial league, although death of drummer Eric Carr from cancer in November 1991 clouded future.

Hit Singles:

	US	UK
Rock And Roll All Nite (Live), 1976	12	—
Beth, 1976	7	—
Hard Luck Woman, 1977	15	—
Calling Dr Love, 1977	16	—
I Was Made For Lovin' You, 1979	11	50
Crazy Crazy Nights, 1987	—	9
Reason to Live, 1987	—	33
Forever, 1990	8	—

Ace Frehley Solo:

	US	UK
New York Groove, 1978	13	—

Albums:
Kiss (Casablanca), 1974
Hotter Than Hell (Casablanca), 1974
Dressed To Kill (Casablanca), 1975
Alive (Casablanca), 1975
Rock And Roll Over (Casablanca), 1976
Destroyer (Casablanca), 1977
Love Gun (Casablanca), 1977
Kiss Alive II (Casablanca), 1977
Dynasty (Casablanca), 1979
Unmasked (Casablanca), 1980
The Best Of The Solo Albums (Casablanca), 1981
The Elder (Casablanca), 1981
Killers (compilation) (Casablanca), 1982
Creatures Of The Night (Casablanca), 1982
Lick It Up (Mercury), 1983
Animalize (Vertigo), 1984
Double Platinum (Casablanca), 1985
Asylum (Vertigo), 1985
Crazy Crazy Nights (Vertigo), 1987
Smashes, Thrashes and Hits (Mercury), 1988
Hot In The Shade (Mercury/Fontana), 1989

Frehley's Comet:
Frehley's Comet (Megaforce/WEA), 1987
Second Sighting (Megaforce), 1988
Live Plus One (Megaforce), 1989

Gladys Knight And The Pips

US vocal group formed 1952

Original line-up: Gladys Knight; Merald (Bubba) Knight; Brenda Knight; William Guest; Elenor Guest.

Career: Gladys Knight (born Atlanta, Georgia, May 28, 1944) was child singing prodigy, winning talent contests and performing with gospel groups; sang with Atlanta gospel group the Morris Brown Choir at four, won *Ted Mack Amateur Hour* TV talent competition at seven. Gladys Knight And The Pips was formed following family celebration when Gladys was only eight; Bubba and Brenda were Gladys' brother and sister, William and Elenor Guest her cousins. Group were soon playing local gigs, and made first national tour (with Sam Cooke and Jackie Wilson) in 1956.

After unsuccessful release on Brunswick, Brenda and Elenor left group, to be replaced by Edward Patten, another cousin, and Langston George. This line-up had major hit with **Every Beat Of My Heart** in 1961. Further hits on Fury followed, and group became sought-after live attraction. George left group and current line-up stabilized. Signing to Maxx Records consolidated R&B success. Following label's demise group signed to Motown in 1966.

Motown started group off on route to international success; version of classic **I Heard It Through The Grapevine** went to No. 2 in US charts in 1967, and was followed by string of major hits. Nevertheless, when Motown deal expired in 1973 group moved to Buddah, and period of unprecedented success followed.

First album, **Imagination**, produced three hit singles and made group America's most successful vocal outfit of 1973. Since then, acclaim and chart honours have been virtually automatic. Vocal prowess of Gladys Knight ensured continued respect of fans. Gladys and her family group managed to straddle both cabaret/ MOR and gutsier, more soul-orientated, fields.

At end of 70s, Knight and Pips drifted apart temporarily, with The Pips cutting two indie albums. Reunited in 1980, group signed with CBS Records debuting with **Touch** album. Despite depletion of hit singles, Knight and entourage maintained status with headline shows and solid recordings. Knight took time out in 1984 for guest spot on Dionne Warwick's **That's What Friends Are For** single, and then teamed with Bill Medley for **Love On Borrowed Time** theme song from movie *Cobra*.

Following **Love Overboard** hit in 1988, which earned a raft of honours including Grammy as Best R&B Single, Knight announced plans for solo career, and signed with MCA; **Silence To Kill** James Bond movie theme-song was debut in same year.

Hit Singles:

	US	UK
Every Beat Of My Heart, 1961	6	—
Letter Full Of Tears, 1962	19	—
Take Me In Your Arms And Love Me, 1967	—	13
I Heard It Through The Grapevine, 1967	2	47
The End Of Our Road, 1968	15	—
The Nitty Gritty, 1969	19	—
Friendship Train, 1969	17	—
If I Were Your Woman, 1971	9	—
I Don't Want To Do Wrong, 1971	17	—
Help Me Make It Through The Night, 1972	33	11
Neither One Of Us (Can Be The First To Say Goodbye), 1973	2	31
Daddy Could Swear, I Declare, 1973	19	—
Midnight Train To Georgia, 1973	1	—
I've Got To Use My Imagination, 1974	4	—
The Best Thing That Ever Happened To Me, 1974	3	7
On And On, 1974	5	—
Try To Remember/The Way We Were, 1975	11	4
Midnight Train to Georgia, 1976	—	10
So Sad The Song, 1976	47	20
Baby Don't Change Your Mind, 1977	52	4
Come Back And Finish What You Started, 1978	—	15
Love Overboard, 1988	13	—
Licence To Kill, 1989	—	6

Albums:
Imagination (Buddah), 1973
Anthology (Tamla Motown), 1974
Best Of (Buddah), 1976
Thirty Greatest (—/K-Tel), 1977
Collection (Buddah), 1978
Memories Of The Way We Were (Buddah), 1979
Touch (Columbia/CBS), 1981
Looking Back — The Fury Years (—/Bulldog), 1982
Neither One Of Us (Motown), 1982
Bless This House (Buddah), 1983
Life (CBS), 1985
Compact Command Performances (Motown), 1986
All I Need (Motown), 1987
About Love (CBS), 1987
Gladys Knight And The Pips (Interpage), 1987
The Early Years (Topline), 1987
All Our Love (MCA), 1988
The Singles Album (RCA), 1989

Kool And The Gang

US group formed 1969

Original line-up: Robert 'Kool' Bell, bass; Robert Mickens, trumpet; Michael Ray, trumpet; Dennis Thomas, alto saxophone; Ronald Bell, tenor saxophone; Clifford Adams, trombone; Amir Bayyan, keyboards; Charles 'Claydes' Smith, guitar; George Brown, drums.

Career: In 1964 Robert 'Kool' Bell formed band called Jazziacs in Jersey City. Band included brother Ronald Bell, Dennis Thomas and Robert Mickens, and played jazz-influenced dance music for local gigs.

During next five years they gained experience, tried out names and expanded line-up. Eventually line-up as above signed as Kool And The Gang with De-Lite in 1969.

They continued policy of funky instrumental R&B with jazz influence, gaining popularity without achieving spectacular success. But fifth album, **Wild And Peaceful**, spawned trio of big-selling singles — **Jungle Boogie, Funky Stuff** and **Hollywood Swinging**.

Although among progenitors of 'whole' style, Kool And The Gang were not among main beneficiaries of mid-70s disco boom. They did, however, feature on best-selling **Saturday Night Fever** soundtrack album. Career finally took off in big way when band took on lead singer James 'J.T.' Taylor and combined forces with producer Eumir Deodato. Result was **Ladies Night** (1979), a major hit album which spawned several smash singles.

The group sustained chart status with a slew of pop dance material until Taylor quit in 1988 for solo career, debuting in 1989 for MCA with **Masters Of The Game**. Bell replaced Taylor with trio of vocalists, Gary Brown, Deen Mays and former Gap Band frontman Skip Martin. Maintaining busy road schedule, Kool And Gang struggled to renew acquaintance with single charts, and 1989 Mercury LP **Sweat** stuck firmly in R&B market.

While the move from funk R&B to mainstream soul was triumphant, it appears that the Bell brothers had Taylor to thank for cross-over success.

Hit Singles:

	US	UK
Jungle Boogie, 1974	4	–
Hollywood Swinging, 1974	6	–
Ladies Night, 1979	8	9
Too Hot, 1980	5	23
Celebration, 1980	1	7
Jones Vs. Jones, 1981	39	17
Take My Heart (You Can Have It If You Want), 1981	17	–
Take It To The Top, 1981	–	15
Steppin' Out, 1981	–	12
Get Down On It, 1982	10	3
Big Fun, 1982	21	14
Let's Go Dancin' (Ooh La La La), 1982	9	6
Straight Ahead, 1983	–	15
Joanna, 1983	2	2
Tonight, 1984	13	–
Fresh, 1985	9	12
Misled, 1985	10	–
Cherish, 1985	2	4
Emergency, 1986	18	–
Stone Love, 1987	13	–
Victory, 1987	13	–

Albums:
Spin Their Top Hits (De-Lite/–), 1978
Ladies Night (De-Lite), 1979
Everybody's Dancing (De-Lite/–), 1979
Celebrate (De-Lite), 1980
Something Special (De-Lite), 1981
As One (De-Lite), 1982
Kool Kuts (De-Lite), 1982
Twice As Kool — The Hits Of (De-Lite/ Phonogram), 1983
In The Heart (De-Lite), 1983
Emergency (De-Lite), 1984
Forever (Club), 1986
Victory (Club), 1986
Everything's Kool And The Gang (Mercury/–), 1988
Sweat (Mercury), 1989

Right: Lauper's unusual stage presence matched her unique talent.

Lenny Kravitz
US vocalist, composer, guitarist
Born New York, 1965

Career: Derivative rock 'n' roller who is almost unbelievably being hailed as 'the new Jimi Hendrix'. Haircut apart, the comparison is invidious. Major claim to fame was short-term marriage to actress Lisa Bonet. Born into show-biz family (mother is Roxie Roker, star of US sitcom *The Jeffersons*, while dad is Sly Kravitz, noted TV producer). After move to Los Angeles, joined California Boys Choir and featured on Zubin Mehta's recording of Mahler's Third Symphony. Quit school (and home) at 16, and adopted 'Romeo Blue' pseudonym in search of record deal.

After enlisting help of innovative engineer Henry Hirsch, who cut demos with Kravitz in New Jersey, he was signed by Virgin America in 1988. Kravitz' archetypal brand of rock was seen to moderate effect on 1989 debut LP **Let Love Rule**, a hotchpotch of funk, space rock and hippie meandering.

Subsequent UK club tour, which included sell-out gigs at London's Town & Country, suggested a bright future, although little progress was made when second album **Mama Said** appeared in May 1991. Only **All I Ever Wanted** track (written with Sean Lennon) justified purchase, and Kravitz might need to restrain his supercharged approach and consider future musical direction.

Hit Singles:

	US	UK
It Ain't Over 'Til It's Over, 1991	2	11

Albums:
Let Love Rule (Virgin), 1989
Mama Said (Virgin), 1991

Cyndi Lauper
US vocalist, composer
Born Queens, New York, June 20, 1953

Career: 'If at first you don't succeed, etc . . .' could well stand as Cyndi Lauper's motto. Behind seeming instant 1984 success with platinum album **She's So Unusual** and superlative singles **Girls Just Want To Have Fun** and **Time After Time** lay years of heartbreak and trauma — the demise of her early band Blue Angel had led her to file for bankruptcy. All this and early background as convent-schooled rebellious product of single-parent home was to shine through in her feminist but fun songmaking.

Perhaps biggest blow was in 1977 when, after several years fronting various poor

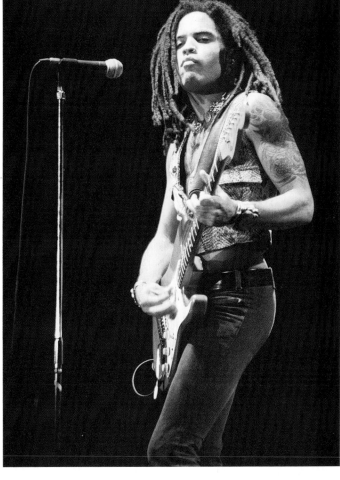

Above: Lenny Kravitz' solid show-biz background has only heightened frustration at artist's limited output.

cover-version bands, her voice failed and she was told she would never sing again. Help from vocal coach Katie Agresta made her singing better than ever and she bounced back from flop of Blue Angel's sole Polygram album in 1980 and a law suit loss against management company to find stardom with Portrait Records.

A slew of hit singles throughout the mid-80s confirmed Lauper as a true original, and genuine talent (**Time After Time** became late jazz great Miles Davis' theme in late 80s and early 90s). Lauper featured on **We Are The World** charity single (where hers was most distinctive contribution!) in 1985, and cut second album **True Colors** in following year, but then took break before **A Night To Remember** surfaced in 1989.

Started new decade with focus on movies, but auspicious debut in *Mother Goose Rock 'N' Rhyme* for Disney Channel

was followed by less-distinguished *Paradise Paved*. Although co-opted for Roger Waters' live production of The Wall in Berlin, Lauper's future musical endeavours look likely to take back seat for time being.

Hit Singles:

	US	UK
Girls Just Want To Have Fun, 1984	2	2
Time After Time, 1984	1	3
She Bop, 1984	3	46
All Through The Night, 1984	5	–
The Goonies 'R' Good Enough, 1985	10	–
True Colors, 1986	1	12
What's Going On, 1987	11	–
Change Of Heart, 1987	4	–
I Drove All Night, 1989	6	7

Albums:
She's So Unusual (Portrait), 1984
True Colors (Portrait), 1986
A Night To Remember (Epic), 1989

Led Zeppelin
UK group formed 1968

Original line-up: Robert Plant, vocals; Jimmy Page, Gibson Les Paul guitar; John Paul Jones, keyboards, Fender Precision bass; John Bonham, drums.

Career: Formed by Jimmy Page upon demise of Yardbirds to complete scheduled dates in northern Europe. Quartet completed by session bass player John Paul Jones, Birmingham drummer John Bonham, and ex-Band Of Joy vocalist Robert Plant.

Page and Jones were both prominent studio players. Page's credits include Kinks, Stones, Georgie Fame and The Who

(featured on **I Can't Explain**). Joined Yardbirds as replacement bass player for departing Paul Samwell-Smith; switched to guitar when Jeff Beck quit. Jones supplied bass and keyboards for Stones, Lulu, Dusty Springfield and many others; formerly bass player for Jet Harris/Tony Meehan, ex-Shadows duo.

As New Yardbirds, band fulfilled Swedish/Finnish dates. With manager Peter Grant, group selected new name Led Zeppelin suggested by Keith Moon (John Entwistle has also been credited). Grant quickly secured recording contract with Ahmet Ertegun of Atlantic (originally turned down by Atlantic's distribution company in UK Polydor); Grant and Ertegun have since arrived at arm's length respect for each other.

First album Led Zeppelin was released in 1968; went gold early following year. Mixture of blues and orchestrated rock riffs filled in void left by Cream; superb musicianship and beginning of Plant's 'macho' bare-to-the-waist image saw them streets ahead of US contemporaries. Album's crisp production set it apart from myriad of ponderous, muddy-sounding heavy metal merchants. Single **Good Times Bad Times** culled from LP earned group first US Top 100 entry.

Reputation secured by **Led Zeppelin II** which included band's anthem **Whole Lotta Love**, a US Top 10. Band has never had singles success in UK, though **Love** was theme for BBC's *Top Of The Pops* TV show for several years; band never officially endorsed singles culled by record company.

Zeppelin completed major tour of US in 1973, compounding success of further albums **III** and **IV**. Tracks **Immigrant Song** (from **III**) and now all-time classic **Stairway To Heaven** (from **IV**) extracted phenomenal reaction from audiences. Band now at peak, with Grant turning down deals which conflicted with long-term strategy.

Assuming Presley/Beatles-type publicity and sales, group spent over a year away from studio after release of **Houses Of The Holy** (1973). Returned in 1975 with **Physical Graffiti**. Album was packaged in 'moveable' sleeve, revealing various objects/individuals in windows of tenement block, and was as impressive musically as visually, attracting more favourable critical reaction; band have always been at loggerheads with 'knowledgeable' music press.

Own label Swan Song launched with release of **Graffiti**; Bad Company, Maggie Bell and Pretty Things also signed to label. Acts distributed by Atlantic and Island. Swan Song office in Kings Road, London, saw much frantic wheeling and dealing by Grant. Reportedly turned down a million pounds for worldwide satellite TV concert of band.

1975 saw Plant injured in car crash during Greek holiday. Second personal tragedy for group's singer occurred in 1977 when his son Karac died of virus infection. Plant's incapacity kept band off road for two years, although album **Presence** (1976) maintained momentum and appeased fans. LP had biggest advance orders ever in US, going platinum upon issue.

In 1976 movie/soundtrack album **The Song Remains The Same** released. Film captured explosive stage act to the full, despite some 'live' footage being shot at Pinewood Studios, England.

Massive US tour saw Zeppelin gross over a million dollars for New York dates (at Madison Square Garden) alone. 10 dates were cancelled, however, when Plant had to fly home on son's death. First rumours of break-up denied by Page. Band had meticulously worked schedule, with periods of inactivity which fuelled 'split' stories.

Ninth album **In Through The Out Door** cut in Sweden at end of 1978 for spring 1979 release. Unlikely hosts in frozen North were Abba, who had invited band to record in their studio.

Major outdoor concert at stately home Knebworth House in August 1979 saw band re-conquer homeland. **In Through The Out Door** LP was released shortly after. Album's unique packaging (wrapped in brown paper and featuring six different covers) won major marketing award in US.

After death of drummer John Bonham in 1980, another victim of rock excesses, band officially called it a day in cursory press release. In intervening years, Plant has forged successful solo career, employing young musicians in upbeat band which captured spirit of 1980s. 1985 saw collaboration of Plant/Page in Honeydrippers, with Nile Rodgers and Jeff Beck; band made US No. 3 with **Sea Of Love**. US success was also

Below: The turning cover of Led Zeppelin III. Courtesy Atlantic Records.

forthcoming for short-lived Page/Paul Rodgers band The Firm.

Having buried the 're-formation' rumours once and for all, Plant continued with solo outings, while Page joined forces in 1991 with David Coverdale, drummer Denny Car-

Above: Led Zeppelin II featured Whole Lotta Love. Courtesy Atlantic Records.

marsi (ex-Heart) and bassist Ricky Phillips (ex-Bad English) for projected tour and album for following year. Coverdale explained that his group Whitesnake was 'deferred, NOT defunct'.

The 'victims' of hip-hop DJs, Zeppelin found their time-honoured riffs featured on several dance cuts in late 80s, while spoof-band Dread Zeppelin enjoyed cult status with their reggae interpretation of group's music during early 1990s.

In 1990, Atlantic Records issued Led Zeppelin 54-track compilation in all formats; testimony to the label's biggest-selling LP act of all time.

Hit Singles:

	US	UK
Whole Lotta Love, 1970	4	—
Immigrant Song, 1971	16	—
Black Dog, 1972	15	—
D'Yer Mak'er, 1973	20	—

Robert Plant Solo:

Big Log, 1983	20	11

Above: Coda, the last Led Zeppelin album. Courtesy Atlantic Records.

Honeydrippers:

Sea Of Love, 1985	3	—

Albums:

Led Zeppelin (Atlantic), 1968
Led Zeppelin II (Atlantic), 1969
Led Zeppelin III (Atlantic), 1970
Led Zeppelin IV (Atlantic), 1971
Houses Of The Holy (Atlantic), 1973
Physical Graffiti (Swan Song), 1975
Presence (Swan Song), 1976
The Song Remains The Same (Swan Song), 1976
In Through The Out Door (Swan Song), 1979

Below (from left to right): Jones, Plant, Page and Bonham form Led Zeppelin.

Above: Houses Of The Holy, Led Zeppelin. Courtesy Atlantic Records.

Below: Ace axeman Page on stage with his trademark 'Les Paul'.

Coda (Swan Song), 1982
Chris Tetley Interviews Led Zeppelin (Music & Media), 1987

Robert Plant Solo:
Pictures At Eleven (Swan Song), 1982
The Principle Of Moments (Es Paranza), 1983
Shaken 'n' Stirred (Es Paranza), 1985
Now And Zen (Es Paranza/Atlantic), 1988
Manic Nirvana (Es Paranza/Atlantic), 1990

Jimmy Page Solo:
Deathwish II (soundtrack) (Swan Song), 1982
Outrider (Geffen), 1988

The Firm:
The Firm (Atlantic), 1985
Mean Business (Atlantic), 1986

Honeydrippers:
Volume One (Es Paranza), 1984

Jimmy Page and Roy Harper:
Whatever Happened To 1214 AD (Beggar's Banquet), 1985

Brenda Lee

US vocalist
Born Brenda Mae Tarpley, Atlanta, Georgia, December 11, 1944

Career: Lee's musical talent was already in evidence at age six when she won local talent contest in home town Nashville. Heard by country star Red Foley at 12, spot on his TV programme *Ozark Jubilee Show* followed. Success was instantaneous, and further TV dates and Decca (later MCA) recording contract followed.

First releases were country-orientated and moderately successful, but when Lee turned to rock 'n' roll her career took off. **Dynamite** was first of several international hits that carried her into mid-60s. Probably the best female white rock singer of her generation, she also showed winning style on pop ballads **I'm Sorry** and **As Usual**.

When chart status began to falter, Lee, like many white rock 'n' rollers from same era (Bob Luman, Conway Twitty, Carl Perkins), returned to roots for moderately successful career in country market, although family commitments precluded high-profile approach. As a legacy from her rocking days, Lee was awarded considerable damages following lawsuit filed against Decca Records for unpaid royalties.

A strong, distinctive stylist, Brenda Lee combined talent with combative personality. Her early 60s classics remain among most evocative discs of period.

Hit Singles:	US	UK
Sweet Nuthins, 1960	4	4
I'm Sorry/That's All You Gotta Do, 1960	1	12
That's All You Gotta Do/I'm Sorry, 1960	6	–
I Want To Be Wanted, 1960	1	31
Rockin' Around The Christmas Tree, 1960	14	–
Let's Jump The Broomstick, 1961	–	12
Emotions, 1961	7	45
You Can Depend On Me, 1961	6	–
Dum Dum, 1961	4	22
Fool No. 1, 1961	3	38
Break It To Me Gently, 1962	4	46
Speak To Me Pretty, 1962	–	3
Everybody Loves You But You, 1962	6	–
Here Comes That Feeling, 1962	–	5
Heart In Hand, 1962	15	–
It Started All Over Again, 1962	29	15
All Alone Am I, 1962	3	7
Rockin' Around The Christmas Tree, 1962	–	6
Losing You, 1963	6	10
I Wonder, 1963	25	14
The Grass Is Greener, 1963	17	–
As Usual, 1964	12	5
Is It True, 1964	17	17
Too Many Rivers, 1965	13	22
Coming On Strong, 1966	11	–

Albums:
Here's Brenda Lee (Vocalion/–), 1967
Let It Be Me (Coral/–), 1968
Brenda (MCA), 1973
Brenda Lee Story (MCA/Decca), 1974
Little Miss Dynamite (MCA/Warwick), 1976
Take Me Back (MCA), 1979
Even Better (MCA), 1980
16 Classic Tracks (–/MFP), 1982
25th Anniversary (MCA), 1982
Greatest Country Hits (–/MCA), 1982
Only When I Laugh (–/MCA), 1982
Very Best Of (MCA), 1985
Wiedersehen Ist Wunderschön (Bear Family), 1986

John Lennon

UK composer, vocalist, guitarist
Born John Winston Lennon, Liverpool, October 9, 1940
Died December 8, 1980

Career: After achieving worldwide success with the Beatles during the 60s, Lennon, under influence of second wife, Yoko Ono, began recording without rest of group in 1968. First LP, recorded with Yoko, featured full frontal nude picture of duo, resulting in LP being sold in brown paper bag, while contents — avant-garde inspired non-music — alienated Beatles fans around the world. Follow-up LP was no better, but, in between, hit single by Plastic Ono Band (John, Yoko and friends), **Give Peace A Chance**, was substantial hit. Several follow-up singles were successful over years until 1976. LPs often unlistenable before **John Lennon/Plastic Ono Band**, released in 1970, in which John, under influence of primal therapy, tried to release all supposedly suppressed feelings about early life.

Next LP, **Imagine**, generally agreed to be Lennon's best solo album. Thereafter output was patchy — Lennon felt to be too easily influenced by those around him,

Below: Mr and Mrs John Lennon at the time of John's comeback.

leading to involvement with peace movement, exotic religions, and many other things which prevented him making classic rock 'n' roll records of which everyone knew he was capable.

On November 28, 1974, Lennon joined Elton John on stage at NY's Madison Square Gardens for three numbers (**Lucy In The Sky With Diamonds**, **I Saw Her Standing There** and **Whatever Gets You Through The Night**); this turned out to be his last live performance.

On birth of second child (first by Yoko), Lennon vowed to cease recording for five years. On return to active service in 1980, produced half LP (other half by Yoko) spawning rather disappointing single hit (**Just Like) Starting Over**. As single began to descend chart, John was murdered by so-called fan outside New York apartment building. The entire world was shocked. Chart was soon deluged with Lennon/Beatles material for several months. While his post-Beatles work was very inconsistent, Lennon is regarded as most notable Beatle by majority of fans, making his quite senseless murder probably *the* ultimate tragedy of rock 'n' roll. A succession of puerile biographies naturally followed his death, of which Albert Goldman's effort (1988) was the nastiest.

Following induction of The Beatles into Rock 'n' Roll Hall Of Fame in 1988, where Lennon was represented by Yoko Ono, plans were formulated for tribute concert celebrating what would have been artist's 50th birthday. In May 1990, a host of international acts performed Lennon material at Pier Head Arena in Liverpool.

Lennon's soundalike son Julian has enjoyed modicum of success since **Too Late For Goodbyes** single in 1984 and **Saltwater** single in 1991, while other offspring, Sean, has also dabbled on fringes of rock biz.

Above: The John Lennon Collection. Courtesy EMI Records/Geffen Records.

Shaved Fish (compilation) (Capitol/Parlophone), 1975
Double Fantasy (Capitol/Parlophone), 1980
The John Lennon Collection (compilation) (Capitol/Parlophone), 1980
Heartplay — Unfinished Dialogues (Polydor), 1983
Milk And Honey (with Yoko Ono) (Polydor), 1984
Live In New York City (Parlophone), 1986
Menlove Ave (Parlophone), 1986

Hit Singles:	US	UK
Give Peace A Chance, 1969	14	2
Cold Turkey, 1969	30	14
Instant Karma, 1970	3	5
Power To The People, 1970	11	7
Imagine, 1971	3	—
Happy Xmas (War Is Over), 1972	—	4
Mind Games, 1973	18	26
Whatever Gets You Thru The Night, 1974	1	36
Number 9 Dream, 1975	9	23
Stand By Me, 1975	20	30
Imagine, 1975	—	6
Happy Xmas (War Is Over), 1980	—	2
Imagine, 1980	—	1
(Just Like) Starting Over, 1981	3	1
Woman, 1981	2	1
Watching The Wheels, 1981	18	30
Nobody Told Me, 1984	5	6

Albums:
Unfinished Music No. 1 — Two Virgins (Apple), 1968
Unfinished Music No. 2 — Life With The Lions, (Capitol/Parlophone), 1969
The Wedding Album (Capitol/Parlophone), 1969
Plastic Ono Band/Live Peace in Toronto, (Capitol/Parlophone), 1969
John Lennon/Plastic Ono Band (Capitol/Parlophone), 1970
Imagine (Capitol/Parlophone) 1971
Some Time In New York City (Captiol/Parlophone), 1972
Mind Games (Capitol/MFP), 1973
Walls and Bridges (Capitol/Parlophone), 1974
Rock 'n' Roll (Capitol/Parlophone), 1975

Level 42
UK group formed 1980

Original line-up: Mark King, vocals, bass; Mike Lindup, keyboards, vocals; Phil Gould, percussion; Boon Gould, guitar.

Career: The early 80s found a number of UK bands exploiting the jazz-funk idiom then expanding own soul style to find major following for their white brand of black music. Level 42 was voted best British group for three years running in *Blues & Soul* magazine whose readers also cited Mark King as best bassist in world.

King and Gould brothers were friends from Isle of Wight days, linking up with Lindup and forming group after moving to London where they found record deal with Polydor.

1985 album **World Machine** went double platinum in UK, while later **Running In The Family** was equally successful. Mid-80s also marked band's development into major stadium filler.

Personnel changes followed **A Physical Presence** LP (1987) and subsequent world tour, with Neil Conti replacing Phil Gould, and Boon Gould quitting. King and Lindup oversaw 1988 album **Staring At The Sun**, which saw further chart action with **Heaven In My Hands** and **Take A Look**.

With rumours of impending label change rife, Level 42 (now just King and Lindup, with hired help) celebrated 10th anniversary with series of UK concerts in 1990. In absence of new album, Lindup cut solo changes in same year, while King maintained status as ace bass man with work for artists such as Nik Kershaw, Midge Ure, Reflex and Robert Palmer.

Having split from Polydor in 1991, band signed deal with RCA Records, with their first LP for that company scheduled for early in 1992.

Hit Singles:	US	UK
The Sun Goes Down, 1983	—	10
Hot Water, 1984	—	18
Something About You, 1985	—	6
Lessons In Love, 1986	14	3
To Be With You Again, 1987	—	10
Running In The Family, 1987	—	6
It's Over, 1987	—	10
Children Say, 1987	—	22
Heaven In My Hands, 1988	—	12
Guaranteed, 1991	—	17

Albums:
Level 42 (Polydor), 1981
The Early Tapes (Polydor), 1982
The Pursuit Of Accidents (Polydor), 1982
Standing In The Light (Polydor), 1983
True Colours (Polydor), 1984
World Machine (Polydor), 1985
Running In The Family (Polydor), 1987
Physical Presence (Polydor), 1987
Staring At The Sun (Polydor), 1988
Level Best (Polydor), 1989

Mark King Solo:
Influences (Polydor), 1984

Mike Lindup Solo:
Changes, 1990

Huey Lewis And The News
US group formed 1982

Original line-up: Huey Lewis, vocals; Chris Hayes, guitar; Sean Hopper, keyboards; Johnny Colla, guitar, saxophone; Mario Cipollina, bass; Bill Gibson, drums.

Career: After graduation, Huey Lewis backpacked round Europe for several years, teaching himself harmonica while waiting for rides. Returning to Marin County, California, he joined country rockers Clover, with whom he played London pub rock scene in late 1970s, featuring on Elvis Costello's debut album **My Aim Is True** and also recording with Phil Lynott.

On Clover's demise, he returned to San Francisco Bay Area to assemble News, Hopper also being ex-Clover while Colla, Cipollina and Gibson all came from local band Soundhole.

Signed worldwide to Chrysalis, group found instant success, quickly becoming biggest-grossing stage act in US and going five-times platinum with superlative **Sports** album (six million sales and 100 weeks on US chart).

If This Is It single brought UK recognition for group's R&B slanted brand of

Below: British funk outfit Level 42, who are led by bassist Mark King (front).

excitement but follow-up surprisingly flopped despite strong airplay.

Single **Power Of Love**, theme from ultra-successful *Back To The Future* movie (in which Lewis appeared) began assault on US and UK single charts which remained unabated until 1989, when **Small World** LP from previous year spawned a couple of Top 50 hits.

Having taken time out, band re-emerged in 1991 with album **Hard At Play** for new label EMI, although early signs were that Huey was no longer News.

Hit Singles:	US	UK
Do You Believe In Love, 1982	7	—
Heart And Soul, 1983	8	—
I Want A New Drug, 1984	6	—
The Heart Of Rock 'n' Roll, 1984	6	—
If This Is It, 1984	6	7
Walking On A Thin Line, 1984	18	—
Power Of Love, 1985	1	11
Hip To Be Square, 1986	1	41
Stuck With You, 1987	1	12
Jacob's Ladder, 1987	1	—
I Know What I Like, 1987	8	—
Doing It All For My Baby, 1987	6	—
Small World, 1988	11	12
Perfect World, 1988	3	48
Couple Days Off, 1991	11	—

Albums:
Huey Lewis And The News (Chrysalis), 1980
Picture This (Chrysalis), 1982
Sports (Chrysalis), 1984
Fore (Chrysalis), 1986
Small World (Chrysalis), 1988
Hard At Play (EMI), 1991

Jerry Lee Lewis
US vocalist, pianist, composer
Born Ferriday, Louisiana, September 29, 1935

Career: Although Lewis made early start playing country-style piano in bars and clubs, recording career did not commence until 1956 with signing to Sun Records in Memphis and first single **Crazy Arms**. Somewhat wilder style surfaced in 1957, with second single **Whole Lotta Shakin' Goin' On** becoming first hit and setting pattern for 'pumpin' piano' style, which rapidly became trademark.

Several hits and tours later, arrived in Britain in May 1958 for nationwide tour just

Above: Huey Lewis (fourth from left) and his loyal News.

as news broke of marriage to 13-year-old cousin, Myra. Resulting publicity effectively stalled career for over two years; made comeback with **What'd I Say** in 1961.

Began recording for Mercury in 1963 and style mellowed considerably over next five years as Lewis turned to country music with increasing success. New career followed with major hits in country charts and occasional excursions into rock 'n' roll.

Continued to tour US and UK regularly, and to appear in headlines as a result of lifestyle in keeping with reputation as wild man of rock. His various drug, booze and gun offences reached climax in 1976 when Lewis was arrested for brandishing a pistol outside Elvis Presley's home in Memphis.

Following signing to Elektra label in 1977, appeared to have adopted quieter lifestyle; relationship with label was strained, however, ultimately leading to lawsuits from both sides. During 1981 was rushed to hospital for extensive stomach surgery, reportedly close to death, but recovered sufficiently to resume stage appearances. 'The Killer' suffered further serious illness in 1985, but recuperative powers were on hand once again. While ill-health has restricted recording, Lewis has become the favourite subject of indie labels in UK.

Recent concerts reveal only slightly reserved stage performance and the same self-confidence — Lewis has always asserted that 'The Killer' is the 'King of Rock 'n' Roll'. This title may have been hotly contested in the 50s, now it would appear to belong to Lewis alone, for he remains one of the few active rock 'n' roll exponents. As testimony to his status, Hollywood saw fit to film the Lewis story for *Great Balls Of Fire* biopic (1989), in which Dennis Quaid starred as our irrational hero.

Hit Singles:

	US	UK
Whole Lotta Shakin' Goin' On, 1957	2	8
Great Balls Of Fire, 1957	3	1
Breathless, 1958	7	8
High School Confidential, 1959	21	12
What'd I Say, 1961	30	10

Albums:
Whole Lotta Shakin' Goin' On (Sun), 1963
Live At The Star Club, Hamburg (Philips), 1964
Best Of The Country Music Hall Of Fame Hits (Mercury), 1969
Jerry Lee Lewis And His Pumping Piano (—/Charly), 1975
Rare Jerry Lee Lewis Volume 1 (—/Charly), 1975
Rare Jerry Lee Lewis Volume 2 (—/Charly), 1975
Good Rockin' Tonite (Sun), 1975
The Original Jerry Lee Lewis (—/Charly), 1976
Nuggets (—/Charly), 1977
Nuggets Volume 2 (—/Charly), 1977
The Essential Jerry Lee Lewis (—/Charly), 1978
Jerry Lee Lewis And Friends — Duets (Sun/Charly), 1978
Jerry Lee's Greatest (—/Charly), 1980
The Sun Years (12 LP box set) (Sun), 1980
Killer Country (Elektra), 1980
Pumpin' Piano Cat (Sun), 1983
The Great Ball Of Fire (Sun), 1983
The Wild One (Sun), 1983
My Fingers Do The Talking (MCA), 1983
I Am What I Am (MCA), 1984
The Killer (12 unit box set: 1963-1968) (Bear Family)
Up Through The Years (1956-63) (Bear Family)
The Session (Mercury), 1985
Collection — Parts 1 and 2 (Castle), 1986
Complete London Sessions Volumes 1 and 2 (Bear Family), 1986
Milestones (Rhino), 1986
18 Original Sun Hits (Rhino), 1986
20 Super Hits (Bellaphon), 1986
Rare And Rockin' (Sun), 1987
Kickin' Up A Storm (Sun), 1987
30th Anniversary (Phonogram), 1987

With Carl Perkins and Johnny Cash:
The Survivors (—/Hallmark), 1985

Lindisfarne
UK group formed 1967

Original line-up: Alan Hull, vocals; Ray Jackson, guitar, mandolin, vocals; Simon Cowe, guitar, mandolin, vocals; Rod Clements, bass, violin, vocals; Ray Laidlaw, drums.

Career: Folk-rock band formed in Newcastle, had various names before signing as Lindisfarne to Charisma in 1969. First album, **Nicely Out Of Tune**, met with good reception, and steady gigging on college and festival circuit during 1969 and 1970 paved way for commercial success.

Next album, **Fog On The Tyne**, was produced by Bob Johnston and became biggest-selling British album of 1970. Also spawned hit single **Meet Me On The Corner**. Earlier unsuccessful single **Lady Eleanor** was re-released and became major hit.

However, band faltered after this success and split in 1973. Clements, Laidlaw and Cowe formed Jack The Lad, whilst Hull and Jackson recorded moderate offerings.

Original line-up re-formed in 1979, and returned to club/festival circuit where they had enjoyed greatest success; scored with dance re-make of classic **Fog On The Tyne** track in 1990 in collaboration with English soccer star Paul Gascoigne, himself an avowed Geordie.

Hit Singles:

	US	UK
Meet Me On The Corner, 1972	—	5
Lady Eleanor, 1972	—	3
Run For Home, 1978	33	10

Albums:
Fog On The Tyne (—/Charisma), 1971
Dingly Dell (—/Charisma), 1972
Lady Eleanor (—/Hallmark), 1976
Back And Forth (Atco/Mercury), 1978
The News (—/Mercury), 1979
The Singles Album (—/Charisma), 1981
Lindisfarne Live (—/Charisma), 1982
Sleepless Nights (—/LMP), 1982
Lindisfarne! Volume 2 (LMP), 1984
C'mon Everybody (Stylus), 1987

Little Feat
US group formed 1969

Original line-up: Lowell George, guitar, harmonica, vocals; Bill Payne, keyboards, vocals; Richard Hayward, drums; Roy Estrada, bass.

Career: Lowell George (born 1945) played in mid-60s folk-rock group Factory (with Hayward and bassist Martin Kibbee) and, two years later, The Standells (**Dirty Water**), then Seeds (**Pushin' Too Hard**) briefly. George left to take over from singer Ray Collins in Mothers Of Invention, playing on both **Weasels Ripped My Flesh** and **Hot Rats** (uncredited).

While in Mothers, wrote/recorded several demos, including **Willing** and **Truck Stop Girl**, the latter being picked up by Clarence White of The Byrds for inclusion on their untitled album. Other covers followed by numerous US acts, including Seatrain, Linda Ronstadt and Commander Cody.

During same period, George teamed up with Bill Payne, and both contributed to Fraternity Of Man's second LP, **Get It On**. Interest in George's demos eventually led to recording deal with Warners. Above line-up was assembled. (Group name apparently came from Mother's drummer Jimmy Carl Black and sarcastically refers to size of George's feet.)

First album **Little Feat**, released in December 1969, was surprisingly mature work for debut and attracted some critical acclaim, though sales were poor. Same fate befell follow-up **Sailin' Shoes**, in spite of increased media coverage. Disillusioned, Estrada left to join Captain Beefheart's Magic Band. The other members re-grouped in new six-piece line-up, including Ken Gradney (bass), Sam Clayton (congas) and Paul Barrere (guitar). Third album **Dixie Chicken** also saw minimal success and members finally lost interest and drifted into other projects.

George was in constant demand as sessioneer/songwriter, but declined invitation to join projected group with John Sebastian and Phil Everly as well as similar request from Jackson Browne. Contributed to albums by The Meters, Jimmy Webb, Carly Simon, John Sebastian, Kathy Dalton, Chico Hamilton, Nilsson, Robert Palmer (**Sneaking Sally Through The Alley**), John Cale (**Paris 1919**) and Van Dyke Parks (**Discover America**). Payne, meanwhile, went on road and appeared on albums with Doobie Brothers (**Toulouse Street** and **The Captain and Me**) and Bonnie Raitt (**Taking My Time** and **Streetlights**).

Little Feat re-formed in 1974 to cut excellent **Feats Don't Fail Me Now**. Followed with critically acclaimed tour of England as part of Warner Bros Music Show in early 1975. Returned to England in May 1976 to support The Who at Charlton Football Ground. Subsequently toured Europe with The Outlaws. During group's final years, Lowell George's role appeared to diminish. Contributed only three songs to **The Last Record Album**, including the memorable **Long Distance Love**.

Hepatitis precluded his extensive involvement in next album, **Time Loves A Hero**, generally regarded as least impressive. Live double, **Waiting For Columbus** (1978), was also poor in relation to earlier work, which was hardly surprising since George was travelling separately during tours. George produced Grateful Dead's **Shakedown Street** in the same year.

Group finally split in April 1979 while recording final album. George, meanwhile, had begun solo career with average **Thanks I'll Eat It Here**, better work being anticipated in the future. On June 29, 1979, Lowell George died, age 34, from drug-induced heart failure in Arlington, Virginia; last gig had taken place at George Washington University in Washington DC the previous evening.

Ironically, posthumously released **Down On The Farm** revealed group's finest moments since early barn-storming days, and prompted release of double album **Hoy Hoy!** (1981).

Plans to re-form band had been rife for almost a decade when Payne, Barrere, Clayton and Hayward took to the road as 'mark two' version of band, with addition of former Pure Prairie League sidekicks Craig Fuller, vocals, and Fred Tackett, guitar. Group's debut LP for Warner Bros, **Let It Roll**, stalled, and 1990 offering **Representing The Mambo** fell foul of critics. However, **Shake Me Up** set for Polydor (December 1991) returned troupe to form; album was a rip-rollicking fusillade of Deep South rock 'n' blues.

Above: Feats Don't Fail Me Now, Little Feat's 1974 release. Courtesy Warner Bros Records.

Albums
Little Feat (Warner Bros), 1971
Sailin' Shoes (Warner Bros), 1972
Dixie Chicken (Warner Bros), 1973
Feats Don't Fail Me Now (Warner Bros), 1974
The Last Record Album (Warner Bros), 1975
Time Loves A Hero (Warner Bros), 1977
Waiting For Columbus (Warner Bros), 1978
Down On The Farm (Warner Bros), 1979
Hoy Hoy! (Warner Bros), 1981
As Time Goes By (compilation) (Warner Bros), 1986
Let It Roll (Warner Bros), 1988

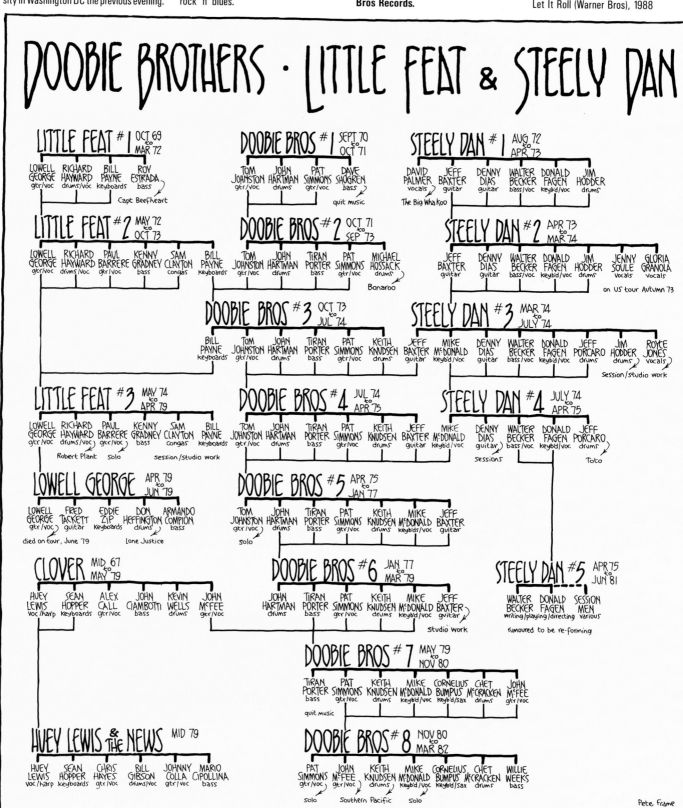

Representing The Mambo (Warner Bros), 1990
Shake Me Up (Polydor), 1991

Lowell George Solo:
Thanks, I'll Eat It Here (Warner Bros), 1979

Little Richard

US vocalist, composer, pianist
Born Richard Wayne Penniman, Macon, Georgia, December 5, 1935

Career: Family had strong religious ties; Richard was Seventh Day Adventist before leaving home for 'medicine show'. Adopted by white Macon couple Ann and Enotris Johnson, who featured as 'Miss Ann' (an intense blues) and as co-writer (Enotris) on **Long Tall Sally** in artist's later career.

Musical career began in 1951. Won talent contest in Atlanta as 'Little Richard'; the prize was a contract with RCA. Two sessions yielded eight songs, mostly ballads and frantic jump-blues. Richard's intense tenor voice was influenced by Roy Brown and gospel blues-wailer Billy Wright.

Success was very limited, and by late 1953 he signed with Peacock Records. During three years recording with the Tempo Toppers vocal group, singles made only local sales. Richard sent demo tape to Art Rupe at Specialty Records. Rupe negotiated release from Peacock, and sent producer Robert 'Bumps' Blackwell to New Orleans to cut some sides with Richard. Results wrote new chapter in annals of rock 'n' roll; debut **Tutti Frutti** charted in late 1955, followed by gems like **Long Tall Sally**, **Rip It Up**, **Ready Teddy**, **Lucille**, **Good Golly Miss Molly** and **The Girl Can't Help It**; latter also became a movie title with Richard in cameo performance. (*Don't Knock The Rock* and *Mr Rock And Roll* also featured him briefly.)

In 1957 Richard suddenly relinquished rock 'n' roll and turned to religion. Career became patchy; Specialty lifted LP tracks for pop hits; he cut gospel songs for various labels, including Coral, End, Goldisc and Mercury (Mercury under the direction of Quincy Jones).

By 1962 Richard's vocals were heard on Little Star singles credited to his band The Upsetters. Then came Mercury single **He Got What He Wanted** with just gospel undertones. 1963 deal with Atlantic yielded gospel sides. 1964 took Richard back to Specialty with storming rocker **Bama Lama Bama Loo**. Moved to Vee Jay to record mixture of soul-tinged new material and crass rehashes of Specialty classics. Among worthwhile singles were **Without Love** and **I Don't Know What You've Got But It's Got Me**, which was his only chart hit on Vee Jay.

Richard then made some interesting raunchy soul sides for Modern and Kent; moved on to OKeh in 1966. Debut for OKeh **Poor Dog** charted briefly. Toured UK and recorded **Get Down With It**, his most torrid rocker in years.

Lean times ensued — brash soul dancers on Brunswick, contemporary production on Reprise; subsequent discs appeared on Green Mountain, Manticore and Mainstream. Richard went from being a refreshingly original baggy-suited stand-up pianist and screamer to an embarrassing poseur in tight pink jumpsuits and effeminate make-up. He then suddenly found religion yet again and rejected his previous homosexuality: 'God made Adam and Eve,

Above: The mercurial Lowell George, another victim in rock 'n' roll heaven.

not Adam and Steve' he quipped in the best-selling biography *The Quasar Of Rock 'n' Roll*, put together by English dentist and rock fan Chas 'Dr Rock' White.

Book put Richard back in limelight, and subsequent documentary for British television about his chequered career showed him in good health and form. With a career resurgence on the cards, WEA signed artist for **Lifetime Friend** LP (1986). Same year saw appearance in *Down And Out In Beverly Hills* movie, from which his single **Great Gosh A Mighty** was Top 50 hit in States. His new-found status saw collaborations with various entertainers, including Beach Boys (**Happy Endings** single), New Edition (**Tears On My Pillow** 45), Philip Bailey (**Twins** movie theme-song) as well as the black nuclear rockers Living Colour (**Time's Up** LP).

Inducted into Rock 'n' Roll Hall Of Fame in 1986, and also recipient of 'star' on Hollywood's Walk Of Fame, Little Richard personifies rebellious spirit of rock 'n' roll, despite (or because of) gay lifestyle and continued religious leanings.

Above: The Georgia Peach, Little Richard. Courtesy Charly Records.

Hit Singles:	US	UK
Tutti Frutti, 1956	17	29
Long Tall Sally, 1956	6	3
Rip It Up, 1956	17	30
She's Got It, 1957	—	15
The Girl Can't Help It, 1957	49	9
Lucille, 1957	21	10
Jenny Jenny, 1957	10	11
Keep A Knockin', 1957	8	21
Good Golly Miss Molly, 1958	10	8
Baby Face, 1959	41	2
By The Light Of The Silvery Moon, 1959	—	17
Bama Lama Bama Loo, 1964	—	20

Albums:
His Biggest Hits (Specialty/London), 1957
The Fabulous Little Richard (Specialty/London), 1959
Well Alright (Specialty/—), 1959
Grooviest 17 Hits (Specialty/—), 1960
The Original (—/Sonet), 1972
All Time Hits (—/Sonet), 1972
22 Original Hits (—/Warwick), 1977
Greatest Hits (—/Embassy), 1977
Tutti Frutti (Accord/—), 1981
Get Down With It (Edsel), 1982
His Greatest Recordings (Ace), 1985
20 Classic Cuts (Ace), 1986
Lifetime Friend (WEA), 1986
Little Richard (The Collection), 1986
The Sessions (Subway), 1987
Rip It Up (Topline), 1987
Rock 'n' Roll Resurrection (Charly), 1987
Little Richard Greatest Hits (MCS), 1988

Living Colour

US group formed 1984

Original line-up: Vernon Reid, guitar; Will Calhoun, drums; Muzz Skillings, bass.

Career: Thunderous rock quartet originally formed by London-born Reid (ex-Defunkt) in New York with Berklee School of Music honour graduate Calhoun and college student Skillings. Vocalist Corey Glover, who appeared in Oliver Stone's movie *Platoon*, was recruited in 1985.

Band's first break was invitation by Mick Jagger to appear on his **Primitive Cool** set, and the Stones' vocalist then produced a demo tape which secured deal with Epic.

Debut album **Vivid** (with Jagger helping production) was potent mix of heavy metal, blues and politics, and this unlikely combination earned Living Colour instant notoriety. Unsure where to place band, they supported such diverse artists as Billy Bragg, Robert Palmer and Anthrax before joining the Stones' Steel Wheels US tour.

Living Colour's frenetic, but musically astute, approach earned a host of MTV awards in the autumn of 1989, and **Cult Of Personality** single (featuring John F.

Kennedy speech) secured Best Hard Rock Performance award at 1990 Grammys.

Second album, **Time's Up** (1990), another Grammy winner, preceded The Miracle Biscuit Tour and first UK dates in the spring of 1991, where critics frantically scrambled for satisfactory description of Living Colour's fiery music. The band would settle for 'rock'.

Hit Singles:	US	UK
Cult Of Personality, 1989	13	—
Love Rears Its Ugly Head, 1991	—	12

Albums:
Vivid (Epic), 1988
Time's Up (Epic), 1990
Biscuits (Epic), 1991

Nils Lofgren

US vocalist, composer, guitarist, pianist
Born Chicago, 1953

Above: I Came To Dance, Nils Lofgren. Courtesy A&M Records.

Career: Lofgren's parents moved to Maryland when he was a teenager. He and his brother began playing in local Washington DC bands. Nils' talents came to attention of Crazy Horse who featured him on their first album. (**Crazy Horse** album remains strong upon hearing even today, thanks in part to Lofgren's lead runs.) This association led to work with Neil Young who used Lofgren on his 1970 album **After The Goldrush**.

18-year-old Lofgren returned to DC to set up own band, Grin. (From this era, LP **1+1** or compilation **The Best Of Grin** are worth a listen.) Grin had split by 1973 and Lofgren was happy to join Neil Young's **Tonight's The Night** tour.

Lofgren spent good part of 1974 reforming Grin and watching it fall apart again. This background ensured modicum of interest when **Nils Lofgren** was released in 1975. Follow-up tour developed cult following and Lofgren seemed ready for stardom. Curious LP, **Back It Up**, appeared, which was 'authorized bootleg' pressed as promo-only item. It became overnight collectors' item.

Despite this, even excellent 1976 **Cry Tough** and tour as opening act for Boston failed to gain expected results. Subsequent LPs are all of interest, **Night After Night** being live. 1979 LP **Nils** managed a lot of US airplay, but didn't chart well. Lofgren again played for Neil Young on 1982 **Trans** LP and joined Young's touring schedule. As expected, Lofgren played with great economy and style, which makes his only slightly successful solo career all the more perplexing, especially since he played guitar for Bruce Springsteen on latter's acclaimed 1985 world tour.

Always the accommodating sideman, Lofgren joined with Ringo Starr for ex-Beatles 1989 US extravaganza Tour For All Generations, and maintained position with Springsteen (featured on **Tunnel Of Love** LP and world tour). Lofgren returned to solo recording (following earlier collapse of Towerbell label for whom he cut **Flip** and **Code Of The Road** LPs) with **Silver Lining** in 1991 for Essential Records. **Valentine** single from album saw Starr and Springsteen make guest appearance.

Guitar: Fender Stratocaster.

Albums:
1+1 (SpinDizzy/Epic), 1971
Nils Lofgren (A&M), 1975
Cry Tough (A&M), 1976
The Best Of Grin Featuring Nils Lofgren (Epic/CBS), 1976
I Came To Dance (A&M), 1977
Night After Night (A&M), 1977
Nils (A&M) 1979
The Best Of (A&M), 1981
A Rhythm Romance (A&M), 1982
Night Fades Away (Backstreet), 1983
Wonderland (MCA), 1983
Code Of The Road (Towerbell), 1986
Silver Lining (Essential), 1991

Love
US group formed 1965

Original line-up: Arthur Lee, vocals, guitar, keyboards; Bryan Maclean, guitar, vocals; Ken Forssi, bass; Alban 'Snoopy' Pfisterer, drums; John Echols, guitar.

Career: Arthur Lee grew up in Memphis but moved to West Coast after British invasion (before it became de rigueur for aspiring American musicians). Was part of nascent music scene in California with several small groups like the LAGs (Los Angeles Group, a name inspired by his hometown success Booker T and The MGs — Memphis Group) and American Four. He saw Byrds perform and decided to explore their style. With Byrds' roadie Bryan Maclean, he lined up Forssi, Echols and drummer Don Conka.

At first they called themselves Grass Roots, but changed to Love when another band appeared with same name (later to become strong US singles band). At some point Conka was thrown out and 'Snoopy' brought in.

**Above: Da Capo, Love.
Courtesy Elektra Records.**

Live Love was always hit or miss and this edge of uncertainty made them a joy to watch. Loyal LA following (group had residency at Bido Lito's in Hollywood) provided strong local reputation. This led Jac Holzman to sign them when he decided Elektra label should expand into growing

rock field. First album was recorded late 1965 and released March 1966. Generally original material, Beatles-Byrds sound and cohesive impact presented very strong debut as well as sounding out growing American response to British rock. **My Little Red Book** became minor hit and **Signed D.C.** (a nod to Don Conka) got some FM play.

Lee already planned to push sound even further on next album. **Da Capo** had two additional players: Tjay Cantrelli on horns and Michael Stuart on drums, with Snoopy on keyboards. They provided the fuller sound Lee sought. Heavy metal had not yet been invented but Lee laid some groundwork with **7 And 7 Is**. He can also take some blame for all magna opera of progressive rock for recording 19-minute **Revelation** over entire second side.

Big-time success failed to come. Uneven live performances and lack of proper tours kept Love an 'underground' band. Love came to be appreciated more in UK than at home (best evidenced by availability of Love albums in UK after US deletion). Size of band also became cumbersome and thrown together make-up took on 'hired hands' atmosphere as Snoopy was fired and Cantrelli disappeared. With remaining members, Lee recorded one of rock's finest albums, **Forever Changes**. It had everything: highs, lows, loud, soft, fast, slow — all mixed into symphonic excitement as fresh today as in 1967. Equally important then, it had lyrics and themes deep enough in year of The Beatles' **Sgt. Pepper** LP. Continued availability confirms the album's timelessness. However, it failed to win the massive audience Lee felt his masterpiece deserved. Within months Love was gone.

In 1968 Lee produced new Love with Jay Donnellan (guitar), Frank Fayad (bass) and George Suranovich (drums). Lee again tried single-handedly to invent heavy metal. This Love lost British-influenced harmonies, replacing them with erratic volume on **Four Sail**. With this album's failure, Lee moved to Blue Thumb Records which later (1969) released double set, **Out Here**. Using recordings from same sessions as Four Sail, it hardly seemed an auspicious start for group on new label.

1970 saw replacement of Donnellan (a.k.a. Jay Lewis) with Gary Rowles, and Love made rare visit to England. This line-up recorded **False Start**, unnotable but for one track, **The Everlasting First**, from Lee's collaboration with Jimi Hendrix during UK visit. (Supposedly an album's worth of material was recorded with Hendrix but results have never been released.) Weakness of **False Start** doomed Love; Lee broke up band before end of 1971. Using old mate Frank Fayad, he released solo album, **Vindicator** (1972), which showed some return to humour and enthusiasm of early Love, but still missed earlier standards and was generally ignored.

In 1973 Elektra released UK compilation **Love Masters**, worth finding for John Tobler's liner notes. Lee recorded another solo album in late 1973 but financial problems prevented its appearance.

Love reappeared in 1974; Lee, Melvan Whittington (guitars), John Sterling (guitars), Joe Blocker (drums), Sherwood Akuna (bass), Robert Rozelle (bass) and some guest/session musicians recorded the poor **Reel-To-Real**. Love deservedly disappeared again. Lee continued to play various one-off dates, trying to live down past.

One musician with whom he worked was John Sterling. In 1977 he got Lee and Maclean to re-form Love with himself, Kim Kesteron (bass) and George Suranovich

(drums). Band tried recapturing the feel of early Love but perhaps should have been more inventive.

Interest in Love never died out as **Forever Changes** remained in Elektra catalogue, and Rhino Records sold a reasonable amount of 1980 compilation, **Best Of Love**. This led Rhino to release **Arthur Lee** in 1981 — interesting but totally out of sync with times. MCA released curious LP in 1982 with one side featuring eight tracks from **Out Here** and live side from Fillmore East with no recording dates or personnel listed. The undying loyalty and unfailing interest in Love is justifiable since they were a brilliant band with several excellent albums, and classic **Forever Changes** LP is a must for any record collection.

As a bizarre footnote, Lee surfaced in 1989 after several years of inactivity, to feature in 'time-warp' Psychedelic Summer festival in Los Angeles with assorted hippies from 'those good old days'.

Albums
Love (Elektra), 1966
Da Capo (Elektra), 1967
Forever Changes (Elektra), 1967
Four Sail (Elektra), 1969
Out Here (Blue Thumb/Harvest), 1969
False Start (Blue Thumb/Harvest), 1970
Love Revisited (Elektra), 1970
Love Masters (—/Elektra), 1973
Reel-To-Real (RSO), 1974
Best Of Love (Rhino/—), 1980
Love Live (Rhino/—), 1982
Love (MCA/—), 1982
Out There (Bigbeat), 1988

Arthur Lee Solo:
Vindicator (A&M), 1972
Arthur Lee (Rhino/Beggar's Banquet), 1982

Lovin' Spoonful
US group formed 1964

Original line-up: John Sebastian, guitar, vocals, harmonica, autoharp; Zal Yanovsky, guitar; Joe Butler, drums; Steve Boone, bass.

Career: Sebastian and Yanovsky were together in folk group Mugwumps. Rest of band went on to form Mamas And Papas. Sebastian travelled south. Upon return to New York in 1965, producer Eric Jacobson suggested Sebastian record his own songs.

Above: The Lovin' Spoonful, 'live' on UK TV show Ready Steady Go.

Lovin' Spoonful became New York club circuit favourites and record deal with Kama Sutra followed.

Band refused to dress or sound like popular English groups of time, although British invasion influence is obvious in band's rock fusion of folk and blues. Sebastian's **Do You Believe In Magic?** reflected excitement and energy of growing rock scene. **Daydream** broke group in UK and **Summer In The City** became classic out-of-school, good-time paean, as well as US No. 1. Establishment wanted to tap rock's enthusiasm and Sebastian found himself in demand for scoring 'with it' movies (Francis Ford Coppola's *You're A Big Boy Now* and Woody Allen's *What's Up Tiger Lily?*).

Drug culture was still hidden side of rock music and Yanovsky's bust in 1967 proved devastating blow to popularity. Worse, Yanovsky went free by naming others involved and band's reputation within rock business was finished. Jerry Yester (brother of Association's Jim Yester) replaced Yanovsky for **Everything Playing** LP. By 1968, group had collapsed.

Subsequent careers have been chequered. Following appearance at Woodstock in 1969, Sebastian carved out living writing TV music, most notably **Welcome Back, Kotter** from series of same name (a US No. 1) and soundtrack for *Care Bears* and *The Jerk II* shows, and occasional gigs. Butler tried to re-form group in early 1970s, while Yester produced Tom Waits' debut LP **Closing Time**. Final word from band came when reunited in 1980 for spot in Paul Simon's *One Trick Pony* movie.

Although Sebastian's songs sound a little airy-fairy now, there is no doubting the class of **Summer In The City** and **Do You Believe In Magic?**. Sadly, Spoonful did not progress and suffered an abrupt exit from the upper echelons of pop's frontrunners.

Hit Singles:	US	UK
Do You Believe In Magic?, 1965	9	—
You Didn't Have To Be So Nice, 1965	10	—
Daydream, 1966	2	2
Did You Ever Have To Make Up Your Mind, 1966	2	—
Summer In The City, 1966	1	8
Rain On The Roof, 1966	10	—
Nashville Cats, 1966	8	26
Darling Be Home Soon, 1967	15	44
Six O'Clock, 1967	18	—

John Sebastian Solo:
Welcome Back, Kotter, 1976   1   —

Albums:
The Best . . . Lovin' Spoonful (Kama
   Sutra/—), 1967
File (—/Pye), 1977
Anthology (Rhino/—), 1990

Worth Searching Out:
Hums (Kama Sutra), 1967
You're A Big Boy Now (Kama Sutra),
   1967
Greatest Hits (Golden Hour), 1975
Golden Hour Of The Lovin' Spoonful's
   Greatest Hits (—/Golden Hour), 1977
Jug Band Music (Edsel), 1986
Collection (Masters), 1986 (Holland)

**Above: Greatest Hits, The Lovin'
Spoonful. Courtesy Kama Sutra.**

Nick Lowe

UK vocalist, bassist, producer
Born Woolridge, Suffolk, March 24, 1949

Career: First significant group was Kipp-
ington Lodge, from Tunbridge Wells area;
also included Brinsley Schwarz, guitar, Bob
Andrews, keyboards. Recorded series of
singles during second half of 60s without
success, so decided at end of decade to
change group name to Brinsley Schwarz.
Management company Famepushers Ltd
tried to launch 'new' group with debut gig
at Fillmore East, New York, to coincide with
release of first LP. This resulted in few taking group seriously, and career blighted
thereafter, despite five more LPs, several
of which were of above average quality,
with many Lowe songs. Group folded in
March 1975.

Lowe worked as songwriter and producer
(for Graham Parker and The Rumour, which
included Schwarz and Andrews) and released pseudonymous singles, then joined new
manager Jake Riviera (real name Andrew
Jakeman) in launch of Stiff Records with
ex-Brinsley manager Dave Robinson.

First Stiff release was Lowe's classic
single **So It Goes**, and much of label's early output involved Lowe either as artist or
producer (for The Damned, Wreckless Eric,
etc) until Riviera signed Elvis Costello,
whose records Lowe produced for several
years with great success. Also worked as
producer for Dr Feelgood plus further
Graham Parker album. Formed alliance with
Dave Edmunds in group Rockpile, featured
with Costello, Edmunds and Ian Dury in Stiff
package tour at end of 1977.

Left Stiff with Riviera and Costello in late
1977, signed with Radar label; made UK
Top 10 with first Radar release; had further hits by end of 1979. Continued to produce Costello, and recorded own albums and
Edmunds albums using Rockpile musicians.
Also produced first single by Pretenders.

Married Carlene Carter (step-daughter of
Johnny Cash).

During 1980, contractual hassles which
had prevented Rockpile recording under
group name resolved, but this only resulted
in group splitting up after single LP. Lowe
made third solo album; produced LPs for
Costello and Dr Feelgood, as well as for wife
during 1981, and in 1982 formed band Noise
To Go, with Paul Carrack (ex-Ace, Squeeze)
who was achieving solo success on his own
account. He produced Carrack and Fabulous
Thunderbirds and cut fourth LP. After much
touring, spent time during first half of 1983
producing John Hiatt and Carlene Carter.
Cut solo **Pinker And Prouder Than
Previous** in 1988, and then, in 1991, teamed
with Ry Cooder, drummer Jim Keltner and
Hiatt for The Little Village project.

Nick Lowe is regarded as a man of many
talents — producer, songwriter, singer, musician — but has only achieved major success consistently as record producer. He
is well known around the world, but conceivably has yet to reach full artistic potential due to diversification. At his best, his
'pure pop for now people' has few equals
in history of rock music.

**Above: Jesus Of Cool, Nick Lowe.
Courtesy Radar Records.**

Hit Singles:	US	UK
I Love The Sound Of Breaking		
Glass, 1978	—	7
Cruel To Be Kind, 1979	12	12

Albums:
Jesus Of Cool (US title: Pure Pop For
   Now People) (Columbia/Radar), 1978
Labour Of Lust (Columbia/Radar), 1979
Nick The Knife (Columbia/F-Beat), 1982
The Abominable Showman (Columbia/
   F-Beat), 1983

Nick Lowe And His Cowboy Outfit
   (RCA), 1984
16 All-Time Lowes (Demon), 1984
Rose Of England (F-Beat), 1985
Pinker And Prouder Than Previous
   (—/Demon), 1988
Basher The Best Of (Columbia/Demon),
   1989
Party Of One (Reprise/Warner Bros), 1990

With Rockpile:
Seconds Of Pleasure (Columbia/F-Beat),
   1980

With Brinsley Schwarz:
Nervous On The Road (Liberty), 1972
New Favourites Of Brinsley Schwarz
   (Liberty), 1974

Worth Searching Out:
Fifteen Thoughts Of Brinsley Schwarz
   (compilation) (UA), 1978

Lynyrd Skynyrd

US group formed 1965

Original line-up: Ronnie Van Zant, vocals;
Gary Rossington, guitar; Allen Collins,
guitar.

Career: Originally formed in Jacksonville,
Florida, as high-school trio, named after their
authoritarian PE teacher, Leonard Skinner.
By 1972, full line-up completed with Leon
Wilkeson (bass), Billy Powell (keyboards) and
Robert Burns (drums). Discovered playing
Southern bars and clubs by Al Kooper, who
immediately signed them to his Sounds Of
The South label. Session bassist Ed King
(ex-Strawberry Alarm Clock) brought in by
Kooper as full-time member. First album,
Pronounced Leh-nerd Skin-nerd, received
favourable response. Closing cut from
album, **Free Bird**, later became group an-
them, achieving minor chart placings in US
and UK following several re-releases.

Career boosted by playing support on The
Who's 1973 US tour. Quickly established
themselves as one of America's most
celebrated boogie bands, boasting three
guitarists. Next album, **Second Helping**,
went gold. Set included US hit single, **Sweet
Home Alabama** their famous riposte to Neil
Young's scathing **Southern Man** and
Alabama put-downs. Third album, **Nuthin'
Fancy** also went gold. Included US Top 30
hit **Saturday Night Special**.

**Above: Lynyrd Skynyrd, who made
another comeback in 1992.**

Extensive touring schedules consistently drained group's energies, prompting Burns'
departure, replaced by Artimus Pyle. Not
surprisingly, seasoned sessioneer Ed King
left shortly afterwards. Undeterred,
Skynyrd kept on boogieing and their increasingly raucous behaviour inspired strong,
devoted following.

On October 20, 1977, a week after the
release of the notable **Street Survivors**
LP, Skynyrd embarked on lengthy US tour.
Their private plane took off from Greenville,
South Carolina, en route for Baton Rouge,
Louisiana; approaching Gillsburg, Mississippi, the plane crashed in a wood, 200 yards
from an open field. Casualties included Ronnie Van Zant, Steve Gaines, roadie Dean
Kirkpatrick, and backing singer Cassie
Gaines. The tragedy shook the rock world,
for the group had always been much loved
for their aggressive, uncompromising ap-
proach: MCA quickly stopped release of
Survivors LP with its prophetic cover. Even
Neil Young sang **Sweet Home Alabama**
at one of his concerts in their memory.

In 1979, spirit of LS was reborn with
Rossington Collins Band, formed by remaining members of group, plus vocalist Dale
Krantz, guitarist Barry Harwood and drummer Dell Hess. Aggregation cut a couple of
albums for MCA before splitting up,
although 1987 saw re-formation for Lynyrd
Skynyrd celebration tour, with Van Zant's
brother Johnny, founder of .38 Special,
fronting the outfit. MCA subsequently
issued a live double album of the concerts,
For The Glory Of The South, although Collins' death in 1990 from respiratory problems further clouded group's history.

Hit Singles:	US	UK
Sweet Home Alabama, 1974	8	—
Free Bird, 1974	19	—

Albums:
Pronounced Leh-nerd Skin-nerd (MCA),
   1974
Second Helping (MCA), 1974
Nuthin' Fancy (MCA), 1975
Gimme Back My Bullets (MCA), 1976
One More From The Road (double live)
   (MCA), 1976
Street Survivors (MCA), 1977
First And Last (MCA), 1978
A Legend (MCA), 1987
Nuthin' Fancy (MCA), 1987
For The Glory Of The South (MCA), 1988

Madness

UK group formed 1978

Original line-up: Suggs, (Graham McPherson), vocals; Chas Smash, vocals, compere, dancer; Chris Foreman, guitar; Lee 'Kix' Thompson, saxophone; Mark Bedford, bass; Dan Woodgate, drums.

Career: Formed in North London as The Invaders, changed name to Madness (after song by ska hero Prince Buster). In 1979, Specials launched 2 Tone records; Madness invited to cut single **The Prince/Madness**, which scored first hit. Group then signed by Stiff and became biggest act on label by far with 13 further consecutive UK hits and five Top 10 LPs by end of 1982, mostly composed within band.

With appealing mixture of ska (now largely abandoned), music hall, pop, R&B, visual comedy and biting yet amusing social comment, Madness became most consistent UK hitmakers of 80s, guaranteed sell-out shows wherever they appear in UK, and to some extent in Europe. American success eluded them until 1983, perhaps because of curiously British lyrical content/humour and appearance. In 1981 made feature film financed by Stiff, *Take It Or Leave It*, which predictably achieved mammoth sales for video medium. **Complete Madness**, TV-advertised hits compilation, topped UK album charts for three weeks during 1982.

Our House (1982) marked US breakthrough, followed by five-week tour including dates as support for both Bowie and The Police.

Following Christmas gig at London's Lyceum, in aid of Greenpeace, Mike Barson announced decision to quit band to live in Holland with Dutch wife Sandra. As six-piece, the band greeted 1984 with **Michael Caine** single on which the actor 'sang'. Also opened own Liquidator studio in London.

After five years and 18 consecutive hit singles, they left Stiff in May 1984 to form own Zarjazz label with Feargal Sharkey single as first release.

Pulling in members of UB40, Specials, General Public, Pioneers and Afrodiziak, Madness put together admirable **Starvation** charity single as their contribution to African famine relief in 1985 but it peaked at 33 on national chart. Meanwhile, a band called The Wayfarers played to packed house at Bull and Gate Pub in Kentish Town, London — and proved to be Madness rehearsing their new album prior to recording. Following hit single, **Uncle Sam**, showed band had lost none of its good, healthy humour.

Band also released **Mad Not Mad** album in same year, which spawned several minor hit singles. However, level of success had

diminished, and difficulties with the Zarjazz operation prompted split within ranks. Suggs, Foreman, Smyth and Thompson resurfaced two years later as The Madness, having signed with Virgin UK. Their eponymous debut LP was released in May 1988. Mark Bedford has since dabbled with television scores, while Graham McPherson (Suggs) found sensible employment as manager of The Fall.

In their prime, Madness' unique blend of ska and British music-hall lit up the British charts. If only the Americans had listened!

Hit Singles:	US	UK
The Prince, 1979	—	16
One Step Beyond, 1979	—	7
My Girl, 1980	—	3
Work Rest And Play, 1980	—	6
Baggy Trousers, 1980	—	3
Embarrassment, 1980	—	4
Return Of The Los Palmas 7, 1981	—	7
Grey Day, 1981	—	4
Shut Up, 1981	—	7
It Must Be Love, 1981	—	4
Cardiac Arrest, 1982	—	14
House Of Fun, 1982	—	1
Driving In My Car, 1982	—	4
Our House, 1982	—	5
Tomorrow's Just Another Day, 1983	—	8
Yesterday's Men, 1985	—	18

Albums:
One Step Beyond (Sire/Stiff), 1980
Absolutely (Sire/Stiff), 1980
Seven (—/Stiff), 1981
Complete Madness (—/Stiff), 1982
The Rise And Fall (—/Stiff), 1982
Keep Moving (Stiff), 1984
Mad Not Mad (Virgin), 1985
Utter Madness (Virgin), 1986
The Madness (Virgin), 1988

Madonna

US vocalist
Born Madonna Ciccone, Detroit, Michigan, 1961

Career: First genuine female 'star' of rock music, whose abilities have been undermined by sexual posturing and provocative outpourings. Madonna's 1991 movie *In Bed With Madonna* (*Truth Or Dare* in US) chronicled her Blond Ambition tour of the previous year, and confirmed that Hollywood's crown does indeed sit comfortably on her oft-tinted head.

After moving from Detroit home to New York in 1978, Madonna worked with choreographer Pearl Lange in Alvin Ailey's dance troupe, and featured in underground movie *Certain Sacrifice*. After a short period in Paris with Patrick Hernandez Revue, she

Left: Madness, Stiff Records' biggest hitmakers, live in London.

Left: Madonna exudes a unique presence in whatever guise she decides to adopt.

returned to the States, signing with Sire Records after a period cutting demos for Adam Alter's Gotham Productions. Alter subsequently sued Madonna (successfully, but for nominal damages). Sire executives Michael Rosenblatt and Seymour Stein provided upbeat club material, **Everybody** and **Physical Attraction**, for her first two hits.

Early albums **Madonna** (producer Reggie Lucas) and **Like A Virgin** (producer Nile Rodgers) contained the mix of a heavy dance beat astride Madonna's trembling vocals, a formula sensibly followed in her self-produced set (with Stephen Bray and Patrick Leonard) **True Blue**.

Marriage to actor Sean Penn (1985) prompted almost daily battle with tabloid press, and Madonna did little to dampen the fire. Early nude shots (from 1977) appeared in *Playboy* and *Penthouse* magazines,

Above: True Blue, Madonna. Courtesy Sire Records.

and the artist (with tempestuous Penn) seemed set on pushing self-destruction button. Flimsy parallel movie career — *Desperately Seeking Susan, Shanghai Surprise, Dick Tracy* — allowed critics full rein. Madonna separated from Penn in 1987, which seemed to lead to a staggering blitz on the pop charts.

Succession of US/UK No. 1 hits and electrifying concerts moved Madonna to the forefront of pop performers, although controversy surrounding the 1989 set **Like A Prayer** (pro-Catholic said Madonna, anti-said the Church) prompted Pepsi Cola to withdraw a commercial featuring the artist.

Similar difficulties befell **The Immaculate Collection** (1990), with Jewish lobbyists concerned about lyrical content which might 'incite anti-Semitism'. The accompanying video (for the single **Justify My Love**) was also clouded in furore with even the liberal MTV declaring a blackout.

As of late 1991, Madonna signed a three-year deal with Time-Warner for an estimated 70 million dollars; however, insiders believe the total accumulation of this deal could well exceed Michael Jackson's billion-dollar contract with Sony.

A champion of feminism, and a surprising heroine of many feminists, the overtly erotic Madonna is an astute individual, who is both trend-setter and trend-follower (when it suits). Furthermore, her music has matured, and her well-produced stage shows and albums indicate a propensity for possible mature reflection in the years (or decades) to come.

Hit Singles:	US	UK
Holiday, 1983*	16	3
Borderline, 1984	10	—
Lucky Star, 1984	4	14

	US	UK
Like A Virgin, 1985	1	3
Material Girl, 1985	1	2
Crazy For You, 1985	1	2
Angel, 1985	5	5
Into The Groove, 1985	1	1
Dress You Up, 1985	5	5
Gambler, 1985	4	4
True Blue, 1986	3	1
Live To Tell, 1986	—	2
Open Your Heart, 1986	1	4
Papa Don't Preach, 1986	1	1
Who's That Girl, 1987	1	1
La Isla Bonita, 1987	3	1
Causing A Commotion, 1987	2	4
Look Of Love, 1987	—	9
Like A Prayer, 1989	1	1
Express Yourself, 1989	2	5
Cherish, 1989	2	3
Dear Jessie, 1989	—	5
Lovesong (with Prince), 1989	1	1
Vogue, 1990	1	1
Hanky Panky, 1990	10	2
Justify My Love, 1990	1	2
Oh Father, 1990	20	—
Crazy For You (re-mix), 1990	—	2
Rescue Me, 1991	9	3
Holiday, 1991	—	5

*1985 in UK

Albums:
Madonna (Sire), 1983
Like A Virgin (Sire), 1984
True Blue (Sire), 1986
You Can Dance (Sire), 1987
Like A Prayer (Sire), 1989
The Immaculate Collection (Sire), 1990
I'm Breathless (from *Dick Tracy*) (Sire), 1990

Below: Hits Of Gold, The Mamas And The Papas. Courtesy ABC Records.

The Mamas And The Papas

US vocal group formed 1965

Original line-up: John Phillips; Michelle Phillips; Cass Elliott; Denny Doherty.

Career: One of first aggregations to make freewheeling, California hippie image commercially acceptable, with series of records that combined strong, memorable melodies with soaring vocal harmonies and distinctive folk-rock sound.

Ex-folkie John Phillips and wife Michelle came together with Cass Elliott and Denny Doherty, former members of New York band The Mugwumps, in Virgin Islands. Almost immediately, guiding light Phillips moved outfit to LA and arranged record deal with Lou Adler's newly formed Dunhill label.

First single was Phillips' **California Dreamin'**, a key flower-power cut almost as evocative as **San Francisco (Be Sure To Wear Flowers In Your Hair)** which Phillips also composed. Top 10 hit in US and

substantial hit elsewhere, it set group on road to success, including three more major hits in 1966.

Despite single success and several gold albums, group was not destined for longevity. John and Michelle Phillip's marriage started teetering in 1966, and this exacerbated break-up two years later. Subsequently, Phillips went into film production and enjoyed life as Californian pop aristocrat before arrest (and then short incarceration) for drug possession. Upon his release, teamed with Doherty for short-lived reunion, and then resurfaced in 1989 with a new Mamas And Papas, the line up comprising Spanky MacFarlane, Scott 'Are You Going To San Francisco' McKenzie, Phillips and his son; also composed **Kokomo** hit for Beach Boys.

Michelle Phillips surfaced occasionally for film roles while providing staple fare for gossip columnists. Mama Cass Elliott died in 1974 of heart attack in London hotel, after patchy solo career; although her solo singles **Dream A Little Dream Of Me** and **It's Getting Better** returned her temporarily to charts.

Despite their brief career with original line-up, The Mamas And Papas exerted considerable influence on 60s music scene, paving way for more heavyweight protagonists of Aquarian Age. Furthermore, they left behind cuts which have become much-played classics, particularly the song **California Dreamin'** which earned accolade as Greatest Pop Single Of All-Time in a prominent 70s media poll.

Hit Singles:

	US	UK
California Dreamin', 1966	4	23
Monday Monday, 1966	1	3
I Saw Her Again, 1966	5	11
Words Of Love, 1966	5	47
Dedicated To The One I Love, 1967	2	2
Creeque Alley, 1967	5	9
Twelve Thirty, 1967	20	—

Albums:
Farewell To The First Golden Era (Dunhill/—), 1968
The Papas And The Mamas (Dunhill/RCA), 1968
Hits Of Gold (ABC), 1969
A Gathering Of Flowers (Dunhill/Probe), 1970
Sixteen Of Their Greatest Hits (Dunhill/—), 1970
Twenty Golden Hits (Dunhill/Probe), 1972
The Best Of The Mamas And The Papas (—/Arcade), 1977
Golden Greats (MCA), 1985

Worth Searching Out:
If You Can Believe Your Eyes And Ears (Dunhill/RCA), 1966

Manfred Mann

UK band formed 1962

Original line-up: Manfred Mann, keyboards; Paul Jones, vocals, harmonica; Mike Vickers, reeds, guitar; Dave Richmond, bass; Mike Hugg, drums.

Career: South African-born Mann and Mike Hugg put together Mann-Hugg Blues Brothers in late 1962 and started gigging on burgeoning London blues circuit. Changing name to Manfred Mann, band signed with HMV and recorded first single, **Why Should We Not**.

Tom McGuinness replaced Dave Richmond on bass on release of third single, **5-4-3-2-1**.

Track, which featured Paul Jones' harmonica, was adopted as theme tune for TV show *Ready Steady Go* and became major hit. From that time until end of 60s, band were rarely out of singles charts, with succession of songs from wide variety of sources, particularly US soul material (**Doo Wah Diddy Diddy**, **Oh No Not My Baby**) and Bob Dylan (**If You Gotta Go, Go Now, Just Like A Woman, Mighty Quinn**).

Changes took place during this period, however; Mike Vickers left at end of 1965, McGuinness switched to lead guitar and Jack Bruce joined on bass; six months later Jones left to pursue solo career as singer (and later actor), and Bruce quit to join supergroup Cream. Their respective replacements were Mike D'Abo from Band Of Angels and Klaus Voorman.

However, by end of decade, after 18 hit singles, members were tired of restrictions of pop formula. Mann folded band, and he and Hugg put together Manfred Mann Chapter Three. More orientated towards albums, outfit lasted for couple of years. Mann then put together Manfred Mann's Earth Band. Original line-up comprised Mann, Colin Pattenden (bass), Mick Rogers (guitar), and Chris Slade (drums).

From beginning, band followed ambitious rock direction, backing album releases with heavy touring schedules in UK and US. In 1973 they had first hit single with **Joybringer** based on theme from Holst's *Planets*, and in mid-70s scored with cover

Above: Extensions, Manhattan Transfer. Courtesy Atlantic Records.

of Bruce Springsteen's **Blinded By The Light**. **Davy's On The Road Again** was also major hit, and band ground on through more moderate times (and frequent personnel changes) until split in 1968.

McGuinness enjoyed brief flurry with McGuinness Flint before pair joined forces with Jones (now a DJ for London radio station Jazz FM) in The Blues Band, with guitarist Dave Kelly and bass player Gary Fletcher. Despite temporary break from 1982, group continues to gig into 90s, with Rob Townshend (ex-Family) now on drums; cut **One More Time** LP in 1989.

In celebration of Tom McGuinness' 50th birthday, both Manfred Mann and McGuinness Flint units re-formed for one-off tribute gig (with Blues Band) at London's Town & Country club in December 1991.

Hit Singles:

	US	UK
5-4-3-2-1, 1964	—	5
Hubble Bubble Toil And Trouble, 1964	—	11
Doo Wah Diddy Diddy, 1964	1	1
Sha La La, 1964	12	3
Come Tomorrow, 1965	50	4
Oh No Not My Baby, 1965	—	11
If You Gotta Go, Go Now, 1965	—	2
Pretty Flamingo, 1966	29	1
Just Like A Woman, 1966	—	10
Semi-Detached Suburban Mr James, 1966	—	2
Ha! Ha! Said The Clown, 1967	—	4
Mighty Quinn, 1968	10	1
My Name Is Jack, 1968	—	8
Fox On The Run, 1968	—	5
Ragamuffin Man, 1969	—	8

Manfred Mann's Earth Band:

	US	UK
Joybringer, 1973	—	9
Blinded By The Light, 1976	1	6
Davy's On The Road Again, 1978	—	6

Albums:
The Best Of Manfred Mann (Mercury/Nut), 1977

Manfred Mann's Earth Band:
Earth Band (Bronze), 1972
Glorified, Magnified (Bronze), 1972
Messin' (Bronze), 1973
Solar Fire (Polydor/Bronze), 1973
The Good Earth (Warner Bros/Bronze), 1974
Nightingales And Bombers (Warner Bros/Bronze), 1975
Mannerisms (—/Sonic), 1976
The Roaring Silence (Warner Bros/Bronze), 1976
Watch (Warner Bros/Bronze), 1978
Angel Station (Warner Bros/Bronze), 1979
The R&B Years (—/See For Miles), 1982
Semi-Detached Suburban (—/EMI), 1979
Chance (Warner Bros/Bronze), 1980
Somewhere In Afrika (—/Bronze), 1983
Budapest (—/Bronze), 1984
The Singles Plus (EMI), 1986

Worth Searching Out:
Manfred Mann Chapter Three:
Chapter Three (Polydor), 1970

Manhattan Transfer

US vocal group formed 1969

Original line-up: Tim Hauser; Janis Siegel; Alan Paul; Laurel Masse.

Career: Originally signed to Capitol Records in 1969; 1971 set **Jukin'** initially failed miserably; Revamped, restyled and with only Hauser remaining, group earned reputation in early 70s in New York.

Hauser had been with R&B vocal group Criterions in 50s; later worked as producer and actor. Paul (with BA in Music and Drama) was film and stage actor; appearing on Broadway in *Camelot, The King And I* and *Oliver*. Masse and Siegel had singing backgrounds — primarily jingles and session vocals. Siegel had recorded for Lieber and Stoller with Young Generation on Red Bird R&B label.

After period in gay bars and bath houses, quartet developed kitsch swing-era image, but vocal ability partially swamped by grandiose stage act. Transfer, however, took good advice on album material, and charted sporadically since **Operator** (1975). Main success was in Europe, particularly France, and UK. Scored eight British Top 50 entries between 1978 and 1980. Lyrical ballad **Chanson D'Amour** made No. 1 in UK.

With Cheryl Bentyne replacing Masse, Transfer entered new era with 1979 set **Extensions**. Produced by guitarist Jay Graydon, album had futuristic air while retaining strong jazz roots. Included stage favourite **Birdland** (used as jingle for Akai stereo), rock-flavoured **Nothin' You Can Do**

About It and electronic **Twilight Zone**, which returned outfit to US charts.

Reputation confirmed by Grammy awards and *Downbeat* magazine honour of Best Vocal Group in 1980 poll. Chart status maintained with 1981 LP **Mecca For Moderns**, which made US Top 40. **Best Of** collection charted following year.

Unit's powerful live act was refined in recent years; camp nostalgia 'feel' was in part replaced by contemporary styling and design. Vocally, the group used perfect mix of jazz, R&B and rock material. Alan Paul's soulful reading of classic doo-wop numbers from the 50s earned him comparisons with leading black performers.

Hit Singles:

	US	UK
Chanson D'Amour, 1977	—	1
Walk In Love, 1978	—	12
On A Little Street In Singapore, 1978	—	20
Boy From New York City, 1981	7	—
Spice Of Life, 1984	40	19

Albums:
Jukin' (with Gene Pistilli) (Capitol/MFP), 1971
Manhattan Transfer (Atlantic), 1975
Coming Out (Atlantic), 1976
Pastiche (Atlantic), 1978
Live (Atlantic), 1978
Extensions (Atlantic), 1979
Mecca For Moderns (Atlantic), 1981
Best Of (Atlantic), 1982
Bodies And Souls (Atlantic), 1984
Bop Doo Wop (Atlantic), 1985
Brazil (WEA), 1987

Barry Manilow

US vocalist, pianist, composer
Born Brooklyn, New York, June 17, 1946

Career: While studying at New York College of Music and Juilliard Academy, Manilow had part-time job in mail room at Columbia Records. After working on *Callback* series of talent shows for WCBS-TV, in 1967 became conductor/arranger for Ed Sullivan TV specials. Met Bette Midler when working as pianist at New York's Continental Baths in 1972. Manilow arranged and co-produced her first two albums as well as joining her 1973 US tour as musical director and pianist. Tour gave him chance to showcase own talents as opening act, leading to own tour in 1974 and recording deal with Arista Records.

Mandy topped US charts in January 1975 within nine months of release, and was first of string of hits which showed crossover between pop and MOR with audiences ranging from young girls to parents.

Manilow's slick and rather schmaltzy stage shows — in the Liberace mould though not quite so extreme — have won him major international audience while at same time nauseating many critics. His records have been consistently well crafted and there is real talent behind the manufactured show-biz image.

Besides his records, Manilow has been prolific writer of TV and radio jingles.

Hit Singles:

	US	UK
Mandy, 1975	1	11
It's A Miracle, 1975	12	—
Could It Be Magic, 1975	6	25*
I Write The Songs, 1976	1	—
Tryin' To Get The Feeling Again, 1976	10	—
Weekend In New England, 1977	10	—
Looks Like We Made It, 1977	1	—
Can't Smile Without You, 1978	3	43
Even Now, 1978	19	—
Copacabana, 1978	8	42
Ready To Take A Chance Again, 1978	11	—
Somewhere In The Night, 1979	1	42
Ships, 1979	9	—
When I Wanted You, 1979	20	—
I Made It Through The Rain, 1980	10	6
Bermuda Triangle, 1981	—	15
Let's Hang On, 1981	32	12
The Old Songs, 1981	15	48
I Wanna Do It With You, 1982	—	8
Read 'Em And Weep, 1983	18	17
*1978 UK		

Albums:
Barry Manilow I (Arista), 1973
Barry Manilow II (Arista/—), 1974
Mandy (—/Arista), 1975
This One's For You (Arista), 1976
Trying To Get The Feeling (Arista/Fame), 1975
Manilow Magic — The Best Of (—/Arista), 1976
Greatest Hits (Arista), 1978
Even Now (Arista), 1978
One Voice (Arista), 1979
All The Best — Barry (Arista), 1980
If I Should Love Again (Arista), 1981
Here Comes The Night (Arista/—), 1981
Barry Live In Britain (Arista), 1982
Oh, Julie! (Arista), 1982
I Wanna Do It With You (Arista), 1982
A Touch More Magic (Arista), 1983
2am Paradise Café (Arista), 1984
Manilow (RCA), 1985
Swing Street (Arista), 1987
Live On Broadway (rec. 1989) (Arista), 1990
Because It's Xmas (Arista), 1990
Showstoppers (Arista), 1991

Marillion

UK group formed 1982

Original line-up: Fish, vocals; Mark Kelly, keyboards; Steve Rothery, guitar; Pete Trewavas, bass.

Career: Origins of Aylesbury-based quintet go back to 1979 when known as Silmarillion from a J.R.R. Tolkien novel. Name changed when various line-up changes saw Scotsman Fish join.

Exposure on Tommy Vance's BBC Radio One show led to extensive UK club tour, record deal with EMI and string of sell-out dates at Marquee club in London.

With just one minor hit single **Market Square Heroes** behind them, Marillion headlined at prestigious Hammersmith Odeon for two sell-out concert dates.

Debut album, **Script For A Jester's Tear** peaked at No. 7 on UK chart, while original drummer was replaced by Ian Mosley, former drummer in *Hair* and *Jesus Christ Superstar* musicals and ex-member of Curved Air.

European and North American tours in 1984 helped build reputation while mushrooming market in Marillion bootlegs prompted release of budget-price **Real To Real** live album.

However, 1985 album **Misplaced Childhood** provided real breakthrough, spawning single **Kayleigh** and occupying upper end of UK charts for greater part of year.

Following **Clutching At Straws** LP, which earned No. 2 on UK chart, charismatic and controversial frontman Fish quit, coming out with 1990 set **Vigil In The Wilderness Of Mirrors**, featuring Mike Simmonds on keyboards and Frank Usher on guitar. The vocalist signed with Polydor Records in 1991, following litigation problems with EMI, debuting for his new label in December of that year with **Internal Exile**.

Fish's replacement was Steve Hogarth (ex-Europeans), who appeared on **Seasons End** and **Holidays In Eden** albums, and featured in European tours of 1989-90.

Undoubtedly a throwback, Marillion have maintained impetus despite loss of the Fishman, who himself looks set to carry all before him.

Hit Singles:

	US	UK
Garden Party, 1983	—	16
Punch And Judy, 1984	—	16
Kayleigh, 1985	—	2
Lavender, 1985	—	5
Incommunicado, 1987	—	6
Sugar Mice, 1987	—	22

Albums:
Script For A Jester's Tear (EMI), 1983
Fugazi (EMI), 1984
Real To Real (live) (EMI), 1984
Misplaced Childhood (EMI), 1985
Clutching At Straws (EMI), 1987
Besides Themselves (EMI), 1987
Brief Encounter (Capitol/—)
The Thieving Magpie (Capitol/EMI), 1988
Seasons End (Capitol/EMI), 1989

Fish Solo:
Vigil In The Wilderness Of Mirrors (Capitol), 1990

Bob Marley

Jamaican vocalist, composer
Born Robert Nesta Marley, St Anns, Jamaica, 1945 (passport gave exact date as February 6, but Marley said this was inaccurate)
Died May 11, 1980

Career: Son of an English army captain and Jamaican mother, Bob Marley was undoubtedly *the* giant figure in the evolution of reggae music.

While at Jamaica's Stepney School, became friendly with Winston Hubert McIntosh and Neville O'Reiley Livingstone; as Peter Tosh and Bunny Wailer they were later to join Marley in forming The Wailers.

Above: Rasta Revolution, Bob Marley. Courtesy Trojan Records.

At 16 cut debut record **Judge Not**, co-written with mentor Joe Higgs, at Ken Khouri's Federal Studio in Kingston. Then with Leslie Kong producing, covered Brook Benton's **One Cup Of Coffee** after seeing the American star in concert with Dinah Washington.

Teaming with Tosh and Wailer, plus Junior Braithwaite and Beverly Kelso, Marley formed The Wailin' Wailers; signed to Clement Coxsone Dodds' Studio One label and sold more than 80,000 copies of first single **Simmer Down**.

Backed by studio band Skatalites, quintet worked through ska and rock-steady eras towards dawn of reggae style. However, they broke up in 1966 following wrangles over payment for their recordings.

Marley joined his mother in Delaware, US, and worked in Chrysler car factory before returning to Jamaica to avoid service in Vietnam. Reuniting with Tosh and Wailer, Marley recorded again with Leslie Kong who, via work with Desmond Dekker, had become island's top producer. Following Kong's death from cancer, trio began work with Lee Perry who helped form Marley's distinctive style. Earned first international hit with **Small Axe**.

Espousing teachings of Jamaican politico/folk legend Marcus Garvey, Marley and friends became devout Rastafarians. In 1968 Marley was busted for possession of marijuana, the first of many subsequent clashes with Jamaican establishment.

Quitting Perry's label, trio took his ace musicians, brothers Carlton and Aston 'Family Man' Barrett, with them and formed own short-lived Wailing Soul label. When Bunny Wailer was sent to prison for a year following another drugs bust, Marley signed as songwriter to American soul star Johnny Nash's Jad label. He helped Nash develop unique blend of soul and reggae which gave the American singer a UK No. 1 with **Stir It Up**.

Marley used resultant income to set up Tuff Gong label with Tosh and Wailer. Subsequent records won them an international deal with Island Records thanks to that company's Jamaican-born boss Chris Blackwell.

Blackwell's carefully orchestrated promotion put Bob Marley and Wailers in vogue with rock critics, musicians and audiences alike. **Catch A Fire** album (1973) led to well-received UK visit and Stateside tour with Sly And The Family Stone. Though not quite so strong, follow-up set **Burnin'** did include **I Shot The Sheriff**, covered very successfully by Eric Clapton.

Wailer and Tosh then quit group, though they remained firm friends with Marley they were unhappy with Island deal. Marley brought in his wife Rita plus Judy Mowatt and Marcia Griffiths (the I-Threes) as back-up vocalists, and in 1975 recorded classic **Natty Dread** album. This set seal on his growing reputation as Jamaica's most important artist. Superb live LP, **Jah Live**, recorded at London's Lyceum, included version of **No Woman No Cry**, which became major UK pop hit, as well as brilliant **Lively Up Yourself**.

Marley's stature as spokesman for Jamaican masses — his songs were often full of social and political comment — made him target of political gangs. In December 1976 he was shot four times in the arm by a group who burst into his home on eve of concert he was to give for then ruling left-wing PNP party led by Michael Manley. Marley appeared in concert but immediately after went into exile in Miami for 18 months. Recorded 1976 album **Exodus** partly in that city, partly in London.

Marley's return to homeland was triumphant. Before 20,000 people at Kingston's National Stadium he joined Manley and political rival (now premier) Edward Seaga in symbolic handshake at concert which

Above: Natty Dread, Marley And The Wailers. Courtesy Island Records.

Below: Reggae crusader Bob Marley was tragically cut down by cancer while still spreading 'the word'.

Towards end of his 1980 world tour he collapsed following performance at NY's Madison Square Gardens and was rushed to hospital. Three years earlier he had had cancerous toe removed, but now it seemed the cancer had spread. Despite treatment at famed Josef Issels Clinic in Bavaria, Marley's condition was incurable. He died during May 1980 at Cedars Lebanon Hospital in Miami where he had flown to visit his mother en-route for Jamaica. Further tragedy befell the Marley clan when both Carlton Bennett and Peter Tosh were killed in 1987.

Marley's son Ziggy has maintained the family name, despite struggle to establish own identity, and has cut albums for EMI and Virgin. A sour note was struck when Marley's estate, which includes Tuff Gong studios (administered by Rita Marley since Bob's death), publishing rights, pressing plant and The Bob Marley Museum, was subject to ownership battle. In November 1991, it appeared that MCA Records would assume control of all assets, despite a matching counter bid by Marley's natural beneficiaries underwritten by former Island Records supremo Chris Blackwell. Happily Marley's camp won the day in early 1992.

Hopefully, Marley's reputation will be sustained by his classic material, and not damaged by the prolonged catfight which threatened to sour the memory of Jamaica's favourite son; island honoured artist with Bob Marley Day on February 6, 1991.

commemorated visit to Jamaica 12 years earlier by Emperor Haile Selassie of Ethiopia, figurehead of the Rastafarian movement. Marley also appeared in a special concert to celebrate birth of the new African nation of Zimbabwe.

Hit Singles:

	US	UK
Exodus, 1977	–	14
Jamming/Punky Reggae Party, 1977	–	9
Is This Love, 1978	–	9
Could You Be Loved, 1980	–	5
No Woman No Cry, 1981	–	8
Buffalo Soldier, 1983	–	4
One Love, 1984	–	5

Albums:
Catch A Fire (Island), 1972
African Herbsman (–/Trojan), 1973
Burnin' (Island), 1973
Rasta Revolution (–/Trojan), 1974
Natty Dread (Island), 1975
Jah Live (Island), 1975
Rastaman Vibration (Island), 1976
Exodus (Island), 1976
Birth Of A Legend (Epic), 1977
Early Music (–/Embassy), 1977
Babylon By Bus (Island), 1978
Kaya (Island), 1978
Bob Marley And The Wailers (–/Hammer), 1979
Survival (Island), 1979
Uprising (Island), 1980
Soul Rebel (–/New Cross), 1981
Chances Are (Warner Bros), 1981
Confrontation (Island), 1983
Legend (Island), 1984
Live At The Lyceum (Island), 1984
Rebel Music (Island), 1984
Bob Marley Intertape, 1985
Mellow Mood (Topline), 1985

Richard Marx
US vocalist
Born Chicago, 1964

Career: Marx recorded his first vocals at the age of five, thanks to his father, a popular jazz pianist and top jingle writer and producer. His songwriting talents were influenced initially by Motown and Earth, Wind And Fire and later Creedence Clearwater Revival and The Eagles. Early songwriting efforts came to the attention of Lionel Richie who had just left The Commodores and was working on his first solo album. Marx contributed vocals to several Richie hits including **You Are**, **All Night Long** and **Running With The Night**.

After introduction to David Foster, Kenny Rogers' producer, Marx started co-writing with Rogers. **And About Me** and **Crazy** were both US hits in 1985, and further songwriting credits included Chicago's **Good For Nothing**, Phillip Bailey's **Love Is Alive** and Durrell Coleman's **Somebody Took My Love**.

Early 1986 Marx signed recording deal with EMI-Manhattan and thanks to his own talent and well-orchestrated marketing campaign has had two US Top 3 hit singles: **Don't Mean Nothing** and **Should've Known Better**. Debut album was a Top 20, and he received a Grammy nomination in the Best Rock Vocal Performance category alongside artists Joe Cocker, Bob Seger and Bruce Springsteen.

Above: Boston hitmaker Richard Marx is not everyone's cup of tea.

Eponymous LP certified platinum in US by February 1988, and major promotional push by EMI brought artist to attention of UK audiences, scoring subsequently with **Right Here Waiting** single (1989) and second album **Repeat Offender**.

In 1990, Marx enjoyed success on adventurous US tour, but also earned scorn from *Rolling Stone* magazine who cited him Worst Male Singer in their critics poll. The view was partially shared by EMI boss Sal Licata, who released artist to join parent label Capitol Records, for which **Rush Street** (December 1991) was Marx's debut.

Hit Singles:

	US	UK
Don't Mean Nothing, 1987	3	–
Should've Known Better, 1987	3	–
Endless Summer Nights, 1988	2	50
Satisfied, 1989	1	52
Right Here Waiting, 1989	1	2
Angelica, 1989	4	45
Too Late To Say Goodbye, 1990	12	38
Children Of The Night, 1990	13	54
Keep Coming Back, 1991	13	–

Albums:
Richard Marx (Manhattan), 1987
Repeat Offender (EMI), 1989
Rush Street (Capitol), 1991

John Mayall

UK vocalist, guitarist, keyboard player, bandleader, composer
Born Manchester, November 23, 1933

Career: Mayall formed his first band, Powerhouse Four, at college after national service, building reputation backing US bluesmen John Lee Hooker and Sonny Boy Williamson on UK tours.

Encouraged by Alexis Korner to move to London in 1962, he formed Bluesbreakers with John McVie (bass) and Bernie Watson (guitar), cutting **Live At Klooks Kleek** 18 months later, Roger Dean replacing Watson and Hughie Flint joining on drums.

Succession of critically applauded singles and exhaustive club tours led to major breakthrough in 1966 when Eric Clapton of Yardbirds joined Mayall's Bluesbreakers. **Bluesbreakers — John Mayall With Eric Clapton** won quick cult-status hitting No. 6 on UK album charts.

Mayall/Clapton/McVie/Flint line-up was arguably best British R&B band of all time. McVie was temporarily replaced by Jack Bruce and Clapton left to join emergent psychedelic movement, forming Cream with Bruce and Ginger Baker. McVie rejoined with Peter Green coming in on guitar and Aynsley Dunbar on drums. Dunbar was soon replaced by Mick Fleetwood, the new line-up lasting until May 1967 when Fleetwood and Green left to form Fleetwood Mac, soon to be joined by McVie.

The then unknown Mick Taylor joined Mayall from The Gods, staying until 1969 when he replaced late Brian Jones in The Rolling Stones.

Changing musical direction, Mayall brought in Keef Hartley's powerhouse drumming and strong brass section for jazz-slanted sound. He also cut back-to-the-roots solo album, **The Blues Alone.**

Chris Mercer, who left for Juicy Luicy, Jon Hiseman and Dick Heckstall-Smith, who formed Colosseum, Andy Fraser, who became member of Free, and Jon Mark and Johnny Almond, who set-up Mark-Almond, all spent time with Mayall before July 1968 when he decided to go back to tighter backing group with new line-up of Mick Taylor, Stephen Thompson (bass) and Colin Allen (drums) from Zoot Money's band. This line-up cut **Blues From Laurel Canyon** set, inspired by brief holiday in Los Angeles. With Taylor leaving, Mayall moved to California,

Above: USA Union, John Mayall. Courtesy Polydor Records.

signed new deal with Polydor (after five years with Decca) and put together first of many American line-ups.

In 1975, Mayall switched to ABC for Allen Toussaint-produced **Notice To Appear** and **Banquet In Blues** albums, which featured artist in dual vocal role with Dee McKinnie. Following unsuccessful stint with former Beatles publisher Dick James' DJM label,

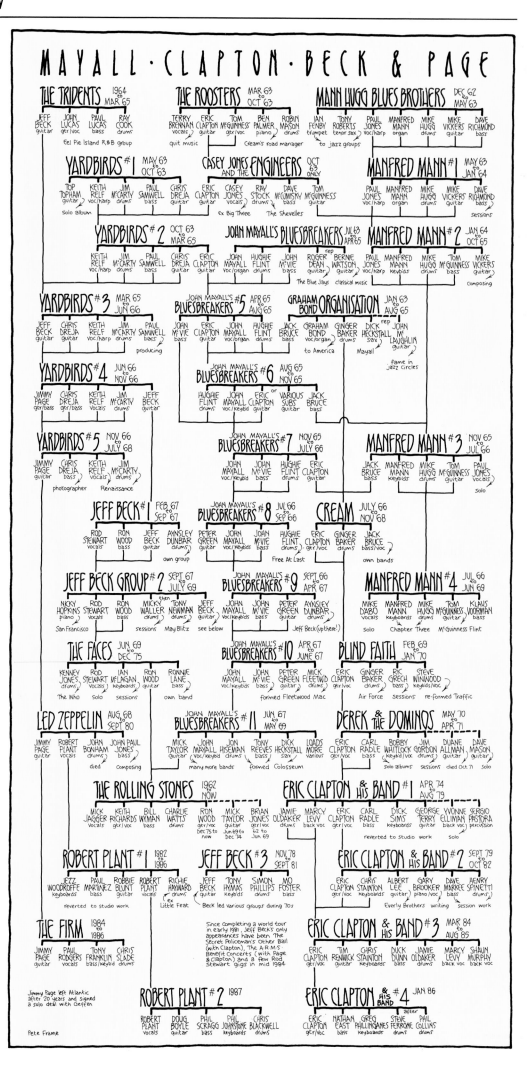

Left: Late 60s Bluesbreakers' line-up, with John McVie and Mick Taylor.

and his solo efforts lacked dynamism of Impressions days.

In 1990, having re-established Curtom label in Atlanta and cut **Superfly 90** rap with Ice-T, Mayfield was victim of tragic accident while performing in New York, leaving him disabled.

Mayfield's high tenor vocals, and choppy guitar style helped distinguish a myriad of quality soul classics, particularly during those heady days with The Impressions.

Hit Singles:

	US	UK
Move On Up, 1971	—	12
Freddie's Dead (theme from *Superfly*), 1972	4	—
Superfly, 1972	8	—

Albums:
Superfly (Buddah/RSO), 1974
Never Say You Can't Survive (Curtom), 1977
Honesty (Epic), 1983
Live In Los Angeles (Capitol), 1986
Live In Europe (Curtom/Ichiban), 1988
Something To Believe In (Curtom), 1989
Take It To The Street (Curtom), 1990

Worth Searching Out:
Roots (Curtom), 1974
Curtis (Curtom), 1974

Above: Back To The Egg, McCartney And Wings. Courtesy Parlophone Records.

which he played to over 180,000 fans at concert in Brazil); tour was filmed for *Get Back* movie (1991). He is also enthusiastic curator of Buddy Holly's musical catalogue, which is administered from artist's MPL offices in London's Soho Square; performed with The Crickets during Buddy Holly Week in 1988 at London club.

He is a conscientious worker for charity, with emphasis on the homeless and animals (like Linda, McCartney is a vegetarian); featured in Live Aid and on **Ferry 'Cross Mersey** single for victims of Hillsborough soccer stadium fire.

He was recipient of countless awards, including NARAS Lifetime Achievement at 1991 Grammys; The Beatles were inducted into Rock 'n' Roll Hall Of Fame in 1988.

The only blot on the mega of all megastars career was abysmal *Give My Regards To Broadway* movie (1985) which earned wrath of critics and flopped at box office. However, the balance was partially redressed by his **Liverpool Oratorio** tribute to Royal Liverpool Philharmonic Orchestra who performed work as part of their 150th anniversary celebration in summer of 1991.

Curtis Mayfield
US composer, vocalist, guitarist
Born Chicago, June 3, 1942

Career: Mayfield led own group, Alphatones, as teenager, then met Jerry Butler in his grandmother's church choir. On moving to north side of Chicago in 1956, he renewed acquaintances with Butler, leaving Alphatones to link up with him and group known as The Roosters.

This team evolved into The Impressions, with Butler as lead singer. Following **For Your Precious Love** smash, Butler went solo. Mayfield had stints as Butler's backing guitarist and wrote material for him while trying to hold Impressions together. With Mayfield elevated to lead singer, Impressions became one of most successful vocal groups in black music history.

In 1968 Mayfield formed own Curtom label and two years later left The Impressions, though he continued to produce them. Debut solo album went gold and single **Move On Up** took him into UK charts. His **Superfly** soundtrack for same-name movie stood up in own right and spawned two gold singles, **Freddie's Dead** and **Superfly**. He also wrote and produced scores for *Claudine* movie (performed by Gladys Knight And The Pips) and Staple Singers (**Let's Do It Again**). He appeared as actor in *Short Eyes*, writing the score, as he did for *A Piece Of The Action* and *Sparkle*, which featured singing of Aretha Franklin.

As record company boss, producer and songwriter, Mayfield continued to be active but Curtom folded (he switched to Epic)

Paul McCartney
UK composer, vocalist, bass player
Born James Paul McCartney, Liverpool, June 18, 1942

Career: As half of the world-dominating Lennon/McCartney songwriting partnership (there were reportedly nearly 2,000 cover versions of their songs by 1965) McCartney seemed particularly alienated when Yoko Ono began exerting strong influence over Lennon in late 60s. Although not first member of Beatles to release solo record, Paul McCartney sued for freedom from all group contracts.

First solo LP released 1970, opening floodgates for virtual barrage of hit singles and inconsistent albums — indicating that break-up of group and particularly of songwriting team was major loss to rock 'n' roll — although singles especially not without controversy. **Give Ireland Back To The Irish** was banned by BBC, and **Hi Hi Hi** suffered the same fate.

In 1971, formed Wings (Paul, vocals, bass; wife Linda McCartney, keyboards, vocals; Denny Laine (ex-Moody Blues) guitar, vocals; Denny Seiwell, drums), which first appeared on **Wild Life** LP. Various personnel changes took place during 1970s — among members were guitarists Henry McCullough, Jimmy McCulloch (who died in January 1979 of drug-related heart failure) and Laurence Juber, drummers Geoff Britton, Joe English and Steve Holley. However Paul, Linda and Denny Laine were ever present until Laine left in 1980, after much publicized arrest of Paul on drug charges at start of planned Japanese tour. Best Wings LP was superb **Band On The Run**.

Subsequently, McCartney has recorded solo or with help from superstar-mates like Stevie Wonder, Michael Jackson and Elvis Costello. He still enjoys life on the road, as witnessed by 1989-90 world tour (during

Mayall slipped quietly from business. After fighting alcohol dependency, he returned in 1982 for Bluesbreakers reunion tour, which saw Mick Taylor and John McVie in the line-up; reconvened band on permanent basis in 1984, cutting **Chicago Line** for Island in 1988, and, in 1990, **A Sense Of Place**, with long-time guitarist Coco Montoya and slide-guitarist Sonny Landreth.

A charismatic catalyst of some of the finest ever multi-racial R&B line-ups, Mayall could fill a rock encyclopedia with the musicians he has nurtured.

Albums:
John Mayall Plays John Mayall (—/Decca), 1965
Bluesbreakers (London/Decca), 1965
A Hard Road (London/Decca), 1967
Crusade (London/Decca), 1967
Blues Alone (London/Ace Of Hearts), 1967
Raw Blues (London/Ace Of Hearts), 1967
Bare Wires (London/Decca), 1968
Diary Of A Band Volume 1 (—/Decca), 1968
Blues From Laurel Canyon (London/Decca), 1969
Looking Back (London/Decca), 1969
Empty Rooms (Polydor), 1970
Turning Point (Polydor), 1970
World Of Volume 1 (—/World Of), 1970
World Of Volume 2 (—/World Of), 1971
Beyond The Turning Point (Polydor/—), 1971
Diary Of A Band Volume 2 (—/Decca), 1972
Jazz Blues Fusion (Polydor), 1972
Through The Years (London/Decca), 1972
Best Of (Polydor), 1973
Notice To Appear (ABC), 1975
John Mayall (Polydor), 1976
A Hard Core Package (MCA/—), 1977
Primal Solos (London/—), 1977
Last Of The British Blues (MCA/—), 1978
No More Interviews (—/DJM), 1979
Bottom Line (—/DJM), 1979
Moving On (—/Polydor), 1985
Behind The Iron Curtain (PRT), 1986
Some Of My Best Friends Are Blues (Charly), 1986
The John Mayall Collection (double album) (Castle), 1986
Crusade (London), 1987
Chicago Line (Island/Charly), 1988
A Sense Of Place (Island), 1990

CURTIS

Left: Curtis, Curtis Mayfield. Courtesy Buddah Records.

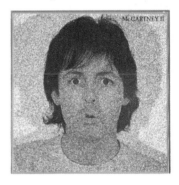

Above: McCartney II, Paul McCartney. Courtesy Parlophone Records.

If there is anything McCartney hasn't done, we don't know about it. And he usually does it better than anybody else.

Hit Singles:

	US	UK
Solo:		
Another Day, 1971	5	2
Uncle Albert/Admiral Halsey, 1971	1	—
Wonderful Christmastime, 1979	—	6
Coming Up, 1980	1	2
Waterfalls, 1980	—	9
Ebony And Ivory (with Stevie Wonder), 1982	1	1
Pipes Of Peace, 1983	—	1
No More Lonely Nights, 1984	6	2
We All Stand Together, 1984	—	3
Spies Like Us, 1986	24	13
Once Upon A Long Ago, 1987	—	10
My Brave Face, 1989	25	18
This One, 1989	—	18

With Michael Jackson:

The Girl Is Mine, 1982	2	8
Say Say Say, 1983	1	2

With McCartney and Wings:

Give Ireland Back To The Irish, 1972	21	16
Mary Had A Little Lamb, 1972	28	9
Hi Hi Hi/C Moon, 1972	10	5
My Love, 1973	1	9
Live And Let Die, 1973	2	9
Helen Wheels, 1973	10	12
Jet, 1974	7	7
Band On The Run, 1974	1	3
Junior's Farm, 1974	3	16
Listen To What The Man Said, 1975	1	6
Venus And Mars/Rock Show, 1975	12	–
Silly Love Songs, 1976	1	2
Let 'Em In, 1976	3	2
Maybe I'm Amazed, 1977	10	28
Mull Of Kintyre/Girls School, 1977	33	1
With A Little Luck, 1978	1	5
Goodnight Tonight, 1979	5	5
Getting Closer, 1979	20	60

Albums:

McCartney (Columbia/Parlophone), 1970
Ram (with Linda) (Columbia/Parlophone), 1971
McCartney II (Columbia/Parlophone), 1980
Tug Of War (Columbia/Parlophone), 1982
Pipes Of Peace (Columbia/Parlophone), 1983
Give My Regards To Broad Street (Columbia/Parlophone), 1984
All The Best (compilation) (Parlophone), 1987
Flowers In The Dirt (Capitol/Parlophone), 1989
Tripping The Light Fantastic (Capitol/Parlophone), 1990
Unplugged — The Official Bootleg (Capitol/–), 1991
Liverpool Oratoria, 1991

McCartney and Wings:

Wild Life (Columbia/Parlophone), 1971
Red Rose Speedway (Columbia/Parlophone), 1973
Band On The Run (Columbia/Parlophone), 1974
Venus And Mars (Columbia/Parlophone), 1975
Wings Over America (triple live) (Capitol/Parlophone), 1976
London Town (Capitol/Parlophone), 1978
Wings' Greatest (compilation) (Capitol/Parlophone), 1978
Back To The Egg (Columbia/Parlophone), 1979
Wings At The Speed Of Sound (Capitol/Fame), 1989

Country Joe McDonald

US vocalist, composer, guitarist
Born Joseph McDonald, El Monte, California, January 1, 1942

Career: Named by leftist parents for Joseph Stalin. Grew up listening to country and folk. Served tour in US Navy and then began working as folk singer in Berkeley, California area. McDonald recorded obscure, unknown solo in 1964, then met guitarist Barry Melton while working in folk band. Like many folk performers, duo turned to rock, forming Country Joe And The Fish

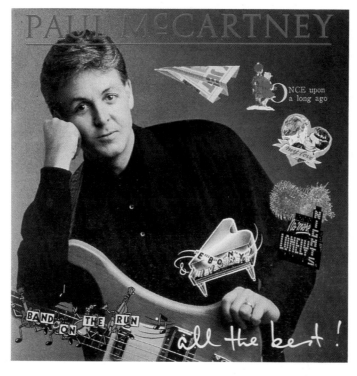

Above: All The Best, Paul McCartney. Courtesy Parlophone Records.

with Barry Melton, guitar; David Cohen, keyboards; Bruce Barthol, bass; and Chicken Hirsch, drums.

Band's first recordings were EPs made to accompany McDonald's self-produced magazine. Gigs at Fillmore attracted folk label Vanguard, who signed band in late 1966. Fish eventually recorded four LPs which at time were highly regarded for political stance, social satire and commitment to counter-culture. First LP, **Electric Music For The Mind And Body**, stands up best. Second LP **Fixin' To Die**, is fondly remembered by nostalgists for Fish cheer ('Give us an 'F'. Give us a 'U', etc.).

Close identification with protest and Berkeley area ultimately backfired and band broke up for good in 1970. McDonald began variety of activities; he wrote music for several movies, briefly worked with Jane Fonda and returned to early style of folk music. Moving to Paris, he played variety of venues and clubs, seeking support for ecological causes.

Above: Here We Are Again, Country Joe And Fish. Courtesy Vanguard Records.

Late 1974 saw brief reunion with Melton for UK gigs, after McDonald had based himself in London. Returned to San Francisco in 1976, and re-formed band for charity concert for disabled vicitms of Vietnam War; cut **Reunion** album for Fantasy Records. In 1978, joined again with Melton in The Barry Melton Band, who reverted to Fish moniker for dates on US West Coast.

Later involved with Save The Whales campaign, during which he appeared with other activists Jackson Browne and Richie Havens for Tokyo concert (1977). After slack period, Country Joe McDonald surfaced in 1991 with **Superstitious Blues** LP for small indie label Rykodisc.

Albums:

Paradise With An Ocean View (Fantasy), 1975
Love Is A Fire (Fantasy), 1976
Goodbye Blues (Fantasy), 1977
Best Of Country (–/Golden Hour), 1977
Rock 'n' Roll Music From Planet Earth (Fantasy), 1978
Leisure Suite (Fantasy), 1979
The Early Years (Piccadily/–), 1980
Animal Tracks (Animus), 1983
Superstitious Blues (–/Rykodisc), 1991

With Fish:

Electric Music For The Mind And Body (Vanguard), 1967
I-Feel-Like-I'm-Fixin'-To-Die (Vanguard), 1967
Here We Are Again (Vanguard), 1969

Michael McDonald

US vocalist, keyboard player
Born St. Louis, Missouri

Career: Began his career as keyboardist with Steely Dan in the early 70s, before joining The Doobie Brothers' line-up for 1975 US tour. He became a fully-fledged member writing several of their hits including **Real Love** and **Minute by Minute**.

In 1980 received Grammy award for penning (with Kenny Loggins) **What A Fool Believes**, a composition that was also named Song Of The Year. Along with The Doobies he received two other Grammy awards for Record Of The Year and Best Group Vocal Performance for **Minute By Minute**. McDonald songs were by now being covered by Aretha Franklin, Carly Simon and Millie Jackson, among others. First solo project, **If That's What It Takes**, included US hit single **I Keep Forgettin'**.

In 1985 released **No Lookin' Back** album which featured material co-written with Kenny Loggins, Ed Sanford and Chuck

Sabatino. LP co-produced by McDonald with Ted Templeman. 1986 saw the release **Sweet Freedom: The Best of Michael McDonald**, digitally re-mastered by Lee Herschberg, which included 12 of his best recordings including **What A Fool Believes**, **Yah Mo B There** and his hit duet with Patti LaBelle, **On My Own**.

Following prolonged hiatus, McDonald finally cut a new solo album, **Take It To Heart** (1990), which struggled commercially. Artist had been active however working with variety of diverse talents including gospel family The Winans (**Decision** LP), Patti LaBelle (**The Winner In You** album), Toto (**I'll Be Over You** single), and Christopher Cross (**Back Of My Mind** set); featured on Roy Orbison benefit in 1989 with Bob Dylan and Bonnie Raitt, and also included in annual Rock And Soul Revue with Donald Fagen and Boz Scaggs.

McDonald's charitable personality might have deflected attention from his own body of work, which, both with The Doobies and solo, remains among the finest soul-styled material around.

Hit Singles:	US	UK
With James Ingram:		
Yah Mo B There, 1985	9	12
Sweet Freedom, 1986	7	12
With Patti LaBelle:		
On My Own, 1987	1	2

Albums:

If That's What It Takes (Warner Bros), 1982
No Lookin' Back (Warner Bros), 1985
Best Of (WEA), 1986
Sweet Freedom (Warner Bros), 1986
Take It To Heart (Reprise/Warner Bros), 1990

Don McLean

US vocalist, guitarist, composer
Born New Rochelle, New York, October 2, 1945

Career: Developed early interest in all forms of American music, particularly folk. On leaving school in 1963 started singing and playing in clubs.

By end of 60s, MacLean had built up excellent reputation within his field and become a prolific songwriter. After spending two years knocking on record company doors, he made album **Tapestry** for small company which soon folded (although record was later re-released by United Artists, who signed him in 1971).

Breakthrough came with late 1971 release of extraordinary single, **American Pie**. Despite McLean's folky background, record was symbolic 'history' of rock 'n' roll, using evocative images tied to highly commercial hook-line. Record was worldwide smash, catapulting McLean to instant stardom. Follow-up, **Vincent**, a highly personal song celebrating genius of painter Vincent Van Gogh, was almost as successful. Both songs were excellent showcases for McLean's attractively plaintive voice.

Career received further boost in 1973 when MOR singer Perry Como had huge hit with **And I Love You So**, another McLean song. In meantime, McLean had become in-demand live performer, years of small-time gigs paying off in controlled, well-paced performances.

During remainder of 70s, McLean consolidated career, although he was never elevated to 'bed-sit philosophy' status of singer-songwriters such as Cat Stevens and Leonard Cohen. Perhaps strangely, he

became more popular in UK than in homeland, and regular tours in Great Britain were always sell-outs.

In 1980, McLean's career entered new phase with massive pop success of cover of Roy Orbison's classic **Crying**. True to form, single entered UK charts before US showed interest.

Artist maintained heavy performing workload, returning to studio during 80s for **Believers** LP (1982) and country-styled **Love Tracks** for Capitol (1988). Various 'greatest hits' packages also surfaced during this period, although McLean will surely be remembered for one greatest hit, the legendary **American Pie**, which returned to UK charts in October 1991, nearly 20 years after first release.

Hit Singles:	US	UK
American Pie, 1972	1	2
Vincent, 1972	12	1
Crying, 1980	5	1
American Pie, 1991	—	10

Albums:
Tapestry (United Artists), 1972
American Pie (United Artists), 1972
Playin' Favourites (United Artists), 1973
Homeless Brother (United Artists), 1974
Solo (United Artists), 1976
Chain Lightning (Arista), 1979
Very Best Of (United Artists), 1980
Belivers (Arista), 1982
Dominion (EMI), 1983
For The Memories Volumes 1 and 2
   (Gold Castle/MFP), 1990
Greatest Hits Live (Gold Castle), 1990
Headroom (Curb), 1991

Meat Loaf

US vocalist, actor
Born Marvin Lee Aday, Dallas, Texas,
September 27, 1948

Career: Bat Out Of Hell was released in 1977 and very slowly began working way up through US/UK charts. Operatic,

Above: Don McLean breaks into American Pie for the zillionth time.

bombastic, with comic-book hero on cover, album seemed to combine pomp of early 70s with enthusiasm of punk. As album settled in for what seemed permanent place in charts, interest grew in larger-than-life figure behind it.

Meat Loaf, as it happened, had been around for sometime. He had released rather weak R&B album for Tamla in 1970; **Featuring Stoney And Meat Loaf** quickly disappeared. So did Meat Loaf as he ventured into theatre. In 1976 he appeared in cult film *Rocky Horror Picture Show*. It was through acting that he met Jim Steinman. Meat Loaf liked Steinman's songs and together they began assaulting record companies with demo tapes. CBS eventually signed them.

After success of first CBS LP (produced by Todd Rundgren), **Bat Out Of Hell**, Meat Loaf toured (with back-up singers and band) until he ruined his voice. Wait for follow-up LP grew to point Steinman released opus **Bad For Good** in May 1981. Meanwhile Meat Loaf appeared in movie *Roadie*.

Dead Ringer finally arrived in 1982 as continuation of gothic texture which made up **Bat**. Some claimed **Dead Ringer** was formalistic repeat while others called it brilliant return. Fans wondered if Meat Loaf

Above: Bad Attitude, Meat Loaf. Courtesy Arista Records.

really underwent rumoured exotic treatments (including drinking his own urine) to save his voice. Whatever the cure, it seems to have worked and **Bad Attitude**, which marked a label switch to Arista and featured a title-cut vocal battle with ex-Who Roger Daltrey, contained some great songs.

More recently, porcine star has continued to gig and record (with producers Tom Dowd and Frank Farian), but has been unable to emulate mega-success of **Bat Out Of Hell**. Also featured in 1988 movie *Out Of Bounds*. Meanwhile, Steinman produced Bonnie Tyler's 1983 hit **Total Eclipse Of The Heart** and cut own **Pandora's Box** (1989) and **The Original Sin** (1990) sets before reuniting with slimmed-down Meatloaf for projected Virgin LP.

Hit Singles:	US	UK
Two Out Of Three Ain't Bad, 1978	11	32
Bat Out Of Hell, 1979	—	15
Dead Ringer For Love, 1982	—	5
Midnight At The Lost And Found, 1983	—	17
Modern Girl, 1984	1	17
Rock 'n' Roll Mercenaries, 1986	—	31

Albums:
Featuring Stoney And Meatloaf (Prodigal), 1970
Bat Out Of Hell (Epic), 1978
Dead Ringer (Epic), 1982
Midnight At The Lost And Found (Epic), 1983
Bad Attitude (Arista), 1984
Hits Out Of Hell (CBS), 1985
Blind Before I Stop (Arista), 1986
Live: Meatloaf (Arista), 1987

John Cougar Mellencamp

US vocalist, composer
Born Seymour, Indiana, October 7, 1951

Career: Married at 17, a father at 19, Mellencamp worked at various jobs before launching himself into music scene in 1975. On strength of demo tapes, was signed by Tony De Fries — then David Bowie's manager — who renamed him Johnny Cougar and signed him to MCA. First album **Chestnut Street Incident** combined new tracks with raw demos; split from De Fries swiftly followed.

Cougar then met up with Billy Gaff (then Rod Stewart's manager), head of Riva Records. Signed to Riva, Cougar achieved some impact with album **A Biography**, which yielded international chart single in **I Need A Lover**, and follow-up **Nothin' Matters And What If It Did**, which made US Top 50. Latter also provided two Top 40 singles, **This Time** and **Ain't Even Done With The Night**.

Steve Cropper produced **Nothin' Matters**, but Cougar decided that time had come to take full musical control. With Don Gehman co-producing, Mellencamp put together **American Fool**; album became one of the sensations of 1982, reaching No. 1 and achieving platinum status. Three singles from the album, which all received heavy MTV airplay, were also hugely successful.

In meantime, Cougar had been touring regularly with band The Zones, and established himself as good live attraction. His music has wide appeal for rock and pop audiences, combining melodic sense,

macho/boyish image, modicum of intelligence and evocative, quintessentially American lyrics.

In intervening years Cougar continued to build reputation as alternative Bruce Springsteen; all-American rocker concerned with subjects like girls, motorbikes and small town life. Artist reverted to real name of Mellencamp along the way.

1985 album **Scarecrow** was mega-selling US No. 1, and **The Lonesome Jubilee** set (1987), which spawned **Paper In Fire** and **Cherry Bomb** hits, confirmed artist's superstar status; featured in Woody Guthrie/Leadbelly tribute LP, **A Vision Shared**, for Folkways label one year later.

Following US Top 10 success of 1989 LP **Big Daddy**, Mellencamp took time out to score *Souvenirs* (in which he also acted) and *Fallen From Grace* movies before returning to studio for autumn of 1991 release **Whenever We Wanted**.

Mellencamp's indifference to music business (he prefers painting) has hardly affected burgeoning career, and more 'mature' image has given this performer credence in all markets.

Above: Maturing John Mellencamp is now carving solid movie career.

Hit Singles:	US	UK
Ain't Even Done With The Night, 1981	17	—
Hurt So Good, 1982	2	—
Jack And Diane, 1982	1	25
Hand To Hold On To, 1983	3	19
Crumblin' Down, 1983	9	—
Pink Houses, 1983	8	—
Authority Song, 1984	15	—
Lonely Ol' Night, 1985	6	—
Small Town, 1985	6	—
Cherry Bomb, 1988	8	—
Check It Out, 1988	14	—
Pop Singer, 1989	15	—
Get A Leg Up, 1991	14	—

Albums:
A Biography (Riva), 1978
John Cougar (Riva), 1979
Nothin' Matters And What If It Did (Riva), 1980
American Fool (Riva), 1982
Uh-Huh (Riva), 1984
Chestnut Street Incident (Mainman), 1984
Scarecrow (Riva), 1985
The Lonesome Jubilee (Riva/Mercury), 1987
Big Daddy (Mercury), 1989
Whenever We Wanted (Mercury), 1991

Metallica

US group formed 1981

Original line-up: Lars Ulrich, drums; James Hetfield, guitar, vocals; Lloyd Grant, guitar; Dave Mustaine, guitar; Ron McGovney, bass.

Career: Riff-laden HM thrash merchants whose response to the refining of rock 'n' roll was a noise bombardment in the finest tradition of punk.

Formed in San Francisco by Danish immigrant Ulrich, who saw time with British HM group Diamond Head, Metallica recorded track for 1981 **Metal Massacre** compilation album. Band's album **Kill 'Em All** saw McGovney and Mustaine replaced by Cliff Burton (ex-Trauma) and Kirk Hammett respectively. Grant had also quit, returning to session work.

1984 set **Ride The Lightning** earned band deal with Elektra Records, and contract with Def Leppard management company Q-Prime.

Heavy touring schedule, including six-month stint supporting Ozzy Osbourne (1986) was temporarily curtailed by death of Burton, killed in road accident involving band's coach. Jason Newstead was chosen as his replacement.

Indifferent studio cuts prompted band to 'return to basics' and **Garage Days Revisited** EP (recorded in Ulrich's workshop) charted in UK after strong support and publicity from Vertigo, Metallica's UK record company.

Group's growing reputation was confirmed when Monsters Of Rock tour (1988) featured outfit headlining with mega-bands The Scorpions and Van Halen; album **And Justice For All** was subsequent Top 10 hit in UK and USA. Successive Grammy awards (1990 and 1991) for Best Metal Performance and dynamic 1990 album **Metallica** have provided Metallica with distinctive profile in the murky and often confusing world of heavy metal.

Hit Singles:

	US	UK
Harvester Of Sorrow, 1988	—	20
One, 1989	35	13
Enter Sandman, 1991	16	5
The Unforgiven, 1991	—	15

Albums:

Ride The Lightning (Elektra/Music For Nations), 1984
Master Of Puppets (Elektra/Music For Nations), 1986
Kill 'Em All (Elektra/Music For Nations), 1987
Garage Days Revisited (Elektra/Vertigo), 1987
The Singles (—/Music For Nations), 1987
And Justice For All (Elektra/Vertigo), 1988
Metallica (—/Vertigo), 1990

George Michael

UK singer/songwriter
Born Georgios Panayiotiou, Finchley, London, June 25, 1963

Career: Met Andrew Ridgeley at school, formed duo Wham! which achieved worldwide success from 1983 to 1986. Michael also scored solo hit singles with **Different Corner** and **Careless Whisper**.

Michael split Wham! partnership in mid-1985 and laid low for a year before launching solo career with controversial **I Want Your Sex** single, which immediately suffered media censorship. Lyrically it recommended sexual fidelity; musically it inspired sexual abandon, employing restrained rockabilly edge that would be more evident on next album and single, **Faith**.

Faith LP spawned further hit singles, including moody title track, and sold 15 million copies. Artist also earned kudos with impressive duet with Aretha Franklin on **I Knew You Were Waiting (For Me)**, which surprised critics expecting 'the glorious one' to be upstaged by veteran soul star; track earned Grammy in 1988.

Michael launched world Faith tour in Japan in 1988, following Best British Artist Award at UK's BRIT ceremonies. Completed arduous tour trek in October 1988, and then saw reward for his endeavour when **Faith** LP earned Album Of The Year Grammy in February 1989.

Second solo LP **Listen Without Prejudice, Volume I**, released in September 1990, debuted at No. 1 in UK, and was later chosen as Best British Album during 1991 BRIT presentations. Began Cover To Cover tour in January, which saw singer perform with old Wham! mate Andrew Ridgeley during show in Rio de Janerio. During same year, Michael's international status confirmed by *Rolling Stone* magazine who voted him both Best and Sexiest Male Artist; ended 1991 at top of UK single charts in live duet with Elton John on **Don't Let The Sun Go Down On Me**. Excellent best-selling biography *Bare* (with Tony Parsons) was published in 1990.

Hit Singles:

	US	UK
Careless Whisper, 1984	1	1
Different Corner, 1986	—	1
Faith, 1987	2	1
I Want Your Sex, 1987	2	3
Father Figure, 1988	1	11
One More Try, 1988	1	8
Monkey, 1988	1	13
Kissing A Fool, 1988	5	18
Praying For Time, 1990	1	6
Freedom, 1990	8	30

Below: George Michael, looking forward to many more years at the top.

With Aretha Franklin:

	US	UK
I Knew You Were Waiting For Me, 1987	1	1

With Elton John:

	US	UK
Don't Let The Sun Go Down On Me, 1991	—	1

Albums:

Faith (CBS), 1987
Listen Without Prejudice Volume 1 (Columbia/Epic), 1990

Below: Faith, George Michael. Courtesy CBS Records.

Steve Miller

US guitarist, vocalist, composer
Born Milwaukee, Wisconsin, November 5, 1943

Career: Began playing guitar at age four under auspices of legendary Les Paul and T-Bone Walker, both friends of Miller's father. Formed first band before teens. This blues outfit, which included Boz Scaggs, was known as The Marksmen Combo.

Returning from adopted home state of Texas, Miller enrolled at University of Wisconsin to study literature, playing guitar part-time in The Ardells and then The Fabulous Knight Train (reuniting Miller with Boz Scaggs).

After studying in Denmark for a year, Miller moved to Chicago's burgeoning blues scene. He got involved with fleeting projects – the Goldberg/Miller Blues Band (with Barry Goldberg) and World War Three Blues Band – but spent most of his time jamming with blues greats Muddy Waters, Buddy Guy, Junior Wells and Otis Rush.

A brief respite back in Texas introduced Miller to recording; working as janitor for a local studio, he cut demos in spare time, before heading for San Francisco in 1966.

Recruiting Lonnie Turner (bass), Tim Davis (drums) and James 'Curly' Cooke (guitar), he formed Steve Miller Band, debuting at the Matrix after frantic period rehearsing in basement on Berkeley University campus.

Band attained strong local following at Avalon Ballroom and Bill Graham's Fillmore Auditorium (where they backed Chuck Berry for a live album). In summer 1967 they appeared at Monterey Pop Festival.

With other San Franciscan outfits Mother Earth and Quicksilver Messenger Service, they made recording debut with **Revolution** soundtrack album.

Signed with Capitol Records in 1967, band released first album **Children Of The Future** in May 1968, with Scaggs re-joining Miller (replacing Cooke) and Jim Peterman providing keyboards. Stunning **Sailor** set (1968), produced by Glyn Johns, included classic material **Living In The USA**, **Gangster Of Love** and haunting **Song For Our Ancestors**, pushing Miller's band to top of West Coast pile.

Various personnel changes (a continuing feature of Miller's outfits) saw Scaggs go solo and Peterman turn to production. Subsequent Miller aggregations have included Nicky Hopkins, Ben Sidran (one-time member of Marksmen) and dextrous bassist Gerald Johnson.

Overcoming serious bout of hepatitis (one of several extended breaks due to health problems), Miller progressed steadily, if not prolifically, through 70s with gold albums **The Joker** and **Fly Like An Eagle**. A four-year hiatus from 1977 to 1981 ended with **Circle Of Love** album, Miller returning from extended period spent farming his estate in Oregon.

1982 set **Abracadabra** returned Miller to pinnacle of charts, when title track topped US listings, although falling one place short in UK. The Miller Band line-up during the mid-80s comprised Johnson, guitarist Kenny Lewis, keyboardist Brian Allred and long-time drummer Gary Mallaver, having lost John Massaro, who toured with group following **Abracadabra** release. The blues set **Living In The 20th Century** was Miller's best work during decade and paid tribute to veteran Jimmy Reed, a major influence on guitarist's style.

Miller's career was resurrected again in 1990 when **The Joker** topped UK singles chart after exposure as theme for a jeans

Below: Children Of The Future, Steve Miller. Courtesy Capitol Records.

commercial. Subsequent **Best Of** set, from his most productive period (1968-73), made Top 50 in British album chart.

Any tendency for critics to trivialize Miller's career should be tempered by acknowledgement of classic **Sailor** and **Brave New World** sets.

Hit Singles:

	US	UK
The Joker, 1974	1	—
Take The Money And Run, 1976	11	—
Rock'n Me, 1976	1	11
Fly Like An Eagle, 1977	2	—
Jet Airliner, 1977	8	—
Swingtown, 1977	17	—
Abracadabra, 1982	1	2
The Joker, 1990	—	1

Albums:
Children Of The Future (Capitol), 1968
Sailor (Capitol), 1969
Brave New World (Capitol), 1969
Your Saving Grace (Capitol), 1970
Number Five (Capitol), 1970
Rock Love (Capitol), 1971
Recall The Beginning (Capitol), 1973
Living In The USA (Capitol), 1973
The Joker (Capitol), 1973
Anthology (Capitol), 1973
Fly Like An Eagle (Capitol/Mercury), 1976
Book Of Dreams (Capitol/Mercury), 1977
Best Of 1968-73 (Capitol), 1977
Greatest Hits 74-78 (Capitol/Mercury), 1978
Circle Of Love (Capitol/Mercury), 1981
Abracadabra (Capitol/Mercury), 1982
Steve Miller Band Live (Mercury), 1983
Italian X Rays (Mercury)
Living In The 20th Century (EMI), 1987
Born 2 B Blue (Capitol), 1988
Best Of (Capitol), 1991

Mr Mister

US group formed 1982

Original line-up: Richard Page, vocalist, bass; Steve George, keyboards; Steve Farris, guitar; Pat Mastelotto, drums.

Career: Band formed in Los Angeles after an initial meeting in a downtown rehearsal studio, although vocalist Page and keyboards player George had been working on same recording sessions before then (with

Donna Summer, Molly Hatchet and Quincy Jones). Guitar player Steve Farris spent three years touring with Eddie Money's band before joining up with Page and George, while drummer Pat Mastelotto had worked with producer Mike Chapman.

Band soon picked up a strong following on the LA club circuit prior to being signed by RCA. Debut album **I Wear The Face** followed by **Welcome To The Real World** in 1985. While touring with Tina Turner in the US, their debut single **Broken Wings** reached No. 1 in the charts.

Their second single was **Kyrie** which also went to No. 1 in US, giving Mr Mister the rare accolade of the No. 1 album, single and video in the US during the same week. Both singles were UK hits, the latter reaching Top 5 at the same time as they played their first London dates.

Their third album **Go On**, engineered, mixed and co-produced (with the band) by Kevin Killen, noted for his work with U2 and Peter Gabriel, was released in March 1988.

Despite band's early promise and pair of US No. 1 singles, they were unable to consolidate early success and drifted into rock oblivion by end of the 80s.

Hit Singles:

	US	UK
Broken Wings, 1985	1	4
Kyrie, 1986	1	5
Is It Love?, 1986	8	—
Something Real, 1987	29	—

Albums:
Welcome To The Real World (RCA), 1985
I Wear The Face (RCA), 1986
Go On (RCA), 1987

Joni Mitchell

US vocalist, composer, guitarist, pianist
Born Roberta Joan Anderson, Fort McLeod, Alberta, Canada, November 7, 1943

Career: Attended Alberta College of Art with intention of becoming commercial artist. Learned to play ukelele for personal enjoyment, then developed serious interest in folk music/songwriting. Securing gig at the Depression coffee-house, Joni gradually gained confidence. Following performance at Mariposa Folk Festival in Ontario, she wrote her first song, **Day After Day**. Professional career began in Toronto, where she quickly became a leading figure of the Yorktown set.

Married Chuck Mitchell in June 1965; couple moved to Detroit, achieving some acclaim as duo on local folk circuit. After break-up of marriage, Joni continued as soloist, securing engagements in New York; signed to Reprise in 1967. Under aegis of Elliot Roberts, she gained widespread reputation as star songwriter with a series of covers by such artists as Judy Collins, Gordon Lightfoot, Johnny Cash, Tom Rush and Fairport Convention.

Employing services of ex-Byrd David Crosby as producer, Mitchell recorded **Songs To A Seagull**, a brilliant debut displaying talent as a singer/songwriter. Early albums were essentially acoustic, melodic works, sharpened by poetic lyrics. Although a product of the singer/songwriter boom of the late 1960s, Mitchell revealed a maturity and incisiveness that separated her from most of her contemporaries. While others wallowed in their own narcissism, Mitchell was careful to bring a cutting edge to many of her lines. She continually struggled to find meaning in her much-publicized broken relationships, without falling into self-indulgence.

Third album, **Ladies Of The Canyon**, provided the breakthrough that Mitchell needed for continued success in the 70s. Sales were boosted by surprise hit single, **Big Yellow Taxi**, and cover versions of **Woodstock** by Crosby, Stills, Nash & Young and Matthew's Southern Comfort (who took song to No. 1 in UK). More importantly, **Ladies Of The Canyon** included piano accompaniment to match her acoustic guitar work.

Successive albums, **Blue**, **For The Roses** and **Court And Spark**, showed greater confidence in her own writing and a willingness to explore new musical ideas. Introduction of Tom Scott on wind instruments on **For**

Left: Masters of AOR, Mr Mister led by Richard Page, standing on left.

Left: The king of comebacks, Steve Miller, who survived a four year rest to return to the top in the early 80s.

The **Roses** LP revealed first recorded signs of an interest in jazz as possible avenue for later work. Significantly, the only non-Mitchell song of the set was a re-make of Annie Ross's **Twisted**.

By 1975, Mitchell was moving too fast for many of her older fans. **The Hissing Of Summer Lawns**, in many respects her best work to date, featured an array of new musical effects, including synthesizer and the African drums of Burundi. The lyrics contained many of the old themes presented from different points of view. By this time, her songwriting talent was probably unmatched by any artist in rock, bar Dylan. In spite of such achievements, her more myopic critics were crying for a return to the folky songs of the late 60s. Instead, Mitchell pushed forward; **Hejira** was another dense work, less tuneful than its predecessor, but still commercially successful.

Her attraction to jazz was fully expressed in late 70s LPs **Don Juan's Reckless Daughter** and, more noticeably, **Mingus**. Realizing, perhaps, that her interests were becoming increasingly incompatible with the mainstream rock audience, Mitchell threatened to retire at the end of decade to devote more energy to her first love, painting. (Virtually all her albums feature her original paintings.)

Just as it seemed that her career was nearing a close, Mitchell returned in 1982 with **Wild Things Run Fast** on David Geffen's label. Surprisingly, it was a return to the more melodic work of the early 70s and fared well chart-wise. Three-year recording

Above: Dog Eat Dog, Joni Mitchell. Courtesy Geffen Records.

break was ended by release of 1985 set **Dog Eat Dog**, whose sharp lyrical content took swipes at everything from US evangelism to domestic bliss.

Now further enmeshed in painting 'career', Mitchell again remained aloof from the recording studio before contractual obligations resulted in critically acclaimed 1988 album **Chalk Mark In A Rain Storm** which marked 20th anniversary of debut LP **Song For A Seagull**.

Despite artistic commitments — her abstracts command high prices in art market, while her photographic endeavours are also considered worthy of exhibition in galleries — Mitchell still feels obliged to complete occasional recording date, and entered 90s with a new album for Geffen, **Night Ride Home**, a typical Mitchell mix of folk, pop and jazz, with emphasis on succinct lyrical content.

Hit Singles:

	US	UK
Big Yellow Taxi, 1970	—	11
Help Me, 1974	7	—

Albums:

Joni Mitchell, aka Songs To A Seagull, (Reprise), 1968
Clouds (Reprise), 1969
Ladies Of The Canyon (Reprise), 1970
Blue (Reprise), 1971
For The Roses (Asylum), 1972
Court And Spark (Elektra/Asylum), 1974
Miles Of Aisles (Asylum), 1974
The Hissing Of Summer Lawns (Asylum), 1975
Hejira (Asylum), 1979
Don Juan's Reckless Daughter (Asylum), 1977
Mingus (Asylum), 1979
Shadows And Light (Asylum), 1980
Wild Things Run Fast (Geffen), 1982
Dog Eat Dog (Geffen), 1985
Chalk Mark In A Rain Storm (Geffen), 1988
Night Ride Home (Geffen), 1991

The Monkees

US group formed 1966

Original line-up: Davy Jones, vocals; Mike Nesmith, guitar, vocals; Peter Tork, bass, vocals; Mickey Dolenz, drums, vocals.

Career: Following conquest by The Beatles, Stones, Kinks and slew of lesser British talents like Herman's Hermits, America was ready for home-grown pop phenomenon. What was needed was group along lines of the Limey invaders — mop-topped, cute and lovable — but *American*. British invasion had spawned imitators like Beau Brummells, but there was still a yawning gap. With typical transatlantic ingenuity, Americans decided to create their own Beatles from scratch — and The Monkees were born.

The Monkees phenomenon, although lasting a scant two years, was a brilliant exercise in marketing. The giant NBC-TV network was prime mover — what it wanted was a TV series that would tap same youth market as The Beatles' phenomenally successful *A Hard Day's Night* and *Help* featuring zany, vaguely anti-establishment 'beat group'. Music featured in the show could be marketed in its own right — the show could promote the records, and vice-versa. It was decided that existing groups could cause too many problems, so after auditioning hundreds of hopeful unknowns, NBC picked Dolenz and English-born Jones, both former child actors, and small-time musicians Tork and Nesmith.

Considering how dire it could have been, the TV series was surprisingly entertaining as well as extremely successful. Music from the show was translated into a series of singles that were worldwide hits.

In fact, The Monkees' music, particularly the singles, stands up as an excellent example of superbly crafted mid-60s pop — not so surprising considering that writing duties were in hands of people like Neil Diamond, Tommy Boyce and Bobby Hart, and back-up production was taken care of by top talents of the day. (Needless to say, band resented not being allowed to play on their first few singles.) Nesmith penned several songs on their later LPs.

Ultimately, it was over as quickly as it had begun. Tork left after badly received movie *Head*, and the others split after hits dried up in 1969. Mike Nesmith went on to forge successful career with own brand of country rock and is now a video/film producer. Dolenz eventually moved to England to become an in-demand TV commercials director. Attempt by Jones and Dolenz to re-create band with Tommy Boyce and Bobby

Above: Pool It, The Monkees. Courtesy Rhino Records.

Hart in 1975 was a failure, Jones going on to star in re-run of *Godspell* stage musical.

Re-runs of group's TV series sparked extraordinary re-formation in 1986 (minus Nesmith), and Jones, Tork and Dolenz enjoyed hysterical US tour, prompting memories nearly 20 years old. And, in June 1990, the anarchic and plotless *Head* movie was released on video, to bemuse a new generation.

Hit Singles:	US	UK
I'm A Believer/(I'm Not Your) Steppin' Stone, 1967	1	1
(I'm Not Your) Steppin' Stone/ I'm A Believer, 1967	20	—
Last Train To Clarksville, 1967	1	23
A Little Bit Me, A Little Bit You, 1967	2	3
Alternate Title, 1967	—	2
Pleasant Valley Sunday/Words, 1967	3	11
Words/Pleasant Valley Sunday, 1967	11	—
Daydream Believer, 1967	1	5
Valleri, 1968	3	12
D. W. Washburn, 1968	19	17

Albums:

Monkees (—/Sounds Superb), 1974
Best Of The Monkees (—/MFP), 1981
The Monkees (Arista), 1981
20 Golden Greats (—/Ronco), 1982
Then And Now (Arista), 1986
Pool It (Rhino), 1987

Moody Blues

UK group formed 1964

Original line-up: Mike Pinder, vocals, keyboards; Denny Laine, vocals, guitar; Ray Thomas, flute, vocals; Clint Warwick, bass, vocals; Graeme Edge, drums.

Career: Line-up above formed R&B group in Birmingham; second single release, cover of classic Bessie Banks' song **Go Now**, leapt to No. 1 in British charts, No. 10 in US.

Although band scored couple more minor hits, after two albums Laine and Warwick both quit (Laine later becoming mainstay of Paul McCartney's Wings). They were replaced by Justin Hayward and John Lodge. Following period of reappraisal, band came up with **Days Of Future Passed**, album which united group with London Symphony Orchestra. Total departure from pattern of previous work, album was heavy on portentous philosophizing, light on rock 'n' roll. However, it caught mood of time (1967) and proved to be total success, re-establishing group in big way and spawning classic single in **Nights In White Satin** (a hit several times over, and since covered by many artists).

From that time on Moodies cornered market in pop-rock; albums generally repeated formula of pop philosophy dressed up in high-flown, often orchestral, arrangements. Occasional hit singles boosted

Below: Moody Blues with their Go Now line-up featuring Denny Laine (right).

sales, which ran into multi-millions all over world. From 1969, Moodies' product was released on own Threshold label, which didn't alter winning formula.

After 1972 album, **Seventh Sojourn**, group did not record any fresh material for six years, spending intervening period on various solo projects. Most viable of these was Lodge/Hayward album, **Blue Jays**, which spawned major hit single **Blue Guitar** in 1975.

Compilation album **This Is The Moody Blues** and collection of bits and pieces called **Caught Live And Five** kept Moodies' public simmering until their return in force in 1978 with **Octave**. Predictably successful album heralded further live work, with ex-Yes keyboard man Patrick Moraz taking place of Mike Pinder. **Long Distance Voyager** LP, featuring Moraz, took Moodies into 80s. It made No. 1 in US, No. 7 in UK, showing that market for group's particular brand of music was far from moribund.

Decade saw series of albums of variable quality, with Tony Visconti-produced **Sur La Mer** (1988) being the most competent. Haywood also retained solo status with LPs **Night Flight** (1990), **Moving Mountains** (1985) and **Classic Blue** (1989), the latter produced by Mike Batt, and featuring the London Philharmonic Orchestra.

1990 US tour preceded release of **Keys Of The Kingdom** LP (with Visconti still at the helm) for Polydor Records, with whom they pacted in 1986.

With a record of longevity equalled by few other groups, the Moodies have defied critics who have questioned approach. What is not in doubt is band's skill and persistence.

Hit Singles:	US	UK
Go Now, 1964	10	1
Nights In White Satin, 1967	—	19
Question, 1970	21	2
Isn't Life Strange, 1972	29	13
Nights In White Satin, 1972	2	9
I'm Just A Singer (In A Rock And Roll Band), 1973	12	36
Nights In White Satin, 1979	—	14
Gemini Dream, 1981	14	—
The Voice, 1981	16	—

Albums:

The Magnificent Moodies (London/Decca), 1966
Days Of Future Passed (Deram), 1967
In Search Of The Lost Chord (Deram), 1968
On The Threshold Of A Dream (Decca), 1969
To Our Children's Children (Threshold), 1969
A Question Of Balance (Threshold), 1970
Every Good Boy Deserves Favour (Threshold), 1971
Seventh Sojourn (Threshold), 1972
This Is The Moody Blues (Threshold), 1974
Caught Live And Five (London/Decca), 1977
Octave (London/Threshold), 1978
Out Of This World (K-Tel), 1979
Long Distance Voyager (Threshold), 1981
Present (Threshold), 1983
Voices In The Sky (Decca), 1984
Sur La Mer (Polydor), 1988
Greatest Hits (Threshold), 1989
Keys Of The Kingdom (Polydor/—), 1991

Worth Searching Out:
Moody Blues:
Go Now (London/—), 1965

Justin Hayward and John Lodge:
Blue Jays (Threshold), 1975

Graeme Edge Band with Adrian Gurvitz:
Kick Off Your Muddy Boots (Threshold), 1975

Above: John Lodge and Justin Hayward, still Moody after all these years.

Ray Thomas Solo:
Hopes, Wishes And Dreams (Threshold), 1976

Michael Pinder Solo:
The Promise (Threshold), 1976

Justin Hayward Solo:
Moving Mountains (Towerbell), 1985
Songwriter (Decca), 1987
Classic Blue (—/Trax), 1989
Night Flight (Polydor/Threshold), 1990

Keith Moon

UK drummer, actor
Born London, August 23, 1946
Died London, September 7, 1978

Career: Moon began musical career in Harrow, playing with local friends in band not serious enough to merit name. Recorded obscure 1963 single, **Mad Goose/You Can't Sit Down**, with The Beachcombers. Later joined Roger Daltrey, John Entwistle, and Pete Townshend in The Who.

Moon quickly earned well-deserved reputation for being one of rock's most exciting, innovative drummers. Entirely self-taught, he had natural gift for using each arm and leg independently. Consequently, he was one of rock's first drummers to employ double bass drums and a myriad of cymbals. Unlike many later imitators with big flashy kits, Moon used all his equipment.

Equally deserved was Moon's growing reputation for crazy, over-the-top antics. His practical jokes, real-life adventures and death-defying feats are legendary. This aspect of Moon's life is detailed in personal

Below: Two Sides Of The Moon, Keith Moon. Courtesy Polydor Records.

manager/minder Peter 'Dougal' Butler's book (co-authored by Chris Trengove), *Moon the Loon* (*Full Moon* in US). However, the larger-than-life image surrounding Moon not only covered up some insecurity and personal unhappiness but also downplayed wide variety of unfortunate incidents which affected those who had to live or work with him. In 1967, The Who had to cancel studio sessions because of injuries suffered by Moon. He was directly involved in the death of his driver during a pub brawl. Such incidents were not nearly so isolated as suggested by the nothing-can-touch-me facade Moon was so fond of projecting.

Moon's growing party reputation soon jeopardized his private life. He had married in 1966, but kept the marriage secret for two years. By early 70s, he had moved his wife and daughter into country estate where they too were caught up with never-ending party atmosphere. Keith's mother, however, recalls his visits home to Harrow when he would arrive alone, and ask only for tea and biscuits. After a few hours of quiet chatter Keith would leave and resume behaviour pattern expected by public.

By mid-1974, Moon's wife Kim could handle no more and left. In many ways, Moon never recovered from the loss. At this particular time, Who reached a two-year hiatus. While Townshend, Daltrey and Entwistle got

Below: Van Morrison's quality output continues unabated.

involved in film or solo LPs, Moon, apart for a brief role in *Tommy* film, had nothing to do. In September 1974, Moon moved to Los Angeles to be near drinking partners Ringo Starr and Harry Nilsson.

Moon convinced MCA he could be solo star, and managed to collect sizeable advance. Using money to party in studio, he began collecting every available LA musician he could and proceeded to record superstar session that defies description. MCA became concerned when single released in October 1974 proved a disaster. **Don't Worry Baby** was a cover of Moon's heroes The Beach Boys, but even expected hard core Who/Beach Boys fans weren't buying. Producer and former Beatles associate Mal Evans was replaced by Skip Taylor and John Stronack, who re-mixed entire album. Released in April 1975, LP's rapid appearance in cut-out bins announced end of Moon's party.

Moon returned to UK in 1978. His pudgy face and generally sloppy appearance were price of his relentless lifestyle. The death of possibly the greatest drummer in rock came as a kind of anticipated shock, but no surprise to those who knew him well. The Who continued with ex-Face Kenney Jones, but magic was lost.

Notable 'session' work includes: **Truth** (Jeff Beck); **Flash Fearless** and **Pussy Cats** (Nilsson); **All This & World War Two** soundtrack; **Sometime In New York** (John Lennon); and **The 20th Anniversary of Rock and Roll** (Bo Diddley).

Drums: Premier.

Albums:
Worth Searching Out:
Two Sides Of The Moon (MCA/Polydor), 1975

Van Morrison

UK vocalist, composer, guitarist
Born George Ivan, Belfast, North Ireland, August 31, 1945

Career: Irish music played little part in Morrison's upbringing. Raised to the sounds of America's Deep South (his mother a blues and jazz singer, his father a fanatical record collector with love for rural blues), Morrison mastered guitar, saxophone and harmonica

while at school, playing in skiffle bands from age 11 at local dance halls.

Leaving school in 1960 for career as professional musician, he joined Monarchs for tour of US air bases in Germany, and in 1963 returned to Belfast to form Them with two Monarchs members and two other friends. Installed as house band at R&B club in Belfast's Maritime Hotel, Billy Harrison (guitar), Ronnie Millings (drums), and Eric Wicksen (piano), fronted by Morrison's vocals, built cult following for frenetic brand of blues-flavoured beat music.

A version of Slim Harpo's **Don't Start Crying Now** was Irish hit and, signed to Decca, band moved base to London and followed through with upbeat version of Big Joe Williams' classic **Baby Please Don't Go** which climbed high into UK national charts.

Ace American producer Bert Berns (co-writer of **Twist And Shout**, **Tell Him**, **Cry Baby** and other 60s soul classics) was brought in for Morrison's own composition **Here Comes The Night**, group's first transatlantic hit. Though never a UK hit, Them's **Gloria**, another Morrison original, helped establish band's reputation and is regarded as true classic. On debut album, session men, including guitarist Jimmy Page (later of Led Zeppelin), were brought in while Jackie McAuley replaced Wicksen.

By second album, band was on verge of collapsing and session men laid down most of tracks behind Morrison's vocals. Following unsatisfactory US tour, Morrison disbanded Them and returned to Ulster.

Having formed own Bang label, Berns sent Morrison air ticket and took him into New York studios to cut solo sides from which sessions **Brown-Eyed Girl** was US hit in mid-1967. Them later re-formed for short period, but without Morrison, whose solo career took full flight.

Berns died of heart attack on December 1, 1967, and Morrison signed to Warner Bros, who gave him complete creative control. Resulting **Astral Weeks** album, cut in New York in just 48 hours, is one of all-time great rock albums; though with no obvious hit singles, it only sold modestly.

Moondance (containing hit single **Into The Mystic**) and **Van Morrison — His Band And Street Choir** (producing **Domino** hit) forged solid reputation and built Morrison into major US concert attraction, touring with large 11-piece band including strings. Close to the mike, eyes half-closed, lips barely parted, chubby face crowned by mass of rust-red hair, his vocals have always oozed soulfulness and personal conviction.

Tupelo Honey (1971), which included suite of love songs to wife Janet Planet, and further albums — especially the exceptionally strong **It's Too Late To Stop Now** live double LP (following hugely successful 1974 US and European tour) which was truly live with no over-dubs — brought Morrison to the zenith of his career.

Personal and professional hassles continued, however. He divorced in 1973 and in 1974 suddenly broke up applauded Caledonia Soul Orchestra, carrying out next European tour with five-piece band, playing sax and harmonica himself.

Morrison had returned to Ireland in 1973 for first time in seven years and songs written there emerged as 1974 album **Veedon Fleece**, arguably his best work since **Astral Weeks**. Followed by several aborted album ventures (including one featuring The Crusaders), it was not until spring 1977 that **A Period Of Transition** surfaced (with Dr John guesting).

Still searching for 'the answer', Morrison's albums during the early 80s, from **Common One** to **No Guru, No Method, No Teacher** were riddled with spiritual assessment. Enjoyed UK Top 20 status with **Inarticulate Speech Of The Heart** (1982) and saw Mark Knopfler guest on 'poppy' **Beautiful Vision**.

Following moderate **Poetic Champions Compose** (1987), Morrison joined forces with Chieftains for wonderful **Irish Heartbeat** set, a heartfelt return to traditional music. In 1989, Morrison co-opted British jazz and blues great Georgie Fame to orchestrate and play on **Avalon Sunset** (1989), which spawned huge British hit single, **Whenever God Shines His Light** duet with Cliff Richard.

Morrison's reticent approach to all facets to the business apart from performing have earned him 'moody' tag. Introspective he may be, but the Belfast native is also a significant purveyor of outstanding modern R&B.

Hit Singles:

	US	UK
Brown-Eyed Girl, 1967	10	—
Domino, 1970	9	—
Whenever God Shines His Light (with Cliff Richard), 1990	—	20

With Them:

Baby Please Don't Go, 1965	—	10
Here Comes The Night, 1965	24	2

Albums:
Astral Weeks (Warner Bros), 1968
Best Of (Bang/President), 1970
Moondance (Warner Bros), 1970
His Band And Street Choir (Warner Bros), 1970
Tupelo Honey (Warner Bros), 1971
St Dominic's Preview (Warner Bros), 1973
Hard Nose The Highway (Warner Bros), 1973
It's Too Late To Stop Now (Warner Bros), 1974
Veedon Fleece (Warner Bros), 1974

Above: Astral Weeks, Van Morrison. Courtesy Warner Bros Records.

Period Of Transition (Warner Bros), 1977
Wavelength (Warner Bros), 1978
Into The Music (Mercury), 1978
Common One (Warner Bros/Mercury), 1980
Beautiful Vision (Warner Bros/Mercury), 1982
Inarticulate Speech Of The Heart (Mercury), 1982
Live At The Grand Opera House Belfast (Mercury), 1984
A Sense Of Wonder (Mercury), 1985
No Guru, No Method, No Teacher (Mercury), 1986
T.B. Sheets (Bellaphon)
Poetic Champions Compose (Mercury), 1987
Avalon Sunset (Mercury/Polydor), 1989
Best Of (Polydor), 1990
Enlightenment (Mercury/Polydor), 1990

With The Chieftains:
Irish Heartbeat (Mercury), 1988

Above: Them, featuring Van Morrison. Courtesy Decca Records.

Mötley Crüe
US group formed 1981

Original line-up: Vince Neil, vocals; Micky Mars, guitar; Nicki Sixx, bass; Tommy Lee, drums.

Career: Outrageous HM group whose inspired name may not have done them justice. Subsequent attention to grooming seems to have mellowed the cacophony emanating from this quartet.

Formed in Los Angeles by Sixx, the band's original moniker was London. They earned sufficient notoriety on LA club scene to justify cutting self-financed album **Too Fast For Love**, released on independent label Leather Records.

Elektra Records were alerted to the spreading Mötley Crüe phenomenon, and signed outfit to contract; hired noted producer Roy Thomas-Baker to re-mix **Too Fast** set. Second LP **Shout At The Devil** (1983) made US Top 20, and nationwide tour with Kiss established unit in metal mainstream.

With spruced-up image evident, Crüe were dealt a desperate blow when Neil was involved in fatal car crash, after being convicted of driving under the influence. Third set **Theatre Of Pain** included a prominent drink-drive warning.

1987 album **Girls Girls Girls** broke the band internationally, and world tour confirm-

Above: Poetic Champions Compose, Van Morrison. Courtesy Mercury.

ed their musical credentials. Unable to entirely escape tabloid headlines, Crüe's comparative period of normality was struck asunder when bass player Matt Tripp (also from LA) claimed he had been depping for Sixx following an earlier car smash. Manager Doc McGhee was then found guilty of drug importation, and the band tussled with Guns N' Roses backstage at the 1989 Grammy Awards. Further incidents included arrest of Lee for lewd behaviour at Georgia concert (he dropped his pants) and show-biz wedding of Sixx to Playboy Playmate.

On the music side, **Dr Feelgood** LP won best HM category at American Music Awards (1991) and *Rolling Stone* magazine named Crüe most popular HM band in their reader's choice. November 1991 greatest hits collection **Decade Of Decadence** nicely summed-up band's career to date.

Hit Singles:

	US	UK
Home Sweet Home/Smokin' In The Boys Room, 1986	16	51
Girls Girls Girls, 1987	12	26
Dr Feelgood, 1989	6	50
Don't Go Away Mad (Just Go Away), 1990	19	—

Albums:
Shout At The Devil (Elektra), 1983
Theatre Of Pain (Elektra), 1985
Girls Girls Girls (Elektra), 1987
Too Fast For Love (re-mix) (Elektra), 1987
Dr Feelgood (Elektra), 1989
Decade Of Decadence, 1991

Motorhead
UK group formed 1975

Original line-up: Ian 'Lemmy' Kilminster; Larry Wallis, guitar; Lucas Fox, drums.

Career: Lemmy worked as roadie for Hawkwind, and, without prior experience, took over group's bass spot. In 1974 he involved band with drug bust at US/Canadian border and got fired. Upon returning to UK, he formed Bastard. Journalist Mick Farren introduced him to ex-Pink Fairies Wallis, and then Fox. Manager Doug Smith convinced trio to pick more viable name. Lemmy came up with Americanism for speed freak, Motorhead.

Band debuted at Camden Town's Roundhouse on July 20, 1975 and promptly went on tour. Opening for Blue Oyster Cult's London October 1975 show, they earned critical assessment as 'worst band in the world'. Motorhead have never looked back.

Trio began recording LP for United Artists in December 1975. Lemmy asked friend Phil Taylor for ride to Rockfield Studios and explained his dissatisfaction with Fox. Taylor volunteered to sit in and found himself re-recording entire album (except for one track). United Artists accepted tapes but refused to release LP. Phil introduced 'Fast' Eddie Clarke to band as second guitarist. Wallis left shortly afterwards and band was back to trio.

Giving up on United Artists, band recorded **White Line Fever/Leavin' Here** for Stiff Records in mid-1976. United Artists, although still refusing to support band, raised contractual objections and killed release. (Both cuts were eventually issued in 1977 on compilation LPs, **Bunch Of Stiffs** and **Hits Greatest Stiffs**.)

Band almost broke up but Ted Carroll of Chiswick Records asked them to record single and provided two days' studio time. Band worked around clock and presented Carroll with 13 backing tracks. He liked them and agreed for band to finish them off. Single **Motorhead/City Kids** and album **Motorhead** both released summer 1977.

Instead of finding success, Lemmy became involved in management problems with in-

Above: Overkill, Motorhead. Courtesy Bronze Records.

terloper Tony Secunda (ex-Move) and band found itself without label in spring 1978. Doug Smith stepped back in and arranged recording contract with Bronze Records. Single **Louie, Louie** was released and paved way for sonic assault of **Overkill** LP.

By now band was developing fanatical following whose loyalty rivals that of any group. Continuing tours opened up new audiences and **Bomber** album made No. 12 in UK charts. Tour supporting this release featured bomber lighting rig with replica of German airplane, and acrobats, which became exciting part of band's performance.

Not too surprisingly, United Artists noted Motorhead's growing stature and released band's first recordings as **On Parole**. Although hardly representative of band's current abilities, it provided insight into early days of Motorhead's history.

April 1980 saw release of live material on EP **The Golden Years**. Motorhead's live shows have always been strong point and EP became band's first Top 10 hit. **Ace of Spades** set became band's biggest seller so far and Motorhead was hot property. Chiswick label released **Beer Drinkers** EP with four tracks recorded at time of **Motorhead** album.

Injury to Taylor caused cancellation of late 1980 tour, while Lemmy and Clarke joined Girlschool to record **Valentines Day**

Massacre EP. Year ended with band being voted No. 1 (as were **Ace of Spades** LP and single) in Sounds Readers Poll.

Band returned to touring in March 1981, and while at Leeds Queen Hall/Newcastle City Hall recorded material for live LP, **No Sleep 'Til Hammersmith**. Described as guaranteed to melt speakers, fuse amps and short circuit turntables, album can claim to be best example of recorded high energy since Who's **Live at Leeds. Hammersmith** went to UK No. 1 within one week of issue. Just prior to its release, Motorhead opened Ozzy Osbourne's US Blizzard Of Oz tour. Band returned again in 1982 and seemed poised to crack US market. Instead, late May 1982 brought announcement that Eddie Clarke was leaving group in the middle of tour (because of disagreement with Lemmy's ongoing plans for Motorhead's involvement in outside activities).

Lemmy's 'try anything once' attitude produced successful **Valentines Day Massacre** release as well as more bizarre single **Don't Do That** featuring himself, Nolan Sisters, Cozy Powell and others. But his disregard for convention reached new heights. He joined Wendy O. Williams of Plasmatics to do send-up version of Tammy Wynette's **Stand By Your Man**. This was too much for Clarke and he left (later to form Fastway). This crisis disrupted band's progression, although Brian Robertson (ex-Thin Lizzy) filled in so band could complete remaining dates on US tour.

Robertson stayed with band until end of 1983, featuring on big-selling album **Another Perfect Day**. Over a year passed before release of next album **No Remorse**, and it featured entirely new line-up apart from Lemmy: Pete Gill, drums, and Michael 'Wurzel' Burston and Phil Campbell, guitars, contributed to sonic mayhem.

In 1986, band signed with GWR for **Orgasmatron** set. Gill quit a year later, to be replaced by former member Taylor. Following **Birthday Party** album in 1990, Lemmy and crew decamped to the States, where they were able to show the Americans the finer points of British decorum; **1916** was US 'debut' in 1991 for WTG Records.

Meltdown greatest (or is that grate-is?) hits package was released in November 1991.

Hit Singles:

	US	UK
The Golden Years (EP), 1980	—	8
Ace Of Spades, 1980	—	15
Motorhead (Live), 1981	—	6

Albums:
Motorhead (—/Chiswick), 1971
Overkill (—/Bronze), 1979
On Parole (—/United Artists), 1979
Bomber (—/Bronze), 1979
Ace Of Spades (Mercury/Bronze), 1980

No Sleep 'Til Hammersmith (Mercury/ Bronze), 1981
Iron Fist (Mercury/Bronze), 1982
What's Words Worth (—/Big Beat), 1983*
Another Perfect Day (—/Bronze), 1983
No Remorse (Bronze), 1984
Anthology (Raw Power), 1986
Orgasmatron (GWR), 1986
Born To Lose (Dojo), 1986
Rock 'N' Roll (GWR), 1987
No Sleep At All (Enigma/Roadrunner), 1988
The Birthday Party (Enigma/GWR), 1990
1916 (WTG), 1991
*Live At The Roundhouse, 1978

Mott The Hoople
UK group formed 1969

Original line-up: Mick Ralphs, guitar; Dale 'Buffin' Griffin, drums; Pete 'Overend' Watts, bass; Verden 'Phally' Allen, organ; Ian Hunter, vocals, guitar, keyboards.

Career: Evolved from Herefordshire group Silence, featuring Ralphs, Griffin, Watts, Allen and vocalist Stan Tippens. Signed to Island by A&R head Guy Stevens, who changed name to Mott The Hoople (from novel by Willard Manus). Following Stevens' suggestion, Tippens reverted to road manager, replaced by Ian Hunter (recruited from auditions).

Debut **Mott The Hoople** relied heavily on Hunter's rasping Dylanesque vocals, recalling sound of **Blonde On Blonde**. Next two albums, **Mad Shadows** (1970) and **Wildlife** (1971), revealed contrasting hard/soft rock styles of Hunter and Ralphs respectively. In spite of loyal following on London club circuit, album sales remained poor. **Brain Capers** (1971) was followed by barren period; group finally split in March 1972. Later that year, recent Hoople fan, David Bowie, encouraged and nurtured re-formation. Following an introduction to Bowie's manager Tony De Fries, a new contract was signed with CBS. Bowie wrote/produced hit single **All The Young Dudes**, which climbed to No. 3. Success of fifth album gave group new lease of life, and, following Bowie's retreat as Svengali, they continued to chart until 1974. During interim, charismatic Hunter took over as leader, resulting in departure of Allen. Original leader Mick Ralphs left shortly afterwards to form Bad Company.

New members were recruited: guitarist Ariel Bender (actually Luther Grosvenor of Spooky Tooth) and keyboards player Morgan Fisher, formerly of Love Affair. 1973 US summer tour proved particularly memorable with an array of costumes and theatrical effects; group subsequently played a week in a

Broadway theatre. New line-up cut one studio album, **The Hoople**, and a Top 50 single, **Saturday Gig**, before Grosvenor left, to be replaced by Bowie sideman Mick Ronson. Shortly afterwards, Hunter was hospitalized in New York suffering from exhaustion, and important British tour was cancelled. Amid rumour and confusion, Hunter and Ronson left to form new group just as **Live** LP was released and became band's biggest seller.

Above: Mott, Mott The Hoople. Courtesy Columbia Records.

Six months later, renamed Mott regrouped with singer Nigel Benjamin and guitarist Ray Major. Two patchy albums appeared before Benjamin quit; CBS then dropped Mott from roster. Remaining members, minus Nigel Benjamin, teamed up with John Fiddler (ex-Medicine Head) for brief career as British Lions. Meanwhile, Hunter/Ronson liaison was short-lived. Hunter issued run of solo albums for Columbia/CBS and Chrysalis and became major influence on British new wave, producing Generation X, among others.

Hunter and Ronson rejoined officially for **Y U I Orta** set in 1989 for Mercury Records, although the guitarist had contributed to Hunter's Columbia work. Pair enjoyed brief but successful UK tour before announcement that Ronson had contracted cancer, throwing future plans into chaos.

Hit Singles:

	US	UK
All The Young Dudes, 1972	—	3
Honaloochie Boogie, 1973	—	12
All The Way From Memphis, 1973	—	10
Roll Away The Stone, 1973	—	8
Golden Age Of Rock And Roll, 1974	—	16

Left: 'We're moving in next door!' The delightful Motorhead with frontman Lemmy, centre.

Above: Head Hoople Ian Hunter, an unfulfilled talent.

Albums:
Mott The Hoople (Atlantic/Island), 1969
Mad Shadows (Island), 1970
Wild Life (Island), 1971
Brain Capers (Island), 1971
All The Young Dudes (Columbia/CBS), 1972
Rock 'n' Roll Queen (Columbia/CBS), 1972
Mott (Columbia/CBS), 1973
Live (Columbia/CBS), 1974
Greatest Hits (Columbia/CBS), 1976

As Mott:
Worth Searching Out:
Drive On (CBS), 1975
Shouting And Pointing (CBS), 1976

The Move
UK group formed 1965

Original line-up: Carl Wayne, vocals; Roy Wood, guitar, vocals; Trevor Burton, guitar, vocals; Ace Kefford, bass; Bev Bevan, drums.

Career: Formed in Birmingham out of some of city's top musicians, The Move first made their mark at London's Marquee Club in 1966. Their exciting stage show/pop-art image created much interest, and band was quickly signed to Deram Records. First single, Roy Wood's **Night Of Fear**, reached No. 2 in UK charts in January 1967.

A troupe of seasoned gigsters, the somewhat fey mantle of psychedelia sat uneasily upon them. However, helped by remarkable songwriting of Roy Wood, The Move took up flower-power banner and produced series of hits which, to many, sum up spirit of 60s.

Above: Something Else From The Move, The Move. Courtesy Harvest Records.

From **Fire Brigade** onwards, Wood began handling lead vocals and it became obvious that band was coming more and more under his influence. 1968 saw first of series of personnel changes — Ace Kefford left, followed in early 1969 by guitarist Trevor Burton (who later went on to Steve Gibbons Band). Rick Price, another Birmingham musician, joined on bass.

Hits continued through the late 60s and early 70s with **Curly**, **Brontosaurus**, **Tonight**, **Chinatown** and **California Man** all charting heavily in UK. Strangely, The Move never made much impact in US, being regarded as cult underground group rather than pop band.

By 1970, however, band was practically falling apart. Jeff Lynne came in to replace Carl Wayne, and by 1971 band was reduced to Wood, Bevan and Lynne. The stage was set for end of The Move and beginning of Electric Light Orchestra, a concept which Wood had been kicking around for some time (Wood/Lynne originally planned to run Move and ELO simultaneously). Wood eventually left ELO to form Wizzard, and achieved considerable success with Spector-influenced sound up to mid-70s.

Always plagued by problem of falling between several stools, not to mention personality clashes and wrangling over musical direction, Move were never likely candidates in longevity stakes. However, they were important influence at a time when rock was beginning to emerge and become a separate form, and they leave behind collection of singles which stand up to repeated listening.

Hit Singles:

	US	UK
Night Of Fear, 1967	—	2
I Can Hear The Grass Grow, 1967	—	5
Flowers In The Rain, 1967	—	2
Fire Brigade, 1968	—	3
Blackberry Way, 1968	—	1
Curly, 1969	—	12
Brontosaurus, 1970	—	7
Tonight, 1971	—	11
California Man, 1972	—	7

Albums:
Best Of (A&M), 1974
Greatest Hits (—/Hallmark), 1978
The Move (Shines On) (—/Harvest), 1979
Platinum Collection (—/Cube), 1981
The Move Collection (double) (Collectors), 1986

Worth Searching Out:
Something Else (live EP) (Regal/Zonophone), 1968

Alison Moyet

UK vocalist
Born Basildon, Essex, June 18, 1961

Career: Alison Moyet has progressed from being a punk rock vocalist, through synth-dominated glam pop, to emerge as a fine jazz-slanted vocalist.

Drifted through series of jobs until she heard punk outfit X-Ray Spex and readily confessed to basing her initial vocal style entirely on Poly Styrene. A fan of soul and blues, she sang with The Vipers, The Vicars and The Screaming Abdabs and furthered her songwriting talents— she had penned **Nobody's Diary**, later to be Yazoo's farewell single.

On point of advertising for new band when Vince Clarke, also from Basildon, left Depeche Mode. They teamed up and recorded **Only You** as a one-off.

Above: Birmingham beatsters The Move, with the great Roy Wood pictured second from left.

An advance from Mute Records and immediate commercial success launched Moyet on to chart scene, sales topping 300,000 and establishing Yazoo (Yaz in the US) overnight as new pop sensation — Moyet's roly-poly yet charismatic image combining admirably with Vince Clarke's technical wizardry.

Upstairs At Eric's album hit No. 1 and Yazoo seemed to be most inspiring of all synth bands which dominated 1982 pop, but they had already decided to split before recording second album **You And Me Both**, due to differences in character and approach to music, Moyet wishing to front real musicians rather than electronic machines.

After some delay, solo career got underway with instant smashes **Love Resurrection** and **All Cried Out** and million-selling debut album **Alf**, produced by Tony Swain and Steve Jolley, established her as one of Britain's premier girl singers.

With her doctrine in place, Moyet's interpretation of Billie Holiday's classic **That Ol'**

Below: Alison Moyet (the former Alf) whose solo career stumbled after string of commendable UK singles. The US has remained unimpressed.

Rick Nelson

US vocalist, guitarist, composer, actor
Born Eric Hilliard Nelson, Teaneck, New Jersey, May 8, 1940
Died January 31, 1985

Career: Joined parents' radio show at four; made transition to television's *Adventures Of Ozzie And Harriet* in early 50s. Signed first record contract as Ricky Nelson with Verve in 1956, scoring first hit **I'm Walkin'**. Signed to Imperial Records 1957; consistently appeared in US and UK charts until early 60s.

Initial appeal was to young teens. He had same good looks as Presley but his clean-cut image was less threatening to middle-American morals. Records were somewhat subdued but well-crafted due to fine musicians, notably guitarist James Burton, who contributed classic solos to sides that would have been classified as rockabilly had they been recorded in Memphis.

Change of image followed shortening of name to Rick in 1961 and recording deal with US Decca in 1963. Later material appealed more to young adults, including effective recording of Dylan's **She Belongs**

Devil Called Love suggested future direction, although a couple of pop hits followed — **Weak In The Presence Of Beauty** and **Is This Love?** before re-make of moody R&B classic **Love Letters**, a hit for Ketty Lester in the mid-60s. 1987 platinum **Raindancing** LP confirmed ability for soulful inflection, and prompted award as Best British Female Singer at 1988 BRIT awards.

A period of self-assessment followed, during which artist was divorced from husband Malcolm Lee. Studio sessions in 1990 finally provided new album **Hoodoo**, although Moyet's only significant live outing in two-year period was The Simple Truth charity concert at Wembley in May 1991.

Hit Singles:

	US	UK
Love Resurrection, 1984	—	10
All Cried Out, 1984	—	8
That Ol' Devil Called Love, 1985	—	2
Weak In The Presence Of Beauty, 1987	—	6
Is This Love?, 1987	—	3
Love Letters, 1987	—	4

Albums:
Alf (CBS), 1984
Raindancing (CBS), 1987
Hoodoo (CBS), 1990

To Me (1969). Formed own group, Stone Canyon Band (1971), with leanings towards country rock. Had major hit in 1972 with autobiographical **Garden Party** summing-up his feelings about audiences who regarded him as a rock 'n' roller and nothing else. Since then Nelson failed to make chart contribution, despite several fine albums, including **Playing To Win** debut for Capitol.

Paucity of hit singles did not diminish reputation, and Nelson continued to gig, happy to provide audiences with older pop material. Also featured on revival packages, and enjoyed successful sortie to UK in 1985 with Del Shannon and Bobby Vee.

In December 1985, the Nelson was killed instantly, along with members of his band and fiancée, when his plane crashed en route to gig in Iowa. The rock 'n' roller who was never allowed to grow up left staggering legacy of hit singles, whose lightweight content belied solid talent. Nelson's sons, Mathew and Gunnar, formed The Nelson rock outfit in 1990.

Hit Singles:

	US	UK
I'm Walkin'/A Teenager's Romance, 1957	2	—
A Teenager's Romance/I'm Walkin', 1957	4	—
Be Bop Baby, 1957	3	—
Stood Up/Waitin' In School, 1958	2	—
Waitin' In School/Stood Up, 1958	18	—
My Bucket's Got A Hole In It/Believe What You Say, 1958	12	—
Believe What You Say/My Bucket's Got A Hole In It, 1958	4	—
Poor Little Fool, 1958	1	4
Lonesome Town/I Got A Feeling, 1958	7	—
I Got A Feeling/Lonesome Town, 1958	10	27
Someday, 1958	—	9
It's Late/Never Be Anyone Else But You, 1959	9	3
Never Be Anyone Else But You/It's Late, 1959	6	14
Sweeter Than You/Just A Little Too Much, 1959	9	19
Just A Little Too Much/Sweeter Than You, 1959	9	11
I Wanna Be Loved, 1959	20	—
Young Emotions, 1960	12	—
Travelin' Man/Hello Mary Lou, 1961	1	2
Hello Mary Lou/Travelin' Man, 1961	9	2
Everlovin'/A Wonder Like You, 1961	16	—
A Wonder Like You/Everlovin' 1961	11	—
Young World, 1962	5	19
Teenage Idol, 1962	5	39
It's Up To You, 1963	6	22
Fools Rush In, 1963	12	12
For You, 1964	6	14
Garden Party, 1972	6	41

Albums:
Ricky (Liberty/London), 1957
Decca Years (MCA/—), 1971
Intakes (Epic), 1977
The Rick Nelson Singles Album (Fame), 1978
Rockin' Rock (MCA), 1979
Playing To Win (Capitol/—), 1981
Best Of (Liberty), 1985
More Songs By Ricky (EMI-Liberty)
Comes Of Age (See For Miles), 1987
Sing Rare Tracks (United Factories), 1987

Worth Searching Out:
Garden Party (MCA), 1974

Neville Brothers
US group formed 1977

Original line-up: Aaron Neville, vocals, percussion; Art Neville, keyboards; Cyril Neville, vocals, keyboards, percussion; Charles Neville, saxophone.

Career: New Orleans-born brothers had diverse musical experiences before combining in late 70s to great effect. Aaron enjoyed classic soul hit **Tell It Like It Is** (later covered by actor Don Johnson), Art was member of Hawkettes and founder of influential The Meters group, session man Charles recorded with B.B. King and Bobby Bland, while Cyril fronted Soul Machine before joining The Meters.

With the brothers (plus uncle George Landry) united in the final months of The Meters (who had enjoyed some success with Alan Toussaint-produced R&B singles in the early 70s), the family changed the group's name and signed with Capitol Records.

Debut set **The Neville Brothers** was well received and group enjoyed notable following among prominent rock and pop stars. Tough touring schedule finally paid dividends when record success was achieved with Daniel Lanois-produced **Yellow Moon** album (1988), which made US Top 100.

Aaron's duet with Linda Ronstadt on million-selling single and Grammy winner **Don't Know Much** (1989) prefaced busy personal schedule and secured wider audience appeal for brothers' unique brand of soul, R&B and funk.

Aaron's parallel solo career included appearance at Super Bowl XXIV for rendition of national anthem, a bit part in Dennis Quaid movie *Everybody's All American*, a further Grammy (with Ronstadt) for **All My Life** single, award as Best Male Singer from *Rolling Stone* magazine and solo album **Warm Your Heart** (1991) for band's label A&M, with Rondstadt co-producer. Aaron cut **Everybody Plays The Fool**, which earned US Top 10 spot in autumn of 1991.

The Neville Brothers live-wire stage show, with Aaron's heaven-sent vocals to the forefront, have finally persuaded mainstream audience to check out band's albums, which now enjoy the chart success they deserve.

Hit Singles:	US	UK
The Neville Sounds:		
Tell It Like It Is, 1967	2	—

Below: They're new, they're kids and they're made out of blocks.

Aaron Neville Solo:

Don't Know Much (with Linda Ronstadt), 1989	—	2
Everybody Plays The Fool, 1991	8	—

Albums:
Neville-ization (Black Top/Demon), 1986
Treacherous, A History Of 1955-85 (Rhino), 1987
Fiyou On The Bayou (A&M/Demon), 1987
Yellow Moon (A&M), 1988
Brothers Keeper (A&M), 1990
Treacherous Too Volume 2 1955-87 (Rhino), 1991
Uptown (EMI/Fame), 1991

Aaron Neville Solo;
Make Me Strong (—/Charly), 1987
Show Me The Way (—/Charly), 1989
Tell It Like It Is (Curb/Ace), 1990
My Greatest Gift (Rounder), 1990
Warm Your Heart (A&M), 1991

New Kids On The Block
US vocal group formed 1985

Original line-up: Donnie Wahlberg; Danny Wood; Jordan Knight; Jonathan Knight; Joey McIntyre.

Career: Brainchild of former New Edition guru Maurice Starr, NKOTB started life as Nynuk, a collection of classmates from Roxbury, near Boston. Curiously signed to CBS Records' soul operation, NKOTB debuted with **Be My Girl** single in 1986.

Hectic period of club dates polished group's abilities, and they were chosen to support Tiffany on US tour when **Please Don't Go** single attracted interest from prominent radio stations. Starr's decision to release heavy **You Got It (The Right Stuff)** as follow-up proved inspired choice, and the NKOTB phenomenon was born with self-titled first LP breaking through.

Second album **Hangin' Tough** contained similar mix of dance and pop cuts, and supplied similar amount of chart ammunition.

Frenetic teenage activity at group's concerts prompted comparisons with Osmonds, but the Kids street image suggested an altogether tougher demeanour. Off-stage activities, avidly recorded by glossy pop magazines, concerned Starr, who felt band's members might be reacting adversely to

Above: New Orleans' own Neville Brothers, who found collective success after inconsistent solo careers. The legendary Aaron Neville is on vocals.

continuing pressures of concerts and studio dates. Wahlberg's arrest in March 1991 (he pleaded guilty to criminal mischief) was symptomatic of ensuing problems, although no serious threat was posed to NKOTB's extra-curricular commercial activities, which include book and comic collection, dolls, and a cartoon series.

Hit Singles:	US	UK
You Got It (The Right Stuff), 1989	3	1
Didn't I (Blow Your Mind), 1989	8	8
Hangin' Tough (re-issue), 1990	—	1
I'll Be Loving You (Forever), 1990	1	5
Cover Girl, 1990	2	4
Step By Step, 1990	1	2
Tonight, 1990	7	3
This One's For The Children, 1990	7	9
Games, 1991	—	14
Call It What You Want, 1991	—	12
If You Go Away, 1991	—	12

Albums:
Hangin' Tough (Columbia/CBS), 1988
New Kids On The Block (Columbia), 1989
No More Games — The Re-mix Album (Columbia), 1990
Step By Step (Columbia/CBS), 1990
Merry Merry Christmas (Columbia/CBS), 1990
Hits (Columbia), 1991

Randy Newman
US composer, pianist, vocalist
Born Los Angeles, November 28, 1943

Career: Born into musical family, took piano lessons from age seven. Graduated from University of California in music composition.

Started career as arranger and songwriter and quickly gained reputation among fellow musicians as perceptive and unusually intelligent writer. Early supporters of his work included Judy Collins, who recorded **I Think It's Going To Rain Today** in 1966, and Alan Price, who hit in 1967 with **Simon Smith And His Amazing Dancing Bear**.

Newman signed with Warner Bros in 1968 and released **Randy Newman**, which featured his striking compositions with large orchestra. It created interest but had little commercial appeal, which could also be said about **Twelve Songs**, his next album (originally a collection of demos recorded before **Randy Newman**). This album contained **Mama Told Me Not To Come**, later a hit for Three Dog Night.

After **Live**, concert versions of songs from first two albums, **Sail Away** and **Good Old Boys**, consolidated Newman's reputation as writer of pointed, oblique songs with sharp edge of satire. His subject matter — nuclear bombs, racism, pollution — although stuff of protest, was dealt with in wry manner that set Newman apart from run-of-the-mill protest singers. Rather than preaching, he has always preferred subtlety.

In 1977 his album **Little Criminals** yielded hit single in **Short People**, a satire on bigotry which nevertheless was mistaken for bigotry itself by many people, including variety of organizations for midgets. Despite controversy, **Little Criminals** won Newman much wider audience.

Never a prolific artist, Newman made further impact with **Born Again** in 1979, then released nothing until **Trouble In Paradise** in early 1983. Regarded by most critics as brilliant return to form of **Little Criminals**, album puts Newman's sardonic voice and spare piano accompaniment into context of LA session-rock ethos.

Although recorded work has become steadily more elaborate (but infrequent), Newman still retained ability to turn out pop anthem, as witnessed by **I Love LA** track from 1983 set **Trouble In Paradise**, now adopted as vocal chant for sports fans on West Coast. After five-year break, returned in 1988 with **Land Of Dreams** LP, co-produced by Mark Knopfler and Jeff Lynne.

His consistent film work has included scores for *Ragtime, The Natural, The Three Amigos* (in which he also appeared) and *Awakenings*. His songs have also appeared in *Performance, Her Alibi* and *Major League*.

A complex, self-effacing man, Newman is one of the few genuine and original talents in the music-biz. However, surprising as it is, he doesn't appear to know it.

Hit Singles:	US	UK
Short People, 1978	2	—

Albums:
Randy Newman (Reprise), 1968
Twelve Songs (Reprise), 1969
Live (Reprise), 1971
Sail Away (Reprise), 1972
Good Old Boys (Warner Bros), 1974
Little Criminals (Warner Bros), 1977
Born Again (Warner Bros), 1979
Trouble In Paradise (Warner Bros), 1983
Lonely At The Top (WEA), 1987
Land Of Dreams (Reprise/Warner Bros), 1988

Harry Nilsson

US vocalist, composer
Born New York, June 15, 1941

Career: Moved to California during teens, started writing songs. After some early success (he wrote **Cuddly Toy** for Monkees), he was signed by RCA in 1968.

Early albums showed Nilsson to be distinctive singer/writer of idiosyncratic promise, but first hit **Everybody's Talkin'** was theme tune of film *Midnight Cowboy* (1969), written by Fred Neil. **Nilsson Schmilsson** became platinum album in US, yielding hit single (No. 1 in both US and UK) in Badfinger-composed song **Without You.** Son Of Schmilsson LP did nearly as well.

Next quirky turn in Nilsson's career came with release of **A Little Touch Of Schmilsson In The Night**, an album of cover versions of standard songs, such as **Makin' Whoopee.** Seemingly aimed somewhere between satire and tribute, album sold well to MOR audiences.

Since mid-70s, however, artist seems to have been casting around for direction. In between bouts of well-publicized partying with friends like Ringo Starr, he has continued to record with varying degrees of success. **The Point**, soundtrack of full-length animated film for TV, was adapted and presented successfully at London's Mermaid Theatre in 1976.

Latterly, Nilsson has maintained generally low profile, although 1980 deal with Mercury should have delivered more than **Flash Harry** project produced by Booker T guitar-god Steve Cropper. In 1991, artist was surprised by news that *The Point* was scheduled as television cartoon series.

Hit Singles:

	US	UK
Everybody's Talkin', 1969	6	23
Without You, 1972	1	1
Coconut, 1972	8	42

Albums:
Pandemonium Shadow Show (RCA), 1967
Aerial Ballet (RCA), 1968
Harry (RCA), 1969
Nilsson Sings Newman (RCA), 1970
Nilsson Schmilsson (RCA), 1971
Son Of Schmilsson (RCA), 1972
Little Touch Of Schmilsson In The Night (RCA), 1973
Du It On Mon Dei (RCA), 1975
Son Of Dracula (RCA), 1974
The Sandman (RCA), 1975
That's The Way It Is (RCA), 1976
Knillssonn (RCA), 1977
Early Times (Mercury/DSM), 1977
Greatest Hits (RCA), 1978
Nilsson's Greatest Music (RCA), 1981
All Time Greatest Hits (RCA/—), 1989
A Touch Of Schmilsson In The Night (—/RCA)

Above: A Little Touch Of Schmilsson In The Night. Courtesy RCA Records.

Ted Nugent

US guitarist, bandleader, vocalist, composer
Born Detroit, December 13, 1949

Career: Self-styled 'wild man of rock', Nugent's antics (including hunting with bow and arrow and wearing a loin cloth) have almost justified first epithet. He acquired first guitar at eight; joined first major band, Amboy Dukes, in 1965. Dukes played quasi-psychedelic music appropriate to times, but with extra Detroit metal quotient. Group scored US Top 20 hit in summer 1968 with **Journey To The Center Of The Mind**, later included on notable **Nuggets** double LP. Early LPs became collectors' items when greater 60s consciousness returned in late 70s.

Group continued through 60s, eventually adopting name of Ted Nugent and The Amboy Dukes — Nugent in typical manner had altered nature of band from democracy to to dictatorship, with himself as dictator. Band's most famous member (other than Nugent) was probably Rusty Day, later in Cactus, although perhaps 10 people were members at one time or another. Despite label changes, group had little success and even a two-year period without record deal. After signing with Epic in 1975, fortunes improved; Amboy Dukes tag dropped. First LP for new label was Nugent's first to make US Top 30, using quite long-lived band (by Nugent standards): Derek St Holmes, rhythm guitar, vocals; Rob Grange, bass; and Cliff Davies, drums.

1976 LP **Free For All** featured Meat Loaf (then a less-than-household name) as guest vocalist and again reached Top 30. By 1978 LP **Weekend Warriors** band was beginning to change again, although Cliff Davies remained as drummer and sometimes producer through 1981 live LP **Intensities In Ten Cities.**

During 1982, Nugent changed labels after seven successful years with Epic, and also formed new band with drummer Carmine Appice (ex-Cactus, Vanilla Fudge), and previous sidemen Dave Kiswiney, bass, and vocalist Derek St Holmes. Decade was less successful for the mad axeman, and following 1988 LP for Atlantic, **If You Can't Lick 'Em . . . Lick 'Em**, he formed Damned Yankees HM combo with Jack Blades (ex-Night Ranger) on bass, Mike Cartellone on drums, and Tommy Shaw (ex-Styx) on guitar; eponymous LP was released in 1990.

The Yankees enjoyed US Top 5 status with single **High Enough** (1991), while album made US Top 20. Nugent also took time out to establish hunting and tracking mail order business — guitarist is avid bow and arrow exponent!

Guitar: Gibson Byrdland.

Hit Singles:

	US	UK
High Enough, 1991	3	—

With Amboy Dukes:

Journey To The Center Of The Mind, 1968	16	—

Albums:
Marriage On The Rocks — Rock Bottom (Polydor), 1970
Call Of The Wild, 1973*
Tooth, Fang And Claw, 1974*
Ted Nugent (Epic), 1975
Free For All (Epic), 1976
Cat Scratch Fever (Epic), 1977
Double Live Gonzo (Epic), 1978
Weekend Warriors (Epic), 1978
State Of Shock (Epic), 1979
Scream Dream (Epic), 1980

Above: Motor City's own mad axeman Ted Nugent, who has recently adopted Davy Crockett persona.

Intensities In Ten Cities (Epic), 1981
Great Gonzos, The Best Of (Epic), 1981
Nugent (Atlantic), 1982
Penetrator (Atlantic), 1984
Little Miss Dangerous (WEA), 1986
Anthology (double) (Raw Power), 1986
If You Can't Lick 'Em . . . Lick 'Em (Atlantic/WEA), 1988
Damn Yankees (Atlantic/WEA), 1990
*Released as double album set (Discreet), 1977

Above: Scream Dream, Ted Nugent. Courtesy Epic Records.

Worth Searching Out:
The Amboy Dukes:
The Amboy Dukes (Mainstream/London), 1967
Journey To The Center Of The Mind (Mainstream/London), 1968
Migration (Mainstream/London), 1969

Ted Nugent and The Amboy Dukes:
Survival Of The Fittest Live (Polydor), 1971

Gary Numan

UK vocalist, instrumentalist
Born Gary Anthony James Webb, London, March 8, 1958

Career: Joined first band The Lasers, a punk outfit, in keeping with times in 1976. By 1977, had assumed control, renaming band Tubeway Army, with trio format; Numan as front man (singer, writer, guitar, keyboards) with Paul Gardiner (bass) and Numan's uncle Jess Lidyard (drums). First single was **That's Too Bad**, recorded later that year.

Signed with small Beggar's Banquet label in 1978.

Gigged around London, with drummer Bob Simmonds replacing Lidyard, then Barry Benn replacing Simmonds; Sean Burke (guitar) added by mid-1978. Second single **Bombers** released, but Numan decided to disband group. Album's worth of demos (recorded before dissolution) impressed record company so much that these were released as debut LP in late 1978.

Early in 1979, Numan, Gardiner and Lidyard cut second and final Tubeway Army LP, **Replicas**, which included No. 1 single **Are Friends Electric?** — as a result, LP topped UK chart. After this, Numan decided to record under own name, and next LP **The Pleasure Principle** also topped chart, as did extracted single **Cars**. Numan's heavily synthesized sound and unworldly material, this time augmented by Chris Payne (keyboards, viola), captured public's imagination. During autumn 1979, first tour as star with stage set of fluorescent tubes was huge success.

In 1980 toured Europe, North America, Japan and Australasia. Hit with three more Top 10 singles in UK, as well as releasing one of earliest rock video cassettes. Cracked US Top 10 with **Cars** single (although American success remained comparatively limited). UK success tailed off, and during 1981, while still scoring hits, Numan was obviously less fashionable.

By this time, drummer Cedric Sharpley (ex-Druid) had joined, replacing Lidyard. Halfway through year, Numan had decided to stop live work but two live LPs (issued separately and as boxed set) were released to coincide, but Numan was seemingly more interested in his flying hobby and gaining private pilot's licence.

Released new LP **Dance** and single **She's Got Claws** in 1981, with help from numerous guest musicians, including Mick Karn (Japan), Roger Taylor (Queen), and Canadian violinist (and Numan discovery) Nash the Slash. Wrote and produced hit single **Stormtrooper In Drag** for ex-colleague Paul Gardiner, as well as singing on hit single **Love Needs No Disguise** by Dramatis, a musical group composed of his ex-band (Russell Bell, guitar; Dennis Haines, keyboards; Chris Payne, keyboards and viola; Cedric Sharpley, drums).

Although success carried on into the 80s, only **We Take Mystery** 45 cracked Top 10, and US still remained diffident. Saw minor resurgence with **The Fury** LP, which spawned hit tracks **This Is Love** and **I Can't Stop.** Re-mix of **Cars** classic also charted during this period. Signed to Illegal after demise of own label for **Metal Rhythm** (1988), which prompted successful UK tour. Later albums **Skin Mechanic** and **Outland** were distributed by IRS.

Still an active flyer, Numan enjoys tinkering with and piloting World War II planes; however, he suffered aborted round-the-world attempt in 1981 when aircraft was grounded in India after violation of airspace regulations.

Hit Singles:	US	UK
Cars, 1979	9	1
Complex, 1979	–	6
We Are Glass, 1980	–	5
I Die, You Die, 1980	–	6
This Wreckage, 1980	–	20
She's Got Claws, 1981	–	6
Music For Chameleons, 1982	–	19
We Take Mystery, 1982	–	9
White Boys And Heroes, 1982	–	20
Warriors, 1983	–	20
This Is Love, 1986	–	28
I Can't Stop, 1986	–	27
Cars (E Reg Model), 1987	–	16

Sharpe and Numan:

Change Your Mind, 1985	–	17

With Tubeway Army:

Are Friends Electric?, 1979	–	1

Albums:
The Pleasure Principle (–/Beggar's
   Banquet), 1979
Telekon (–/Beggar's Banquet), 1980
Dance (Atco/Beggar's Banquet), 1981
I Assassin (Atco/Beggar's Banquet), 1982
Warriors (Beggar's Banquet), 1983
White Noise (Numa), 1985
The Fury (Numa), 1985
Strange Charm (Numa), 1986
Numa Records Year 1 (Numa), 1986
Exhibition (Beggar's Banquet), 1987
Metal Rhythm (–/Illegal), 1988
The Skin Mechanic Live (IRS), 1988
Outland (IRS/–), 1991

With Tubeway Army:
Tubeway Army (–/Beggar's Banquet), 1979
Replicas (–/Beggar's Banquet), 1979
The Plan (Beggar's Banquet), 1984

Billy Ocean
UK vocalist
Born Trinidad, January 21, 1952

Career: Growing up in London's East End, Ocean joined Shades Of Blue who played at local Bluecoat Boy pub. Signing solo, first off with Spark label, Ocean had various releases and supplemented income by working on Ford Motor assembly line. Sub-license deal with GTO saw **Love Really Hurts Without You** kept off top of UK charts only by Brotherhood Of Man's million-seller **Save Your Kisses For Me**. Further hits followed, including **Red Light Spells Danger** (1977) which also made No. 2. At this time Ocean signed new management deal with Laurie Jay but demise of GTO and switch to its distributors, CBS, saw Ocean pushed to back of long artist queue. Several frustrating years followed before Jay landed new deal for his artist with Clive Calder's Jive label.

Jay had worked tirelessly for years to make his artist overnight success in US and breakthrough came when Keith Diamond, a Trinidadian resident in US was brought in as writer and arranger. Mutt Lange, successful with The Cars, Foreigner, AC/DC and Def Leppard was brought in to produce.

Released **African Queen** in Africa and **European Queen** in UK where it bombed at first, **Caribbean Queen** came out with different vocal track as well as title in US and was instant smash, crossing over from soul and dance charts to national listings. Re-issued in UK in **Caribbean Queen** format, record was instant success and **Suddenly** album also yielded further hits, leading to 1985 American tour and Grammy award for Best Male Vocal Performance in R&B for **Caribbean Queen**.

Ocean enjoyed his greatest success to date in 1986, when **When The Going Gets Tough, The Tough Get Going** theme from Michael Douglas/Danny DeVito/Kathleen Turner movie *The Jewel Of The Nile*, scored in all territories east and west of the Irrawaddy River. Ocean's promotional video, featuring the esteemed lead players from the flick, was unquestionably a better piece of entertainment than the film.

Although further hits followed through 1989, Ocean's chart status was in decline. The only notable piece of news during the early 90s was his wrongful arrest for alleged drug importation offence (September 1991). However, his previous reversal of fortune should serve him well, and he has sufficient talent as vocalist and writer to resurface at any time.

Hit Singles:	US	UK
Love Really Hurts Without You,		
1976	22	2
L.O.D. (Love On Delivery),		
1976	–	19
Stop Me (If You've Heard It		
All Before), 1976	–	12
Red Light Spells Danger, 1977	–	2
Caribbean Queen, 1984	1	6
Lover Boy, 1985	2	15
Suddenly, 1985	4	4
When The Going Gets Tough		
(The Tough Get Going), 1986	1	1
There'll Be Sad Songs To Make		
You Cry, 1986	1	12
Love Zone, 1986	10	49
Get Outta My Dreams Get		
Into My Car, 1988	1	3
The Colour Of Love, 1988	17	–

Albums:
City Limit (GTO), 1980
Inner Feelings (Epic), 1982
Suddenly (Jive), 1984
Billy Ocean (Epic), 1985
Love Zone (Jive), 1986
Greatest Hits (RCA/Jive), 1989
Tear Down These Walls (Jive), 1988

Sinéad O'Connor
Irish vocalist, composer
Born Glenageary, Ireland, December 12, 1966

Career: Androgynous Irish singer whose single-minded approach has caused chasm between herself and the rock industry, and which also resulted in period of mutual suspicion with audiences.

Difficult childhood prompted early escape to Dublin College Of Music, where O'Connor was recruited to back band Ton Ton Macoute. Their manager (and her future boyfriend) suggested her powerful vocals would be ideal augmentation for U2 guitarist The Edge's soundtrack for *The Hostage* movie, from which **The Heroine** (with O'Connor) was selected promotional single.

Artist's debut album **The Lion And The Cobra** (1987) followed release of cuts **Troy** and chart-destined **Mandinka**. Second LP **I Do Not Want What I Haven't Got** included breakthrough single **Nothing Compares 2 U**, a strident cover version of an early Prince R&B track.

O'Connor's indomitable spirit was neither bent nor broken during various verbal and vocal tirades, including support of IRA (now retracted) and strong anti-police stance. On first US tour in spring of 1990, performers as diverse as Frank Sinatra and controversial comedian Andrew Dice Clay were reported to have slammed her political standpoint, and certain radio stations implemented O'Connor boycott following her refusal to allow playing of American National Anthem at concert in New Jersey.

With the world and it's brother joining the anti-O'Connor drive, the singer collected umerous awards for the **I Do Not Want** set, and **Nothing Compares** single, and found time to guest on Roger Waters' live interpretation of The Wall in Berlin. Appearance on AIDS benefit album Red Hot & Blue and memorable Royal Albert Hall concert brought eventful 1990 to a close.

Further aggravation was caused when O'Connor questioned validity of the music business in letter to National Academy of Recording Arts and Sciences (NARAS), benefactors of prestigious Grammy Awards. Ironically, she was slighted when her peers chose **I Do Not Want** as best 'alternative' performance of year. Further evidence of O'Connor's reputation was revealed when *Rolling Stone* magazine named her both Best and Worst Female Artist in their readers' poll in 1990. O'Connor's threat to quit business was fuelled by prolonged period of inactivity, and rumour of acting lessons, which should give this tempestuous Dubliner a further target to aim at. At press time, she was mooted for role as Charlotte Brontë in *Wuthering Heights* re-make.

Hit Singles:	US	UK
Mandinka, 1988	–	17
Nothing Compares 2 U, 1990	1	1

Albums:
The Lion And The Cobra (Chrysalis/Ensign),
   1987
I Do Not Want What I Haven't Got
   (Chrysalis/Ensign), 1990

Mike Oldfield
UK composer, multi-instrumentalist
Born Reading, Berkshire, May 15, 1953

Career: Started at age 14 in folk duo with sister Sally. Released acoustic **Sallyangie** in 1968 on Transatlantic. After forming short-lived Barefeet, joined Kevin Ayers and the Whole World as bassist/guitarist in 1970-71. Composed 50-minute demo, which was rejected by most major companies. Work was eventually chosen to launch Richard Branson's new label, Virgin. Oldfield overdubbed all the instruments in the studio, creating collage of melodies and instrumental lines that formed basis of **Tubular Bells**, released in May 1973. Album was critically acclaimed and sold in extraordinary quantities, much to amazement of the rock business. US success was assured when **Tubular Bells** was chosen as theme for horror film *The Exorcist*.

The less instantly appealing **Hergest Ridge** covered similar ground. Oldfield received critical backlash but survived intact to produce best-selling **Ommadawn**, a more ambitious work incorporating African drums and Celtic pipes.

Friendship with avant-garde composer David Bedford, from Kevin Ayers days, led to work on **The Orchestrated Tubular Bells** with Royal Philharmonic Orchestra. In addition, Virgin released four-album set **Boxed**, which included all previous work, plus **Collaborations**. Meanwhile, Oldfield spent three years preparing **Incantations**, his most epic project to date.

Moving to London in 1978, he began experimenting with dance music, producing single **Guilty** with a New York rhythm section. First-ever tour followed, backed by 50 musicians, including string players and choir. Music was accompanied by set of films by Ian Eames; live double LP **Exposed** was culled from shows.

1980's **Platinum** was lighter work than its predecessors and included punk-rock

Below: Gary Numan, perhaps the first superstar of the synthesizer.

parody **Punkadiddle**, juxtaposed alongside an Irish jig. To promote **Platinum**, Oldfield Music was formed; British debut (July 1981) was followed by extensive European tour. New work, **QE2**, quickly followed and immediately went gold. World sales of **Tubular Bells** hit 10 million in 1981 and Oldfield was awarded The Freedom Of The City Of London in recognition of sales to exports and charity works. Further distinction came when he was entered in *Who's Who*, the only rock musician, bar McCartney, to achieve recognition there.

May 1982 saw formation of the Mike Oldfield Group (Maggie Reilly, vocals; Morris Pert, percussion, keyboards; Rick Fern, bass; Tim Cross, keyboards; and Pierre Moerlen, drums), Eighth album **Five Miles Out** signalled end of decade of extraordinary sales, although **Crises** LP (1983) did make UK Top 10.

Oldfield flittered through later part of 80s, which saw his soundtrack for *The Killing Fields* movie receive good notices, and release of singles featuring guest vocalists — former Welsh choirboy Aled Jones sung **Pictures In The Dark** (1985), while fiery Bonnie Tyler fronted **Islands** (from Oldfield's 1987 LP of same name).

The 1989 set **Earth Moving** saw collaboration with regular vocalist Maggie Reilly and former Manfred Mann Earth Band frontman Chris Thompson. Subsequent **Amarok** album (1990) seemed to stretch artist's resources, and provided disappointing sales and only short tenure in charts. Nonetheless, mega-talent is unlikely to have ground to a permanent halt.

Hit Singles:

	US	UK
In Dulce Jubilo/On Horseback, 1975	—	4
Portsmouth, 1976	—	3
Blue Peter, 1979	—	19
Moonlight Shadow (with Maggie Reilly), 1983	—	4

Albums:
Tubular Bells (Virgin), 1973
Hergest Ridge (Virgin), 1974
Ommadawn (Virgin), 1975
The Orchestrated Tubular Bells (Virgin), 1975
Boxed (Virgin), 1975
Incantations (Virgin), 1978
Exposed (Virgin), 1979
Platinum (Virgin), 1980
QE2 (Virgin), 1980
Five Miles Out (Virgin), 1982
Crises (Virgin), 1983
Discovery (Virgin), 1984
The Killing Fields (soundtrack) (Virgin), 1984
The Complete Mike Oldfield (Virgin), 1985
Islands (Virgin), 1987
Earth Moving (Virgin), 1989
Amarok (Virgin), 1990

Roy Orbison

US vocalist, composer, guitarist
Born Vernon, Texas, April 23, 1936
Died November 6, 1988

Career: Formed first group, The Wink Westerners, at 13. Appeared on local radio talent shows, then formed Teen Kings while at North Texas State University. First recordings made (after encouragement from college friend Pat Boone) at Norman Petty's Clovis, New Mexico, studio in 1955, including first version of **Ooby Dooby** released on Jewel. During 1956 recorded for Sun in Memphis; re-recording of **Ooby Dooby** reached lower part of US charts.

Above: One of rock's few genuine superstar talents, the late Roy Orbison.

Encouraged by some success as songwriter, mostly stemming from Everly Brothers' version of **Claudette**, Orbison moved to Nashville and signed with RCA. Two singles failed to make impression and in 1959 signed with Monument Records, beginning long partnership with producer Fred Foster. Although first two releases were not hits, Orbison and Foster found right formula with **Only The Lonely** in summer 1960; many hits followed in similar style.

Orbison's records were characterized by romantic themes and vocal crescendos, making best use of distinctive high tenor delivery. Although he could rock 'n' roll with the best of them (**Oh Pretty Woman**, **The Man**), his subtle delivery was seen to best effect on pop anthems like **Crying** and **In Dreams**. His dramatic stage presence was heightened by almost motionless delivery and black outfits. And he never removed those dark glasses!

Having established reputation with slew of majestic hits during 60s, Orbison found he had to trade on his name and reputation when chart status disappeared. Suffered appalling personal tragedy during decade when wife Claudette died in motorbike accident (1966), and then two sons perished in house fire (1968).

Continued to record during the 70s, but without notable success, although duet with Emmylou Harris on **That Lovin' Feeling Again** in 1979 earned Grammy award. Later featured on **Insignificance** and **Blue Velvet** soundtracks, which prompted **In Dreams** collection of re-recordings of classic hits. Relentless touring schedule brought the classic Orbison catalogue to a new generation, and 1987 televised concert, with prominent rock stars Bruce Springsteen, Bonnie Raitt, Elvis Costello and Jackson Browne, reminded audiences of the 'quiet one's' abilities. Cut **Mystery Girl** album with Jeff Lynne (ELO) as producer, and joined Lynne, George Harrison, Tom Petty and Bob Dylan in Traveling Wilburys troupe.

In November 1988, Orbison, who had a history of coronary problems, suffered fatal heart attack. Posthumous single release **You Got It** made UK Top 10, while **Mystery Girl** LP returned artist to Top 5 album listing in both UK and US. Slew of 'greatest hits' packages also enjoyed chart action.

With interest in Orbison higher than it had been for nearly two decades, soundtrack

A Black And White Night (from 1987 concert) was released, and later took Grammy when **Oh Pretty Woman** single from set won Best Male Vocal Performance. Artist had previously been honoured by Roy Orbison Day in home state, and was inducted into Rock 'n' Roll Hall Of Fame in 1987.

If he had wiggled his hips, Orbison might have enjoyed equal stature with Presley. But as an interpreter of teen dilemmas, Orbison had no peer, and had arguably the finest pop 'voice' of all his contemporaries.

Hit Singles:

	US	UK
Only The Lonely, 1960	2	1
Blue Angel, 1960	9	11
Running Scared, 1961	1	9
Crying, 1961	2	25
Dream Baby, 1962	4	2
In Dreams, 1963	7	6
Falling, 1963	22	9
Blue Bayou/Mean Woman Blues, 1963	29	3
Pretty Paper, 1963	15	6
Mean Woman Blues/Blue Bayou, 1963	5	3
Borne On The Wind, 1964	—	15
It's Over, 1964	9	1
Oh Pretty Woman, 1964	1	1
Goodnight, 1965	21	14
Crawlin' Back, 1965	46	19
Lana, 1966	—	15
Too Soon To Know, 1966	—	3
There Won't Be Many Coming Home, 1966	—	18
You Got It, 1989	9	3

Albums:
Greatest Hits (Monument), 1972
All-Time Greatest Hits (Monument), 1973
The Big O (Charly), 1975
At The Rockhouse (Charly), 1980
Golden Days (Monument), 1981
Big O Country (Decca), 1983
The Roy Orbison Collection (Castle), 1986
In Dreams (Virgin), 1987
Roy Orbison And Sonny James (Bear Family), 1987
Go Go Go, (Charly)
The Other Side (Muskateer), 1987
Mystery Girl (Virgin), 1988
The Singles Collection (Polydor), 1989

Orchestral Manoeuvres In The Dark (OMD)

UK group formed 1978

Original line-up: Paul Humphreys and Andy McCluskey, various electronic instruments, vocals.

Career: Humphreys and McCluskey, both from Merseyside, formed first band, VCL XI, in 1976, when pair were 16. Interest stimulated by early German synthesizer bands like Kraftwerk. Group never got beyond rehearsals, but duo joined Hitlers Underpantz, described as 'an assortment of musicians into doing things differently', although this band was no more successful than VCL XI had been. By the end of 1977, duo became nucleus of The Id, an eight-piece band which soon folded.

In 1978, Humphreys and McCluskey adopted name of Orchestral Manoeuvres In The Dark (later abbreviated to OMD), using backing tapes played on tape recorder known as 'Winston'. Played debut gig in this formation at end of 1978 at 'Eric's' in Liverpool, then approached trendy independent label Factory Records of Manchester, who released single of **Electricity** as limited edition in June 1979. Signed by Virgin records subsidiary Dindisc, and supported Gary Numan on UK tour. With proceeds duo built own recording studio, where they cut first LP, **Orchestral Manoeuvres In The Dark** (1980). After retiring 'Winston', expanded line-up by adding drummer Malcolm Holmes (ex-The Id) and David Hughes (ex-Dalek I) on bass and keyboards.

Below: Orchestral Manoeuvres In The Dark, who shortened name to OMD.

1980 saw two minor hit singles followed by first Top 10 single **Enola Gay** (titled after name of plane which dropped first atom bomb) from second LP **Organisation**. Hughes left during year, replaced by multi-instrumentalist (keyboards, saxophone) Martin Cooper. 1981 was big year for band — two Top 5 singles plus Top 3 LP, **Architecture And Morality**. Impetus continued into early 1982 with another Top 5 single. Rest of year spent recording fourth LP **Dazzle Ships**, which was less well received than earlier work; it seemed needlessly self-indulgent, although it contained another hit single, **Genetic Engineering**.

OMD continued to turn out hits, but mid-80s output became increasingly self-indulgent, with over-reliance on effects. 1985 album **Crush** was return to simpler formula, but recent output has continued to attract critical obloquy. **The Pacific Age**, for example, was almost universally dismissed, and prompted barren period broken only by **In The Dark — The Best Of OMD** greatest hits package (1988). With likelihood of terminal split within ranks, Humphreys formed The Listening Pool; McCluskey ploughed on, cutting **Sugar Tax** for April 1991 release.

Hit Singles:

	US	UK
Enola Gay, 1980	–	8
Souvenir, 1981	–	3
Joan Of Arc, 1981	–	5
Maid Of Orleans, 1982	–	4
Genetic Engineering, 1983	–	20
Locomotion, 1984	–	5
Talking Loud And Clear, 1984	–	11
So In Love, 1985	16	–
If You Leave, 1986	–	48
Live and Die (Forever), 1986	19	–
Dreaming, 1988	16	50
Pandora's Box, 1991	–	7

Albums:
Orchestral Manoeuvres In The Dark (–/Virgin), 1980
Organisation (–/Virgin), 1980
Architecture And Morality (Virgin-Epic/Virgin), 1981
Dazzle Ships (Virgin-Epic/Virgin), 1983
Junk Culture (Virgin), 1984
Crush (Virgin), 1985
Pacific Age (Virgin)
Best Of (A&M/Virgin), 1988
Sugar Tax (Virgin), 1991

Ozzy Osbourne
UK vocalist
Born John Osbourne, Birmingham, December 3, 1948

Career: Ozzy Osbourne first won acclaim as Black Sabbath vocalist. Following Osbourne's departure in 1978 (under unpleasant terms), Black Sabbath fans have been delighted with both sides trying to outdo each other professionally.

Formed permanent band called Blizzard Of Ozz; signed to Jet on strength of past history. Strong debut album released in 1980 featured Lee Kerslake (ex-Uriah Heep) on drums, Bob Daisley on bass and Randy Rhoads on guitar; **Blizzard Of Ozz** showed Osbourne had no intention of avoiding confrontation with old mates. **Ozz** featured same hard rock approach of Sabbath and provided impetus for that band to re-form and work again.

Diary Of A Madman indicated Ozzy and Rhoads had special talent for creating exciting, riveting heavy metal. But just as it seemed as if Ozzy would leave Sabbath in

the dust, his luck turned sour. Publicity stunt of biting the head off a dead bat thrown on stage backfired when Ozzy had to undergo painful rabies innoculations. Worse, Randy Rhoads was killed in freak airplane accident and Blizzard Of Ozz crumbled around Osbourne. Kerslake and Daisley left band and went to Uriah Heep.

Refusing to give in, Ozzy recruited Brad Gillis, guitar; Rudi Sarzo, bass; and Tommy Aldridge, drums. This line-up recorded blistering double live set **Talk of the Devil**, which included versions of early Sabbath material. By 1982 Osbourne had become one of biggest headliners on American concert circuit.

Make-up artist Greg Cannon, who worked on movies *The Howling* and *American Werewolf In London*, spent eight hours making Osbourne up for bizarre sleeve to 1983's **Bark At The Moon** album, artwork costing staggering £50,000 to produce. Platinum stature of album repaid investment and gave Osbourne first solo Top 30 singles in UK with title track and ballad **So Tired**.

Rewriting album twice helped account for two-year delay before next album **The Ultimate Sin**, the first on which Osbourne has used an outside producer (ex-Led Zeppelin and Survivor man, Ron Nevison). **Ultimate Sin** was Ozzy's most successful chart album. In 1987 he approved the issue of an album of five-year-old material featuring Randy Rhoads' **Tribute**, originally intended for release on Jet.

During the same year, guitarist Jake E. Lee, who had contributed heavily to Osbourne's last two studio albums, quit band; replacement was New Jersey-born Zakk Wylde. Toured US in 1988 with Wylde, drummer Geezer Butler and bassist Randy Castillo who featured on **No Rest For The Wicked** set in same year.

Still battling an alcohol problem and most of middle America, Osbourne took time out to resolve marital problems (he was arrested after threats to kill his wife) and participate in charity gigs. He featured at Moscow Peace Festival (August 1989), having previously donated earnings from concerts for AIDS research.

Just Say Ozzy Album in 1989 preceded departure of Butler, leaving the wild one to

Below: 'Who brought the bats?' asks the one and only Ozzy Osbourne.

ponder possible Hollywood career; featured as manic preacher in HM spoof movie *Trick Or Treat* in 1987, for which he received encouraging notices. Two-year hiatus in career was broken by Epic set **No More Tears** in November 1991.

Hit Singles:

	US	UK
So Tired, 1984	–	20
Shot In The Dark, 1986	–	20
Close My Eyes Forever (with L. Ford), 1989	8	–

Albums:
Blizzard Of Ozz (Jet), 1980
Diary Of A Madman (Jet), 1981
Talk Of The Devil (Jet), 1982
Bark At The Moon (Jet), 1983
The Ultimate Sin (Epic), 1986
Tribute (Epic), 1987
No Rest For The Wicked (CBS/Epic), 1988
Just Say Ozzy (EP) (CBS/Epic), 1990
No More Tears (Epic), 1991

The Osmonds
US vocal group formed 1960

Original line-up: Alan Osmond; Wayne Osmond; Merrill Osmond; Jay Osmond.

Career: Encouraged by parents, brothers were taught to sing and play several instruments. They first started performing at various Mormon Church functions. Professional career started with residency at Disneyland. Walt Disney TV show led to regular spot on Andy Williams' show where they were mainly featured doing barber shop quartet-type numbers, which lasted from 1962 to 1966. That year group became regulars on *Jerry Lewis Show*, and younger brother Donny (then nine) joined group. Further TV work and touring followed.

In 1970 brothers signed with MGM, and following year scored US No. 1 with **One Bad Apple**. Record initiated string of hits (mainly cover versions) that lasted into mid-70s, and elevation of group into 'teenybopper sensation' worldwide. Success of group also spawned solo careers for Donny, younger brother Jimmy and sister Marie, as well as launching Donny and Marie as duo.

At best, group were pale imitation of Jackson Five, although their professionalism and polish could not be denied. Religious background ensured clean-living image, and in many quarters The Osmonds became byword for safe, slick, show-biz approach to rock and pop music.

Towards end of 70s appeal faded, and members pursued different career directions with varied success. Donny and Marie being the most successful with own TV show in late 70s. Jimmy acted in films and TV, most recently featured in *Fame* series.

In recent years family (without Donny) has regrouped as country-style outfit, swiftly becoming fixture at UK's Wembley Country Music Festival. Marie Osmond has also pursued career in country music with degree of success.

Donny has followed solo path, developing into competent 'Vegas-style' vocalist, and endeavours in late 80s to develop AOR following met with some success; **Soldier Of Love** single (1988) making US No. 2, and also breaking into UK Top 30. Follow-up **Sacred Emotion** also earned prominent chart berth in US.

As a footnote, a quartet of Alan Osmond's children formed group and cut **Osmond Boys** LP for Reprise in 1990, threatening Osmond-mania all over again.

Hit Singles:

	US	UK
One Bad Apple, 1971	1	43
Double Lovin', 1971	14	–
Yo-Yo, 1971	3	–
Down By The Lazy River, 1972	4	40
Hold Her Tight, 1972	14	–
Crazy Horses, 1972	14	2
Going Home, 1973	36	4
Let Me In, 1973	36	2
I Can't Stop, 1974	–	12
Love Me For A Reason, 1974	10	1
The Proud One, 1975	22	5
Donny Osmond:		
Sweet And Innocent, 1971	7	–
Go Away Little Girl, 1971	1	–
Hey Girl, 1971	9	–
Puppy Love, 1972	3	1
Too Young, 1972	13	5
Why, 1972	13	3
Twelfth Of Never, 1973	8	1
Young Love, 1973	23	1
When I Fall In Love, 1973	14	4
Are You Lonesome Tonight, 1974	14	–
Where Did All The Good Times Go, 1974	–	18
Soldier Of Love, 1989	2	29
Sacred Emotion, 1989	13	–
Marie Osmond:		
Paper Roses, 1973	5	2
Donny And Marie Osmond:		
I'm Leaving It All Up To You, 1974	4	2
Morning Side Of The Mountain, 1974	8	5
Make The World Go Away, 1975	44	18
Deep Purple, 1976	14	25
Jimmy Osmond:		
Long-Haired Lover From Liverpool, 1972	38	1
Tweedle Dee, 1973	59	4
I'm Gonna Knock On Your Door, 1974	–	11

Albums:
Our Best To You (MGM), 1974
Christmas Album (Polydor), 1976
Greatest Hits (Polydor), 1976

Donny Osmond:
Donald Clark Osmond (Polydor), 1977
Eyes Don't Lie (Capitol), 1990

Marie Osmond Solo:
This Is The Way That I Feel (Polydor), 1977
There's No Stopping Your Heart (Capitol), 1986
I Only Wanted You (Capitol), 1987
All In Love (Capitol), 1988
Steppin' Stone (Capitol), 1989
Best Of (Curb/—), 1990

Donny And Marie Osmond:
Goin' Coconuts (MGM), 1974
Deep Purple (Polydor), 1976
Winning Combination (Polydor), 1978

Osmond Boys:
Osmond Boys (Curb/—), 1990

Robert Palmer

UK vocalist, composer, guitarist
Born Batley, Yorkshire, January 19, 1949

Career: Developed taste for American R&B as teenager; first band (at 15) was Mandrakes. After year working as graphic designer, Palmer decided to go for musical career. In 1968 he took vocalist job with Alan Brown Set; next year he moved on to group DaDa, which provided his first visit to US. DaDa eventually transformed into Vinegar Joe, for whom he played rhythm guitar and shared vocals with Elkie Brooks. By 1974 Palmer and Brooks were off on solo careers.

Palmer approached Chris Blackwell (Island Records) with some of his demos and Blackwell immediately packed him off to New Orleans and New York to record first LP. **Sneakin' Sally Thru The Alley** was released in September 1974 and won Palmer enough US audience support to convince him to move to America. (In 1976 he transferred to Nassau.)

Pressure Drop was released a little over a year later and was lead-in to Palmer's first US nationwide tour. True US success came in 1978-79 when singles **Every Kinda People** (from **Double Fun**) and **Bad Case of Lovin' You** (from **Secrets**) won approval of national audience.

Follow-up album **Clues** provided minor hits **Johnny & Mary** and **Looking For Clues**. Palmer then put his own career on hold to branch into independent production, and subsequently worked with reggae legend Desmond Dekker, former Tangerine Dream keyboard player Peter Baumann and Palmer-soundalike Moon Martin. Returned with **Maybe It's Alive** LP (1982), and later teamed with moonlighting members of Duran Duran (John and Andy Taylor), plus session drummer Tony Thompson for Power Station group, which provided **Power Station** album and hit singles **Some Like It Hot**, **Get It On** and **Communications**.

Although short-lived, Power Station revived Palmer's own career and **Riptide** set (1985) provided major success with **Addicted To Love** 45, for which sexy video won MTV award in following year.

In 1988, Palmer signed with EMI Records after 10 years tenure with Island. Debut set for company **Heavy Nova** made US/UK Top 30 album listings, while singles **Simply Irresistible** (a Grammy winner) and **She Makes My Day** also charted. Following **Don't Explain** collection (1990), artist revived Marvin Gaye's classic **Mercy Mercy Me** and **I Want You** (1991) tracks for inspired medley which made UK Top 10; toured UK in same year.

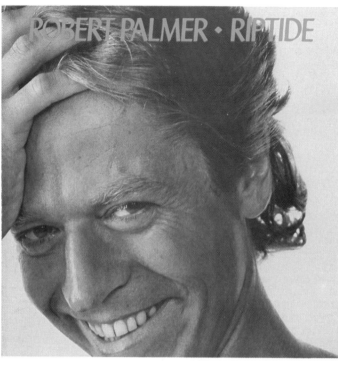

A laconic performer, Palmer is not interested in recording for it's own sake. His considered approach to the business has seen a fair amount of success — probably as much as he wants.

Hit Singles:	US	UK
Every Kinda People, 1978	16	53
Bad Case of Lovin' You (Doctor, Doctor), 1979	14	—
Some Guys Have All The Luck, 1982	—	16
I Didn't Mean To Turn You On, 1986	3	9
Addicted To Love, 1986	—	5
Simply Irresistible, 1988	2	44
She Makes My Day, 1988	—	6
Early In The Morning, 1989	19	—
Mercy Mercy Me — I Want You, 1991	16	9

With Power Station:		
Some Like It Hot, 1985	6	14
Get It On, 1985	9	—

Below: Authentic blue-eyed soul stylist Robert Palmer, whose 1991 tribute to Marvin Gaye was the 'real thang'.

Left: Riptide, Robert Palmer. Courtesy Island Records.

Albums:
Sneaking Sally Through The Alley (Island), 1974
Pressure Drop (Island), 1975
Some People Can Do What They Like (Island), 1976
Double Fun (Island), 1978
Secrets (Island), 1979
Clues (Island), 1980
Maybe It's Alive (Island), 1982
Pride (Island), 1983
Riptide (Island), 1985
The Early Years (with Alan Brown) (C5), 1987
Addictions Volume 1 (Island), 1988
Heavy Nova (EMI), 1988
Don't Explain (EMI), 1990

With Power Station:
Power Station (Parlophone), 1985

Alan Parsons Project

UK group formed 1975

Original line-up: Alan Parsons, guitars, keyboards, vocals, producer, engineer; Eric Woolfson, keyboards.

Career: Parsons was assistant engineer at EMI studios in 1968 when he worked on Beatles' **Abbey Road**. His involvement impressed Paul McCartney, who subsequently used him to engineer several Wings LPs. Parsons also engineered various albums for The Hollies as well as Pink Floyd's **Dark Side Of The Moon**. Turning to production, he cut Cockney Rebel, Pilot and Al Stewart.

Woolfson also worked at Abbey Road Studios where he met Parsons and together they began plans to create own music. Woolfson's previous experience had been as writer; became Project's idea man.

Woolfson's first idea seemed to borrow from Rick Wakeman, who had begun electronic symphonic album concept in 1972 with **Six Wives Of Henry VIII**. Woolfson turned his attention to writing mood pieces to describe stories of Edgar Allen Poe. **Tales Of Mystery And Imagination** appeared in 1975 with highly innovative packaging scheme which almost caused music within to be overlooked.

Science fiction was motif of **I Robot** while **Pyramid** was based on then popular pyramid power cult. **Eve** looked at relations with women, and bears close hearing as well as close look at surprising cover. **The Turn Of A Friendly Card** dealt with gaming and the role of fate in modern society. **Eye In The Sky** continued the concern with modern high-tech society by dealing with 80s surveillance concepts; LP featured vocalists Colin Blunstone, Steve Harley and Peter Straker.

Mid-80s saw repeat formula, with **Ammonia Avenue** (1984) and **Vulture Culture** (1985) enjoying significant chart action. **Stereotomy** (1986), with Gary Booker (Procol Harum) on vocals and **Gaudi** (1987) maintained 'theme' formula. Parsons then re-mixed debut **Tales** album with added narrative by Orson Welles.

The Project's no-risk approach has acquired loyal following intrigued by choice of subject matter and lush production, although shouts of 'bland' are not without foundation.

Hit Singles:	US	UK
Eye In The Sky, 1982	3	—

Above: Alan Parsons (right) and Eric Woolfson (left) of the enigmatic Alan Parsons Project.

Albums:
Tales Of Mystery And Imagination (20th Century/Arista), 1975
I Robot (Arista), 1977
Pyramid (Arista), 1978
Eve (Arista), 1979
The Turn Of A Friendly Card (Arista), 1980
Eye In The Sky (Arista), 1982
Best Of (Arista), 1983
Ammonia Avenue (Arista), 1984
Vulture Culture (Arista), 1985
Stereotomy (Arista), 1986
Gaudi (Arista), 1987

Dolly Parton
US vocalist, guitarist, composer
Born Locust Ridge, Tennessee,
January 19, 1946

Career: Born into large, poor rural family; showed early interest in music-making. Appeared on Grand Ole Opry at age 12; moved to Nashville after leaving high school at 18.

Contract with Monument Records led to little success, but break came when Parton formed partnership with country superstar Porter Wagoner in 1967. She became integral part of Wagoner's live show, and also recorded and made TV appearances with him. Under Wagoner's aegis Parton developed vivid 'blonde bombshell' persona that was to become her stock-in-trade.

In 1973 Parton left Wagoner show, although he continued to produce her solo records. In 1976 she split from Wagoner altogether, having signed contract with Los Angeles-based management company. In meantime, solo career began to take off, helped by endorsement of other female artists such as Linda Ronstadt, Emmylou Harris and Maria Muldaur. (All three recorded Parton compositions on albums.)

Seeking to broaden appeal, Parton moved into rock territory with **New Harvest — First Gathering** in 1977. Featuring numbers like **My Girl** and **Higher And Higher**, album alienated country stalwarts but gained artist many new fans. Audience-widening process bore fruit when Parton scored platinum album with **Here You Come Again** in 1978. Elaborate West Coast production was far removed from country roots.

By beginning of 80s Parton had achieved dream of all-round stardom, with major role in successful movie *9 To 5* (self-penned title song from film was US No. 1), string

Right: Dolly Parton. From C&W to rock and movies and back to country again.

of awards, and ability to draw capacity crowds at virtually any type of venue. A chat-show favourite, Parton showed that lively and witty intelligence lurked beneath her spectacular Mae-West-meets-Barbie-Doll appearance.

Parton enjoyed mixed fortunes in further movie roles, with success of *Steel Magnolias* tempered by critical thumbs-down for *Best Little Whorehouse In Texas* and *Rhinestone Cowboy*. Enjoyed platinum single with Barry Gibb-produced duet with Kenny Rogers on **Islands In The Stream** (1983) and later enjoyed country smash with 1987 **Trio** LP (a Grammy winner) in collaboration with Linda Ronstadt and Emmylou Harris. 1989 LP **White Limozeen** (produced by ace multi-instrumentalist and vocalist Ricky Skaggs) also saw singer return to roots.

Apart from film and record career, Parton's entrepreneurial instincts prompted 'Dollywood' theme park in Tennessee and subsequent purchase of local radio station, which, she claimed, first fired her show-biz ambitions.

An established cross-over artist, Parton will nonetheless be best remembered for her

Above: Carl Perkins, composer of rock 'n' roll gem Blue Suede Shoes.

classic country recordings, which appear in countless 'best of' packages.

Hit Singles:	US	UK
Jolene, 1976	60	7
Here You Come Again, 1978	3	—
Two Doors Down, 1978	19	—
9 to 5, 1980	1	46

Albums:
Best Of (with Porter Wagoner) (RCA), 1969
Best Of (RCA), 1970
My Tennessee Mountain Home (RCA), 1973
Jolene (RCA), 1974
Best Of Volume 2 (RCA), 1975
Love Is Like A Butterfly (RCA), 1975
Bargain Store (RCA), 1975
New Harvest — First Gathering (RCA), 1977
Here You Come Again (RCA), 1978
Both Sides Of (—/Lotus), 1979
The Dolly Parton Collection (Monument), 1980
9 to 5 And Odd Jobs (RCA), 1981
Very Best Of (RCA), 1981

Greatest Hits (RCA), 1982
Heartbreak Express (RCA), 1982
The Winning Hand (with K. Kristofferson, W. Nelson, Brenda Lee) (Monument), 1983
The Great Pretender (RCA), 1984
Once Upon A Christmas (with Kenny Rogers) (RCA), 1984
Real Love (RCA), 1985
Just Because I'm A Woman (RCA), 1986
Rainbow (Columbia/CBS), 1988
White Limozeen (CBS), 1989
Eagle When She Flies (Columbia/CBS), 1991

With Linda Ronstadt and Emmylou Harris:
The Trio (WEA), 1987

Carl Perkins
US vocalist, guitarist, composer
Born Lake City, Tennessee, April 9, 1932

Career: Began performing country and blues material in Tennessee in late 1940s. By early 1950s had evolved own style, apparent in first recordings for Flip and Sun labels in Memphis in 1955. At first encouraged to record country material by Sun's Sam Phillips, but turned to rockabilly and achieved distinction of first national rockabilly hit with own composition **Blue Suede Shoes** in 1956. Major setback to career came when hospitalized following serious car crash on way to first major television appearance; unable to consolidate chart success.

Despite quality material and distinctive vocal and guitar style, Perkins was overshadowed by Elvis Presley (who covered **Blue Suede Shoes** with some success) and was neglected at Sun in favour of Jerry Lee Lewis. Moved to US Columbia with fellow Sun artist Johnny Cash in 1958 in joint deal, only to find himself overshadowed again, this time by Cash, and, despite minor hit with **Pointed Toe Shoes**, star status eluded him.

Death of elder brother Jay in 1958 was further setback, and Perkins turned increasingly to drink. Signed to US Decca in 1963, toured Europe and recorded with Beatles who regarded him as hero. Cut good material for various labels during 60s and became integral part of Johnny Cash Road Show, touring extensively. Encouraged by Cash, turned towards Christianity and away from pills and booze. Perkins split with Cash in 1976 in order to return to touring and recording independently.

Highly regarded as guitarist, Perkins still impresses with live performances (his back-up band now features sons Greg and Stanley), although recorded material is less frequent, despite instigation of own Suede label in late 70s. During the 1980s, Perkins was frequent 'guest' on albums and at concerts, and worked with Paul McCartney (**Tug**

Of War LP), Johnny Cash and Jerry Lee Lewis (The Survivors album), and George Harrison, Ringo Starr, Eric Clapton and Dave Edmunds for Carl Perkins And Friends show to commemorate 30th anniversary of Blue Suede Shoes. Inducted into Rock 'n' Roll Hall Of Fame in 1987.

A perennial back-up musician, Perkins can consider himself unlucky not to have shared in the success of contemporaries like Presley and Roy Orbison.

Guitars: Gibson Switchmaster, Fender Telecaster.

Hit Singles:

	US	UK
Blue Suede Shoes, 1956	2	10

Albums:
The Rocking Guitar Man (Charly), 1975
The Original Carl Perkins (Charly), 1976
Sun Sound Special (Charly), 1978
The Carl Perkins Dance Album (Charly), 1981
The Sun Years (3 LP box set) (Sun), 1982
Survivors (with Johnny Cash and Jerry Lee Lewis) (CBS), 1982
Carl Perkins (MCA), 1986
Dixie Fried (Charly)
Up Through The Years (Bear Family)

Pet Shop Boys

UK vocal/instrumental duo formed 1983

Original line-up: Neil Tennant, vocals, born London, 1954; Chris Lowe, instruments, born London, 1959.

Career: Ex-UK pop magazine *Smash Hits* music journalist Tennant and ex-architecture student Lowe met and discovered mutual love for Euro-disco rhythms in 1983. Contacted underground producer Bobby O, who produced West End Girls; released as one-off deal and became minor hit in Europe, receiving extensive radio play in UK.

Spent all of 1984 extracting themselves from contract with Bobby O and unable to record elsewhere. Subsequently signed to Parlophone Records and released Oppor-

Below: Precious they may be, but we concede the talent of the Pet Shop Boys.

tunities Let's Make Lots Of Money produced by Art Of Noise which failed to chart. Re-recorded West End Girls with Stephen Hague, which became worldwide No 1.

Debut album, Please, featured both these, plus Love Comes Quickly and Suburbia, also Top 20 hits, as PSB established winning formula that blended sardonic lyrics with hypnotic synthesizer melodies and stomping dance beat.

Disco was specially re-mixed version of debut album. Next new release was What Have I Done? single featuring Tennant duet with 60s star Dusty Springfield, which reached No. 2. Follow-up It's A Sin, reached No. 1 despite allegations that it plagiarized Cat Stevens' 1970s hit Wild World. Second album Actually contained both singles plus Rent, which became minor hit later in year. Album sleeve maintained PSB's image of refusing to smile for camera.

Recorded electro-disco version of Always On My Mind for Elvis Presley TV special, which became surprise UK chart topper. Duo also produced single for Patsy Kensit and Eighth Wonder.

Despite reluctance to gig, the Boys enjoyed burgeoning reputation and continued success during 80s, although movie *It Couldn't Happen Here* floundered. Rejoined with Dusty Springfield in 1989 to produce her UK Top 20 single Nothing Has Been Proved.

After much persuasion, PSB undertook debut tour in 1989, with dates in Far East and UK. Visual graphics and appreciative audiences eased duo through tenative early shows. During same year, pair produced Liza Minnelli for her Losing My Mind chart 45 and Tennant formed part-time Electronic aggregation with Johnny Marr (ex-Smiths) and Bernard Sumner (New Order).

1990 saw release of Behaviour album and US concert debut, although American fans were bemused by idiosyncratic antics of Tennant and Lowe. Subsequent gigs in 1991 were more successful.

Discography 'greatest hits' package released in autumn of 1991 is testament to an unlikely coupling who have won over fickle dance crowd.

Hit Singles:

	US	UK
West End Girls, 1985	1	1
Opportunities, 1986	11	11
Suburbia, 1986	—	8
Love Comes Quickly, 1986	—	19

Pet Shop Boys, actually.

Above: Actually, Pet Shop Boys. Courtesy Parlophone Records.

Its A Sin, 1987	9	1
What Have I Done To Deserve This, 1987	2	2
Rent, 1987	—	8
Always On My Mind, 1987	4	1
Heart, 1988	—	1
Domino Dancing, 1988	—	7
Left To My Own Devices, 1988	—	4
It's Alright, 1989	—	5
So Hard, 1990	—	4
Being Boring, 1990	—	20
Where The Streets/Seriously, 1991	—	4
Jealousy, 1991	—	12
DJ Culture, 1991	—	13

Tennant with Electronic:

Getting Away With It, 1989	38	12

Albums:
Please (Parlophone/EMI America), 1986
Actually (Parlophone), 1987
Disco (compilation) (EMI), 1988
Introspective (EMI/Parlophone), 1988
Behaviour (EMI/Parlophone), 1990
Discography (EMI/Parlophone), 1991

Peter, Paul And Mary

US group formed 1961
Peter Yarrow, vocalist, guitarist; born New York City, May 31, 1938
Paul (Noel) Stookey, vocalist, guitarist; born Baltimore, Maryland, November 30, 1937
Mary Travers, vocalist; born Louisville, Kentucky, November 7, 1937

Career: Although PP&M were manufactured in 1961 by Bob Dylan's manager Albert Grossman to emulate success of Kingston Trio, each had strong folk roots. Yarrow was exposed to folk scene at NY's High School of Music and Art, then studied and taught folklore while getting BA degree in psychology. Stookey led rock 'n' roll band while at school, competed and sang at student events at Michigan State, then came to NY for job in industry. Performing

weekends as singer and comedian in Greenwich village clubs, met and was influenced by Tom Paxton, Dave Van Ronk and others, becoming full-time performer in 1960. Travers grew up in progressive NY family, and at 14 belonged to Songswappers.

With Milt Okun as musical director, trio's strong stage personality combined with intelligent material and arrangements to make them style-setters during 1960s. Programme mixed Yarrow/Stookey originals with traditional songs and compositions by others. First album Peter, Paul And Mary (1962) gave double-sided hit single of Seeger's If I Had A Hammer and Lemon Tree.

There were two 1963 albums, Moving and In The Wind, from which Dylan's Blowin' In The Wind went to No. 2 in US and No. 13 in UK, won Grammy and brought Dylan to public notice. Trio sang Dylan's song with him at 1963 Newport Festival.

Other major hits included Puff The Magic Dragon and John Denver's 1969 Leaving On A Jet Plane. Of ten albums, eight went gold; five of these were platinum. Then, after 1970 peace rally in Washington, DC, trio split.

Each made solo albums and each managed Top 100 single; but no spectacular success followed. Yarrow co-produced Mary MacGregor's 1976 album Torn Between Two Lovers, from which his title track composition became major 1977 chart-topper. Stookey produced folk albums then formed Neworld Media, running a recording studio and doing film editing. Mary Travers hosted US radio chart show in 1975 and wrote her autobiography.

In 1978 trio reunited for anti-nuclear rally in California, then gradually began performing together more frequently. During 1983 they played a heavy schedule of concerts, including a European tour, and received high praise from critics and full-capacity audiences who found that old songs hadn't gone stale. Group can now find considerable audience whenever it tours.

Hit Singles:

	US	UK
If I Had A Hammer, 1962	10	—
Puff The Magic Dragon, 1973	2	—
Blowin' In The Wind, 1963	2	13
Don't Think Twice, It's Alright, 1963	9	—
I Dig Rock And Roll Music, 1967	9	—
Leavin' On A Jet Plane, 1969	1	2

Albums:
Peter Paul And Mary (Warner Bros), 1962
In Concert (Warner Bros), 1965
Album 1700 (Warner Bros), 1967
Peter Paul And Mommy (Warner Bros), 1970
Ten Years Together (Warner Bros), 1974
Reunion (Warner Bros), 1978

Tom Petty And The Heartbreakers
US group formed 1976

Original line-up: Tom Petty, vocals, Fender Stratocaster, Rickenbacker 12-string guitars; Stan Lynch, drums, vocals; Mike Campbell, guitar; Benmont Tench, keyboards, vocals; Ron Blair, bass.

Career: Petty grew up in Gainsville, Florida, and played for local group Epics in high school. He quit when band began posing instead of playing. After finishing high school, he held variety of low-paid jobs while playing bass in Gainsville's premier band Mudcrutch, where he came across Mike Campbell and Benmont Tench.

Mudcrutch elected to seek fortune in Los Angeles and moved there in April 1974. One single flopped and band folded. Trio kept in touch and in early 1976 were working on some of Tench's demos with Lynch and Blair (also from Gainsville) when they decided to try again. Group interested Shelter Records and released first LP, which received critical praise for Byrds-like feel with 70s technology. (Single from album, **American Girl** was covered by Jim McGuinn.)

Exciting live shows and plenty of radio play ensured quick success for band, who responded by recording even stronger LP, **You're Gonna Get It!.** Just as it seemed they were making it (**Don't Do Me Like That** single gave them first Top 10 hit), Shelter Records collapsed. Band became deeply involved in legal problems (Petty himself filing bankruptcy) and lost momentum.

Damn The Torpedoes reflected the band's tenacity and resilience in both title and sound. Doing much to pick up band again, album also brought approval of fellow musicians. Stevie Nicks, taking break from Fleetwood Mac used band on **Bella Donna** solo LP; Petty produced excellent, Del Shannon LP; and Tench worked with Dylan.

The double album **Pack Up The Plantation** emanated from band's gigs at Los Angeles' Wiltern Theatre but also included two vocal duets of Tom Petty with Stevie Nicks from an LA Forum dating back to 1981.

Petty continued to gather momentum throughout 80s, albums like **Long After Dark, Southern Accents** and **Let Me Up, I've Had Enough** confirming position near top of rock tree. Double-header tour with Bob Dylan and formation of Traveling Wilburys (with George Harrison, Jeff Lynne, Roy Orbison and Bob Dylan) showed Petty's ability to hold his own against brightest stars of music firmament.

1989 set **Full Moon Fever** saw Petty at artistic peak; album made UK Top 10 and spawned **I Won't Back Down, Running Down A Dream** and **Free Fallin'** hit singles. Petty followed multi-platinum **Moon** with **Great Wide Open** set in August 1991, which saw fellow-Wilbury Lynne co-producing. He then set up own label Gone Gator to oversee release of first two LPs on CD; also issued Del Shannon's last album **Rock On** before that artist's suicide in 1991.

The Heartbreakers, who had been used sparingly since **Let Me Up**, embarked on individual projects. Campbell co-wrote and co-produced Don Henley's **Boys Of Summer**, and Tench worked with Elvis Costello, Feargal Sharkey and Bonnie Raitt. Stan Lynch composed with Henley and Byrdman Roger McGuinn, while bassist (since 1982) Howie Epstein produced tracks for John Prine's proposed 1991 LP.

Since early financial problems, Petty has adopted focused approach to the business and straight-ahead rock 'n' roll delivery.

Below: Tom Petty, an assured performer who has endured for over 16 years.

Above: He missed his big day out on The Commitments movie set, but Wilson Pickett's influence was still apparent.

Hit Singles:	US	UK
Don't Do Me Like That, 1979	10	—
Refugee, 1980	15	—
The Waiting, 1981	19	—
You Got Lucky, 1983	20	—
Don't Come Around, 1985	13	—
I Won't Back Down, 1989	12	28
Free Fallin', 1990	7	—

With Stevie Nicks:

	US	UK
Stop Draggin' My Heart Around, 1981	3	—

Albums:
Tom Petty And The Heartbreakers (Shelter/Island), 1976
You're Gonna Get It! (Shelter/Island), 1978
Damn The Torpedoes (Backstreet), 1979
Hard Promises (Backstreet), 1981
Long After Dark (Backstreet), 1982
Southern Accents (MCA), 1985
Pack Up The Plantation Live! (MCA), 1986
Let Me Up (I've Had Enough) (MCA), 1987
Full Moon Fever (MCA), 1989
Into The Great Wide Open (MCA), 1991

Wilson Pickett
US vocalist, composer
Born Prattville, Alabama, March 18, 1941

Career: First made impression as lead singer for Detroit-based vocal group The Falcons; Falcons' releases demonstrated full-blooded vocal style that was to become Pickett's stock-in-trade. After group split Pickett recorded **If You Need Me** and **It's Too Late** for Lloyd Price's Double L label; both were R&B hits.

Pickett signed with Atlantic in 1964, and, after a couple of unsuccessful releases, company recorded him at Stax Studios in Memphis with Steve Cropper and Stax session mafia. Result was first major hit, the classic **In The Midnight Hour** (co-written by Cropper), which went to No. 21 in the US, 12 in the UK. **Hour**'s irresistible dance beat coupled with Pickett's cocky, macho vocalizing established him as soul star on a par with 60s heroes such as Otis Redding.

The next four years saw slew of exciting soul hits, firmly based on solid dance beat (Pickett was underrated as an interpreter of soul ballads). He also toured extensively, with large soul revue show, and was particularly popular in UK.

Towards end of 1960s, Pickett's popularity waned as new flower-power ethos began to take effect (although strangely one of his biggest hits was cover of The Beatles' mock-gospel ballad **Hey Jude**). He signed with RCA in 1972, and continued to record with varied success. Although there has been no diminution in the power of his voice, since

the early 1970s Pickett seems to have been searching for a direction that could open up a place for him.

Pickett has continued to work live, but his aggressive personality has made him a less than bankable proposition; two recent trips to UK have been cancelled at last minute amid rumours of fisticuffs and/or ludicrous monetary demands.

One of the great soul performers of the 60s, Wilson Pickett summed up for many what soul was all about. Sly, sexy, macho and aggressive, he had all the vocal equipment required to wring the last ounce out of a song. His hit singles collections demonstrate perfectly the raw exhilaration of 1960s soul, and are essentials for any well-rounded record collection. Pickett recently signed to Motown, a company well placed to engineer Tina Turner-style regeneration of career. **American Soul Man** was well received, while re-recording of **Midnight Hour** enjoyed brief sojourn in UK charts. Pickett was inducted into Rock 'n' Roll Hall Of Fame in 1991.

Hit Singles:	US	UK
In The Midnight Hour, 1965	21	12
634-5789, 1966	13	23
Land Of 1000 Dances, 1966	6	22
Funky Broadway, 1967	8	43
She's Lookin' Good, 1968	15	—
Hey Jude, 1969	23	16
Engine Number 9, 1970	14	—
Don't Let The Green Grass Fool You, 1971	17	—
Don't Knock My Love — Part 1, 1971	13	—

Albums:
If You Need Me (—/Joy), 1974
I Want You (United Artists), 1979
The Right Track (EMI), 1981
Best Of (Atlantic), 1982
American Soul Man (Motown), 1988

Pink Floyd
UK group formed 1966

Original line-up: Syd Barrett, vocals, guitar; Roger Waters, bass; Richard Wright, keyboards; Nick Mason, drums.

Career: Barrett and Waters attended Cambridge High School for boys, along with future member Dave Gilmour. Barrett moved to art college in London, playing in Geoff Mott And The Mottos and The Hollering Blues, before forming short-lived duo with Gilmour. Waters, meanwhile, was studying architecture in London and had formed Sigma 6 with Mason and Wright.

Group evolved into T. Set, Meggadeath and Screaming Abdabs, finally bringing in jazz guitarist Bob Close and Barrett. Latter dubbed group The Pink Floyd Sound, a name said to have been inspired by Georgia bluesmen Pink Anderson and Floyd Council. As they moved towards psychedelic music, Close was ousted.

Group spent late 1966 playing at variety of early underground haunts, including The Marquee, the London Free School's Sound/Light Workshop in All Saint's Church Hall, Notting Hill and, most notably, The Roundhouse. By end of year they were regular headliners at UFO, London's foremost hippie club. With new managers Peter Jenner and Andrew King, secured contract with EMI, recording first single in January 1967. **Arnold Layne**, written by Barrett, was amusing tale of transvestite who steals underwear. Novel sound and theme ensured Top 20 placing in UK charts, establishing Floyd as most successful group to emerge from Britain's underground scene.

During May 1967, ambitious **Games For May** was staged at London's Queen Elizabeth Hall, complete with quadrophonic sound system. **Games For May**, re-titled **See Emily Play**, was released as single and reached UK No. 6 in July.

In August, first LP **Piper At The Gates Of Dawn** demonstrated Barrett's dominant role in group. Songs were full of childlike images, subtly echoing work of Lewis Carroll, combining the innocent and the menacing. Barrett's lead guitar work was impressive, neatly complementing Wright's unusual keyboard style. Prior to first US tour, Barrett's behaviour became increasingly erratic, possibly a side-effect of over-use of hallucinogens. In succeeding months, condition worsened; at some performances he would not play at all, remaining motionless on stage. By February 1968, Gilmour was brought in as replacement, Barrett finally leaving in April.

Without Barrett's lyrics, group had little chance of succeeding as singles act. Instead they concentrated on live work, appearing regularly at Middle Earth, and headlining free concert in London's Hyde Park in July. Second album, **A Saucerful Of Secrets**, demonstrated ability to survive. Used Waters' instrumental, electronic and choral work to great effect, particularly during **Set The Controls For The Heart Of The Sun**.

Subsequent concerts revealed increasing professionalism and imagination in use of lighting and sound. At Royal Festival Hall their presentation More Furious Madness From The Massed Gadgets Of Auximenes featured the innovatory Azimuth Coordinator, a PA system that ingeniously projected the sound around auditorium. Increasing interest in soundtrack music led to scores **More** (1969), **The Committee** (1969), **Zabriskie Point** (1979), **The Body** (1970) and **Obscured By Clouds** (1972).

Released double album **Ummagumma**, featuring two live sides (recorded at Mothers Club, Birmingham, and Manchester College of Commerce, in June 1969) backed by studio contributions from every member. Work was self-indulgent in parts and erratic in quality. A period of relative quiet ended with release of **Atom Heart Mother** (1970) which topped UK LP charts. In spite of commercial success, it was least impressive offering to date. Successful concerts followed, including free concert in Hyde Park.

Early in 1971, Floyd appeared at Crystal Palace Garden Party amid fireworks and rain. Premiered **Return To The Son Of Nothing**, an extended melodic rock improvisation

that finally emerged as **Echoes**, the key track on their 1971 LP **Meddle**. Extra-curricular work was undertaken frequently during the early 70s. A film of group at Pompeii (directed by Adrian Maben) was premiered at Edinburgh Festival, while they worked industriously on next album.

The Dark Side Of The Moon LP, the culmination of various ideas over the years, centred on death and emotional breakdown caused by fear, loneliness and spiritual impoverishment. Work also underlined dark pessimism evident in Waters' songwriting, perhaps consciously rejecting the escapist romanticism that had characterized and destroyed Barrett. Bleakness of theme was offset by stunning production, unparalleled for its period. An aesthetically rewarding venture, album also became their biggest seller. Remained in UK lists for over two years; stayed in US charts for over a decade, making it the longest running LP in recording history.

Following album's release, group played to London's Earls Court, then retired for six months. Re-emerged briefly for Robert Wyatt benefit. For most of 1974 group members embarked on various projects, but they returned to the States for another tour in 1975, before playing badly received set in UK at Knebworth.

Wish You Were Here finally appeared in September 1975 after two and a half years. Work was rather anti-climactic and press reaction proved unfavourable. Sales-wise, it was another triumph. During 1976 group toured Europe and States, and completed work on **Animals**, released January 1977. Further solo projects followed amid rumours of impending dissolution. The release of **The Wall** in 1979 provided another phenomenal seller, including a Christmas single chart-topper, **Another Brick In The Wall**. Spin-off film *The Wall*, starring Bob Geldof of Boomtown Rats received mixed review, but fared no worse than others in the genre.

Prophetically titled **The Final Cut** emphasized Waters' dominance of group with further bleak visions of present day society. From early underground following, group had gone on to worldwide acclaim, but after Mason quit to pursue motor-racing, they lapsed into inactivity.

Legal wrangles over entitlement of group name ensued. In 1987 Wright, Gilmour and Mason toured with Floyd paraphernalia,

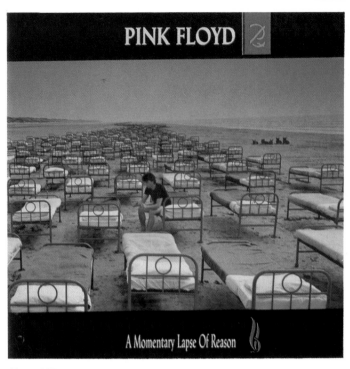

Above: A Momentary Lapse Of Reason, Pink Floyd. Courtesy EMI Records.

including their inflatable pig. Waters also gigged, using archive Floyd film footage as visual back-up. Waters released aptly-titled second solo set **Radio KAOS** before staging triumphant 'live' interpretation of The Wall in 1990, before audience approaching 250,000. Show included guest performances from Cyndi Lauper, Van Morrison, Sinéad O'Connor, The Band and Bryan Adams. Proceeds from international television sales were donated to the British-based Memorial Fund For Disaster Relief. Subsequent album **The Wall — Live In Berlin** charted in both US and UK.

With litigation still threatened, Floyd (without Waters) cut **A Momentary Lapse Of Reason** (1987) and **The Delicate Sound Of Thunder** (1988) LPs, but this venture was proving a shallow, albeit successful, exercise, if unlikely to damage Floyd's estimable reputation.

Hit Singles:

	US	UK
Arnold Layne, 1967	—	20
See Emily Play, 1967	—	6
Money, 1973	13	—
Another Brick In The Wall, 1979	1	1

Albums:
Piper At The Gates Of Dawn (Columbia), 1967
A Saucerful Of Secrets (Columbia), 1968
More (Columbia), 1969
Ummagumma (Harvest), 1969
Atom Heart Mother (Harvest), 1970
Relics (Regal Starline), 1971
Meddle (Harvest), 1971
Obscured By Clouds (Harvest), 1972
The Dark Side Of The Moon (Harvest), 1973
A Nice Pair (Harvest), 1973
Wish You Were Here (Harvest), 1975
Animals (Harvest), 1977
The Wall (Harvest), 1979
The Final Cut (EMI), 1983
Works (Capitol), 1983
A Momentary Lapse Of Reason (EMI), 1987
Delicate Sound Of Thunder (Columbia/EMI), 1988

With Various Artists:
Zabriskie Point (soundtrack) (MGM), 1970

Above: Original Pink Floyd line-up, circa 1966, with (from left and clockwise) Nick Mason, Roger Waters, Richard Wright and Syd Barrett.

Syd Barrett Solo:
The Madcap Laughs/Barrett (Harvest), 1974
About Face (Harvest), 1984

David Gilmour Solo:
David Gilmour (Columbia/CBS), 1978

Nick Mason Solo:
Fictitious Sports (Columbia/CBS), 1981

Roger Waters Solo:
The Body (soundtrack with Ron Geesin) (—/Harvest), 1970
The Pros And Cons Of Hitchhiking (Columbia/Harvest), 1984
Radio K.A.O.S. (Columbia/Harvest), 1987
The Wall: Berlin (Mercury), 1990

Below: Piper At The Gates Of Dawn, Pink Floyd, was released in 1967 and shows Syd Barrett's influence. Courtesy EMI/Columbia Records.

Gene Pitney

US vocalist, composer
Born Rockville, Connecticut, February 17, 1941

Career: Began as songwriter; first record **I Wanna Love My Life Away** was made as song demo and only released after several music publishers had rejected song. Track featured Pitney playing all instruments and multi-track vocals; it reached No. 39 in US charts, becoming first of many chart appearances throughout 60s.

Wrote several hits for other artists, including Roy Orbison, Ricky Nelson, and The Crystals. Most of own recordings were self-penned and later published by own company.

Pitney's distinctive tenor vocals made records immediately identifiable, and regular tours consolidated position in UK as major US solo artist of 60s, second only to Orbison. The Beatles liked Pitney and they toured the UK with him.

In late 60s, Pitney turned to country music, and enjoyed liaison with George Jones for two LPs, while continuing regular visits to Britain where he satisfied audiences with his no-frills approach to his classic material. Reprised magnificent **Something's Gotten Hold Of My Heart** (1989) in collaboration with flamboyant English warbler Marc Almond for surprise UK No. 1 hit, which ensured another decade of bill-topping.

Hit Singles:

	US	UK
Town Without Pity, 1962	13	–
(The Man Who Shot) Liberty Valance, 1962	4	–
Only Love Can Break A Heart, 1962	2	–
Half Heaven-Half Heartache, 1963	12	–
Mecca, 1963	12	–
24 Hours From Tulsa, 1963	17	5
That Girl Belongs To Yesterday, 1964	49	7
It Hurts To Be In Love, 1964	7	36
I'm Gonna Be Strong, 1964	9	2
I Must Be Seeing Things, 1965	31	6
Last Chance To Turn Around, 1965	13	–
Looking Through The Eyes Of Love, 1965	28	3
Princess In Rags, 1965	–	9
Backstage, 1966	–	4
Nobody Needs Your Love, 1966	–	2
Just One Smile, 1966	–	8
Something's Gotten Hold Of My Heart, 1967	–	5
Somewhere In The Country, 1968	–	19
She's A Heartbreaker, 1968	16	–

Albums:
Best Of (Piccadilly/–), 1981
Greatest Hits Of All Time (–/Phoenix), 1982
20 Golden Pieces Of (–/Bulldog), 1983
20 Greatest Hits (Spectrum)
22 Greatest Hits (Bescol)
Backstage – The Greatest Hits And More, 1990

The Platters
US vocal group formed 1953

Original line-up: Tony Williams; Alex Hodge; David Lynch; Herb Reed.

Career: Perhaps the best-known of many vocal harmony groups who trod fabled 'rags-to-riches' path during rock 'n' roll years of the 50s, Platters climbed from obscurity of regional R&B charts to worldwide stardom. Original quartet met entrepreneur Buck Ram in Los Angeles in 1953; signed to Federal Records, but met little success. Ram made some inspired personnel changes, replacing Hodge with Paul Robi and recruiting Zola Taylor as contrasting female voice.

Continued to record for Federal, picking up local sales. Ram placed them with Mercury as virtual 'make-weights' in deal involving The Penguins, who had just scored pop

hit with **Earth Angel**. Platters' first four records on Mercury all reached national Top 5 between 1955 and late 1956. **Only You, The Magic Touch, The Great Pretender** and **My Prayer** were fine, lyrical ballads; latter two topped charts, led by Tony Williams' clear, soaring tenor.

Hits continued to flow during next five years; chart-toppers **Twilight Time** and **Smoke Gets In Your Eyes** became 'pop' standards in Platters' distinctive ballad styling and lush orchestrations.

In 1961 Tony Williams quit to pursue solo career; auditions yielded Sonny Turner as replacement. Despite maintaining similar mode of performance, hits did not come as readily. Group made good living on cabaret circuit, though, and continued steady output of LPs until leaving Mercury in 1965.

Change of musical direction followed more personnel changes; Sandra Dawn replaced Zola, Nate Nelson took over from Paul Robi. Group pacted with Musicor in 1966, taking more soulful inclination and switching up-tempo; scored with **I Love You 1000 Times** and **With This Ring**. Albums contained reworkings of their Mercury hits.

Subsequent years brought further personnel changes, record label switches, and profusion of lawsuits. Buck Ram Platters became touring minions of their ageing manager, who slapped injunctions on any original member who dared to quote Platters' name in show billings. As testimony to classic hits, group were inducted into Rock 'n' Roll Hall Of Fame in 1990.

Hit Singles:

	US	UK
Only You, 1955	1	–
The Great Pretender, 1956	1	–
The Great Pretender/Only You, 1956	–	5
(You've Got) The Magic Touch 1956	4	–
My Prayer, 1956	1	4
You'll Never Know/It Isn't Right, 1956	11	23
It Isn't Right/You'll Never Know, 1956	13	23
On My Word Of Honor/One In A Million, 1957	20	–
One In A Million/On My Word Of Honor, 1957	20	–
Only You, 1957	–	18
I'm Sorry/He's Mine, 1957	11	18
He's Mine/I'm Sorry, 1957	16	–
Twilight Time, 1958	1	3
Smoke Gets In Your Eyes, 1959	1	1
Harbor Lights, 1960	8	11

Albums:
Best Of Volume 1 (–/Philips), 1973
Best Of Volume 2 (–/Philips), 1973
Encore (Mercury/–), 1976
More Encore Of Greatest Hits (Mercury), 1976
19 Hits (King/–), 1977
20 Greatest Hits (Bescol)
Golden Hits (Mercury)

The Pogues
UK group formed 1983

Original line-up: Shane McGowan; guitar, vocals; James Fearnley, accordion; Andrew Ranken, drums; Spider Stacy, penny whistle; Jem Finer, banjo.

Career: Anarchic Irish combine (although McGowan born in Kent) whose affinity for indigenous folk music has proved heavy influence on recorded output.

Originally Pogue Mo Chone (unprintable Gaelic expression), the quintet added Caitlin O'Riordan after early gigs in north London pubs. Debut single **Streets Of London** (1984) was cut for own indie Pogue Mahone label, with distribution by Rough Trade.

Group's moniker caused sufficient furore to forestall airplay on mainstream radio stations, a situation resolved when Stiff Records signed band after agreement to abbreviate name to The Pogues.

After first album **Red Roses For Me** (1984) attracted good reviews and minor chart action, Elvis Costello was recruited to produce **Rum, Sodomy And The Lash** LP which made UK Top 20.

With addition of Philip Chevron on guitar, Pogues embarked on first US dates (January 1986), making limited impact. **Poguetry In Motion** EP was lone recorded output for year which saw O'Riordan quit (after marrying Costello) and remainder of group featured in *Straight To Hell* Western spoof movie. Those who saw it concurred with title.

Celebration concert for The Dubliners in March 1987, featuring The Pogues and U2, prompted recording of traditional **The Irish Rover** single, teaming band with Dublin's most famous export (after Guinness). To their mutual astonishment, single made UK Top 10. Terry Woods was then added to line-up. Band ended eventful year back in hit parade when **A Fairytale Of New York** (with Kirsty MacColl on vocals) made No. 2.

With MacColl's husband Stephen Lillywhite producing, **If I Should Fall From Grace With God** set peaked at No. 3 in UK album listings (1988), by which time Pogues (with ex-Clash guitarist Joe Strummer now in line-up) were cracking American market, where LP made Top 100. Prior to scheduled US tour in July, McGowan was taken ill, although band maintained road schedule.

The Pogues have consolidated reputation with **Peace And Love** and **Hell's Ditch** LPs, despite McGowan's erratic contribution. McGowan was absent for autumn 1991 UK tour and was permanently replaced by bass player Darryl Hunt.

Hit Singles:

	US	UK
Fairy Tale Of New York, 1987	–	2

With The Dubliners:

	US	UK
The Irish Rover, 1987	–	8

Albums:
Red Roses For Me (Enigma/Stiff), 1984
Rum, Sodomy And The Lash (–/Stiff), 1987
If I Shall Fall From Grace With God (Island/WEA), 1988
Yeah Yeah Yeah Yeah Yeah (Island/Pogue Mahone), 1988
Peace And Love (Island/Pogue Mahone), 1989
Hell's Ditch (Island/Pogue Mahone), 1990
Best Of (Warner Bros), 1991

Below: The Pointer Sisters, now successful as a trio.

Pointer Sisters
US vocal group formed 1973

Original line-up: Bonnie Pointer; Anita Pointer; Ruth Pointer; June Pointer.

Career: Group formed of four genuine sisters, daughters of church ministers; and born in Oakland, California. Started singing in church, and formed Pointer Sisters after

Above: Retrospect, The Pointer Sisters' 1981 album, depicting all four sisters. Courtesy MCA Records.

leaving school. Through acquaintance with producer David Rubinson, they became involved with session work on West Coast, singing behind such artists as Boz Scaggs, Grace Slick and Esther Phillips. Eventually they decided to pursue career in own right and Rubinson negotiated deal with ABC/Blue Thumb in 1973.

Initially the sisters concentrated on jazzy nostalgia material and featured close-harmony scat singing; 40s image was followed through in clothes and presentation. They achieved considerable success in this mode, and showed versatility by scoring country hit with Grammy award-winning single **Fairy Tale**. The sisters also featured in movie *Car Wash*.

Eventually musical frustration set in, and the sisters left ABC/Blue Thumb in 1977. They disbanded for short period, Bonnie branching out to pursue moderately successful solo career. Remaining three regrouped in 1978 and signed deal with producer Richard Perry's Planet label.

First album **Energy** and hit single **Fire** both achieved gold status and showed total change in direction, the girls now finding inspiration from writers like Bruce Springsteen and Becker/Fagen from Steely Dan. With career now firmly based in rock mainstream, Sisters enjoyed slew of Perry-inspired chart records from early 80s, of which **Jump** (a Grammy winner) and **I'm So Excited** were most notable.

A label change (to RCA) in 1985 saw trio sustain success for a couple of years (debut for label Contact went platinum) before diminishing chart return. Anita then cut solo album **Love For What It Is** for notable

soul/R&B producer Preston Glass, which suggested disappointment at current return from AOR market. Seemingly frustrated by musical direction, The Pointer Sisters signed to Motown in 1990 for **Right Rhythm** LP.

Hit Singles:

	US	UK
Yes We Can Can, 1973	11	—
Fairy Tale, 1974	13	—
How Long (Betcha' Got A Chick On The Side), 1975	20	—
Fire, 1979	2	34
Heaven Must Have Sent You, 1979	11	—
He's So Shy, 1980	3	5
Slow Hand, 1981	2	10
Should I Do It, 1982	13	50
American Music, 1982	16	—
Automatic, 1984	5	2
Jump (For My Love), 1984	3	6
I'm So Excited, 1984	9	11
Neutron Dance, 1985	6	—
Dare Me, 1985	11	17
Be There, 1987	42	—

Albums:

Live At The Opera House (ABC), 1974
Best Of (Blue Thumb/ABC), 1976
Energy (Planet), 1978
Priority (Planet), 1979
Special Things (Planet), 1980
Black And White (Planet), 1981
Retrospect (MCA/—), 1981
So Excited (Planet), 1982
Greatest Hits (Planet), 1982
Black And White (Planet), 1984
Break Out (Planet), 1984
Contact (RCA)
Hot Together (RCA), 1987
Pointer Sisters (Planet)
Right Rhythm (Motown), 1990

Below: Despite short-lived tenure, The Police were an arresting influence.

The Police

UK group formed 1977

Original line-up: Sting (Gordon Sumner), vocals, Ibanez bass; Henri Padovani, guitar; Stewart Copeland, drums.

Career: Band was formed by drummer Copeland, previously with moderately successful UK outfit Curved Air. Idea was to combine post-punk principles of simplicity and spontaneity with coherence and melodic sense. Copeland recruited Sting from Newcastle jazz and rock scene, and pair pulled in Padovani on guitar.

Band's first single was **Fall Out**, released in January 1977 on Illegal Records, an independent label formed by Copeland with brother Miles. (Miles Copeland had also served as manager throughout band's career.) Padovani's tenure was short-lived; he left in August 1977 to form Flying Padovani Brothers; replacement was Andy Summers, veteran of Zoot Money's Big Roll Band, The Animals, Soft Machine, Kevin Ayers and Kevin Coyne.

It was with re-release of **Roxanne** on A&M in 1979 that band started to attract attention. Combining reggae-styled verse with rocking harmony chorus, single eventually went silver. It was first of string of major hit singles, each distinctive yet recognizable Police. By end of 1980 band was firmly established in UK and was making major inroads into US and international market.

Albums were as successful as singles. **Outlandos D'Amour** went double platinum in UK and gold in US, **Regatta De Blanc** made triple platinum in UK and gold in US, and third album, **Zenyatta Mondatta**, had massive sales figures all over the world —

Above: Synchronicity, The Police. A No. 1 album in both the US and UK. Courtesy A&M Records.

it achieved triple platinum status in UK, platinum status in US and went either gold or platinum in virtually every other territory.

Meanwhile, band had gained reputation as exciting live act and toured throughout world to wild acclaim during 1980-81. **Six Pack**, a package of the first five Police singles plus new release **The Bed's Too Big Without You** on A&M Records, went to No. 17 in the UK singles charts, a rather unique accomplishment.

1982 saw **Ghost In The Machine** LP riding high in charts, and hit singles from album soaring; **Every Little Thing She Does Is Magic** gave them their fourth UK No. 1, and **Invisible Sun** reached No. 2 in the UK despite BBC banning of accompanying video which depicted troubled streets of Belfast. Band kept relatively low profile as members went about various solo projects. Sting, natural frontman of band, had already had major acting parts in The Who film *Quadrophenia* and BBC-TV film *Artemis '81*, and received further acclaim for his lead role in Dennis Potter-written movie

Brimstone And Treacle. As if that were not enough, he scored hit with **Spread A Little Happiness**, the song featured in film. Andy Summers recorded moderately successful instrumental LP, **I Advance Masked**, with Robert Fripp in 1982.

Return to group work came in spring 1983. **Synchronicity** LP and single **Every Breath You Take** flew to No. 1 both sides of the Atlantic. **Synchronicity** was third Police LP in a row to enter UK album charts at No. 1.

With awards and hit singles still flying around, and interest in group hardly diminished despite relative low profile, trio abandoned plans for follow-up to **Synchronicity** when Sting elected to pursue solo career (started with **Dream Of The Blue Turtles** LP). In 1986 A&M released greatest hits package **Every Breath You Take — The Singles**, another UK No. 1.

Sting's extra-curricular activities (see separate entry) squashed any hope of a re-formation, and Summers and Copeland began to shape their own destinies. Summers slipped quietly into jazz-styled recording career, belying early criticism of his lightweight, albeit creative, input. Reunited with Fripp for 1984 release **Bewitched**, before cutting **XYZ** for MCA in 1987, an oddity given guitarist's vocal contribution. Enjoyed good reviews for 1991 set **World Gone Strange** featuring bassist Tony Levin and drummer Chad Wackerman.

Copeland scored Francis Ford Coppola movie *Rumblefish* (1984), and then cut **The Rhythmatist** LP, an amalgam of African and Western musical styles. Continued with film and TV work, most notably *Wall Street* flick. His **The Equalizer And Other Cliff Hangers** LP (1988) included celluloid themes and incidental music. Formed short-lived Animal Logic with virtuoso bassist Stanley Clarke and vocalist Debbie Holland who cut self-titled album for Virgin in 1989.

Hit Singles:	US	UK
Roxanne, 1979	32	12
Can't Stand Losing You, 1979	–	2
Message In A Bottle, 1979	–	1
Walking On The Moon, 1979	–	1
So Lonely, 1980	–	6
Six Pack, 1980	–	17

Below: The usually subdued Andy Summers in exuberant mood. Summers is now carving a career in jazz field.

	US	UK
Don't Stand So Close To Me, 1980	10	1
De Do Do Do, De Da Da Da, 1980	10	5
Invisible Sun, 1981	–	2
Every Little Thing She Does Is Magic, 1981	3	1
Spirits In The Material World, 1982	11	12
Every Breath You Take, 1983	1	1
Wrapped Around Your Finger, 1983	–	7

	US	UK
Synchronicity II, 1983	16	17
King Of Pain, 1984	3	17

Albums:
Outlandos D'Amour (A&M), 1978
Regatta De Blanc (A&M), 1979
Zenyatta Mondatta (A&M), 1980
Ghost In The Machine (A&M), 1981
Synchronicity (A&M), 1983
Every Breath You Take – The Album (A&M), 1986

Stewart Copeland Solo:
The Rhythmatist (A&M), 1985
The Equalizer (IRS/MCA), 1988

Below: The trio take in what's left of the clean outdoor air.

Above (from left to right): Stuart Copeland, Andy Summers and Sting — their own men since 1986.

Stewart Copeland with Animal Logic:
Animal Logic (MCA/Virgin), 1989

Andy Summers Solo:
XYZ (A&M), 1987
Mysterious Barricades (Private Music), 1989
The Golden Wire (Private Music), 1989
Charming Snakes (Private Music), 1990
World Gone Strange (Private Music), 1991

Andy Summers with Robert Fripp:
I Advance Masked (A&M), 1982
Bewitched (A&M), 1984

Elvis Presley

US vocalist, guitarist, composer, actor
Born Tupelo, Mississippi, January 8, 1935
Died Memphis, Tennessee, August 16, 1977

Career: Early influences included gospel concerts, church singing, R&B radio shows in hometown, and country singers of 40s. In first public appearance at age 10, came second singing **Old Shep** in State Fair talent contest. Following family move to Memphis and some experience singing with gospel groups, visited Sun Studios to cut acetate as gift to mother.

Sun's Sam Phillips recognized potential and eventually in 1954 teams Presley with Scotty Moore, guitar, and Bill Black, bass. Resulting first single, **That's All Right**, became big enough hit locally for trio to begin touring Southern US and eventually appear on *Louisiana Hayride* radio show.

Further Sun singles consolidated popularity and reports of excitement generated at live appearances prompted Colonel Tom Parker to become manager and RCA-Victor Records to purchase contract from Sun for $35,000. In retrospect, sum paid seems minimal, but was astronomical in 1955.

With better distribution and promotion than Sun could provide, coupled with controversial television appearances, Presley rapidly became most important artist in rock 'n' roll field and major threat to 'establishment' singers. First major hit, **Heartbreak Hotel**, in summer 1956 was rapidly followed by succession of No. 1s in similar style, mostly introduced on major TV shows.

Fan fervour resulted in unprecedented merchandising of Presley products and hysterical scenes at concerts and public appearances. Although management policy was criticized later, Colonel Parker successfully promoted hysteria while building solid career for Presley, typified by first movie contract guaranteeing advances of $450,000 for first three films.

Career interrupted for two years by draft into US Army in 1958. However, Presley's popularity was scarcely affected by lack of public appearances thanks to stockpile of recordings and continuing publicity resulting from Colonel Parker's activities on his behalf. By 1960, when Presley returned from service in Germany, rock 'n' roll had ceased to rule the charts. Subsequent releases followed the pattern set by **It's Now Or Never**, an almost-MOR ballad.

First movies had shown some acting promise coupled with fairly natural musical content, but as demand for anything featuring Presley increased, less importance was placed on scripts. Aim was to maintain flow of glossy films with box-office appeal. Thus best films *Love Me Tender, Jailhouse Rock* and *Loving You* quickly degenerated to opportunist pap of *Girls Girls Girls* and *Paradise Hawaiian Style*.

Presley was undoubtedly capable of succeeding with better acting parts, as in *Flaming Star*, but more money could be made linking soundtrack album with teen-appeal films. Resulting 'assembly line' material bored Presley and accelerated decline as movie actor. At same time recorded material became less adventurous, with movie soundtrack providing singles releases to exclusion of stronger unrelated material.

Following marriage in 1967 to Priscilla Beaulieu, daughter of Army officer, hoped-for return to former greatness confirmed by first TV appearance since 1960, an NBC Special. Both material and physical appearance raised hopes of fans who had watched their idol decline. Unfortunately, early promise of single **If I Can Dream** and live appearances in Las Vegas with distinguished band, including guitarist James Burton, failed to sustain momentum. During the 70s, records and stage shows again declined, although faithful fans maintained following.

In mid-70s Presley increasingly withdrew to safety of Graceland estate in Memphis with family and bodyguards. He became dependent on drugs to control basic functions, and gained weight. Record releases were irregular and stage appearances a parody of former self. Many were convinced that drugs were major factor in death from 'natural causes' at age 42. Presley's doctor is believed to be somewhat suspect.

As news of death spread, there were hysterical scenes outside home in Memphis and at funeral. RCA was unable to cope with demand for Presley product as sales broke all previous records. Cult following since death has continued unabated. Books,

Below: His Hand In Mine. Courtesy RCA Records. Presley holds the record for the most weeks at No. 1 in the UK.

articles, films and TV documentaries on Presley's life abound; many attempt to investigate cause of demise.

Despite criticism of later career, it is undeniable that Presley's influence on others has been and remains enormous. He was first rock 'n' roll artist to successfully blend black and white musical influences and retain appeal to broad audience. Presley holds nearly every rock record in UK, including Most Hits, Most Weeks In Charts and Most Top 10 Hits. The 10th anniversary of artist's death in 1987 stimulated plethora of retrospectives and tributes, although later authorized (by Priscilla Presley) TV series about The King's early career failed.

With his good looks, vocal talent and sex appeal, Presley was a 'natural' pop idol, and it is a measure of his greatness that he remains the most important and adulated performer of the rock 'n' roll era.

Hit Singles:	US	UK
Heartbreak Hotel/I Was The One, 1956	1	2
Blue Suede Shoes (EP in US), 1956	20	9
I Was The One/Heartbreak Hotel, 1956	19	–
I Want You, I Need You, I Love You, 1956	1	14
Don't Be Cruel/Hound Dog, 1956	1	2
Hound Dog/Don't Be Cruel, 1956	1	2
Love Me/When My Blue Moon Turns To Gold (EP), 1956	2	–
When My Blue Moon Turns To Gold/Love Me, 1956	19	–
Love Me Tender/Any Way That You Want Me, 1956	1	11
Any Way That You Want Me/Love Me Tender, 1956	20	–
Blue Moon, 1956	–	9
Too Much, 1957	1	6
All Shook Up, 1957	1	1
(Let Me Be Your) Teddy Bear/Loving You, 1957	1	3
Loving You/(Let Me Be Your) Teddy Bear, 1957	20	–
Paralysed, 1957	–	8
Party, 1957	–	2
Got A Lot O' Livin' To Do, 1957	–	17
Trying To Get To You, 1957	–	16
Lawdy Miss Clawdy, 1957	–	15
Santa Bring My Baby Back To Me, 1957	–	7
Jailhouse Rock/Treat Me Nice, 1957	1	1
Treat Me Nice/Jailhouse Rock, 1957	18	–
Don't/I Beg Of You, 1958	1	2
I Beg Of You/Don't, 1958	8	–

Above: It Won't Seem Like Christmas Without You — just part of Presley's vast discography. Courtesy RCA Victor.

Below: Elvis Presley, The king of rock 'n' roll, who remains a true legend. Photograph from the late 1950s.

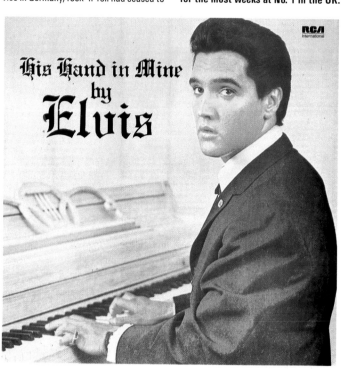

Wear My Ring/Doncha Think It's Time, 1958	2	3
Doncha Think It's Time/Wear My Ring, 1958	15	—
Hard Headed Woman, 1958	1	2
King Creole, 1958	—	2
One Night/I Got Stung, 1958	4	1
I Got Stung/One Night, 1958	8	—
A Fool Such As I/I Need Your Love Tonight, 1959	2	1
I Need Your Love Tonight/A Fool Such As I, 1959	4	—
A Big Hunk O' Love/My Wish Came True, 1959	1	4
My Wish Came True/A Big Hunk O' Love, 1959	12	—
Stuck On You/Fame And Fortune, 1960	1	3
Fame And Fortune/Stuck On You, 1960	17	—
It's Now Or Never, 1960	1	1
A Mess Of Blues, 1960	—	2
Are You Lonesome Tonight/I Gotta Know, 1960	1	1
I Gotta Know/Are You Lonesome Tonight, 1960	20	—
Surrender, 1961	1	1
Wooden Heart, 1961	—	1
Flaming Star (EP), 1961	14	—
I Feel So Bad/Wild In The Country, 1961	5	—
Wild In The Country/I Feel So Bad, 1961	—	4
(Marie's The Name) His Latest Flame/Little Sister, 1961	4	1
Little Sister/(Marie's The Name) His Latest Flame, 1961	5	—
Can't Help Falling In Love/Rock A Hula Baby, 1962	2	—
Rock A Hula Baby/Can't Help Falling In Love, 1962	—	1
Good Luck Charm, 1962	1	1
Follow That Dream (EP), 1962	15	34
She's Not You, 1962	5	1

Return To Sender, 1961	2	1
One Broken Heart For Sale, 1963	11	12
(You're The) Devil In Disguise, 1963	3	1
Bossa Nova Baby, 1963	8	13
Kiss Me Quick, 1963	—	14
Viva Las Vegas, 1964	29	17
Kissin' Cousins, 1964	12	10
Such A Night, 1964	16	13
Ask Me/Ain't That Loving You Baby, 1964	12	—
Ain't That Loving You Baby/Ask Me, 1964	16	15
Blue Christmas, 1964	—	11
Do The Clam, 1965	21	19
Crying In The Chapel, 1965	3	1
Easy Question, 1965	11	—
Tell Me Why, 1965	33	15
I'm Yours, 1965	11	—
Puppet On A String, 1965	14	—
Love Letters, 1966	19	6
All That I Am, 1966	41	18
If Every Day Was Like Christmas, 1966	—	13
Guitar Man, 1968	43	19
US Male, 1968	28	15
If I Cant Dream, 1969	12	11
In The Ghetto, 1969	3	2
Clean Up Your Own Back Yard, 1969	35	2
Suspicious Minds, 1969	1	2

Don't Cry Daddy, 1970	6	8
Kentucky Rain, 1970	16	21
I've Lost You, 1970	32	9
The Wonder Of You, 1970	9	1
You Don't Have To Say You Love Me, 1970	11	9
There Goes My Everything, 1971	—	6
Rags To Riches, 1971	—	9
I Just Can't Help Believin', 1971	—	6
Until It's Time For You To Go, 1972	40	5
American Trilogy, 1972	—	8
Burning Love, 1972	2	7
Separate Ways/Always On My Mind, 1973	20	—
Always On My Mind/Separate Ways, 1973	—	9
Steamroller Blues/Fool, 1973	17	—
Fool/Steamroller Blues, 1973	—	15
If You Talk In Your Sleep, 1974	17	40
Promised Land, 1974	14	9
My Boy, 1975	20	5
Girl Of My Best Friend, 1976	—	9
Suspicion, 1976	—	9
Moody Blue, 1977	—	6
Way Down, 1977	18	1
My Way, 1977	—	9
It Won't Seem Like Christmas Without You, 1979	—	13
It's Only Love, 1980	—	3

Albums:

Rock 'n' Roll (RCA), 1956
Elvis Presley (RCA), 1956
Elvis (RCA), 1956
Loving You (RCA), 1957
King Creole (RCA), 1958
For LP Fans Only (RCA), 1959
A Date With Elvis (RCA), 1959
Elvis Is Back (RCA), 1960
His Hand In Mine (RCA), 1960
Something For Everybody (RCA), 1961
Blue Hawaii (RCA), 1961
Pot Luck (RCA), 1962
It Happened At The World's Fair (RCA), 1963
Roustabout (RCA), 1964
Harem Holiday (RCA), 1965
Paradise, Hawaiian Style (RCA), 1966
How Great Thou Art (RCA), 1967
Clambake (RCA), 1967
Double Trouble (RCA), 1967
Speedway (RCA), 1968
Elvis — NBC Special (RCA), 1968
That's The Way It Is (RCA), 1970
I'm 10,000 Years Old, Elvis Country (RCA), 1971
Elvis Sings The Wonderful World Of Christmas (RCA), 1971
Elvis Live At Madison Square Garden (RCA), 1972
Aloha From Hawaii (RCA), 1973
Hits Of The 70s (RCA), 1974
Pictures Of Elvis (RCA), 1975
The Elvis Presley Sun Collection (RCA), 1975
Elvis In Demand (RCA), 1977
Elvis, Scotty and Bill — The First Year (Very Wonderful Golden Editions), 1979
Elvis Aaron Presley (RCA), 1980
Guitar Man (RCA), 1980
Elvis Presley Sings Leiber and Stoller (RCA), 1980
The Million Dollar Quartet (Sun), 1981
This Is Elvis (RCA), 1981
Rocker (RCA), 1983
The Legend (RCA), 1983
32 Film Hits (RCA), 1984
G.I. Blues (RCA), 1984
Loving You (RCA), 1984
Collection Volume 3 (RCA), 1985
Collection Volume 4 (RCA), 1985
Reconsider Baby (RCA), 1985
Collection Volume 1 (RCA), 1986
Collection Volume 2 (RCA), 1986
Essential Elvis (RCA), 1986

Right: The early Elvis Presley, whose brilliance has never been surpassed by any other solo singer.

Below right: Elvis in decline — shots from his 'cabaret period' during the 70s.

Below: One of the few 1960s artists who rivalled The Beatles in popularity.

Pretenders

UK group formed 1978

Original line-up: Chrissie Hynde, vocals; James Honeyman-Scott, vocals, keyboards, guitar; Pete Farndon, bass; Martin Chambers, drums.

Career: In 1974, American-born Chrissie Hynde quit job on London-based rock paper *New Musical Express* to sing with French band, which flopped; returned to US to join R&B group Jack Rabbit. Giving France another try, she joined rock 'n' roll band The Frenchies before returning to London again. Then worked as back-up singer on Stiff Records' national tour.

Impressed with her work, bosses of Real label introduced her to group of musicians from Hereford and groomed them as The Pretenders. Just cracking UK Top 30 with debut single, a re-make of Kinks' **Stop Your Sobbing**, band toured UK, released second single **Kid** (1979). With third record, catchy **Brass In Pocket** (highlighting Hynde's sensual vocals), topped chart.

Well-balanced debut album **Pretenders** went straight to No. 1. Appearance on all-star Kampuchean refugee charity concert heightened reputation; three of their songs appeared on resultant double album.

Tours of Europe and America (received accolade as Best New Artists in *Rolling Stone* magazine) and release of another single, **Message Of Love**, and **Extended Play** (a five-track EP) preceded **Pretenders II** album (1981). Recorded in Paris and London and produced by Chris Thomas, nine of 12 songs were penned by Chrissie Hynde. She co-wrote two more with James Honeyman-Scott, but his death (drug-related) in mid-1982 put future of band in question. Soldiered on, and late 1982 single **Back On The Chain Gang**, featuring Billy Bremner (guitar) and Tony Butler (bass), became Top 5 hit in US, with heavy airplay on MTV. Then

Below: The multi-talented Chrissie Hynde, soldiering on after the tragic deaths of Honeyman-Scott and Farndon.

suddenly, in April 1983, Farndon died. Two new members, Rob McIntosh (ex-Night) and Malcolm Foster (ex-Foster Brothers), were recruited in time for performance at US festival in May 1983, but in 1985 band broke up for good, Chrissie Hynde concentrating on raising family with Simple Minds' Jim Kerr, who she married in May 1984. She resurfaced to join UB40 on 1985 hit re-make of Sonny and Cher's original **I Got You Babe**.

More recently, Hynde returned with Pretenders mark two, featuring MacIntosh, bassist Tom Stevens, drummer Blair Cunningham and keyboard player Bernie Worrell; world tour in 1987 preceded **My Baby** single. Band released **Packed** album in 1990, while a further collaboration with UB40 resulted in **Breakfast In Bed** UK hit single.

A committed vegetarian, Hynde's tirades against the likes of McDonalds has kept her firmly in public eye. Her admittance to firebombing one of the hamburger chain's restaurants in more radical days prompted compromise over future statements concerning the company.

Hit Singles:

	US	UK
Brass In Pocket, 1979	14	1
Talk Of The Town, 1980	—	8
Message Of Love, 1981	—	11
I Go To Sleep, 1981	—	7
Back On The Chain Gang, 1982	5	17
2000 Miles, 1983	—	15
Middle Of The Road, 1984	17	—
Don't Get Me Wrong, 1986	5	10
Hymn To Her, 1986	—	8

Chrissie Hynde (with UB40):

I Got You Babe, 1985	28	1
Breakfast In Bed, 1988	—	6

Albums:

Pretenders (Sire/Real), 1980
Pretenders II (Sire/Real), 1981
Learning To Crawl (Sire/Real), 1984
Get Close (WEA), 1986
The Singles (Real), 1987
Packed! (Sire/Warner Bros), 1990

Right: The prodigious talent of Prince seen during a concert at Rio De Janeiro.

Prince

US vocalist, guitarist
Born Minneapolis, Minnesota, June 7, 1961

Career: Christened Prince Rogers Nelson after jazz bandleader father who used stage name Prince Rogers, Prince was fronting band, called first Grand Central then Champagne, at high school dances when only 12 years old.

Prince and Champagne's bass player André Cymone wrote bulk of group's material over five year period and when Champagne split, Prince went into studios to cut demos showcasing his material, but trip to New York failed to yield record deal. Undeterred, he cut further songs and took tape to Warner Bros in Los Angeles, finally securing a long-term contract.

A powerful catalyst for the Minneapolis music scene, Prince was quick to develop his charisma and individual flamboyant dress style, together with an extensive entourage which included the funky group Time, headed by Champagne's one-time drummer Morris Day, and girlie group Vanity 6, later replaced by Apollonia 6.

Switch of management to high-powered Steve Fargnoli (who previously took Little Feat into big time) helped propel Prince's career into major league.

Debut album, which he wrote, produced, and arranged, and on which he sang and played all 27 instruments, led to string of often outrageous LPs and eventually to semi-biographical movie *Purple Rain* which showcased international hit single **When Doves Cry**.

Album of movie showed signs of broadening of musical appeal, and movement continued in 1985 set **Around The World In A Day**. Psychedelic influence was now apparent, and reflected in album sleeve.

Continuing to pursue celluloid ambitions, Prince then directed and starred in *Under The Cherry Moon*, one of most critically lambasted productions of all time. On music front, however, he further extended his horizons with 1987 double set **Sign 'O' The Times**, an eclectic set which pleased music critics and went on to achieve double platinum status.

In 1988 artist cut majestic **Lovesexy**, a feast of musical erotica. Album was substitute for LP tentatively titled **Black Album**, which was withdrawn after concern about lyrical content. **Lovesexy** spawned **Alphabet Street** hit single, and became theme for world tour in same year.

Prince returned to film work for score of *Batman* flick in 1989, a dark, moody offering which topped both US and UK LP charts. His own *Graffiti Bridge* movie opened a year later to good critical notices, and soundtrack album made No. 1 in UK chart.

Following controversial cancellation of Blenheim Palace gig scheduled for August 1991 (artist cited bad organization, money problems, etc), Prince saw sixth LP **Diamonds And Pearls** make immediate impact, with video for **Cream** single showing no sign of mellowing from rock's answer to Russ Meyer.

While he is undoubtedly taken seriously as a performer, Prince's capabilities spread further than sexy posturing. He formed own Paisley Park label in 1987, and has produced The Family, Sheila E, Mica Paris and Mavis

Staples. Also featured in unlikely duet with Scottish vocalist Sheena Easton on singles **U Got The Look** and **The Arms Of Orion**.

Hit Singles:

	US	UK
I Wanna Be Your Lover, 1979	11	—
1999, 1983	12	25
Little Red Corvette, 1983	6	—
Delirious, 1983	8	—
When Doves Cry, 1984	1	4
Let's Go Crazy, 1984	1	7
Purple Rain, 1984	2	8
I Would Die 4 U, 1985	8	—
Little Red Corvette/1999, 1985	—	2
Raspberry Beret, 1985	2	26
Paisley Park, 1985	—	18
Pop Life, 1985	7	—
Kiss, 1986	—	6
Mountains, 1986	—	45
I Could Never Take The Place Of Your Man, 1987	10	29
If I Was Your Girlfriend, 1987	—	20
Sign 'O' The Times, 1987	6	10
Alphabet Street, 1988	8	9
Batdance, 1989	1	2
Partyman, 1989	18	14
Thieves In The Temple, 1990	6	7
Gett Off, 1991	21	4
Cream, 1991	1	15

With Sheena Easton:

U Got The Look, 1987	2	11

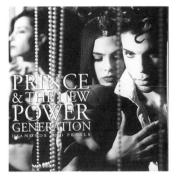

Above: Diamonds And Pearls, Prince. Courtesy Paisley Park Records.

Albums:
Prince (Warner Bros), 1980
Dirty Mind (Warner Bros), 1981
Controversy (Warner Bros), 1982
1999 (double) (Warner Bros), 1983
Purple Rain (Warner Bros), 1984
Around The World In A Day (Warner Bros), 1985
For You (Warner Bros), 1986
Parade (Warner Bros), 1986
Sign 'O' The Times (double) (Paisley Park), 1987
Lovesexy (Warner Bros), 1988
Batman (soundtrack) (WEA), 1989
Graffiti Bridge (Paisley Park), 1990
Diamonds And Pearls (Paisley Park), 1991

Procol Harum

UK group formed 1967

Original line-up: Gary Brooker, vocals, piano; Ray Royer, guitar; Matthew Fisher, organ; David Knights, bass; Bobby Harrison, drums.

Career: Brooker was singer with R&B group The Paramounts, who worked club circuit between 1962-66 and had minor hit with re-working of Coasters' **Poison Ivy**. On break-up of group, Brooker started collaboration with lyricist Keith Reid and recruited above line-up to record songs.

Under aegis of producer-entrepreneur Denny Cordell, band released **A Whiter Shade Of Pale** in summer 1967. This highly individualistic cut featuring surrealistic lyrics against cantata-like organ part struck chord with record buyers; **Pale** became enormous hit both sides of Atlantic.

Almost immediately line-up was reshuffled; Royer and Harrison quit to form short-lived Freedom, and were replaced by ex-Paramount Robin Trower on guitar and B. J. Wilson on drums. This line-up hit with **Homburg** and cut first three Procol albums.

In UK band was regarded as something of a one-hit wonder, but US audiences took Procol to heart and American tours were successful. Meanwhile, Matthew Fisher quit band to pursue solo career, followed by David Knights. Bassist Chris Copping, another ex-Paramount, replaced latter and **Home** and **Broken Barricades** were made as quartet. Heavier rock direction was in evidence at this time.

Trower left in 1971, finding band too restricting for guitar heroics, and eventually formed highly successful Robin Trower Band. Copping switched to organ and in came bassist Alan Cartwright and guitarist Dave Ball. In November 1971 band went to Canada to gig with Edmonton Symphony Orchestra. Resulting live album was huge success, especially in US.

In 1973 Mick Graham replaced Dave Ball, and line-up remained stable until 1976 when Cartwright left. Copping returned to bass and Pete Solley joined on organ.

Final albums suffered from lack of direction and provided only few gems compared to earlier output. Procol Harum eventually disbanded in 1977; Gary Brooker surfaced with solo album **Lead Me To The Water** in 1982.

Following barren decade for PH's principal movers Brooker, Fisher and Trower, trio rejoined in 1991 for **The Prodigal Stranger** album, which featured new material by Brooker and Reid. Suggestions are that Procol Harum mark two might have a future.

Hit Singles:

	US	UK
A Whiter Shade Of Pale, 1967	5	1
Homburg, 1967	34	6
A Whiter Shade Of Pale, 1972	—	13
Conquistador, 1972	16	22
Pandora's Box, 1975	—	16

Albums:
Procol Harum (Known as A Whiter Shade of Pale) (A&M/Regal Zonophone), 1967*
A Salty Dog (A&M/Regal Zonophone), 1969*
Shine On Brightly (A&M/Regal Zonophone), 1969*
Home (A&M/Regal Zonophone), 1970*
Broken Baricades (A&M/Chrysalis), 1971
Live In Concert (A&M/Chrysalis), 1972
Grand Hotel (Chrysalis), 1973
Exotic Birds And Fruit (Chrysalis), 1974
Ninth (Chrysalis), 1975
Platinum Collection (—/Cube), 1981
Procol Harum (greatest hits) (—/Impact), 1982
Collection (Collector)
The Prodigal Stranger (RCA), 1991

Gary Brooker Solo:
Lead Me To The Water (Mecury), 1982
Echoes In The Night (Mecury), 1985
*Available as double set (—/Cube), 1975

Right: Waiting for the Apocalypse. Public Enemy have earned the wrath of middle America, but have no intention of diluting their political message.

Public Enemy

US group formed 1986

Original line-up: Hank Shocklee and Chuck D, producers, DJs.

Career: Pioneering hip-hoppers from New York whose seminal recordings attracted Def Jam CE Rick Rubin. Following early cuts, outfit added DJs Terminator X, Professor Griff and Flavor Flav.

Premier album **Yo! Bum Rush The Show** attracted attention in US R&B market, and cut **Rebel Without A Pause** edged into UK charts. Subsequent promotional tour was notable for its large security presence. Headstrong political message and wildfire rhythms placed Public Enemy at the head of burgeoning rap scene, with **It Takes A Nation of Millions To Hold Us Back** album confirming international acceptance with notable chart placing in US/UK markets.

Following anti-Semetic outburst in *Washington Times*, Professor Griff was expelled from unit, prompting Chuck D to consider band's future. With Griff pursuing solo career on Skywalker Records, Chuck D saw material for Spike Lee movie *Do The Right Thing* attract mainstream attention.

Following *Rolling Stone* award as Best Rap Group (1991), Chuck D again clouded Public Enemy's future with fatalistic statements, although **Apocalypse '91 . . . The Enemy** album (a US Top 5) forestalled any immediate bust-up.

Hit Singles:

	US	UK
Don't Believe The Hype, 1988	—	18
Welcome To The Terrordome, 1990	—	18

Albums:
Yo! Bum Rush The Show (Def Jam/—), 1987

It Takes A Nation Of Millions To Hold Us Back (Def Jam), 1988
Fear Of A Black Planet (Columbia/Def Jam), 1990
Apocalypse '91 . . . The Enemy (Def Jam), 1991

Suzi Quatro

US vocalist, bass player, guitarist, actress
Born Detroit, June 3, 1950

Career: Made debut at eight playing bongos in father Art Quatro's jazz band. Left school at 14 to appear on TV as go-go dancer Suzi Soul. Formed all-girl group Suzi And The Pleasure Seekers at 15 with sisters Pattie, Nancy and Arlene. They played all over US and visited Vietnam for tour of bases.

Changing name to Cradle, they performed at Detroit dance hall and were seen by British producer Mikie Most (in town to record Jeff Beck Group at Motown studios). Suzie's aggressive stage presence — despite her diminutive size — struck Most as star quality. He expressed interest in bringing her to Britain to sign for his Rak label.

Suzi toured UK working as support act. Most encouraged her songwriting, but, after 1972 debut single **Rolling Stone** flopped, decided to call on services of songwriters Nicky Chinn and Mike Chapman.

Encased in black leather jump suit, blatantly sensual legs astride her bass guitar, she thumped away aggressively. Her small figure fronted band of tough guys; this image as trend-setting raunchy female rock star provided perfect showcase for Chinn and Chapman's propulsively direct rockers like chart-toppers **Can The Can**, **48 Crash** and **Devil Gate Drive**.

Put together at time of her 1972 tour as support for Slade, Quatro's band compris-

ed: Len Tuckey, guitar; Dave Neal, drums; and keyboard player Alastair McKenzie (soon replaced by Mike Deacon from Vinegar Joe).

Efforts to break in America — had a hit single there with **All Shook Up** and toured widely — caused her to lose grip on UK charts. She remained major personality of rock scene thanks to wide TV exposure via chart shows, variety shows, panel games and appearances as actress, initially through *Happy Days* comedy series as character based on self, Leather Tuscadero, friend of The Fonz and, more recently, as Annie Oakley in stage production of *Annie Get Your Gun*.

Combines hectic work and domestic schedule with husband, guitarist Len Tuckey, with whom she has two children.

Guitar: Fender Precision bass.

Hit Singles:

	US	UK
Can The Can, 1973	56	1
48 Crash, 1973	—	3
Daytona Demon, 1973	—	14
Devil Gate Drive, 1974	—	1
Too Big, 1974	—	14
The Wild One, 1974	—	7
If You Can't Give Me Love, 1978	—	4
She's In Love With You, 1979	—	11

Albums:
Suzi Quatro (Bell/Rak), 1973
Aggro-phobia (—/Rak), 1977
If You Knew Suzie (—/Rak), 1978
Greatest Hits (—/Rak), 1980
Main Attraction (—/Polydor), 1982
Wild One — The Greatest Hits (—/EMI), 1990

Queen
UK group formed 1972

Original line-up: Brian May, self-made 'May Axe' guitar; Roger Meadows Taylor, drums; Freddie Mercury, vocals; John Deacon, bass.

Career: Evolved from college group Smile, featuring Brian May, Tim Staffell and Roger Meadows Taylor. Smile lasted long enough for series of gigs and one single, **Earth/Step On Me**, released only in US on Mercury. When group folded, Staffell persuaded flatmate Freddie Mercury to join May and Taylor in new venture. Several months later Deacon was added.

Group underwent strenuous rehearsals, playing occasionally at Imperial College, while Mercury masterminded flamboyant satin and silk image. Lucrative contract with EMI was quickly followed by debut single **Keep Yourself Alive**, which flopped. A month prior to its release, Mercury had recorded cover of Beach Boys' **I Can Hear Music** under pseudonym Larry Lurex, another rare cut.

First album **Queen** revealed group negotiating clever balance between early 70s glam rock and late 60s Zeppelin-style heavy metal. With EMI publicity campaign in full swing, group eventually hit charts in early 1974 with **Seven Seas Of Rhye**. By end of 1974 two further LPs were issued, **Queen II** and **Sheer Heart Attack**. Latter attracted critical commendation from certain section of rock press, who praised group

for aggressive rock and ingenious arrangements, courtesy of producer Roy Thomas Baker. Success of fifth single **Killer Queen** placed Queen in enviable position of achieving following from both Top 20 fans *and* heavy-metal enthusiasts.

Most of 1975 spent preparing **A Night At The Opera**, one of the most extravagant and expensive albums of era. Pilot single **Bohemian Rhapsody** was ultimate kitsch epic, an elaborate production brilliantly highlighting group's harmonies and guitar work as well as Mercury's falsetto vocal. Single became Christmas chart-topper for nine weeks, the longest stay at top since Paul Anka's **Diana** in 1957. From that point on, Queen were established in top echelon of rock biz.

Success of **Bohemian Rhapsody** encouraged quartet to pursue even more elaborate and grandiloquent works in complete contrast to their HM-styled early albums. Determined not to be dismissed as 70s glam rock refugees, Queen seemed to change image and musical style with every cut. Witness pop-styled **Another One Bites The Dust** (penned by Deacon) and rockabilly spoof single **Crazy Little Thing Called Love** from the late 70s. Earlier, band scored with **We Are The Champions**, a song later adopted by sports fans (and politicians) across the world.

Staggering array of hits during 80s, of which **Flash** (from *Flash Gordon* movie which group scored), **Radio Ga Ga** and **I Want To Break Free** became pop classics, further enhanced band's burgeoning reputation. Members also embarked on various solo

projects. Taylor cut **Fun In Space** LP (1981), May collaborated with Eddie Van Halen on **Star Fleet** project, Mercury contributed to Girgio Moroder's soundtrack for updated *Metropolis* movie and enjoyed UK Top 20 single with **I Was Born To Love You** (1985), while Deacon formed The Immortals, who featured on score for *Biggles* film.

Prodigious performers, Queen were kings of stadium circuit during early 80s, and broke then world record with paid attendance of over 130,000 at Sao Paulo concert in Brazil; dominant performance at Live Aid ex-

Above: A Kind Of Magic, Queen. Courtesy Elektra/EMI Records.

travaganza in 1985 was considered highlight of show. However, following European tour in 1986, group temporarily disbanded to allow a slew of outside interests. Taylor formed The Cross, and signed to Virgin for **Shove It** LP, from which **Cowboys And Indians** single enjoyed a chart tickle. Mercury recorded passionate version of The Platters' immortal **The Great Pretender**, duetted with Spanish opera diva Montserrat Caballe on **Barcelona** opus, a contender as theme for 1992 Olympic Games in that city, and penned theme for *Time* musical; signed multimillion dollar deal with Hollywood Records in 1990. May produced spoof **Bohemian Rhapsody** single by Bad News and tracks for girlfriend Anita Dobson, star of UK soap *East Enders*.

Queen rejoined in 1989 for **The Miracle** LP, which spawned a trio of hit singles, although concern about Mercury's health clouded outfit's future. May took time out to write music for stage production of *Macbeth*, and also joined with Ian Gillan, Robert Plant and Bruce Dickinson to record **Walk On The Water** for Armenian Aid charity; the 45 made US Top 50. Charted again in December 1991 with **Driven By You** single, theme from popular British television advertisement.

With tabloid speculation about Mercury's fitness rife, Queen's 1991 release **Innuendo** was surprise. Album debuted at No. 1 in UK album charts, while six-minute-plus title track topped single listings.

With Queen enjoying a chart renaissance, serious concerns were being voiced about their enigmatic vocalist. On Saturday, November 23, 1991, a terse press release announced that Mercury had contracted AIDS. Two days later, he was dead, victim of broncho-pneumonia exacerbated by the killer disease. The remaining members of Queen soon announced that they would celebrate his life 'in the style to which he was accustomed'. Ironically, at time of Mercury's demise, Queen's current single was **The Show Must Go On**.

Left: Queen members Brian May, the late Freddy Mercury, John Deacon and Roger Taylor. Mercury succumbed to AIDS after a prolonged struggle against the debilitating illness.

Hit Singles:	US	UK
Seven Seas Of Rhye, 1974	—	10
Killer Queen, 1974	12	2
Now I'm Here, 1975	—	11
Bohemian Rhapsody, 1975	9	1
You're My Best Friend, 1976	16	7
Somebody To Love, 1976	13	2
Queen's First EP, 1977	—	17
We Are The Champions, 1977	18	2
Bicycle Race/Fat Bottomed Girls, 1978	—	11
Don't Stop Me Now, 1979	—	9
Crazy Little Thing Called Love, 1979	—	2
Save Me, 1980	—	11
Play The Game, 1980	—	14
Another One Bites The Dust, 1980	1	7
Flash, 1980	—	10
Las Palabras de Amor, 1982	—	17
Body Language, 1982	11	25
Radio Ga-Ga, 1984	16	2
I Want To Break Free, 1984	—	3
It's A Hard Life, 1984	—	6
Hammer To Fall, 1985	—	13
One Vision, 1985	—	7
Who Wants To Live Forever, 1986	—	24
Friends Will Be Friends, 1986	—	14
A Kind Of Magic, 1986	—	3
I Want It All, 1989	50	3
Breakthru, 1989	45	7
The Invisible Man, 1989	—	12
Innuendo, 1991	—	1
Headlong, 1991	—	14
The Show Must Go On, 1991	—	18
Bohemian Rhapsody, 1991	—	1

With David Bowie:

	US	UK
Under Pressure, 1981	29	1

Brian May Solo:

Driven By You, 1991	—	10

Freddie Mercury Solo:

Love Kills, 1984	—	10
I Was Born To Love You, 1985	—	11
Great Pretender, 1987	—	4

Freddie Mercury and Montserrat Caballé:

Barcelona, 1987	—	8

Albums:
Queen (Elektra/EMI), 1973
Queen II (Elektra/EMI), 1974
Sheer Heart Attack (Elektra/EMI), 1974
A Night At The Opera (Elektra/EMI), 1975
A Day At The Races (Elektra/EMI), 1976
News Of The World (Elektra/EMI), 1977
Jazz (Elektra/EMI), 1978
Live Killers (Elektra/EMI), 1979
The Game (Elektra/EMI), 1980
Flash Gordon (soundtrack) (Elektra/EMI), 1980
Greatest Hits (Elektra/EMI), 1981
Hot Space (Elektra/EMI), 1982
The Works (Elektra/EMI), 1984
The Miracle (Capitol/Parlophone), 1989
Innuendo (Hollywood/Parlophone), 1991
Greatest Hits II (Parlophone), 1991

Brian May Solo:
Star Fleet Project (EMI), 1983

Freddie Mercury Solo:
Mr Bad Guy (CBS), 1985

Roger Taylor Solo:
Fun In Space (Elektra), 1981
Strange Frontier (EMI), 1984

Roger Taylor and The Cross:
Shove It (Virgin), 1988

Left: One of the numerous Rainbow line-ups led by Ritchie Blackmore (second from right).

Gerry Rafferty
UK vocalist, composer, guitarist
Born Paisley, Scotland, April 16, 1947

Career: Original member of Scottish folk trio Humblebums (with Billy Connolly and Tam Harvey), cutting two albums for ethnic UK label Transatlantic.

Debut solo album **Can I Have My Money Back**, released 1971, featured Joe Egan and Rab Noakes on guitars, and Roger Brown on bass, founding members of Stealers Wheel (with bassist Ian Campbell). However, this original unit quickly disbanded. Rafferty and Egan then recruited Paul Pilnick, guitar, Tony Williams, bass, and Rod Coombes, drums, to supply additional instrumentation for 1973 self-titled **Stealers Wheel** album.

LP included **Stuck In The Middle**, a US and UK Top 10 single, and an excellent example of legendary producers Leiber/Stoller's ear for a hit. Still under aegis of Leiber/Stoller, band recorded **Ferguslie Park** (1974) and then **Right Or Wrong** (1975), a Mentor Williams production which marked end of Rafferty/Egan partnership.

Shackled by legal problems resulting from Stealers Wheel contract, Rafferty did not resurface until 1977, when **City To City** album was released. **Baker Street** cut from LP earned artist million-selling Top 3 hit in both US and UK, and set subsequently topped US charts. Follow-up **Night Owl** also provided successful singles, the title track making No. 5 in UK.

Rafferty's flirtation with pop listings ended after release of **Snakes And Ladders** LP (1982), although later **Sleepwalking** album eased into UK Top 40. Artist's reticent approach to promotional activities (he has never toured USA) saw shelf-life expire. Following contribution to Mark Knopfler's score for *Local Hero* movie, Rafferty disappeared until 1987 when he produced fellow-Scots The Proclaimers' UK hit **Letter From America**. Re-recorded track earned the Reid brothers' LP, **This Is The Story**, a gold album. A year later, singer cut **North And South** album for London Records.

A major talent, Rafferty never came to terms with rock music's unwritten laws — find a manager (like it or not), and leave everything to him.

Hit Singles:	US	UK
Baker Street, 1978	2	3
Right Down The Line, 1978	12	—
Days Gone Down, 1979	17	—
Night Owl, 1979	—	5

With Stealers Wheel:

	US	UK
Stuck In The Middle, 1973	6	8

Albums:
Can I Have My Money Back (Blue Thumb/Transatlantic), 1971
Gerry Rafferty Revisited (—/Transatlantic), 1974
Gerry Rafferty (Visa/Logo), 1978
City To City (Liberty/United Artists), 1978
Night Owl (Liberty/United Artists), 1979
Snakes And Ladders (Liberty/United Artists), 1980
Sleepwalking (Liberty), 1982
Early Collection (Transatlantic)
North And South (Polydor/London), 1988
Best Of Right On Down The Line (EMI/United Artists), 1989

Rainbow
UK group formed in 1975

Original line-up: Ritchie Blackmore, Fender Stratocaster guitar; Ronnie James Dio, vocals; Mickey Lee Soule, keyboards; Craig Gruber, bass; Gary Driscoll, drums.

Career: Virtuoso guitarist Blackmore was founder-member of Deep Purple, but left amid much speculation in 1975. Joined forces with New York band Elf to form first version of Rainbow. Eponymous album released 1975.

Summer of 1976 saw first of succession of personnel changes. Blackmore sacked entire band except Dio, and brought in Jimmy Bain on bass, Tony Carey on keyboards and Cozy Powell on drums. Line-up released **Rainbow Rising**, including tracks with Munich Philharmonic Orchestra. For **Long Live Rock 'n' Roll** LP, group added bassist Bob Daisley and keyboards man was David Stone.

The next album heralded reunion with former Purple bassist Roger Glover, while Don Airey replaced Stone and Graham Bonnet (ex-Marbles) took over on vocals. This line-up was the most successful so far, scoring two major hit singles. These showed Rainbow to be masters of pop-metal sub-genre, able to combine heavy rock power with commercial melody lines. By 1980 band had also become top-line live attraction, headlining that summer's hugely successful Castle Donington Festival.

However, further personnel changes were in store. Powell and Bonnet left to pursue solo careers and were replaced by Bob Rondinelli on drums and Joe Lynn Turner on vocals. Run of success continued with album **Difficult To Cure** and hit singles **I Surrender** and **Can't Happen Here**.

Record success continued throughout 1982, with **Straight Between The Eyes** making US album charts. After American tour in same year, Rondinelli quit, being replaced by Chuck Burgi.

UK tour in 1983 preceeded rumblings of group's demise. This was confirmed with reformation of Deep Purple, with Blackmore as instigator, although unit came close to a new beginning in 1988 before Turner replaced Gillan in Purple.

Hit Singles:	US	UK
Since You've Been Gone, 1979	57	6
All Night Long, 1980	—	5
I Surrender, 1981	—	3
Can't Happen Here, 1981	—	20

Albums:
Ritchie Blackmore's Rainbow (Polydor), 1975
Rainbow Rising (Polydor), 1976
On Stage (Polydor), 1977
Long Live Rock 'n' Roll (Polydor), 1978
Down To Earth (Polydor), 1979
Difficult To Cure (Polydor), 1981
Jealous Lover (Polydor/—), 1981
Best Of (Polydor), 1981
Straight Between The Eyes (Polydor), 1982
Bent Out Of Shape (Polydor), 1983
Finyl Vinyl (Polydor), 1986

Bonnie Raitt
US guitarist, vocalist, composer
Born Los Angeles, California, November 8, 1949

Career: Grew up in musical family in LA, moved to Cambridge, Boston, area in 1967. Raitt selected Dick Waterman as manager because of his association with various blues artists, her childhood heroes.

1971 debut LP set pattern of using wide variety of material and musicians for each recording. Subsequent LPs showed maturity, understanding and warmth in Raitt's reading of good contemporary material. Notable examples are: Jackson Browne's **Under The Falling Sky** and Eric Kaz's **Love Has No Pride** from second LP; Allen Toussaints' **What Is Success** on **Streetlights** LP; and Hayes-Porter's **Your Good Thing** from **The Glow** album.

Raitt's performances and regular touring finally earned a little US success with **Sweet Forgiveness** album (1977), from which revival of Del Shannon's classic **Runaway** was Top 40 hit. **The Glow** was carefully conceived follow-up, and included more original material. Following **Green Light** set (1982), Raitt spent four years in wilderness before prophetic **Nine Lives** was issued.

Frustration at lack of success and self-confessed 'excesses' saw artist in virtual exile until Don Was-produced **Nick Of Time** (1989) for Capitol Records earned two million sales, the US No. 1 spot and a handful of Grammys, including Album Of The Year. A plethora of guest musicians, including Herbie Hancock, David Crosby and Graham Nash, prompted Raitt into superlative performance, and renewed status earned spot on John Lee Hooker's excellent **The Healer** set. She went on to work with Emmylou Harris and B.B. King.

Following US tour and several charity gigs, Raitt returned to studios and cut **Luck Of The Draw**, which she supported with sell-out dates in UK during autumn of 1991.

Raitt is one of the few female rock musicians to command respect from peers. Having been a favourite 'guest artist', she is now capable of re-establishing own career without help of others.

Hit Singles:

	US	UK
Something To Talk About, 1991	5	—

Albums:
Bonnie Raitt (Warner Bros), 1971
Give It Up (Warner Bros), 1972
Takin' My Time (Warner Bros), 1973
Streetlights (Warner Bros), 1974
Home Plate (Warner Bros), 1975
Sweet Forgiveness (Warner Bros), 1977
The Glow (Warner Bros), 1979
Green Light (Warner Bros), 1982
Nine Lives (Warner Bros), 1986
Nick Of Time (Capitol), 1989
The Bonnie Raitt Collection (Warner Bros), 1990
Luck Of The Draw (Capitol), 1991

Ramones
US group formed 1974

Original line-up: Joey Ramone (Jeffrey Hyman), drums; Dee Dee Ramone (Douglas Coldin), bass; Johnny Ramone (John Cummings), guitar.

Career: Began as a trio, first appearing at New York's Performance Studio in March 1974. Four months later, manager Tommy Ramone (Tommy Erdelyi) became drummer, with Joey switching to lead vocals (original and later members all changed from real names to 'Ramone'). Residency at CBGBs (new wave club in NY's Bowery) in summer allowed group to develop stage act, but on first attempt to spread wings — opening Johnny Winter concert — they were booed from stage. Danny Fields took over management in late 1975, having already worked with MC5, The Stooges and Lou Reed.

Record deal with Sire led to recording of debut **Ramones**, released in April 1976. Album served as catalyst by encouraging other companies to sign many of New York's up-and-coming young acts. Prototype new wave rockers, group received rapturous welcome in UK in summer of 1976, heavily influencing emerging punk movement with their distinctive dress (leather jackets and torn jeans) and high-speed minimalist rock (17 song sets played in half an hour!).

Next two albums, **Leave Home** and

Below: Plug 'em in and watch 'em rock. The Ramones in action.

Above: Bonnie Raitt seen without her trademark Fender Stratocaster guitar.

Rocket to Russia, established familiar pattern of high-powered rock based on late 50s/early 60s themes. Singles were uniformly impressive, but neither **Sheena Is A Punk Rocker** nor **Swallow My Pride** cracked Top 20. Having championed pinheads, cretins and glue-sniffing during 1977, group were swiftly becoming redundant following first flowering of punk. In May 1978, Tommy departed to become producer, playing memorable farewell gig at CBGBs. New drummer Marc Bell (Marty Ramone) debuted on 1978's **Road To Ruin** and LP proved most commercially successful to date, though met with mixed response from critics, disturbed by mid-tempo material. Following in England was underlined by release of double **It's Alive** from Rainbow gigs of 1979.

Very much the spirit of CBGBs, Ramones have modified original formula to a minimal degree over the years, though union with producer Phil Spector resulted in less raucous material in **End Of The Century**. Group only finally broke into UK charts late in 1980 with uncharacteristic but memorable violin-steeped cover of Ronettes' 1964 hit, **Baby I Love You**, a complete contrast to earlier head-banging material. 1980 also saw release of Ramones' first feature film *Rock 'n' Roll High School*, the title of a track from **End Of The Century**.

Dismissed as unintelligent and ephemeral, Ramones survived the 70s intact. 1981 LP **Pleasant Dreams** (with former Mindbenders and 10cc member Graham Gouldman producing) and **Subterranean Jungle** sets received strong support from critics. For **Too Tough To Die** album (1985), Bell was replaced by ex-Velveteen Richard Beau (now Ricky Ramone). Set saw wide variety of producers, including Eurythmics' Dave Stewart.

Bell later re-joined outfit, and featured on both **Halfway To Sanity** and **Brain Drain** albums, the latter which included theme from Stephen King's *Pet Sematary* movie (1990). Following departure of Coldin (C.J. Ramone was replacement), Ramones embarked on US tour with Tom Tom Club and Debbie Harry. Later European dates resulted in **Loco Live** LP (1991), recorded at gig in Barcelona. Whether the 'trash with flash' can maintain impetus into new decade remains questionable, and Hyman's solo endeavours (producer/actor) could prove fatal for group.

Hit Singles:

	US	UK
Baby I Love You, 1980	—	8

Albums:
Leave Home (Sire), 1977
Rocket To Russia (Sire), 1977
Road To Ruin (Sire), 1978
It's Alive (—/Sire), 1979
End Of The Century (Sire), 1980
Pleasant Dreams (Sire), 1981
Subterranean Jungle (Sire), 1983
Too Tough To Die (Beggar's Banquet), 1985
Animal Boy (Beggar's Banquet), 1986

Halfway To Sanity (Sire/Beggar's Banquet), 1987
Ramones Mania (Sire), 1988
Brain Drain (Chrysalis), 1989
All The Stuff (Sire), 1990
Loco Live (Chrysalis), 1991

Worth Searching Out:
Ramones (Sire), 1976

Johnnie Ray
US vocalist, pianist, actor
Born John Alvin Ray, Dallas, Oregon, January 10, 1927
Died February 24, 1990

Career: First professional appearance at age 15 with Jane Powell on Portland, Oregon, radio talent show. Moved south to California in 1949 and for next two years worked night clubs and bars in Hollywood. Moved to Detroit in 1951; discovered by DJ Robin Seymour who obtained record deal with Columbia Records. Following success of double-sided hit **Cry/The Little White Cloud That Cried**, many presumed singer was black, as single was released on Columbia's R&B subsidiary Okeh.

Ray's vocal histrionics earned him nickname 'The Prince of Wails', and he rapidly became one of the most popular artists of the early 1950s. Inspired a fanatical, sometimes hysterical, fan following; near-riots resulted when he toured Britain just prior to the rock 'n' roll explosion.

First film with Ethel Merman, *There's No Business Like Show Business*, led to further film roles and theatre productions. Sales waned in US but hits continued into rock 'n' roll era in UK, with **Yes Tonight Josephine** almost making permanent transition.

An avid charity worker, particularly for deaf children (he had worn a hearing aid since age 15), Ray retained reputation with concert tours and cabaret work before death in 1990.

Hit Singles:

	US	UK
Cry/The Little White Cloud That Cried, 1951	*	*
Please Mr Sun/Here I Am Brokenhearted, 1952	*	*
What's The Use, 1952	*	*
Walking My Baby Back Home, 1952	*	
Faith Can Move Mountains, 1952	*	*
Somebody Stole My Gal, 1953	*	*
Such A Night, 1954	*	*
If You Believe, 1955	—	*
Paths Of Paradise, 1955	—	20
Hey There, 1955	—	5
Song Of The Dreamer, 1955	—	10
Who's Sorry Now, 1956	—	17
Ain't Misbehavin', 1956	—	17
Just Walkin' In The Rain, 1956	2	1
You Don't Owe Me A Thing/ Look Homeward Angel, 1957	10	12
Look Homeward Angel/You Don't Owe Me A Thing, 1957	36	7
Yes Tonight Josephine, 1957	12	1
Build Your Love (On A Strong Foundation), 1957	58	18

*No official charts existed prior to 1955. Asterisks denote records which generated sufficient sales to be considered hits

Albums:
Best Of (—/Hallmark), 1968
Greatest Hits (Columbia/Embassy), 1977
An American Legend (—/Embassy), 1979
20 Golden Greats (—/MSD), 1979
Yesterday, Today And Tomorrow (RCA), 1981

Chris Rea

UK vocalist, songwriter
Born Middlesbrough, 1951

Career: Sometimes cited as 'the English Springsteen', Rae has likeable personality and knack for writing evocative songs.

Of half-Irish half-Italian descent, he entered music business after hearing a Joe Walsh record, and in 1975 formed Magdelene which quickly changed name to Beautiful Losers and won *Melody Maker* Best New Band award. David Coverdale, who later fronted Whitesnake, was also in group.

Signed to Magnet as solo in 1976, Rea wrote **Fool If You Think It's Over** for his sister. His recording charted both sides of Atlantic while Elkie Brook's cover was also big UK hit.

Advent of punk made his style unfashionable but he came back strongly in 1983 with **I Can Hear Your Heartbeat** hit and half-million-selling **Watersign** album; also collaborated with Bill Wyman on Willie And The Poor Boys project, having previously cut **Deltics** LP with fellow keyboard players Pete Wingfield and Rod Argent.

Maintained status during 80s with series of critically acclaimed LPs — **Shamrock Diaries** made UK Top 20, **On The Beach** edged towards Top 10, while **Dancing With Strangers** earned No. 2 spot in British album listings. The latter album was artist's first for Motown in US.

Rea finally topped LP charts with **The Road To Hell** (1989), where relentless advertising campaign paid dividends. 1991 follow-up **Auberge** debuted at No. 1 in UK, and preceded run of sell-out European dates. Rea's laid-back attitude and melodic approach have provided artist with serious funds in which to indulge his hobby of racing Lotus 7 sports cars (one of which appears on **Auberge** cover). It appears to be the only thing he does quickly.

Hit Singles:

	US	UK
Fool If You Think It's Over, 1978	12	30
Let's Dance, 1987	—	12
On The Beach Summer 88, 1988	—	12
The Road To Hell, 1989	—	10
Auberge, 1991	—	16

Albums:
Whatever Happened To Benny Santini (Magnet), 1978
Deltics (Magnet), 1979
Tennis (Magnet), 1980
Chris Rea (Magnet), 1982
Watersign (Magnet), 1983
Shamrock Diaries (Magnet), 1985
Wired To The Moon (Magnet), 1985
On The Beach (Magnet), 1986
Dancing With Strangers (Magnet), 1987
Best Of New Light Through Old Windows (Geffen/WEA), 1988
The Road To Hell (Geffen/WEA), 1989
Auberge (Atco/Eastwest), 1991

Otis Redding

US vocalist, composer
Born Macon, Georgia, September 9, 1941
Died December 10, 1967

Career: All-time soul great, Redding started musical career in time-honoured fashion, singing in local church choir and at gigs around his home town of Macon. Through school-friend Phil Walden (later to head up

Capricorn Records), Redding was introduced to local band Johnny Jenkins And The Pinetoppers, and in 1959 joined them on the road as assistant and occasional vocalist.

Redding recorded various sides over the next few years for several small labels, but did not taste success until 1962 when he cut **These Arms Of Mine** and **Hey Hey Baby** at the end of a Jenkins recording session at Stax Studios. Stax boss Jim Stewart was impressed by Redding's style and composing talent, releasing **These Arms Of Mine** in November 1962.

The single made impression on US charts, and paved way for succession of successful singles over next few years. Master of the soul ballad, Redding was particularly affecting on slow numbers like **Pain In My Heart**, **That's How Strong My Love Is**, the classic **I've Been Loving You Too Long** and the much-loved **My Girl**, but was capable of whipping up a storm of excitement on up tempo material. Classic Redding stompers include **Respect**, **I Can't Turn You Loose**, Sam Cooke's **Shake**, **Hard To Handle** and **Love Man**.

Many soul albums feature one or two hits and a lot of mediocre padding, but Redding's albums were of consistently high standard. The definitive Redding album is **Otis Blue**, a superbly balanced set of ballads and uptempo material which includes a version of B.B. King's **Rock Me Baby**.

Otis Redding also excelled as live performer, and toured regularly between 1964 and 1967. He headed the 1965 Stax-Volt tour of Europe and made other trips to UK with own band, and during this period was probably appreciated more in Britain than in his native country. Never giving less than 100 per cent of himself, Otis Redding was the performer for whom the term 'soul' might have been invented. Dancing, dropping to his knees, running on the spot, urging on members of his band, he radiated energy and emotional commitment.

In 1967 Redding's career looked set to achieve new levels of success. His appearance at Monterey Pop Festival, recorded on 1970 Reprise LP **Monterey International Pop Festival: Otis Redding/The Jimi Hendrix Experience**, on bill which featured heavy rock acts like Jimi Hendrix and The Who, was hailed by critics and fans alike. European tour later the same year won him more friends, so much so that he was voted top international male singer by *Melody Maker* readers. But just as everything seemed to be coming together for the soul star, Redding was killed when his plane crashed into Lake Monona in Wisconsin in 1967. Several members of his band, The Bar-Kays, also perished.

As often happens, Redding's tragic death seemed to improve his marketability. Posthumous single **Dock Of The Bay** reached top of American charts and became a million-seller, and made No. 3 in Britain. It was easily his biggest hit.

One of the most important and best-loved of the 60s soul heroes, Redding had an inimitable vocal style and ability to get to the heart of a song, particularly ballads. Scorned during the psychedelic and heavy rock eras, he is now revered as one of the major influences of black music.

Hit Singles:

	US	UK
My Girl, 1965	—	11
Tramp (with Carla Thomas), 1967	—	18
Dock Of The Bay, 1968	1	3
Hard To Handle, 1968	51	15

Albums:
Otis Blue (Atco/Atlantic), 1966
Otis Redding Live In Europe (Volt/Atlantic), 1966
The Immortal Otis Redding (Atco/Atlantic), 1968
Love Man (Atco/Atlantic), 1969
History Of Otis Redding (Atco/Atlantic), 1969
History Of Otis Redding (Volt/Atlantic), 1970
Best Of (Atco/Atlantic), 1972
Pure Otis (Atco/Atlantic), 1979
Recorded Live (Atlantic), 1982
The Dock Of The Bay — The Definitive Collection (Atlantic), 1987

Worth Searching Out:
Pain In My Heart (Atco/Atlantic), 1965
Dictionary Of Soul (Volt/Atlantic), 1966
Sings Soul Ballads (Atco/Atlantic), 1970

Lou Reed

US vocalist, guitarist, composer
Born Long Island, New York, March 2, 1943

Career: Born into rich middle-class family. Spent much of adolescence 'rebelling' in various punk/garage groups (Pasha And The Prophets, The Eldorados, The Shades and The Jades). Later attended Syracuse University, but dropped out; dabbled in journalism, acting and music. Record companies refused songs because of their bizarre nature, so for time he wrote conventional love songs, but eventually organized new group with another disenchanted performer, John Cale. Velvet Underground achieved some measure of fame and notoriety, mainly in New York, but albums were too controversial for mass consumption; group eventually folded in 1970, after which their influence on other musicians was increasingly felt.

Reed drifed for a year, even taking up employment at father's accountancy firm in Long Island, before signing RCA contract in late 1971. Moved to Britain to work on solo debut with aid of New York writer Richard Robinson. **Lou Reed** was effective in parts, but spoiled by uninspired production.

Luck changed when David Bowie took interest in Reed's career. With Bowie in producer's chair, sessions were completed for **Transformer**; Reed was invited to appear at Royal Festival Hall alongside the androgenous one. Album received great publicity, sold well, and spawned memorable and controversial hit **Walk On The Wild Side**. The appearance of Reed in eye liner, singing deliberately risqué songs, yet minus the true menace of his Velvet Underground work, led to accusations of commercial sell-out. Reed was clearly parodying himself, and has continued to do so frequently over the years. **Berlin** was attempt to recapture power of Velvets' work, but in spite of some critical approbation, failed commercially. Nevertheless it remains Reed's most harrowing album in its analysis of sado/masochism.

Following **Berlin** sessions, Reed assembled touring group comprising Dick Wagner and Steve Hunter on guitars, Prakash John on bass, and Whitey Glan on drums. One of their better performances, at NY's Academy Of Music, released as **Rock 'n' Roll Animal**. Having partially restored credibility, Reed faltered with next work, **Sally Can't Dance**, his least inspired to this point. Another average effort followed before horrendous **Metal Machine Music**, a double album of 'electronic music', consisting almost entirely of tape hum. Rock's premier candidate for 'the worst album ever made', **Metal Machine Music** was ultimate example of artistic suicide.

Coney Island Baby was reasonable, yet hardly sufficient to repair damage done to career. Since then, Reed has had mixed fortunes, and Arista albums, including **Street Hassle** (co-produced by Richard Robinson), **The Bells** and **Growing Up In Public**, received merely lukewarm response from critics and public. In October 1981, Reed recorded a new work with producer Sean Fuller at RCA's New York studios; **The Blue Mask**, released in 1982, proved surprise return to form.

Both **New Sensations** and **Mistrial** albums maintained artist's reputation in 80s, although duet with Sam Moore (of Sam & Dave) on re-working of soul duo's **Soul Man** (1987) emphasized his vocal limitations. Stunning 1989 **New York** set saw critics

Left: New York's favourite son Lou Reed, founder of sonorous Velvet Underground.

thumb through their Thesauri for correct phrase. LP featured Michael Rathke (guitar), Fred Maher (drums), Maureen Tucker (vocals) and Rob Wasserman (bass), the latter of whom used Reed on own **Duets** LP in 1988. Long Islander then re-teamed with John Cale for performance at Brooklyn Academy Of Music of *Songs For Drella — A Fiction* composition as a tribute to Andy Warhol. Music later included in **Songs For Drella** LP (1990).

A legend in UK, where his work usually fares better than US, Reed stole show with manic performance during Nelson Mandela tribute concert at Wembley Stadium during April 1990. Later staged News Aid benefit gig for workers on New York *Daily News* before that paper's 'rescue' by UK press baron Robert Maxwell. Also regular participant in Amnesty International bashes.

The 'mad monk' of rock has travelled a unique and bizarre trail since his debut with Velvet Underground over two decades ago. He'll hate us for saying so, but Reed has become part of the rock establishment despite his idiosyncratic approach.

Hit Singles: US UK
Walk On The Wild Side, 1973   16   10

Albums:
Lou Reed (RCA), 1972
Transformer (RCA), 1972
Berlin (RCA), 1973
Rock 'n' Roll Animal (RCA), 1973
Sally Can't Dance (RCA), 1974
Lou Reed Live (RCA), 1975
Coney Island Baby (RCA), 1976
Rock And Roll Heart (Arista), 1976
Walk On The Wild Side — The Best Of Lou Reed (RCA), 1977
Street Hassle (Arista), 1978
Live — Take No Prisoners (Arista), 1978
The Bells (Arista), 1979
Growing Up In Public (Arista), 1980
Rock 'n' Roll Diary 1967-1980 (Arista), 1980
The Blue Mask (RCA), 1982
Legendary Hearts (RCA), 1983
New Sensations (RCA), 1984
Mistrial (RCA), 1986
New York (Sire/WEA), 1989
Songs For Drella (with John Cale) (—/WEA), 1990
Magic And Loss (Sire/Warner Bros), 1992

Above: Life's Rich Pageant, R.E.M. Courtesy IRS Records.

R.E.M.
US band formed in 1981

Original line-up: Bill Berry, drums, backing vocals; Peter Buck, guitars; Mike Mills, bass, backing vocals, keyboards; Michael Stipe, vocals, words.

Career: Band started in Macon, Georgia when Mike Mills and Bill Berry teamed up at High School. Together they moved to Athens, Georgia to attend university and there met up with Peter Buck and Michael Stipe, fellow students.

The four formed R.E.M., playing gigs in Athens performing covers of **Needles And Pins**, The Sex Pistols' **God Save The Queen** and **California Sun**. After dropping out of university, group members made an independent single **Radio Free Europe/Sitting Still**, on the strength of which IRS signed the band and released the already-recorded EP **Chronic Town**.

Reckoning followed in 1984, and in 1985 the band arrived in London to record their third album **Fables Of The Reconstruction**, produced by Joe Boyd. The harder-edged **Life's Rich Pageant** followed.

R.E.M.'s fifth album **Document**, recorded in Nashville and mixed in Los Angeles, was released in autumn 1987, coinciding with their UK gig at Hammersmith Odeon. Band co-produced with Scott Litt, and LP achieved strong reviews.

In 1988 band signed with Warner Bros in a million-dollar deal, and debuted for that label with **Green** in October of same year; world tour commenced four months later.

The rock press's favourite outfit — *Rolling Stone* voted R.E.M. Best American Band in 1988, while influential UK mag *Q* saw fit to declare quartet World's Best Act in 1991 — enjoyed critical and commercial success with 1991 set **Out Of Time**, which topped both US and UK album charts.

Solo projects have not hindered R.E.M.'s enviable reputation: Buck contributed to Byrds' tribute LP **Time In Between** with Robyn Hitchcock, and with Mills, Berry and Warren Zevon cut **Hindu Love Gods** set. Stipe produced **White Dirt** LP for The Chickasaw Mudpuppies, featured on Syd Straw LP **Surprise** and became prominent voice for AIDS and environmental issues.

R.E.M. seem to be in the right place at the right time in the 1990s. Their work for charity enhanced their reputation.

Hit Singles: US   UK
The One I Love, 1987   9   —
Stand, 1989   6   48
Losing My Religion, 1991   4   19
Shiny Happy People, 1991   10   6
The One I Love, 1991   —   16

Albums:
Murmur (IRS/A&M), 1983
Reckoning (IRS), 1984
Chronic Town (EP) (IRS), 1984
Fables Of The Reconstruction (IRS), 1985
Life's Rich Pageant (IRS), 1986
Dead Letter Office (IRS), 1987
Document (IRS), 1987
Green (Warner Bros), 1988
Eponymous (IRS/MCA), 1988
Out Of Time (Warner Bros), 1991
Best Of (IRS), 1991

REO Speedwagon
US group formed 1971

Original line-up: Gary Richrath, Gibson Les Paul guitar, vocals; Neil Doughty, keyboards; Alan Gratzer, drums; Gregg Philbin, bass; Barry Luttnell, vocals.

Career: Formed in Champaign, Illinois, REO Speedwagon began years of local, then national, touring. Owing much to Ted Nugent and Bob Seger, REO played highly competent rock with no frills.

Stripped-down sound underwent various changes: Luttnell left after first album and

Above: REO Speedwagon, the self-titled first album. Courtesy Epic Records.

Kevin Cronin brought more laid-back, almost country, feel when he took over vocals. (He was replaced by Michael Murphy in 1974-75 before returning to resume lead vocals.)

You Get What You Play For was live recording and attempted to translate energy of live REO on to vinyl. Widespread success continued to elude band until self-produced **Nine Lives** LP. With new bass player Bruce Hall, REO consolidated its growing popularity through another live album **A Decade Of Rock And Roll 1970-1980**.

Nothing suggested REO would ever produce massive hit, but **Hi Infidelity** roared to top of US charts and became REO's ticket to headlining large concerts. Unexpected success took REO by surprise and band spent over two years following up with next release. It could hardly match its predecessor and **Good Trouble** attracted criticism that REO was Frampton-like one-LP wonder.

Despite criticism that band was producing 'music by numbers', success was sustained until mid-80s with singles **Can't Fight This Feeling** (a US No. 1, like 1980's **Keep On Lovin' You**) and **One Lonely Night**. Having fallen out of favour in UK, interest was maintained in USA when **That Ain't Love** and **In My Dreams** from **Life As We Know It** set charted in 1987, although band subsequently disappeared.

Hit Singles: US   UK
Keep On Lovin' You, 1981   1   7
Take It On The Run, 1981   5   19
Keep The Fire Burnin', 1982   7   —
Can't Fight This Feeling, 1985   1   16
One Lonely Night, 1985   19   —
That Ain't Love, 1987   16   15
In My Dreams, 1987   19   19

Albums:
REO Speedwagon (Epic), 1971
R.E.O. T.W.O. (Epic), 1972
Ridin' The Storm Out (Epic), 1973
Lost In A Dream (Epic), 1974
This Time We Mean It (Epic), 1975
REO (Epic), 1976
You Get What You Play For (live) (Epic), 1977
You Can Tune A Piano But You Can't Tuna Fish (Epic), 1978
Nine Lives (Epic), 1979
A Decade Of Rock 'n' Roll 1970-1980 (live) (Epic), 1980
Hi Infidelity (Epic), 1980
Good Trouble (Epic), 1982
Speedwagon (Epic), 1984

Left: Macon, Georgia quartet R.E.M., for whom the 90s looked mighty enticing.

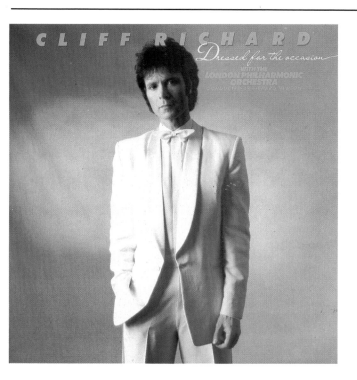

Wheels Are Turnin' (Epic), 1985
Best Foot Forward (—/Epic), 1985
Life As We Know It (Epic), 1987
The Hits (Epic), 1988
The Earth, A Small Man, His Dog And A
  Chicken (Epic), 1990

Cliff Richard

UK vocalist, guitarist, composer
Born Harry Rodger Webb, Lucknow, India,
October 14, 1940

Career: Spent childhood in colonial India
where English father worked for catering
company; returned to UK in 1948. Following early racial problems due to sunburnt
skin, soon became integrated into post-war
British life, discovering rock 'n' roll via Bill
Haley and Elvis Presley; played in local skiffle groups. Formed The Drifters in 1958,
which included Terry Smart (drums), Norman Mitham (guitar) and Richard himself
(guitar, vocals). Mitham then replaced by Ian
Samwell. After impressing agent with neo-
Presley style, signed to EMI's Columbia label
in August 1958. First single **Move It**, written by Samwell, recorded with session musicians, is now regarded as first British rock
'n' roll record.

Booked to appear on national tour, Richard
recruited new band — Smart, Samwell
(bass), plus guitarist Hank B. Marvin (real
name Brian Marvin) and Bruce Welch, both
from Newcastle. After tour, Smart and
Samwell were replaced by Jet Harris (bass)
and Tony Meehan (drums) — entire band (including Cliff) was spawned by early London
rock 'n' roll coffee bar, '2Is'. Cliff and The
Drifters became original British rock superstars, with ten Top 10 singles; by end of
1960, Drifters (changing name to Shadows
to avoid confusion with black US vocal
group) were chart-topping act in own right.

Cliff and Shadows appeared in several very
popular films during 60s, including *Expresso
Bongo, The Young Ones, Summer Holiday,
Wonderful Life* and *Finders Keepers*. By
mid-1962 Harris and Meehan had left group
for short-lived solo success, replaced by
Brian Bennett (drums) and first Brian Locking, later John Rostill (bass). Hits continued
in UK: 43 for Cliff, including eight No. 1's,
plus 24 for Shadows, including five No. 1's,

Shadows, joined Marvin, Welch and Farrar
group in 1970 and cut two albums. Farrar
joined Shadows in 1972.

Cliff appeared close to retirement by
mid-70s; returned with strong material and
arrangements **Miss You Nights** and **Devil
Woman** in 1976; latter was first US Top 10
hit. 1977 compilation LP **40 Golden Greats**
was a huge seller which topped UK charts.
Rest of 70s continued with 20th anniversary celebrations by Cliff and Shadows, with
end of decade providing Cliff's tenth No. 1
single, **We Don't Talk Anymore** (first since
1968), and growing US following.

In 1980 Richard was awarded OBE by
Queen Elizabeth II. Charted with duet **Suddenly** from film *Xanadu*, with Olivia Newton-
John, whom he had helped to fame via his
early 70s TV series. In 1983, Cliff celebrated
25 years as a rock star, having scored over
80 British hit singles, including ten No. 1's,
plus numerous big-selling LPs.

Cut self-deprecating single **Living Doll**
in 1986 in collaboration with manic English
comics The Young Ones, which belied staid
reputation, and artist took further risk with
starring role in Dave Clark's (of Dave Clark
Five) *Time* musical in London's West End.

Late 80s saw collaboration with noted
British production trio of Stock/Aitkin/Water-
man for **I Just Don't Have The Heart** 45
and unlikely chart duet with Van Morrison
on **Whenever God Shines His Light**. 30th
anniversary of first hit **Move It** was
celebrated by major sell-out UK tour, and,
in 1989, Richard enjoyed triumphant concert, Cliff Richard — The Event, staged at
Wembley Stadium, and supported by over
140,000 loyal fans.

Now over 50 years old, but with mysti-
que of Dorian Gray, Cliff Richard has been
written-off, castigated for religious beliefs
and satirized by every mimic in the UK.
Despite lack of US success, enjoys an international reputation which has even attracted sections of AOR crowd.

**Above: Dressed For The Occasion, Cliff
Richard. Courtesy EMI Records.**

by 1968, but still very little US success. By
end of 1960s, Shadows had disbanded, but
Cliff's success continued; his early rock 'n'
roll was toned down to become 'family entertainment' and withstood Merseybeat/
R&B crazes of early and mid-60s. However,
conversion to Christianity in 1966 blunted
his pop sensibility.

Continued (sometimes with re-formed
Shadows, including Marvin, Welch and Bennett) as prime cabaret attraction with own
TV series, but seemed generally out of touch
with youth during progressive rock years,
although twice representing UK in Eurovision
Song Contest. Rostill died in November 1973
from accidental electrocution. John Farrar,
member of an Australian group based on

**Below: Cliff with three-quarters of
The Shadows, circa 1960.**

Hit Singles:	US	UK
Move It, 1958*	—	2
High Class Baby, 1958*	—	7
Livin' Lovin' Doll, 1959*	—	20
Mean Streak/Never Mind, 1959*	—	10
Living Doll, 1959*	30	1
Travellin' Light, 1959+	—	1
Dynamite, 1959+	—	16
Expresso Bongo (EP), 1960+	—	14
A Voice In The Wilderness, 1960+	—	2
Fall In Love With You, 1960+	—	2
Please Don't Tease, 1960+	—	1
Nine Times Out Of Ten, 1960+	—	3
I Love You, 1960+	—	1
Theme For A Dream, 1961+	—	3
Gee Whiz It's You, 1961+	—	4
A Girl Like You, 1961+	—	3
When The Girl In Your Arms Is The Girl In Your Heart, 1961+	—	3
The Young Ones, 1962+	—	1
I'm Looking Out The Window/ Do You Wanna Dance, 1962	—	2
It'll Be Me, 1962+	—	2
The Next Time/Bachelor Boy, 1962+	—	1
Summer Holiday, 1963+	—	1

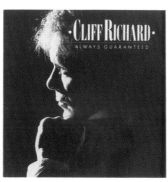

**Above: Always Guaranteed, Cliff
Richard. Courtesy EMI Records.**

	US	UK
Lucky Lips, 1963+	—	4
It's All In The Game, 1963	25	2
Don't Talk To Him, 1963+	—	2
I'm The Lonely One, 1964+	—	8
Constantly, 1964	—	4
On The Beach, 1964+	—	7
The Twelfth Of Never, 1964	—	8
I Could Easily Fall, 1964+	—	9
The Minute You're Gone, 1965	—	1
On My Word, 1965	—	12
Wind Me Up (Let Me Go), 1965	—	2

Blue Turns To Grey, 1966+	—	15
Visions, 1966	—	7
Time Drags By, 1966+	—	10
In The Country, 1966+	—	6
It's All Over, 1967	—	9
The Day I Met Marie, 1967	—	10
All My Love, 1967	—	6
Congratulations, 1968	—	1
Good Times (Better Times), 1969	—	12
Big Ship, 1969	—	8
With The Eyes Of A Child, 1969	—	20
Goodbye Sam, Hello Samantha, 1970	—	6
Sunny Honey Girl, 1971	—	19
Sing A Song Of Freedom, 1971	—	13
Living In Harmony, 1972	—	12
Power To All Our Friends, 1973	—	14
(You Keep Me) Hangin' On, 1974	—	13
Miss You Nights, 1976	—	15
Devil Woman, 1976	6	9
I Can't Ask For Anything More Than You Babe, 1976	—	17
My Kinda Life, 1977	—	15
We Don't Talk Anymore, 1979	7	1
Carrie, 1980	34	4
Dreamin', 1980	7	8
A Little In Love, 1981	11	15
Wired For Sound, 1981	—	4
Daddy's Home, 1981	23	2
The Only Way Out, 1982	—	10
Little Town, 1982	—	11
True Love Ways, 1983	—	8
Never Say Die, 1983	—	15
Please Don't Fall In Love, 1983	—	7
She's So Beautiful, 1985	—	17
Living Doll (with the Young Ones), 1986	—	1
Mistletoe And Wine, 1988	—	1
The Best Of Me, 1989	—	2
I Just Don't Move The Heart, 1989	—	3
Lean On You, 1989	—	17
Stronger Than That, 1990	—	14
Silhouettes, 1990	—	10
From A Distance, 1990	—	11
Saviours Day, 1990	—	1

With Hank Marvin:
Throw Down A Line, 1969	—	7

With Olivia Newton-John
Suddenly, 1980	20	15

With Phil Everly:
She Means Nothing To Me, 1983	—	9

With Sarah Brightman:
All I Ask Of You, 1986	—	3
Some People, 1987	—	3
My Pretty One, 1987	—	6

*with Shadows (As Drifters)
+with Shadows

Albums:
The Young Ones (—/Columbia), 1961
Summer Holiday (Epic/Columbia), 1963
I'm Nearly Famous (Rocket/EMI), 1976
40 Golden Greats (—/EMI), 1977
Rock 'n' Roll Juvenile (—/EMI), 1979
Wired For Sound (EMI America/EMI), 1981
Dressed For The Occasion (—/EMI), 1983
Silver (EMI), 1983
Now You See Me Now You Don't (EMI), 1985
Walking In The Light (Myrrh), 1985
Always Guaranteed (EMI), 1987
Best Of (Maybelline), 1987
Cliff (EMI), 1987
Private Collection (—/Charly), 1988
Stronger (—/Capitol), 1989
Together (—/EMI), 1991

Above: Bill Medley (second from left) and Bobby Hatfield (second from right), The Righteous Brothers, with Mitch Ryder, Tommy James and David Clayton-Thomas.

Lionel Richie

US vocalist, composer, producer
Born June 20, 1949

Career: Former economics major at Alabama's Tuskegee Institute who had considered career as Episcopal priest, Richie was founder member, saxophonist and subsequent lead singer of Commodores. Developed writing/production talents while with band, penning and producing **Lady** for Kenny Rogers; cut **Endless Love** duet with Diana Ross from Franco Zeffirelli film of same title — single stayed at top of US single charts for nine weeks.

In 1981 released first solo album **Lionel Richie**. Set included hit singles **Truly**, **You Are** and **My Love**. Richie combined soul music background with a healthy regard for easy-listening country-flavoured ballads to emerge as one of Motown's solo megastars. Cross-over appeal was rewarded with country as well as black music awards.

In 1983, cheerful calypso-flavoured sound of **All Night Long** showed further dimension to Richie's talents and was that year's major dance-floor success, propelling subsequent album to No. 1 on both sides of Atlantic. Hit single **Say You, Say Me** (1985) was taken from movie *White Nights*.

Can't Slow Down LP became Motown's all-time best seller, logging more than 14 million sales worldwide, spawning no fewer than five Top 20 singles in UK where he has consistently commanded strong following.

His efforts for African famine relief with the Grammy award-winning **We Are The World** (co-written with Michael Jackson)

Above: Dancing On The Ceiling, Lionel Richie. Courtesy Motown Records.

showed a further dimension to an artist who is amongst a select handful of 'bankable' music stars, despite lack of output since **Dancing On The Ceiling** LP.

Hit Singles:	US	UK
My Love, 1983	5	—
All Night Long, 1983	1	2
Running With The Night, 1983	7	9
Hello, 1984	1	1
Stuck On You, 1984	3	12
Penny Lover, 1984	8	18
Say You, Say Me, 1985	1	8
Ballerina Girl, 1986	9	17
Love Will Conquer All, 1987	9	45
Dancing On The Ceiling, 1987	1	—
Sela, 1987	20	43

Albums:
Lionel Richie (Motown), 1982
Can't Slow Down (Motown), 1983
Say You, Say Me (Motown), 1986
Dancing On The Ceiling (Motown), 1987

Left: Lionel Richie enjoyed solo success in the charts after leaving Commodores.

The Righteous Brothers

US vocal duo formed 1962
Bill Medley born Los Angeles, September 19, 1940
Bobby Hatfield, born Wisconsin, August 10, 1940

Career: Bill Medley and Bobby Hatfield came together as blue-eyed soul duo in 1962. They undertook club gigs around California, and had a small hit in 1963 with Medley-penned **Little Latin Lupe Lu** on Moonglow. Originally called The Paramounts, duo changed name because early black fans called their music 'righteous'.

Although increasingly popular on home ground, they didn't gain national prominence until noticed by TV producer Jack Good who gave them regular spot on pop show *Shindig*. At this point Phil Spector stepped in. Already hot, with big hits by Crystals and Ronettes under his belt, Spector took The Brothers into the studio and worked with them for three solid weeks on one song. The result of this concentrated effort was **You've Lost That Loving Feeling**.

Feeling was released on Spector's own Philles label, and by January 1965 had reached No. 1 spot on both sides of Atlantic. The combination of Bill Medley's Ray Charles-influenced baritone, Bobby Hatfield's impassioned high tenor and Spector's inspired production provided pop masterpiece and perennial favourite. A slew of successful, if not quite so brilliant, singles followed.

The Brothers eventually parted company in 1968 after farewell concert in Los Angeles. Bill Medley pursued solo career, making series of undistinguished and not particularly successful albums. Bobby Hatfield recorded solo and also attempted to keep Brothers act together with new partner, Billy Walker, but with little success.

In 1974, however, Medley and Hatfield got together again and scored US Top 10 hit with **Rock 'n' Roll Heaven**, a novelty death disc, following it with **Give It To The People**. A couple of albums also ensued before they split again.

Without doubt, their best testimony is early work, particularly of re-issued **You've Lost That Loving Feeling**, magnificent **Unchained Melody** and underrated **Ebb Tide**.

Rare among blue-eyed soul artists in that their delivery was 100 per cent convincing,

The Righteous Brothers offered unique, instantly recognizable sound with perfect harmonies and helped to assimilate 'soul' approach into mainstream of pop music.

A surprise postcript to The Brother's career was co-incidentally provided by success of two films starring Patrick Swayze. *Dirty Dancing* saw Medley team with Jennifer Warnes for US chart-topping and subsequent Grammy winner **(I've Had) The Time Of My Life**, while re-issued **Unchained Melody** (which ironically features Hatfield singing solo), topped UK charts following inclusion in 1990's successful flick *Ghost*. Pair also guested (at different times) on hit US TV show *Cheers*.

Hit Singles:

	US	UK
You've Lost That Loving Feeling, 1965	1	1
Just Once In My Life, 1965	9	—
Unchained Melody, 1965	4	14
Ebb Tide, 1965	5	48
(You Are My) Soul And Inspiration, 1966	1	15
He, 1966	18	—
You've Lost That Loving Feeling, 1969	—	10
Rock 'n' Roll Heaven, 1974	3	—
Give It To The People, 1974	20	—
Cruisin', 1979	4	—
Unchained Melody, 1990	13	1
You've Lost That Loving Feeling/ Ebb Tide (re-issue), 1990	—	3

With Jennifer Warnes:

(I've Had) The Time Of My Life, 1991	—	8

Albums:
Greatest Hits (MGM), 1987*

Best Of (Curb), 1990
Very Best Of (Verve), 1990
Reunion (Curb), 1991

Worth Searching Out:
Soul And Inspiration (Verve), 1966
Two By Two (MGM), 1973*
*Originally issued on Verve label

Smokey Robinson

US vocalist, composer, executive
Born William Robinson, Detroit, February 19, 1940

Career: Formed Miracles (then called the Matadors) as high-school vocal group in 1955 with Bobbie and Emerson Rogers and Warren 'Pete' Moore; when Claudette Rogers replaced brother, became The Miracles. Met up with Berry Gordy in 1957 while latter was still working as independent producer. Collaboration led to release of **Got A Job**, through End Records, and **Bad Girl**, through Chess. Moderate success of group encouraged Gordy to set up Tammie — later Tamla — Records, with Robinson and Miracles as first signing. Group consisted of Robinson (lead vocals), Claudette and Bobbie Rogers (first and second tenors), Ronnie White (baritone), Warren More (bass) and Marvin Tarplin (guitar).

1960 saw first major success for Miracles and Tamla. **Shop Around**, written by Gordy and Robinson, reached No. 2 in US charts. Group was on its way, and next few years saw clutch of hit singles that included classics like **You've Really Got A Hold On Me** (covered by Beatles) and **Mickey's Monkey** (actually written by Holland/Dozier/Holland team).

At the same time Robinson started writing for and producing other artists. Mary Wells scored with **Two Lovers** and **What's So Easy For Two**, and had her finest hour with **My Guy** in 1964. That same year Robinson began two-year collaboration with Temptations, which resulted in memorable classics such as **Get Ready, The Way You Do The Things You Do, It's Growing, Since I Lost My Baby** and evocative **My Girl** (covered by Otis Redding and many others). Incredibly, Robinson found time to work with other Motown artists like Marvin Gaye (**I'll Be Doggone, Ain't That Peculiar**) and The Marvellettes.

During second half of 1960s, Miracles continued to release hit after hit, including **Tracks Of My Tears**, considered one of all-time great singles. Robinson was by now regarded as important creative force, attracting particular attention for his lyrics. Although most of his songs (apart from straight dance tunes) were about hackneyed subject of love, unrequited or otherwise, fresh, vivid imagery, and felicitous turn of phrase ensured memorable impact. At same time, Robinson had established himself as one of pop's great voices, his plaintive high tenor providing some of its most moving moments. Group became known as Smokey Robinson And The Miracles.

However, Motown's impetus was being provided more and more by writing/production team of Holland/Dozier/Holland and their artists Supremes and Four Tops. And by end

Below: Smokey Robinson leads The Miracles in a well-drilled dance routine. His solo career confirmed 'legend' status.

of decade Robinson was thinking of leaving Miracles. In 1971, after series of farewell concerts, he did split from group, and started to concentrate on position as Vice-President of Motown Records with special responsibility for new talent.

Initially, Robinson continued to produce Miracles, but they were soon handed over to other Motown 'house' producers and eventually left label for Columbia. Robinson himself worked on series of solo albums, which continued to make impression on black American market while being largely ignored by general pop audience. Often more experimental than his previous output, Robinson's 70s albums repay listening and contain gems that are worth searching out.

In 1981, Robinson made surprise return to pop charts with **Cruisin'** and **Being With You** singles, the latter of which topped both UK and US charts. Repeated success in 1987 when **Just To See Her** (a Grammy winner) and **One Heartbeat** made US Top 10.

Composer of nearly 70 hit songs and possessor of unique pop voice, Robinson is capable of taking his special formula well into the 90s; he was inducted into Rock 'n' Roll Hall Of Fame in 1987 and Songwriters Hall Of Fame in 1990.

Hit Singles:

	US	UK
Cruisin' 1979	4	
Being With You, 1981	1	1
Just To See Her, 1987	9	—
One Heartbeat, 1987	10	—

With The Miracles:

Shop Around, 1961	2	—
You Really Got A Hold On Me, 1963	8	—
Mickey's Monkey, 1963	8	—
Ooh Baby Baby, 1965	16	—
Tracks Of My Tears, 1965	16	—
My Girl Has Gone, 1965	14	—
Going To A Go-Go, 1966	11	44
(Come 'Round Here) I'm The One You Need, 1966	17	34
The Love I Saw In You Was Just A Mirage, 1967	20	—
I Second That Emotion, 1967	4	27
If You Can Want, 1968	11	50
Baby Baby Don't Cry, 1969	8	—
Tracks Of My Tears, 1969	—	9
Tears Of A Clown, 1970	1	1
(Come 'Round Here) I'm The One You Need, 1971	—	13
I Don't Blame You At All, 1971	18	11

The Miracles:

Do It Baby, 1974	13	—
Love Machine, 1976	1	3

Albums:
Smokey (Tamla/Motown), 1973
Smokin' (Tamla/—), 1978
Being With You (Motown), 1981
Yes It's You Lady (Motown), 1982
Essar (Motown), 1984
22 Greatest Hits (Motown)
Greatest Songs (Motown)
Smoke Signals (Motown/Ace), 1986
One Heartbeat (Motown), 1987
Where There's Smoke (Motown/—), 1989
Love, Smokey (Motown/—), 1990

With The Miracles:
Anthology (Motown), 1974
Greatest Hits (Tamla/Motown), 1977
18 Greatest Hits (Motown)
Compact Command Performance Volume 4 (Motown)
Going To A Go-Go/Tears Of A Clown (Motown)

With Marvin Gaye:
Love Songs (Telstar), 1988

The Rolling Stones

UK group formed 1963

Original line-up: Mick Jagger, vocals; Keith Richard, guitar, vocals; Brian Jones, guitar, vocals; Bill Wyman, bass; Ian Stewart, piano; Charlie Watts, drums.

Career: Jagger and Richard first met at primary school in Kent, then went their separate ways. In 1960, when Richard was attending Dartford Art School and Jagger the London School Of Economics, they discovered mutual interest in blues and R&B. Pair moved in and out of ever-changing group line-ups that made up London's infant blues scene of the time.

Line-up that was to become first version of Rolling Stones came together around

Alexis Korner's Blues Incorporated, pioneer British blues outfit that had regular gig at Ealing Blues Club. Occasional sitter-in with outfit was Cheltenham-born guitarist Brian Jones. By early 1962 Jagger was regular singer with band, and was also rehearsing with Jones, Richard, and other like-minded musicians, such as pianist Ian Stewart.

In June 1962, Blues Incorporated were booked for radio broadcast; budget only allowed for six players, so Jagger stepped down and instead deputized for Blues Incorporated at gig at London Marquee Club; band was billed as Brian Jones And Mick Jagger And The Rollin' Stones. Line-up as above did not coalesce until following year when Charlie Watts made move from Blues Incorporated, and Bill Wyman joined on bass after audition.

Turning-point was residency at Crawdaddy Club in Richmond. Reputation quickly

spread by word of mouth, and band came to attention of former PR man Andrew Loog Oldham; he became band's manager and negotiated record contract with Decca. (First move was to oust pianist Stewart on the grounds that he looked too 'normal' — although he was to remain 'sixth Stone' throughout band's career, playing on records, and at gigs.)

First release, version of Chuck Berry's **Come On**, came out in June 1963, and although not a major hit brought band to notice of public and, particularly, of media. Oldham pushed Stones as 'bad boys' compared to 'lovable moptop' Beatles, and band swiftly became cult figures among youth. First album **The Rolling Stones**, largely covers of R&B material, reached top of UK charts in April 1964. June that year saw first US tour and first UK chart-topper, their version of Womack's **It's All Over Now**.

From this time onwards band quickly gathered momentum. From 1965 all singles were Jagger/Richard compositions, and band developed distinctive pop-rock style that still kept strong blues undertones. **The Last Time** made US Top 10, and paved way for first No.1 on both sides of the Atlantic, the classic **(I Can't Get No) Satisfaction**.

By end of 60s, Stones had become international attraction, second only to Beatles in importance. They were surrounded by almost permanent aura of publicity and notoriety: **Let's Spend The Night Together** was censored by the Ed Sullivan TV show; Jagger, Richard and Jones were all busted for drugs; Jagger's relationship with Marianne Faithfull provided gossip-column titillation; and virtually every 'pillar of decency' from Bournemouth to Wagga Wagga denounced band as corrupters of youth, tramplers on moral values, etc. End of decade

Below: Mick Jagger on stage at Leeds during 1982 UK tour.

Right: Wembley Stadium gets ready for the return of The Rolling Stones in 1982.

Above: The posturing Mick Jagger (left) and Ron Wood (right) on stage in 1976.

Inset above: Goat's Head Soup, Rolling Stones. Courtesy Rolling Stones Records.

also saw tragedy of Brian Jones' death, following his exit from group. Mick Taylor, formerly with John Mayall Band, replaced Brian Jones.

Musically, apart from 1967 flirtation with psychedelia manifested by **Their Satanic Majesties Request** album and **We Love You** single, band had gone from strength to strength. **Beggars Banquet** and **Let It Bleed** were both classic rock albums, regarded by many critics as together making up Stones' finest hour.

In 70s Stones became something of a rock 'n' roll institution, living life of jet-setting tax exiles and establishing new records for massively attended live performances. In 1974 Mick Taylor quit, to be replaced by Ron Wood, a member of Faces. There was some toning down of former 'rebel' image, as members eased into mature years; their former stance being taken over by 70s punk outfits like Sex Pistols. Record-wise, band continued to put out worthwhile albums (after 1971, on their own Rolling Stones label) that generally contained a couple of classics each, and maintained standard of singles with releases like **Brown Sugar** and **It's Only Rock And Roll**.

Although it was assumed that The Stones would coast into the 80s, a flurry of album releases laid to rest all talk of a break-up. **Emotional Rescue** (1980) and **Tattoo You** (1981) saw band in solid but uninspiring mood, although the latter LP topped US chart and preceded record-breaking American tour. Following mediocre **Undercover**, quintet signed with CBS for **Dirty Work** set (1986) which spawned authentic version of Bob & Earl's R&B classic **Harlem Shuffle**. A long break until **Steel Wheels** LP and tour (1989) allowed group members to consolidate solo ambitions, although 1991 'live' LP **Flashpoint** maintained collective profile.

Jagger cut **She's The Boss** (1985) and **Primitive Cool** (1987), and enjoyed chart duet with David Bowie on **Dancing In The Street** (from Live Aid) in 1985; married Jerry Hall in 1990. Wyman enjoyed hit single with **Si Si Je Suis Un Rock Star** ditty (1983), but subsequently suffered at hands of British tabloid press after marriage to model Mandy Smith (later annulled); autobiography *Stone Alone* published in 1990.

Richards, now officially with an 's', recorded **Talk Is Cheap** for Virgin in 1988, and acted as musical director for Chuck Berry's *Hail Hail Rock 'n' Roll* concert video; toured US in 1988. Watts appeared frequently with his jazz quintet and cut one big-band LP, **The Charlie Watts Orchestra Live**.

Woods pursued painting career, and enjoyed exhibition of work in autumn of 1987. Solo set **1,2,3,4** was released in 1981. Guitarist suffered severe leg injuries in 1990 after car accident. Stones' long-term keyboard player Ian Stewart died in 1984.

Never far from the front pages, The Stones caused controversy with anti-Gulf War single, **High Wire**, in March 1991, and signed a 30 million-pound deal with Virgin Records, UK, in December of same year with album releases to commence 1993; by then, Mick Jagger will be 50.

Inset above: The classic Aftermath. Courtesy Decca Records.

Left: Thank Your Lucky Stars TV show, 1965. From left are Jones, Jagger, Wyman, Watts and Richard.

Inset left: Still Life LP, 1982. Courtesy Rolling Stones Records.

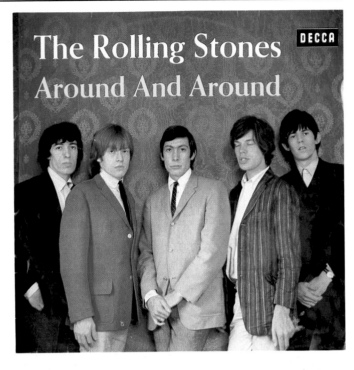

Above: Around And Around, an early Rolling Stones' album sleeve reproduced courtesy of Decca Records.

Below: The sleeve for Some Girls, which resulted in several law suits. Courtesy Rolling Stones Records.

Hit Singles:

	US	UK
I Wanna Be Your Man, 1963	–	12
Not Fade Away, 1964	48	3
It's All Over Now, 1964	26	1
Little Red Rooster, 1964	–	1
Time Is On My Side, 1964	6	–
Heart Of Stone, 1965	19	–
The Last Time, 1965	9	1
(I Can't Get No) Satisfaction, 1965	1	1
Get Off My Cloud, 1965	1	1
As Tears Go By, 1966	6	–
19th Nervous Breakdown, 1966	2	2
Paint It Black, 1966	1	1
Mother's Little Helper, 1966	8	–
Have You Seen Your Mother Baby (Standing In The Shadows), 1966	9	5
Ruby Tuesday/Let's Spend The Night Together, 1967	1	3
Let's Spend The Night Together/ Ruby Tuesday, 1967	55	3
We Love You/Dandelion, 1967	14	8
Jumping Jack Flash, 1968	3	1
Honky Tonk Woman, 1969	1	1
Brown Sugar/Bitch/Let It Rock, 1971	1	2
Tumbling Dice, 1972	7	5
Angie, 1973	1	5
Doo Doo Doo Doo Doo (Heartbreakers), 1974	16	–
It's Only Rock And Roll, 1974	16	10
Ain't Too Proud To Beg, 1974	17	–
Fool To Cry, 1976	10	6
Miss You/Far Away Eyes, 1978	1	3
Beast Of Burden, 1978	8	–
Emotional Rescue, 1980	3	9
Start Me Up, 1981	2	7
Waiting On A Friend, 1982	13	50
Hang Fire, 1982	20	–
Undercover Of The Night, 1983	9	11
Just Another Night, 1985	–	9
Harlem Shuffle, 1986	–	13
Mixed Emotions, 1989	5	36

Mick Jagger (with David Bowie):

Dancing In The Street, 1985	7	1

Bill Wyman Solo:

Si Si Je Suis Un Rock Star, 1983	–	14

Albums:

The Rolling Stones (London/Decca), 1964
12x5 (London/–), 1965
The Rolling Stones Now (London/–), 1965
Out Of Our Heads (London/Decca), 1965
December's Children (London/–), 1965
Aftermath (London/Decca), 1966
Big Hits (High Tide And Green Grass), (London/Decca), 1966
Got Live If You Want It (London/–), 1967
Between The Buttons (London/Decca), 1967
Flowers (London/Decca), 1967
Their Satanic Majesties Request (London/ Decca), 1967
Beggars Banquet (London/Decca), 1968
Let It Bleed (London/Decca), 1969
Through The Past Darkly (Big Hits Volume 2) (London/Decca), 1969
Get Yer Ya Yas Out (London/Decca), 1970
Sticky Fingers (Rolling Stones), 1971
Stone Age (–/Decca), 1971

Gimme Shelter (—/Decca), 1971
Milestones (—/Decca), 1971
Exile On Main Street (Rolling Stones), 1972
Hot Rocks: 1964-71 (London/—), 1972
More Hot Rocks (Big Hits And Fazed Cookies) (London/—), 1972
Goat's Head Soup (Rolling Stones), 1973
No Stone Unturned (—/Decca), 1973
It's Only Rock 'n' Roll (Rolling Stones), 1974
Rolled Gold (—/Decca), 1975
Metamorphosis (London/Decca), 1975
Made In The Shade (Rolling Stones), 1975
Black And Blue (Rolling Stones), 1976
Love You Live (Rolling Stones), 1977
Some Girls (Rolling Stones), 1978
Emotional Rescue (Rolling Stones), 1980
Sucking In The Seventies (Rolling Stones), 1981
Tattoo You (Rolling Stones), 1981
Still Life (Rolling Stones), 1982
Undercover (Rolling Stones), 1983
Dirty Work (CBS), 1986
Singles Collection London Years (Abkco/London), 1989
Steel Wheels (Columbia), 1989
Flashpoint (Columbia), 1991

Mick Jagger Solo:
She's The Boss (CBS), 1985
Primitive Cool (CBS), 1987

Keith Richards Solo:
Talk Is Cheap (Virgin), 1988

Charlie Watts Orchestra:
Live At Fulham Town Hall (CBS), 1986

Ron Wood Solo:
(See Faces entry)

Bill Wyman (With Buddy Guy and Junior Wells):
Drinkin' T.N.T. 'N' Smoking' Dynamite (Red Lightnin'), 1983

Bill Wyman Solo:
Bill Wyman (A&M), 1982

Worth Searching Out:
Monkey Grip (Rolling Stones), 1974
Stone Alone (Rolling Stones), 1976

Linda Ronstadt

US vocalist
Born Tucson, Arizona, July 15, 1946

Career: Daughter of guitar player; had musical upbringing. After attending Arizona State Univeristy, headed for California in 1964 to try luck in music business. She teamed up with old friend Bob Kimmel and LA musician Ken Edwards to form folk-rock group Stone Poneys. Band made three albums for Capitol between 1966 and 1968, scoring hit single with Mike Nesmith's **Different Drum**.

Encouraged by Capitol, Ronstadt decided to go solo in 1969. First two albums created considerable interest, and second, **Silk Purse**, provided first solo hit single **Long, Long Time**.

In 1971 she recruited Don Henley, Glenn Frey and Randy Meisner to form new backing band. All played on **Linda Ronstadt**, but split within six months to form Eagles.

Career really began to take off when Ronstadt joined country-rock-orientated West Coast label Asylum in 1973. Debut album **Don't Cry Now**, co-produced by Peter Asher, made US album charts. (Asher became manager and has produced all

Above: Linda Ronstadt sports nifty Latino outfit and earings.

albums since.) 1974 album **Heart Like A Wheel** (contractually obligated to Capitol) eventually went platinum, spawning three gold singles including No. 1's **You're No Good** and **When Will I Be Loved**. At end of year Ronstadt had become top-selling female artist in US.

Further albums confirmed superstar status and Ronstadt became major concert attraction. Her private life also prompted attention, particularly during relationship with California Governor Jerry Brown.

Having enjoyed flurry of single successes with covers of pop classics, such as **It's So Easy** and **Ooh Baby Baby**, Ronstadt's teaming with legendary arranger Nelson Riddle for trio of albums (from 1983) featuring standards by George Gershwin, Rodgers & Hart and Irving Berlin was unexpected career move. During same period, vocalist appeared in both stage and film versions of *Pirates Of Penzance* and also featured in off-Broadway production of *La Boheme*.

1987 marked return to roots with heralded **Trio** country album with Emmylou Harris and Dolly Parton. Also guested on Paul Simon's **Graceland** before cutting brilliant Spanish-language **Canciones De Mi Padre** (1988) as tribute to her Mexican-born father.

Added further string to bow after successful collaboration with soul artists James Ingram (on **Somewhere Out There** 45) and Aaron Neville, the latter featuring on her **Cry Like A Rainbow** LP, which spawned **Don't Know Much** Grammy-winning single. She later produced Neville's **Warm Your Heart** LP with George Massenburg, and also toured

US with Neville Bros. Further duet with Neville on **All My Life** single earned pair 1991 Grammy.

A passionate and versatile vocalist, Ronstadt has not suffered the fate of others who move uneasily between various musical styles. In fact, her career has thrived on it.

Hit Singles:	US	UK
You're No Good, 1975	1	—
When Will I Be Loved, 1975	1	—
Heat Wave, 1975	5	—
That'll Be The Day, 1976	11	—
Blue Bayou, 1977	3	35
It's So Easy, 1977	5	—
Back In The USA, 1978	16	—
Ooh Baby Baby, 1979	17	—
How Do I Make You, 1980	10	—
Hurt So Bad, 1980	8	—

With The Stone Poneys:		
Different Drum, 1968	13	—

With James Ingram:		
Somewhere Out There, 1987	9	18

With Aaron Neville:		
Don't Know Much, 1989	2	2
All My Life, 1990	11	—

Albums:
Hand Sown, Home Grown (Capitol), 1969
Silk Purse (Capitol), 1970
Linda Ronstadt (Capitol), 1972
Don't Cry Now (Asylum), 1974
Heart Like A Wheel (Capitol), 1974
Different Drum (Capitol), 1975
Stone Poneys Featuring Linda Ronstadt (Capitol), 1975
Prisoner In Disguise (Asylum), 1975
Hasten Down The Wind (Asylum), 1976
Greatest Hits (Asylum), 1976
Simple Dreams (Asylum), 1977
Retrospective (Capitol), 1977
Living In The USA (Asylum), 1978
Greatest Hits Volume 2 (Asylum), 1980
Mad Love (Asylum), 1980
Beginnings (Capitol/—), 1981
Get Closer (Asylum), 1982
Lush Life (Asylum), 1984
For Sentimental Reasons (Asylum), 1986
Canciones De Mi Padre (Asylum), 1987
Cry Like A Rainstorm, Howl Like The Wind (Elektra), 1989
Mas Canciones (Elektra), 1991

With Dolly Parton:
Trio (WEA), 1987

Diana Ross

US vocalist, actress
Born Detroit, March 26, 1944

Career: Following endless speculation, Ross left record-breaking vocal group Supremes in December 1969. First solo single, **Reach Out And Touch**, was released in June 1970 and started string of hits which has continued to present.

Right from beginning, however, Ross and Motown label boss Berry Gordy collaborated to project Ross as more than merely successful pop singer. Pair envisaged all-round super-stardom à la Streisand. To this end Ross was presented as centrepiece of series of elaborately staged concerts and TV specials, at same time making debut in *Lady Sings The Blues*, a Motown-produced film about Billie Holiday.

While movie was not universally well received, it was commercially successful and Ross won general acclaim for her portrayal of the tragic jazz singer. Second foray into film acting was in the less successful *Mahogany* (1975), although film did give Ross opportunity to wear variety of high-fashion costumes.

In meantime, hits continued apace — generally highly arranged ballads which allowed Ross to emote to good effect. In 1976, however, she surprised everyone with **Love Hangover**, a genuinely exciting upbeat disco stomper.

For third film, Ross played part of Dorothy in re-make of *Wizard Of Oz* called *The Wiz*. Again, movie was less than ecstatically received by critics but Ross herself garnered generally good reviews.

By 1980 relations with Motown were becoming strained, and Ross split from the company, signing with RCA for US and with Capitol for rest of world. However, this was not before artist had reasserted her dance floor-filling credentials with Chic-produced album **Diana**, which yielded three hit singles.

Since changing companies, Ross has consolidated reputation. Enjoyed swan-song for Motown with **Endless Love** duet with Lionel Richie; hit with disco-styled **Muscles** in 1984, and also saw success with Barry Gibb-produced **Eaten Alive** LP a year later.

Although now firmly entrenched in pop idiom, Ross showed could still handle soul material with Tom Dowd-produced **Red Hot Rhythm And Blues** (1987) and fiery **Workin' Overtime** (1989) with Nile Rodgers producing. The latter album was first for artist's own Ross label.

Ross is now a glossy soul diva whose triumphant personal appearances owe more to reputation than current output. Nonetheless, she can hold court whenever she wants, as witnessed by 1991 UK tour.

Hit Singles:	US	UK
Reach Out And Touch (Somebody's Hand), 1970	20	33
Ain't No Mountain High Enough, 1970	1	6
Remember Me, 1970	16	7
I'm Still Waiting, 1971	—	1
Surrender, 1971	38	10
Doobedood'ndoobe Doobedood'ndoobe, 1972	—	12
Touch Me In The Morning, 1973	1	9
All Of My Life, 1974	—	9
Last Time I Saw Him, 1974	14	35

Left: Diana Ross has developed from Motown contract player into international superstar, although her current reputation is based on past work.

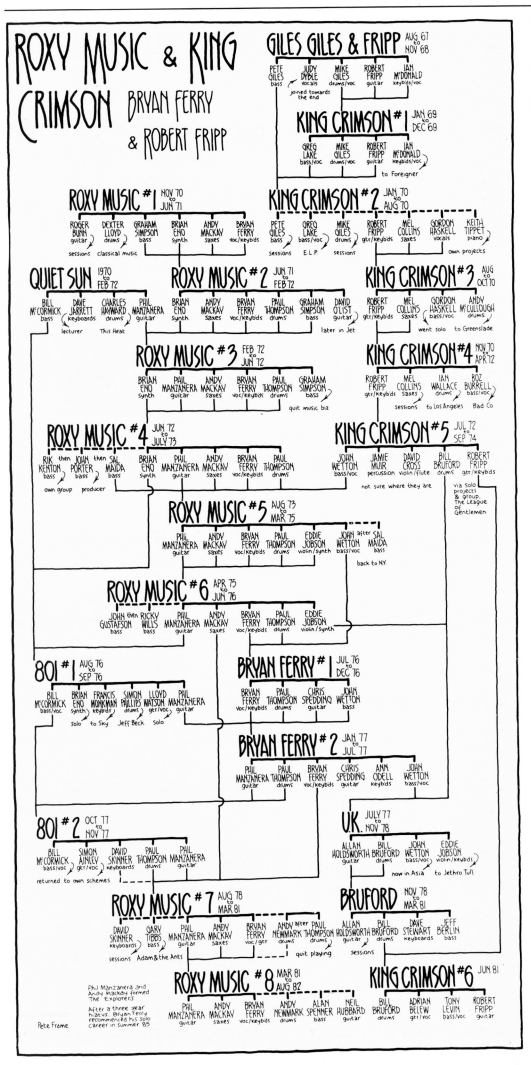

Do You Know Where You're
Going To (Theme from
Mahogany), 1976   1   5
Love Hangover, 1976   1   10
The Boss, 1979   19   40
Upside Down, 1980   1   2
My Old Piano, 1980   —   5
I'm Coming Out, 1980   5   13
It's My Turn, 1981   9   16
Why Do Fools Fall In Love?,
1981   7   4
Mirror Mirror, 1982   8   36
Work That Body, 1982   44   7
Muscles, 1982   10   15
Swept Away, 1984   19   —
Missing You, 1985   10   —
Chain Reaction, 1986   —   1
Experience, 1986   —   47

With Marvin Gaye:
You're A Special Part Of Me,
1973   12   —
You Are Everything, 1974   —   5
My Mistake (Was To Love
You), 1974   19   —

With Lionel Richie:
Endless Love, 1982   1   7

Albums:
Diana Ross (Motown), 1970
Everything Is Everything (Motown), 1971
I'm Still Waiting (Motown), 1971
Lady Sings The Blues (Motown), 1972
Original Soundtrack Of *Mahogany*
(Motown), 1975
Diana Ross (Motown), 1976
Greatest Hits (Motown), 1976
Greatest Hits Volume 2 (Motown), 1976
Baby It's Me (Motown), 1977
The Wiz (MCA), 1978
Ross (Motown), 1978
20 Golden Greats (Motown), 1979
The Boss (Motown), 1979
Diana (Motown), 1981
To Love Again (Motown), 1981
All The Great Hits (Motown), 1981
Why Do Fools Fall In Love? (RCA/Capitol),
1981
Silk Electric (RCA/Capitol), 1982
Ross (RCA/Capitol), 1983
Swept Away (Capitol), 1984
An Evening With (Motown), 1985
Eaten Alive (Capitol), 1985
Touch Me In The Morning/Baby It's Me
(Motown), 1973/1977
25th Anniversary (double) (Motown), 1986
Red Hot Rhythm 'N' Blues (EMI), 1987
Workin' Overtime (Motown/EMI), 1989
Greatest Hits Live (—/EMI), 1989
The Force Behind The Power (EMI), 1991

With Marvin Gaye:
Diana and Marvin (Motown), 1974

With M. Jackson, G. Knight and S. Wonder:
Diana, Michael (Priority), 1986

Diana and Michael Ross:
Their Very Best Back To Back (Priority),
1982

Roxy Music

UK group formed 1970

Original line-up: Bryan Ferry, vocals,
keyboards; Graham Simpson, bass; Andy
Mackay, bass; Brian Eno, synthesizer; Dex-
ter Lloyd, drums; Roger Bunn, guitar.

Career: While working as teacher, Bryan
Ferry spent free-time learning, playing and
composing music. By 1970 he had decided

to pursue full-time music career and sought out college friend Simpson to form band. MacKay was located in January 1971 through trade advert and he subsequently introduced Brian Eno.

Original line-up lasted only few months. Paul Thompson (drums) answered *Melody Maker* ad, following Lloyd's departure. Phil Manzanera wanted to join as second guitarist. He settled for sound-mixer when Ferry sought out ex-Nice guitarist, David O'List. Manzanera got his chance when Bunn, then O'List, left band.

Roxy Music tried to interest record companies with fully textured sound rather than relying on then standard lead guitar and over-emphasized bass. Island finally took chance and was rather surprised when debut LP was both critical and commercial success. Band's image and sound projected cool, calculating approach to rock as yet unseen.

Next bold move for early 70s was to release single which was not intended to be included on any LP. **Virginia Plain** made UK No. 4 and won band broad audience. This release also featured first of many new bass players, Rik Kenton. Within a few months, his place was taken by John Porter who lasted only first two months of 1973 while band recorded **For Your Pleasure**. During 1973 Europe and UK tours, Sal Maida filled in on bass.

Roxy Music took vacation for second half of 1973 due to Eno's departure for solo career and Ferry's growing interest in developing parallel solo venture. Eddie Jobson (ex-Curved Air) assumed Eno's spot on keyboards and Roxy Music returned to stage work in autumn 1973. This time Ferry pushed 'cool' image to extreme by cutting long hair and wearing tuxedo on stage.

Above: Avalon, Roxy Music. Courtesy Polydor Records.

sophisticated lyrics with melodic background. Somehow Roxy achieved sound which fitted into 80s without destroying roots from 60s.

By now Roxy Music had lost Thompson and remaining core used various session players to produce their finest effort, **Avalon. More Than This** and **Take A Chance With Me** are two classic cuts from LP which surpass bounds of rock and encourage hope that, though Roxy Music has split, its work will remain strong influence on today's newer bands.

Hit Singles:	US	UK
Virginia Plain, 1972	—	4
Pyjamarama, 1973	—	10
Street Life, 1973	—	9
All I Want Is You, 1974	—	12
Love Is The Drug, 1975	30	2
Virginia Plain, 1977	—	11
Dance Away, 1979	—	2
Angel Eyes, 1979	—	4
Over You, 1980	—	5
Oh Yeah (On The Radio), 1980	—	5
The Same Old Scene, 1980	—	12
Jealous Guy, 1981	—	1
More Than This, 1982	—	6
Avalon, 1982	27	13

Albums:
Roxy Music (Reprise/Island), 1972
For Your Pleasure (Warner Bros/Island), 1973
Stranded (Atco/Island), 1973
Country Life (Atco/Island), 1974
Siren (Atco/Island), 1975
Viva Roxy Music (live) (Atco/Island), 1976
Greatest Hits (Polydor), 1977
Manifesto (Polydor), 1979
Flesh And Blood (Polydor), 1980
The First Seven Albums (boxed set) (Polydor), 1981
Avalon (Polydor), 1982
The High Road (live mini-LP) (Polydor), 1983
The Atlantic Years 1973-80 (EG), 1983
Heart Still Beating (EG), 1990

Andy Mackay Solo:
In Search Of Eddie Riff (—/Island), 1974
Resolving Contradictions (—/Bronze), 1978

Phil Manzanera Solo:
Diamond Head (Atco/Island), 1975
Quiet Sun: Mainstream (Antilles/Island), 1975
801: Live (Polydor/Island), 1976
Listen Now (Polydor), 1977
K Scope (Polydor), 1978
Southern Cross (—/Expression), 1990

Manzanera and Mackay:
Manzanera And Mackay (—/Expression), 1990

Above: Greatest Hits, Roxy Music. Courtesy Polydor Records.

Roxy's live efforts helped boost **Stranded** LP to UK No. 10. John Gustafson played bass on this album (and next two) but did so as session player and didn't tour with Roxy. John Wetton took on this role from autumn 1974 until April 1975 when he suddenly left for Uriah Heep and Gustafson at last went on the road. In late 1975 he was replaced by Rick Wills (later Small Faces).

Although **Country Life** and **Siren** were big success in UK and garnered critical praise in US, Ferry wanted to try solo tour. Roxy Music's break-up was never formally announced but band no longer truly existed after June 1976. Various solo projects failed to produce new careers for Roxy members but public interest in band remained high.

In late 1978, Ferry gathered nucleus of MacKay, Manzanera and Thompson for Roxy Music Reunion. Using ex-Vibrator Gary Tibbs (bass) and ex-Ace Paul Carrack (keyboards), band recorded **Manifesto**.

After extensive touring, Roxy Music entered new stage of career with **Flesh And Blood**. Although not radically different from past, this album marked new level of

Right: A Wizard, A True Star, Todd Rundgren. Courtesy Bearsville Records.

Todd Rundgren

US vocalist, composer, producer, guitarist
Born Upper Darby, Pennsylvania, June 22, 1948

Career: Greatly influenced by 'British Invasion' spearheaded by Beatles and Rolling Stones; acquired first electric guitar at 17. First band was Woody's Truck Stop (for less than a year); by 1968 had left to form The Nazz, legendary Philadelphia band who made three LPs between 1968 and 1970 now regarded as prime collectors' items (re-issued in 1983 by Rhino Records, Los Angeles). However, Todd left group by mid-1969 to perfect ability as producer/engineer.

Produced only minor acts early on, but engineered for such as The Band, Paul Butterfield Blues Band and Jesse Winchester, as well as embarking on personal solo career.

Had great success with 1972 LP **Something/Anything?**, plus production of debut LP by Sparks (then known as Halfnelson) and Badfinger.

1973 productions included New York Dolls, Grand Funk Railroad and Fanny. In 1974 he formed Utopia.

Musically and vocally, Rundgren has experimented with several styles; equally proficient backed solely by own guitar or by piano. His lyrics have also been varied, sometimes poignant, often witty, but always perceptive.

During 70s, he was probably best known as producer, while own performing/recording career has largely retreated into cult status. Among notable productions during this period are those for Hall And Oates, Tom Robinson, Tubes, Patti Smith and **Bat Out Of Hell** by Meat Loaf.

Rundgren reduced production schedule during 80s, electing to direct music videos. Maintained sporadic personal output, although demise of Bearsville saw Rundgren switch to Warner Bros. His debut for label was **A Cappella** (1985). Utopia endured through **Swing To The Right** (1982) and **Oblivion** (1983) before splitting.

Hit Singles:	US	UK
We Gotta Get You A Woman, 1971	20	—
I Saw The Light, 1972	16	36
Hello It's Me, 1973	5	—

Albums:
With The Nazz:
Nazz (Screen Gems-Columbia/—), 1968
Nazz Nazz (Screens Gems-Columbia/—), 1969
Nazz III (Screen Gems-Columbia/—), 1970

Solo and with Utopia:
Something/Anything (Bearsville), 1972
A Wizard, A True Star (Bearsville/Island), 1973
Todd (Bearsville), 1973
Todd Rundgren's Utopia (Bearsville), 1974
Initiation (Bearsville), 1975
Another Life (Bearsville), 1975
Faithful (Bearsville), 1976
Ra (Bearsville), 1977
Oops! Wrong Planet (Bearsville), 1977
Hermit Of Mink Hollow (Bearsville/Island), 1978
Back To The Bars (Bearsville), 1978
Adventures In Utopia (Bearsville), 1980
Deface The Music (Bearsville), 1980
Healing (Bearsville), 1981
Swing To The Right (Rhino/Bearsville), 1982

Above: Hemispheres, Rush. Courtesy Mercury Records.

Utopia (Bearsville), 1982
The Ever Popular Tortured Artist Effect (Bearsville), 1983
Oblivion (WEA/Warner), 1983
A Cappella (Rhino/Warner Bros), 1985
Nearly Human (—/WEA), 1989
Utopia (Rhino/—), 1989
2nd Wind (Warner Bros), 1991

Worth Searching Out:
Runt (Bearsville), 1970
The Ballad Of (Bearsville), 1971

Rush

Canadian group formed 1973

Original line-up: Alex Lifeson, guitar; Geddy Lee, bass, keyboards, vocals; John Rutsey, drums.

Career: band began playing bars in Toronto, using hard rock/heavy metal sound to project gothic images of sci-fi future. Privately produced first LP was rejected by major labels but received extensive airplay in Seattle. This led to some American bookings in Pacific Northwest and group caught attention of Mercury Records.

Mercury released first album and set up national tour when Rutsey decided to leave. Neil Peart joined and expanded band's potential by adding lyric-writing and vocal talents.

Next two LPs spread band's reputation for hard rock; more importantly began expounding Rush's vision of the individual winning out against high-tech in some distant society. This approach culminated in extended work covering entire first side of **2112**, which tells the tale of a young man who discovers an electric guitar and suddenly finds himself an outlaw for inventing music to go with it.

At this point, band stepped back from studio commitments and released live set **All The World's A Stage**. Subsequent LPs dabbled in sci-fi motifs.

Established burgeoning reputation with early 80s albums **Permanent Waves** and **Exit: Stage Left** and solid stage presence, although band seemed reluctant to delve far from studio sound. Maintained output for Mercury until 1989 and **A Show Of Hands** set; company then released **Chronicles**. Signed with WEA in 1990.

Hit Singles:

	US	UK
Spirit Of Radio, 1980	–	13

Albums:
Rush (Mercury), 1974
Fly By Night (Mercury), 1975
Caress Of Steel (Mercury), 1975
2112 (Mercury), 1976
All The World's A Stage (double live), (Mercury), 1976
A Farewell To Kings (Mercury), 1977
Archives (Mercury), 1978*
Hemispheres (Mercury), 1978
Permanent Waves (Mercury), 1980
Rush Through Time (Mercury), 1980
Moving Pictures (Mercury), 1981
Exit: Stage Left (live) (Mercury), 1981
Signals (Mercury), 1982
Grace Under Pressure (Vertigo), 1984
Power Windows (Vertigo), 1985
Hold Your Fire (Mercury), 1987
A Show Of Hands (Mercury/Vertigo), 1988
Presto (Atlantic), 1989
Chronicles (Mercury/Vertigo), 1990
*Re-issue of first three LPs

Leon Russell

US composer, vocalist, pianist, guitarist
Born Lawton, Oklahoma, April 2, 1941

Career: Studied classical piano from early age; at 14 took up trumpet and formed own band. Other experience included playing with Ronnie Hawkins and Jerry Lee Lewis.

In 1958 Russell moved to Los Angeles and became session musician, working with artists like Glen Campbell, Byrds, Herb Alpert, Crystals, and Righteous Brothers. In late 60s became friendly with blue-eyed soul duo

Delaney And Bonnie, and in 1969 joined Delaney And Bonnie's Friends for touring and recording.

Most of Friends eventually became part of Joe Cocker's touring band, Mad Dogs And Englishmen, which Russell led. Exposure made him cult figure, and solo career started to take off in 1970 with **Leon Russell**.

Although technically limited singer, Russell made up for this with excellent production, superstar session line-ups and good, largely self-penned material. Russell came up with several much-covered classics, notably **A Song For You**, **Superstar** and **This Masquerade**. Recording career peaked with gold album **Carney** and triple album **Live**.

Despite striking stage personality, Russell's career quietened down in late 70s. Following an earlier country album in 1973, artist turned to country roots.

Hit Singles:

	US	UK
Tight Rope, 1972	11	–
Lady Blue, 1975	14	–

Albums:
Leon Russell (MCA), 1970
Leon Russell And The Shelter People (MCA), 1971
Carney (MCA), 1972
Will O' The Wisp (MCA), 1975
Best Of Leon Russell (MCA), 1976
Leon Russell And New Grass Revival Live (Paradise), 1981

Sade

UK group formed 1982

Original line-up: Sade Adu, vocals; Stuart Matthewman, saxophone; Paul Denman, bass; Andrew Hale, keyboards.

Career: Though singer Sade Adu holds the spotlight, Sade insist they are not an individual but a four-strong group, augmenting itself with such extra musicians as drummer Dave Early and percussionist Martin Ditchman to produce music described as 'soul with a jazz feel'.

Asked by manager Lee Barrett if she could sing, Sade auditioned for London funk band Pride. When Matthewman and Denman came down from Hull to join Pride they instantly got on with Adu and ballads penned by her and Matthewman soon became high spot of Pride's otherwise pungent funk set. Sade developed into an opening act for Pride, then a separate band in own right.

Adding Hale and linking with producer Robin Millar, act signed to Epic and reworked old Pride number **Smooth Operator** into smash hit, concurrent **Diamond Life** album also making major impact, with group's total sales figures topping six million

Below: Promise, Sade's second album. Courtesy Epic Records.

Left: Rush front-men Alex Lifeson (left) and Geddy Lee.

before release of second, chart-topping album **Promise**.

Following last gig in December 1988 at Wembley, band emarked on prolonged hibernation, and Sade informed public that no new recordings were to be released until summer of 1992.

To date, group has subsequently sold half-million CDs of first two albums, and Sade herself remains a national heroine to the French, who have taken the sultry jazz vocalist to their collective heart.

Hit Singles:

	US	UK
Your Love Is King, 1984	–	6
Smooth Operator, 1984	5	19

Albums:
Diamond Life (Epic), 1984
Promise (Epic), 1985
Stronger Than Pride (Epic), 1987

Above: Santana's first album, self-titled. Courtesy CBS Records.

Carlos Santana

US guitarist, bandleader, composer
Born Autlan, Jalisco, Mexico, July 20, 1947

Career: Emerged as major local rock musician during San Francisco's Haight-Ashbury flower-power era; guested on seminal **The Live Adventures Of Mike Bloomfield And Al Kooper** album, then put together own band. Brought Latin flavour to rock through use of conga player Mike Carrabello and award-winning Central American percussionist José 'Chepito' Areas alongside Gregg Rolie, keyboards, vocals, David Brown, bass, and Mike Shrieve, drums.

Reputation was already made before 1969 debut album **Santana** which sold a million copies (most after Woodstock) in US alone. Band's appearing in *Woodstock* concert and film, performing **Soul Sacrifice**, was one of the great moments of rock.

Oye Como Va, penned by Latin-music great Tito Puente, helped second album **Abraxas** (1970) to equally big sales. **Santana 3** (1972) brought Santana's guitarist protégé Neil Schon and Coke Escovedo into band. Live album jamming with Buddy Miles was less satisfying. Its release coincided with disbanding of original Santana group in wake of Santana's espousal of teachings of guru Sri Chinmoy at instigation of friend Mahavishnu John McLaughlin; Santana adopted name Devadip.

Latin/jazz/rock fusion **Caravanserai** album used Rolie and Schon, along with studio musicians; they were not included in new band in 1973. This placed Santana originals Areas and Shrieve alongside Tom Coster, keyboard, James Mingo Lewis and Armando Peraza, percussion, and Doug Rauch, bass. Besides own band's work,

Santana recorded **Love, Devotion, Surrender** album in partnership with John McLaughlin, and **Illuminations** album with Alice Coltrane.

Various line-up changes saw Santana band return from heady experimentation to simpler roots, which put albums back among best-sellers.

In 1977 Santana ditched existing band, except Coster; Schon and Rolie formed Journey. Guitarist then signed management deal with former Woodstock and Fillmore promoter Bill Graham. Maintained prodigious output, which, by 1982, had resulted in 14 LPs in 15 years.

Carlos Santana enjoyed single success with **Winning** (1981) and **Hold On** (1982), and also renewed collaborative work. Cut **Havana Moon** with Willie Nelson (1983) and rejoined with Buddy Miles for **Beyond Appearances** (1985). Guested on Wayne Shorter's 1988 US tour, and also featured on John Lee Hooker's Grammy-winning LP, **The Healer**.

Following 20th anniversary concert at San Francisco, Santana toured US with line-up comprising Rolie, Coster, Graham Lear, percussionists Armando Perez, Orestes Vilato and Raul Rekow, with Miles on vocals.

In solo vein, Santana earned Grammy for 1987 LP **Blues For Salvador** before further group effort with **Spirits Dancing In The Flesh** (1990), the line-up for which was Thompson, Perez, bassist Benny Reitveld, Scottish vocalist Alec Ligertwood and drummer Wilfredo Reyes.

A revered musician, Santana's fluid solos and pure tone have marked him as the Latin voice of rock.

Guitar: Gibson 335.

Hit Singles:	US	UK
Evil Ways, 1970	9	—
Black Magic Woman, 1970	4	—
Oye Como Va, 1971	13	—
Everybody's Everything, 1971	12	—
She's Not There, 1977	27	11
Winning, 1981	17	—
Hold On, 1982	15	—

Albums:
Santana (Columbia/CBS), 1969
Abraxas (Columbia/CBS), 1970
Santana III (Columbia/CBS), 1972
Caravanserai (Columbia/CBS), 1972
Welcome (Columbia/CBS), 1973

Above: Carlos Santana, one of the finest guitarists to emerge from San Francisco in the 1960s.

Greatest Hits (Columbia/CBS), 1974
Borboletta (Columbia/CBS), 1976
Amigos (Columbia/CBS), 1976
Moonflower (Columbia/CBS), 1977
Inner Secrets (Columbia/CBS), 1978
Marathon (Columbia/CBS), 1979
Swing Of Delight (Columbia/CBS), 1980
Zebop! (Columbia/CBS), 1981
Shango (Columbia/CBS), 1982
Havana Moon (Columbia/CBS), 1983
Beyond Appearances (CBS), 1985
Freedom (CBS), 1987
Blues For Salvador (Columbia/CBS), 1987
Viva Santana (Columbia/CBS), 1988
Spirits Dancing In The Flesh (Columbia/CBS), 1990
Lotus (Columbia/CBS), 1991

With John McLaughlin:
Love, Devotion, Surrender (Columbia), 1973

With Alice Coltrane:
Illuminations (—/CBS), 1974

Boz Scaggs

US vocalist, guitarist, composer
Born William Royce Scaggs, Ohio, June 8, 1944

Career: William 'Boz' Scaggs was brought up in Texas, and met Steve Miller at high school in Dallas. Joined Miller's band, The Marksmen, in 1959.

Scaggs and Miller moved on to University of Wisconsin; formed band (The Ardells)

Above: Silk Degrees, Boz Scaggs. Courtesy CBS Records.

to play local gigs. Scaggs quit college in 1963 to return to Texas and put together short-lived outfit called The Wigs, playing R&B. From 1964 to 1966 Scaggs was in Europe, scraping living as solo act (as folk singer). First album, **Boz**, was recorded in Stockholm.

In 1967 Scaggs returned to America to join Steve Miller in San Francisco, collaborating on two highly acclaimed albums, **Children Of The Future** and **Sailor**. Left in late 1968, citing musical differences.

After one Atlantic album, Scaggs signed with CBS and started to move towards R&B stylings that would eventually make his name. During early 70s Scaggs continued to build following with albums like **My Time** and **Slow Dancer**, but it was not until **Silk Degrees** that he hit big time.

Featuring musicians to become famous as members of Toto, **Degrees** was soul-influenced without being slavishly imitative, and full of memorable songs. Album contained several hit singles, including much-covered semi-standard **We're All Alone**, and went on to sell over five million copies.

Two Down Then Left followed similar musical pattern and scored comparable

success. Scaggs consolidated position by touring extensively (material performed even better live) throughout US and rest of world. 1980 album **Middle Man** featured guest guitarist Carlos Santana, and was followed by compilation **Hits!**.

However, Scaggs retreated suddenly after chart duet with Lisa Dal Bello on **Miss Sun**. Ensconced in restaurant/bar in San Francisco, artist did not materialize again until **Other Roads** album was released in 1988. The success of **Heart of Mine** single from LP did not prompt Scaggs into full-scale comeback, and he remains reluctant to add rock 'n' roll to his menu.

Hit Singles:	US	UK
Lowdown, 1976	3	28
What Can I Say, 1977	42	10
Lido Shuffle, 1977	11	13
Breakdown Dead Ahead, 1980	15	—
Jojo, 1980	17	—
Look What You've Done To Me, 1980	14	—
Miss Sun, 1980	14	—

Albums:
Boz Scaggs (Atlantic), 1969
Moments (Columbia/CBS), 1971
Boz Scaggs And Band (Columbia/CBS), 1971
My Time (Columbia/CBS), 1972
Slow Dancer (Columbia/CBS), 1974
Silk Degrees (Columbia/CBS), 1976
Two Down Then Left (Columbia/CBS), 1977
Middle Man (Columbia/CBS), 1980
Hits! (Columbia/CBS), 1980
Other Roads (Columbia/CBS), 1988

Michael Schenker Group

European group formed 1980

Original line-up: Michael Schenker, guitar; Gary Barden, vocals; Simon Phillips, drums; Mo Foster, bass; Don Airey, keyboards.

Career: Schenker (born Saustedt, West Germany, January 10, 1955) joined brother's band, Scorpions, who opened for UFO on one of their early German tours. UFO was impressed enough to ask Schenker to join them. From 1974 until 1979, helped develop UFO into excellent hard rock band, culminating in brilliant live LP, **Strangers In The Night**.

By time of its release in early 1979, Schenker had left group. Briefly touring with Scorpions again, he then guested on their **Long Drive** LP before finally going solo.

Following jamming sessions with Aerosmith in September 1979, Schenker was free to work on solo LP. Rehearsals began with Gary Barden and Denny Carmassi (ex-Montrose) on drums, as well as Billy Sheehan on bass. Schenker then went into hospital because of personal problems and project fell apart. Within a year, had formed line-up above; hired Roger Glover as producer, and released first solo LP. (Drummer Simon Phillips' previous notable work included sessions for Jack Bruce, Nazareth, Roger Glover, Art Garfunkel, Jeff Beck, Roxy Music and Pete Townshend.)

Although strong, line-up was never meant to be permanent and Schenker recruited touring unit of Barden, Chris Glen on bass, famous session drummer Cozy Powell and his own replacement in UFO, Paul Raymond.

In 1981, this line-up struggled to produce second studio LP. **MSG** was expensive flop and, as expected, line-up again changed.

However, old line-up was featured on double-live LP, **One Night At Budokan**.

Raymond left for full-time duties with UFO and Graham Bonnet stepped in for vocalist Barden. Bonnet helped band present a very strong Reading Festival performance, then recorded **Assault Attack**. For some reason, Bonnet's vocals failed to live up to either his earlier solo work or live efforts with Schenker. Barden returned on vocals and Ted McKenna replaced Cozy Powell. Further dissension in group saw quick-fire changes — Barden returned, Andy Nye joined on keyboards and, after **Built To Destroy** LP, guitarist Derek St. Holmes was recruited. Barden was then replaced by Ray Kennedy, and then bassist Chris Glen said goodbye, with Dennis Feldman taking his place. In epitaph to the upheavals, Nye, McKenna and Feldman all then left.

MSG broke up in 1984, and then Michael forged a new working relationship with Irish singer/songwriter Robin McAuley, formerly of Grand Prix and Far Corporation. The new McAuley Schenker Group featured German drummer Bodo Schopf, bassist Rocky Newton and second guitarist Mitch Perry. After several months of rehearsal, the band made their debut at the European Monsters Of Rock Festival in 1987 and released their album **Perfect Timing** in October, with a subsequent single **Love Is Not A Game**. The band toured America, uncomfortably billed with Rush, and later toured the UK with British group Whitesnake. Schenker was happy to reduce his 'guitar hero' role to allow room for McAuley to develop as writer and performer.

Following disappointing 1989 set **Save Yourself** for Capitol Records, Schenker guested with pick-up outfit Contraband (not the Aussie band of same name) for 1991 self-titled LP in a line-up comprising drummer Bobby Blotzer (ex-Ratts), guitarist Tracii Guns (ex-LA Guns), vocalist Richard Black (ex-Shark's Island) and bassist Share Pederson (ex-Vixen).

Albums:
The Michael Schenker Group (Chrysalis), 1980
MSG (Chrysalis), 1981
One Night At Budokan (Chrysalis), 1981
Dancer (Chrysalis), 1982
Assault Attack (Chrysalis), 1983
Built To Destroy (Chrysalis), 1983

Above: German-born guitar star Michael Schenker, who worked with both The Scorpions and UFO before embarking on his own successful career.

Portfolio (Chrysalis), 1987
Perfect Timing (Capitol), 1987
Rock Will Never Die (Chrysalis), 1988
Save Yourself (Capitol), 1989

Left: German HM crunchers The Scorpions have finally made top flight after a 20-year bash.

Scorpions
German group formed 1970

Original line-up: Michael Schenker, guitar; Rudolph Schenker, guitar; Klaus Meine, vocals; Lothar Heimbeer, bass; Wolfgang Dziony, drums.

Career: Long-established German heavy-metal crew who have survived major changes in personnel to remain in front-line of head-banging fraternity.

Schenker brothers united in 1970 after stints in low-key groups and cut **Lonesome Crow** album for label Brain. Michael left band to join UFO (replacement Ulrich Roth) before second album **Fly To The Rainbow** for RCA (1974), which also saw Jürgen Rosenthal on drums and new bassist Francis Buchholz. Rosenthal's stint was brief, and the drum chair was occupied, in turn, by Rudy Lenners and Herman Rarebell.

After period of inactivity, but with German and Japanese markets clamouring for more product, settled line-up (Rudy Schenker, Meine, Buchholz, Matthias Jabs on guitar and Rarebell) embarked on sustained period of success, commencing with **Lovedrive** (1979), when Michael Schenker guested, then **Animal Magnetism**, **Blackout** (US Top 10 in 1982) and **Love At First Sting.**

Persistent gigging (including Russian tour in 1988 and Roger Waters' The Wall spectacular) maintained Scorpions presence, although lack of studio material was appeased when **Crazy World** album was released in 1990, with Whitesnake producer Keith Olsen at the helm.

Hit Singles:

	US	UK
Wind Of Change, 1991	4	2

Albums:
Lonesome Crow (Brain), 1972
Fly To The Rainbow (RCA), 1974
In Trance (RCA), 1976
Virgin Killer (RCA), 1977
Taken By Force (RCA), 1978
Best Of (RCA), 1979
Tokyo Tapes (RCA), 1979
Animal Magnetism (Harvest), 1980
Rock Galaxy (RCA), 1980
Love At First Sting (Mercury/Fame), 1984
World Wide Live (Mercury/Harvest), 1985
Crazy World (Mercury/Vertigo), 1990
Hot And Heavy (RCA), 1990

The Searchers
UK group formed 1962

Original line-up: Mike Pender, vocals, guitar; John McNally, vocals, guitar; Tony Jackson, vocals, bass; Chris Curtis, drums.

Career: On Merseyside in early 60s The Searchers were second only to Beatles in terms of local popularity; they specialized in high, keening harmonies and immaculate stage presentation.

National attention came after signing to Pye in 1963; group's cover of Drifters' **Sweets For My Sweet** soared to No. 1 spot and made group integral part of Merseybeat boom.

Group did not write own material and generally relied on covering suitable American hits like Jackie De Shannon's **Needles And Pins** (co-written by Sonny Bono), Orlons' **Don't Throw Your Love Away**, and **When You Walk In The Room**, also a hit for De Shannon. Group had considerable American success on Kapp label, making Top 40 on five occasions in 1964.

By 1965 group seemed unable to find right material and hits dried up. Jackson left to form Tony Jackson And The Vibrations (one minor hit), and was replaced by Frank Allen, formerly with Cliff Bennett's Rebel Rousers.

Band subsequently moved into lucrative club and cabaret circuit, during which time they signed two-album deal with American label Sire, which saw release of **The Searchers** (1980) and **Play For Today** (1981).

Following 21st anniversary celebrations, The Searchers lost guitarist and founder Pender, who formed his own band Mike

Below: Meet The Searchers, The Searchers. Courtesy Pye Records.

Pender's Searchers. The remaining members, including new addition Spencer James (guitar), subsequently sued Pender, who, they claimed, had no right to the use of group's name.

Hit Singles:

	US	UK
Sweets For My Sweet, 1963	—	1
Sugar And Spice, 1963	44	2
Needles And Pins, 1964	13	1
Don't Throw Your Love Away, 1964	16	1
Some Day We're Gonna Love Again, 1964	34	11
When You Walk In The Room, 1964	35	3
Love Potion No. 9, 1964	3	—
What Have They Done To The Rain, 1964	29	13
Goodbye My Love, 1965	52	4
He's Got No Love, 1965	—	12
Take Me For What I'm Worth, 1966	—	20

Albums:
Meet The Searchers (Kapp/Pye), 1963
Sugar And Spice (—/Pye), 1963
When You Walk In The Room (—/Pye), 1964
It's The Searchers (—/Pye), 1964
Sounds Like The Searchers (—/Pye), 1964
Take Me For What I'm Worth (—/Pye), 1965
Needles And Pins (—/Hallmark), 1971
The Searchers File (—/Pye), 1977
The Searchers (Sire), 1980
Play For Today (Sire), 1981
100 Minutes (—/Pye), 1982
Silver Searchers (Nouveou), 1986
Hits Collection (PRT), 1987

Neil Sedaka
US vocalist, composer, pianist
Born Brooklyn, New York, March 13, 1939

Career: Piano prodigy at eight, this son of a taxi driver studied at prestigious Juilliard School and had promising future as classical pianist. At 13 began writing songs with neighbour Howard Greenfield, who remained lyric-writing partner for over 20 years (until replaced by Phil Cody after 1973). Sedaka and Greenfield were one of several teams working at Brill Building in New York, turning out high-quality music which bridged gap between Tin Pan Alley and rock 'n' roll for teen market's top performers. Then, in 1958, Connie Francis had hit with their **Stupid Cupid.**

Sedaka began recording own songs, and between 1959 and 1963 hits like **The Diary, Calendar Girl, Oh Carol** (dedicated to friend and fellow Brill Building writer Carole King), **Stairway To Heaven, Breaking Up Is Hard To Do** and **Happy Birthday Sweet Sixteen** sold over 20 million copies. Never succumbing to pitfalls of stardom, Sedaka lived and worked in father's unpretentious Brooklyn apartment, writing over 500 songs before Beatles-influenced music caused his popularity as performer to fade. Composing talent was still in demand, however, and he wrote for Tom Jones, The Fifth Dimension and Andy Williams.

Always popular in Britain (his second record, **I Go Ape**, made No. 5 in UK), Sedaka was persuaded in 1971 to do comeback concert at Albert Hall in London; show successfully combined new songs with oldies. While in Britain he recorded two albums with group called Hot Legs (who became

10cc), then returned to Los Angeles to record third album — all for Britain. When Elton John realized Sedaka had no US record company, he signed him to own label, Rocket Records. Gold-rated **Sedaka's Back** and **The Hungry Years**, combining songs from three British LPs, was well received in US and Sedaka had his first US No. 1 hit single in ten years with **Laugher In The Rain** (1975) followed by hit **Bad Blood**, which featured Elton John on backing vocals. **Breaking Up Is Hard To Do** single returned to charts in 1976 after 14 years.

Sedaka's songs for Captain And Tenille, **Love Will Keep Us Together** and **You Never Done It Like That**, further enhanced revived reputation. first NBC-TV special in 1976 received both critical and popular acclaim. Since then, Sedaka has continued to write, record, appear on television and play to full houses in Las Vegas, Lake Tahoe and around the world. His autobiography *Laughter In The Rain* was published in 1988.

A star at 20 and a has-been at 25, Sedaka has accepted ups and downs with equanimity. His new songs remain fresh and original, and his music is enjoyed by the widest possible audience.

Above: Oh! Carol, Neil Sedaka. The album and single were dedicated to Carole King. Courtesy RCA Records.

Hit Singles:	US	UK
The Diary, 1959	14	–
I Go Ape, 1959	42	5
Oh! Carol, 1959	9	3
Stairway To Heaven, 1960	9	8
You Mean Everything To Me, 1960	17	45
Calendar Girl, 1961	4	8
Little Devil, 1961	11	9
Happy Birthday, Sweet Sixteen, 1961	6	3
Breaking Up Is Hard To Do, 1962	1	7
Next Door To An Angel, 1962	5	29
Alice In Wonderland, 1963	17	–
Oh Carol/Breaking Up Is Hard To Do/Little Devil, 1972	–	19
That's When The Music Takes Me, 1973	27	18
Laughter In The Rain, 1974	1	15
Bad Blood, 1975	1	–
Breaking Up Is Hard To Do, 1976	8	–
Love In The Shadows, 1976	16	–

With Daria Sedaka:
Should've Never Let You Go, 1982	19	–

Albums:
Oh! Carol (–/Camden), 1970
Stupid Cupid (–/Camden), 1972
Tra-La Days Are Over (Polydor), 1974
Live At The Royal Festival Hall, With The Royal Philharmonic Orchestra (Polydor), 1974
Laughter In The Rain (Polydor), 1974

Below: Laughter And Tears, Neil Sedaka. Courtesy Polydor Records.

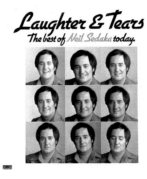

Let's Go Steady Again (–/Pickwick), 1975
Laughter And Tears (Polydor), 1976
And Songs — A Solo Concert (Polydor), 1977
Sedaka 50s and 60s (RCA), 1977
A Song (Elektra/Polydor), 1977
All You Need Is The Music (Polydor), 1978
Many Sides Of (RCA), 1979
Neil Sedaka's Greatest Hits (RCA), 1980
In The Pocket (Elektra/Polydor), 1980
Now (Elektra/Polydor), 1981
Singer, Songwriter, Melody Maker (Accord/–), 1982
20 Golden Pieces Of (–/Bulldog), 1982
Good Times (PRT), 1986
The Rare Sedaka (RCA/–), 1990

Bob Seger
US vocalist, composer, guitarist
Born Detroit, Michigan, 1947

Career: Seger grew up in Detroit and played in local band, Last Heard. 1966 saw release of solo material. Several tracks received good critical notice or became regional hits (**Heavy Music** (1966), **2+2=?** (1967) and **Ramblin' Gamblin' Man** (1968). After four LPs and many, many Mid-Western gigs, Seger quit music in 1969 and went to college. By 1971 he was on the road again, with same results; critical praise, regional hits — and always just out of the running.

Third phase of career began when he formed permanent backing group, The Silver Bullet Band. This aggregation produced **Beautiful Loser**, but again national success just eluded Seger. He decided to try Frampton's approach of using live LP to sell sound rather than collection of old hits.

Live Bullet proved to be key and Seger was sudden overnight success some 12 years after first attempts. He quickly followed up with **Night Moves** and both albums stayed in US charts for some time (**Night Moves** went platinum).

Anxious to give fans same musical diet, Seger finally found time in heavy touring schedule to record **Stranger In Town**, which went triple platinum.

Against The Wind went to No. 1 in US LP charts, but seemed to suffer from platinum overdosage. Seger sensed this and offered another live set, **Nine Tonight**, a collection of old hits, giving him time to rejuvenate his creative forces for his personal masterpiece, **The Distance**.

Although follow-up **Like A Rock** (1986) also achieved platinum status, Seger was becoming rock music's most renowned recluse. Apart from **Shakedown** single in 1987 (from *Beverley Hills Cop II* movie) and

Right: Never Mind The Bollocks, Here's The Sex Pistols. Courtesy Virgin.

guest spot on Little Feat's **Let It Roll** LP a year later, Seger was nowhere to be seen.

Citing personal difficulties (said to be due to failed marriage) for lengthy hiatus, Seger returned to studios in 1991 for **The Fire Inside** set, which also led to re-formation of Bullet Band and a neat new haircut.

Hit Singles:	US	UK
Ramblin' Gamblin' Man, 1969	17	–
Night Moves, 1977	4	–
Still The Same, 1978	4	–
Hollywood Nights, 1978	12	42
We've Got Tonite, 1979	13	41
Fire Lake, 1980	6	–
Against The Wind, 1980	5	–
You'll Accomp'ny Me, 1980	14	–
Tryin' To Live My Life Without You, 1981	5	–
Shame On The Moon, 1983	2	–
Even Now, 1983	12	–
Understanding, 1985	17	–
Shakedown (From *Beverley Hills Cop II*), 1987	1	–

Albums:
Ramblin' Gamblin' Man (Capitol), 1969
Noah (Capitol/–), 1969
Mongrel (Capitol), 1970
Smokin' O.P.'s (Reprise), 1972
Seven (Reprise), 1974
Beautiful Loser (Capitol), 1975
Live Bullet (Capitol), 1976
Night Moves (Capitol), 1976
Stranger In The Town (Capitol), 1980

Above: Stranger In Town, Bob Seger. Courtesy Capitol Records.

Against The Wind (Capitol), 1980
Nine Tonight (Capitol), 1982
The Distance (Capitol), 1983
Greatest Hits (Capitol), 1984
Like A Rock (Capitol), 1986
The Fire Inside (Capitol), 1991

The Sex Pistols
UK group formed 1975

Original line-up: Steve Jones, guitar, vocals; Glen Matlock, bass; Paul Cook, drums; Johnny Rotten, vocals.

Career: Jones, Cook and Matlock used to hang around Malcolm McLaren's clothes store; there they met John Lydon whom McLaren suggested as band's vocalist. McLaren became manager and began developing strong image by encouraging tough, ragged street dress (which rebelled against decadent glam look of 70s acts). He renamed Lydon 'Rotten' and coined moniker Sex Pistols.

Early gigs were hardly professional but full of explosive energy. McLaren capitalized on group's inexperience and used it to promote image of angry young men, only refused to copy established rock stars (megabands in particular).

1976 gigs not only enhanced band's reputation for being 'anti' everything but began involving audience in violence on regular basis. November 1976 turned Sex Pistols loose on centre of rock world. A few days after signing EMI contract, and readying **Anarchy In The UK** single, Pistols were provoked into swearing on live Thames TV programme. Uproar made them front page items of all newspapers, not just music weeklies. Kids loved it and the 'punk' revolution was on.

EMI dropped band in January 1977, losing £40,000 advance . A&M stepped in to sign band, but gave up £75,000 advance a few days later. By time Virgin offered £50,000 advance in May 1977, band had collected over £150,000 for one single.

In interim, Rotten replaced Matlock with friend Sid Vicious. Pistols were banned practically everywhere, which meant there was no way to follow up notoriety with a little rock 'n' roll. Subsequent recordings ensured Pistol's place in chart histories, but on concluding first American tour, Rotten announced group's break-up. Other three carried on temporarily, even using infamous Great Train Robber, Ronald Biggs, for vocal or two. All this was pointless; it became macabre when Vicious was arrested for murder of girlfriend. He died in ugly overdose incident while awaiting trial.

Several post-Pistols solo projects (Rich Kids, Professionals, Public Image Ltd.) have all failed to win either wide critical acclaim

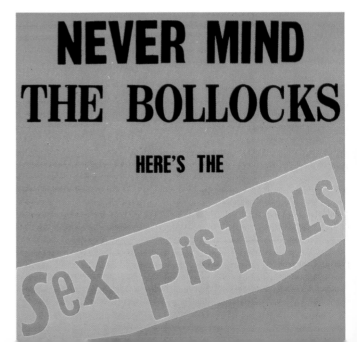

NEVER MIND THE BOLLOCKS

HERE'S THE

Sex Pistols

or the popular support afforded Pistols. Ironically, Pistols influenced entire rock industry but accomplished little musically.

The Sex Pistols' raw style inspired many young musicians/singers, previously inhibited by lack of money or finesse, to form back-to-the-basics bands. The Pistols were not only a shot in the arm to the music industry, but (with McLaren's foresight) helped bring back the fashion/music connection that had been so exciting in the 60s. Most importantly, The Sex Pistols encouraged audiences and performers to question the music scene.

Very much a creation of manager Malcolm McLaren's publicity-hype machine, The Sex Pistols lived out their role as punk radicals to the fullest extent and are likely to be remembered more for their image and their charisma than for their musical contribution.

Tenth anniversary of Summer Of Punk in 1986 brought resurgence of interest in proto-typical punksters, and further controversy when McLaren was sued by Lydon, Cook, Jones and Vicious's mother. Well-received Vicious biopic *Sid And Nancy* was released in same year.

McLaren resurfaced in 1991 with TV project *The Ghosts Of Oxford Street*, featuring Sinéad O'Connor, Screaming Lord Sutch, Tom Jones and Kirsty MacColl.

Hit Singles:

	US	UK
God Save The Queen, 1977	–	2
Pretty Vacant, 1977	–	6
Holidays In The Sun, 1977	–	8
No One Is Innocent/My Way, 1978	–	7
Something Else/Friggin' In The Riggin', 1979	–	3
Silly Thing/Who Killed Bambi, 1979	–	6
C'mon Everybody, 1979	–	3

Albums:

Never Mind The Bollocks, Here's The Sex Pistols (Warner Bros/Virgin), 1977*
The Great Rock 'n' Roll Swindle (–/Virgin), 1978
Some Produce (–/Virgin), 1979
Carry On Sex Pistols (–/Virgin), 1979
Flogging A Dead Horse (–/Virgin), 1979
Original Pistols Live (Dojo), 1986
Live At Chelmsford Top Security Prison (Restless/–), 1990
*Only LP released while band was working as unit

The Shadows
UK group formed 1959

Original line-up: Hank Marvin, Fender Stratocaster guitar; Bruce Welch, Fender Telecaster guitar; Jet Harris, bass; Tony Meehan, drums.

Career: In 1958 Marvin and Welch were members of Cliff Richard's backing group The Drifters. By following year personnel had stabilized as above, and group had changed name to Shadows to avoid confusion with American Drifters.

Although band continued to back Richard, they started to record independently from 1959. During a 1960 British tour, Jerry Lordan, artist on same bill, gave them instrumental piece he had written called **Apache**. Their version of song reached No. 1 in July 1960, and set pattern for instrumental hits that would last until psychedelia era of 1967. Formula for success was simple yet effective; Marvin's guitar would carry melody, while other members provided clipped, efficient backing.

Above: The very lovely Sex Pistols (from left), Sid Vicious, Paul Cook, Johnny Rotten and Steve Jones.

Almost completely arranged, Shadows music could be clinical; yet it provided example for thousands of young instrumentalists, especially, of course, guitar players. Image-wise, Shadows relied on matching mohair suits and laid-back non-chalance; wildness of R&B era was, in many cases, reaction to their uniformed neatness.

During this period several personnel changes took place. Tony Meehan left in 1961 to be replaced by Brian Bennett. Jet Harris quit in 1962 and almost immediately joined up with Meehan again – duo produced three Top 10 singles in 1963 before Harris retired from scene due to ill health. For short while Harris was replaced in Shadows by Brian 'Liquorice' Locking; he in turn was followed by John Rostill.

In 1968, after hits had dried up, outfit ceased to exist as regular working aggrega-

Below: The surviving Shadows (left to right), Bruce Welch, Brian Bennett and Hank Marvin in the 1980s.

tion. During 70s members got involved in other musical activities; among many other projects, Bruce Welch wrote for and produced Cliff Richard, John Farrar produced Olivia Newton-John, and Brian Bennett became in-demand session musician. However, band continued to record and work together sporadically, with various bass players.

In 1977 **20 Golden Greats** compilation album topped UK charts, and in following year group returned to singles chart in big way with version of show tune **Don't Cry For Me Argentina**. Since that time group has made sporadic chart appearances, and tours continue to be sell-outs.

Although their music has not been that influential – few rock guitarists actually play *like* Hank Marvin – Shadows encouraged generation of young men to take up instruments and make music for themselves. Many current axe heroes point to Hank Marvin as their first role model. Now elder statesmen of rock and pop, The Shadows will undoubtedly clock up more hits before drawing final curtain.

Hit Singles:

	US	UK
Apache, 1960	–	1
Man Of Mystery/The Stranger, 1960	–	5
F.B.I., 1961	–	6
Frightened City, 1961	–	3
Kon-Tiki, 1961	–	1
The Savage, 1961	–	10
Wonderful Land, 1962	–	1
Guitar Tango, 1962	–	4
Dance On!, 1962	–	1
Foot Tapper, 1963	–	1
Atlantis, 1963	–	2
Shindig, 1963	–	6
Geronimo, 1963	–	11
Theme For Young Lovers, 1964	–	12
The Rise And Fall Of Flingel Bunt, 1964	–	5
Genie With The Light Brown Lamp, 1964	–	17
The Next Time I See Mary Anne, 1965	–	17
Stingray, 1965	–	19
Don't Make My Baby Blue, 1965	–	10
War Lord, 1965	–	18
Let Me Be The One, 1975	–	12
Don't Cry For Me Argentina, 1978	–	5
Theme From *The Deer Hunter* (Cavatina), 1979	–	9
Riders In The Sky, 1980	–	12

Albums:

The Shadows (–/Columbia), 1962
Greatest Hits (–/Columbia), 1963
Dance With The Shadows (–/Columbia), 1964
The Sound Of The Shadows (–/Columbia), 1965
More Hits (–/Columbia), 1965
Shadow Music (–/Columbia), 1966
Jigsaw (–/Columbia), 1967
Established 1958 (–/Columbia), 1968
Something Else (–/Columbia), 1969
Shades Of Rock (–/Columbia), 1970
Rockin' With Curly Leads (–/EMI), 1973
Specs Appeal (–/EMI), 1975
The Shadows (–/Ember), 1975
Live At Paris Olympia (–/EMI), 1975
Rarities (–/NUT), 1976
Tasty (–/EMI), 1977
20 Golden Greats (–/EMI), 1977
At The Movies (–/MFP), 1978
String Of Hits (EMI), 1979
Change Of Address (–/Polydor), 1980
Another String Of Hot Hits (–/EMI), 1980
Hits Right Up Your Street (–/Rollover), 1981

Live (–/MFP), 1981
Life In The Jungle (–/Polydor), 1982
Guardian Angel (Rollover), 1984
Compact Shadows (Polydor)
Moonlight Shadows (Polydor)
Simply Shadows (Polydor), 1987
XXV (Polydor), 1987
20 Golden Greats (EMI), 1987
Steppin' To The Shadows, 1989
At Their Very Best, 1989
Reflections (–/Rollover), 1990

Simon And Garfunkel

US duo formed 1957

Career: During late 50s, a bouncy little guy named Paul Simon was hustling for fraternity party gigs around Forest Hills High School in New York. Unfashionable and uncool, his vocal harmony duo Tom And Jerry had few takers. (When he and partner Art Garfunkel became famous in 1965 as Simon And Garfunkel, lots of people were kicking themselves.) As Paul And Jerry they actually reached No. 54 in charts with late 1957 **Hey Schoolgirl** but, despite appearance on *American Bandstand*, follow-ups failed to take off. They then went their separate ways, Paul Simon to Queens College and Art Garfunkel to New York's Columbia University.

While at college, Simon and fellow-student Carole King made demo tapes for publishers, which taught him techniques like overdubbing. Single **The Lone Teen Ranger** (recorded in 1962 as Jerry Landis) got to 97 in US charts. Dropping out of law school in 1964, Simon left for England to perform on folk circuit. Another single **He Was My Brother** (recorded as Paul Kane) was heard in New York by Columbia Records, who agreed to produce Simon And Garfunkel album. Simon returned to US where **Wednesday Morning 3 AM** was recorded under real names. Garfunkel had recorded for Octavia, then Warwick, as Arty Garr. Mixing traditional and modern folk songs, plus original numbers by Simon, album was less than successful. Simon returned to UK, where he recorded solo album **The Paul Simon Songbook**, containing own material, including **I Am A Rock**, and using only guitar accompaniment.

Producer Tom Wilson, who had helped electrify Dylan, saw possibilities in one track on **3 AM**. Adding electric guitar, bass and drums, Wilson released **Sounds Of Silence** as single, which shot to US No. 1. Hearing of success while in Europe, Simon again returned to US. In 1966 he and Garfunkel recorded **Sounds Of Silence** album, including material from **Songbook**, but with rock backing. **Homeward Bound**, written while waiting for train in Lancashire, became duo's first UK hit single, reaching No. 9 (No. 5 in US).

Simon's literate, poetic, yet aggressive, lyrics, filled with introspection, isolation and ironic protest, combined perfectly with Garfunkel's delicate vocal arrangements to create a sound that appealed to increasingly sophisticated young listeners. Tour of US and UK was followed by **Bookends**, then **The Graduate** soundtrack album which won Grammy for Best Original Motion Picture Score. Also received Grammy for **Mrs Robinson** (Best Record), supposedly written almost by accident while working on film score: new song had gap which, by chance, had same number of beats as name of character in Mike Nichols'

film, so Simon jokingly used her name to fill gap. When Nichols heard there was song called Mrs Robinson, he demanded to hear it, and it went straight into film.

By now Simon and Garfunkel were so popular that **3 AM** was finally released in UK. In 1970 **Bridge Over Troubled Water** became extraordinarily successful, title track reaching No. 1 in US and UK, and album selling over 9 million copies. Despite success, duo felt constrained by partnership, so split up after final concert in Forest Hills. Although Garfunkel occasionally did guest numbers with Simon, it was 11 years before they reunited for 1981 free concert in New York's Central Park. Nearly half a million people, including the Mayor, gathered there to be reminded of, as *New York Times* said, 'distinct musical identities that complement each other in a very special way'. Double-record, video and six-week European tour followed, giving much-needed boost to solo careers.

Hit Singles:

	US	UK
The Sounds Of Silence, 1966	1	–
Homeward Bound, 1966	5	9
I Am A Rock, 1966	3	17
A Hazy Shade Of Winter, 1966	13	–
At The Zoo, 1967	16	–
Scarborough Fair (Canticle), 1968	11	–
Mrs Robinson, 1968	1	4
Mrs Robinson (EP), 1969	–	9
The Boxer, 1969	7	6
Bridge Over Troubled Water, 1970	1	1
Cecilia, 1970	4	–
El Condor Pasa, 1970	18	–
My Little Town, 1975	9	–

Albums:

Wednesday Morning 3 AM (Columbia/CBS), 1966
The Sounds Of Silence (Columbia/CBS), 1966
Parsley, Sage, Rosemary And Thyme (Columbia/CBS), 1966
Bookends (Columbia/CBS), 1968
The Graduate (soundtrack) (Columbia/CBS), 1968

Below: Greatest Hits, Simon And Garfunkel's 60s classics. Courtesy CBS Records.

Bridge Over Troubled Water (Columbia/CBS), 1970
Greatest Hits (Columbia/CBS), 1972
Collected Works (Columbia/–), 1981
Collection (–/CBS), 1981
Concert In Central Park (Warner Bros), 1982

Carly Simon

US vocalist
Born New York, June 25, 1945

Career: Carly Simon emerged on New York folk scene in mid-60s with sister Lucy as Simon Sisters. Enjoyed minor hit on Kapp in 1964 with **Winkin', Blinkin' And Nod** while still studying at exclusive Sarah Lawrence College.

When Lucy got married, Carly went to France; did not return to singing until she met Bob Dylan's manager Albert Grossman. He brought in Dylan's producer Bob Johnson, and his regular backing musicians, including The Band, Al Kooper and Mike Bloomfield. He persuaded Dylan himself to write one song for 1966 New York session aimed at establishing Carly as 'the female Dylan'. The pair fell out, however, and tracks

Above: Carly Simon has not stopped the music since her debut in 1971.

were never released. Carly was rediscovered by Elektra Records' boss Jac Holzman at party in late 1969.

Esquire magazine film critic and screenplay writer Jacob Brackman had been writing material with her for some time. This provided content for debut album which included smash single **That's The Way I've Always Heard It Should Be**, a pensive song about difference between childhood dreams and adult realities. Theme was fully exploited in subsequent albums, notably on follow-up set **Anticipation**.

1972's **No Secrets** album made Simon international star thanks to classic single **You're So Vain** (featuring Mick Jagger on backing vocals). Reportedly, its anonymous non-hero was film star Warren Beatty, though Carly refused to confirm this.

Married to singer/songwriter James Taylor in 1973, the couple duetted on 1974 hit single **Mockingbird**, a mirror copy of Inez and Charlie Foxx's original. Following that year's **Hotcakes** album, had 18-month hiatus before appearance of **Playing Possum**, Simon's third LP with ace producer Richard Perry. After **Another Passenger** album (produced by Ted Templeman in 1976), Simon returned to Richard Perry in following year for Oscar and Grammy nominated song **Nobody Does It Better**, theme for James Bond film *The Spy Who Loved Me*.

Carly finished long contract with Elektra in 1979, then sojourned briefly with Warner Bros and Epic before settling at Arista in 1987. **Coming Around Again** album and single revitalized career which had been flagging since break up with James Taylor.

Simon won Grammy for *Working Girl* movie theme **Let The River Run** in 1990, and saw issue of two albums in same year, **My Romance**, an uncomfortable collection of standards, and **Have You Seen Me Lately?**, a more considered and largely self-composed set.

Daughter of founder of Simon & Schuster publishing empire, Carly herself enjoyed success with children's books *Amy And The Dancing Bear* and *The Boy Of The Bells* during early 90s.

Hit Singles:

	US	UK
That's The Way I've Always Heard It Should Be, 1971	10	–
Anticipation, 1972	13	–
You're So Vain, 1972	1	3

	US	UK
The Right Thing To Do, 1973	17	17
Haven't Got Time For The Pain, 1974	14	—
Nobody Does It Better, 1977	2	7
You Belong To Me, 1978	6	—
Jesse, 1980	11	—
Why, 1982	—	10
Coming Around Again, 1987	—	10

With James Taylor:

	US	UK
Mockingbird, 1974	5	34

Albums:

Carly Simon (Elektra), 1971
Anticipation (Elektra), 1971
No Secrets (Elektra), 1972

Above: Coming Around Again, Carly Simon. Courtesy Arista Records.

Hot Cakes (Elektra), 1974
Playing Possum (Elektra), 1975
Best Of (Elektra), 1976
Another Passenger (Elektra), 1976
Boys In The Trees (Elektra), 1978
Spy (Elektra), 1979
Come Upstairs (Warner Bros), 1980
Torch (Warner Bros), 1981
You're So Vain (—/Hallmark), 1981
Spoiled Girl (Epic), 1985
Hello Big Man (Elektra), 1986
Coming Around Again (Arista), 1987
My Romance (Arista), 1990
Have You Seen Me Lately? (Arista), 1990

Paul Simon

US composer, vocalist, guitarist
Born Newark, New Jersey, October 13, 1941

Career: Musical career began as schoolboy with, in 1964, startlingly successful partnership of Simon And Garfunkel. Far from remaining with Garfunkel throughout early years, Simon recorded on his own as Paul Kane, Jerry Landis and True Taylor, toured European folk circuit and made solo album of own material in London before duo's hit single **Sounds Of Silence** became US No. 1 in 1966. Pair then continued to record and toured together until splitting up amicably in 1970, at height of success.

Freed from constraints of partnership, Simon became more musically complex, incorporating variety of influences, including South American group Los Incas, jazz violin of Stephane Grapelli and Jamaican reggae. 1972 album **Paul Simon** not only provided US and UK hit single, **Mother And Child Reunion**, but reached No. 1 in UK. Dixie Hummingbirds gospel group and top quality session musicians were added to second LP **There Goes Rhymin' Simon**. Lyrically more relaxed, simpler and funkier, album gave Simon hit singles on both sides of Atlantic. Concert album **Live Rhymin'** from 1973 tour featured Jesse Dixon gospel group and South American band Urubamba performing new versions of his old songs.

In 1975, **Still Crazy After All These Years** blended musical changes with starkly precise personal songs. Containing US No. 1 single **50 Ways To Leave Your Lover**, album won two Grammys (Best Album and Best Male Pop Vocal Performance), bringing Simon's Grammy award total to 12. Disappointed that critical attention still focused on lyrics rather than musical ideas, Simon toured again with group of top-rated session musicians.

In 1980, following acting debut in *Annie Hall*, Simon produced, starred in and scored disappointing **One Trick Pony**. Film soundtrack, artist's first original release in five years, fared as badly as the movie.

Temporary reunion with Garfunkel for Central Park Concert seemed to give Simon new impetus, although 1983 release **Hearts And Bones** failed to generate prolonged appeal for artist.

Simon's interest in world music resulted in classic 1987 **Graceland** album, an anathema to certain anti-apartheid organizations because of it's involvement with South African musicians. Subsequent world tour prompted audience to remember the stature of this giant of pop music.

Graceland, which spawned hit single **You Can Call Me Al**, subsequently earned Grammy as Album Of The Year, and prompted similar examination of indigenous music in follow-up **The Rhythm Of The Saints** (1990). Simon's exploration of the percussive mood of South American music resulted in authentic collection, aided by collaboration of leading Brazilian musicians, including 14-piece Olodum drum troupe.

During 1991, Simon embarked on world Born At The Right Time pilgrimage, with band including South African and Brazilian musicians, plus noted jazz players Michael Brecker (tenor sax) and Steve Gadd (drums). Recording of free concert held in New York's Central Park in August during US leg of tour was released in November 1991 as **Concert In The Park** LP. The event attracted 750,000 fans, 500,000 more than had rejoiced in Simon And Garfunkel's reunion a decade earlier.

Below: Paul Simon, whose 1992 concerts in South Africa were threatened by factions of the anti-apartheid movement despite artist's honourable intentions.

Hit Singles:	US	UK
Mother And Child Reunion, 1972	4	5
Me And Julio Down By The Schoolyard, 1972	22	15
Take Me To The Mardi Gras, 1973	—	7
Kodachrome, 1973	2	—
Love Me Like A Rock, 1973	2	39
50 Ways To Leave Your Lover, 1976	1	23
Slip Slidin' Away, 1977	5	36
(What A) Wonderful World (with Art Garfunkel and James Taylor), 1978	17	—
Late In The Evening, 1980	6	—
Boy In The Bubble, 1986	—	33
The Obvious Child, 1990	—	15

Albums:

Paul Simon (Columbia/CBS), 1972*
There Goes Rhymin' Simon (Columbia/CBS), 1973*
Live Rhymin' (Columbia/CBS), 1974
Still Crazy After All These Years (Columbia/CBS), 1975*
Greatest Hits (Columbia/CBS), 1977
One Trick Pony (soundtrack) (Warner Bros), 1980
Hearts And Bones (Warner Bros), 1983
Graceland (Warner Bros), 1986
Negotiations And Lovesongs (1971-86) (Warner Bros), 1988
The Rhythm Of The Saints (Warner Bros), 1990
Paul Simon's Concert In The Park (Columbia), 1991
*Available as 5 LP set Collected Works (Columbia/—), 1981, with Paul Simon Songbook LP

Simple Minds

UK group formed 1977

Original line-up: Jim Kerr, vocals; Charlie Burchill, guitar; Brian McGee, drums; Mick MacNeil, keyboards; Derek Forbes, bass.

Career: Scottish outfit began reaping commercial rewards after years building following on pub, club and university tour circuit. Formed from remains of punk outfit Johnny And The Self-Abusers, band was quickly signed by Arista for national distribution of Edinburgh label Zoom.

Three albums later, Arista and band parted company, with Virgin promptly offering quintet new contract. 1981 LP **Sons And Fascination**, produced by Steve Hillage, entered UK Top 20, before McGee left to be replaced (temporarily) by Kenny Hyslop. Mike Ogletree took the drum chair for **New Gold Dream (81-82-83-84)**.

With percussionist Mel Gaynor recruited early 1983, band undertook series of festival gigs to further broaden ever-widening market. US tour in 1984 (supporting Pretenders) provided sufficient media attention — not least the marriage of Pretenders' vocalist Chrissie Hynde and Jim Kerr — to spur single **Don't You** to one million sales. Band subsequently featured in Live Aid concert at Philadelphia.

In 1985 band topped UK LP charts with **Once Upon A Time**, which featured new bass player John Giblin who had replaced Forbes, later to start Propaganda with McGee. Album spawned **Alive And Kicking** single which broke into Top 10 in both US and UK.

Following **Live In The City Of Light** (1987) and **Street Fighting Years** (1989) LPs, MacNeil quit, leaving Simple Minds in some disarray. Group had enjoyed further 45 chart action with poignant Belfast Child and cutting **This Is Your Land**, but retreated upon MacNeil's departure to ponder future.

In 1990 Kerr, with Burchill, Gaynor, Pete Vitesse (keyboards) and Malcolm Foster (bass) returned to studios to cut **Real Life** set, released in May 1991. The album reflected difficulties Kerr was having with his marriage to Chrissie Hynde and, with love as it's central theme, was in contrast to cutting content of previous work.

Simple Minds began world tour in April 1991, and showed no signs of previous upheaval which had threatened their future.

Following divorce from Chrissie Hynde, Kerr confirmed his taste for show-biz liaisons by marrying British starlet Patsy Kensit in January 1992.

Hit Singles:	US	UK
Promised You A Miracle, 1982	—	13
Glittering Prize, 1982	—	16
Waterfront, 1983	—	13
Speed Your Love To Me, 1984	—	20
Don't You Forget About Me, 1985	1	7
Alive And Kicking, 1985	11	7
All The Things She Said, 1986	—	9
Ghostdancing, 1986	—	13
Promised You A Miracle, 1987	—	19
Belfast Child, 1989	—	1
This Is Your Land, 1989	—	13
Kick It In, 1989	—	15
The Amsterdam (EP), 1989	—	18
Let There Be Love, 1991	—	6
See The Lights, 1991	40	20
Stand By Love, 1991	—	13

Albums:

Sons And Fascination (Virgin), 1981
New Gold Dream (81-82-83-84) (Virgin), 1982
Life In A Day (Virgin), 1982
Real To Real Cacophony (Virgin), 1982
Empire And Dance (Virgin), 1983
Celebration (Virgin), 1983
Sparkle In The Rain (Virgin), 1984
Once Upon A Time (Virgin), 1985
In The City Of Light (Virgin), 1987
Street Fighting Years (A&M/Virgin), 1989
Simple Minds (CD set) (—/Virgin), 1990
Real Life (A&M/—), 1991

Simply Red
UK group formed 1982

Original line-up: Mick 'Red' Hucknall, vocals; Chris Joyce, drums; Tony Bowers, bass; Tim Kellet, keyboards, trumpet; Fritz McIntryre, keyboards, vocals; Sylvan Richardson, guitars.

Career: Brought up in Manchester, ex-art student Hucknall formed excellent indie punk band called Frantic Elevators, who released 3 singles including early version of **Holding Back The Years**.

Formed first version of soul-influenced Simply Red in 1982 and was immediately offered a million-dollar deal by Seymour Stein, who owned Sire Records, to turn solo. Hucknall refused and Stein signed an unknown called Madonna instead! Three months later, Hucknall fired the rest of the band anyway. Recruited Joyce, Bowers and Kellet from fellow Manchester band Durutti Column, added McIntryre and later Richardson, before recording impressive demos and securing deal with Elektra in early 1985.

Teamed up with soul producer Stewart Levene and recorded version of **Money's Too Tight** by Valentine Brothers as first single, which created media interest but failed to chart in US. Released second single **Come To My Aid**, supported James Brown in London and recorded debut album **Picture Book** which featured further near-miss singles **Jericho** and **Red Box**. Then came hit single **Holding Back The Years**.

Supported UB40 in UK tour, then headlined own world tour throughout 1986. Hucknall, with instant image of curly red hair and walking cane, became media personality, writing songs for Diana Ross and co-composing with Lamont Dozier.

Recorded second album **Men And Women** with late Alex Sadkin, covering songs by Sly Stone, Bunny Wailer and Cole Porter! Musically, the blend was both melodic and rhythmic, topped off by Hucknall's distinctive 'white soul' vocals.

Further hits followed, notably the cool, sparsely arranged version of Cole Porter's **Everytime We Say Goodbye**, and Hucknall and crew played another sell-out world tour through 1987, despite vocalist's serious throat problem.

A New Flame album (1989) debuted at No. 1 in UK charts in February 1989, and spawned Hucknall's hit interpretations of soul standards **It's Only Love** and **If You Don't Know Me By Now**, the latter of which topped US listings and won Grammy as Best R&B Single Of The Year.

With producer Stewart Levene still at the helm, Simply Red cut **Stars** LP for 1991 release, from which **Something Got Me Started** and title track were chart cuts.

Hit Singles:

	US	UK
Holding Back The Years, 1985	1	2
Money's Too Tight, 1985	—	13
The Right Thing, 1987	—	11
Ev'rytime We Say Goodbye, 1987	—	11
If You Don't Know Me By Now, 1989	1	2
A New Flame, 1989	—	17
It's Only Love, 1989	—	13
Something Got Me Started, 1991	—	11
Stars, 1991	—	8

Albums:
Picture Book (Elektra), 1985
Men And Women (WEA/Elektra), 1987
A New Flame (Elektra/—), 1989
Stars (Eastwest), 1991

Above: Picture Book, Simply Red. Courtesy Elektra Records.

Siouxsie And The Banshees
US group formed 1976

Original line-up: Siouxsie Sioux, vocals; Steve Severin, bass; Sid Vicious, drums; Marco Pirroni, guitar.

Career: Siouxsie had closely followed Sex Pistols attack on polished, professional sound of established rock bands; without rehearsal formed above line-up for one gig. Within two months Vicious and Pirroni were gone, Vicious to Sex Pistols and Pirroni to play in The Motels, then with Adam And The Ants. Kenny Morris took over drums and Peter Fenton assumed guitar.

Refusal to sign standard recording contract meant band was ignored by major firms. Plans to sign with Kit Lambert's Track label fell through when Track folded. By July 1977 Fenton was replaced by John McKay.

Polydor finally signed Siouxsie but found itself in confrontation with band. Following release of two LPs, McKay and Morris quit in autumn 1979 just as band started extensive tour. Ex-Slits member, Budgie, was quickly taken on as permanent drummer and Cure guitarist Robert Smith was 'loaned' to meet tour dates. John McGeoch (ex-Magazine) then joined as permanent guitarist. **Kaleidoscope** LP also featured great guitar work from Steve Jones (ex-Pistols, Professionals), yet studio work never matched live enthusiasm of Siouxsie on stage. Despite strong LP **Ju Ju**, spirit of band is best experienced on **Once Upon A Time/The Singles**.

The Banshees remained a viable proposition through the 80s, despite Siouxsie and Budgie's parallel venture The Creatures, formed in 1981; enjoyed UK hit singles with **Mad-Eyed Screamers**, **Miss The Girl** and **Right Now**. Despite loss of McGeoch, who quit after **A Kiss In The Dreamhouse** (1982), Banshees made UK Top 10 with cover of Beatles' **Dear Prudence** (1983). Robert Smith returned to Cure duty in 1984, his replacement being Johnnie Carruthers (ex-Clock DVA) who featured on **Hyena** in same year. Signed to Geffen Records in the States, Siouxsie and the boys eventually cracked US charts with 1986 set **Tinderbox**, from which **Candy Man** single also made hit listings.

Carruthers left unit in 1987, following recording of unique **Through The Looking Glass** album, a collection of classic pop material from which Dylan's **This Wheel's On Fire** was UK hit. Band added guitarist John Klein and keyboard player Martin McCarrick for subsequent UK tour and LP **Peepshow** the following year; **Superstition** set was released in June 1991.

Hit Singles:

	US	UK
Hong Kong Garden, 1978	—	7
Happy House, 1980	—	17
Dear Prudence, 1983	—	3
Candyman, 1986	—	34
This Wheel's On Fire, 1987	—	14
Peek-A-Boo, 1988	53	16

Creatures:

	US	UK
Right Now, 1983	—	7

Albums:
The Scream (—/Polydor), 1978
Join Hands (—/Polydor), 1979
Kaleidoscope (Gem/Polydor), 1980
Ju Ju (Gem/Polydor), 1981
Once Upon A Time/The Singles (Gem/Polydor), 1981
A Kiss In The Dreamhouse (Polydor), 1982
Nocturne (Geffen/Polydor), 1983
Hyena (Polydor), 1984
Tinderbox (Wonderland), 1986
Through The Looking Glass (Wonderland), 1987
Peepshow (Geffen/Wonderland), 1988
Superstition (Geffen/—), 1991

Siouxsie and Budgie as The Creatures:
Wild Thing (EP) (—/Polydor), 1981
Feast (—/Polydor), 1983

Skid Row
US group formed 1987

Original line-up: Dave Sabo, guitar; Rachel Bolan, bass; Sebastian Basch, vocals; Scott Hill, guitar; Rob Affuso, drums.

Career: Latest in a line of East Coast rock 'n' rollers, whose first headline tour (Japan in autumn of 1991) and thumping second LP **Slave To The Grind** promised a secure future in this flourishing musical genre; album debuted at No. 1 in US charts.

Signed to Atlantic Records in 1988, and with the backing of Bon Jovi manager Doc McGhee, Skid Row had short apprenticeship before basking in 'the stadium effect'. Debut self-titled album was skippered by Mötley Crüe producer Mike Wagner, and critics seized on similarities between bands. Like the Crüe, Skid Row also have ambition in the 'seek and destroy' department.

Coast to coast US tour with Bon Jovi in 1989 pushed album to platinum status, and band quickly outgrew 'supporting act' tag.

Hit Singles:

	US	UK
18 And Life, 1990	—	12
Monkey Business, 1991	—	19

Albums:
Skid Row (Atlantic), 1989
Slave To The Grind (Atlantic), 1991

Left: Old 'Simply' himself, the ubiquitous Mick 'The Greatest' Hucknall.

Slade

UK group formed 1966

Original line-up: Noddy Holder, vocals, guitar; Dave Hill, guitar; Jimmy Lea, bass, piano; Don Powell, drums.

Career: Group started out playing routine material in Midlands clubs as 'N Betweens. Changed name to Ambrose Slade; discovered in 1969 at Rasputin's Club in London's Bond Street by Chas Chandler, during era of original skinhead cult. Chandler, who had been member of Animals and had already turned Jimi Hendrix into a superstar, decided on cash-in image. Short-cropped hair 'bovver boots', rolled-up jeans, etc., were adopted. Audiences saw it as pure marketing ploy and gambit failed.

Chandler persevered, hanging on to Polydor contract while shortening band's name to Slade. Re-make of Bobby Marchan's **Get Down And Get With It**, also a US R&B hit for Little Richard, got them into the hit chart. Image now was of aggressive glitter, heavy stomping and loud guitar. Adopting gimmick of misspelt song titles, band were projected as teen working-class heroes. **Look Wot You Dun, Take Me Bak 'Ome, Mama Weer All Crazee Now, Cum On Feel The Noize**, and others made them Britain's top pop band of 1972-74. Between October 1971 and October 1974 released 12 singles, all of which made UK Top 5, six of them reaching No 1. 1973 Christmas hit **Merry Xmas Everybody** also made No. 1 and charted again in December 1980, 1981, 1982 and 1983.

Songwriting partnership of Lee and Holder now mentioned in same breath as Lennon/McCartney, while band were touted as new Beatles. However, despite success, songs elicited few cover versions and Slade never showed Beatles' diversity of musical talent.

Attempts to broaden base of appeal served only to dampen fires of Slade fever. Spent tail-end of 1974 working on *Flame* movie project in which they starred as mythical band. Despite some flair for acting and good script, movie made little impact, though yielded hit semi-ballad **Far Far Away**. Time spent trying to crack Stateside market served only to further weaken grasp on UK. 1975 was bad year, but Slade bounced back in 1976 with stomping **Let's Call It Quits**. Slade didn't listen to own message and revived career on back of heavy metal boom with **Lock Up Your Daughters**.

Quartet enjoyed further revival in mid-80s, when **Keep Your Hands Off My Power Supply** cracked US album charts; spawned single **Run Runaway**, which earned place in US Top 20. **My Oh My** 45 also scored, making Top 2 in UK charts.

Above: Slade, one of the UK's most popular rock bands.

Slade celebrated 20th anniversary in 1986, although **You Boyze Make Big Noize** LP in following year spelled a temporary halt to group's career. Unit regrouped for cover of Chris Montez's twist opus **Let's Dance** in 1988 before venturing into solo projects, Holder enjoying particular success as DJ for prominent Northern UK radio station Radio Piccadilly.

Following three-year break, Slade reformed for **Radio Wall Of Sound** single in 1991, another UK hit which prompted album and new greatest hits collection, which included group's first British No. 1, **Coz I Love You**, cut 20 years previously.

Hit Singles:

	US	UK
Get Down And Get With It, 1971	—	16
Coz I Luv You, 1971	—	1
Look Wot You Dun, 1972	—	4
Take Me Back 'Ome, 1972	—	1
Mama Weer All Crazee Now, 1972	—	1
Good Buy T' Jane, 1972	—	2
Cum On Feel The Noize, 1973	—	1
Skweeze Me Pleeze Me, 1973	—	1
My Friend Stan, 1973	—	2
Merry Xmas Everybody, 1973	—	1
Everyday, 1974	—	3
Bangin' Man, 1974	—	3
Far Far Away, 1974	—	2
How Does It Feel, 1975	—	15
Thanks For The Memory (Wham Bam Thank You Mam), 1975	—	7
In For A Penny, 1975	—	11
Let's Call It Quits, 1976	—	11
We'll Bring The House Down, 1981	—	10
My Oh My, 1983	37	2
Run Run Away, 1984	20	7
All Join Hands, 1984	—	15

Albums:

Slade Alive (Polydor), 1972
Slade Alive Volume 2 (–/Barn), 1978
Return To Base (–/Barn), 1979
We'll Bring The House Down (–/Cheapskate), 1981
Lock Up Your Daughters (–/RCA), 1981
Slade On Stage (–/RCA), 1982
The Amazing Kamikaze Syndrome (RCA), 1983
Slade's Greats (Polydor), 1984
Crackers (Telstar), 1985
Rogues Gallery (RCA), 1985
You Boyz Make Big Noise (RCA), 1987
Wall Of Hits (Polydor), 1991

Right: Greatest Hits, a Small Faces re-issue, released in 1977. Courtesy Immediate Records.

Sly And The Family Stone

US group formed 1966

Original line-up: Sly Stone, vocals, keyboards, guitar; Freddie Stone,, guitar; Cynthia Robinson, trumpet; Jerry Martini, saxophone; Rosie Stone, piano, vocals; Larry Graham, bass; Greg Errico, drums.

Career: The history of Sly And Family Stone is virtually the history of founder and guiding light Sly Stone. Born Sylvester Stewart in 1944 in Dallas, Texas, he played in various bands with brother Freddie after family had moved to California. As lead singer for group called The Viscanes, he made his recording debut with **Yellow Moon**, which became small local hit.

In late teens and early twenties Sly gained experience in many areas of the music business, writing and producing successfully for artists like Bobby Freeman, Mojo Men and Beau Brummels, and working as DJ on San Francisco radio. In 1966 he put together own band, The Stoners, which was forerunner of Family Stone.

Formation of Family Stone coincided with upsurge of psychedelia centred in San Francisco. An interracial, male and female band, Family Stone pioneered acid-soul-rock, combining punch brass riffs and stinging rock guitar with wild vocal harmonies and an irresistible dance beat.

Success came in early 1968. Signed to Epic, band released LP **A Whole New Thing**, and single **Dance To The Music**. **Dance** was an exhilarating rock-soul amalgam that brought breath of fresh air to charts both sides of Atlantic.

Follow-up single **M'Lady** did better in UK than US, where it only just made Top 100, but third single, **Everyday People**, topped American charts. **Stand**, the album from which it was taken, went gold, and title track was also hit.

Sly And The Family Stone become in-demand concert act, and were a high point of 1969 Woodstock Festival. Sly's **I Want To Take You Higher** became Festival's anthem, but the Festival turned out to be zenith of band's career. More record success was still to come, but personality clashes and drug problems led to band (in particular Sly, who often failed to show up at scheduled concerts) becoming increasingly unreliable. Sly's darker side was reflected in pessimistic vision of 1971 album **There's A Riot Going On**.

Following years saw band undergo various personnel changes. Collection of Sly's old hits, **Back On The Right Track**, was issued in 1979, and in 1982 he surfaced in partnership with George Clinton. Seminal cultural figure of his time, Sly Stone showed that rock could be funky as well as heavy.

As a footnote, Sly Stone was incarcerated in 1989 for cocaine possession; later ordered to complete sentence in drug rehabilitation centre.

Hit Singles:

	US	UK
Dance To The Music, 1968	8	7
Everyday People, 1969	1	36
Hot Fun In The Summertime, 1969	2	—
Thank You Falettinme Be Mice Elf Agin, 1970	1	—
Family Affair, 1971	1	15
Runnin' Away, 1972	23	17
If You Want Me To Stay, 1973	12	—

Albums:

Dance To The Music (Epic/Direction), 1968
Life (Epic), 1968
A Whole New Thing (Epic), 1970
High Energy (Epic), 1975
Back On The Right Track (Warner Bros), 1979
Recorded 64/67 (Sculpture), 1979
Greatest Hits (Epic), 1981
Ain't But The One Way (Warner Bros), 1983
Fresh (Edsel), 1987
Free (Edsel), 1987

Worth Searching Out:
Stand (Epic), 1969
There's A Riot Going On (Epic), 1971

Small Faces

UK group formed 1965

Original line-up: Steve Marriott, vocals, guitar; Jimmy Winston, organ; Ronnie 'Plonk' Lane, bass; Kenny Jones, drums.

Career: The Who were group that adopted mod image as sales ploy; the Small Faces were mods who became a group.

Formed in London's East End, Small Faces (so called because of members' diminutive size, 'faces' being flash mods) were built round lead singer, former child actor Marriott. Wearing razor-sharp clothes, group initially set out to re-create the American R&B soul music espoused by fellow mods. Borrowing riff from Solomon Burke's **Everybody Needs Somebody To Love** they came up with potent **Watcha Gonna Do About It?** to crash chart in September 1965. Ian MacLagan replaced Winston for follow-up **I've Got Mine**, which flopped but was quickly followed by successes, **Sha La La La Lee**, **Hey Girl**, the chart-topping **All Or Nothing** and **My Mind's Eye**. All were co-written by Marriott and Lane (one of the strongest songwriting duos of the 1960s), moving increasingly into straight pop vein.

Switching to Immediate label, set up by Rolling Stones' manager Andrew Loog Oldham, and Tony Calder, Small Faces came up with more interesting material with clever and evocative **Itchycoo Park** (1967), their only US Top 20 record, and the perceptive **Lazy Sunday** (1968). Then came superlative **Ogden's Nut Gone Flake** album (1968), its classic circular fold-out sleeve a replica of the familiar UK tobacco brand.

Marriott left in early 1969 to join Peter Frampton in formation of Humble Pie. Lane, Jones and MacLagan soldiered on. Went through very rough patch but turned down offers to work as backing band for solo artists, linking up with Jeff Beck Group emigrés Rod Stewart and Ron Wood, later the next year as The Faces. Wood was eventually invited to join Rolling Stones and Stewart concentrated increasingly on solo image, leading to Faces' early demise.

Small Faces re-formed in 1976 with following line-up: Marriott; Jones; MacLagen; Rick Wills (ex-Roxy Music) on bass. Cut two mediocre LPs **Playmates** and **78 In The Shade** in attempt to cash in on then extant mod revival, but, despite new generation following, Small Faces' fortunes could not be regenerated.

Lane, a multiple sclerosis victim, formed Slim Chance and in 1985 was catalyst for charity record to help fellow sufferers. Steve Marriott was killed in house fire in 1991.

Hit Singles:

	US	UK
Watcha Gonna Do About It?, 1965	—	14
Sha La La La Lee, 1966	—	3
Hey Girl, 1966	—	10
All Or Nothing, 1966	—	1
My Mind's Eye, 1966	—	4
Here Comes The Nice, 1967	—	12
Itchycoo Park, 1967	16	3
Tin Soldier, 1967	—	9
Lazy Sunday, 1968	—	2
Universal, 1968	—	16
Itchycoo Park, 1975	—	9

Albums:

Small Faces (—/Decca), 1966
Ogdens Nut Gone Flake (Immediate), 1967
Rock Roots: The Small Faces (—/Decca) 1976*
Greatest Hits (—/Immediate), 1977
Playmates (Atlantic), 1977
78 In The Shade (Atlantic), 1978
Big Hits (—/Virgin), 1980
For Your Delight (—/Virgin), 1981
By Appointment (Accord/—), 1981
Sha La La La Lee (—/Decca), 1981
Collection (Collector), 1985
*Features all Decca A&B sides

With Amen Corner:

Amen Corner And Small Faces (—/New World), 1975

Worth Searching Out:

There Are But Four Small Faces (Immediate), 1967
Autumn Stone (Castle), 1969

The Smiths

UK group formed 1982

Original line-up: Johnny Marr, guitar; Stephen Morrissey, vocals; Andy Rourke, bass; Mike Joyce, drums.

Career: Some would say wimpish and fragile, others poetic and concise, but while opinion was divided The Smiths established a loyal and substantial following early in their career.

After a handful of gigs, group signed to Rough Trade, who fought off (so their press office says) six-figure offers from several major record companies. First single **Hand In Glove** (1983) preceded sessions for

Above: Meat Is Murder, The Smiths. Courtesy Rough Trade Records.

Below: Morrissey (centre) seen during harmonious times with The Smiths.

debut album produced by ex-Teardrop Explodes/Fashion member Troy Tate. Tate's efforts were subsequently dumped when group met John Porter, who re-recorded material for **The Smiths**. Extensive UK tour hurried LP to instant No. 2 position in Britain, with gold status quickly following.

Bizarre coupling of Smiths with Sandie Shaw (Morrissey's favourite female singer) earned **Hand In Glove** single a UK Top 30 entry in spring of 1984.

Following year saw **Meat Is Murder** album expound band's vegetarian lifestyle; LP entered UK charts at No. 1. Succession of British hit singles following **What Difference Does It Make** (1984) seemed certain to establish Smiths at forefront of pop

Above: Strangeways Here We Come, The Smiths. Courtesy Rough Trade Records.

circus, but rumblings of discontent within group placed a question mark over their long-term future.

In 1987 Morrissey/Marr conflict split band. Marr subsequently adopted 'have guitar, will travel' approach and gigged with Pretenders, Bryan Ferry, Midge Ure, Talking Heads and Paul McCartney, among others. Later joined The The, and collaborated in temporary Electronic aggregation with Neil Tennant from Pet Shop Boys and New Order's Bernard Sumner. Their 1990 single **Getting Away With It** made UK Top 20.

Stephen Morrissey launched solo career with **Suedehead** single in 1988, and saw debut LP **Viva Hate** break into UK charts at No. 1. Subsequent sets **Bona Drag** (1990) and **Kill Uncle** (1991), the latter produced by former Madness duo Clive Langer and Alan Winstanley, were swathed by Morrissey's oblique and morbid message. Artist gained popularity in US throughout early 90s and returned to live gigs in 1991 with mega-shows in Dublin and London as part of UK tour.

Morrissey's haunting but ephemeral compositions have a certain compulsive quality. We say he's the Emily Bronte of the 90s.

Hit Singles:

	US	UK
What Difference Does It Make, 1984	—	12
Heaven Knows I'm Miserable Now, 1984	—	10
William It Was Really Nothing, 1984	—	17
The Boy With The Thorn In His Side, 1985	—	15
Ask, 1986	—	14
Panic, 1986	—	11
Girlfriend In A Coma, 1987	—	13
Shoplifters Of The World, 1987	—	12
Sheila Take A Bow, 1987	—	10
I Started Something I Couldn't Finish, 1987	—	23

Johnny Marr (In Electronic):
Getting Away With It, 1990   38   12

Morrissey Solo:
Suedehead — Nowhere   —   28

Albums:

The Smiths (Rough Trade), 1983
Meat Is Murder (Rough Trade), 1984
Hatful of Hollow (Rough Trade), 1985
Louder Than Bombs (Rough Trade), 1987
The World Won't Listen (Rough Trade), 1987
Sheila Take A Bow (Pacific), 1987
The Queen Is Dead (Rough Trade), 1987
Big Mouth Strikes Again (Rough Trade), 1987

Strangeways Here We Come (Rough Trade), 1987
'Rank' Live (Sire/Rough Trade), 1988

Morrisey Solo:
Viva Hate! (Parlophone), 1988
Bona Drag (Sire), 1990
Kill Uncle (Sire), 1991

Soul II Soul
UK group formed 1982

Original line-up: Jazzie B, vocals, arranger; Philip Harvey, mixer, DJ, arranger.

Career: London based rap/DJ outfit whose tuned ear for commercial sounds thrust them swiftly into mainstream of UK's burgeoning dance scene.

Duo, with friends, built a solid following at African Centre in London's Covent Garden and, with addition of Nellee Hooper (electronics), signed deal with Virgin Records club label 10 Records. Early singles **Fairplay** and **Feel Free** generated moderate chart action, before breakthrough cut **Keep On Moving** (with Caron Wheeler on vocals) made UK Top 10, and later US Top 20.

Soul II Soul established unique mix of dance/soul/rap rhythms with 1989 UK No. 1 **Back To Life (However Do You Want Me)**, whereupon Wheeler quit to establish solo career.

US and UK tours in 1990 confirmed infectious following for the aggregation, whose stage presentation successfully re-created studio work. Confirmation of Soul II Soul's ability arrived in welter of *Soul Train* TV show and *Rolling Stone* magazine awards.

With the Soul II Soul empire now including retail fashion outlets and thriving merchandising business, Jazzie B and Hooper expended further energy on production/arrangement jobs for Sinéad O'Connor, Fine Young Cannibals and Neneh Cherry.

After serious car accident caused cancellation of 1991 US tour, with Jazzie B hospitalized with back injuries, new label venture with Motown Records, **Funki Dred** (April 1991), put Soul II Soul back on course for extended chart action.

Hit Singles:	US	UK
Keep On Moving, 1989	11	5
Back To Life (However Do You Want Me), 1989	4	1
Get A Life, 1989	54	3
A Dream's A Dream, 1990	—	6

Albums:
Keep On Moving (Virgin/Ten), 1989
A New Decade (Virgin/Ten), 1990
Club Classics Volume 1 (Virgin/Ten), 1990
Funki Dred (Motown), 1991

Spandau Ballet
UK group formed 1979

Original line-up: Tony Hadley, vocals; Gary Kemp, guitar; Martin Kemp, bass; Steve Norman, saxophone; John Keeble, drums.

Career: Formed by young Londoners to provide soundtrack for 'futurist'/'new romantic' activities in ultra fashion-conscious London night clubs. Early on managed by

Right: Spandau Ballet in the early 1980s, dismissed as hype at first but came through with numerous hits.

Above: Jazzie B from Soul II Soul jives to the rap beat.

Steve Strange, before latter formed Visage. Band refused to publicize early gigs other than by word of mouth, creating elitist image which led to exposure on TV documentary about London scene. Played gig on HMS Belfast moored on River Thames.

Signed with Chrysalis Records in mid-1980, given own label identity, Reformation Records — such a distinction for unknown band that success was assured.

First single and album both made Top 5. Third single showed that band could provide more than 'futurist' sound. One side, **Glow**, using jazz funk, provided new direction for next single, **Chant No. 1**, which reached Top 3, using black London horn section Beggar And Co. Bubble seemed to be bursting in early 1982, but second LP was released in normal form and as boxed set of 12-inch singles. Worked live in Europe and America, while **Instinction** and **Lifeline** were both re-mixed from LP to become Top 10 singles.

Success continued in 1983 with release of third LP, **True**; title track topped UK singles chart in first half of year. Despite cries of 'hype', Ballet had earned distinction as major UK act, vying with fellow glamsters Duran Duran as most popular band in Britain.

Following **Parade** LP (1984), Ballet sought release from Chrysalis and then signed long-term million-dollar deal with CBS in 1986. **Through The Barricades** was first collection for new company, the title track making UK Top 10.

In 1988, the Kemp Brothers were cast as notorious 60s London gangsters Ronald and Reggie Kray for movie *The Krays*, which received critical acclaim and generally good reviews for Gary and Martin.

Heart Like A Sky set (1989) proved final outing for CBS, who appeared unhappy at Spandau Ballet's pure 'British' sound. LP was not released in USA, and band have since disappeared.

Hit Singles:	US	UK
To Cut A Long Story Short, 1980	—	5
The Freeze, 1981	—	17
Muscle Bound/Glow, 1981	—	10
Chant No. 1 (I Don't Need This Pressure On), 1981	—	3
Instinction, 1982	—	10
Lifeline, 1982	—	7
Communication, 1983	—	12
True, 1983	—	1
Gold, 1983	29	2
Only When You Leave, 1983	34	3
I'll Fly For You, 1984	—	9
Highly Strung, 1984	—	15
Round And Round, 1985	—	18
Fight For Ourselves, 1986	—	15
Through The Barricades, 1986	—	6

Albums:
Journeys To Glory (Chrysalis), 1981
Diamond (—/Chrysalis), 1982
True (—/Chrysalis), 1983
Parade (Chrysalis), 1984
Singles Collection (Chrysalis), 1985
Through The Barricades (CBS), 1986
Twelve Inch Mixes (Reformation), 1986
Heart Like A Sky (—/CBS), 1989

The Specials
UK group formed 1977

Original line-up: Terry Hall, vocals; Lynval Golding, guitar, vocals; Jerry Dammers, keyboards; Roddy Radiation, guitar; Horace 'Gentleman' Parker, bass; Neville Staples, percussion, vocals; John Bradbury, drums.

Career: Exploited Jamaican ska style, which pre-dated reggae, The Specials struck a chord with British youth — black and white — and especially, the unemployed. Dubbed their up-dated and racially integrated dance music style 'Two-Tone'. Band, formed in Coventry during middle of 1977, seemed set to lead nationwide ska revival with **Message To You Rudy** hit. Instead they evolved own lyrically strong 'lounge music' style, featuring veteran trombone player Rico Rodriguez as regular guest.

Too Much Too Young, **Rat Race**, **Do Nothing** and other hits showed way for UB40, Madness, Bad Manners, and other like-conceived groups. As keyboard player Jerry Dammers increasingly dominated proceedings as songwriter and producer, discontent flared. In summer 1981 singers Neville Staples and Terry Hall and guitarist

Lynval Golding were already preparing to split and form Fun Boy Three. They laid down tracks for debut album while The Specials' superb **Ghost Town** — which summed up riot-torn summer — was soaring to UK No. 1.

Remnants of The Specials, now totally Dammers-dominated, revived earlier name, Specials AKA. Backed girl singer Rhoda on controversially acidic **The Boiler** before re-emerging in chart with effective **Free Nelson Mandela** single.

However, unit was short-lived as Dammers drifted into variety of projects including charity **Starvation** single and collaboration with Robert Wyatt for **Winds Of Change** 45; he helped organize Nelson Mandela's 70th Birthday Party tribute at Wembley in 1988.

Hit Singles:	US	UK
Gangsters, 1979	—	6
A Message To You Rudy/Nite Club, 1979	—	10
Too Much Too Young (EP), 1980	—	1
Rat Race/Rude Boys Outa Jail, 1980	—	5
Stereotype/International Jet Set, 1980	—	6
Do Nothing/Maggie's Farm, 1981	—	4
Ghost Town, 1981	—	1
Free Nelson Mandela, 1984	—	9

Albums:
Specials (Chrysalis), 1979
More Specials (Chrysalis/Two Tone), 1980
The Singles Collection (Chrysalis), 1991

Dusty Springfield

UK vocalist
Born Mary O'Brien, London, April 16, 1939

Career: First made impression as part of pop-folk trio The Springfields which had handful of hits in early 1960s. Group broke up in September 1963, and Springfield embarked on solo career. Forsaking folksiness for more soulful style (then being popularized by Motown), she was responsible for series of hit singles which combined commercial catchiness with distinctive vocalizing. More than any other British female singer of the time she impressed the US market; five singles made US Top 20.

Well-received by critics and fellow professionals, Springfield was better equipped vocally than most of her contemporaries, and could make creditable job of more demanding soul material. This ability was best displayed on 1969 LP **Dusty In Memphis**, produced by Jerry Wexler, featuring Memphis session mafia. Although in retrospect not as brilliant as made out to be at the time, it remains one of the best soul efforts of this era.

Son Of A Preacher Man in late 1968 was Springfield's last major chart success; she then began to fade from sight amid rumours of personal problems. During 1970s she lived somewhat reclusively in America, occasionally recording and acting as back-up for other singers. A flurry of activity in 1978-79 resulted in a couple of LPs.

More recently, Springfield has returned to the public eye in a number of incarnations, most particularly as guest vocalist on Pet Shop Boys' Top 10 single **What Have I Done To Deserve This**. The Boy's Tennant and Lowe then wrote and produced Springfield's 1989 Top 20 offering **Nothing Has Been Proved** (from *Scandal* movie)

and **In Private**. 1990 album **Reputation**, featuring further new material by Tennant and Lowe, made UK Top 20.

In 1991 Springfield added to her coffers when awarded substantial damages pertaining to portrayal as drunk by noted British impressionist Bobby Davro.

Hit Singles:	US	UK
I Only Want To Be With You, 1963	12	4
Stay Awhile, 1964	38	13
I Just Don't Know What To Do With Myself, 1964	—	3
Wishin' And Hopin', 1964	6	—
Losing You, 1964	—	9
In The Middle Of Nowhere, 1965	—	8
Some Of Your Lovin', 1965	—	8
Little By Little, 1966	—	17
You Don't Have To Say You Love Me, 1966	4	1
Going Back, 1966	—	10
All I See Is You, 1966	20	9
I'll Try Anything, 1967	40	13
I Close My Eyes And Count To Ten, 1968	—	4
Son Of A Preacher Man, 1968	10	9
Am I The Same Girl, 1969	—	9
Nothing Has Been Proved, 1989	—	16
In Private, 1989	—	14

With Pet Shop Boys:

	US	UK
What Have I Done To Deserve This?, 1987	2	2

Albums:
Golden Hits (Philips), 1966
This Is Dusty Springfield Volume 2 — The Magic Garden (—/Philips), 1973
You Don't Have To Say You Love Me (—/Contour), 1976
It Begins Again (Liberty/Mercury), 1978
Greatest Hits (Mercury/Phonogram), 1979
Living Without Your Love (Liberty/Mercury), 1979
Memphis Plus (Mercury), 1980
Very Best Of (—/K-Tel), 1981
Whiteheat (Casablanca/—), 1982
Reputation (—/Parlophone), 1990

Worth Searching Out:
Dusty In Memphis (Atlantic/Philips), 1969
Love Songs (Philips), 1984
Beautiful Feelings (Mercury), 1985
Dusty — The Silver Collection (Philips), 1988

American critic Jon Landau had become acquainted with Springsteen and liked his shows. In May 1974 he wrote review citing Springsteen as 'rock and roll future'. The phrase caught and, aided by Columbia, pushed Springsteen into glare of publicity.

Landau and Springsteen became friends and when sessions for next LP bogged down, Springsteen asked Landau to help out production. **Born To Run** finally justified media hype and deservedly became instant success. It also continued maturation process begun on second album.

The LP ensured sell-out tours for 1975, during which Springsteen honed down live act to professional perfection. It was obviously time to start on follow-up album. Instead, Springsteen's career came to halt when he and Appel became involved in contract dispute. This delayed new releases until 1978, when **Darkness On The Edge Of Town** appeared. Springsteen's vision of everyman's future continued on excellent album **The River**.

Deciding that studio tapes had lost raw edge, Springsteen instead released demos. Decision vindicated when **Nebraska** hit No. 1 in US charts. With Miami Steve Van Zandt, revived Gary 'US' Bonds' career with raw-edged LPs in early 1980s. Van Zandt subsequently quit E-Street line-up, although continued to collaborate with Springsteen notably on **We Are The World** 45, **USA For Africa** LP and **Sun City** anti-apartheid single in 1985.

Springsteen returned to the road (with former Crazy Horse member Nils Lofgren on guitar) for Born In The USA world tour, titled after 1984 set, **Born In The USA**, which topped both US and UK album charts; LP spawned five hit singles and totalled over 10 million sales. In mid-tour, artist took time out to marry Julie-Ann Phillips in Oregon. As testimony to his awesome stage presence, **Live 1975-85** was 1986 release, a five-album collection which generated single chart action with **War** and **Fire** cuts.

Springsteen returned to studios in 1987 for **Tunnel Of Love**, a less frenetic offering, but which still earned mega-sales and Top 20 singles with title track and **Brilliant**

Bruce Springsteen

US composer, vocalist, guitarist
Born Freehold, New Jersey, September 23, 1949

Career: Springsteen grew up watching Beatles revolutionizing rock 'n' roll and decided he wanted to be a rock star. Started gigging in New York clubs, formed various bands, went to California. Then returned to East Coast, but failed to hit success.

In 1972 he hired Mike Appel to manage him. Appel took him to John Hammond of Columbia Records who supposedly was as impressed with Springsteen as he had been years ago with Bob Dylan. Result was recording of folkish **Greetings From Asbury Park, New Jersey**. But Bruce still failed to make it.

Second LP, **The Wild, The Innocent And The E-Street Shuffle**, carried the seeds for developing back-up group, the E Street Band. It also marked Springsteen as original talent rather than another Dylan soundalike.

Live shows began to take on marathon proportions of epic tales, true-life ballads, whispered intimacies and buckets of sweat.

Below: Born In The USA, Bruce Springsteen. Courtesy CBS Records.

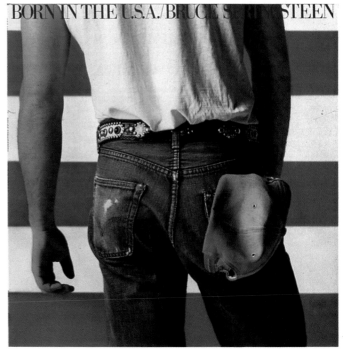

Disguise. Album prompted Tunnel Of Love Express Tour, which saw Springsteen perform in US and Europe.

Latterly artist has immersed himself in charity work. A notable inclusion for Live Aid, Springsteen has also gigged for the Rainforest Foundation and Amnesty International, and contributed to **The Last Temptation Of Elvis** album for Nordoff-Robbins Music Therapy.

Divorced in March 1989, Springsteen's relationship with E-Street vocalist Patti Scialfa maintained high profile. Two new albums were due for simultaneous release in spring 1992.

Hit Singles:

	US	UK
Hungry Heart, 1980	5	—
Fade Away, 1981	20	—
Dancing In The Dark, 1984	2	4
Cover Me, 1984	38	16
Born In The U.S.A., 1985*	9	—
I'm On Fire, 1985*	6	5
Glory Days, 1985	5	17
I'm Going Down, 1985	9	—
Santa Claus Is Coming To Town, 1985	—	9
My Home Town, 1986	16	—
War, 1986	12	18
Brilliant Disguise, 1987	5	20
Tunnel Of Love, 1987	9	—
Tougher Than The Rest, 1988	—	13
One Step Up, 1988	13	—

*Double A side in UK

Albums:

Greetings From Asbury Park, New Jersey (Columbia/CBS), 1973
The Wild, The Innocent And The E-Street Shuffle (Columbia/CBS), 1973
Born To Run (Columbia/CBS), 1975
Darkness On The Edge Of Town (Columbia/CBS), 1978
The River (Columbia/CBS), 1980
Nebraska (Columbia/CBS), 1982
Born In The U.S.A. (Columbia/CBS), 1984
Live (1975-85) (CBS), 1986
Tunnel Of Love (CBS), 1987

Squeeze

UK group formed 1974

Original line-up: Jools Holland, keyboards; Harry Kakoulli, bass; Gilson Lavis, drums; Chris Difford, guitar, vocals; Glenn Tilbrook, guitar, vocals.

Career: Squeeze (known as UK Squeeze in US until American band of same name split up) have had long-time reputation for successfully rewriting the teenage anthem songbook expounding love in the back seat.

The enterprising South East London quintet first recorded for independent Deptford Fun City label with EP **Packet Of Three** in 1974. The EP helped them carve out a solid local reputation.

First album **Squeeze** released in 1978 contained hit single **Take Me I'm Yours**, first in series of cockney, adolescent anecdotes from Difford and Tilbrook.

Personnel changes (John Bentley replacing Kakoulli, Paul Carrack (ex-Ace) coming in for Holland) established line-up which scored with such singles as **Up The Junction**, **Another Nail In My Heart** and **Pulling Mussels**.

Fourth album **East Side Story** earned group breakthrough in States, and included new keyboard player Don Snow following departure of Carrack to Carlene Carter's band. Carrack then toured with Nick Lowe and pursued solo career.

Above: East Side Story, Squeeze. Courtesy A&M Records.

Ironically, soon after American success, band went into swift demise. Difford and Tilbrook cut album together, and wrote play *Labelled With Love* in which they featured. Jools Holland formed Millionaires and became popular front man for UK TV music show *The Tube*.

Squeeze re-formed in 1985 for **Cosi Fan Tutti Frutti** LP, with a line-up comprising Difford, Tilbrook, Holland, Lavis and Keith Wilkinson on bass. This aggregation (with temporary addition of keyboard player Andy Metcalfe), scored in US with **Babylon And On** LP (1987), from which **Hourglass** was single; toured US in same year.

Following **Frank** album (1989), Holland took his leave once again, later cutting **World Of His Own** LP. Remaining quartet have subsequently stuck together, and signed major deal with Warner Brothers, for which excellent set **Play** was debut.

Although unlikely to regain lost 'pop' status, Squeeze have an outstanding vocalist in Tilbrook, and a seemingly limitless source of material which should ensure acceptable level of success.

Hit Singles:

	US	UK
Take Me I'm Yours, 1978	—	19
Cool For Cats, 1979	—	2
Up The Junction, 1979	—	2
Another Nail In My Heart, 1980	—	17
Labelled With Love, 1981	—	4
Hour Glass, 1987	15	16
853-5937, 1987	32	—

Albums:

Squeeze (A&M), 1978
Cool For Cats (A&M), 1979
Argy Bargy (A&M), 1980
East Side Story (A&M), 1981
Singles (A&M), 1982
Sweets From A Stranger (A&M), 1982
Cosi Fan Tutti Frutti (A&M), 1985
Babylon And On (CDA), 1987
Frank (A&M), 1989
A Round And A Bout (IRS/Deptford Fun City), 1990
Play (WEA/Warner), 1991

Difford and Tilbrook:
Difford And Tilbrook (A&M), 1984

Jools Holland Solo:
World Of His Own (IRS), 1990

Lisa Stansfield

UK vocalist
Born Rochdale, 1965

Career: Breathy soul-styled vocalist who had brief tenure with Coldcut (UK dance hit with **People Hold On**), own Blue Zone band and stint as presenter of UK TV show *Razzamatazz* before signing with former Wham! manager Jazz Summers.

Debut solo single **This Is The Right Time**, written by Stansfield and former Blue Zone members Ian Devaney and Andy Morris, made UK Top 20 (1989), while follow-up **All Around The World** secured No. 1 spot. In US, **World** reached No. 3, and created almost unique situation when topping R&B chart, confirming Stansfield's superb vocal delivery. Debut **Affection** (recorded at her studio in Rochdale) has now sold in excess of 4 million copies.

This sudden chart activity led to US and European tours, where doubts were raised over artist's dormant stage personality and limited repertoires. Appearances at The Prince's Royal Gala Trust and The Simple Truth charity concerts were hardly riveting spectacles.

However, a BRIT award in 1991 as Best British Female Artist was matched in the States by *Rolling Stone* critics' Best New Female Singer category and suggested career longevity with the right material.

Hit Singles:

	US	UK
This Is The Right Time, 1989	21	13
All Around The World, 1989	3	1
Live Together, 1990	—	10
You Can't Deny It, 1990	14	—
Change, 1991	—	8

Albums:

Affection (Arista), 1989
Real Love (Arista), 1991

Ringo Starr

UK drummer, vocalist, composer, actor
Born Richard Starkey, Liverpool, July 7, 1940

Career: The only member of the Beatles to have played in other bands (notably Rory Storme and The Hurricanes) before Beatles; Ringo only joined famous group immediately before first Parlophone recording session (which produced **Love Me Do**). Throughout Beatles era, was never taken seriously as writer, although occasional songs were set aside for him to sing, like **Honey Don't** on **Beatles For Sale** and especially singalong **Yellow Submarine**. Shortly before Beatles split, he released extremely poor LP of standards **Sentimental Journey**, supposedly recorded because his mother liked such songs as **Night And Day** and **Bye Bye Blackbird**.

Ringo continued to work with both John Lennon and George Harrison after split, appearing on most of their early solo records. In 1970 released second solo effort, country and western-flavoured **Beaucoups Of Blues**, produced by Nashville star Pete Drake. It was major improvement over debut, if still somewhat obscure. During this period, made several appearances in films. Next LP, excellent **Ringo**, produced by Richard Perry,

was incredibly successful, spawning two US chart-topping singles, plus participation from other ex-Beatles (although not altogether). Follow-up LP, **Goodnight Vienna**, used same recipe, but with fewer hits.

1976's **Ringo's Rotogravure** LP was far less interesting; subsequent LPs showed little sign of return to mid-70s form. Own label Ognir proved unsuccessful. Seemingly, Ringo has now outlived the advantages of being a Beatle, and while his drumming remains object lesson in unostentatious brilliance, as a vocalist he is now regarded as merely adequate. He looks unlikely to return to chart contention unless he teams up with Richard Perry (or someone like him).

Latterly Starr has remained in public eye as rock's 'odd-job' man. Narrated popular UK television cartoon series *Thomas The Tank Engine*, fronted US TV show *Shining Time Station*, featured in dismal *Give My Regards To Broadway* movie and also provided voice for own character in *The Simpsons* cartoon series. Musically, toured US in summer of 1990 with Tour For All Generations show, featuring Billy Preston, Dr John, Joe Walsh (with whom he cut **Old Wave** set), Nils Lofgren 'and many others'. Had previously worked with Carl Perkins on *Blue Suede Shoes* TV special and appeared on Prince's Trust charity bill at Wembley.

Hit Singles:

	US	UK
It Don't Come Easy, 1971	4	4
Back Off Boogaloo, 1972	9	2
Photograph, 1973	1	8
You're Sixteen, 1974	1	4
Oh My My, 1974	5	—
Only You, 1974	6	28
No No Song, 1976	3	—

Albums:

Sentimental Journey (Apple), 1970
Beaucoups Of Blues (Apple), 1970
Ringo (Apple), 1973
Goodnight Vienna (Apple), 1974
Blast From Your Past (compilation) (Apple), 1975
Ringo's Rotogravure (Atco/Polydor), 1976
Ringo The 4th (Atco/Polydor), 1977
Bad Boy (Portrait/Polydor), 1978
Stop And Smell The Roses (Boardwalk/RCA), 1981
Ringo Starr And His All Starr Band (Rykodisc/EMI), 1990

Status Quo

UK group formed 1967

Original line-up: Rick Parfitt, guitar, vocals; Francis Rossi, guitar, vocals; Alan Lancaster, bass, vocals; John Coghlan, drums; Roy Lynes, organ, vocals.

Below: Quo, from left are Lancaster, Kirchner, Parfitt, Rossi and Bown.

Career: Rossi (originally known as Mike) met Lancaster at school in spring 1962. As young 12-year-olds, they formed first band, Scorpions. Within four months, band's guitarist quit. Rossi and Lancaster recruited another schoolmate to carry on. This second band came across Coughlan in September 1962 when his own group was practising next door.

Going through several personnel changes in the merge, The Spectres, as they called themselves, began playing holiday camps. In April 1965 Roy Lynes took over organ spot. The line-up of Rossi, Lancaster, Coghlan and Lynes actually recorded three flop singles for Pye. Parfitt was added in May 1967.

Group changed name to Traffic, then to Traffic Jam because of Winwood's group. Another single flopped and to earn living band had to assume backing duties for US artists.

In August 1967, group took new name of Status Quo. They recorded Rossi number, **Pictures Of Matchstick Men**, and quietly resumed duties as back-up band. Early 1968 found Status Quo sudden pop stars as single became international hit, but subsequent work failed to maintain success.

Lynes left in 1970 and when Quo was at nadir of career. A year later band moved to Vertigo Records with no noticeable change in fortunes. Instead, they began building up following by playing relentless (some say, repetitious) boogie. Despite critical write-off, Status Quo's audience put band back in UK Top 10 with **Paper Plane. Piledriver** LP charted shortly after and everything band did seemed to go gold. Single **Down, Down** went to No. 1 in UK and album **On The Level** charted in late 1974. Andy Bown played keyboards from 1974-79. Since 1974 every new LP on Vertigo made UK Top 5.

Above: In The Army Now, Status Quo. Courtesy Vertigo Records.

Arduous touring and approaching veteran status appeared to have little effect on Quo, and 1982 announcement that Coghlan had retired was genuine surprise. His replacement was Pete Kirchner (ex-Original Mirrors) who featured on subsequent chart albums **1982** and **From The Makers Of . . .** live set.

Temporary hiatus prompted by Lancaster's move to Australia almost spelled finish for outfit, but the Quo must go on, and the bassist returned for Live Aid gig in 1985. However, trouble was afoot when band returned to studios without Lancaster, who subsequently issued high court proceedings to prevent other members continuing without his presence.

With all squabbles resolved, Quo regrouped in 1986 with a line-up comprising Rossi, Parfitt, Bown and former Climax Blues members Jeff Rich and John Brown, on drums and bass respectively. This quintet cut **In The Army Now** set, from which title track made No. 2 in UK charts.

With group's chart run proceeding unabated, Status Quo entered 90s in solid shape and fast-approaching 25 years in the biz.

Hit Singles:

	US	UK
Pictures Of Matchstick Men, 1968	12	7
Ice In The Sun, 1968	—	8
Down The Dustpipe, 1970	—	12
Paper Plane, 1973	—	8
Mean Girl, 1973	—	20
Caroline, 1973	—	5
Break The Rules, 1974	—	8
Down, Down, 1974	—	1
Roll Over Lay Down, 1975	—	9
Rain, 1976	—	7
Mystery Song, 1976	—	11
Wild Side of Life, 1976	—	9
Rockin' All Over The World, 1977	—	3
Again And Again, 1978	—	13
Whatever You Want, 1979	—	4
Living On An Island, 1979	—	16
What You're Proposing, 1980	—	2
Lies/Don't Drive My Car, 1981	—	11
Something 'Bout You Baby I Like, 1981	—	7
Rock 'n' Roll, 1981	—	8
Dear John, 1982	—	10
Caroline (live), 1982	—	13
Ol' Rag Blues, 1983	—	9
A Mess Of Blues, 1983	—	15
Marguerita Time, 1983	—	3
Going Downtown Tonight, 1984	—	20
The Wanderer, 1984	—	7
Dreamin', 1986	—	15
In The Army Now, 1986	—	2
Ain't Complaining, 1988	—	19
Running All Over The World, 1988	—	17
Burning Bridges (On And Off Again), 1988	—	5
The Anniversary Waltz — Part 1, 1990	—	2
The Anniversary Waltz — Part 2, 1990	—	16

Albums:
Ma Kellys Greasy Spoon (PRT), 1970
Dog Of Two Heads (PRT), 1971
Piledriver (A&M/Vertigo), 1973
Hello (A&M/Vertigo), 1973
Quo (A&M/Vertigo), 1974
On The Level (Capitol/Vertigo), 1975
Blue For You (—/Vertigo), 1976
Status Quo Live (Capitol/Vertigo), 1977
Rockin' All Over The World (Capitol/Vertigo), 1977
Status Quo File (—/Pye), 1977
If You Can't Stand The Heat (—/Vertigo), 1978
Whatever You Want (—/Vertigo), 1979
Twelve Gold Bars (Vertigo), 1980
Just Supposin' (—/Vertigo), 1980
Never Too Late (—/Vertigo), 1981
1982 (Vertigo), 1982
From The Makers Of . . . (—/Vertigo), 1982
Spare Parts (PRT), 1983
Twelve Gold Bars Volumes I & II (Vertigo), 1984
In The Army Now (Vertigo), 1986
Back To Back (Vertigo), 1987
Ain't Complaining (—/Vertigo), 1988
Rock 'Til You Drop (—/Vertigo), 1991

Steely Dan
US group formed 1972

Original line-up: Donald Fagen, keyboards, vocals; Walter Becker, bass, vocals; Denny Dias, guitar; Jeff 'Skunk' Baxter, guitar, pedal steel guitar; Jim Hodder, drums; David Palmer, vocals.

Career: Formed around dual writing and performing talents of Fagen and Becker, both former students at Bard College, New York. First band included Denny Dias; joined Jay And Americans back-up band when group split. First recorded work was soundtrack for off-beat Zalman King movie *You Gotta Walk It Like You Talk It (Or You'll Loose That Beat)*. Took name Steely Dan from a William Burroughs novel.

Moved to West Coast at insistence of producer Gary Katz; signed as writers to ABC/Dunhill Records. Katz/Fagen/Becker assembled group comprising Dias, fellow New Yorker Palmer, and Bostonians Baxter and Hodder.

Debut album **Can't Buy A Thrill** (1972) set pattern for jazz-structured melodies and succinct, Runyonesque lyrics. Singles from LP **Do It Again** and **Reelin' In The Years** made US Top 20.

Palmer quit (forming Wha Koo in 1977) before second album **Countdown To Ecstasy**, leaving vocals exclusively to Fagen. Quintet completed **Pretzel Logic** with notable session musicians, such as Michael Omartian, Jeff Porcaro (Toto), Chuck Rainey, Dean Parks, Vic Feldman and Crusaders' Wilton Felder. Album included classic **Rikki Don't Lose That Number**, a US Top 10 single.

With Fagen and Becker deriving more pleasure from recording than touring, Baxter and Hodder departed; Baxter subsequently joined Doobie Brothers. For **Katy Lied**, group added Michael McDonald (also later to join Doobies) on vocals, and Jeff Porcaro on drums. McDonald had previously toured both US and UK with band.

By now almost permanent studio unit, group cut **The Royal Scam** with addition of session players but without departed Dias. Chart success maintained with track **Haitian Divorce**.

Below: Only the flares remain. Donald Fagen (right) and Walter Becker.

Aja (1977) saw Fagen and Becker firmly in control; musicians included drummer Bernard Purdie, guitarists Larry Carlton and Lee Ritenour, guest appearance by Dias, veteran Feldman on percussion and keyboards, and surprisingly Chuck Rainey on bass, depriving Becker of his role for all but one track. McDonald supplied back-up vocals.

Officially Steely Dan's final album to date, **Gaucho** (1980), returned duo to singles chart with track **Babylon Sisters**. Becker again limited on bass contribution, with Rainey and Anthony Jackson stepping in.

Band's tenuous story further confused by Donald Fagen solo set **Nightfly** (1982); songs were exclusively Fagen's (except Leiber/Stoller's **Ruby Baby**) but sound was definitive Steely Dan.

Nightfly explored fantasies of teen America; sound complemented by Porcaro, Brecker Bros on trumpet and sax, Carlton, Hugh McCracken on guitar, and Rainey Jackson, Marcus Miller, Abe Laboriel and Will Lee. Becker could take heart from the talent it took to replace him.

1985 double album set **Best Of** went platinum, and further fuelled rumours of re-formation. Becker and Fagen did work together again on Rosie Vela's debut LP **Zazu**, but Becker's self-confessed drug abuse and subsequent incarceration halted any further speculation. Fagen contributed to *Bright Lights, Big City* movie soundtrack, and featured on **New York Rock And Soul Revue — Live At The Beacon** (1991). Becker moved to Hawaii and set up own studio complex, where he produced China Crisis' **Flaunt The Imperfection** album and Ricki Lee Jones' **Flying Cowboys** set.

A decade after release of **Nightfly**, Fagen announced plans for new solo LP in 1992. Citing 'writer's block' for lengthy absence, Fagen summoned his old pal Becker to produce, but the pair are now adamant that Steely Dan should be buried 'once and for all'.

Hit Singles:

	US	UK
Do It Again, 1973	6	39
Reelin' In The Years, 1973	11	–
Rikki Don't Lose That Number, 1974	4	–
Haitian Divorce, 1976	3	17
FM (No Static At All), 1978	7	49
Peg, 1978	11	–
Deacon Blues, 1978	19	–
Babylon Sisters, 1980	2	–

Albums:
You Gotta Walk It (Visa/—), 1969
Can't Buy A Thrill (MCA), 1972
Countdown To Ecstasy (MCA), 1973
Pretzel Logic (MCA), 1974
Katy Lied (MCA), 1975
The Royal Scam (MCA), 1976
Aja (MCA), 1977
Greatest Hits (MCA), 1979
Gaucho (MCA), 1980
Gold (MCA), 1982
Reelin' In The Years (MCA), 1985
Best Of (MCA), 1985
Berry Town (Belaphon), 1986
Old Regime (Thunderbolt), 1987

Donald Fagen Solo:
The Nightfly (Warner Bros), 1982

Steppenwolf
US group formed 1967

Original line-up: John Kay, guitar, vocals; Jerry Edmonton, drums; Goldy McJohn, organ; Michael Monarch, guitar; Rushton Moreve, bass.

Career: East German-born John Kay and his family fled to Canada when he was 14. There he discovered Western music and formed blues group Sparrow. Realizing limited chances in Toronto, Kay took band to New York, then California.

Sparrow began adapting style to blues-based gritty rock made popular by English bands. By mid-1967 they had become Steppenwolf and the first of many bass player changes occurred as John Russell Morgan replaced Moreve.

When band recorded debut LP in late 1967, they had several years of road experience and original material stored up. **Born To Be Wild** single was released as crisis in Czechoslovakia led to Russian invasion. Rough vocals, outrageous lyrics and grinding music epitomized political atmosphere of tanks in the street and worldwide call to break free. **Magic Carpet Ride**, released barely three months later, enhanced image of bold, creative force at large.

Albums by Steppenwolf were patchy and uneven until 1969 release, **Monster**. This

represented band at its most political as well as its most cohesive musically. Instead of pushing ahead, frenzied past few years caught up and group began more extensive personnel changes. Monarch's guitar spot was taken by Larry Byrom, then Kent Henry. Bass player duties were handed over to Nick St. Nicholas, then to George Biondo. This caused break-up of tight-knit sound forged by early band, and in February 1972 came announcement of Steppenwolf's demise.

When Kay's solo career failed to take hold, he reorganized band in 1974 with McJohn, Edmonton, Biondo and guitarist Bobby Cochran. After **Slow Flux** LP Wayne Cook replaced McJohn. **Hour Of The Wolf** album proved band could sometimes recapture old sound, but Kay failed to come up with material that matched magic days of 1967-69. Despite further efforts, including 1987 set **Rock And Roll Rebels**, band never regained old form.

Steppenwolf's place in rock history depended as much on political climate of 60s as on music. As memories fade, band's music seems less potent, less a call to arms. Nevertheless, underlying sound still has powerful hold as seen by many successful greatest hits and compilation releases.

Hit Singles:

	US	UK
Born To Be Wild, 1968	2	30
Magic Carpet Ride, 1968	3	–
Rock Me, 1969	10	–

Albums:
Steppenwolf (Dunhill/Stateside), 1968
Steppenwolf The Second (Dunhill/Stateside), 1968
Monster (MCA/—), 1969
For Ladies Only (MCA/—), 1970
Live Steppenwolf (Dunhill/Probe), 1970
Steppenwolf 7 (Dunhill/Probe), 1970
Steppenwolf Gold (MCA), 1971
16 Greatest Hits (ABC), 1973
Slow Flux (Epic), 1974
Hour Of The Wolf (Epic), 1975
Gold (MCA), 1981
Golden Greats (MCA), 1985
Rock And Roll Rebels (Epic), 1987
Rise And Shine (IRS), 1990

Cat Stevens
UK vocalist, composer, guitarist
Born Steven Georgiou, London, July 21, 1947

Career: Son of a Greek restauranteur father and Swedish mother, Stevens enjoyed two distinct musical careers, first as straightforward folk-influenced pop artist then, following time off seriously ill, as folk-rock album star experimenting heavily with ethnic Greek instruments which gave his style unique dimension.

He became involved in folk scene while studying at Hammersmith College and met former Springfields' folk group member Mike Hurst, then working as independent record producer. Instead of emigrating to America as intended, Hurst invested his savings in recording Stevens' own composition, **I Love My Dog**, which he then licensed to Tony Hall for Decca's newly formed Deram (progressive music subsidiary) as label's debut release. The record charted and follow-up **Matthew And Son** did even better, reaching No. 2 in early 1967.

Stevens toured with both Jimi Hendrix and Englebert Humperdinck and his perceptive songs were snapped up by other recording

Left: John Kay, lead singer of US hard rock band Steppenwolf.

Above: Cat Stevens, a chart star of two decades, but now retired.

stars (notably P.P. Arnold with **The First Cut Is The Deepest** and The Tremeloes with **Here Comes My Baby**). In early 1968 he scored third Deram hit with **I'm Gonna Get Me A Gun**.

After contracting TB, Stevens spent year recuperating, using the time to develop new ideas and songs in almost classical manner. Taking time to get everything just right, Stevens eventually signed to Island and released the landmark **Mona Bone Jakon** in 1970. From that set, **Lady d'Arbanville** (written about a former girlfriend) emerged as hit single, but Stevens had truly matured into album artist and subsequent sets made him a superstar on both sides of Atlantic.

Massive earnings from records and concerts led to tax exile in Brazil during which time he became heavily involved with UNESCO and various charities.

By mid-70s, Stevens had become very much the recluse, developing a passionate interest in mysticism. He converted to the Moslem faith and married girl he had seen at a London mosque but never spoken to. **The Old School Yard** (1977) was his last hit single; subsequently he retired completely from music scene, devoting himself to religious studies and adopting the name Yusef Islam; he acted as intermediary in 1990 Gulf War between British representatives seeking release of hostages and Saddam Hussein's government.

Hit Singles:

	US	UK
Matthew And Son, 1967	–	2
I'm Gonna Get Me A Gun, 1967	–	6
A Bad Night, 1967	–	20
Lady D'Arbanville, 1970	–	8
Wild World, 1971	11	–
Peace Train, 1971	7	–
Morning Has Broken, 1972	6	9
Can't Keep It In, 1972	–	13
Sitting, 1972	16	–
Oh Very Young, 1974	10	–
Another Saturday Night, 1974	6	19

Albums:
Matthew And Son (—/Deram), 1967
New Masters (—/Deram), 1968
World Of (—/Decca), 1970
Mona Bone Jakon (A&M/Island), 1970
Tea For The Tillerman (A&M/Island), 1971
Teaser And The Firecat (A&M/Island), 1971
Catch Bull At Four (A&M/Island), 1972
Foreigner (A&M/Island), 1973
Buddha And The Chocolate Box (A&M/Island), 1974
View From The Top (—/Deram), 1974

Numbers (A&M/Island), 1975
Greatest Hits (A&M/Island), 1975
Izitso (A&M/Island), 1977
Back To Earth (A&M/Island), 1978
The First Cut Is The Deepest (—/Decca), 1980

Rod Stewart
UK vocalist, composer
Born London, January 10, 1945

Career: London born, but eternally proud of Scottish ancestry (his brothers were born north of the border). Attended same school as Ray and Dave Davies of The Kinks.

After spells as fence-erector and grave-digger, signed apprentice forms with Brentford Football Club but was soon disillusioned by poor pay and having to clean boots of senior players. However, he is still a soccer fanatic.

While travelling around Europe, met folk singer Wizz Jones in Spain who taught him to play harmonica. Repatriated as destitute, Stewart learned guitar and joined Birmingham outfit Jimmy Powell And Dimensions; sang and played harmonica.

In 1964 Stewart recorded obscure but superb version of R&B classic **Good Morning Little Schoolgirl** for Decca. Joined Long John Baldry's band The Hoochie Coochie Men as second vocalist. Fronted Soul Agents for while before joining Brian Auger, Julie Driscoll and Reginald Dwight (better known as Elton John) in Steampacket in mid-65. Also had spell in Steampacket's next form, Bluesology. Backed by Auger's organ playing, Stewart cut version of his hero Sam Cooke's **Shake** for Columbia in 1966. Quit to sing alongside Beryl Marsden in Shotgun Express, with Peter Green (guitar), Peter Bardens (keyboards), Dave Ambrose (bass) and Mick Fleetwood (drums). Despite classy line-up, band failed. While continuing as-yet-unsuccessful solo recording career, Stewart joined Jeff Beck Group.

After disastrous London concerts, band found feet in America. Stewart featured on lauded albums **Truth** (1968) and **Beck-Ola** (1969). This led to solo contract with Mercury in 1969.

Stewart quit Beck's band when latter wanted to fire Ronnie Wood with whom Stewart had struck up friendship and strong working relationship. Soon after, Stewart and Wood were added to line-up of Faces.

While Faces, with Stewart singing lead, turned out patchy albums, Stewart's solo efforts for Mercury were outstanding. After initial break in US via **An Old Raincoat Won't Ever Let You Down** (the **Rod Stewart Album** in US) and **Gasoline Alley** LP in 1970, he quickly built similar reputation in homeland. Hit big with **Maggie May** from dynamic 1971 album **Every Picture Tells A Story**. In September 1971, Stewart achieved distinction of topping both album and singles charts on both sides of the Atlantic in same week.

Fronting Faces for live appearances, Stewart built band into massive concert attraction. Generated frenetic atmosphere and built legion of fanatical followers who followed him in adopting the tartan symbol — and espousing football. Group regularly kicked footballs into audience and Stewart always took time out to attend major games.

In 1972, **Never A Dull Moment** LP and **You Wear It Well** single struck gold. An astute minor label dug out an old track Stewart had recorded, for session fee alone, with studio group Python Lee Jackson back in 1968. They could not use Stewart's name but his reputation was enough and **In A Broken Dream** made No. 3 in UK charts.

Recording material first made famous by his heroes in rock 'n' roll, soul and R&B (ranging from Jerry Lee Lewis to Chuck Berry to Sam Cooke), Stewart always added his own inimitable touch. Cover versions and new material alike showed Stewart's enormous creativity and fully exploited merits of his gravelly vocals.

Court wrangles between Mercury and Warner Bros (to whom Faces were signed) led to delays in release of next album. Time was filled in by **Sing It Again, Rod**, a compilation set of old tracks which also included Stewart's version of **Pinball Wizard** from Lou Reizner's Rainbow Theatre stage presentation of The Who's Pete Townshend's rock musical *Tommy* in which Stewart had appeared.

Below: Rod The Mod is now the favourite son of the British tabloids, who follow his attempted conquest of every blonde in the US with microscopic interest.

Issued late in 1974, Stewart's **Smiler** album was disappointing. In December 1975 he announced he was leaving Faces to give solo career more impetus. Debut Warner Brothers' album, Tom Dowd-produced **Atlantic Crossing**, recorded largely in Muscle Shoals, Alabama (he had moved home base to Hollywood), was good start. 1976 followup, **A Night On The Town**, appeared on manager Billy Gaff's Riva label (through Warner Bros) and was hugely successful, yielding three US chart-topping singles: **Tonight's The Night**, **The Killing Of Georgie** and **The First Cut Is The Deepest**. The first equalled achievement of the Beatles' **Hey Jude** in topping US charts for eight weeks.

Sailing brought another UK No. 1, but on personal front Stewart had problems. His long-standing but tempestuous relationship with actress Britt Ekland broke up amid acrimony and 'kiss and tell' stories. He later married actor George Hamilton's ex-, Alana, but they also parted company. Stewart also severed partnership with manager Gaff, relinquishing his one-third share of Riva Records.

Stewart enjoyed greatest success when strutting before good old-fashioned rock outfit, and the late 70s aggregation including guitarist Jim Cregan and nuclear drummer Carmine Appice provided a perfect foil for singer's posturing. With Appice, Stewart wrote mega-hit **D'Ya Think I'm Sexy** which featured on multi-platinum **Blondes Have More Fun** set (1978).

Maintained hectic touring schedule during 1980s, occasionally returning to home territory for sell-out concerts, although chart action was more sporadic. Revived classic soul cut **If Loving You Is Wrong (I Don't Want To Be Right)** and rock standards **How Long, Some Guys Have All The Luck** and **All Right Now**. Paired with old mate Jeff Beck on that artist's Grammy-winning **Flash** LP (1985) and then organized re-release of **Sailin'** for bereaved families of Zeebrugge ferry disaster. Provided music for movies *Night Shift* (**That's What Friends Are For**), *Legal Eagles* (**Love Touch**) and *Innerspace*

(his version of **Twistin' The Night Away**). Returned to album Top 20 with **Out Of Order** (1988), produced by Andy Taylor from Duran Duran and ace bassist Bernard Edwards, prime mover behind Chic.

Married again in 1990 (to model Rachel Hunt) as rumours of multi-million dollar palimony suit surfaced. In 1991, Stewart was confronted by former live-in girlfriend Kelly Emberg (where does he find them all?) who claimed 25 million-dollar settlement for her years spent with the veteran rocker.

Enjoyed better luck with **Vagabond Heart** LP (his 18th solo outing), a massive hit in US and UK, and which spawned **Rhythm Of The Heart** chart cut.

The tabloid press's favourite loin lizard, Stewart has confounded critics with his durability, although those poor tonsils should now be ground to dust.

Hit Singles:

	US	UK
Reason To Believe/Maggie May, 1971	–	19
Maggie May/Reason To Believe, 1971	1	1
You Wear It Well, 1972	13	1
Angel/What Made Milwaukee Famous, 1972	40	4
Oh No Not My Baby, 1973	59	6
Farewell/Bring It On Home To Me/You Send Me, 1974	–	7
Sailing, 1975	58	1
This Ole Heart Of Mine, 1975	–	4
Tonight's The Night, 1976	1	5
The Killing Of Georgie, 1976	30	2
Get Back, 1976	–	11
I Don't Want To Talk About It/The First Cut Is The Deepest, 1977	21	1
You're In My Heart, 1977	4	3
Hotlegs/I Was Only Joking, 1978	28	5
Ole Ola (Muhler Brasileira), 1978	–	4
Do Ya Think I'm Sexy?, 1978	1	1
Ain't Love A Bitch, 1979	22	11
Passion, 1980	5	9
Tonight I'm Yours (Don't Hurt Me), 1981	–	8
Young Turks, 1981	5	11
Baby Jane, 1983	15	1
What Am I Gonna Do, 1983	35	3
Infatuation, 1984	6	27
Some Guys Have All The Luck, 1984	10	15
Every Beat Of My Heart, 1986	–	2
Love Touch, 1987	5	–
Forever Young, 1988	12	57
My Heart Can't Tell You No, 1988	4	–
Crazy About Her, 1989	11	–
Downtown Train, 1990	3	10
Rhythm Of My Heart, 1991	5	3
Motown Song, 1991	10	10

With Tina Turner:

	US	UK
It Takes Two, 1990	–	5

Albums:

An Old Raincoat Won't Ever Let You Down (Vertigo), 1970*
Gasoline Alley (Mercury/Vertigo), 1970
Every Picture Tells A Story (Mercury), 1971
Never A Dull Moment (Mercury), 1972
Sing It Again Rod (Mercury), 1973
Smiler (Mercury), 1974
Atlantic Crossing (Warner Bros/Riva), 1975
A Night On The Town (Warner Bros/Riva), 1976
Foot Loose And Fancy Free (Warner Bros/Riva), 1977

Above: The Best Of Rod Stewart. Courtesy Mercury Records.

Best Of (double compilation) (Mercury), 1977
Best Of, Volume II (double compilation) (Mercury), 1977
Blondes Have More Fun (Warner Bros/Riva), 1978
Greatest Hits (Warner Bros), 1979
Foolish Behaviour (Warner Bros/Riva), 1980
Tonight I'm Yours (Warner Bros/Riva), 1981
Rod The Mod (Accord), 1981
Maggie May (–/Contour), 1981
Absolutely Live (Warner Bros/Riva), 1982
Body Wishes (WEA), 1983
Camouflage (Warner Bros), 1984
Greatest Hits Volume 2 (CBS), 1986
Every Beat Of My Heart (Warner Bros), 1987
Out Of Order (Warner Bros), 1988
Vagabond Heart (Warner Bros/–), 1991
*Titled Rod Stewart Album, aka Thin, (Mercury) in US

Stephen Stills

US guitarist, vocalist, songwriter
Born Dallas, Texas, January 3, 1945

Career: Moved about Southern US as child, attending variety of schools, eventually entering University of Florida. After playing part-time in local folk circles, Stills quit college and moved to New York for its reputed folk scene. Perceiving changing musical climate, he left for Los Angeles. After several projects (one of which was to fail audition for Monkees) he helped found Buffalo Springfield. Stills wrote band's major hit, **For What It's Worth**.

Following Buffalo's demise, Stills recorded **Supersession** with Al Kooper and Mike Bloomfield; toured with girlfriend Judy Collins and played on one of her albums; did sessions for Joni Mitchell.

End of 1968 brought announcement of Crosby, Stills And Nash supergroup (CSN). Still's ode to Judy Collins became their first hit, **Suite: Judy Blue Eyes**. When CSN reunited Stills with old Buffalo Springfield mate Neil Young, band became top heavy with egos, and Stills began working on first solo LP, recorded while he was living in London. Stills employed number of major musicians, including Jimi Hendrix, who died before album's release; LP was dedicated to him. Second solo album used CSN&Y sidemen whom Stills organized into loose confederation he called Manassas. After two releases, part of band left with Chris Hillman who formed Souther-Hillman-Furay Band.

Stills reorganized back-up band but broke off acitivity for 1974 CSN&Y reunion tour. Since then Stills has released several LPs, most notable being joint venture with Neil Young as Stills-Young Band. He also rejoins CSN periodically, but of late his influence is diminishing.

Hit Singles:

	US	UK
Love The One You're With, 1971	14	37

Albums:
Stephen Stills (Atlantic), 1970
Stephen Stills II (Atlantic), 1971
Stills (Columbia/CBS), 1975
Stills Live (Atlantic), 1976
Illegal Stills (Columbia/CBS), 1976
Best Of Stephen Stills (Atlantic), 1976
Long May You Run (with Stills-Young Band) (Reprise), 1976
Thoroughfare Gap (Columbia/CBS), 1978
Right By You (WEA), 1984

Manassas:
Manassas (Atlantic), 1975
Down The Road (Atlantic), 1973

Worth Searching Out:
Supersession (with Al Kooper and Mike Bloomfield) (Columbia/CBS), 1968

Sting

UK vocalist, bass player, composer, producer
Born Gordon Sumner, Wallsend, Tyne & Wear, October 2, 1951

Career: Former Police front-man, whose infrequent solo musical output has been rock's equivalent of the 'one-note samba'. His tireless commitment to environmental matters stalled hugely successful solo career, but commanded front-page attention, particularly for plight of Brazilian rainforests.

Three-pronged attack — music, movies and ecology — has seen Sting stretch his fragile resources wide. Well-received debut album **The Dream Of The Blue Turtles**, which featured all-star studio/stage band comprising Wynton Marsalis, trumpet, Branford Marsalis, saxophone, Darryl Jones, bass, Kenny Kirkland, keyboards, and Omar Haikim, drums, has been pick of recorded material since **Synchronicity**, the last roll-call for The Police.

Live double album **Bring On The Night** (1986), with accompanying documentary directed by Michael Apted, preceded final live gig for Police at Amnesty International event in Georgia. Plans to re-form trio were abandoned during rehearsals for contracted LP with Sting's personal schedule the major distraction. Guested on Dire Strait's **Money For Nothing** in same year.

Third solo LP, **Nothing Like The Sun** (1987), earned berth on top of UK album charts and BRIT award as Best British Album. Sting was further honoured when **Bring On The Night** took Best Male Vocal Performance at 1988 Grammy celebrations.

Hectic concert outings were almost exclusively for charity, with Conspiracy Of Hope tour (plus Bryan Adams, U2, Bob Dylan, Peter Gabriel, Tom Petty) a major coup for Amnesty International. Sting also featured on album of same name. Other benefit events included 1988 concert for Nelson Mandela's 70th Birthday Party and Human Rights Now world tour (with Bruce Springsteen, Tracy Chapman and Peter Gabriel), Rainforest Foundation gigs (1990-91) and The Simple Truth extravaganza in 1991 at Wembley Arena, London.

On theatre and club dates (including 1991 UK tour), Sting used quality trio comprising drummer Vinnie Colaiuta (ex-Zappa, Joni Mitchell, Juice Newton), guitarist Dominic Miller (ex-Pretenders) and long-time Springsteen and Stanley Clark sideman David Sancious on keyboards.

Although immersed in critical global issues, Sting also pursued fitful movie career, which had seen an unfortunate choice of material (*Dune, Brimstone & Treacle, The Bride, Plenty, Stormy Monday, Julia Julia*) unlikely to strain cash registers at the box office. His Broadway debut in *Threepenny Opera* (September 1989) fared worse, although survied critical battering from New York heavies to approach 150 performances.

After three-year hiatus, A&M Records released **Soul Cages** collection in 1991, an uncomfortable mix of rock and, dare we say it, jazz, with Sting seemingly going through the motions. The *Sunday Times* suggested it sounded like the work of a man who would rather be doing something else. Which he is for most of the time.

Hit Singles:

	US	UK
Spread A Little Happiness, 1982	–	16
Russians, 1985	16	12
If You Love Somebody Set Them Free, 1985	3	26
Fortress Around Your Heart, 1985	8	–
Love Is The Seventh Wave, 1985	17	–
We'll Be Together, 1987	7	–
Be Still My Beating Heart, 1988	15	–
An Englishman In New York (re-mix), 1990	–	15
All This Time, 1991	5	22

Albums:
Dream Of The Blue Turtles (A&M), 1985
Bring On The Night (A&M), 1986
Nothing Like The Sun (A&M), 1987
Igor Stravinsky's The Soldier's Tale (–/Pangaea), 1988
Soul Cages (A&M), 1991

Stone Roses

UK group formed 1985

Original line-up: Gary Mountfield, bass; Ian Brown, vocals; John Squire, guitar; Alan Wren, drums.

Career: Manchester quartet who developed 'punkadelic' new wave sound on early gigs in Sweden. Controversial musical and personal approach has already landed band in 'who is trashing what' columns of pop press.

With New Order's Peter Hook at the production helm, Stone Roses cut trio of indie singles before Top 10 chart success with **Fool's Gold** (1989). Eponymous self-titled first album (on Silvertone Records) sent critics into an orgy of superlatives. The LP's success renewed interest in group's previous material, and FM Revolver label bore brunt when band initiated paint attack on company's offices when unsolicited video was issued to promote **Sally Cinnamon** cut.

With major labels waiting to tempt Stone Roses into long-term, mega-buck deal, Silvertone shrewdly maintained re-issue of old product. Subsequent litigation between the label and band prevented recording for period in excess of 12 months.

Hit Singles:

	US	UK
What The World Is Wating For/ Fool's Gold, 1989	–	8
Elephant Stone, 1990	–	8
Made Of Stone, 1990	–	20
One Love, 1990	–	4
I Wanna Be Adored, 1991	–	20

Albums:
Stone Roses (Silvertone), 1989
What A Trip (–/Baktabak), 1991

The Stranglers

UK group formed 1975

Original line-up: Hugh Cornwell, vocals, Fender Telecaster guitar; Jean-Jacques Burnel, vocals, bass; Dave Greenfield, keyboards; Jet Black, drums.

Career: Following formation in village near Guildford, Surrey, supported Patti Smith on 1975 UK tour. During 1976 played more

than 200 gigs, mainly around London, and built up reputation as powerful live act. Benefited from interest in 'new wave' despite having little in common with punk outfits.

Two years live work paid off with release of first album **Rattus Norvegicus**, which leapt to No. 4 in UK charts. Simultaneously, single **Peaches/Go Buddy Go** reached No. 8 in singles charts.

Winning streak continued throughout 1977 and 1978, but from 1979 to beginning of 1981 band seemed to slip from limelight somewhat. Had no major solo success during this time, but continued touring regularly. Low point came when, following series of legal wrangles, band was imprisoned in Nice, France.

Although successful within their field, band seemed destined to remain something of unknown quantity to average record buyer. Some were already beginning to dismiss Stranglers as 'punk revivalists' when band bounced back in 1981 with two major albums, **The Meninblack** and **La Folie**. More surprising was single from **La Folie**, **Golden Brown**. In contrast to tough black leather visual image and usual output it was gentle, floating summery waltz that appealed to many who had never before bought Stranglers' records. Single was huge hit all over the world; few months later band followed with almost as successful **Strange Little Girl** single.

Unpredictable tag finally wore thin, as band became increasingly reliant on clichéd philosophizing and media shenanigans. Near ten-year chart standing looked likely to end after series of uninspired singles in mid-80s, although note-for-note cover of Kinks' class, **All Day And All Of The Night**, gave group temporary reprive. The latter prompted 1988 album **All Live And All Of The Night**, a collection of concert and club recordings. A further revival and Mysterions' **96 Tears** provided a solid start to the 90s, although Hugh Cornwell's departure in same year following recording of **Ten** LP clouded Stranglers' future.

Hit Singles:

	US	UK
Peaches/Go Buddy Go, 1977	–	8
Something Better Change/ Straighten Out, 1977	–	9
No More Heroes, 1977	–	8
Five Minutes, 1978	–	11
Nice 'n' Sleazy, 1978	–	18
Duchess, 1979	–	14
Golden Brown, 1982	–	2
Strange Little Girl, 1982	–	7
European Female, 1983	–	9
Skin Deep, 1984	–	15
Always The Sun, 1986	–	30
Nice In Nice, 1986	–	30
Big In America, 1986	–	49
All Day And All Of The Night, 1988	–	7
96 Tears, 1990	–	17

Albums:
Rattus Norvegicus (A&M/United Artists), 1977
No More Heroes (A&M/United Artists), 1977
Black And White (A&M/United Artists), 1978
Live (A&M/United Artists), 1979
The Raven (A&M/United Artists), 1979

Left: The original members of The Stranglers. From left, Dave Greenfield, Jet Black, Jean-Jacques Burnel and Hugh Cornwell.

The Meninblack (EMI), 1981
La Folie (EMI), 1981
The Collection 1977-1982 (–/Liberty), 1982
Feline (Epic), 1983
Dreamtime (Epic), 1986
Off The Beaten Track (Liberty), 1986
Aural Sculpture (Epic), 1987
All Live And All Of The Night (Epic), 1988
The Singles (EMI), 1989
10 (Epic), 1990
Greatest Hits 1977-90 (Epic), 1990

Style Council

UK group formed 1983

Original line-up: Paul Weller, vocals, guitar, composer; Mick Talbot, keyboards, composer.

Career: When The Jam disbanded in December 1982, Paul Weller linked up with former Merton Parkas, Dexys Midnight Runners and Bureau member Talbot to form Style Council, an outfit heavily influenced by Weller's long-time interest in soul in general and Motown in particular.

Highly politically motivated, Style Council played first gig at May Day concert in Liverpool for Campaign for Nuclear Disarmament and Merseyside Unemployment Centre and later in year captured mood of a rare British summer with **Long Hot Summer** EP.

Released in March 1983, debut single **Speak Like A Child** peaked at No. 4 on UK chart. Further hits carried group through 1984 leading to Best Debut Group Of The Year award in America's New Music Awards.

Raising money for striking British coal miners and widow of taxi-cab driver David Wilkie, killed during miners' dispute, Weller and Talbot put together Council Collective with aid from Steve White, Junior Giscombe, Dizzy Heights, Animal Nightlife's Leonardo Chignoli, Heaven 17's Martin Ware, Vaughn Toulouse, American soul singer Jimmy Ruffin and Weller's girlfriend D.C. Lee to cut version of **Soul Deep**.

Weller's political stance was reflected in his election as president for Britain of International Youth Year in 1985 and participation in the Red Wedge tour in aid of UK Labour Party in early 1986.

In 1987, Weller further established credibility when Curtis Mayfield and The Valentinos featured as guest vocalists on 1987 set **The Cost Of Loving**. Band then released ironic **Confessions Of A Pop Group** amid reports of acrimony between Weller and Talbot.

Following release of greatest hits package, **Singular Adventures Of The Style Council**, duo split, Weller going on to form Paul Weller Movement, which toured UK in spring of 1991.

Hit Singles:	US	UK
Speak Like A Child, 1983	–	4
Money Go Round, 1983	–	11
Long Hot Summer, 1983	–	3
Solid Bond In Your Heart, 1983	–	11
My Ever Changing Moods, 1984	29	5
Groovin', 1984	–	5
Shout To The Top, 1984	–	7
Walls Come Tumbling Down, 1985	–	6
The Lodgers, 1985	–	13
Have You Ever Had It Blue, 1986	–	14
It Didn't Matter, 1987	–	9
Wanted, 1987	–	20

Above: Our Favourite Shop, The Style Council. Courtesy Polydor Records.

Albums:
Café Bleu (Polydor), 1984
Our Favourite Shop (Polydor), 1985
Home And Abroad (Polydor), 1986
Cost Of Loving (Polydor), 1987
Introducing The Style Council (Polydor), 1987
Confessions Of A Pop Group (Polydor), 1988
Singular Adventures Of The Style Council (Polydor), 1989

Supertramp

UK group formed 1969

Original line-up: Roger Hodgson, vocals, bass, keyboards; Richard Davies, vocals, keyboards; Dave Winthrop, reeds; Richard Palmer, guitar; Bob Miller, drums.

Career: Hodgson and Davies formed band with aid of wealthy benefactor and convinced A&M to take chance on recording them. A&M wasn't particularly impressed with first effort and didn't release it in US. Miller left and was replaced by Kevin Currie. Frank Farrell joined on bass to allow Hodgson's

Below: Final line-up of The Supremes. Mary Wilson is at rear.

move to guitar on second album. Band broke up after LP failed to dent charts and Scandinavian tour met with indifferent audiences.

Hodgson and Davies regrouped with Douglas Thompson on bass and John Anthony Helliwell on reeds (both ex-members of Alan Brown set). Bob Benberg (ex-Bees Make Honey) took over drums. Using production talents of Ken Scott, band recorded million-selling 1974 release **Crime Of The Century**.

In 1977, band moved lock stock and barrel to US, relocation artistically reflected in mega-selling album **Breakfast In America**, which spawned a handful of hit singles. Low-key persona ensured that cutback to four-piece (Davies, Helliwell, Thompson and Benberg) did not lower band in public estimation. 1985 set **Brother Where You Bound** was tenth of career, although rumours were then rife of permanent split.

Hodgson rejoined quartet for promotion of greatest hits package **The Autobiography Of Supertramp** in 1986, cutting solo **Hai Hai** a year later.

Supertramp's apparent studio finale was 1987 set **Free As A Bird**, which failed to make US Top 100 albums. Live offering **Supertramp Live 88** was released in October 1988.

Hit Singles:	US	UK
Dreamer, 1975	–	13
Give A Little Bit, 1977	15	29
The Logical Song, 1979	6	7
Goodbye Stranger, 1979	15	–
Take The Long Way Home, 1979	10	–
Breakfast In America, 1979	–	9
Dreamer, 1980	–	15
It's Raining Again, 1983	11	26

Albums:
Supertramp (A&M), 1970
Indelibly Stamped (A&M), 1971
Crime Of The Century (A&M), 1974
Crisis? What Crisis? (A&M), 1975
Even In The Quietest Moments (A&M), 1977
Breakfast In America (A&M), 1979
Paris (A&M), 1980

Famous Last Words (A&M), 1982
Brother Where You Bound (A&M), 1985
Autobiography Of Supertramp (A&M), 1986
Free As A Bird (A&M), 1987
Live 1988 (A&M), 1988

The Supremes

US vocal group formed 1959

Original line-up: Diana Ross; Mary Wilson; Florence Ballard; Barbara Martin.

Career: Originally known as Primettes, formed by Mary Wilson, Florence Ballard, Diana Ross and Betty Anderson in Detroit. Anderson quickly replaced by Barbara Martin. Group did local gigs with male group The Primes (later The Temptations) and recorded for Lupine without great success.

In 1960 they came to attention of emerging local entrepreneur Berry Gordy, who signed them to Tamla Motown. Over the next few years group acted as back-up singers and recorded handful of moderately successful singles. Barbara Martin dropped out in 1962 and group carried on as trio.

Turning-point came when Gordy assigned writing and production team Holland/Dozier/Holland to group in 1963; **Where Did Our Love Go** became US No. 1 and massive worldwide hit in 1964. Next three years saw trio become most successful female vocal group in pop history, with slew of international chart-toppers.

From 1966 group was billed as Diana Ross And The Supremes, Gordy already singling out Ross as potential solo superstar. Florence Ballard left to pursue unsuccessful solo career (ending in untimely death by heart attack in 1976). Replacement was Cindy Birdsong, formerly of Pattie LaBelle and Bluebelles. Hits continued, although not on such a massive scale, until Diana Ross left group in 1969 to achieve superstardom. Between 1964 and 1969 group had notched up 12 No. 1 hits.

Although Ross's departure (she was replaced by Jean Terrell) was expected to deal mortal blow to group's success, more major hits were forthcoming, starting with **Up The Ladder To The Roof** in 1970. Couplings with Temptations and Four Tops also helped keep Supremes at forefront during this period.

After 1972 group began to look slightly old-fashioned against new, more militant stance of black music; it also suffered from personnel changes. Mary Wilson continued to tour and record with various line-ups until 1977 when group broke up.

Supremes' 60s output with Holland/Dozier/Holland ranks among finest pop music ever. They were also influential in making black music a major international force, combining glamour, real talent and touch of soul hitherto missing from many female vocal line-ups. In retrospect, group may appear simply as launch pad for Diana Ross, but Supremes' records still stand up as classics.

The Supremes were inducted into Rock 'n' Roll Hall Of Fame in 1988. Motown tribute **Love Supreme** subsequently made it into the US charts.

Hit Singles:	US	UK
Where Did Our Love Go, 1964	1	3
Baby Love, 1964	1	1
Come See About Me, 1964	1	27
Stop! In The Name Of Love, 1965	1	7
Back In My Arms Again, 1965	1	40
Nothing But Heartaches, 1965	11	–
I Hear A Symphony, 1965	1	39

My World Is Empty Without You, 1966	5	–
Love Is Like An Itching In My Heart, 1966	9	–
You Can't Hurry Love, 1966	1	3
You Keep Me Hangin' On, 1966	1	8
Love Is Here And Now You're Gone, 1967	1	17
The Happening, 1967	1	6
Reflections, 1967	2	5
In And Out Of Love, 1967	9	13
Love Child, 1968	1	15
I'm Livin' In Shame, 1969	10	14
Some Day We'll Be Together, 1969	1	13
Up The Ladder To The Roof, 1970	10	6
Stoned Love, 1970	7	3
Nathan Jones, 1971	16	5
Floy Joy, 1972	16	9
Automatically Sunshine, 1972	37	10
Baby Love, 1974	–	12

With The Four Tops:

River Deep Mountain High, 1971	14	4

With The Temptations:

I'm Gonna Make You Love Me, 1969	11	3
I Second That Emotion, 1969	–	18

Albums:
Live At The Talk Of The Town (Motown), 1968
Greatest Hits (Motown), 1968
Love Child (Motown), 1969
Greatest Hits Volume 2 (Motown), 1970
Baby Love (–/MFP), 1973
Anthology (Motown), 1974
At Their Best (Motown), 1978
Stoned Love (–/MFP), 1979
Greatest Hits (featuring Mary Wilson) (Motown), 1981
Motown Superstars Series Volume 1 (Motown/–), 1982

With The Four Tops:
The Magnificent Seven (Motown), 1971

With The Temptations:
TCB (Motown), 1969

Mary Wilson Solo:
Mary Wilson (Motown), 1979

Below: Talking Heads before they all went their separate ways.

Talking Heads

US group formed 1976

Original line-up: David Byrne, vocals, guitar; Chris Frantz, drums; Tina Weymouth, vocals, bass, synthesizer; Jerry Harrison, vocals, guitar, keyboards.

Career: Byrne, Frantz and Weymouth met at Rhode Island School of Design in early 70s. Trio began working, living, and then playing music together. In 1976 they decided to expand line-up and asked Harrison (ex-Modern Lovers) to join. Harrison had grave doubts about any further involvement with music business and had applied for graduate school, but later agreed to join provided he could finish semester.

Band cashed in on Sire Records' search for 'new wave' groups and recorded **Talking Heads: 77**. Upon release it was clear Heads didn't fit into neat category.

Next album, **More Songs About Buildings And Food**, may have overloaded on ideas Byrne picked up while studying design (cover was modern mosaic of band made up of polaroid prints), but it also contained music which moved mind and soul. Single **Take Me To The River** earned heavy radio play and opened up audience. Band had become intellectual favourites. **Fear Of Music** LP was instant critical success and won notice in UK.

Band members became involved in variety of private projects. Byrne worked on albums with Brian Eno; Harrison released solo LP. Weymouth and Frantz enjoyed outside success with Tom Tom Club.

This activity alone could have caused a delay before next release, but **Remain In Light** was soon out, and went beyond sparse sound of previous LPs. **Light** explored African rhythms, added side group of musicians, and generally destroyed any possible preconceptions about band. Supporting tour included expanded line-up so audiences could hear new efforts. Band emphasized change by including live material going back to early days, as well as new material for LP **The Name Of This Band Is Talking Heads** (1982).

1983 set **Speaking In Tongues** provided Talking Heads with first US Top 10 single, **Burning Down The House**. Band then teamed with director Jonathan Demme (the man behind *The Silence Of The Lambs*) for *Stop Making Sense* concert movie, which provided outstanding soundtrack. Subsequent albums, **Little Creatures** (which included majestic single **Road To Nowhere**) and **True Stories** consolidated Byrne's growing reputation as both writer and musician.

Taking time out from Talking Heads, Byrne recorded **Theatre In The Knee Plays** LP (later adapted for stage) before scoring *True Stories* flick, an intensely personal vision of small-town America which he narrated. The movie provided Talking Heads with another chart LP. Follow-up **Naked** (1988), recorded in Paris with producer Steve Lillywhite, proved band's swan-song when Byrne declared himself 'out' of future group activities. The remaining trio toured US in 1990, while Weymouth and Frantz also revived Tom Tom Club. Harrison had previously formed Casual Gods outfit, who cut eponymous debut LP in 1988 and followed this up with the **Walk On Water** set in 1990.

Byrne composed music for Bernardo Bertolucci's magnificent epic *The Last Emperor*, and also recorded solo albums **Rei Momo** (1989) and **The Forest** (1991); has also compiled series of anthologies of Brazilian and Cuban music, and composed 'Ile Aiye' for public television in the US.

Unpredictable and imaginative, Byrne is likely to crop up in anything unusual, while subsequent endeavours of his former teammates confirms all-around ability of Talking Heads.

Hit Singles:	US	UK
Once In A Lifetime, 1981	–	14
Burning Down The House, 1983	9	–
Road To Nowhere, 1985	–	6
And She Was, 1986	–	17
Wild Wild Life, 1986	–	43

Albums:
Talking Heads: 77 (Sire), 1977
More Songs About Buildings And Food (Sire), 1978
Fear Of Music (Sire), 1979
Remain In Light (Sire), 1980
The Name Of This Band Is Talking Heads (Sire), 1982
Speaking In Tongues (Sire), 1983
Stop Making Sense (EMI), 1984
Little Creatures (EMI), 1985
True Stories (EMI), 1986
Naked (EMI), 1988

David Byrne Solo:
Music For The Knee Plays (EMI), 1985
Songs From Catherine Wheel (Sire), 1981
Rei Momo (Sire/WEA), 1989
The Forest (Luaka Bop/–), 1991
Brazil Classics 3 (WEA), 1991

The Tom Tom Club Albums (Frantz And Weymouth):
Tom Tom Club (Sire/Island)
Close To The Bone (Sire), 1983
Boom Boom Chi Boom Boom (Sire), 1989

Left: True Stories, Talking Heads. Courtesy EMI Records.

Jerry Harrison:
Casual Gods (Sire), 1988
Walk On Water (Sire), 1990

James Taylor

US vocalist, composer, guitarist
Born Boston, Massachusetts, March 12, 1948

Career: Taylor's mother passed interest in music on to her children — thus Taylor's decision to try musical career following high school. In 1987 he recorded some tapes with friend Danny Kortchmar in New York as the Flying Machine. He moved to Notting Hill area of London and passed demos of work to new Beatles company, Apple Ltd. **James Taylor** was released and ignored, though it included his excellent **Carolina In My Mind**.

With Apple falling into disarray, Taylor returned to US. After bouts of depression, and another round of mental institutions (his first had been while still in high school), with support of producer Peter Asher, he finally signed with Warner Bros. Taylor's painful expression, deep introspection and laid-back delivery began selling well. **You've Got A Friend** single reached No. 1 in US and his popularity peaked in 1972. In 1973 he married Carly Simon (they divorced in late 70s). He branched out and encouraged siblings Livingston and Kate Taylor in their musical careers.

Surprisingly, in view of his writing credentials, Taylor chose to finish decade with reworking of Sam Cooke's **Wonderful World** and The Drifters' **Up On The Roof**, which nonetheless maintained his chart status. Although 1980s saw sporadic album releases, but selective high-profile concert appearances (July 4 Disarmament Festival in the USSR, Prince's Trust gala in UK, both 1987) have done more to keep Taylor in the public eye.

Latterly, Taylor has devoted energies to charitable work, although 1988 album **Never Die Young** enjoyed modicum of success. In 1990, artist undertook coast-to-coast US tour, before joining forces with new American sensation, Marc Cohn, on that performer's self-titled debut LP.

Hit Singles:	US	UK
Fire And Rain, 1970	3	42
You've Got A Friend, 1971	1	4
Don't Let Me Be Lonely Tonight, 1973	14	–
Mockingbird (with Carly Simon), 1974	5	34
How Sweet It Is, 1975	5	–
Handy Man, 1977	4	–
Your Smiling Face, 1977	20	–
(What A) Wonderful World, 1978	17	–

With J.D. Souther:

Her Town Too, 1981	11	–

Albums:
James Taylor (Apple), 1968
Sweet Baby James (Warner Bros), 1970
James Taylor And The Original Flying Machine (Springboard/DJM), 1971
Mud Slide Slim* (Warner Bros), 1971
One Man Dog (Warner Bros), 1972
Walking Man (Warner Bros), 1974
Rainy Day Man (Trip/DJM), 1975
Gorilla (Warner Bros), 1975
In The Pocket (Warner Bros), 1976

169

Best Of (Warner Bros), 1976
JT (Columbia/CBS), 1977
Greatest Hits (Warner Bros), 1977
Flag (Columbia/CBS), 1979
Dad Loves His Work (Columbia/CBS), 1981
That's Why I'm Here (Columbia/CBS), 1986

Above: Mud Slide Slim, James Taylor. Courtesy Warner Bros Records.

Classic Songs (WEA), 1987
Never Die Young (Columbia/CBS), 1988
Absolute (Biglife), 1991
*Released as double album, UK only, 1975

Tears For Fears
UK group formed 1980

Original line-up: Roland Orzabel, guitar, vocals; Curt Smith, bass, vocals.

Career: Pretentious pop duo who have acquired more accomplished talents after a rather lightweight start.

Orzabel and Smith first met in early 1970s, and played in variety of nondescript bands before signing with Phonogram as Tears For Fears (name comes from Arthur Yanoff's book *Prisoners Of Pain*). First single **Suffer The Children** was recorded with David Lord on synthesizers.

Temporary alliance with producer Mike Howlett (Flock Of Seagulls, China Crisis, Thompson Twins, etc), before Chris Hughes (Adam And The Ants, Wang Chung, etc) took charge. Debut LP **The Hurting** was released in 1983.

However, it was **Songs From The Big Chair** set, which propelled them to inter-

Below: James Taylor, a major 1970s star still active in the 1990s.

national superstardom. Album spawned three major hits, including worldwide No. 1 **Everybody Wants To Rule The World** (later theme-song, as **Run The World**, for hunger relief in Africa). Duo subsequently

decided to take indefinite sabbatical, which was broken by re-working of old hits at the beginning of 1988.

Duo returned to studios for **The Seeds Of Love** (1989), an instant UK No. 1, which spawned hit singles **Sowing The Seeds Of Love** and **Woman In Chains**. Toured USA the following year, with Debbie Harry enlisted as support.

Latterly, Smith and Orzabel have enjoyed success as producers of **Circle Of One** LP for their former vocalist Oleta Adams (who guested on **Big Chair** set).

Hit Singles:

	US	UK
Mad World, 1982	—	3
Change, 1983	—	4
Pale Shelter, 1983	—	5
Mother's Talk, 1984	—	14
Shout, 1985	1	4
Everybody Wants To Rule The World, 1986	1	5
Head Over Heels, 1985	3	12
Sowing The Seeds Of Love, 1989	2	5

Albums:
The Hurting (Mercury), 1983
Songs From The Big Chair (Mercury), 1985
The Seeds Of Love (Fontana), 1989

The Temptations
US vocal group formed 1961

Original line-up: Otis Williams; Melvin Franklin; Eldridge Bryant; Eddie Kendricks; Paul Williams.

Career: Formed in Detroit in 1961 from amalgam of elements from Otis Williams and The Distants (Otis Williams, Franklin, Bryant) and The Primes (Kendricks, Paul Williams). Temptations were recording for Tamla Motown a year later but it was not until David Ruffin replaced Bryant in 1963 (his brother Jimmy Ruffin had been offered job but declined) that breakthrough came. The contrast between lead vocals of Kendricks — high, sweet and soft — and Ruffin — gritty and emotion-laden — provided formula for success: thanks were also due to promising young songwriter and producer Smokey Robinson.

The Robinson-penned, Kendricks-led **The Way You Do The Things You Do** gave them 1964 hit. Two years later, with Ruffin singing lead, **My Girl** brought them to forefront among black vocal groups, overtaking Curtis Mayfield's Impressions in mass popularity.

In 1966 group started working with writer/producer Norman Whitfield, who exploited more biting version of Motown sound with **Ain't Too Proud To Beg, I Know (I'm Losing You)** and others, counter-balanced by smooth ballad efforts.

After Ruffin split for solo career, Dennis Edwards was brought in from Contours and Whitfield took opportunity to push Temptations in new musical direction. So-called 'psychedelic soul' style evolved with dramatic use of recording effects and rock-influenced arrangements which made **Cloud Nine, Runaway Child, Running Wild, Can't Get Next To You, Psychedelic Shack** and **Ball Of Confusion** such totally distinctive hits.

A return to soft balladry saw **Just My Imagination** earn The Temptations' first platinum single award, and marked last appearance of solo-bound Kendricks; now seriously ill, Paul Williams also left (he died

soon after). Their replacements were Damon Harris (ex-Vandals) and Richard Street (ex-Monitors).

Further Whitfield-produced progressive soul hits came with **Superstar, Take A Look Around, Papa Was A Rolling Stone** and the monumental **Masterpiece** album.

Following departure of Harris (replaced by Glenn Leonard in 1975) and Edwards (in 1979), group seemed to lose much of its fire. Whitfield having moved on to mastermind Undisputed Truth, then Rose Royce, plus his own label, Temptations' subsequent work lacked sense of direction.

After unsuccessful stint with Atlantic, group returned to home base at Motown for **Power** set with Edwards temporarily back in line-up. Subsequent **Reunion** LP saw brief return of Kendricks and Ruffin, although further personnel changes ensued when Ron Tyson and Ollie Woodson joined.

Group then enjoyed chart success as backing vocalists on Bruce Willis's painful rendition of their classic **Up On The Roof**, which made No. 2 in UK charts. Minor revival prompted another return for Edwards, who appeared on **Together Again** LP. The Temptations were inducted into Rock 'n' Roll Hall Of Fame in 1989.

Kendrick and Ruffin began working as duo following successful 1985 collaboration with Hall And Oates. Their **Live At The Apollo** LP, recorded at re-opening of legendary venue, charted in both US and UK. Pair subsequently signed with RCA for **Ruffin And Kendricks** album, and were enjoying renaissance before Ruffin, who had history of drug abuse, died in June 1991. Five months later, Kendricks underwent surgery for removal of a lung.

Hit Singles:

	US	UK
The Way You Do The Things You Do, 1964	11	—
My Girl, 1965	1	43
It's Growing, 1965	18	45
Since I Lost My Baby, 1965	17	—
My Baby, 1965	13	—
Ain't Too Proud To Beg, 1966	13	21
Beauty Is Only Skin Deep, 1966	3	18
(I Know) I'm Losing You, 1966	8	19
All I Need, 1967	8	—
You're My Everything, 1967	6	26
(Loneliness Made Me Realize) It's You That I Need, 1967	14	—
I Wish It Would Rain, 1968	4	45
I Could Never Love Another (After Loving You), 1968	13	47
Cloud Nine, 1968	6	15
Run Away Child, Running Wild, 1969	6	—
Get Ready, 1969*	29	10
Don't Let The Joneses Get You Down, 1969	20	—
I Can't Get Next To You, 1969	1	13
Psychedelic Shack, 1970	7	33
Ball Of Confusion (That's What The World Is Today), 1970	3	7
Just My Imagination (Running Away With Me), 1971	1	8
Superstar (Remember How You Got Where You Are), 1971	18	32
Take A Look Around, 1972	30	13
Papa Was A Rollin' Stone, 1972	1	14
Masterpiece, 1973	7	—
*In 1966, US		

With Diana Ross and Supremes:

	US	UK
I'm Gonna Make You Love Me, 1969	2	3
I Second That Emotion, 1969	—	18

Albums:
Greatest Hits (Gordy/Motown), 1967

Cloud Nine/Puzzle People (Motown), 1969/1970
Psychedelic Shack (Gordy/Motown), 1970
Psychedelic Shack/All Directions (Motown), 1970/1972
Puzzle People (Gordy/Motown), 1970
Greatest Hits Volume II (Gordy/Motown), 1972
All Directions (Gordy/Motown), 1972
Masterpiece (Gordy/Motown), 1973
Anthology Vols 1 And 2 (Motown), 1977
Temptations (—/Motown), 1977
Sing Smokey (—/Motown), 1979
Power (Gordy/Motown), 1980
20 Golden Greats (—/Motown), 1980
Reunion (Gordy/—), 1981
All The Million Sellers (Gordy/Motown), 1982
Get Ready (—/Pickwick), 1982
Give Love At Christmas (—/Motown), 1982
Surface Thrills (Motown), 1983
Back To Basics (Motown), 1983
Truly For You (Motown), 1984
Touch Me (Motown), 1985
17 Greatest Hits (Motown), 1985
Song For You (Motown), 1986
25th Anniversary (Motown), 1986
To Be Continued (Motown), 1986
Live At The Copa/With A Lot O Soul (Motown), 1987
Together Again (Motown), 1987
Milestone (Motown), 1991

With The Supremes:
TCB (Tamla Motown), 1969

David Ruffin And Eddie Kendricks:
Live At The Apollo (with Hall And Oates) (RCA), 1985

Above: Sheet Music, 10cc. Courtesy Mercury Records.

10cc
UK group formed 1972

Original line-up: Eric Stewart, guitar, vocals; Graham Gouldman, bass, vocals; Lol Creme, guitar, vocals; Kevin Godley, drums, vocals.

Career: In June 1970, Stewart, Creme and Godley had worldwide hit as Hotlegs with **Neanderthal Man**. Godley and Creme had first met at art school; Stewart had been in Mindbenders (who had 1966 UK Top 5 Hit with **Groovy Kind Of Love**). Graham Gouldman, another Mindbender, joined Hotlegs for 1970 UK tour supporting Moody Blues, and wrote Yardbirds' hit **For Your Love**. Stewart had set up Strawberry Studios in Cheshire, and in 1971 Neil Sedaka recorded his comeback album **Solitaire** there with Stewart, Gouldman, Godley and Creme. Sedaka returned following year to cut **The Tra La Days Are Over** (Gouldman

Above: 10cc's debut album with Rubber Bullets. Courtesy UK Records.

had met Sedaka while he was working as a songwriter for the Kasenatz-Katz organization in New York's Brill Building).

Godley and Creme came up with **Donna**, a clever parody (as much of their work is) of US 50s hits, and took song to Jonathan King who released it on his new UK label, King, changing band's name to 10cc. Record made No. 2. First chart-topper **Rubber Bullets** scored in 1973.

Following debut album **10cc**, band played first live gigs at Douglas, Isle Of Man, in August 1973, adding Paul Burgess on drums; toured US twice in 1974.

Switching to Phonogram early in 1975 for third album, **The Original Soundtrack**, group continued run of hits; peaked creatively with classic single **I'm Not In Love**.

After guesting with Rolling Stones at Knebworth in August 1976, band was depleted in October when Godley and Creme decided to leave for career as duo.

With Stewart and Gouldman now firmly in control of creative aspect, Stuart Tosh, Rick Fenn and Tony O'Malley joined 10cc in April 1977, debuting on May UK tour. Duncan Mackay was added on keyboards 10 months later.

Group's planned Japan/Australia tour was cancelled after motorcycle accident to Gouldman in Japan. He was soon back in action writing and recording score for that year's *Animalympics* movie and title song for movie *Sunburn*. Stewart produced Sad Cafe's second album as well as songs for French movie *Girls*, recorded own solo album in 1981. Further outside production work came for Gouldman with The Ramones and Gilbert O'Sullivan in 1981.

Godley and Creme went on to become successful artists in own right. Pair also developed parallel career as video makers, becoming much in demand as video became essential part of pop promotion process. Gouldman also formed Wax duo with US AOR artist Andrew Gold.

Hit Singles:

	US	UK
Donna, 1972	—	2
Rubber Bullets, 1973	—	1
The Dean And I, 1973	—	10
Wall Street Shuffle, 1974	—	10
Life Is A Minestrone, 1975	—	7
I'm Not In Love, 1975	1	1
Art For Art's Sake, 1975	—	5
I'm Mandy Fly Me, 1976	60	6
Things We Do For Love, 1976	5	6
Good Morning Judge, 1977	—	5
Dreadlock Holiday, 1978	44	1
Under Your Thumb, 1981	—	3
Wedding Bells, 1981	—	7

Godley and Creme:

Cry, 1985	17	19

Albums:
10cc (UK), 1973
Sheet Music (UK), 1974

The Original Soundtrack (Mercury), 1975
How Dare You (Mercury), 1976
Deceptive Bends (Mercury), 1977
Live And Let Live (Mercury), 1977
Bloody Tourists (Mercury), 1978
Greatest Hits (Mercury), 1979
Things We Do For Love (Mercury), 1979
Look Hear (Warner Bros/Mercury), 1980
Greatest Hits, 71-78 (Polydor/—), 1981
Ten Out Of Ten (Warner Bros/Mercury), 1981
In Concert (—/Contour), 1982
Windows In The Jungle (Mercury), 1983

Godley and Creme:
Consequences (Mercury), 1977
'L' (Mercury), 1978
Freeze Frame (Polydor), 1979
Ismism (Polydor), 1981
Birds Of Prey (Polydor), 1983
The History Mix (Polydor), 1986
Goodbye Blue Sky (Polydor), 1988

Ten Years After
UK group formed 1967

Original line-up: Alvin Lee, Gibson ES 335 guitar, vocals; Chick Churchill, keyboards; Leo Lyons, bass; Rick Lee, drums.

Above: Alvin Lee, leader of Ten Years After and the inferior Ten Years Later.

Career: One of major bands to emerge from mid-60s blues revival movement in UK. Formed by Lee and Lyons who met in Nottingham and worked together in Hamburg for a time. On returning to Britain, met music scholar Rick Lee while working in West End production and formed Jaybirds. Adding Chick Churchill, changed name and came to critics' attention via appearances at London's Marquee Club. Group signed to Decca's Deram subsidiary who put out first album without waiting to score any hit singles (an unusual move in those days).

Famed American promoter Bill Graham heard album and booked group for his Fillmore Auditorium venues in US. Subsequent albums and appearance at massive Woodstock rock festival (and in the *Woodstock* movie in which their 11-minute opus **Goin' Home** scored heavily) established world reputation for fast and furious blend of blues and heavy rock.

Introduced electronic effects for **A Space In Time** and moved into more pensive direction; album was US smash. But, by 1973, Lee was disillusioned with group's direction and exhaustive tour schedules (a record 28 US tours before they broke up, and describing band as 'a travelling jukebox'.

Members took time off for solo projects and Lee retired to 15th-century country home to build studio and record gospel singer Mylon Lefevre. Churchill's solo album **You And Me** appeared in 1973. **Ten Years After** set that year was live album compiled from concerts in Amsterdam, Rotterdam, Frankfurt and Paris.

A month before band's scheduled spring 1974 UK tour, Lee appeared at London's Rainbow with own hastily assembled nine-piece band. Show was released on disc as **Alvin Lee And Co In Flight**.

Ten Years After's own Rainbow appearance a month later was sell-out. It proved to be their last British stage appearance as Lee set off to tour world as Alvin Lee And Co.

In May 1975, Alvin Lee declared Ten Years After defunct, and Rick Lee formed own band. However, just one month later Ten Years After were back on road for US tour to fulfill contractual obligations before final split. Lee formed Ten Years Later in 1977 with Tom Compton on drums and Mick Hawksworth on bass; released two LPs, **Rocket Fuel** (1978) and **Ride On** (1979). Since then, Alvin Lee has recorded further solo efforts; Chick Churchill has become professional manager at Chrysalis Music; and Leo Lyons has worked as producer, notably with UFO.

Band did reconvene in late 80s when **About Time** LP made some minor noises in US chart. Unit also appeared at a couple of German HM festivals during same year.

Hit Singles:

	US	UK
Love Like A Man, 1970	—	10

Albums:
Ten Years After (Deram), 1967
Undead (Deram), 1968
Stonehenge (Deram), 1969
Ssssssh (Chrysalis), 1969
Cricklewood Green (Chrysalis), 1970
Watt (Chrysalis), 1970
Alvin Lee And Co (Deram), 1972
A Space In Time (Columbia/Chrysalis), 1972
Rock 'n' Roll To The World (Columbia/Chrysalis), 1972
Recorded Live (Columbia/Chrysalis), 1973
Positive Vibrations (Columbia/Chrysalis), 1974
Goin' Home (Deram/Chrysalis), 1975
Classic Performances (Columbia/Chrysalis), 1977
Hear Me Calling (—/Decca), 1981
Goin' Home, Their Greatest Hits (London/—), 1975
Original Recordings Volume 1 (See For Miles), 1987
Original Recordings Volume 2 (See For Miles), 1987

Below: Phil Lynott (left) and Scott Gorham of Thin Lizzy.

About Time (Chrysalis), 1989

Ten Years Later:
Rocket Fuel (Polydor), 1978
Ride On (Polydor), 1979

Alvin Lee Solo:
Free Fall (—/Avatar), 1980
RX5 (Atlantic/—), 1981

With Mylon Lefevre:
Road To Freedom (Columbia/CBS), 1973

Above: Vagabonds Of The Western World, Thin Lizzy. Courtesy London Records.

Thin Lizzy
UK group formed 1970

Original line-up: Phil Lynott, Fender Precision, Ibanez basses, lead vocals; Eric Bell, lead guitar; Brian Downey, drums.

Career: Hard-rocking group equally at home with blues ballads, Thin Lizzy was accessible and electric on record.

First hit was **Whiskey In The Jar**. Hard-driving 1973 version of traditional folk song reached No. 6, staying in charts for eight weeks, but next three singles flopped. By then Eric Bell, disturbed by Irish troubles, left group after Belfast concert, to be briefly replaced by Gary Moore, until Scott Gorham and Brian Robertson were added.

In summer 1974, band signed with Vertigo label and made Reading Festival debut. More albums followed and UK, European and US tours, but three more singles failed to make charts. Then, five years and five LPs after first release, **Jailbreak** album provided **The Boys Are Back In Town** single, which entered Top 10 in UK and US charts. Title single also made charts, and album reached Top 10 on both sides of Atlantic. *Melody Maker*'s readers' poll voted band 'brightest hope'. However, summer 1976 US tour was cancelled when Lynott contracted hepatitis and winter US tour was postponed when Robertson injured hand in brawl.

Next two singles made 1977 charts. Band headlined Reading Festival, topped bill on

US tour, and **Bad Reputation**, their eighth album, reached No. 4. Video of Rainbow Theatre concert in March 1978 was shown on television in many countries but not in Britain. Albums and singles continued to reach charts; pick-up band called Greedy Bastards formed and Robertson left the group going on to Motorhead, to be replaced by Gary Moore. Moore's single, **Parisienne Walkways** co-written by Lynott, reached No. 8 in 1979. **Black Rose**, released same month, topped album charts.

Tours still beset by troubles; three European dates were cancelled when Lynott got food poisoning and Moore was sacked for missing two US dates. Ex-Pink Floyd guitarist Snowy White joined group in 1980. The same year Lynott's solo album **Solo In Soho** reached No. 28. Band toured Japan and Australia, and further albums and singles made UK Top 30. In 1981 **The Adventures Of Thin Lizzy**, compilation of a decade of hits, was successful (helped by television advertising campaign). With Darren Warton, keyboards, and John Sykes, guitar, band played farewell gig at Reading Festival in August 1983.

Lynott and Downey then formed five-piece Grand Slam, which attracted less attention than Lynott's well documented personal problems (marriage, drinks, drugs). Phil Lynott eventually succumbed to indulgent lifestyle, dying in January 1986. Moore went on to enjoy success with his own band, and later cut magnificent **Still Got The Blues** LP in 1990 with Albert Collins and Albert King.

Hit Singles:	US	UK
Whiskey In The Jar, 1973	—	6
The Boys Are Back In Town, 1976	12	8
Don't Believe A Word, 1977	—	12
Dancin' In The Moonlight (It's Caught Me In The Spotlight), 1977	—	14
Rosalie — Cowgirl's Song, 1978	—	20
Waiting For An Alibi, 1979	—	9
Do Anything You Want To, 1979	—	14
Killer On The Loose, 1980	—	10
Killer Live (EP), 1981	—	19

Phil Lynott and Gary Moore:

Out In The Fields, 1985	—	5

Phil Lynott Solo:

Yellow Pearl, 1981	—	14

Gary Moore Solo:

Parisienne Walkways, 1979	—	8

Above: Thin Lizzy's eponymous debut album, released in 1971. Courtesy London Records.

Albums:
Thin Lizzy (London/Decca), 1971
Shades Of A Blue Orphanage (—/Decca), 1972

Vagabonds Of The Western World (London/Decca), 1973
Night Life (Mercury/Vertigo), 1974
Fighting (Mercury/Vertigo), 1975
Jailbreak (Mercury/Vertigo), 1976
Johnny The Fox (Mercury/Vertigo), 1976
Remembering (—/Decca), 1976
Bad Reputation (Mercury/Vertigo), 1977
Live And Dangerous (Warner Bros/Vertigo), 1978
Rocker (1971-1974) (London/—), 1978
Black Rose (Warner Bros/Vertigo), 1979
Chinatown (Warner Bros/Vertigo), 1980
Renegade (Warner Bros/Vertigo), 1981
Adventures Of (—/Vertigo), 1981
Thunder And Lightning (Warner Bros/Vertigo), 1983
Collection (Castle Collectors)
Lizzy Killers (Vertigo)
Dedication — The Very Best Of (Mercury), 1991

Phil Lynott Solo:
Solo In Soho (Warner Bros/Vertigo), 1980
The Philip Lynott Album (Warner Bros/Vertigo), 1982
Making Love From Memory (MCA/—), 1982

Gary Moore Solo:
Run For Cover (Relativity/Ten), 1986
Wild Frontier (Virgin), 1987
After The War (with Ozzy Osbourne) (Virgin), 1989
Rockin' Every Night (Live In Japan) (Virgin), 1989
We Want Moore (Virgin), 1989
Still Got The Blues (Charisma/Virgin), 1990

Three Dog Night
US group formed 1968

Original line-up: Danny Hutton, vocals; Cory Wells, vocals; Chuck Negron, vocals; Joe Schermie, bass; Floyd Sneed, drums; Jim Greenspoon, keyboards; Mike Allsop, guitar.

Career: Original members were all LA-based musicians passing through small local groups and doing session work. Hutton instigated ideas of group based on three lead vocalists and recruited Wells and Negron. According to Eskimo lore, the colder the night, the more dogs are brought in to sleep with, coldest being 'three dog night'. Despite name, however, band was far from cold and began picking up US gold records.

Although albums sold extremely well, group remained primarily a singles factory. **Joy To The World** was *the* No. 1 US single of 1971. By 1972 when hits stopped, band became disjointed. Jack Ryland replaced Schermie, and second keyboards player, Skip Konte, joined. Then band disappeared.

Nova-like career came at time when singles were disdained by 'serious' rock crowd, so it was easy to dismiss band as having little or no impact. Yet Three Dog Night must be fondly remembered for turning non-original material into joyful celebration all their own.

Hit Singles:	US	UK
One, 1969	5	—
Easy To Be Hard, 1969	4	—
Eli's Coming, 1969	10	—
Celebrate, 1970	15	—

Right: 'Close but no cigar'. Boston-based band Throwing Muses are still searching for mainstream success.

Mama Told Me (Not To Come), 1970	1	3
Out In The Country, 1970	15	—
One Man Band, 1970	19	—
Joy To The World, 1971	1	24
Liar, 1971	7	—
An Old Fashioned Love Song, 1971	4	—
Never Been To Spain, 1971	5	—
The Family Of Man, 1972	12	—
Black And White, 1972	1	—
Pieces Of April, 1972	19	—
Shambala, 1973	3	—
Let Me Serenade, 1973	17	—

Albums:
Joy To The World — Greatest Hits (MCA/Anchor), 1974
Best Of (MCA/—), 1975

Worth Searching Out:
It Ain't Easy (Dunhill/Stateside), 1970
Harmony (Dunhill/Probe), 1971

Throwing Muses
US group formed 1988

Original line-up: Kristin Hersh, guitar, piano, vocals; Tanya Donnelly, guitar, vocals; Leslie Langston, bass, vocals; David Narcizo, drums.

Career: Once described as the 'Cinderellas' of the US indie scene, Boston-based Muses have never quite attained the commercial success they undoubtedly deserve.

Based around writing abilities of Kristin Hersh and Tanya Donnelly, band's rough edge did not do material full justice on early albums, following debut self-titled LP (1986), released on 4AD. However, solid workload (particularly on US East Coast) and potent political message maintained Muses' role as mainstay of New York's alternative music scene.

Group finally look to have discovered cross-over answer with 1991 LP **The Real Ramona**, which saw Fred Abong replace San Francisco-bound Leslie Langston. The smoother sound of **Ramona** did not aggravate critics, and also made musical approach more accessible. Ironically, Donnelly quit Muses in autumn of 1991, which,

coupled with Hersh's domestic problems, threw veil over outfit's future activities.

Albums:
Throwing Muses (Sire/4AD), 1986
The Fat Skier (Sire/4AD), 1987
Horse Tornado (Sire/4AD), 1988
Humkpapa (Sire/4AD), 1989
The Real Ramona (Sire/4AD), 1991

Toots And The Maytals
Jamaican group formed 1962

Original line-up: Toots Hibbert, vocals; Raleigh Gordon, vocals; Jerry Matthias, vocals.

Career: Legendary ska/rock-steady/reggae vocal exponents whose contribution to West Indian music has been at least the equal of Bob Marley And Wailers.

Toots (real name Frederick) formed group (originally known as Vikings) in 1962, and cut first records at Clement Coxsone Dodd's Brentford Road studios. Group's debut single for Studio One label was **Hallelujah**, a local hit, followed by similar gospel-styled **Six And Seven Books Of Moses** and **Never Grow Old**.

Trio then switched allegiance to sound-system pioneer Prince Buster, before signing with Byron Lee's BMN operation. A slew of Jamaican hits followed, but the group's activities were curtailed when Toots was jailed for two years after admitting marijuana possession.

Upon release, Toots placed his future in the hands of notable producer Leslie Kong, for whom **54-46 That's My Number** single charted in UK. Further Kong-inspired hits included **Do The Reggay**, considered the first citing of the term (albeit with different spelling) used to describe Jamaica's indigenous pop music, **Pressure Drop**, **Monkey Man** and **Water Melon**.

Following death of Kong, Toots And Maytals returned to Lee for notable **Funky Kingston** album (Island Records), which included ripping cover of Kingsmen's 60s R&B classic **Louie Louie**. Band later toured States and UK, and enjoyed chart single in

Britain with **Reggae Got Soul** from album of same name, on which Steve Winwood contributed. A 1980 show at London's Hammersmith Odeon was used for **Toots Live** set which appeared in shops a miraculous 24 hours after concert.

With Hibbert and Matthias now considered superfluous, Toots continued to weave his magic, despite lack of international success. His endeavours to cross-over were nearly rewarded when 1988 album **Toots In Memphis** attracted much critical acclaim.

Albums:
Funky Kingston (Mango/Island), 1973
From The Roots (–/Trojan), 1973
In The Dark (–/Island), 1974
Reggae Got Soul (Mango/Island), 1978
The Maytals (State), 1978
Pass The Pipe (Mango/Island), 1979
Live (Mango/Island), 1980
Just Like That (Mango/Island), 1980
Best Of (–/Trojan), 1984
An Hour Live (Genes), 1990

Peter Tosh

Jamaican vocalist, composer, guitarist
Born Peter McIntosh, Kingston, Jamaica, October 19, 1944
Died September 11, 1987

Career: A fervent preacher of Rastafarian ethic, Peter Tosh established himself as leading figure of Jamaica's alternative culture, first as member of influential Wailers, alongside Bob Marley and Bunny (Wailer) Livingstone, then as solo artist, allied — in somewhat unlikely fashion — to Mick Jagger and Keith Richards via Rolling Stones Records.

An adept musician by early teens, playing steel guitar, acoustic guitar and keyboards, Tosh met fellow Wailers in Kingston ghetto suburb Trenchtown, sharing socially aware songwriting, taking themes from politics, religion, poverty and social repression. Among his songs for Wailers were **Get Up**, **Stand Up**, **One Foundation** and **400 Years**.

When trio split up in 1974 Tosh's work took on increasingly revolutionary nature which led to beating by Jamaican police in 1975. From this experience came his banned **Mark Of The Beast** and an ever more radical stance, as in **Legalise It** (also banned, but big Jamaican hit nonetheless) which called for legalization of marijuana. 1977 album **Equal Rights** summed up Tosh's crusade against racism and oppression with his outspoken demand for recognition by blacks of Africa as the true homeland.

Switching from Virgin to Rolling Stones Records in 1978 brought Tosh support of Jagger and Richards. He teamed with revered reggae sidemen Sly Dunbar (bass) and Robbie Shakespeare (drums) to guest on Stones' American tour. His classic **Bush Doctor** album of 1978 included the superb **(You Gotta Walk) Don't Look Back** single which, in limited-release dub version, featured Jagger and Richards on back-up vocals to Smokey Robinson composition.

Two more LPs and 1981 appearance at London's Rainbow Theatre furthered Tosh's international appeal, while love-song duet with Gwen Guthrie on **Nothing But Love** showed a softening lyrical approach.

Tosh looked to re-form Wailers with Bunny Livingstone and the pair had re-recorded classic cuts before Tosh was brutally murdered in an attempted burglary at his home in September, 1987.

Albums:
Legalise It (Columbia/Virgin), 1976
Equal Rights (Columbia/Virgin), 1978
Bush Doctor (Rolling Stones), 1978
Mystic Man (Rolling Stones), 1979
Wanted Dread And Alive (EMI/Rolling Stones), 1981
Captured Live (EMI), 1984
No Nuclear War (Parlophone), 1987
The Toughest (Capitol/Parlophone), 1988

Toto

US group formed 1978

Original line-up: Bobby Kimball, vocals; Steve Lukather, guitar; David Paich, keyboards; Steve Porcaro, keyboards; David Hungate, bass; Jeff Porcaro, drums.

Career: All original line-up, bar Kimball, were notable Los Angeles session musicians — credits for various members include Steely Dan, Boz Scaggs, Aretha Franklin, Leo Sayer, Earth, Wind And Fire, Jackson Browne, Barbra Streisand and many more. Group named either after Dorothy's dog in *Wizard Of Oz* film, or Kimball's real surname (supposedly 'Toteaux'). Succesful first LP featured in US album chart for most of 1979 and spawned three US hit singles, but second and third LPs were rather less notable; due, according to Lukather, to fame arriving too quickly for group to adapt to it.

However, 1982 LP gave group highest placing in album chart in US, plus three US and two UK hit singles. Resulted in domination of 1983 Grammy Award Ceremony, winning seven categories; group also returned to UK charts. This coincided with another Porcaro brother, Mike, replacing David Hungate as bass player.

Toto's involvement with **Dune** soundtrack album in 1984 saw band as instrumental outfit, Kimball having left for solo career. Replacement on vocals was Fergie Frederiksen (ex-Trillion).

Band's reduced commitment saw minimal output through 80s, with albums **Fahrenheit** (featuring vocalist Joe Williams) and **The Seventh One** struggling to emulate previous success. After two-year absence, Toto regrouped, the personnel comprising

Above: Like Bob Marley, former Wailer Peter Tosh died in tragic circumstances, but his son continues the music.

Lukather, Paich, Jeff and Michael Porcaro and J.M. Byron, vocals. Greatest hits package **Past To Present 1977-90** (1990) also included material cut with new line-up.

The epitome of AOR, Toto nonetheless have had some inspired moments; **Hold The Line** is now rightly regarded as a pop classic.

Hit Singles:	US	UK
Hold The Line, 1978	5	14
Rosanna, 1982	2	12
Africa, 1982	1	3
I'll Be Over You, 1986	8	—

Albums:
Toto (Columbia/CBS), 1978
Hydra (Columbia/CBS), 1979
Turn Back (Columbia/CBS), 1981
Toto IV (Columbia/CBS), 1982
Isolation (Columbia/CBS), 1984
Fahrenheit (CBS), 1986
The Seventh One (Columbia/CBS), 1988

Below: Pete Townshend with his favoured Rickenbacker guitar.

Pete Townshend

UK guitarist, composer, vocalist, multi-instrumentalist
Born London, May 19, 1945

Career: Townshend grew up in Ealing, West London, son of singer Betty Dennis and sax player Cliff Townshend, who played with The Squadronaires. Spent summers at holiday camps where father played in bands. His grandmother bought him his first guitar when he was 12.

Townshend wrote his first song, **It Was You**, at 16 (actually recorded by very early Who, in 1963, before Keith Moon joined, but was never released). In 1965 he began 20-year career writing for The Who.

Townshend's first departure from the band came in 1972 when he released **Who Came First**, an album of songs either about his Indian master Meher Baba, or included because Baba liked them. (Various Baba-orientated LPs done with other Baba-lovers were previously recorded, but these were never intended as official Townshend releases.) **Who Came First** gave the public a very different taste of Townshend. Playing guitar without vengeance known as trademark in Who, Townshend created an atmosphere of relaxation with excellent acoustic sound accompanied by a clear and sincere, if not technically magnificent, voice. Up until this point, Townshend's voice was not often heard at length, as Roger Daltrey handled Who vocals.

Next official solo release, **Rough Mix**, didn't come until 1977, when Townshend teamed up with singer, composer and bass player Ronnie Lane (ex-Small Faces, Faces). Though LP had a 'Baba flavour', the references were quite subtle, and the sound was more upbeat. Only mildly successful initially, it has remained a steady seller, and has been re-released several times.

In 1980 Townshend truly made his mark as solo artist with **Empty Glass**. The single, **Let My Love Open The Door**, made it into the US Top 10 (matching most successful Who single in US. **I Can See For Miles**), and several other tracks received massive US airplay. Townshend's voice, under producer Chris Thomas, had improved dramatically. Lyrical content was more intellectual and more personally revealing than Daltrey would have agreed had the material been offered to The Who. Many expected great things from Townshend's future solo

work; there was no doubt about who was the main creative force behind The Who.

Unfortunately, the much-anticipated **All The Best Cowboys Have Chinese Eyes** LP in 1982 didn't quite measure up to **Empty Glass**. A bit too heady and abstract for some, it confused the general public with its experimental song structure, and sometimes bizarre lyrics. The stream-of-consciousness effect was balanced by a couple of energetic, almost Who-style

Above: Scoop, Pete Townshend's demos. Courtesy Atco Records.

tracks, but overall the LP lacked cohesiveness. When, around the time of its release, Townshend gave several confessional interviews attesting to personal confusion and unhappiness, and even alcohol and drug addiction during much of its recording, this was understandable.

Early 1983 brought new LP of old material, a double LP collection of Townshend's personal demos, some done for The Who, some just for himself, entitled **Scoop**. In February 1983, Townshend received the Lifetime Achievement Award from the British Record industry.

An ardent charity worker, Townshend has gigged for Rock Against Racism and Amnesty International, and also attracted headlines with his anti-drug drive in 1985. Following The Who's re-formation for US tour in 1989, Townshend returned to the front pages when admitting homosexuality to British press.

Guitars: Rickenbacker 6 and 12 strings (1964-66); Fender Stratocaster, Telecaster (1967-68); Gibson SG/(1969-71); Gibson Les Paul Deluxe (1972); Schecters (1979).

Hit Singles:	US	UK
Let My Love Open The Door, 1980	9	—

Albums:
Who Came First (Decca/Track), 1972

Rough Mix (MCA/Polydor), 1977
Empty Glass (Atco/WEA), 1980
All The Best Cowboys Have Chinese Eyes (Atco/WEA), 1982
Pete Townshend Scoop (Atco/Atco), 1983
White City (Atco), 1985
Iron Man (Atlantic/Virgin), 1989

T'pau
UK band formed 1980

Original line-up: Carole Decker, vocals; Ronnie Rogers, guitar; Paul Jackson, bass; Mike Chetwood, keyboards; Taj Wyzgowski, guitar; Tim Burgess, drums.

Career: Group was formed in England's Midlands territory. Carole Decker and Ronnie Rogers were members of The Lazers before offer of contract from Virgin UK. Adopted new moniker for group from alien featured in *Star Trek* TV series.

Debut single **Heart And Soul** was surprising US and UK Top 10 entry, and band subsequently enjoyed British No. 1 45 with **China In Your Hand**. First album **Bridge Of Spies** made US Top 50 and topped British charts, earning 3 million sales. Follow up **Rage** (like **Bridge**, produced by Roy Thomas Baker) failed to sustain America's interest but peaked at No. 4 in the UK.

Steady diet of stadium work (toured with Bryan Adams, among others), failed to sustain success, and band then lost guitarist Wyzgowski (replaced by Dean Howard).

In 1990, T'pau quit Virgin, but failed to produce new material. Rumours of conflict within group spread like bush fires, and Decker subsequently announced solo plans in early 1992.

Hit Singles:	US	UK
Heart And Soul, 1987	4	4
China In Your Hand, 1987	—	1

Albums:
Bridge Of Spies (Siren/Virgin), 1987
Rage (Siren/Virgin), 1988
The Promise (Siren), 1989

Traffic
UK group formed 1967

Original line-up: Steve Winwood, guitar, keyboards, vocals; Dave Mason, guitar; Jim Capaldi, drums; Chris Wood, saxophone, flute.

Career: Traffic emerged following Winwood's departure from Spencer Davis Group, in which Winwood played dominant role. Mason and Capaldi previously played in Birmingham group Deep Feeling. Wood had played sax in ska-influenced Locomotive. In spring 1967, retired to a Berkshire cottage in Aston Tirrold, coining cliché 'getting it together in the country'.

Six months later, debut **Paper Sun**, a powerful and evocative summer single, climbed to No. 5 in UK charts. Follow-up **Hole In My Shoe**, with its dream-like imagery and schoolgirl's voice, was even more commercial and reached No. 2.

First album **Mr Fantasy** revealed individual talents of all members, indicating this was no one-man band. Another Top 10 single, film theme **Here We Go Round The Mulberry Bush**, revealed Mason's ability to pen commercial tunes, in contrast to others' heavy jazz leanings. This apparently caused incompatibility, culminating in Mason's departure in December 1967. Within six months he returned, contributing four songs to **Traffic**, but left again in October 1968 and group folded. Live/studio album **Last Exit** (1969) was erratic and unsatisfactory finale.

After short stay in ill-fated Blind Faith, Winwood worked on projected solo album **Mad Shadows**, which ended up as Traffic reunion, minus Mason. Re-formed trio released **John Barleycorn Must Die** in April 1970, a superb fusion of jazz, rock, R&B and folk. Unit was bolstered by induction of Rick Grech (ex-Family, Blind Faith), and later Jim Gordon (session drummer) and Reebop Kwaku-Baah (congas). Mason again returned temporarily and this short-lived aggregation played six gigs, captured for posterity on **Welcome To The Canteen**,

Left: Traffic line-up, from left to right, Steve Winwood, Chris Wood, Jim Capaldi, and Dave Mason — the original quartet. Mason left in 1967 but occasionally reappeared.

a surprisingly impressive live album.

During December 1971 US tour, **The Low Spark Of High Heeled Boys** met critical acclaim. However, Grech and Gordon quit and Winwood fell ill with peritonitis amid rumours of Traffic's imminent dissolution. During lull in group activity, Capaldi cut solo **Oh How We Danced** at Muscle Shoals. Formed partnership with rhythm section David Hood and Roger Hawkins, who joined Traffic for Jamaican-recorded **Shoot Out At The Fantasy Factory**. Muscle Shoals sessioneer Barry Beckett was added on keyboards for 1973 world tour, which included some of the band's finest live performances as evidenced on German-recorded album **On The Road**.

When Shoalsmen returned to States in autumn 1973, Rosko Gee from Gonzalez was brought in as bassist. As quartet (Winwood, Wood, Capaldi and Gee) cut final album **When The Eagle Flies**, which revealed Winwood concentrating heavily on keyboards/synthesizer. Period of indecision ended in December 1974 with Capaldi and Winwood pursuing solo careers. Chris Wood died in July 1983 of liver failure.

Traffic were responsible for some of the finest music to emerge from Britain in the late 60s and early 70s. While many contemporaries fell into self-parody or became victims of self-indulgent art-rock, Traffic continued to produce music of increasing complexity, originality and quality.

Hit Singles:	US	UK
Paper Sun, 1967	—	5
Hole In My Shoe, 1967	—	2
Here We Go Round The Mulberry Bush, 1967	—	8
Jim Capaldi Solo:		
Love Hurts, 1975	—	4
(see also Winwood entry)		

Albums:
Mr Fantasy (Island), 1967
Traffic (Island), 1968

Left: Transvision Vamp's Wendy James, hoping her career begins to smell more like roses than manure entering 1992.

Last Exit (Island), 1969
Best Of (Island), 1969
John Barleycorn Must Die (Island), 1970
Welcome To The Canteen (Island), 1971
Low Spark Of High Heeled Boys
  (Island), 1971
Shoot Out At The Fantasy Factory
  (Island), 1973
On The Road (Island), 1973*
Where The Eagle Flies (Island), 1974
*Issued in single *and* double LP form

Jim Capaldi Solo:
Oh How We Danced (—/Island), 1972
Short Cut Draw Blood (Antilles/Island), 1975
The Contender (—/Polydor), 1978
Electric Nights (Polydor), 1979
Sweet Smell Of Success (—/Carrere), 1980
Let The Thunder Cry (WEA), 1981
Fierce Heart (WEA), 1983
One Man Mission (WEA), 1984
Some Come Running (with Clapton,
  Harrison, Winwood) (Island), 1988

Transvision Vamp
UK group formed 1988

Original line-up: Wendy James, vocals; Nick Sayer, guitar; Dave Parsons, bass; Tex Axile, drums.

Career: Reincarnation of Blondie (whatever happened to the first?), Transvision Vamp is vehicle for Wendy James who claims 'fame, fortune and an Oscar are just around the corner'.

Former drama student and aspiring opera singer James put group together with Sayer in London's Notting Hill Gate after move from South Coast resort of Brighton. Signed to MCA, group debuted with **Pop Art** album in 1988, from which **Revolution Baby** made noises in UK charts. Band then had flurry of British hits, of which **I Want Your Love** (1988) and **Baby I Don't Care** (1989) both made Top 5.

James subsequently exploited music press to full, ranting on about 'inevitable stardom' and being 'bigger than Madonna'. To date, prophecies remain pipedream, but James and Vamps maintained notoriety with two subsequent LPs, **Velveteen** (1989) and **Little Magnets Vs The Bubble of Babble** (1991), as well as a major UK tour in the spring of 1991.

Hit Singles:	US	UK
I Want Your Love, 1988	—	5
Baby I Don't Care, 1989	—	3
The Only One, 1989	—	15
Landslide Of Love, 1989	—	14

Below: Debut album, Terence Trent D'Arby. Courtesy CBS Records.

INTRODUCING THE HARDLINE ACCORDING TO
TERENCE TRENT D'ARBY

Albums:
Pop Art (MCA), 1988
Velveteen (MCA), 1989
The Little Magnets Vs The Bubble Of
  Babble (MCA/-), 1991

Terence Trent D'Arby
US singer, composer
Born New York, 1962

Career: Son of Pentecostal Minister father and gospel singer mother, raised in Chicago, played drums at church meetings. Took up boxing, then enlisted in US army at 18, posted to Germany, where he bought bass guitar and joined local rock band, The Touch, who split up just as they were about to hit big time.

Secured worldwide deal with CBS on strength of tape of own songs and made sensational live appearances on UK TV pop show *The Tube* which catapulted him into public attention. Immediately dubbed 'The New Prince Of Pop' by influential UK magazine *New Musical Express* and undertook several interviews where he proclaimed himself to be 'a genius'.

Finding an audience in UK, Trent D'Arby's debut single **If You Let Me Stay** was fiery, pleading soul ballad. Follow-up **Wishing Well** was much rockier.

Debut album **Introducing The Hardline According to Terence Trent D'Arby** mixed R&B, pop and soul with a hard-edged modern production from Heaven 17's Martyn Ware, yielding two more hit singles in UK in **Dance Little Sister** and **Sign Your Name.** In early 1988, he finally gained success in America with release of **Wishing Well** single.

Following Grammy for **Hardline** set in 1987, Trent D'Arby was brought back to earth when second album **Neither Fish Nor Flesh** was lambasted by critics. Maintained profile during 1990 with appearances at Nelson Mandela and John Lennon tribute

Above: Terence Trent D'Arby suffered ignominy of diffidence following outstanding debut album and singles hits Wishing Well and Sign Your Name.

concerts in London and Liverpool respectively. However, aggravation with management company over unpaid commission left TTD bereft of new product going into 1992.

An unquestioned talent, with influences from Michael Jackson to Rolling Stones (covered two Jagger/Richards songs on B side of **Sign Your Name** single), but who needs to take himself a little less seriously.

Hit Singles:	US	UK
If You Let Me Stay, 1987	—	7
Wishing Well, 1987*	1	4
Dance Little Sister, 1987	30	20
Sign Your Name, 1987	5	2
*1988 in US		

Albums:
Introducing The Hardline According To
  (CBS), 1987
Neither Fish Nor Flesh (Columbia/CBS),
  1989

The Troggs
UK group formed 1966

Original line-up: Reg Presley, vocals; Chris Britton, guitar; Pete Staples, bass; Ronnie Bond, drums.

Career: Formed in Andover, Hampshire, The Troggs were discovered by record producer Larry Page who signed them to management deal and secured recording contract with Fontana.

After debut in BBC Radio show *Saturday Club* and TV show *Thank Your Lucky Stars*, they recorded American writer Chips Taylor's **Wild Thing.** Featuring Reg Presley's moody vocal and ocarina playing, the record lived up to title, being one of wildest records ever cut in UK. Its originality was rewarded with a million sales and US

chart-topping status (where it was, most unusually, available on two record labels — Fontana and Atco).

Presley himself penned the follow-up **With A Girl Like You**, a UK chart-topper which also went gold, and again available on both Fontana and Atco in US.

The classic **I Can't Control Myself** and **Any Way That You Want Me** gave them four UK Top 10 hits in very first year. Another million-seller came in 1967 with **Love Is All Around.**

Peter Staples was replaced by Tony Murray in 1969 and group's recording career went into decline despite mini-hit with novel version of Beach Boys' **Good Vibrations.**

However, stunning stage act created fanatically loyal following in Germany, France, Holland, Britain and, particularly, in America, which sustained them throughout the 70s despite lack of activity.

With no further line-up changes, group today continues to earn good money on cabaret and club circuits, despite lack of recording success.

Hit Singles:	US	UK
Wild Thing, 1966	1	2
With A Girl Like You, 1966	29	1
I Can't Control Myself, 1966	43	2
Any Way That You Want Me, 1966	—	8
Give It To Me, 1967	—	12
Night Of The Long Grass, 1967	—	17
Love Is All Around, 1967	7	5

Albums:
The Troggs Tapes (Private Stock/Penny
  Farthing), 1975
Live At Max's Kansas City (Max's
  Kansas City), 1979
Golden Hits (Astan), 1984

Worth Searching Out:
Wild Thing (Atco/Fontana), 1966
Best Of (Rhino), 1985

Above: Wild Thing, The Troggs. Courtesy Fontana Records.

Robin Trower
UK guitarist, composer
Born London, March 9, 1945

Career: Trower began in a Southend band, The Paramounts. Co-member Gary Brooker went on to form Procol Harum. After recording **Whiter Shade Of Pale**, Brooker asked Trower to join Harum and he stayed from 1967-71. He left because of dissatisfaction with limited guitar sound.

Trower had become a great admirer of Jimi Hendrix, as evidenced by his **Song For A Dreamer**, which he contributed to his final Harum LP, **Broken Barricades.** Instead of going for guitar hero role, Trower tried to form group to be called Jude. This effort failed, but introduced him to bassist and vocalist Jim Dewar. In mid-1972, he and Dewar formed Robin Trower Band with drummer Reg Isadore. First LP, **Twice Removed From Yesterday**, produced some spacy riffs which some found exhilarating, but others considered a Hendrix rip-off.

Band was ignored in UK, but did well in the US. Unfortunately, each subsequent release pushed Trower further into axe hero role. Ex-Sly Stone drummer Bill London replaced Reg Isadore on third LP, **For Earth Below**. This line-up recorded next five LPs, by which time recycled Hendrix lines were no longer interesting.

Trower then teamed up with London and Jack Bruce to form BLT. LP made US Top 40 in 1981. Isadore joined band for **Truce** LP.

Despite success of BLT project, Trower slipped quietly into semi-retirement before one-off deal with GNP Records saw release of **Passion** set. Later Trower signed with Atlantic (debut **Take What You Need**) and then re-joined Procul Harum for their 1991 LP **The Prodigal Stranger**.

Guitar: Fender Stratocaster.

Albums:
Twice Removed From Yesterday
 (Chrysalis), 1973
Bridge Of Sighs (Chrysalis), 1974
For Earth Below (Chrysalis), 1975
Robin Trower Live (Chrysalis), 1975
Long Misty Days (Chrysalis), 1976
In City Dreams (Chrysalis), 1977
Caravan To Midnight (Chrysalis), 1978
Victim Of Fury (Chrysalis), 1980
Time Is Short (Chrysalis), 1983
Back It Up (Chrysalis), 1983

Above: Twice Removed From Yesterday, Robin Trower. Courtesy Chrysalis Records.

Beyond The Mist (Music For Nations), 1985
Passion (GNP), 1986
Take What You Need (Atlantic), 1988
In The Line Of Fire (Atlantic), 1990

Bruce, London, Trower:
BLT (Chrysalis), 1981

Bruce, Trower:
Truce (Chrysalis), 1982
No Stopping Anytime (compilation of BLT and Truce) (Chrysalis), 1989

The Tubes
US group formed 1972

Original line-up: Fee Waybill, vocals; Bill Spooner, guitar; Vince Welnick, keyboards; Rich Anderson, bass; Michael Cotten, synthesizer; Roger Steen, guitar; Prairie Prince, percussion.

Above: The outrageous Tubes toned down their act to find success.

Career: Formed by Bill Spooner with art school friends, group immediately gained devoted following in San Francisco's Bay Area. Combined often heavy rock with outrageous satire and became known for bizarre creations such as Quay Lude (drugged-out superstar) and Dr Strangekiss (a crippled Nazi, sounding not unlike Tom Jones). Semi-clad girls were also well to the fore.

Signed record deal with A&M in 1975, releasing **The Tubes** same year. With Al Kooper as producer, set included Rocky Horror-style classics, notably **White Punks On Dope**, later a Top 30 UK hit.

By third album **Now**, Tubes had recruited Minge Lewis to produce more mainstream work. Late 70s also saw them tempering theatrical outrage by limiting appearances of dancing girls, possibly to avoid accusations of blatant sexism. Braved a purely musical, non-theatrical, club tour in 1980, which was only partially successful.

Fourth album **Remote Control**, produced by Todd Rundgren, failed to break any new ground and caused renewed friction with record company. Finally recorded unreleased album for A&M, for which Waybill refused to contribute vocals. Reputedly left their record company following finance dispute.

Signed deal with Capitol, which led to 1981-82 tour, taking in Sweden, Norway, Germany, France, Holland, Portugal, Italy and Britain. **The Completion Backward Principle** (a phrase borrowed from the methodology of salesmanship) saw group assigned to producer David Foster (Boz Scaggs, Hall And Oates) in attempt to record hit album. Although work showed flashes of old humour, it was obvious compromise, and Tubes seemed part of the very system they once parodied so effectively, as confirmed by hit **She's A Beauty** (1983).

The return of Rundgren for **Love Bomb** (1986) saw a partial return to anarchy, but subsequent loss of Welnick (who joined Grateful Dead) and solo endeavours of Waybill, commencing with 1984 set **Read My Lips**, stifled band's progress.

Hit Singles:	US	UK
She's A Beauty, 1983	10	—

Albums:
The Tubes (A&M), 1975
Young And Rich (A&M), 1976

Now (A&M), 1977
What Do You Want From Live (A&M), 1978
Remote Control (A&M), 1979
The Completion Backward Principle
 (Capitol), 1981
Outside Inside (Capitol), 1983
Trash (A&M), 1986
Love Bomb (A&M/—), 1986

Tina Turner
US vocalist
Born Annie Mae Bullock, Brownsville, Tennessee, November 26, 1938

Career: When Ike and Tina Turner's long-term working and marital relationship split amidst much acrimony, it seemed like end of the line for one of soul music's most gifted vocalists. For while Tina had fronted the steady flow of hits, everyone knew that Ike Turner was the key to it all, writing much of the material, heading the band, playing superb guitar and keyboards, choreographing the dazzling stage shows and making all the business deals. Tina seemed destined to end her days singing the old hits at second-rate cabaret venues.

But in 1982 an invitation to join Heaven 17 for joint vocals on **Ball Of Confusion** for the UK group's new album, brought Tina to London. Heaven 17's Greg Walsh and Martin Ware then produced Tina on version of Al Green's **Let's Stay Together** which went to the Top 10 and spawned a sell-out European tour. Record hit in US too, and sold a million.

With Capitol Records now 100 per cent behind her revived career, Tina scored in 1984 with **Private Dancer** album, and subsequent crop of hit singles, including Grammy-winning **What's Love Got To Do With It?**.

Tina started her long career very much in the R&B vein. Her sister had been dating member of Ike Turner's Kings Of Rhythm in St Louis and Tina eventually persuaded Ike to let her sing. Ousting Ike's first wife and pianist Bonnie Turner, both in the band and at home, Tina sang lead on **A Fool In Love** single when another of Ike's vocalists failed to make the session. The result was an R&B hit at No. 2.

Ike, who had helped earlier careers of B.B. King, Bobby Bland and Howlin' Wolf (among others), masterminded stunning Ike And Tina Turner Revue featuring The Ikettes backing group (of which P.P. Arnold, Merry

Clayton and Bonnie Bramlett were all one-time members).

The all-singing, all-dancing revue, plus records on wide range of labels, including milestone **River Deep Mountain High**, produced by Phil Spector, took Ike and Tina from R&B 'chitlin' circuit' to highest realms of rock, helped by the endorsement of The Rolling Stones.

Linking with major Liberty/Minit/United Artists set-up, Ike and Tina veered heavily toward rock while also cutting heavy blues-oriented material, and Tina appeared as the Acid Queen in screen version of The Who's rock opera *Tommy*.

Ike's bizarre behaviour finally split the relationship, Tina walking out in 1974 with nothing but clothes she stood up in.

Many traumas and a whole decade later she was right back on top while Ike, the man on whom she had seemed totally dependent, lost his fortune and passed into obscurity. Ike was incarcerated in the late 80s following parole violation and drunk-driving offence. In one of rock-biz's little ironies, both Ike and Tina Turner were inducted into Rock 'n' Roll Hall Of Fame in January 1991.

Upon success of **Private Dancer** album, Tina enraptured audiences with revitalized concert appearances. Always a vivid and imaginative performer with Ike, and fully accustomed to exotic posturing while fronting the Revue, Turner's stage assault on initially European audiences confirmed her re-found superstardom.

Apart from almost permanent chart status from 1983, Turner broadened her horizons with well-received movie debut with *Mad Max (Beyond The Thunderdome)*. The artist threatened to return to films, having announced, in 1991, withdrawal from concert dates. Following success of studio set **Foreign Affair**, Turner enjoyed multi-platinum sales of heavily TV-advertised compilation **Simply The Best**.

Turner's glowing personality should now simplify cross-over to whatever medium she subsequently chooses. Those who enjoyed her final barnstorming appearances will rue the day artist quit live work. Aficionados can get full lowdown on this rock diva's eventful life in best-selling autobiography *I Tina*.

Hit Singles:	US	UK
Let's Stay Together, 1983	26	6
What's Love Got To Do With It?, 1984	1	3
Better Be Good To Me, 1984	5	—
Private Dancer, 1985	7	26
We Don't Need Another Hero, 1985	2	3
One Of The Living, 1985	15	—
Typical Male, 1986	1	33
Two People, 1986	—	43
What You Get Is What You See, 1987	15	—
The Best, 1989	15	5
I Don't Wanna Lose You, 1989	—	8
Steamy Windows, 1990	39	13
Way Of The World, 1991	—	11

With Bryan Adams:

	US	UK
It's Only Love, 1985	19	29

Albums:
Private Dancer (Capitol), 1984
Break Every Rule (Capitol), 1986
So Fine (Entertainers), 1987
Too Hot To Handle (Thunderbolt), 1987
Live In Europe (Capitol), 1988
Foreign Affair (Capitol), 1989
Rough (Parlophone), 1990
Simply The Best (Capitol), 1991

Above: Tina Turner salvaged career with help of manager Roger Davies.

The Turtles

US group formed 1965

Original line-up: Howard Kaylan, vocals; Mark Volman, vocals; Al Nichol, guitar; Chuck Portz, bass; Jim Tucker, guitar; Don Murray, drums.

Career: While still at Westchester High School, Los Angeles, in 1962, Kaplan (change to Kaylan came later), Nichol and Portz formed surf band, The Nightriders. Murray, who attended nearby school, joined on drums. In February 1963 band added Volman, and changed name to Crossfires.

With various rhythm guitarists, this line-up recorded some obscure singles, and played at local high-school dances. Jim Tucker eventually took rhythm guitar spot. (Band occasionally billed itself as folk group, Crosswind Singers.) The new, but very small, White Whale label offered a contract on condition that name be changed yet again. Band's manager suggested 'Tyrtles' to cash in on UK-sounding name; band agreed on 'Turtles'.

The Byrds had just hit with Dylan cover, **Mr Tambourine Man**, so Turtles' first release, **It Ain't Me, Babe**, sounded like perfect progression in folk-rock fusion. **Let Me Be** and **You Baby**, both written by 'protest' songwriter P.F. Sloan, followed debut into charts. First LP was released in 1965 and, as was typical of time, carried lots of covers and some filler. The surprise is that the jangling sound on **Wanderin' Kind** and **Love Minus Zero** sounds as fresh and novel today as it did then.

Next single was self-penned **Grim Reaper Of Love**; being different in texture and sound from expected Turtles mould, it barely made charts. White Whale regrettably put pressure on Kaylan/Volman to stop releasing original material. Next release, **Outside Chance**, missed completely, but included new drummer John Barbata (later of Jefferson Starship). Then Portz left; Jim Pons (ex-Leaves) joined.

By early 1967, band had been a year without a hit, a bad sign in the golden age of singles. However, **Happy Together** went to US No. 1, and put band back in spotlight. Turtles' next release, **She'd Rather Be With Me**, made No. 3 in US.

By 1968, band wanted to assume self-production. After two misses, they came up with US No. 6 **Elenore**, but the public seemed to miss ironic mockery of song, so band overloaded potshots on next LP. **The Turtles Present The Battle Of The Bands** was unequalled in its snipes at rock styles, until the release of Nick Lowe's **Jesus Of Cool/Pure Pop For Now People**.

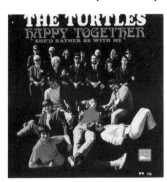

Above: Happy Together, The Turtles. Courtesy White Whale Records.

The Turtles lost Tucker while touring UK, (he wasn't replaced). As sessions were to begin for new LP, Barbata also quit and John Seiter (ex-Spanky And Our Gang) came in. Line-up of Kaylan, Volman, Nichol, Pons and Seiter lasted rest of band's lifetime. New LP was to be straight-ahead rock, and admirer Ray Davies agreed to produce it. Despite strong material and Davies credentials, album failed to hit at a time when LPs were beginning to determine music groups' success and status.

Band continued to tour with greatest hits package, making 'unhip' decision to play White House at Tricia Nixon's request. Failure to produce hit records caused growing problems with White Whale, which led to legal hassles; band quietly disappeared in 1970.

Kaylan and Volman have most interesting Turtles history. Unable to record under their own name because of lawsuits, the duo took names of two Turtles roadies and joined Frank Zappa as Phlorescent Leech and Eddie. Their appearance in *200 Motels* was promising and promoted comic image. As Flo And Eddie, they released several LPs, backed Marc Bolan, promoted a radio show, and maintained zany side of Turtles into 70s and 80s, including reggae album **Rock Steady With Flo And Eddie** (1982).

Considering their brilliant sound and good sense of humour, it is puzzling that the Turtles have not exerted greater influence. They remain a highly underrated cult band; though recordings during their heyday have become somewhat collectable.

Hit Singles:

	US	UK
It Ain't Me Babe, 1965	8	—
You Baby, 1966	20	—
Happy Together, 1967	1	12
She'd Rather Be With Me, 1967	3	4
You Know What I Mean, 1967	12	—
She's My Girl, 1967	14	—
Elenore, 1968	6	7
You Showed Me, 1969	6	—

Albums:

As The Crossfires:
Out Of Control (Rhino/—), 1981

As The Turtles:
Happy Together Again (—/Philips), 1975
It Ain't Me Babe (Rhino/—), 1982
Great Hits Of (Rhino/—), 1982

Worth Searching Out:
You Baby (White Whale/—), 1966
Happy Together (White Whale/London), 1967
Golden Hits (White Whale/—), 1967
Battle Of The Bands (White Whale/London), 1968
Turtle Soup (White Whale/—), 1969
Wooden Head (White Whale/—), 1970
20 Greatest Hits (Rhino), 1986

U2

UK group formed 1979

Original line-up: Bono 'Vox' Hewson, vocals; Dave 'The Edge' Evans, guitar, keyboards; Adam Clayton, bass; Larry Mullen, drums.

Career: Inspired by London's new, young bands in 1976, Bono and the The Edge decided to form own group in Dublin. Fellow mates Clayton and Mullen joined, and name U2 was taken, with implication that every fan could join in the music as well.

Bono described band as beginning with three chords, but with special enthusiasm. Pub gigs led to local record contract with CBS. Two singles, released in Ireland only, gained cult status in UK. Island Records became interested and took over band, releasing **11 O'clock Tick Tock** in 1980.

UK critics began falling over themselves to cite U2 as next big thing. When **Boy** LP was released, U2 were hailed as *the* hope of rock's future. Band ignored press and pushed on, establishing close rapport with audiences. **I Will Follow** was issued as strong single.

Touring in US brought band into contact with producer Sandy Pearlman (Blue Oyster Cult, Dictators, Clash) and for time he was considered for second LP. Some New York sessions were produced, but ultimately band returned to Steve Lillywhite.

1981 single **Gloria** received heavy airplay and made UK Top 40. When **October** LP was released, expected revisionism set in and critics carped that U2 was really just another 1960s band because of basic guitar, bass, and drum sound. Band continued to ignore press and found audiences growing everywhere.

1982 tour introduced music from forthcoming **War** album, which subsequently entered UK listings at No. 1, and established credentials in US. First chart single **New Years Day** made UK Top 10 in January, 1983. Evangelical outlook did not restrict U2's development, although group were still struggling to impress critics sceptical of 'message' contained in their music. **Red Sky** set (1985) saw journalistic 'about face', and preceded appearance in Live Aid concert which further spread international appeal.

By 1987, U2 were generally considered premier band of the moment, and 18 month world tour promoting **Joshua Tree** album left very little geographically for them to conquer. Obligatory cover of *Time* magazine confirmed acceptance from mainstream of rock business. U2's biography *Unforgettable Fire* written by former professional soccer player Eamon Dunphy (published 1987) quickly became surprise best-seller, despite band's subsequent distancing from project.

U2 won Grammys in 1988 for Best Album and Best Group, and were also honoured at BRIT awards for Best International Group. During same year, Bono and The Edge featured on Roy Orbison's final album **Mystery Girl**.

Double set **Rattle And Hum** (1989), which mixed live and studio recordings, confirmed band's position at pinnacle of rockbiz. Produced by Jimmy Iovine, the album topped both US and UK charts in achieving multi-platinum status, while the accompanying movie, directed by Philip Joanou, was also critically and commercially acclaimed. The LP spawned hit singles **Desire**, **Angel Of Harlem** and funky **When Love Comes To Town** (with B.B. King).

Group toured Australia in 1989, and also featured in televised New Year's Eve concert in Dublin. Further Grammy and BRIT awards preceded arrest of Clayton for drug possession, although he avoided conviction after making charitable donation to the Woman's Aid Group of Ireland.

In the absence of any new material, U2 members took time out in 1990 to embark upon solo projects. The Edge contributed to score of Royal Shakespeare Company's *A Clockwork Orange 2004*, an updating of now-banned movie, while Mullen's national pride prompted composition of official team song for Irish soccer side. Unit rejoined for Cole Porter anthology **Red Hot And Blue** and associated video to benefit international AIDS charity.

Returning to the production team of Daniel Lanois (Bob Dylan, Neville Bros, Robbie Robertson, Peter Gabriel) and Brian Eno, who had worked with band on **The Unforgettable Fire** and **The Joshua Tree**, U2 completed eighth album **Achtung Baby** for November 1991 release. The LP was recorded at the Hansa studios in Berlin (where Eno had worked with David Bowie) and at Dublin's Windmill Lane studio, the first sessions having commenced in October 1989. Lanois described the album as 'rougher and harder than anything they've done before'. Needless to say, **Achtung Baby** left some critics cold, while others raved, and the cover art, featuring a naked Clayton, attracted adverse comment.

U2 were formulating plans for world tour to commence in spring 1992 at press-time, although fans of band could amuse themselves in the meantime by checking out **The Joshua Trio**, a satirical triumvirate dedicated to the life and work of their music heroes.

Hit Singles:	US	UK
New Years Day, 1983	—	10
Two Hearts Beat As One, 1983		18
Pride, 1984	—	3
The Unforgettable Fire, 1985	—	6
With Or Without You, 1987	1	4
I Still Haven't Found What I'm Looking For, 1987	1	6
Where The Streets Have No Name, 1987	13	4
Desire, 1988	3	1
Angel Of Harlem, 1988	14	9
When Love Comes To Town, 1989	—	6
All I Want Is You, 1989	—	4
Mysterious Ways, 1991	—	10

Albums:
Boy (Island), 1980
October (Island), 1981
War (Island), 1983
The Unforgettable Fire (Island), 1984
Under A Blood Red Sky (Island), 1985
The Joshua Tree (Island), 1987
Rattle And Hum (Island), 1988
Achtung Baby (Island), 1991

UB40

UK group formed 1977

Original line-up: Ali Campbell, vocals, guitar; Robin Campbell, guitar, vocals; Brian Travers, saxophone; Earl Falconer, bass; Jimmy Lynn, keyboards; Jim Brown, drums; Norman Hassan, percussion; 'Yomi' Babayemi, percussion.

Above: Early incarnation of Ireland's premier export, U2.

Career: Band came together in West Midlands; as most members were unemployed, took name from unemployment benefit form.

Interracial outfit, UB40 pioneered specifically British brand of melodic reggae, combining smooth vocals and liquid saxophone fill-ins with relaxed reggae beat. At first amateurish band quickly tightened up sound and by 1979 were undertaking gigs. That same year Lynn left, replaced by Michael Virtue, Babayemi returned to his native Nigeria and Astro joined as resident toaster/vocalist. That year group also signed to local Graduate label; second single, **King/Food For Thought**, took them into Top 5. Debut album **Signing Off** was also major hit, prompting band to form their own Dep International label in 1981.

Relatively quiescent couple of years passed until band released **Labour Of Love** in 1983. Album featured slick covers of reggae classics, and struck major chord with

Above: The Best Of UB40. Courtesy Dep Records.

public; former Neil Diamond/Tony Tribe hit **Red Red Wine** became UK No. 1 and established band internationally. Further hit singles ensued, reinforcing outfit's position as foremost pop-reggae outfit. In 1985 Ali Campbell duetted with Pretenders' Chrissie Hynde on re-make of Sonny and Cher's **I Got You Babe**, again hitting No. 1 spot.

Band maintained chart action with **Sing Our Own Song** (1986), **Rat In The Kitchen** and **Maybe Tomorrow** (both 1987). A further collaboration (in 1988) with Chrissie Hynde saw UB40 make UK Top 10 with **Breakfast In Bed**. Outfit also teamed with Robert Palmer in 1990 for **I'll Be Your Baby Tonight** hit.

In 1988, group undertook world tour (without Earl, who had been jailed for drunken driving), which saw appearance at

Nelson Mandela tribute concert at London's Wembley Stadium; **UB40** LP was released in same year. Band then enjoyed US No. 1 single when **Red Red Wine** was re-issued in the States, spurring five-year-old **Labour Of Love** album into US Top 20.

1990 saw issue of **Labour Of Love II** LP, which prompted usual flurry of 45 action including tidy re-make of Temptations' **The Way You Do The Things You Do**, a further US hit.

UB40's seemingly chanceless choice of material, whether it be cover versions or original material, has given them enviable portfolio of hits and has failed to dent their street credibility.

Hit Singles:	US	UK
King/Food For Thought, 1980	—	4
My Way Of Thinking/I Think It's Going To Rain, 1980	—	6
The Earth Dies Screaming/Dream A Lie, 1980	—	10
Don't Slow Down/Don't Let It Pass You By, 1981	—	16
One In Ten, 1981	—	7
Red Red Wine, 1983	34	1
Please Don't Make Me Cry, 1983	—	10
Many Rivers To Cross, 1983	—	16
Cherry Oh Baby, 1984	—	12
If It Happens Again, 1984	—	9
Don't Break My Heart, 1985	—	3
I Got You Babe (With Chrissie Hynde), 1985	28	1
All I Want To Do, 1986	—	41
Sing Our Own Song, 1986	—	5
Maybe Tomorrow, 1987	—	14
Rat In The Kitchen, 1987	—	12
Red Red Wine, 1988	1	—
Breakfast In Bed, 1988	—	6
Homely Girl, 1989	—	6
Kingston Town, 1990	—	4
The Way You Do The Things You Do, 1991	6	49
Here I Am (Come And Take Me), 1991	7	—

Albums:
Signing Off (—/Graduate), 1980
Present Arms (—/Dep International), 1981
Present Arms In Dub (—/Dep International), 1981
The Singles Album (—/Graduate), 1982
UB44 (—/Dep International), 1982
Live (—/Dep International), 1983
Labour Of Love (—/Dep International), 1983
Geffery Morgan (—/Dep International), 1984
Baggariddim (—/Dep International), 1985
The UB40 File (—/Dep International), 1985
Rat In The Kitchen (Dep), 1986
More Music (Sound), 1986
Best Of (Dep), 1987
UB40 With Chrissie Hynde (A&M/—), 1988
Labour Of Love II (Virgin), 1990

UFO

UK group formed 1970

Original line-up: Phil Mogg, vocals; Pete Way, bass; Andy Parker, drums; Mick Bolton, guitar.

Career: When UFO formed, their style of music was called hard rock. **UFO 1** and **Flying** were totally ignored in UK and US, but became popular in Germany and Japan. Bolton left and remaining trio became core of UFO through various personnel changes.

Michael Schenker met UFO while with Scorpions, who opened one of their early German tours. He took guitar spot on **Phenomenon** which became underground cult LP in US.

Force It and **No Heavy Petting** LPs showed off Schenker's growing heavy-metal guitar abilities; the latter album also saw band expand range by adding Danny Peyronel on keyboards. **Lights Out** album provided stage favourites **Love To Love** and title song. Paul Raymond was now on keyboards and band developed highly competent stage show. In UK they had become major draw without compromising to punk or new wave.

Growing reputation was boosted by **Obsession**, but live **Strangers In The Night** finally broke band in US. For exciting heavy metal, this LP is excellent introduction. Unfortunately, it marked departure of Schenker who left to form Michael Schenker Group. Paul Chapman, who had guested on LP, took over his spot full time.

In hindsight, this period began demise of band. **No Place To Run** saw Raymond replaced by Neil Carter. LP was too slickly produced by George Martin and missed edge given by Schenker. **The Wild, The Willing And The Innocent** album met fair reviews but did nothing new or exciting. Worse, Mogg's stage performances were becoming erratic because of personal problems and pressures. Way managed to contend with deteriorating situation for one

Above: Strangers In The Night, UFO. Courtesy Chrysalis Records.

more LP, but mid-1982 brought announcement he was leaving to form Fastway with ex-Motorhead guitarist, Fast Eddie Clarke.

Band recorded **Making Contact** in 1983 with Carter doubling on keyboards and bass. UFO set off on European tour with Billy Sheehan as guest bassist. Then, at February 1983 Athens show, Mogg collapsed, and audience nearly rioted. Cutting short European tour, group returned to UK. A month later plans were announced for UK tour, following which UFO disbanded.

During 1987 Phil Mogg recorded a series of demos in America with Atomik Tommy M on guitar, Jim Simpson on drums, and Paul Gray on bass, which they hoped would lead to a major record deal. When this wasn't forthcoming, the tracks were released by UK label FM Revolver as a 'musical scrapbook' in April 1988. On December 23, 1987 UFO played for rock magazine *Metal Hammer*'s Christmas Party at London's Astoria. A few months later Phil Mogg began writing new material with Pete Way hoping to re-form UFO with its original line-up, although this plan was eventually aborted and future of UFO left in tatters when Mogg joined The Quireboys.

Albums:
UFO 1 (—/Beacon), 1971
Flying (—/Beacon), 1972

Phenomenon (Chrysalis), 1973
Force It (Chrysalis), 1975
No Heavy Petting (Chrysalis), 1976
Lights Out (Chrysalis), 1977
Obsession (Chrysalis), 1978
Strangers In The Night (double live)
  (Chrysalis), 1979
No Place To Run (Chrysalis), 1979
The Wild, The Willing And The
  Innocent (Chrysalis), 1981
Mechanix (Chrysalis), 1982
Making Contact (Chrysalis), 1983
Misdemeanor (Chrysalis), 1985
Anthology (Raw Power), 1987

Ultravox

UK group formed 1975

Original line-up: John Foxx (real name Dennis Leigh), vocals; Billy Currie, violin, keyboards, synthesizer; Chris Cross (Chris St John), bass; Stevie Shears, guitar; Warren Cann, drums.

Career: Foxx, from Chorley, Lancashire, met Cross when latter moved from London to join Preston band Stoned Rose. After recruiting other three (Cann born in Canada, others British), formed band named Tiger Lily, with intention of playing like early Roxy Music. Signed with small Gull label, and

released version of Fats Waller's **Ain't Misbehavin'**, title music to X-rated film of same name. No success, but single was re-issued in 80s on even smaller Scottish label, Dead Good Records.

Band also known in early days by such names as The Zips, The Innocents, London Soundtrack and Fire Of London, but by 1976 had settled on name of Ultravox! (exclamation mark later dropped).

Signed with Island in 1976, releasing three LPs and numerous singles, all unsuccessful, despite growing cult following. In 1978, Shears left, replaced until 1979 by Robin Simon. That same year, Foxx departed to embark on partially successful solo career. Currie, Cross and Cann decided to stay together, even though group dropped by Island at this time. Recruited James 'Midge' Ure as singer and guitarist — Ure had played with Currie in Visage, part-time band for both, led by Steve Strange. Ure's previous career had included Slik, a Scottish pop band who topped UK charts in 1976 with

Left: Ultravox, masters of synthesized sound. From left, Chris Cross, Billy Currie, Midge Ure and Warren Cann.

Forever And Ever, Rich Kids, formed by ex-Sex Pistol bassist Glen Matlock (Ure was also invited at one point to join Sex Pistols, but declined), and temporary work with hard-rockers Thin Lizzy.

When Ure joined Ultravox, group adopted fresh direction with synthesizers, which had started when Foxx was singer, and signed with Chrysalis. They enjoyed success in UK, and to a lesser extent in other countries, with unbroken run of hit singles, plus several successful LPs.

While working on outside projects (Currie with Visage until early 1983, Ure also with Visage, as well as solo records and 1983 collaboration with Mick Karn of Japan, Cross making videos with Ure, and Cann writing film music), consensus was that band were drifting to conclusion. 1986 release **U-Vox** proved Ultravox' final recording, although band later regrouped for Nelson Mandela's 70th Birthday Party gig at Wembley Stadium in 1988.

Following creditable endeavour with Bob Geldof for Band/Live Aid, Midge Ure enjoyed UK No. 1 single with **If I Was** (1985), and cut own **Answer To Nothing** LP in 1988 and **Midge Ure** set in 1991. Billy Currie also saw release of solo album **Stand Up And Walk** in 1991.

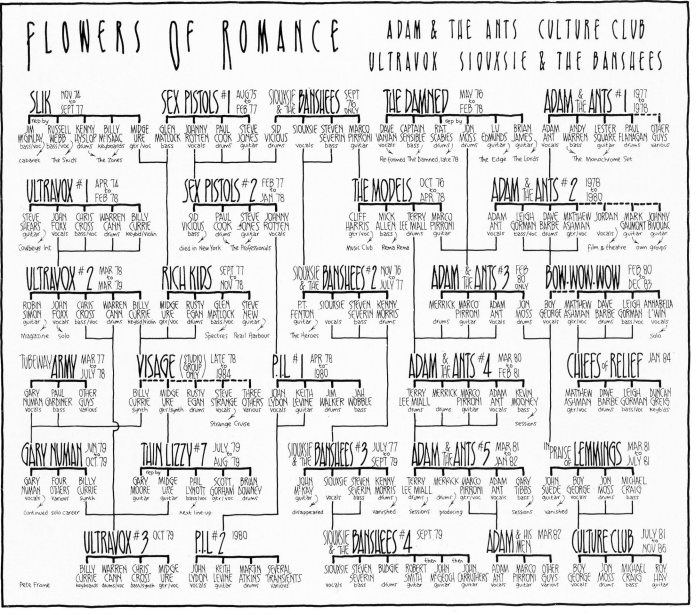

Hit Singles:

	US	UK
Vienna, 1981	—	2
All Stood Still, 1981	—	8
The Thin Wall, 1981	—	14
The Voice, 1981	—	16
Reap The Wild Wind, 1982	—	12
Hymn, 1982	—	11
Visions In Blue, 1983	—	15
We Came To Dance, 1983	—	18
Dancing With Tears In My Eyes, 1984	—	3
Love's Great Adventure, 1984	—	12
Same Old Story, 1986	—	31
All Fall Down, 1986	—	30

Midge Ure Solo:

	US	UK
No Regrets, 1982	—	9
If I Was, 1985	—	1
Call Of The Wild, 1986	—	27
Cold Cold Heart, 1991	—	17

Albums:
Ultravox! (Island), 1977
System Of Romance (Antilles/Island), 1978
Vienna (Chrysalis), 1980
Three Into One (Antilles/Island), 1980*
Rage In Eden (Chrysalis), 1981
Quartet (Chrysalis), 1982
Monument (soundtrack) (Chrysalis), 1983
Lament (Chrysalis), 1984
Collection (Chrysalis), 1985
U-Vox (Chrysalis), 1986
*compilation

Midge Ure Solo:
The Gift (Chrysalis), 1985
Answer To Nothing (Chrysalis), 1988

Billy Currie Solo:
Transportation (IRS/Island), 1988
Stand Up And Walk (—/Hot Food), 1991

John Foxx Solo:
Metamatic (—/Virgin), 1980
The Garden (—/Virgin), 1981
In Mysterious Ways (—/Virgin), 1985

Worth Searching Out:
Ha! Ha! Ha! (Island), 1977

Undertones
UK group formed 1975

Original line-up: Feargal Sharkey, vocals; John O'Neill, guitar; Damian 'Dee' O'Neil, guitar; Mike Bradley, bass; Billy Doherty, drums.

Career: Formed in Derry, Northern Ireland, band went unnoticed until mid-1978 when UK press discovered Irish music scene. **Teenage Kicks** EP was put out on independent label; John Peel played a role in getting band exposure by including EP on his radio show.

Undertones' first LP captured brash, young sound. With a cover deliberately derivative of The Who's **My Generation** LP, Undertones struck pose of a 1980s band aware of rock music's past. Critics praised band's freshness, and UK concerts won large audiences.

Focus of band was Sharkey's quavering vocals, which always seemed ready to break down but just managed to last to end of each song. This kept concerts interesting, but band stalled on record. **Hypnotised** was termed average by critics but **Positive Touch** was condemned as repetitive.

Undertones retreated to Northern Ireland in 1982 to re-work sound, as evident from **The Sin Of Pride** set. With band now on

crest of a wave, Sharkey's solo aspirations prompted group's demise.

First success for Sharkey was 1983 hit **Never Never**, released under name of Assembly, outfit co-led by former Yazoo and later Erasure maestro Vince Clarke.

But major breakthrough was not to come until 1985, when fervent **A Good Heart Is Hard To Find** touched chord with British public, taking No. 1 spot. Debut album **Feargal Sharkey** went on to sell more than two million copies worldwide.

Latterly, Feargal Sharkey has become purveyor of contemporary pop with hint of soul, as exemplified by Alison Moyet, Level 42 and others. However, lack of product — only **Wish** LP (1988) and **I've Got News For You** 45 (1991) have surfaced since initial album — could hinder the Sharkey phenomenon.

Hit Singles:

	US	UK
Jimmy, Jimmy, 1979	—	16
My Perfect Cousin, 1980	—	9
Wednesday Week, 1980	—	11
It's Going To Happen, 1981	—	18

Feargal Sharkey Solo:

	US	UK
A Good Heart Is Hard To Find, 1985	—	1
You Little Thief, 1986	—	5
I've Got News For You, 1991	—	12

Feargal Sharkey with Vince Clarke in Assembly:

Never Never, 1983	—	4

Albums:
Undertones (Fame), 1979
Hypnotised (Sire), 1980
Positive Touch (Harvest/EMI), 1981
The Sin Of Pride (—/Ardeck), 1983
Cher O'Bowlies (compilation) (EMI)

Feargal Sharkey Solo:
Feargal Sharkey (Virgin), 1985
Wish (Virgin), 1988

Uriah Heep
UK group formed 1969

Original line-up: Mick Box, guitar; David Byron, vocals; Ken Hensley, keyboards; Alex Napier, drums; Paul Newton, bass, vocals.

Career: Box and Byron asked Ken Hensley to leave Toe Fat and formed Uriah Heep.

Above: Feargal Sharkey fronts The Undertones before their early demise.

Napier and Newton had been with Box and Byron in their old band Spice; Newton had known Hensley in earlier band, Gods, and introduced him to Heep. While recording first LP, Napier left, to be replaced by Nigel Olsson, who quit after recording sessions for Elton John. Heep auditioned Keith Baker as new drummer.

Following second LP, Baker left. Ian Clarke joined for one year and one album. Hensley finally convinced Toe Fat mate, Lee Kerslake, to take drums. Band also replaced Newton with Mark Clarke who quit after few months. Throughout this flux, band was object of critical attack rivalled only by that directed towards Grand Funk Railroad. Gary Thain joined on bass and band took off as international stars. Based on vague sorcery, **Demons And Wizards** and **The Magician's Birthday** LPs were full of mystic connotations. The same line-up also recorded highly underrated **Uriah Heep Live** LP which pre-dates heavy metal without the boring repetition that sometimes plagues the genre.

Thain developed drug problems which led to his firing in early 1975 (he died in December 1975). John Wetton (later of

Below: Uriah Heep must be termed survivors, despite continual line-up changes in the band.

Asia) joined for 18 months. **Return To Fantasy** and **High And Mighty** were recorded during this period.

Even though LPs were as strong as ever, Heep lost audience and internal dissent began tearing band apart. Wetton and Byron left in August 1976. Box, Hensley and Kerslake signed up John Lawton for vocals and Trevor Bolder (ex-David Bowie) on bass. This line-up recorded **Firefly**, **Innocent Victim** and **Fallen Angel** as band continued downward slide. Reshuffle again occurred before recording of excellent **Abominog**, which appeared after most fans assumed band was gone for good.

Despite being dropped by Bronze label, Uriah Heep continued to work and secured deal with CBS subsidiary Portrait in 1984, from which liaison saw release of **Equator** album (1985).

Band still suffered from personnel problems, the HM disease, losing vocalist Pete Goalby and keyboard player John Sinclair (both featured on **Abominog**). Their replacements were Stef Fontaine and Phil Lanzon, respectively. A further adjustment saw Bernie Shaw oust Fontaine prior to **Live In Europe '87** set.

Uriah Heep joined with Legacy label in 1988, debuting for company with **Live In Moscow**, recorded at historic series of gigs which took place in city during the winter of 1987. The unit later returned to the Eastern Bloc for concerts in Russia, Poland and East Germany.

Despite being a chronicler's nightmare, Heep have endured remarkably well, and their inventive touring schedule has seen fan support grow in the oddest of places.

Albums:
Very 'Eavy, Very 'Umble (—/Vertigo), 1970
Uriah Heep (Mercury/—), 1970
Salisbury (Mercury/Vertigo), 1971
Demons And Wizards (Mercury/Bronze), 1972
The Magician's Birthday (Mercury/Bronze), 1972
Sweet Freedom (Warner Bros/Bronze), 1973
Wonderworld (Warner Bros/Bronze), 1974
The Best Of (Mercury/Bronze), 1975
Innocent Victim (Warner Bros/Bronze), 1977
Fallen Angel (Chrysalis/Bronze), 1978
Conquest (—/Bronze), 1980
Dreamer (—/Bronze), 1982
Head First (Mercury/Bronze), 1983
Abominog (Castle Classics)
Equator (Portrait), 1985
Anthology (Raw Power)

Live In Europe '87 (−/Raw Power), 1987
Live In Moscow (−/Legacy), 1988
Look At Yourself (Mercury/Castle
    Classics), 1989
Live (Mercury/Raw Power), 1989

Richie Valens
US vocalist, guitarist, composer
Born Los Angeles, California, May 13, 1941
Died February 3, 1959

Career: Took up guitar age nine; became popular entertainer while in high school, appearing at school functions and local dances with own group, The Silhouettes. Spotted by Bob Keene of Del-Fi Records and signed to contract. First single **Come On Let's Go** was moderate success in US with cover version by Tommy Steele reaching UK Top 10.

Mexican background apparent in many recordings, with adaptation of traditional Mexican song **La Bamba** becoming best-known example; song was released with **Donna**, and became Valens' biggest hit. Valens made film debut in late 1958 singing **Ooh My Head** in rock 'n' roll teen drama movie *Go Johnny Go*.

Embarked on first major tour through Mid-West US in January 1959. Halfway through tour, co-star Buddy Holly chartered plane to fly to next engagement; Valens won seat on aircraft by flipping coin with guitarist Tommy Allsup. Valens died with Holly and Big Bopper when plane crashed into snow-covered cornfield.

Death at age 17 cut short promising career, and Valens left relatively few recordings. However, he established chicano strain of rock, paving way for artists like Chris Montez. Interest in Valens leapt following success of 1987 biopic *La Bamba*, and fellow LA denizens Los Lobos took Valens' hits into charts all over again.

Hit Singles:

	US	UK
Donna/La Bamba, 1958	2	−

Albums:
His Greatest Hits (−/President), 1970
Rock Lil' Darlin (−/Joy), 1971
History Of (Rhino), 1985
The Best Of 1958-59 (Rhino/−), 1987

Van Halen
US group formed 1974

Original line-up: David Lee Roth, vocals; Edward Van Halen, Gibson Flying V guitar; Mike Anthony, bass; Alex Van Halen, drums.

Career: Netherlands-born Van Halen brothers originally trained as concert pianists; family relocated in Pasadena, California. Formed group (originally known as Mammoth) with Roth and Anthony (both born in Mid-West), and became popular local attraction through combination of loud and energetic heavy metal and Roth's very tight trousers. Due to inability to attract record deal, began promoting own gigs; used every possible attention-grabbing trick − like parachuting into stadium in successful attempt to upstage the headlining band.

By 1977, group were attracting audiences of 3,000. Warners Bros' A&R man Ted Templeman saw them playing in Hollywood club and signed them immediately.

Subsequent albums, all produced by Templeman, achieved major US chart success. **1984** LP contained superb **Jump**.

At end of 1985 Roth left to pursue solo ambitions, scoring considerable success. Van Halen reconstituted with veteran metal merchant Sammy Hagar and went on to record biggest album of career, multi-platinum-selling **5150**. Disc also spawned US hit single **Why Can't This Be Love?**.

Band took two years off before returning with 1988 set **OU812**, which topped US album chart, although Hagar (see separate entry) has maintained successful parallel career. Van Halen returned to road in September of same year for two-month American tour.

Eddie and the boys went into voluntary exile once again after mega-US hike, but reprised success of **OU812** when June 1991 LP **For Unlawful Carnal Knowledge** debuted at No. 1 in *Billboard* album chart. Surprisingly, collection did not overwhelm critics, although single cuts **Top Of The World** and **The Dream Is Over** saw unit in prime form.

Pyrotechnic guitar-playing of Eddie Van Halen has kept band in forefront of HM units, but he owes a debt to solid front-men Roth and Hagar.

Hit Singles:

	US	UK
Dance The Night Away, 1979	15	−
Pretty Woman, 1982	12	−
Jump, 1984	1	7
I'll Wait, 1984	13	−
Panama, 1984	13	−
Why Can't This Be Love, 1986	−	8
Love Walks In, 1987	14	−
Just Like Paradise, 1988	6	27
When It's Love, 1988	5	28
Finish Whatcha Started, 1988	13	−

David Lee Roth Solo:

	US	UK
California Girls, 1985	3	−
Just A Gigolo/I Ain't Got Nobody, 1985	12	−

Albums:
Van Halen (Warner Bros), 1978
Van Halen II (Warner Bros), 1979
Women And Children First (Warner Bros), 1980
Fair Warning (Warner Bros), 1981
Diver Down (Warner Bros), 1982
1984 (Warner Bros), 1984
5150 (WEA), 1986
OU812 (Warner Bros), 1988
For Unlawful Carnal Knowledge (Warner Bros/−), 1991

David Lee Roth Solo:
Crazy From The Heat (Warner Bros), 1985
Eat 'Em And Smile (Warner Bros), 1986
Skyscraper (Warner Bros), 1988
A Little Ain't Enough (WEA), 1991

Above: Guitar god Eddie Van Halen (right), now the ultimate HM axeman.

Vanilla Ice
US rap artist
Born Robert Van Winkle

Career: Authentic bad-mouth rapper whose WASPish good looks raised questions about residence in almost uniquely black musical environment.

Raised in middle-class suburb of Dallas, his reputed hell-fire teenage days turned out to be a figment of record company's imagination. A solid citizen and member of local church choir, Ice Baby's only tickle from the law came when he was unable to produce his driving licence when stopped by the cops.

Discovered at City Lights disco in downtown Dallas, where his novelty value as only white act prompted visits from inquisitive record company executives. Signed by SBK, **To The Extreme** debut album spawned **Ice Ice Baby** multi-million-selling single following support on MC Hammer's 1990 US tour.

Second album **Extremely Live** (1991) received better reviews than Ice's movie debut in *Cool As Ice* for Universal Pictures, which received as savage a reception as the Christians in Rome. Plans to distribute the film in UK were subsequently abandoned, although soundtrack was scheduled for early 1992 release.

Hit Singles:

	US	UK
Ice Ice Baby, 1990	−	1
Play That Funky Music, 1991	18	10

Albums:
To The Extreme (SBK), 1990
Extremely Live (SBK), 1991

Bobby Vee
US vocalist
Born Robert Veline, Fargo, North Dakota, April 30, 1943

Career: Formed first band The Shadows in 1959. Made first appearance in hometown as direct result of Buddy Holly's death in plane crash on February 3. Holly and rest of 'Winter Dance Party' had been due to appear in Fargo that evening; Vee's group brought in as replacement. First record on local label, **Suzy Baby**, became local hit and was released nationally on Liberty, who signed Vee to long-term deal. In attempt to take over where Buddy Holly had left off, producer Snuff Garrett had Vee cover Adam Faith's UK hit **What Do You Want**, which in turn had been inspired by Holly's last recordings with pizzicato strings. Release failed but next single, **Devil Or Angel**, made Top 10, followed by Hollyish **Rubber Ball** which became first of many UK hits.

During next three years, Vee became established as purveyor of Brill Building pop songs, with best material from Gerry Goffin and Carole King who wrote biggest hit **Take Good Care Of My Baby**. Although records and image were 'manufactured' to appeal to same market as Frankie Avalon and Fabian, Vee's records had more lasting appeal due to careful production. Collaboration with Crickets in 1962 resulted in excellent **Bobby Vee Meets Crickets** album and sell-out tour of UK, with guest spots in *Just For Fun* teen-movie. Appeal faded in mid-60s despite attempts to score with material and comeback in 1967 with **Come Back When You Grow Up**.

Attempted further comeback in 70s under real name, but, despite interesting album, failed to make impression. Became Bobby Vee again in order to capitalize on old hits in nostalgia market.

Hit Singles:

	US	UK
Devil Or Angel, 1960	6	−
Rubber Ball, 1960	6	4
How Many Tears, 1961	−	10
Take Good Care Of My Baby, 1961	1	3
Run To Him, 1961	2	6

Below: Catch him while you can. The Iceman suffered serious decline in 1991.

	US	UK
Please Don't Ask About Barbara, 1962	15	29
Sharing You, 1962	15	10
Punish Her, 1962	20	—
A Forever Kind Of Love, 1962	—	13
The Night Has A Thousand Eyes, 1962	3	3
Charms, 1963	13	—
Come Back When You Grow Up, 1967	3	—

Albums:
Golden Greats (Liberty/—), 1968
Singles Album (—/Fame), 1982
Bobby Vee Meets The Crickets (EMI/Liberty), 1991

Suzanne Vega

US composer, vocalist
Born New York

Career: Encouraged into arts background by Puerto Rican father, she attended New York High School of Performing Arts studying dance.

Grew up reading Sylvia Plath's introspective poetry and listening to Leonard Cohen and early (acoustic) Bob Dylan. Began performing self-composed songs in NY club scene and attracted attention of lawyer Ron Fierstein and studio engineer Steve Addabbo who immediately offered to manage her. Addabbo also became her record producer when a deal with A&M records was signed.

Vega soon gained image as 80s version of Joni Mitchell — cute, fey and lonely, clutching acoustic guitar for support — but insisted on still wearing battered old leather jacket on stage and refused to wear dresses.

Debut LP **Suzanne Vega** established her as strong songwriter in traditional vein but only reached wider audience in 1986 when **Left Of Center** featured in *Pretty In Pink* brat-pack movie and became surprise hit.

Following **Marlene On The Wall** hit, sell-out world tour and **Solitude Standing**

Above: Solitude Standing, Suzanne Vega. Courtesy A&M Records.

album showed sharper, more modern approach. Finally achieved true star status with hit single **Luka**, which concerned child cruelty, forcing even critics to view Vega with respect and admiration.

After surprising two-year gap, Vega finally got around to recording new album, although finished product **Days Of Open Hand** did not appear until spring of 1990. Toured US and Europe later in year during which time she received jolt when **Tom's Diner** formed basis of DNA hit single in UK. Re-mixed by the two DJs, the track (taken from **Solitude Standing**) had the British dance crowd hopping, which was hardly Vega's original intention. Ironically, the single was released by A&M, her own label.

Hit Singles:	US	UK
Marlene On The Wall, 1985	—	21
Left Of Center, 1986	—	32
Luka, 1987	—	3

Albums:
Suzanne Vega (A&M), 1985
Solitude Standing (A&M), 1987
Days Of Open Hand (A&M), 1990

The Velvet Underground

US group formed 1966

Original line-up: Lou Reed, guitar, vocals; John Cale, guitar, bass, viola; Maureen Tucker, drums, percussion.

Career: Ill-assorted group of talented subversives came together in New York's fertile and bustling 'alternative' music scene in 1966 — Cale, a Welsh child prodigy, Reed, a classically trained trumpet player, and Tucker, one of few female drummers to succeed in rock.

Outlook was direct and dramatic opposite of the 'flower power' scene that was burgeoning at that time. Group mercilessly spotlighted drugs, death and the bizarre. Struggled in NYC's underground clubs until discovery by Andy Warhol. He added Nico, one of his protégées, promoted the group, and designed cover of first album, **The Velvet Underground And Nico** (1967).

Group's image, outlook and sound were shocking and incomprehensible at times. Literate, half-spoken vocals and dark slashing sound did not suit audience looking for peace and love, and connection with Warhol led some to view them as publicity stunt. Their pervading influence is now obvious in punk, new wave and Euro-pop.

Nico left after first album. Group recorded two more albums on Verve/Polydor, **White Light/White Heat** (1968) and **The Velvet Underground** (1969), but they were too controversial to meet with commercial success. In 1970 Cale and Reed left, both to pursue solo careers. Morrison was joined by Bill and Doug Yule briefly, but the Velvets' natural life had ended by 1972.

Above: Suzanne Vega has been favourably compared to Joni Mitchell.

Footnote: Nico died from a brain haemorrhage in July 1988 following a bicycle accident; remaining VU members regrouped two years later in Paris at exhibition of Andy Warhol paintings: Reed, Cale and Morrison featured on Tucker's 1992 LP.

Albums:
White Light/White Heat (Verve), 1968
The Velvet Underground (MGM), 1969
Loaded (Cotillion/Atlantic), 1970
Live (with Lou Reed) (Mercury), 1969
Velvet Underground Live (Cotillion/Atlantic), 1970
VU (Polydor), 1985
Another View (Polydor, Germany)

Below: The charismatic Gene Vincent in Capitol Studios during the 1950s.

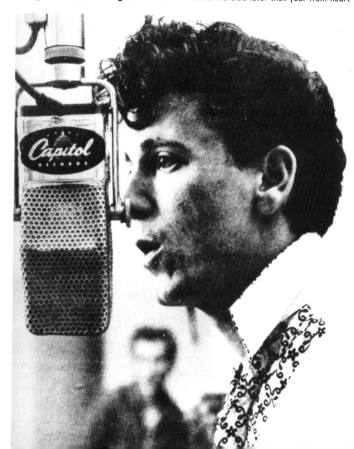

Worth Searching Out:
The Velvet Underground And Nico (Verve), 1967

Gene Vincent

US vocalist, composer
Born Vincent Eugene Craddock, Norfolk, Virginia, February 11, 1935
Died Hollywood, California, October 12, 1971

Career: Took up music seriously following disablement due to leg injuries received in motorcycle accident at Norfolk Naval Base while merchant seaman. By 1956 secured regular spot on country music station WCMS with DJ 'Sheriff' Tex Davis acting as manager. Recorded demo of **Be-Bop-A-Lula** at WCMS studio and won contract with Capitol Records, who regarded Vincent as 'answer' to Elvis Presley. **Lula** rapidly became hit, but, despite making charts again in 1957, Vincent's popularity declined in US.

During short-lived road career with Blue Caps, Vincent was regarded as wildest rock 'n' roll act on and off stage, leaving wrecked hotels and dressing rooms in wake. Poor management and money problems with group forced him to cease touring in US. Continued to record for Capitol, occasionally producing classic tracks. Generally recording career lacked direction, with producer Ken Nelson veering towards MOR standards in attempt to broaden appeal.

During 1960 found new popularity in Britain with appearances on Jack Good's *Boy Meets Girl* TV show. Despite setback of further injuries received in April 1960 car crash that killed Eddie Cochran, continued to tour UK regularly and became hero of teddy-boy movement; scored several minor UK hits on Capitol before final decline to smaller labels and smaller club dates.

By 1969 Vincent was shadow of former self, beset by personal problems and alcoholism. Returned to California in 1971, where attempts to revive career once again failed. He died later that year from heart failure, undoubtedly related to his chronic drink problems.

Cult following established during lifetime shows no sign of diminishing and echoes of Vincent's style are still found in many rockabilly revival groups, such as the New York trio Stray Cats.

Hit Singles:

	US	UK
Be-Bop-A-Lula, 1956	7	16
Bluejean Bop, 1956	–	16
Lotta Lovin', 1957	13	–
My Heart, 1960	–	16
Pistol Packin' Mama, 1960	–	15

Albums:
Gene Vincent's Greatest (Fame), 1977
The Gene Vincent Singles Album (Capitol), 1981
Gene Vincent and Eddie Cochran – Together Again (Capitol), 1980
Gene Vincent and Eddie Cochran – Rock 'n' Roll Heroes (Rockstar), 1981
The Bop They Couldn't Stop (Magnum Force), 1981
Dressed in Black (Magnum Force), 1982
Ain't That Too Much (Everest), 1982
Birddoggin' (Bulldog), 1982
For The Collectors Only (Magnum Force), 1984
I'm Back And I'm Proud (Nightlife)
Songs Of The James Dean Era (Capitol)
Born To Be A Rolling Stone (Charly), 1987

Gene Vincent and Shouts:
Shakin' Up A Storm (EMI), 1983

Loudon Wainwright III

US composer, guitarist, vocalist
Born Chapel Hill, North Carolina, September 5, 1947

Career: Wainwright began appearing in East Coast clubs and bars in the late 60s. He clearly emphasized the folk side of rock by relying on acoustic guitar and funny between songs patter. In 1971 Atlantic brought out **Album I** which continued folk trend with macabre subject matter. **Album II** emphasized outrage for sake of outrage à la Lenny Bruce.

Switching to Columbia, Wainwright found sense of balance between humour and making a point. **Album III** captured Wainwright at his best; **Red Guitar** tipped hat to Pete Townshend's stage antics, and **Dead Skunk** got into US Top 20. Wainwright also had realized limits of self-accompaniment and on this LP began using session musicians for recording and as back-up group on stage. He married Kate McGarrigle in 1973 and she appeared on **Unrequited** LP. (They had separated by 1978).

Always a minority taste, Wainwright nonetheless maintained output throughout the 80s, recording for variety of indie labels. He joined with ex-Fairport Convention guitarist/vocalist Richard Thompson for trio of LPs for country/folk label Rounder: **Fame And Wealth**, **I'm Alright** and **More Love Songs**. Artist featured as resident troubadour on British comedian Jasper Carrot's TV series, and also appeared in *MASH* (in similar role), plus movie *Jacknife* (1989), which starred Robert De Niro.

Hit Singles:

	US	UK
Dead Skunk, 1973	16	–

Albums:
Album I (Atlantic), 1971
Album II (Atlantic), 1972
Album III (Columbia/CBS), 1973
Attempted Moustache (Columbia/CBS), 1974
Unrequited (Columbia/CBS), 1975
T-Shirt (Arista), 1976
Final Exam (Arista), 1978
Live One (–/Radar), 1979
Fame And Wealth (–/Demon), 1983
I'm Alright (Rounder), 1988
More Love Songs (Rounder), 1988
Therapy (Silvertone), 1989

Tom Waits

US composer, vocalist, pianist
Born Pomona, California, December 7, 1949

Career: Waits entertained small audiences on West Coast in early 70s. His rough voice and sparse back-up (usually piano, stand-up bass, drums and sax) evoked atmosphere of 50s beatniks rather than 60s rock. Waits' tales of survival on other sides of tracks drew attention of Elektra, who signed him in 1973.

Waits' compositions started to get recorded by other artists and he opened for variety of acts from Charlie Rich to Frank Zappa. He continued working throughout US and Europe, but, despite rave critical approval, remained cult figure on outskirts of rock. Waits' songs about lowlife are perceptive and poignant observations rather than critical judgements, and his music seems best suited to dark, smoke-filled basement clubs and Bohemian cafés. This perhaps limits his potential for mass appeal, though he did contribute to score of Francis Ford Coppola's movie *One From The Heart*, and also appeared in that director's movies *Rumble Fish* and *Cotton Club*. Further film roles during 80s included *Ironweed* and *Cold Feet*.

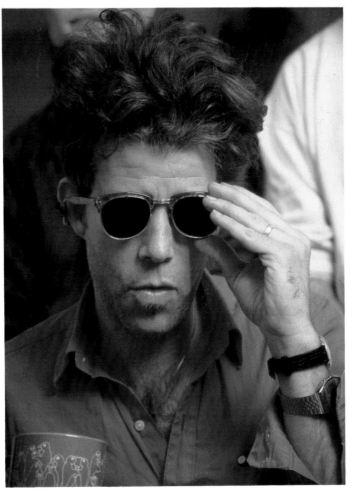

Above: Cult figure Tom Waits has shied away from popular acclaim.

Above: Frank's Wild Years, Tom Waits. Courtesy Island Records.

Waits sneaked into US Top 40 with album **Rain Dogs** (1985), but follow-up **Frank's Wild Years** failed to crack Hot 100, confirming 'minority' tag. However, continued to enjoy success with covers of his songs, particularly Rod Stewart's re-working of **Downtown Train**, which made US Top 5 singles chart.

Artist returned to studios in 1991 after four-year break to record soundtrack to *The Black Rider* theatre opus he co-wrote with William Burroughs and Robert Wilson. Also resumed relationship with Coppola when selected for *Dracula* flick scheduled for 1992 release. Other movie activities in same period included part in *At Play In The Fields Of The Lord* and musical contribution to Jim Jarmusch's *Night On Earth*.

Waits' planned new LP for April 1992 release, having supplied vocals for tenor saxophonist Teddy Edward's 1991 collection **Mississippi Lad.**

Albums:
Closing Time (Elektra), 1973
The Heart Of A Saturday Night (Elektra/Asylum), 1974
Nighthawks At The Diner (Asylum), 1975
Small Change (Asylum), 1976
Foreign Affairs (Elektra), 1977
Blue Valentine (Asylum), 1978
Heartattack And Vine (Asylum), 1980
Bounced Checks (Asylum), 1981
Swordfish Trombones (Island), 1983
Asylum Years (Asylum), 1984
Rain Dogs (Island), 1985
Frank's Wild Years (Island), 1987
Big Time (Island), 1988

Rick Wakeman

UK keyboard player, composer
Born London, May 18, 1949

Career: Born into musical family; father was professional pianist. Studied piano from age four. On leaving school attended Royal College of Music when he started to make mark as session musician. Eventually gave up studies in favour of recording world. Provided keyboards expertise for many top artists, including David Bowie, T. Rex and Cat Stevens during late 60s and early 70s.

In 1970 Wakeman was asked to join emergent Strawbs, and stayed with band

Below: Keyboard maestro Rick Wakeman, an electro-pop pioneer.

for 16 months. But after Yes lost keyboards man Tony Kaye, they persuaded Wakeman to quit Strawbs and join them, which he did in summer 1971.

While with Yes, Wakeman became keyboard star, adding prodigious technique and classical influence. But, having already released one solo album, **Six Wives Of Henry VIII**, Wakeman split to pursue solo career in 1974.

Next album, **Journey To The Centre Of The Earth**, was huge success on both sides of Atlantic, and Wakeman built spectacular stage show around it. With following album, **The Myths And Legends Of King Arthur**, he went step further and produced musical spectacular on ice at London's Empire Pool, complete with 45-piece orchestra and 48-piece choir.

Continuing to make solo records, Wakeman nevertheless rejoined Yes in 1976, staying with group until end of 1979.

Quitting long-time label A&M in 1979, Wakeman did not record for two years until he came up with elaborate visionary work **1984** for Charisma. This became Top 30 UK album, and put Wakeman back on path of success. Following earlier excursions into film music **Lisztomania** (1975) and **White Rock** (1976), he scored horror movie *The Burning* in 1982, following it with **G'Olé**, music for World Cup movie in 1983.

Wakeman kept relatively low profile during 80s, with albums such as **Beyond The Planets** (with Kevin Peek) and **The Gospels**, although interest in New Age music returned him to radio playlists.

In 1989, Wakeman rejoined with Bill Bruford, Jon Anderson and Steve Howe for reincarnation of Yes and cut eponymous album for CBS; toured US in same year. Offical Yes re-formed in 1991, giving Wakeman opportunity to return to stadium gigs he must have thought were a thing of the past.

Albums:
Six Wives Of Henry VIII (A&M), 1973
Journey To The Centre Of The Earth
(A&M), 1974
Myths And Legends Of King Arthur
(A&M), 1975
Lisztomania (soundtrack) (A&M), 1975
No Earthly Connection (A&M), 1976
White Rock (soundtrack) (A&M), 1976
Criminal Record (A&M), 1977
Best Known Works (A&M), 1978
Rhapsodies (A&M), 1979
1984 (Charisma), 1981
The Burning (soundtrack) (Charisma),
1982
G'Olé (soundtrack) (Charisma), 1983
Silent Night (TBG), 1985
Country Airs (Coda), 1986
The Family Album (President), 1987
The Gospels (President), 1987
New Age Collection (President), 1987
Live At Hammersmith (President),
Crimes Of Passion (soundtrack)
(President), 1987

Joe Walsh

US guitarist, vocalist, composer
Born Wichita, Kansas, November 20, 1947

Career: First gained attention as star of The James Gang, a Cleveland-based band who toured with The Who gathering critical raves. Walsh was propelling force of group, providing songs and fierce hard-rock guitar. Quit in 1971 and, with drummer Joe Vitale and bassist Kenny Passarelli, recorded solo LP, **Barnstorm**. After idea of developing Barnstorm into a working band fell apart,

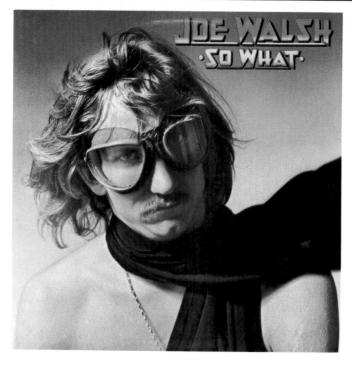

he recorded two albums. One, **The Smoker You Drink, The Player You Get**, went gold in 1973; from it came Top 30 single **Rocky Mountain Way**.

Signed with MCA in 1974. Released fairly interesting live LP, **You Can't Argue With A Sick Mind** (1976). Joined The Eagles same year, becoming part of that group's best line-up, Walsh's guitar adding bite to band's progressive LA harmonies. Continued with his solo projects; contributed theme song for movie *The Warriors* in 1978, and played on sessions for Randy Newman, Emerson, Lake and Palmer and Warren Zevon, among others. Had hit single with **Life's Been Good To Me** from **But Seriously Folks** LP.

In 1982 The Eagles announced their break-up. Walsh worked with John Entwistle on his **Too Late The Hero** album, then began major US tour opening for Stevie Nicks the following year. Continues to record solo with limited success.

Hit Singles:	US	UK
Life's Been Good To Me, 1978	12	14
All Night Long, 1980	19	—

Albums:
Barnstorm:
Barnstorm (Dunhill/Probe), 1972

Solo:
The Smoker You Drink, The Player You
Get (Dunhill/Probe), 1973
So What (Dunhill/Probe), 1974
You Can't Argue With A Sick Mind
(ABC-MCA/Anchor), 1976

Above: Famous Blue Raincoat, Jennifer Warnes. Courtesy RCA.

Above: So What, Joe Walsh. Courtesy ABC Records.

But Seriously Folks . . . (Asylum), 1978
Best Of (ABC-MCA/—), 1978
There Goes The Neighborhood (Asylum),
1981
You Bought It You Name It (Warner
Bros), 1983
The Confessor (Warner Bros), 1985
Got Any Gum (WEA), 1987
Live (MCA), 1986
Ordinary Average Guy (Epic/—), 1991

Jennifer Warnes

US singer
Born Orange County, California

Career: Made her professional debut at seven wrapped in an American flag singing the national anthem accompanied by 300 accordions. Weaned on the Los Angeles folk circuit, Warnes took the female lead in West Coast production of *Hair*, and also had a weekly stint on the *Smothers Brothers Comedy Hour* television programme.

She made one album for Warner Brothers produced by John Cale before signing to Arista. Single **Right Time Of The Night** reached the UK charts in 1975 followed by **I Know A Heartache When I See One** from **Shot Through The Heart** album.

Associated next with a number of major film themes, including the Oscar-winning **It Goes Like It Goes** from *Norma Rae* (1979) and **One More Hour** from Randy Newman's *Ragtime* score (1981). Her association with movies provided greatest success when duets with Joe Cocker — **Up Where We Belong**, from *An Officer And A Gentleman* — and Bill Medley — **(I've Had) The Time Of My Life** from *Dirty Dancing* — both earned Grammy and Academy Award tropies.

Cut third set **Famous Blue Raincoat** for RCA in 1987; featured material by Leonard Cohen, who also contributed vocals on **Joan Of Arc** track. Now signed to Private Music, the company planned a debut album for Warnes in 1992. Meanwhile, singer continued her extra-curricular activities with appearance on Tanita Tikaram's 1991 LP **Everybody's Angel**.

Hit Singles:	US	UK
(With Joe Cocker)		
Up Where We Belong, 1985	1	1
(With Bill Medley)		
The Time Of My Life, 1987	1	

Albums:
Shot Through The Heart (Arista), 1979
Best Of (Arista), 1982
Famous Blue Raincoat (RCA/Cypress),
1987

Dionne Warwick

US vocalist
Born East Orange, New Jersey,
December 12, 1941

Career: Studied music from age six. Sang with family gospel group Drinkard Singers. After further music training at Hart College of Music in Connecticut, Warwick (she has gone back and forth between Warwick and Warwicke spellings) moved to New York and became back-up singer. Often worked with sister Dee Dee, and aunt Cissy Houston.

Songwriters/producers Burt Bacharach and Hal David were impressed by her work on Drifters' session and arranged contract with Sceptre Records. Warwick's first solo release, written by them, was **Don't Make Me Over**; it became US hit and started huge run of success for Bacharach-David-Warwick partnership. Team created some of classiest romantic pop music ever recorded; Bacharach's distinctive and often subtle melodies, David's above-average lyrics and Warwick's ethereal but soulful voice combined to produce clutch of classics.

Nevertheless, by late 1960s formula was wearing thin and Warwick attempted to revive flagging career by switching to Warner Bros. Arrived back in limelight through pairing with Spinners on **Then Came You**.

Second major phase of career started with signing to Arista. Barry Manilow-produced 1979 LP **Dionne** was million-seller, and further Arista albums have also scored heavily. Enjoyed US No. 1 with **That's What Friends Are For** in 1985 in collaboration with Gladys Knight, Stevie Wonder and Elton John, and was featured on **We Are The World** in same year. Further liaison, with Jeffrey Osbourne, on **Love Power** single, also proved US success.

A talented artist with truly distinctive vocal approach, Warwick has managed to avoid worst excesses of MOR while steering clear of disco route. Her perfectionist approach ensures that she will be able to pursue successful career for years to come.

Hit Singles:	US	UK
Anyone Who Had A Heart, 1964	8	42
Walk On By, 1964	6	9
You'll Never Get To Heaven, 1964	34	20
Reach Out For Me, 1964	20	23
Message To Michael, 1966	8	—
Alfie, 1967	15	—
I Say A Little Prayer/Valley Of The Dolls, 1967	4	—
Valley Of The Dolls/I Say A Little Prayer, 1968	2	28
Do You Know The Way To San Jose, 1968	10	8
Promises Promises, 1968	19	—
This Girl's In Love With You, 1969	7	—
You've Lost That Lovin' Feeling, 1969	16	—

I'll Never Fall In Love Again, 1970	6	–
I'll Never Love This Way Again, 1979	5	–
Deja Vu, 1979	15	–
Heartbreaker, 1982	10	2
All The Love In The World, 1983	–	12
That's What Friends Are For, 1985	1	16

With Detroit Spinners:

Then Came You, 1974	1	9

With Jeffrey Osbourne:

Love Power, 1987	12	–

Albums:
Greatest Hits Volume 1 (–/Hallmark), 1973
Greatest Hits Volume 2 (–/Hallmark), 1973
Greatest Hits Volume 3 (–/Hallmark), 1974
Greatest Hits Volume 4 (–/Hallmark), 1975
Collection (–/Pickwick), 1976
Dionne (Arista), 1979
No Night So Long (Arista), 1980
Golden Collection (–/K-Tel), 1981
Hot Live And Otherwise (Arista), 1981
Friends In Love (Arista), 1982
Heartbreaker (Arista), 1982
Golden Hits Volume 1 (–/Phoenix), 1982
Golden Hits Volume 2 (–/Phoenix), 1982
So Amazing (Arista), 1983
Without Your Love (Arista), 1985
Reservations For Two (Arista), 1987
Walk On By And Other Favourties (Charly), 1988
20 Greatest Hits (Bescol), 1988
Greatest Hits 1979-90 (Arista), 1989
Sings Cole Porter (Arista), 1990

Waterboys
UK group formed 1982

Original line-up: Michael Scott, guitar, vocals; Anthony Thistlethwaite, saxophones, keyboards.

Career: Edinburgh-born Scott teamed with Thistlethwaite in 1982 after participating with slew of unsuccessful rock groups, although secured deal with Virgin while featuring in Another Pretty Face line-up.

Eponymous Rupert Hine-produced debut album was released in 1983 on Ensign label, with Scott and Thistlethwaite supplemented by a handful of session musicians. Duo subsequently added keyboard player Karl Wallinger and drummer Kevin Wilkinson prior to issue of 1984 set, **A Pagan Place**.

Having tickled critic's fancy with first two LPs, Waterboys made commercial breakthrough with **This Is The Sea** album (1985), from which single **Whole Of The Moon** made US Top 30. Band then lost Wallinger, who formed World Party.

1988 saw notable change of direction when Scott, now resident in Galway Bay, Ireland, cut folky **Fisherman's Blues**, which featured short-term signing Steve Wickham on violin. Scott and Thistlethwaite were then joined by Trevor Hutchinson on bass, Sharon Shannon on violin and squeezebox, and Colin Blakey on keyboards and flute for another traditional-styled album, **Room To Roam** (1990), which earned band position in UK Top 10.

Despite success of **Roam**, chameleon-like tactics of Scott and Thistlethwaite saw

Below: Dionne Warwick is approaching 30 years in show business.

reversion to more rock-orientated approach for UK tour in 1990, with Hutchinson and drummer Kevin Blevins. Band then earned their highest chart placing for **Best Of** package which made No. 3 in UK album charts.

Hit Singles:	US	UK
Whole Of The Moon (re-issue), 1991	–	3

Albums:
The Waterboys (Chrysalis/Ensign), 1983
A Pagan Place (Chrysalis/Ensign), 1984
This Is The Sea (Chrysalis/Ensign), 1985
Fisherman's Blues (Chrysalis/Ensign), 1988
Room To Roam (Chrysalis/Ensign), 1990
Best Of 1981-91 (Chrysalis/Ensign), 1991

Muddy Waters
US vocalist, guitarist, composer
Born McKinley Morganfield, Rolling Fork, Mississippi, April 4, 1915
Died April 30, 1983

Career: Raised on a plantation in Clarksdale, Mississippi, where he was discovered and recorded by folklorist Alan Lomax for the Library of Congress in 1941, Waters joined the great wartime black exodus to the Northern cities, settling in Chicago in 1943 and establishing himself in its blues circuit.

Leonard and Phil Chess signed Waters to their Aristocrat label (soon renamed Chess) in 1945. He became company's musical father figure, helping to nurture many careers, including those of his sidemen Otis Spann (his half-brother), Little Walter, Jimmie Rodgers and emergent R&B/rockers Bo Diddley and Chuck Berry.

Waters, a true giant of the blues, was indisputably the major figure of Chicago blues scene through the 50s (when he logged 12 American R&B chart hits) and into 60s. Some of his best-known songs, **Rollin' Stone**, **Got My Mojo Working**, and **Mannish Boy**, became fodder for countless British and American R&B/rock bands, most notably the Rolling Stones (named after Waters' hit) and Johnny Winter. In recent years he recorded for Winter's Blue Sky label, and still showed enormous musical powers despite ailing health, which culminated in death from heart failure.

Above: UK band The Waterboys broke through in 1991.

Albums:
Can't Get No Grinding (Chess), 1973
Back In The Early Days (–/Syndicate), 1977
Hard Again (Blue Sky), 1977
I'm Ready (Blue Sky), 1977
Live (Blue Sky), 1977
Chess Masters (Chess), 1981
King Bee (Blue Sky), 1981
Hoochie Coochie Man (Blue Sky), 1983
Rare And Unissued (Chess), 1985
Collection (De-Ja Vu), 1985
On Chess Volume 1 (1948-1951), 1986
On Chess Volume 2 (1951-1959), 1986

Worth Searching Out:
Electric Mud (Cadet), 1968

Wax
UK/US duo formed 1986

Original line-up: Andrew Gold, vocals, keyboards; Graham Gouldman, guitar, bass, vocals.

Career: American Gold (son of Hollywood composer Ernest Gold, former keyboard player with Linda Ronstadt and Jackson Browne, but also successful solo artist himself) and Englishman Gouldman (songwriter and former member of Mindbenders and Hotlegs) were introduced in 1982; Gold then co-wrote three tracks with Gouldman and fellow 10cc member Eric Stewart for band's **Ten Out Of Ten** album.

When 10cc dissolved in 1984, Gold joined Gouldman in UK to continue writing material with no clear aim as to use. After two months' work together, christened themselves Wax, signed record deal with RCA and released 1986 debut album, **Magnetic Heaven** to indifference. Two singles **Right Between The Eyes** and **Hear No Evil** failed to chart.

1987 saw release of second album, **American English**, spawning deserved UK Top 10 hit single **Bridge To Your Heart**, followed by minor hit of title track.

Given duo's backgrounds in high-quality pop music, their success was no surprise,

but the career approach of both artists always threatened long-term future of the Wax amalgam.

Following third album, **A Hundred Thousand In Fresh Notes**, Gouldman and Gold went their separate ways, adding to successful production resumes.

Hit Singles:

	US	UK
Bridge To Your Heart, 1987	—	12

Albums:
Magnetic Heaven (RCA), 1986
American English (RCA), 1987
A Hundred Thousand In Fresh Notes
 (RCA), 1988

Weather Report
US group formed 1970

Original line-up: Josef Zawinul, keyboards, synthesizer; Wayne Shorter, saxophones; Miroslav Vitous, bass; Alphonse Mouzon, drums; Airto Moreira, percussion.

Career: Most durable of all jazz/rock aggregations that sprung to life in late 1960s. Formed by Austrian (born Vienna) Zawinul and Shorter (born Newark, New Jersey).

Members held impressive jazz credentials: Zawinul worked with Cannonball Adderley

Left: Joe Zawinul, founder member of jazz-rockers Weather Report.

Above: Wax duo Graham Gouldman (left) with his partner Andrew Gold.

and Miles Davis (recorded **Bitches Brew**); composed standards **Mercy Mercy Mercy** and **In A Silent Way**; earned Grammy in 1967 for best instrumental performance. Shorter (ex-Art Blakey, Miles Davis) was prominent tenor player before switching affection to alto sax. Czech-born Vitous had recorded and performed with Art Farmer, Freddie Hubbard, Brookmeyer-Terry Quintet, Miles Davis, Stan Getz and Herbie Mann. Brazilian Moreira worked with Lee Morgan and Miles Davis. South Carolinan Mouzon recorded and performed with Roy Ayers and did sessions for Roberta Flack and Gene McDaniels.

Moreira quit shortly after release of debut **Weather Report** (1970). LP earned plaudits from jazz and rock critics alike; set recording pattern of tight percussive music with emphasis on interplay between Zawinul and Shorter. Tracks were totally melodic, opening new musical avenues for those usually reluctant to listen to normal complexity of jazz.

Unit subsequently went through various personnel changes: Vitous left in 1974 after release of **Mysterious Traveller**. Replacement Jaco Pastorius remained until 1979 and **Mr Gone** set. Bass duties were taken over by Abe Laboriel. Mouzon moved to McCoy Tyner group in 1972, and then Larry Coryell's 11th House. Mouzon then became prominent session player and sometime leader of own band. Drum seat was filled by Pete Erskine (ex-Stan Kenton and Maynard Ferguson) in 1978. Percussionists

who have graced group's work include Alex Acuna, Ishmael Wilburn, Tony Williams, Steve Gadd and Eric Garratt, group drummer from 1972-76.

Weather Report earned various poll honours throughout world before band split in 1987, also the year that former member Jaco Pastorius was killed. They were regular recipients of *Downbeat* magazine's Best Group plaudit. Debut album also won Downbeat award. Unit's popularity exended worldwide, particularly to Japan. They were infrequent but welcome visitors to Europe. With Erskine and and guitarist Steve Khan, Zawinul went on to form Weather Update, while Shorter guested with various artists as well as fronting own quartet.

Albums:
Weather Report (Columbia/CBS), 1970
I Sing The Body Electric (Columbia/
 CBS), 1972
Sweetnighter (Columbia/CBS), 1973
Mysterious Traveller (Columbia/CBS),
 1974
Tail Spinnin' (Columbia/CBS), 1975
Black Market (Columbia/CBS), 1976
Heavy Weather (Columbia/CBS), 1977
Mr Gone (Columbia/CBS), 1978
8.30 (Columbia/CBS), 1979
Night Passage (Columbia/CBS), 1980
Weather Report (Columbia/CBS), 1981
Procession (Columbia/CBS), 1983
Domino Theory (Columbia/CBS), 1984
Sportin' Life (Columbia/CBS), 1985

Jaco Pastorius Solo:
Word Of Mouth (Warner Bros), 1981
Jazz Street (Timeless), 1989

Joe Zawinul Solo:
Zawinul (Atlantic), 1974
Dialects (CBS), 1986

Wham!
UK duo formed 1982
George Michael, vocals; born Georgios Panayotiou, London, June 25, 1963
Andrew Ridgeley, guitar; born January 1963

Above: Make It Big, Wham! Courtesy Epic Records.

Career: Michael and Ridgeley as teenage North Londoners had been in various no-hope groups before joining forces in summer 1982 and recording as duo, co-writing material. First single **Wham! Rap (Enjoy What You Do)** was well received by pop press and in clubs, but not played on daytime radio due to so-called contentious lyrics concerning problems faced by jobless youth.

Second single **Young Guns (Go For It)** covered same lyrical ground, but achieved radio play to become Top 3 hit at end of 1982. Follow-up **Bad Boys**, released March 1983, made No. 2 in UK; first LP **Fantastic** followed.

Above: George Michael (left) and Andrew Ridgeley of Wham! before their farewell concert. Michael has since eclipsed his old buddy in solo stakes, and is arguably rock's major teen icon.

Early part of 1984 was spent writing material for **Make It Big** LP, which was recorded in South of France. Set contained Wham!'s first UK No. 1 single **Wake Me Up (Before You Go Go)**.

Group established international following in 1985, touring China and breaking through in States. Wham! claimed Chinese tour had cost them £1m; publicity value was further heightened when member of support band stabbed himself on flight to Canton.

Subject to frivolous gossip-mongering in Britain's tabloid press, duo found it hard to be taken seriously, despite undoubted talent; Michael was recipient of 1985 Ivor Novello Songwriter of the Year award. Pair also featured in Band Aid and Live Aid events, 1985, but in early 1986 there were reports of split between the two because of management problems.

Inevitable split came in 1986, with Ridgeley going on to do little other than attract attention of gossip columnists, Michael embarking on hugely successful solo career (see separate entry). Inevitably, Ridgeley has been less successful. Always the butt of adverse critical comment, his first solo LP **Son Of Albert** (1990) prompted reams of vitriolic abuse from erstwhile reviewers.

As final postcript, duo reunited for concert in Rio de Janeiro in 1991 during Michael's solo world tour.

Hit Singles:	US	UK
Young Guns (Go For It), 1982	–	3
Bad Boys, 1983	–	2
Club Tropicana, 1983	–	4
Club Fantastic Megamix, 1983	–	15
Wake Me Up (Before You Go Go), 1984	1	1
Freedom, 1984*	3	1
Last Christmas, 1984	–	1
Everything She Wants, 1985	1	2
I'm Your Man, 1985	20	1
Edge Of Heaven, 1987	9	–
*1985 in US

Albums:
Fantastic (–/Innervision), 1983
Make It Big (Epic), 1984
The Final (Epic), 1986

Whitesnake
UK group formed 1978

Original line-up: David Coverdale, vocals; Micky Moody, guitar; Bernie Marsden, guitar; Jon Lord, keyboards; Neil Murray, bass; David Dowle, drums.

Career: Coverdale joined 1973 Deep Purple line-up and stayed with band until its demise in 1976. 1977 saw release of solo LP, **Whitesnake**. It disappeared, but Coverdale had more success with next solo project, **Northwinds**. Once legal problems were sorted out (allowing him to play live again), Coverdale formed stable line-up. Band released **Trouble** while undertaking extensive UK tour. Sound was basic R&B-influenced rock, pioneered decade before by Deep Purple and others.

Snakebite and **Love Hunter** continued in same style with danger of Whitesnake becoming cliché. Dowle was replaced by Purple-mate Ian Paice to roughen up edges of band's backbeat.

Fool For Your Loving single proved band could reach mass appeal. **Ready An' Willing** sold well enough to encourage recording of double live set, **Live In The Heart Of The City** (title reflected place of origin: Hammersmith Odeon, London). **Come An' Get It** was next release and revealed basic problem: music was loud and energetic, but it sounded as if everyone could play it in their sleep. **Saints An' Sinners** saw revised line-up, and continuing personnel changes have bugged band. Most significant was departure of Lord upon re-formation of Deep Purple in 1984.

Latterly, however, reconstituted band has gone from strength to strength, conquering US and rest of the world with platinum set **Whitesnake**, their first for EMI. Line-up during this period was Coverdale, guitarists Adrian Vandenberg and Viv Campbell, bassist Rudy Sarzo and drummer Tom Aldridge. With permed locks and erotic posturing, quartet enjoyed extravagant MTV video exposure and hysterical scenes on major US tour. Group lost Campbell for **Slip Of The Tongue** LP (1989); album made both US and UK Top 10.

1990 world binge saw unit recruit frenzy-fingered Steve Vai as replacement for Campbell; topped bill at Donnington Park Monsters Of Rock HM festival in same year. Subsequent lack of product and Coverdale's involvement with Jimmy Paige in new project saw band take break, although vocalist insists Whitesnake are still ready, willing and able.

Hit Singles:	US	UK
Fool For Your Loving, 1980	53	13
Don't Break My Heart Again, 1981	–	17
Still Of The Night, 1987	–	16
Here I Go Again, 1987	1	9
Is This Love?, 1987	2	9
Give Me All Your Love, 1988	48	18

Above: Whitesnake, 1987's eponymous album. Courtesy EMI Records.

Albums:
Trouble (United Artists), 1978
Love Hunter (United Artists), 1979
Ready An' Willing (Mirage/United Artists), 1980
Live In The Heart Of The City (Mirage/United Artists), 1980
Come An' Get it (Atlantic/Liberty), 1981
Saints An' Sinners (–/Liberty), 1982
Lovehunter (Fame), 1984
Slide It In (Liberty), 1985
Whitesnake (EMI), 1987
Slip Of The Tongue (Geffen/EMI), 1989

Below: David Coverdale (right) enjoys the camaraderie of Whitesnake axemen during excitement of live concert.

187

The Who

UK group formed 1964

Original line-up: Pete Townshend, guitar, keyboards, vocals; Roger Daltrey, vocals; John Entwistle, bass, horns, vocals; Keith Moon, drums.

Career: While at Acton County Grammar School, Townshend and Entwistle joined Daltrey's band The Detours in 1962. Townshend's mother got boys audition with Commercial Entertainments Ltd's Bob Druce; they were soon doing gigs on his club circuit, playing mostly R&B and Top 10 covers. Originally a five-piece, Detours went through several singers and guitarists until Daltrey switched from guitar to vocals; they then stayed a four-piece with Townshend on lead, Entwistle on bass, and Dougie Sandom on drums. Became Who when they saw another band named Detours on TV. Were introduced to Helmut Gorden, an enterprising door-knob manufacturer; he became manager, took all earnings and put band on weekly wage.

More influential, however, was Pete Meaden, a fast-talking, pill-popping, freelance publicist enamoured with the world of 'mods' — Meaden decided Who were perfect for mod audience; convinced band to change name to High Numbers (a 'number' being a mod). He introduced them to fashions of Carnaby Street. Wrote and produced a mod single for them, **I'm The Face/Zoot Suit**, on Fontana in July 1964; it flopped, despite widespread publicity, probably because Meaden had simply written new lyrics to Slim Harpo's **Got Love If You Want It**.

Band didn't really arrive at the perfect formula until one night at the Royal Oldfield Hotel. A cocky young kid in the audience announced he could play drums better than their drummer (a substitute — Sandom had left band), and proved it by demolishing the drum kit in the interval; Keith Moon was in.

Meaden had ideas, but no money, so when Kit Lambert stopped by the Railway Hotel in Harrow to see High Numbers, he persuaded them to let him, and his partner Chris Stamp, take over management. Meaden was dropped, and band became Who again. It was at the Railway that Townshend smashed his first guitar: he accidentally broke the neck of his 12-string Rickenbacker on a very low ceiling; mishap getting no reaction from audience, Townshend proceeded to smash it to smithereens. This got such a reaction that Lambert encouraged Townshend (and Moon, who followed suit and kicked over his drum kit) to continue

instrument-destroying as a publicity stunt. The stunt became the traditional ending to a Who performance.

Lambert bought Townshend two Vortexian tape recorders; he came up with first demo, **I Can't Explain**, which later sold itself to Kinks' producer Shel Talmy. Talmy became Who producer; got band recording contract with US Decca, then UK Decca. While in residency Tuesday nights at Marquee Club in Soho in early 1965, still playing mostly R&B covers, Who recorded **I Can't Explain** at Pye Studios. Helped by first *Top Of The Pops* appearance, single went to No. 8 in UK. From then on Townshend continued to write 90 per cent of Who material (Entwistle contributed remainder).

Four months later, a second single, **Anyway, Anyhow, Anywhere**, which featured feedback (then so revolutionary that their record company sent it back, convinced strange noises were a mistake), went to No. 10 in the UK and became signature tune for TV's music show *Ready, Steady, Go*. Third single that year not only surpassed others in sales, reaching No. 2 in UK, but also in notoriety. **My Generation** was soon adopted as anthem for the young with its controversial angry, stuttered lyric, 'Hope I die before I get old'.

With three hit singles and first LP, **My Generation (The Who Sing My Genera-**

tion in US), doing well, bookings were up. Earnings trebled, yet Who remained in debt because of continued instrument smashing. On top of financial worries, there were personality clashes, internal power struggles, constant threats to split up (which continued for 20 years), and management and producer problems. With conflict on all sides, Who ended up in legal battle with Shel Talmy over **Substitute**, their next single. Despite being released on two different labels, it reached No. 5 in Britain, and Talmy bowed out for a percentage. Lambert produced single that followed, **I'm A Boy**, which climbed to No. 2 in UK. Later that year, band had first US hit, **Happy Jack**, followed by success with seemingly innocent song about masturbation, **Pictures of Lily**, and slightly psychedelic Top 10 hit both sides of the Atlantic, **I Can See For Miles**. The Who had moved away from mod, and after brief pop art phase (Union Jack jackets, target T-shirts, slightly longer hair) they dabbled briefly in semi-hippie look until late 1960s.

First live dates in America were with Murray The K show in New York. Later that year toured extensively in US as support for Herman's Hermits; a tour that made them rather unpopular with hotel managers. It was their appearance at Monterey Pop Festival, aided by first national US TV appearance on

**Top: The triptych cover of The Who's Tommy. Courtesy Polydor records.
Left: The Who, circa 1965 — what youthful innocence!**

Above: A feature of early Who shows was an instrument-destroying finale, apparently conceived by the group in order to avoid encores.

the *Smothers Brothers Show*, that sold them to America. Both shows made use of smoke bombs and self-destruction.

Until **Tommy**, The Who were basically a singles band. Neither **A Quick One** nor **The Who Sell Out** LPs did particularly well. Though **Sell Out** had brilliant basis for an album — a radio station format with adverts and jingles between tracks — the cover, with Daltrey sitting in bath of baked beans, drew more attention.

In 1969 Who released their long-awaited double LP **Tommy**. A 'rock opera' concept album chronicling the adventures of a deaf, dumb and blind boy; with spiritual overtones, it was dedicated to Townshend's Indian master Meher Baba. From now on Who music was more obsessed with problems of adolescent males, as lyrics grew more politically, socially and spiritually thought-provoking. Daltrey became more of a front-man; band spent two years performing **Tommy** live in its entirety, taking it eventually to several European opera houses. Received 14-minute standing ovation at NY's Metropolitan Opera House. One of the most familiar Who images of era was Daltrey in long blonde curls and leather fringe twirling his mike, and Townshend in white boiler suit doing scissor leaps. **Tommy** was part of the Woodstock festival and Woodstock absolutely confirmed The Who's future success in US.

In 1970 released **Live at Leeds**; many critics regard it as fine example of live Who concert. The Who have long been considered one of the top live acts in rock 'n' roll. Few have matched their intensity and versatility, and few moments in rock have been more universally moving than the **See Me, Feel Me** finale.

After very trying work on another ambitious concept LP, **Lifehouse**, failed, remains were salvaged to make **Who's Next**, the first LP produced by Glyn Johns, and the first to feature synthesizers, used frequently thereafter.

The next major project, **Quadrophenia**, returned to sound of band's early days, and again used mod culture as vehicle to address adolescence. **Quadrophenia** was vastly underrated (criticized mostly for over-

orchestration), and only fully appreciated in 1979 when repackaged as movie soundtrack for Who film of same name, which coincided with the UK rebirth of the mod movement.

By 1975, all four Who members had made at least one solo album. Entwistle put together **Odds And Sods**, an LP of old Who rarities to appease fans, but no new Who material was being recorded.

It seemed that nothing could match the success of **Tommy**; in 1975 it was Ken Russell's *Tommy* film, with Daltrey in leading role, and soundtrack LP, which brought band whole new following, rather than new album, **Who By Numbers**. Poorly received, melancholy **Numbers** addressed problems of ageing; single **Squeeze Box** made US Top 20 and UK Top 10.

Back on the road in 1975-76, The Who were selling out soccer stadiums; May 1976 concert at Charlton Athletic Ground earned them a place in the *Guinness Book of World Records* for loudest concert.

After problems with Lambert and Stamp, Bill Curbishley stepped in as manager. There was a long lull in recording until 1978 when **Who Are You** was completed. The LP and single of the same name were Who's biggest sellers since original **Tommy**.

Untimely death of drummer Keith Moon on September 7, 1978 forced Who to consider folding, but by early 1979 pressed on with ex-Small Faces and Faces drummer Kenney Jones. Jones made live debut with new Who at London's Rainbow; soon press was hailing 1979 'Year of the Who'. Extensive touring and two successful Who films *The Kids Are Alright*, a film biography of the band, and *Quadrophenia* with accompanying Who soundtracks put Who back in business. However, year ended in tragedy when 11 fans were crushed to death at Cincinnati concert on December 3, 1979. Devastated, Who again considered disbanding, but continued US tour well into 1980.

Face Dances in 1981, the first new material in three years, was produced by Bill Szymcyzk. Some thought it innovative, but most considered it wrong for The Who. Single **You Better, You Bet** made US Top 20, but at this point Who were being large-

Above: The Quadrophenia album, The Who. Courtesy Polydor Records.

ly ignored in UK. Worry over responsibility of the band and the efforts of balancing stardom with family life drove Townshend to drink and drugs. Some felt Who were finished. But Townshend pulled himself together, going completely straight in early 1982. Much relieved, the other members were anxious to contribute to next LP (returning to producer Glyn Johns) **It's Hard**, which erased bad press of **Face Dances**; in conjunction with tours in US, LP proved band was still strong.

In 1982, band decided to call it a day, going out in style with US Farewell Tour, which was hottest concert ticket of year, grossing 40 million dollars. Band regrouped for Live Aid in 1985 at Wembley Stadium, and also when occasion demanded (1988 BPI Awards ceremony, for example). Townshend and Daltrey maintained busy solo careers (see separate entries), while Entwistle joined with Joe Walsh for Entwistle's 1981 **Too Late The Hero** set.

After four-year gap, when it seemed certain that The Who were consigned to rock's historic chronicles, Daltrey, Townshend and Entwistle rejoined for triumphant American tour in 1989, and also completed four dates at London's Wembley Arena later in the year.

Below: Awaiting the limo to take them to collect their pensions are (from left to right) John Entwhistle, Kenney Jones, Roger Daltrey and Pete Townshend.

Above: The Kids Are Alright soundtrack compilation. Courtesy Polydor Records.

With a line-up augmented by guitarist Stevie Bolton (ex-Headstone), drummer Simon Phillips and noted session keyboard player 'Rabbit' Bundrick (Free, Donovan, John Cale, Jim Capaldi, etc), all gigs were sold-out, confirming band's reputation for explosive creativity and rebellious instinct.

Hit Singles:	US	UK
I Can't Explain, 1965	–	8
Anyway, Anyhow, Anywhere, 1965	–	10
My Generation, 1965	–	2
Substitute, 1966	–	5
I'm A Boy, 1966	–	2
Happy Jack, 1966	24	3
Pictures Of Lily, 1967	51	4
I Can See For Miles, 1967	9	10
Pinball Wizard, 1969	19	4
The Seeker, 1970	44	19
See Me Feel Me/Overture From Tommy, 1970	12	–
Won't Get Fooled Again, 1971	15	9
Let's See Action, 1971	–	16
Join Together, 1972	17	9
5.15, 1973	45	20
Squeeze Box, 1975*	16	10
Substitute (re-issue), 1976	–	7
Who Are You, 1978	14	18
You Better, You Bet, 1981	18	–

*1976 in UK

Albums:
Tommy (Decca/Track), 1969
Live At Leeds (Decca/Track), 1970
Who's Next (Decca/Track), 1971
Meaty, Beaty, Big And Bouncy
  (compilation) (Decca/Track), 1971
Quadrophenia (MCA/Track), 1973
Odds And Sods (MCA/Track), 1974
A Quick One/Sell Out (double re-issue)
  (MCA/Track), 1974
Magic Bus/My Generation (double
  re-issue), 1974
Tommy (soundtrack) (Polydor), 1975
The Who By Numbers (MCA/Polydor),
  1975
The Story Of The Who (compilation)
  (—/Polydor), 1976
Who Are You (MCA/Polydor), 1978
The Kids Are Alright (soundtrack)
  (MCA/Polydor), 1979
Quadrophenia (soundtrack)   (Polydor),
  1979
My Generation (re-issue) (—/Virgin),
  1979
Live At Leeds/Who Are You (double
  re-issue) (—/Polydor), 1980
Face Dances (Warner Bros/Polydor),
  1981
Hooligans (compilation) (MCA/—), 1981
It's Hard (Warner Bros/Polydor), 1982
Who's Greatest Hits (compilation)
  (MCA/—), 1983
Rarities (—/Polydor), 1983
Once Upon A Time (Polydor), 1983
The Singles (Polydor), 1984

Kim Wilde

UK vocalist
Born Kim Smith, London, November 18, 1960

Career: Daughter of seminal UK rock 'n' roller Marty Wilde, Kim embarked on training for non-musical career at Hertfordshire Art College. After singing on demos made by brother Ricky, attracted attention of notable producer and record company owner Mickie Most. He supervised mixing of **Kids In America**, produced by Ricky and written by Marty and Ricky. Single was released on Most's RAK label in early 1981 reached No. 2; hit with three further singles in UK Top 20 during 1981 — **Chequered Love**, **Water On Glass** and **Cambodia**.

First LP reached Top 3 in UK in 1981; less successful in US when released there in 1982, although **Kids In America** was sizeable US hit 18 months after UK release. 1982 was far less successful — two smaller hit singles and **Select** LP minor chart item — but Kim embarked on first tour which was generally well received.

Artist remained in public eye during mid-80s, but achieved major US breakthrough in 1987 by time-honoured method of covering classic Motown hit. **You Keep Me Hanging On** hit No. 1 spot at end of May that year. Maintained Tamla connection as support for Michael Jackson on his meritorious European tour in 1988, during which year her **Close** LP earned berth in UK Top 10; LP spawned trio of chart singles.

Despite continued exposure on television, Wilde slipped somewhat during early 90s, with **Love Moves** LP (1990) making relatively little impact. While there is no doubting Wilde's stunning visual presence, her competent, but hardly inspirational, vocals could prove her undoing. Movies here we come!

Hit Singles:

	US	UK
Kids In America, 1981	25	2
Chequered Love, 1981	—	4
Water On Glass, 1981	—	11
Cambodia, 1981	—	12
View From A Bridge, 1982	—	16
Rage To Love, 1985	—	19
You Keep Me Hanging On, 1986	1	2
Another Step, 1987	—	6
Say You Really Want Me, 1987	—	29
Rocking Around The Xmas Tree (with Mel Smith), 1987	—	1
You Came, 1988	41	3
Never Trust A Stranger, 1988	—	7
Four Letter Word, 1988	—	6

Albums:
Kim Wilde (EMI/RAK), 1981
Select (—/RAK), 1982
Catch As Catch Can (—/RAK), 1983
Best Of (—/RAK), 1984
Teases And Dares (MCA), 1984
Very Best Of (EMI), 1984
Another Step (MCA), 1987
Close (MCA), 1988
Love Moves (—/MCA), 1990

Jackie Wilson

US vocalist
Born Detroit, June 9, 1934
Died 1984

Career: Possessor of one of the finest tenor voices in popular music, Wilson's hit record career spanned three decades. During spell as boxer in late 1940s, won amateur title.

Singing began in church. Performed with Ever Ready Gospel Singers before taking secular path in 1951 for session with Dizzy Gillespie's Dee Gee label. Later that year sang in talent show at Paradise Theatre, Detroit; heard by Billy Ward, whose group, The Dominoes, were then hot with **Sixty Minute Man**. Ward, impressed, took phone number, then called months later when Clyde McPhatter quit Dominoes. Wilson replaced him to sing lead/second tenor; sang with group for four years on King/Federal Records; his soaring tenor tones distinctive in of ballads like **Rags To Riches**.

When Dominoes moved to Decca in 1956, Wilson stayed with them for while, then left for solo career. Sang in local clubs until spotted by Al Green, manager of Johnny Ray and LaVern Baker. Signed with Brunswick Records under supervision of house bandleader Dick Jacobs. Wilson was mainstay of roster for more than a decade with lengthy succession of hits, adapting style to keep up with times. Hits included **Reet Petite** (1957), **Lonely Teardrops** and classy ballad **To Be Loved** (1958).

Wilson maintained stylistic variations and fought with orchestration over the years until 1963, when he injected R&B feeling with **Baby Workout**.

In 1966 Wilson began recording in Chicago (instead of New York); with move came transfusion of new ideas from producers Carl Davis and Sonny Sanders. More mainstream soul output of danceable songs like **Whispers**, **Higher and Higher** and **I Get The Sweetest Feeling** resulted. Wilson was transformed into soul star.

Formula lost commercial impact by early 70s, and Wilson began searching for new ideas and material. Brief liaison with Eugene Records and Chi-Lites was unsuccessful.

On September 29, 1975, Jackie suffered heart attack while singing at Latin Casino in Camden, New Jersey; lapsed into coma, suffered severe brain damage and was confined to Cherry Hills Medical Center in New Jersey before death in 1984.

Ironic postcript to career was provided when re-issued **Reet Petite** topped UK charts for four weeks in 1987, success almost equalled by re-issued **Higher And Higher**. Wilson was also portrayed in hit movie about Richie Valens, *La Bamba*.

Hit Singles:

	US	UK
Reet Petite, 1957	—	6
Lonely Teardrops, 1959	7	—
That's Why (I Love You So), 1959	13	—
I'll Be Satisfied, 1959	20	—
Night/Doggin' Around, 1960	4	—
Doggin' Around/Night, 1960	15	—
(You Were Made For) All My Love/A Woman, A Lover, A Friend, 1960	12	—
A Woman, A Lover, A Friend/ (You Were Made For) All My Love, 1960	15	—
Alone At Last, 1960	8	50
My Empty Arms, 1961	9	—
Please Tell Me Why, 1961	20	—
I'm Comin' On Back To You, 1961	19	—
Baby Workout, 1963	5	—
Whispers (Gettin' Louder), 1966	11	—
(Your Love Keeps Lifting Me) Higher And Higher, 1967	6	—
I Get The Sweetest Feeling, 1972*	35	9
(Your Love Keeps Lifting Me) Higher And Higher, 1969	—	11
Reet Petite (re-issue), 1987	—	1
Higher And Higher, 1987	—	15
*Charted in US in 1968		

Albums:
My Golden Favourites (Brunswick/Coral), 1962
My Golden Favourites Volume 2 (Brunswick/Coral), 1962
Higher And Higher (Brunswick), 1967
Greatest Hits (Brunswick), 1968
Classic (Skratch), 1984
Reet Petite, (Ace)
Very Best Of (Ace)

Worth Searching Out:
Baby Workout (Brunswick/—), 1964
Higher And Higher (Brunswick/MCA), 1967

Above: Johnny Winter And, Johnny Winter. Courtesy CBS Records.

Johnny Winter

US guitarist, vocalist, composer
Born Leland, Mississippi, January 23, 1944

Career: Fluid guitarist who lived for traditional blues and R&B; spent teens playing with younger brother Edgar in local Texan bands. Later began working as session player and recorded several LPs for regional release in the South. **Austin**, **Texas**, **About Blues**, **Early Times**, **Before The Storm**, **First Winter**, **The Johnny Winter Story** and **The Progressive Blues Experiment** all contain material from this period.

One of these albums was mentioned in *Rolling Stone* article covering local scene in Texas; New York club owner Steve Paul then located Winter and signed him to management contract. He proclaimed Winter next rock 'superstar'.

Columbia offered one of largest recording contracts ever given new talent and promptly packed Winter off on national tour. When Winter's atmospheric blues did not transfer to large concert halls, he overhauled his back-up band. Steve Paul took the club's house band and reorganized The McCoys (**Hang On Sloopy**) to back Winter; key figure in line-up was Rick Derringer.

Columbia was faced with competition from Winter's old material, which had been bought up and re-issued by various cash-in outfits. As a result, Winter's new material failed to mark up expected sales. More importantly, music tastes began to change in US as younger kids failed to support blues revival. Despite several excellent LPs (**Johnny Winter And**, **Johnny Winter And Live**), strain on Winter exceeded his ability to cope and rock's 'next superstar' retired with drug habit.

Still Alive And Well didn't appear until 1973 but showed Winter was still talented and capable of recording strong effort. However, its critical success failed to produce significant sales and next two LPs began to sound as if he was desperately trying to produce a commercial success.

In 1977, Winter extended collaboration with Muddy Waters. If this signalled end of Winter's hopes for superstardom, it also marked return to true strength as blues guitarist: simple, clean and traditional music which helped revitalize interest in Muddy Waters' career.

Artist maintained blues connection with trio of LPs for indie Alligator label, **Guitar Slinger** (1984), **Serious Business** (1985), and the Grammy-winning **Third Degree** (1987), which featured Mac 'Dr John' Rebbenack. Later Winter signed with MCA, for whom **Winter Of '88** (1988) was outstanding debut. In December 1991, **Let Me In** collection appeared on Pointblank, and included covers of Robert Johnson's **Barefootin'** and Jimmy Reed's stylish single **Shame Shame Shame**. Johnny Winter undertook national US tours in both 1988 and 1990, thus completing a career rehabilitation of sorts.

Albums:
Johnny Winter (Columbia/CBS), 1969
Second Winter (Columbia/CBS), 1969
Johnny Winter And (Columbia/CBS), 1970
Johnny Winter And . . . Live (Columbia/CBS), 1971
Still Alive And Well (Columbia/CBS), 1973
Saints And Sinners (Columbia/CBS), 1974
Captured Live (Blue Sky), 1976
Nothin' But The Blues (Blue Sky), 1977
White, Hot, And Blue (Blue Sky), 1978
Ready For Winter (Accord/—), 1981
Raised On Rock (Blue Sky), 1981
Third Degree (Alligator/Sonet), 1983
Early Winter (President), 1984
Serious Business (Sonet), 1985
The Winter Of '88 (MCA), 1988
The Winter Scene (Pair/—), 1990
Let Me In (Pointblank), 1991

With Edgar Winter:
Together Live (Blue Sky), 1976

Worth Searching Out:
The Johnny Winter Story (double) (Blue Sky), 1980

Stevie Winwood

UK vocalist, composer, multi-instrumentalist
Born Birmingham, May 12, 1948

Career: Generally acclaimed as one of Britain's greatest white R&B vocalists. Career began in 1961, playing with trombonist Rico, and later the Muff Woody Jazz Band (featuring his brother Muff Winwood).

Above: Steve Winwood, man of many bands and persistent solo star.

Above: Arc Of A Diver, Steve Winwood. Courtesy Island Records.

At 15, Steve and Muff joined Spencer Davis Rhythm 'n' Blues Quartet.

Professional career began following year, by which time Winwood had assimilated many musical influences, including folk, jazz, pop, blues and soul. Newly named Spencer Davis Group achieved some lowly chart placings before breaking big in 1965-66 with string of hits and two No. 1s, **Keep On Running** and **Somebody Help Me**. In spite of title, it was Winwood who gained attention and approval for powerhouse vocals and impressive guitar and piano work; it came as no surprise when he announced his decision to form new unit in 1967.

Traffic (see separate entry) provided Winwood with greater freedom to develop his musical ideas. Two highly acclaimed albums, **Mr Fantasy** and **Traffic**, were boosted by three hit singles: **Paper Sun**, **Hole In My Shoe** and **Here We Go Round The Mulberry Bush**. By early 1969, Winwood was tempted by a more ambitious plan and formed world's first supergroup, Blind Faith, with Cream's Eric Clapton and Ginger Baker, and Family's Rick Grech. Group were hyped

to ludicrous proportions and individual egos suffocated natural talents. After recording one album, and touring America (following much-publicized appearance in Hyde Park), Faith folded.

Winwood began 1970s guesting with Ginger Baker's Air Force, but soon began work on solo album **Mad Shadows**, which finally emerged as Traffic re-formation. Over next four years, Traffic recorded four more studio albums, all critically acclaimed.

Winwood's solo career was preceded by two years of silence, punctuated by appearances on albums by Viv Stanshall, Jim Capaldi, Sandy Denny, Toots And Maytals, and George Harrison. Such eclectic musical activities proved sufficient inspiration for first solo, finally released in 1977. Ever restless, Winwood continued with related projects, including concert with Georgie Fame and appearances on Stomu Yamashta's **Go Live From Paris** and Marianne Faithful's **Broken English**.

Second solo **Arc Of A Diver**, a US Top 5 hit, revealed imaginative use of electronic keyboard instruments and synthesizer, continuing experiments begun on first effort. Lyrical contributions by Will Jennings, George Fleming and Viv Stanshall seemed erratic in quality, but hit single **While You See A Chance** made US Top 10. 1982 work, **Talking Back To The Night**, consolidated rather than improved solo reputation. Winwood undertook his first tour as solo artist during summer 1983. However, in spite of illustrious history, the once precocious teenager had yet to produce the work of genius which had appeared his birthright.

The outstanding **Back In The High Life** (1986) certainly had its moments; the title track earning two Grammys in following year for Record Of The Year and Best Pop Vocal. Winwood subsequently signed with Virgin, cutting **Roll With It** (title track made No. 1 in US charts) in 1988 and **Refugees Of The Heart** (1990), but both albums confirmed frustration at artist's inconsistency.

The 'boy wonder' tag has proved an almost insufferable burden for Winwood, especially as he approaches middle-age. Nonetheless, he should appreciate that the expectations are high because of his unique abilities.

Hit Singles:

	US	UK
While You See A Chance, 1980	9	—
Higher Love, 1986	1	13
Valerie, 1987	9	19
Freedom Overspill, 1987	16	—
The Finer Things, 1987	4	—
Back In The High Life Again, 1987	10	—
Valerie (re-issue), 1987	—	19
Roll With It, 1988	1	53

Left: Bill Withers can afford to smile after charting for over ten years.

Don't You Know What The Night Can Do, 1988	6	—
Holding On, 1989	11	—
One And Only Man, 1990	18	—

Albums:
Steve Winwood (Island), 1977
Arc Of A Diver (Island), 1980
Talking Back To The Night (Island), 1982
Back In The Highlife (Island), 1986
Chronicles (Island), 1987
Roll With It (Virgin), 1988
Refugees Of The Heart (Virgin), 1990

Bill Withers

US vocalist, composer, guitarist
Born Slab Fork, West Virginia, July 4, 1938

Career: Born into rural family, Withers showed no particular aptitude for music as child. Served in US navy for nine years, only started singing and playing guitar afterwards, in 1964.

While working in aircraft factory he began composing songs, and was eventually signed by independent Sussex label in 1971. First album **Just As I Am**, was produced by Booker T. Jones and featured clutch of sensitive and original songs. Single from album, **Ain't No Sunshine**, eventually went gold and has since become a standard, recorded by everyone from Michael Jackson to Roland Kirk.

Second album, **Still Bill**, confirmed emergence of major new talent and notched up even greater success. By now Withers was also performing live with superb rhythm section (guitarist Benorce Blackman, bass player Melvin Dunlan and drummer James Gadson), winning over audiences with

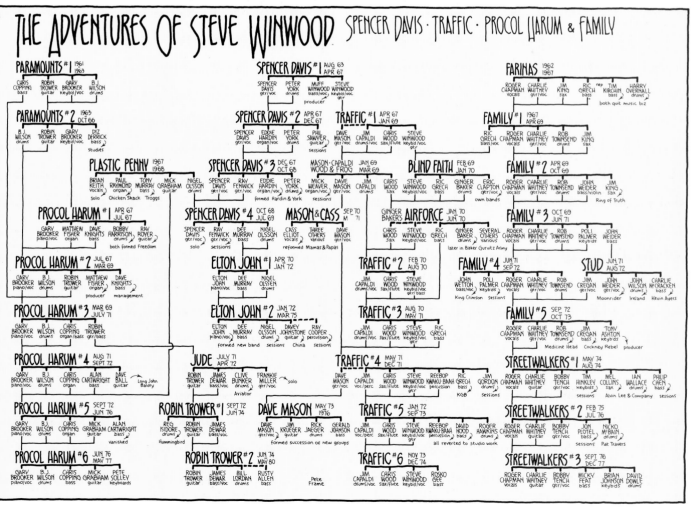

combination of appealingly unstylized voice, distinctive material and modest, almost diffident, manner. Style coalesced the best elements of black music and singer/songwriter tradition.

After a superb live double album and further studio set, Withers split from Sussex to join mighty CBS roster. Although **Lovely Day** provided company with Top 10 hit in 1979, Withers' career has since progressed in fits and starts.

Guested on two superb singles, The Crusaders' **Soul Shadows** (1980) and Grover Washington's **The Two Of Us** (1981), and later enjoyed revivals of re-mixed **Lean On Me** (1987), which earned Grammy, and **Lovely Day** (1988). The popular Withers returned to UK for major tour in 1988 to capitalize on regeneration, and reminded audiences of all-round quality.

Hit Singles:

	US	UK
Ain't No Sunshine, 1971	3	—
Lean On Me, 1972	1	18
Use Me, 1972	2	—
Lovely Day, 1978	30	7
Just The Two Of Us (with		
Grover Washington Jr.), 1981	2	34
Lovely Day (re-mix), 1988	—	4

Albums:
Best Of (Sussex), 1975
Menagerie (Columbia/CBS), 1978
'Bout Love (Columbia/CBS), 1978
Greatest Hits (Columbia/CBS), 1980
Watching You Watching Me (CBS), 1985

Worth Searching Out:
Just As I Am (Sussex), 1971
Still Bill (Sussex), 1972
Live At Carnegie Hall (Sussex), 1973

Right: Still sporting a sensible haircut, the teenage Stevie Wonder became soul veteran before voting age.

Stevie Wonder

US vocalist, composer, multi-instrumentalist
Born Stevland Morris, Saginaw, Michigan, May 3, 1950

Career: One of the most important and consistent of contemporary artists, Stevie Wonder showed early interest in music. Although blind since birth, by age eight he was proficient on piano, harmonica, drums and bongos.

Family moved to Detroit when Wonder was child; at age 10 he was introduced to nascent Tamla Motown label by family friend Ronald White, one of the Miracles. Period of grooming followed, during which time several moderately successful singles were released. Wonder gained experience of live work on Motown's touring 'revues', quickly winning reputation as exciting vocal/instrumental act.

First major success came in 1963 with **Fingertips**, recorded live and featuring Stevie's urgent vocalizing and harmonica playing against jumping brass background. Record made No. 1, as did album from which it was taken, **Twelve Year Old Genius**. Nevertheless, next few singles were not particularly successful: right format for youthful prodigy had not yet been found.

Wonder solved problem himself with **Uptight**, released in 1966. Self-penned, and featuring vocals without harmonica, it made No. 3 in US and became massive international hit. It heralded string of international

successes, most of them self-written, others taken from incredibly wide range of sources, including Bob Dylan (**Blowin' In The Wind**) and cabaret repertoire (**For Once In My Life**).

By end of 60s Wonder was becoming somewhat restless within confines of Motown 'family', although reluctant to make break completely. He was already producing other artists, and felt capable of taking full control of his career. Crucial point was release of album **Signed, Sealed And Delivered** in 1970. Entirely produced by Wonder, it won award for best soul album of 1970 and gave him confidence to pursue own path.

In 1970 Wonder met and married Syreeta Wright (marriage later broke up). Syreeta contributed to **Where I'm Coming From** album, which heralded new phase of Wonder music in experimental direction.

Following year saw Wonder attain majority, at which time all previous earnings became available to him. Artist then set up Taurus Productions. Although Wonder was gaining independence from Motown, company remained as distributor of all Wonder products.

New freedom prompted important musical leap forward with **Music Of My Mind**, a one-man tour-de-force featuring variety of electronic keyboards. Album alienated some old fans, but brought Wonder to attention of new rock audience, and eventually went gold. It also paved way for album which established commercial viability of new

Left: Little Stevie Wonder cranks out his harmonica opus Fingertips, the Motown artist's debut single in 1963.

Wonder music, **Talking Book**. Full of songs which have since become standards — **You Are The Sunshine Of My Life**, **You've Got It Bad, Girl**, **Superstition**, **I Believe (When I Fall In Love It Will Be Forever)** — **Talking Book** was first in series of award-winning platinum albums that became synonymous with name Stevie Wonder in the 1970s.

Wonder signed record-breaking financial agreement with Motown — a guaranteed 13-million dollars between 1975 and 1982. He became one of most often-awarded artists, with 14 Grammys between 1974 and 1977 alone. He gained reputation for keen socio-political awareness (particularly of black issues) and became symbol of spirit of liberation. Double album **Songs In The Key Of Life**, was regarded by many as one of *the* albums of the decade.

Entering 80s as strongly as ever with **Hotter Than July**, Wonder continued to exert huge influence. In 1982 he was given Award of Merit by American Music Awards, a citation which only does scant justice to enormous contribution he has made to popular music. Revered by his peers as much as by public, Wonder continued to push back boundaries, and saw deserved critical acclaim for funky **Characters** album (1987). Artist also enjoyed duets with Paul McCartney (**Ebony And Ivory**), Michael Jackson (**Get It**) and unlikely teaming with Julio Iglesias (**My Love**). Also featured on work by Dionne Warwick (**That's What Friends Are For**), Elton John, Eurythmics and others, as well as contributing to charity disc **We Are The World** and scoring movie *The Woman In Red*. At end of decade Wonder was inducted into The Rock 'n' Roll Hall Of Fame.

Following hectic 1990, which was mostly spent fund-raising for variety of charitable causes, including education, the homeless and diabetes, Wonder resumed recording career with soundtrack for Spike Lee's film *Jungle Fever*.

It is difficult to add a satisfactory testament to Stevie Wonder's extraordinary career other than to say that he has hardly faltered in the thirty-plus years since signing with Motown.

Hit Singles:

	US	UK
Fingertips Part 2, 1963	1	—
Uptight (Everything's Alright), 1966	3	14
Nothing's Too Good For My Baby, 1966	20	—
Blowin' In The Wind, 1966	9	36
A Place In The Sun, 1966	9	20
I Was Made To Love Her, 1967	2	5
I'm Wondering, 1967	12	22
Shoo-Be-Doo-Be-Doo-Da-Day, 1968	9	46
For Once In My Life, 1968	2	3
I Don't Know Why, 1969	39	14
My Cherie Amour, 1969	4	4
Yester-Me, Yester-You, Yesterday, 1969	7	2
Never Had A Dream Come True, 1970	26	6
Signed, Sealed, Delivered, I'm Yours, 1970	3	15
Heaven Help Us All, 1970	9	29
We Can Work It Out, 1971	13	27
If You Really Love Me, 1971	8	20
Superstition, 1973	1	11

Below: Stevie Wonder, loyal Motown recording artist of 30 years and inspiration to myriad of soul stars.

	US	UK
You Are The Sunshine Of My Life, 1973	1	7
Higher Ground, 1973	4	29
Living For The City, 1974	8	15
He's Misstra Know It All, 1974	—	10
Don't You Worry 'Bout A Thing, 1974	16	—
You Haven't Done Nothing, 1974	1	30
Boogie On Reggae Woman, 1975	3	12
I Wish, 1976	1	5
Sir Duke, 1977	1	2
Send One Your Love, 1979	4	52
Masterblaster (Jammin'), 1980	5	2
I Ain't Gonna Stand For It, 1980	11	10
Lately, 1981	—	3
Happy Birthday, 1981	—	2
That Girl, 1982	4	39
Do I Do, 1982	13	10
I Just Called To Say I Love You, 1984	1	1
Love Light In Flight, 1985	17	—
Part-time Lover, 1985	1	3
Go Home, 1986	22	—
Overjoyed, 1986	—	17
Skeletons, 1987	19	—

With Paul McCartney:

	US	UK
Ebony And Ivory, 1982	1	1

Albums:

Tribute To Uncle Ray (Motown), 1963
Jazz Soul Of Little Stevie (Motown), 1963
Twelve Year Old Genius Recorded Live (Motown), 1963
With A Song In My Heart (Motown), 1964
Uptight (Motown), 1966
Down To Earth (Motown), 1966
I Was Made To Love Her (Motown), 1967

Some Day At Christmas (Motown), 1967
For Once In My Life (Motown), 1969
My Cherie Amour (Motown), 1969
Live At The Talk Of The Town (Motown), 1970
Where I'm Coming From (Motown), 1971
Greatest Hits (Motown), 1972
Greatest Hits Volume 2 (Motown), 1972
Music Of My Mind (Motown)
Talking Book (Motown), 1972
Innervisions (Motown), 1973
Fullfillingness First Finale (Motown), 1974
Songs In The Key Of Life (Motown), 1976
The Secret Life Of Plants (Motown), 1979
Hotter Than July (Motown), 1980
Signed (Motown), 1981
Stevie Wonder's Original Musiquarium 1 (Motown), 1982
People Move Music Play (Motown), 1983
Woman In Red (Motown), 1984
In Square Circle (Motown), 1985
Original Musiquarium Volume 2, 1985
Essential Stevie Wonder (Motown), 1987
Characters (Motown), 1987
Where I'm Coming From (Motown), 1991

Roy Wood

UK vocalist, composer, multi-instrumentalist
Born Ulysses Adrian Wood, Birmingham, November 8, 1946

Career: Learned guitar in early teens. Joined and formed numerous groups, including Falcons, Lawmen, Gerry Levene and The Avengers, and Mike Sheridan and The Nightriders (who recorded Wood's composition **Make Them Understand**). Following expulsion from Mosely College of Art, Wood became more involved in group work, finally forming The Move in 1964. Impressive line-up of Bev Bevan (drums), Carl Wayne (vocals), Chris 'Ace' Kefford (bass) and Trevor Burton (guitar) was enlisted from cream of small-time Birmingham groups. Signed to opportunist manager Tony Secunda, they established themselves via residency at London's Marquee Club. Burgeoning interest in group led to recording contract with Deram.

First single, **Night Of Fear**, reached No. 2 in early 1967, and was followed by eight other hits, all composed by Wood, one of the cleverest and most appealing songwriters of the era. Psychedelia, flower power, early rock 'n' roll and classical pastiche were some of the themes explored on successive single releases.

As years passed, Wood's influence over group increased. From **Fire Brigade** onwards he assumed lead vocals as well as songwriting credits.

Following two essentially pop albums, **The Move** and **Shazam**, Wood was anxious to undertake more ambitious work. Acknowledged as a singles group in Britain, Move were gradually accepted as serious musicians in the States (despite limited popularity). Musical direction became increasingly diverse and uncertain towards end of decade; during final stage of career they flirted with heavy metal (**Brontosaurus, When Alice Comes Back To The Farm**) and rock revivalism (**California Man**). Wood's desire for music of greater complexity resulted in creation of Electric Light Orchestra, whose creative aim was to continue the exploratory work begun by the Beatles on such innovative songs as **Strawberry Fields Forever** and **I Am The Walrus**.

After recording one hit album and single (**10538 Overture**), the ever-restless Wood left ELO in the hands of Jeff Lynne in order

to pursue another new project. Soon a new group, Wizzard, emerged, comprising Rick Price (guitar), Bill Hunt (piano, harpsichord, French horn), Hugh McDowell (electric cello), Nick Pentelow (sax), Mike Burney (sax), Keith Smart (drums) and Charlie Grima (drums). Wood took lead role with new image, including multi-coloured hair and war-paint. First single, **Ball Park Incident**, was an intriguing production, echoing Phil Spector's Wall Of Sound.

Subsequent singles were even more impressive and included two celebrated No. 1's, **See My Baby Jive** and **Angel Fingers**. These and the haunting Spector-like festive hit, **I Wish It Could Be Christmas Everyday**, confirmed Wood's ability to write and produce hits that were the equal of his finest 60s work. Nevertheless, inability to produce albums of equivalent interest remained a failing from the early days. A brave attempt at rock revivalism, **Eddy And The Falcons**, proved commercially unsuccessful, causing Wood to lose interest.

In mid-70s he revived the pseudo-heavy metal experimentation of **Brontosaurus** in a revamped Wizzo, but this work was ill-timed. A simultaneous shot at solo fame produced the impressive hit **Forever**, an affectionate tribute to Neil Sedaka and the Beach Boys. Solo albums **Boulders** (1970) and **Mustard** (1975) were again erratic, though they demonstrated his total control as producer, engineer and designer (he even painted the cover!).

Late 70s and 80s proved barren for Wood, while his protégé Lynne has reaped a fortune with ELO. Wood's great strength and weakness has always been his peripatetic nature, but his past record remains exemplary: composer of all Move's hits; the mastermind behind the original ELO; and the creator of some of early 70s finest UK singles via Wizzard. A multi-talented producer, arranger, singer, songwriter and manipulator of pop genres, it would be a mistake to write him off despite his inconspicuous profile on the current scene.

Postscript: influential UK rock journal *Vox* reported in their Missing In Action series (January 1992) that Wood was busy recording at own studio for proposed new album, as well as providing incidental music for British television.

Hit Singles:

	US	UK
Dear Elaine, 1973	—	18
Forever, 1973	—	8
Going Down The Road, 1974	—	13
Oh What A Shame, 1975	—	13

With Wizzard:

	US	UK
Ball Park Incident, 1972	—	6
See My Baby Jive, 1973	—	1
Angel Fingers, 1973	—	1
I Wish It Could Be Christmas Everyday, 1973	—	4
Rock 'n' Roll Winter (Looney's Tune), 1974	—	6
Are You Ready To Rock, 1974	—	8

Albums:

Boulders (Harvest), 1973
Mustard (Jet), 1975
The Roy Wood Story (Harvest), 1976
On The Road Again (Automatic), 1979
The Best Of (70-74) (MFP), 1985
Starting Up (Legacy), 1987

With Wizzard:

Wizzard Brew (Harvest), 1973
Eddy And The Falcons (Warner Bros), 1974
See My Baby Jive (Harvest), 1974

Roy Wood Wizzo Band:

Super Active Wizzo (Warner Bros), 1977

XTC

UK group formed 1977

Original line-up: Andy Partridge, guitar, vocals; Colin Moulding, bass, vocals; Barry Andrews, keyboards; Terry Chambers, drums.

Career: Partridge organized XTC as punk band in Swindon, near London. **This Is Pop?** single attracted some attention and revealed XTC to be power-pop group in punk clothing. This became more apparent by time solid third album, **Drums And Wires**, appeared in 1979.

Next LP yielded minor hit, **Sergeant Rock**, which earned some US airplay and write-off as lightweight by UK press. In 1982 **Senses Working Overtime** put band back in UK charts, and double LP **English Settlement** (cut to single LP for US market) received critical approval. End of 1982 produced singles compilation (UK only) **Waxworks**. In promotional move, this album was issued for limited time with second LP, **Beeswax**, comprising B-side.

Above: Oranges And Lemons, XTC. Courtesy Virgin Records.

After illness hit leader Partridge, band gave up heavy touring schedule while continuing to record. Subsequent albums were well received by critics (particularly Todd Rundgren-produced 1986 offering **Skylarking**), but major commercial breakthrough continued to elude band, although 1988 set **Oranges And Lemons** came close. XTC were now trio, having seen Chambers depart after Partridge's terse announcement about quitting live work.

Partridge, who produced The Mission's **Hands Across The Ocean** single in 1990, has also had fun with outfit when using The Dukes Of Stratosphere tag, cutting eponymous EP in 1985 and 1987 LP **Psonic Psunspots**.

Hit Singles:

	US	UK
Making Plans For Nigel, 1979	–	17
Sergeant Rock, 1981	–	16
Senses Working Overtime, 1982	–	10

Albums:
White Music (Virgin-Epic/Virgin), 1978
Go 2 (Virgin-Epic/Virgin), 1978
Drums And Wires (Virgin-Epic/Virgin), 1979
Black Sea (Virgin), 1980
English Settlement (Virgin), 1982
Waxworks: Some Singles 1977-1982 (–/Virgin), 1982
Beeswax: Some B-sides 1977-1982 (–/Virgin), 1982
Mummer (Virgin), 1983
Go Too (Virgin), 1984
Big Express (Virgin), 1984
Compact XTC (Virgin), 1986

Skylarking (Virgin), 1986
Oranges And Lemons (Geffen/Virgin), 1988

Andy Partridge and The Dukes Of Stratosphere:
Psonic Psunspots (Geffen/Virgin), 1987
Chips From The Chocolate Fireball (Geffen/Virgin), 1987

The Yardbirds

UK group formed 1963

Original line-up: Keith Relf, vocals, harmonica; Anthony 'Top' Topham, guitar; Chris Dreja, guitar; Paul Samwell-Smith, bass; Jim McCarty, drums.

Career: First version of Yardbirds grew out of Kingston Art School band, the Metropolitan Blues Quartet. Eric Clapton replaced Topham in late 1963, before band took over residency vacated by Rolling Stones at Crawdaddy Club in Richmond. Band generated strong cult following on London and Home Counties club circuit, and toured Europe with blues legend Sonny Boy Williamson.

Signed by Columbia, they released **Five Live Yardbirds** in 1964 (only in UK), essential listening for anyone wanting to know what British R&B was all about. Album increased their following, as did **Sonny Boy Williamson And The Yardbirds**, released same year. 1965 saw shift in direction when band recorded **For Your Love**, written by Graham Gouldman, then of Mindbenders, later of 10cc. An unusual yet thoroughly commercial rock-pop song, far removed from band's R&B orientation, it catapulted The Yardbirds into charts on both sides of Atlantic, making No. 3 in UK and No. 6 in US.

Success was consolidated by release of two more Graham Gouldman singles, **Heart Full Of Soul** and **Evil Hearted You**. Clapton, however, quit after **For Your Love**, unable to reconcile himself to move away from band's roots, and joined John Mayall's Bluesbreakers. Jimmy Page was asked to

Below: UK quartet XTC who caused a minor flurry during the 1980s.

replace Clapton, but declined and recommended Jeff Beck, another ex-art college musician, who accepted.

1966 saw further stresses and personnel changes. Now a hot live act, band was continually touring, which didn't suit Paul Samwell-Smith. He pulled out to concentrate on production. Chris Dreja moved to bass, and Jimmy Page, then an in-demand session musician, agreed to second offer, joining Beck on guitar. Relatively minor hit **Happenings Ten Years Time Ago** was only single with this line-up.

By end of year Beck had also left. Following fairly disastrous album produced by Mickey Most, and a couple of unsuccessful American singles, Relf, McCarty, Page and Dreja called it a day in July 1968.

Relf and McCarty formed folk duo Together, then founded Renaissance, but their post-Yardbirds career was not particularly auspicious. Relf died in accident at home in 1976. Dreja became a photographer, while Page formed New Yardbirds which metamorphosed into supergroup Led Zeppelin (managed by former Yardbirds road manager Peter Grant).

Yardbirds' influence was greater than their actual success and paved the way for guitar-dominated psychedelic/heavy rock bands of 60s and 70s. Now, virtually all recordings have become collectors' items, and Yardbirds are regarded as one of all-time legendary rock bands.

Hit Singles:

	US	UK
For Your Love, 1965	6	3
Heart Full Of Soul, 1965	9	2
Evil Hearted You/Still I'm Sad, 1965	–	3
I'm A Man, 1965	17	–
Shapes Of Things, 1966	11	3
Over Under Sideways Down, 1966	13	10

Albums:
Yardbirds With Sonny Boy Williamson (Mercury/Fontana), 1964
Five Live Yardbirds (–/Charly), 1964
The Yardbirds (–/CBS), 1966
Great Hits (Epic/–), 1967
Remember (–/Starline), 1971
Eric Clapton And The Yardbirds (Springboard/–), 1972
Yardbirds Favourites (Epic), 1972

Above: Five Live Yardbirds, The Yardbirds. Courtesy EMI Records.

Yardbirds Featuring Eric Clapton (–/Charly), 1975
Yardbirds Featuring Jeff Beck (–/Charly), 1975
Shapes Of Things (Springboard/Charly), 1977
Single Hits (–/Charly), 1982
Afternoon Tea (Rhino/–), 1982
For Your Love (Accord/–), 1982
Classic Cuts (Topline)
First Recordings (Bellaphon)
Roger The Engineer (Edsell)
Greatest Hits (Charly)

Worth Searching Out:
Having A Rave-Up With The Yardbirds (Epic/–), 1971
Live Yardbirds Featuring Jimmy Page (Epic), 1971*
*withdrawn

Yes

UK group formed 1968

Original line-up: Jon Anderson, vocals; Chris Squire, bass; Peter Banks, guitar; Tony Kaye, organ; Bill Bruford, drums.

Career: After 12 years in nowhere bands, Anderson chanced upon Squire in Soho night-club; line-up of Yes was completed by members of their previous bands. Debut LP **Yes** took Beatles and Byrds originals and expanded them into almost unrecognizable baroque extravaganzas; sound deliberately emulated classical influence of ELP's Keith Emerson.

Follow-up **Time And A Word** LP added superfluous strings and did not sound as innovative as intended. In 1971 Banks left; he was replaced by Steve Howe (ex-Syndicate, In Crowd, Budast, Tomorrow). This line-up produced **The Yes Album**, which showed that original intention to fuse rock and classical music remained band's driving force. Significantly, Banks added synthesizer and Yes recorded completely original music for the LP.

Kaye was replaced by Rick Wakeman (ex-Strawbs) whose classical training coincided with band's direction. **Fragile** LP took on symphonic sound closely associated with Yes. In 1972 Alan White (ex-Plastic Ono Band) took over drums for what many consider best Yes line-up.

Growing integration of technological advances and classical idioms exploded on **Close To The Edge** (recorded before Bruford had left drum slot to play with King Crimson). New line-up proved that complex, orchestral compositions translated well on stage with live set, **Yessongs**. This triple set also betrayed problem with Yes music: the line between innovative exploration and overblown pretension.

Next double LP **Topographic Oceans** sank under its own weight and convinced Wakeman to jump ship. (He had released successful solo album **Six Wives Of Henry VIII** in 1973.) Patrick Moraz (keyboards) joined August 1974. His classical training allowed him to assume Wakeman's mantle with little difficulty, as evidenced on **Relayer** LP and in live shows. Wakeman rejoined in 1976 when Moraz quit Yes as fans were flooded with plethora of various solo efforts and spin-offs.

1977's **Going For The One** dredged up same old Yes conventions and music seemed slightly foolish in light of new wave. Wakeman left after **Tormato** and then — a shock to Yes fans — so did Anderson; Anderson went on to solo work and Vangelis. Buggles duo Trevor Horn (guitars) and Geoff Downes (keyboards) joined in 1980 for US and UK tours and recording of **Drama** LP. Then, not with a bang, but with a short press announcement, Yes folded altogether. Howe and Downes reappeared in Asia, with Carl Palmer and John Wetton in 1981.

Although it seemed that the techno-rock maestros had packed their last stadium, band rejoined in 1983 for **91025** set which spawned tuneful **Owner Of A Lonely Heart** single. Line-up included Anderson, Squire, White, Kaye and Trevor Rabin, guitar. Group toured US in 1987 following release of **Big Generator** set.

Anderson maintained solo career, cutting **3 Ships** (1985) and **In The City Of Angles** (1988) as well as guesting on LPs by Tangerine Dream and Mike Oldfield. He then quit band once again, before recruiting former Yes-men Bruford, Wakeman and Howe for 1989 album. Quartet fooled audience on 1989 American tour with obvious supposition that this was current Yes outfit, despite legal wrangle which had prevented them using moniker.

1991 saw official Yes in action once again, the band comprising Anderson, Squire, Wakeman, Kaye, White and Howe. Unit undertook Yesshows world tour in same year, as well as completing **The New Union** album. In order to appease rock journalists, Yes have agreed to stick together for the next decade!

Hit Singles:	US	UK
Roundabout, 1972	13	—
Wonderous Stories, 1977	—	7
Owner Of A Lonely Heart, 1983	1	—
Love Will Find A Way, 1987	30	—
Rhythm Of Love, 1988	40	—

Albums:
Yes (Atlantic, 1969)
Time And A Word (Atlantic), 1970
The Yes Album (Atlantic), 1971
Fragile (Atlantic), 1971
Close To The Edge (Atlantic), 1972
Yessongs (Atlantic), 1973
Tales From Topographic Oceans (Atlantic), 1973
Relayer (Atlantic), 1974
Yesterdays (Atlantic), 1975
Going For The One (Atlantic), 1977
Tormato (Atlantic), 1978
Drama (Atlantic), 1980
Yesshows (Atlantic), 1980
Classic Yes (Atlantic), 1981
90125 (Atlantic), 1983
Big Generator (Atlantic), 1987
Anderson, Bruford, Wakeman, Howe (Arista), 1989
The New Union (Arista/—), 1991

Bill Bruford Solo:
Feels Good To Me (Polydor), 1978

Neil Young
Canadian vocalist, composer, guitarist
Born Toronto, Ontario, November 12, 1945

Career: Son of a well-known Toronto sports writer, who gave Neil ukelele for Christmas, 1958. Graduated to banjo, then guitar soon after. Early influence was Hank Marvin of the Shadows. After short-lived group The Jades, joined first real band Squires in 1963. By late 1964 began to arrange and write for them. During this period, met Stephen Stills and Richie Furay, whom he would later join in Buffalo Springfield. Became coffee-bar folk singer in New York, then met Bruce Palmer, a member of Mynah Birds (led by Rick Matthews, who later found fame as Rick James in 80s). Mynah Birds, with Young a member, cut several unreleased tracks for Motown Records, but arrest of James as deserter from US Navy effectively killed group.

Young moved to Los Angeles with Palmer in early 1966; reunited with Stills and Furay in freeway traffic jam. Quartet decided to form group The Herd, with drummer Dewey Martin (ex-Dillards). Changed group name to Buffalo Springfield after steamroller of same name; began gigging in spring 1966. After meeting Byrds, became embroiled in LA folk-rock and country-rock scenes.

With several line-up changes in rhythm section (Palmer departed and later returned, Young left and rejoined, Jim Messina joined early 1968), Buffalo Springfield lasted until May 1968, leaving three excellent LPs and five hit singles, only one of which, **For What It's Worth**, made US Top 10.

After working as folkie, Young acquired record deal with Reprise. First solo LP was released in 1969. Then formed band Crazy Horse, who provided backing for second classic LP, **Everybody Knows This Is Nowhere**. After recording third LP, Young was invited to join Crosby, Stills And Nash, and briefly group became Crosby, Stills, Nash And Young for **Déjà Vu** LP, double live album and performance at Woodstock Festival. Personality clashes led Young back to solo career; **After The Goldrush** and **Harvest** were commercially and artistically successful. But Young turned back on success with 1973 release of **Journey Through The Past**, soundtrack to film produced by Young. Subsequent three LPs permeated by melancholy songs and performances, as Young refused to follow easy commercial path.

Late 1975 LP **Zuma** saw return to form of earlier LPs, with attacking guitar solos and instantly recognizable vocals from Young. Briefly worked with Stephen Stills, but union short-lived. Next LP, **American Stars 'n' Bars**, included assistance from Linda Ronstadt and Emmylou Harris, joining stellar list of guests on previous Young records, such as Crosby, Stills, Nash, Jack Nitzsche, Rick Danko and Levon Helm (The Band), Nils Lofgren, and others. Three-LP set **Decade**, a self-compiled retrospective, released in late 1977, almost whole year before **Comes A Time**, which encountered many delays due to track changes, re-mixes, cover art alteration, etc. New era arrived with **Rust Never Sleeps** and **Live Rust**, once again with backing from Crazy Horse, to whom Young returned several times in his career. Concept included major tour, made into film *Rust Never Sleeps*.

Young then worked at length on film project *Human Highway*. Directed and acted in movie, along with Dean Stockwell, Russ Tamblyn and Devo. During this period (1980-81) also released two more albums.

In 1982, began using synthesizers and electronic instruments; eventually invited many of past friends from backing bands to assist him in making **Trans**, including: Nils Lofgren, guitar; Ben Keith, pedal steel, keyboards; Bruce Palmer, bass; Joe Lala, percussion; and Ralph Molina, drums. Group toured in support of **Trans** album. While new electronic direction admirable in some ways, peculiar sounds of album tended to alienate long-standing Young fans, who preferred his earlier work.

However, faithful following were hoping electro-indulgence was temporary, and were pleased with return to more traditional output with **Landing On Water** (1986) and **Ragged Glory** (1990), the latter seeing further rejoining with Crazy Horse. Young maintained liaison with his old back-up band for bizarre live double album **Weld** (taken from Ragged Glory tour) in 1991, an anarchic thrash through troubled waters, in which artist asked plaintively 'Why Do I Keep F...... Up?'.

Young has always been out of step with rock mainstream, unfazed by trends or demands. His sojourn with CSN&Y (with whom Young temporarily regrouped in 1988) saw most creative period, although his almost maniacal solo output has never been less than interesting.

Hit Singles:	US	UK
Heart Of Gold, 1972	1	10

Crosby, Stills, Nash And Young:

	US	UK
Woodstock, 1970	11	—
Teach Your Children, 1970	16	—
Ohio, 1970	14	—

Above: Neil Young, Canadian megastar who survived Woodstock and various CSN&Y regroupings.

Albums:
Neil Young (Reprise), 1968
Everybody Knows This Is Nowhere (Reprise), 1969
After The Goldrush (Reprise), 1970
Harvest (Reprise), 1971
Journey Through The Past (Reprise), 1972
Time Fades Away (Reprise), 1973
On The Beach (Reprise), 1974
Tonight's The Night (Reprise), 1975
Zuma (Reprise), 1975
Long May You Run (Stills/Young Band), 1976
American Stars 'n' Bars (Reprise), 1977
Decade (compilation) (Reprise), 1977
Comes A Time (Reprise), 1978
Rust Never Sleeps (Reprise), 1979 ·
Live Rust (Reprise), 1979
Hawks And Doves (Warner Bros), 1980
Re-ac-tor (Warner Bros), 1981
Trans (Warner Bros), 1982
Everybody's Rockin' (Geffen), 1983
Landing On Water (Geffen), 1986
Best Of (Warner Bros), 1987
Freedom (Reprise/Warner Bros), 1988
Ragged Glory (Reprise/—), 1990
Weld (Reprise), 1991

Crosby, Stills, Nash And Young:
Deja Vu (Atlantic), 1970
Four Way Street (Atlantic), 1971
So Far (compilation) (Atlantic), 1974

With Crazy Horse:
Life (Geffen), 1987

195

Paul Young

UK vocalist
Born November 30, 1955

Career: More than 700 shows up and down Britain from 1979 to 1982, fronting the fondly remembered eight-piece soul review Q-Tips, provided perfect grounding for the talents of Paul Young who had become leading British exponent of 'blue-eyed soul'.

When Q-Tips broke up, Young retained services of keyboard player Ian Kewley, his regular songwriter partner, and began work on **No Parlez** album which built on chart-topping success of **Wherever I Lay My Hat** single — CBS's most successful domestic release in its 18 year history.

A sell-out debut tour of UK and lengthy European tour plus six weeks in US caused vocal strain and temporary loss of top six notes in his range. Therefore planned major Wembley concert with Elton John was cancelled, and another US tour was deferred. There was a gap of over 18 months between **No Parlez** and follow-up album **The Secret Of Association** which featured superlative version of Ann Peebles' soul classic single **I'm Gonna Tear Your Playhouse Down**.

Above: From Time To Time, Paul Young. Courtesy Columbia Records.

During hiatus, Young revamped his Royal Family backing outfit, Johnny Turnbull replacing Steve Bolton on guitar, Matt Irving joining as second keyboard player, and respected black singers George Chandler, Jimmy Chambers and Tony Jackson replacing the Fabulous Wealthy Tarts (Maz Roberts and Kim Leslie). Drummer Mark Pinder, bass player Pino Palladino and Ian Kewley completed line-up.

1987 album **Between Two Fires** achieved platinum status in UK, but latterly Young's career seems to have stalled slightly. Although highly successful, artist seemed unsure of best direction to take.

1990 set **Other Voices** (with Chaka Khan and Stevie Wonder) saw return to form; album spawned excellent cover version of Chi-Lites' classic **Oh Girl** which made US Top 10. Young then enjoyed success when collaboration with Italian vocalist Zucchero on **Senza Una Donna** single charted in UK.

Young's apparent uncertainty of own talent has prevented mega-stardom, despite majestic voice and appealingly unpretentious personality. Someone should tell him to stand on his own two feet.

Hit Singles:

	US	UK
Wherever I Lay My Hat (That's My Home), 1983	—	1
Come Back And Stay, 1983*	22	4
Love Of The Common People, 1983	—	2
I'm Gonna Tear Your Playhouse Down, 1984†	13	9
Everything Must Change, 1985	—	9
Everytime You Go Away, 1985	1	4
Tomb Of Memories, 1985	—	16
Wonderland, 1986	—	24
Calling You, 1991	—	57
Don't Dream It's Over, 1991	—	20

*1984 in US
†1985 in US

Albums:
No Parlez (CBS), 1983
The Secret of Association (CBS), 1985
Between Two Fires (CBS), 1986
Live At Last (CBS), 1986
Other Voices (Columbia/CBS), 1990
From Time To Time (Columbia), 1991

Paul Young and The Q-Tips:
Live (Hallmark), 1985

Frank Zappa

US composer, guitarist, vocalist
Born Francis Vincent Zappa Jr., Baltimore, Maryland, December 21, 1940

Career: Raised on East Coast until age 10, then moved to West Coast with family, which may explain schizoid musical career. Early interests ranged from Edgar Varese to R&B to 1950s doo-wop. Practical experience included high-school band Blackouts, recording Don Von Vliet (also ex-Blackout and renamed Captain Beefheart by Zappa), and producing naughty sex tape for local vice squad (which earned light jail sentence and draft exemption).

Zappa joined group Soul Giants which, according to legend, played first gig on Mothers Day. MGM couldn't cope with name 'The Mothers' so added 'Of Invention'. Original line-up of Ray Collins, Jimmy Carl 'Token Indian' Black, Roy Estrada and Dave Coranda immediately went for record number of personnel changes. Coranda left in horror at Zappa's master plan for world domination through music.

Tom Wilson (Dylan and Velvet Underground producer) recorded debut **Freak Out** in early 1966. Double bonanza of over-the-top social commentry, **Freak Out** demanded a little thinking to get behind satire to strange music underlying it. Zappa became touted as rock's sharpest sociologist. The highly intelligent interviews he gave revealed distaste for any trends or fashions. With further personnel changes, Zappa recorded **Absolutely Free** which questioned lack of freedom in modern society. If rock fans felt smug, claiming to be outside that society, they missed point of **We're Only In It For The Money** which lampooned Beatles' **Sgt. Pepper** and rock's under-30 audience in one blow.

Claiming all his work was one extended piece, Zappa overloaded his modern classical influences into free-form solo **Lumpy Gravy** LP. Zappa's band seemed to disappear although he continued to use many of the same musicians. In late 1967 he started work on two simultaneous recording projects. **Cruising With Ruben And The Jets** appeared first and provided return to satire of early albums. In fact, Zappa reproduced 50s feel so faithfully from cover and liner notes to sound itself, it's questionable whether he intended a put-down or tribute; Sha-Na-Na or Rocky And The Replays never did better. **Uncle Meat**, soundtrack for never-made-movie, indicated Zappa's fascination for all forms of media. **Burnt Weeny Sandwich** proved to be Mothers' last album. **Weasels Ripped My Flesh** (1970) was released under Mothers

Above: Underrated but influential musical talent Frank Zappa had to face battle with cancer in late 1991.

name but was compilation of old and live material. Zappa formally announced Mothers' demise in October 1969 press release, and promptly buried himself in running two new labels (Bizarre and Straight) while producing groups on outer fringe of rock respectability (early Alice Cooper, GTO's, Beefheart, Wild Man Fischer). Old Mothers Lowell George and Roy Estrada went on to form Little Feat. Jimmy Carl Black and Bunk Gardner formed Geronimo Black, while Art Tripp left to join Captain Beefheart.

Zappa kept Ian Underwood (guitar, keyboards) for second solo album **Hot Rats**. When released, it was hard to tell difference between Zappa alone and Zappa with Mothers. This was apparent when next LP, **Chunga's Revenge**, featured many musicians who eventually made up the Mothers used in **200 Motels** soundtrack and movie. These last two projects made particular use

of vocalists Howard Kaylan and Mark Volman (ex-Turtles).

Zappa jammed with John Lennon, and appeared on **Sometime In New York** LP (1972). Then he took Mothers (who, of course had undergone several more personnel changes) on tour and released two live albums: **The Mothers: Fillmore East June 1971** and **Just Another Band From LA**. End of 1971 saw poor European tour (band's equipment lost in Montreux fire) and serious injury to Zappa when pushed from stage at Rainbow Theatre, London. Zappa continued to release (some say grind out) material, either solo (**Waka Jawaka**) or with Mothers (**Grand Wazoo**). Although assured of certain level of sales, Zappa seemed to want wider approval of his ideas. His writing moved closer to simple rock. Lyrics began to lose bite and became more scatological. If shock tactics didn't get him into Top 10, he'd titillate his way there.

Below: The classic cover of Weasels Ripped My Flesh, Mothers Of Invention. Courtesy Bizarre/Reprise Records.

New record deal with Warners emphasized efforts to make hit record. **Overnite Sensation** missed mark, but **Apostrophe** finally rose high in US charts. In gratitude Zappa hired marching band to play past Warners' office. Next two LPs, **Roxy And Elsewhere** and **One Size Fits All**, took step back to live recordings as if Zappa was content to resume his role outside mainstream rock. **Bongo Fury** was also primarily live but featured reunion with old friend Captain Beefheart. Beefheart's appearance signalled end of dispute between the two stretching back to Zappa's production of the Captain in late 1960s.

One year passed before **Zoot Allures** appeared. Then, as if possessed, Zappa began releasing albums every few months. **Sheik Yerbouti** (1979), **Joe's Garage Act 1** (1979) and **You Are What You Is** (1981) are all excellent. **Ship Arriving Too Late To Save A Drowning Witch** (1982) contains **Valley Girl** single by Zappa and Moon Unit (his daughter). It was counter-culture's answer to Frank and Nancy Sinatra duet of 60s, comprised of Southern California's teenage jargon, a language of its own.

Latterly, Zappa has involved himself in struggle against right wing/fundamentalist moves to censor rock lyrics; joined with Czech president Vachlev Havel as 'trade consultant' as well as cutting occasional album; **Jazz From Hell** (1987) earned artist Grammy for Best Rock Instrumental. However, unsettling news filtered through in winter of 1991 of Zappa's battle with prostate cancer, preventing him appearing in planned 'Zappa's Universe' event.

Below: Dusty Hill (left) and Billy Gibbons from Texas boogie band ZZ Top.

The Zappa offspring have also enjoyed notoriety; Moon Unit as frothy VJ for MTV and guitarist Dweezil for session work.

Guitars: D'mini-Les Paul, the Strato.

Albums:
Uncle Meat (Bizarre/Reprise), 1969
Hot Rats (Bizare/Reprise), 1969
Burnt Weeny Sandwich (Bizarre/Reprise), 1969
Weasels Ripped My Flesh (Bizarre/Reprise), 1970
Chunga's Revenge (Bizarre/Reprise), 1970
The Mothers: Fillmore East, June 1971 (Bizarre/Reprise), 1971
200 Motels (United Artists), 1971
Just Another Band From LA (Bizarre/Reprise), 1972
Waka Jawaka — Hot Rats (Bizarre/Reprise), 1972
Grand Wazoo (Bizarre/Reprise), 1972
Overnite Sensation (DiscReet), 1973
Apostrophe (DiscReet), 1974
Roxy And Elsewhere (DiscReet), 1974
One Size Fits All (DiscReet), 1975
Bongo Fury (DiscReet), 1975
Zoot Allures (DiscReet), 1976
Zappa In New York (DiscReet), 1978
Studio Tan (DiscReet), 1978
Sheik Yerbouti (DiscReet), 1979
Sleep Dirt (DiscReet), 1979
Orchestral Favourites (DiscReet), 1979
Joe's Garage Act I (Zappa/CBS), 1979
Joe's Garage Acts II And III (Zappa/CBS), 1979
Tinsel Town Rebellion (Barking Pumpkin/CBS), 1980
You Are What You Is (Zappa/CBS), 1981
Shut Up And Play Yer Guitar (Barking Pumpkin/CBS), 1981

Ship Arriving Too Late To Save A Drowning Witch (Barking Pumpkin/CBS), 1982
The Man From Utopia (Barking Pumpkin/CBS), 1983
Rare Meat — Early Productions of Frank Zappa (Del Fi/—), 1983
Them Or Us (EMI), 1984
Thing Fish (Capitol), 1985
Does Humour Belong In Music (EMI), 1986
Jazz From Hell (Barking Pumpkin/Music For Nations), 1987
One Size Fits All (Barking Pumpkin/WEA), 1988
Zoot Allures (Rykodisc/WEA), 1990
Make A Jazz Noise Here (Barking Pumpkin), 1991
Beat The Boots (8 LP set) (Foo-Eee), 1991

Worth Searching Out:
Freak Out (MGM/Verve), 1966
Absolutely Free (MGM/Verve), 1967
We're Only In It For The Money (DiscReet), 1968
Lumpy Gravy (MGM/Verve), 1968
Cruising With Ruben And The Jets (MGM/Verve), 1968
Mothermania — The Best Of The Mothers (MGM/Verve), 1968

ZZ Top
US group formed 1970

Original line-up: Billy Gibbons, Gibson Les Paul guitar, vocals; Dusty Hill, Fender Telecaster bass, vocals; Frank Beard, drums.

Career: Gibbons was exciting guitarist in local Houston, Texas, band of late 60s,

Moving Sidewalks. When that project fell apart, he and manager Bill Ham planned new group. Beard joined and, after failure to find right combination through auditions, recommended Hill. Drawing on traditional country blues and delta music, ZZ Top added hard

Above: Afterburner, ZZ Top. Courtesy Warner Bros Records.

white rock to come up with own version of high-energy music. Band quickly established reputation as powerful act, challenging headliners to match their performance.

First Album received only local interest but **Rio Grande Mud** reflected growing audience by eventually going gold. **Tres Hombres** in 1973 put band into big time and provided US hit single **La Grange**. Forever touring as boogie band, ZZ Top now headlined massive concerts and **Fandango!** quickly followed **Tres Hombres** to platinum. From studio side of LP **Tush**, with its raunchy euphemisms, merited heavy airplay. Following **Téjas** LP and massive World Wide Texas Tour (1976-77), ZZ Top decided to take a vacation which turned into a three-year hiatus in career.

Dequello LP returned trio to prominence in 1979 and group subsequently enjoyed international chart success with 1983 set **Eliminator** and 1985 album **Afterburner**. Single **Gimme All Your Lovin'** heralded renewed single chart action, and accompanying videos for selected 45s became permanent fixture on MTV. Band then took further break before release of **Recycler** album in 1990, during which time it was announced that **Eliminator** and **Afterburner** had combined sales approaching 15 million. Trio also featured in *Back To The Future III* movie during their 'hot' period.

Re-paying debt to their roots, ZZ Top provided funding for Delta Blues Museum in Clarksdale, Mississippi, and were feted by town council during Memphis leg of 1991 American tour.

Hit Singles:	US	UK
Tush, 1974	20	—
Gimme All Your Lovin', 1984	37	10
Legs, 1984	8	16
Sleeping Bag, 1985	8	27
Rough Boy, 1986	—	23
Doubleback, 190	—	29
My Head's In Mississippi, 1991	—	37

Albums:
First Album (Warner Bros), 1971
Rio Grande Mud (Warner Bros), 1972
Tres Hombres (Warner Bros), 1973
Fandango! (Warner Bros), 1974
Téjas (Warner Bros), 1976
Best Of (Warner Bros), 1977
Dequello (Warner Bros), 1979
El Loco (Warner Bros), 1981
Eliminator (Warner Bros), 1983
Afterburner (Warner Bros), 1985
Sixpack (Warner Bros)
Recycler (Warner Bros), 1990

APPENDIX

This section recognizes the one-hit wonders, the has-beens, the never-haves, the once-weres, the could-bes and the you-never-knows in the rock world.

A

ACE – Short-lived British soul-influenced group. Topped US charts in 1975 with moody **How Long** from **Five-A-Side** album.

ADAM ANT – British singer who came to prominence with New Romantic Movement of late 70s and early 80s. Went on to pursue career as actor.

KING SUNNY ADE – Nigerian performer of good-time African music whose 'juju' sounds have attracted large audiences in both the US and UK.

AIR SUPPLY – Australian band who scored well in the American singles chart in the early 80s, most notably with **All Out Of Love** and **The One That You Love**, both penned by vocalist, UK-born Graham Russell.

JAN AKKERMAN – Former lead guitarist of Dutch band Focus which enjoyed success during 70s. A reticent, introverted character, he has since cut selection of excellent solo albums.

ALABAMA – Consistent performers who broke into the US pop charts with **Feels So Right** in 1981 after a decade in the country listings. Went on to enjoy platinum status with albums.

ALARM – Welsh rock quartet who debuted with odd acoustic punk set **Declaration** in 1984 on IRS label. Musical diversity has, as yet, failed to secure mega-audience, although fifth album **Raw** (1991) did at least see a stabilization of musical style.

MOSE ALLISON – Highly individual white blues/jazz singer and pianist. Much recorded and a major influence on British stars such as Georgie Fame.

CARLOS ALOMAR – US guitarist and highly regarded leader of David Bowie's stage band for many years. He also worked with John Lennon, Bette Midler, Chuck Berry and R&B greats Wilson Pickett and James Brown. Married to former Chic vocalist Robin Clark.

ALTERED IMAGES – UK synth band behind cutesy, squeaky, goo-goo vocals of Clare Grogan (who had part in film *Gregory's Girl*). Had promising start with 1981 hits **Happy Birthday** and **I Could Be Happy**.

AMEN CORNER – Cardiff-based mod band which topped UK charts with **Half As Nice** (1969) and enjoyed four other Top 20 records. Name changed to Fairweather (after lead singer Andy Fairweather-Low) in 1970 when they had Top 5 hit with **Natural Sinner**.

AMERICA – US trio who peaked with lilting **Horse With No Name** in 1972. CSN&Y soundalike formula surprisingly returned outfit to US Top 10 in 1982 with **You Can Do Magic**.

TORI AMOS – Potential superstar of 90s, Carolina-born Tori Amos is a vigilant pro-feminist vocalist whose cutting style reminds one of early 70s wunderkind Melanie. Powerful debut LP **Little Earthquakes** was released in 1992.

LAURIE ANDERSON – US sculptress whose turgid excursions into electro/techno 'music' almost incredibly provided UK Top 10 spot in 1981 with wistful **O Superman**. Has also worked with mainstream rock performers Nile Rodgers (**Home Of The Brave** LP) and Peter Gabriel (**Mr Heartbreak** album).

PAUL ANKA – Canadian teen idol who topped US and UK charts in 1957 with **Diana**. Subsequently scored 35 further Top 60 entries in America before settling down on nightclub circuit. Wrote English lyrics to **My Way**, which assured already wealthy artist royalties in old age.

ANTHRAX – New York thrash quintet whose 1985 collection **Spreading The Disease** put them in forefront of zap merchants. Collaborated with notorious Public Enemy for **Bring The Noise** (1991).

APRIL WINE – Canadian HM outfit from Nova Scotia who cracked US LP listings in 1980.

ARGENT – Former member of Zombies, Rod Argent is a first division keyboard performer who has settled nicely into film and studio work after a couple of decent hit singles from the early 70s, notably rock anthem **Hold Your Head Up**.

ARRIVAL – Liverpool pop band who scored in 1970 with **Friends** and **I Will Survive**, but folded three years later. Three of the members became nucleus of Kokomo.

ART OF NOISE – Electro invention of notable producer Trevor Horn. Success of **Beat Box** and **Close (To The Exit)** achieved by dynamic videos rather than muted group image.

ASHFORD AND SIMPSON – Premier US songwriters (**Ain't No Mountain High Enough, You're All I Need To Get By, Ain't Nothing Like The Real Thing, Reach Out And Touch**) who found chart success as performers with dynamic **Solid** in 1985.

ASIA – Superstar aggregation featuring John Wetton (ex-King Crimson, Family, Roxy Music), Steve Howe (ex-Yes), Geoff Downes (ex-Buggles, Yes) and Carl Palmer (ex-ELO). Enjoyed modicum of success in early 80s for Geffen label.

ASSOCIATION – Slick pop group who featured their five-part harmonies on series of major hits throughout late 60s. Topped US charts twice with **Windy** (1967) and **Cherish** (1966).

CHET ATKINS – Country guitarist whose influence permeates all kinds of American guitar music. Became head of RCA Records in Nashville.

ATLANTA RHYTHM SECTION – Distinguished band of session musicians (featuring guitarist Barry Bailey) who scored five US Top 20 hits in late 70s. Re-make of **Spooky**, originally recorded by Classics IV, was group's last major success.

BRIAN AUGER – From jazz pianist to R&B organist. He featured John McLaughlin in his first group, then formed Brian Auger Trinity which, by 1965, had become Steampacket with Long John Baldry, Rod Stewart and Julie Driscoll fronting on vocals. After band split, Auger and Driscoll had 1968 hit with **This Wheel's On Fire**.

FRANKIE AVALON – US teen idol from late 50s who scored with succession of teen anthems, most notably US No. 1 **Venus** in 1959.

AVERAGE WHITE BAND – Scottish outfit led by Hamish Stuart and Alan Gorrie whose potential was unfulfilled after series of exciting hit singles, of which **Pick Up The Pieces** topped the US charts in 1975.

HOYT AXTON – Best known as songwriter with hits for Steppenwolf, Three Dog Night, Ringo Starr, Tiny Tim and Joan Baez. Cut series of fine country rock albums in own right. His mother wrote Elvis Presley's hit **Heartbreak Hotel**, and was partner in formation of Stax label.

AZTEC CAMERA – Vehicle for talented Scottish guitarist/vocalist Roddy Frame who enjoyed UK Top 10 status with **Love** LP (1987).

B

BURT BACHARACH – Enormously successful New York-based songwriter, notably in partnership with Hal David. On Staff at Scepter/Wand Records they wrote hits for Chuck Jackson, Tommy Hunt, Maxine Brown and Dionne Warwick – including classics **Anyone Who Had A Heart, Walk On By** and **You'll Never Get To Heaven**. Partnership dissolved after *Promises, Promises* musical. From 1963 on, Bacharach recorded own albums for MCA and A&M and starred in countless TV specials. 1986 chart-topping hit was Michael McDonald/Patti LaBelle duet **On My Own**.

THE BACHELORS – Irish balladeer group (brothers Declan and Con Clusky, plus Dean Stokes). Their old-hat 'Tin Pan Alley' format competed successfully with Merseybeat explosion; had ten Top 20 hits between 1963-67.

BACHMAN-TURNER OVERDRIVE – Formed from the remnants of Guess Who, Canadians Randy Bachman and Fred Turner have earned a place in rock history if for nothing but staying power. Topped US singles chart in 1975 with oft-revised **You Ain't Seen Nothing Yet**.

BAD MANNERS – Notable part of British ska revival (along with Specials and Madness) from early 80s led with gusto by Buster Bloodvessel (Doug Trendle). Enjoyed handful of UK hits of which 'good-time' rendition of **Can Can** made No. 3.

BADFINGER – Beatles' protégés; scored in 1970 with McCartney's **Come And Get It**. Founder songwriter Peter Ham committed suicide in 1975.

JOAN BAEZ – Peacenik from the early 60s whose magnificent vocal style enhanced folk and rock protest scene. Ironically, the country classic **The Night They Drove Old Dixie Down** provided her with her only Top 10 success. Continues touring and recording in the 90s to faithful audiences.

ANITA BAKER – Detroit-born soul diva whose mellifluous vocals have graced chart singles such as **Sweet Love** (1986) and **Giving You The Best That I've Got** (1988). Earned Grammy with **Ain't No Need To Worry** collaboration with The Winans.

Below: 'Buster' Bloodvessel leads Bad Manners with aggression and wit.

GINGER BAKER – Best known as drummer for Cream. Upon band's demise, formed short-lived Blind Faith, then Airforce, then Baker-Gurvitz Army. Other ventures have included Ginger Baker's Nutters and Bakerland.

LONG JOHN BALDRY – Seminal figure on British R&B scene. Served with Cyril Davies R&B All Stars, taking over band and re-naming it Hoochie Coochie Men on Davies' death in January 1964. Gave Rod Stewart his first break (as second singer) and then joined Steampacket, also with Stewart. From Bluesology (which included Elton John) moved into pop with 1967 UK chart-topper **Let The Heartaches Begin**. Sports anthem **Mexico** marked by big, full voice.

BANANARAMA – UK all-girl trio paired with Fun Boy Three for 1982 hit **Really Saying Something**. Hit chart several times more in 80s with **Shy Boy** and **Guilty**.

BARCLAY JAMES HARVEST – Manchester-based British cult band with critically acclaimed albums for EMI's Harvest label and Polydor.

BOBBY BARE – First hit, **The All-American Boy**, a parody on Elvis Presley, made US No. 2 in 1958 but label credit went to his friend Bill Parsons. Subsequently became major pop/country artist with classic **Detroit City** and **500 Miles Away From Home**, plus brilliant reading of **Me And Bobby McGee**.

LEN BARRY – Had big hit as member of Dovells with **Bristol Stomp** (1961), then became successful blue-eyed soul singer on own with Philadelphia classics **1-2-3** and **Cry Like A Baby**.

SHIRLEY BASSEY – Welsh-born daughter of West Indian seaman. Made UK charts with cover of Harry Belafonte's **Banana Boat Song**. After two-year chart hiatus, London Palladium appearances helped establish her as major recording, concert and cabaret star with torch-ballad successes **As Long As He Needs Me, You'll Never Know, What Now My Love** and **I (Who Have Nothing)**.

BAUHAUS – Post-punk British outfit, pioneers of gothic rock who achieved cult following in early 80s.

BAY CITY ROLLERS – 70s manufactured phenomenon, this Scottish band were never out of the UK singles chart for nearly seven years, and even topped US listings with **Saturday Night** in 1975.

BEASTIE BOYS – Over-hyped US punk crew whose re-hashed Sex Pistols-styled antics in late 80s were a decade too late. Scored with three UK Top 20 singles, of which **Fight For Your Right To Party** (1987) also made US listings. Topped US chart with debut LP **Licensed To Kill** in 1987.

THE BEAT – Enterprising UK group whose quirky lyrics endeared UK fans. Upon demise, band spawned Fine Young Cannibals and General Public.

THE BEAU BRUMMELS – Launched as 'America's answer to the British invasion', their soft-rock approach paved way for The Byrds, Turtles and others with 1965 hits **Laugh Laugh** and **Just A Little**.

FREDDIE BELL AND THE BELLBOYS – Pioneer rock 'n' rollers who appeared with Bill Haley in 1955 *Rock Around The Clock* movie and were first US rockers to visit UK, touring with Tommy Steele in 1956.

MAGGIE BELL – Blues and soul-laced Scottish singer. Fronted admirable Stone The Crows which featured Les Harvey on lead guitar. After band split, following Harvey's death from electrocution on-stage at Swansea, she released superb if uncommercial solo albums.

BELLESTARS – Seven-piece all-girl group evolved from Bodysnatchers who make funky, brassy dance music. Early hit singles were covers **Iko Iko** and **The Clapping Song**. **Sign Of The Times** (1983) indicated some originality. 1986 line-up was reduced to trio.

BROOK BENTON – Gospel-rooted black rock 'n' roll balladeer. With Belford Hendricks and producer Clyde Otis he co-wrote his first three big hits, **It's Just A Matter Of Time, Endlessly** and **Thank You Pretty Baby**, in 1959. Consistently in charts with million-selling duets **Baby (You've Got What It Takes)** and **Rockin' Good Way** (with Dinah Washington) until 1963. Bounced back in 1970 with classic rendition of Tony Joe White's **Rainy Night In Georgia**.

BIG AUDIO DYNAMITE – Quintet formed by Mick Jones following his departure from The Clash in 1984. Enjoyed critical acclaim until Jones was struck down by pneumonia in 1989, although guitarist/vocalist recovered sufficiently to re-group the following year; comeback LP **The Globe** was released in 1991.

BIG BOPPER – One-hit wonder J. P. Richardson, alias The Big Bopper, was top Texan DJ during the late 1950s. Scored worldwide with rock 'n' roll novelty **Chantilly Lace** (1958). Had minor success with follow-up **The Big Bopper's Wedding**, but died February 3, 1959, in air crash (with Buddy Holly and Richie Valens). Also a successful songwriter, he penned Johnny Preston's **Running Bear** hit.

BIG BROTHER AND THE HOLDING COMPANY – The San Francisco-based group which springboarded Janis Joplin to superstardom.

BIG OZZIE BAND – Australian rockers with concern over ecology in the 80s. Single **Midnight Oil** placed them in the spotlight.

ELVIN BISHOP – Emerged from Paul Butterfield Blues Band to form own highly respected funky rock band highlighting his delicious guitar style and solid vocals.

BILL BLACK – American stand-up bassist featured on Elvis Presley's early Sun recordings. Moving to electric bass, formed Bill Black Combo in 1959 and enjoyed six US Top 20 hits. After his death in 1965, the Combo continued with Willie Mitchell replacing Black.

CILLA BLACK – Friend and close associate of The Beatles, launched to stardom by Brian Epstein with covers of US soul hits, then veered towards MOR via cabaret and regular TV shows.

BLACK CROWES – This HM crew from Georgia earned instant notoriety when 1990 debut LP **Shake Your Money Maker** topped US charts. Original? Hardly. Enthusiastic? You Bet!

BLACK OAK ARKANSAS – Raunchy Southern US boogie band. Group earned gold in 1974 for **High On The Hog** album.

BLANCMANGE – UK duo Neil Arthur and Stephen Luscombe make lighthearted pop in style of biggest hit **Living On The Ceiling**. Check out 1982 single **God's Kitchen/I've Seen The World**.

BOBBY BLAND – Classic blues vocalist, whose smooth styling has kept him continually in the public eye over a 30-year career.

THE BLASTERS – Los Angeles-based outfit formed by brothers Phil and Dave Alvin who have been on verge of mega-success since early punk-styled albums.

BLIND FAITH – Archetypal 'supergroup' formed in 1969 featuring Eric Clapton, Steve Winwood, Ginger Baker and Rick Grech. London Hyde Park concert which attracted 100,000 was highlight of this short-lived venture.

BLOOD SWEAT AND TEARS – Bombastic but innovative brass-rock aggregation from late 60s who survived a decade on the back of million-selling singles **You've Made Me So Very Happy**, **Spinning Wheel** and **And When I Die**.

MIKE BLOOMFIELD – American Blues guitarist whose greatest success came from partnership with Al Kooper. Unfulfilled talent who died in 1981.

BLUES PROJECT – New York white blues band formed by Danny Kalb and featuring Al Kooper and Steve Katz (who went on to create Blood Sweat And Tears). Influence far exceeded their record sales.

COLIN BLUNSTONE – Classy British singer/songwriter remembered as lead singer of Zombies and for 1971 solo hit **Say You Don't Mind**.

GRAHAM BOND – Early days as modern jazz alto-sax player led him into British R&B boom of early 60s. Switching to organ, he replaced the deceased Cyril Davies in Blues Incorporated before forming own group which included Ginger Baker, Jack Bruce, and John McLaughlin. After demise of Graham Bond Organization he was involved in several bands, including Ginger Baker's Airforce before falling to death under London Underground train in 1974.

GARY 'US' BONDS – Influential R&B shouter whose soul anthems **New Orleans** and **Quarter To Three** launched a zillion dance bands. Enjoyed mini-revival with **Dedication** LP in 1981 under aegis of Bruce Springsteen and Miami Steve Van Zandt.

BONEY M – West Indian vocal/instrumental group with several semi-religious UK pop hits, including **Daddy Cool**, **Sunny**, **Ma Baker**, **Rivers of Babylon/Brown Girl In The Ring** (a No. 1), **Rasputin**, **Mary's Boy Child** (also a No. 1) and **Hooray! Hooray! It's A Holi Holiday** in the late 70s.

BONZO DOG (DOODAH) BAND – British rock band with penchant for humorous material, led by Viv Stanshall, Neil Innes and Roger Ruskin Spear. Had outrageously funny stage act and UK Top 45 single with **The Urban Spaceman** in 1968.

BOOKER T AND THE MG'S – Influential Memphis-based quartet featuring the best of the Stax session men Booker T. Jones (organ), Steve Cropper (guitar), Duck Dunn (bass) and Al Jackson Jr (drums). Their classic instrumental **Green Onions** became a firm dance favourite.

PAT BOONE – Next to Elvis, the most successful US singer of the rock 'n' roll era (though his music was somewhat right of MOR and relied on clean-cut all-American image). Raised in Nashville and married to daughter of country star Red Foley; came to prominence with bland cover versions of black rock 'n' roll hits by Fats Domino (**Ain't That A Shame**) and Little Richard (**Tutti Frutti**, **Long Tall Sally**). Then switched to romantic ballads with **Love Letters In The Sand**, **April Love** and others. Had 24 Top 20 hits of which novelty item **Speedy Gonzales** was best credential for his inclusion in a rock book. Daughter Debbie had major hit in 1977 with **You Light Up My Life**.

Above: David Gates, lead singer of Bread, solo artist and songwriter.

BOSTON – American East Coast band led by Tom Scholz who revelled in two bites of cherry. In 1976, self-titled mega-album provided two multi-million-selling singles (including **More Than A Feeling**) and in 1987 re-formed unit scored with **Third Stage** set.

BOW WOW WOW – One of Malcom McLaren's rare failures, this effete quartet led by vocalist Annabella Lwin nonetheless made UK charts in 1982 with **Go Wild In The Country** and **I Want Candy**.

THE BOX TOPS – Super Memphis-based soul band. Topped charts in 1967 with **The Letter**. As much a vehicle for songwriting/arranging/producing talents of Dan Penn, Spooner Oldham and Chips Moman as for Alex Chilton's distinctively husky lead vocals.

BOYZ II MEN – Motown's hope for the 90s, arguably a latter-day Jackson 5. This teenage quartet (from Philadelphia School of Music) scored in US during 1991 with **It's Hard To Say Goodbye** 45 and **CooleyHighHarmony** LP.

PAUL BRADY – Former member of traditional groups Planxty and The Johnstons, this Irish singer/songwriter turned to rock mainstream in early 80s, although has not quite achieved deserved success to date.

BREAD – Sugary American pop outfit led by David Gates whose ear for a weepy ballad kept group in charts for most of the 70s.

BRINSLEY SCHWARZ – Launched with biggest PR hype of all-time (a complete jet-load of UK journalists being flown out to see them perform at New York's Filmore East; backlash worked against them). Despite some fine mixtures of blues-rock and soft-rock harmonies they could not fight way into major league and broke up in 1975.

DAVID BROMBERG – American guitarist, also dobro player (though inferior vocalist), who has worked with Bob Dylan, Willie Nelson, Gordon Lightfoot, Rick Derringer, and Sha Na Na among others. Large selection of solo LPs recorded for Columbia and Fantasy (from 1971-77) feature many live recordings.

ELKIE BROOKS – Superior smokey-voiced songstress. Emerged from Da Da and Vinegar Joe to become major solo concert attraction and notch massive-selling albums, notably **Pearl**.

ARTHUR BROWN – Zany UK rock personality who scored with powerful **Fire** (1968). The Crazy World Of Arthur Brown was staggering in-concert spectacle but was never properly captured on disc.

BOBBY BROWN – Solid American soul performer whose career has stuttered somewhat since heady days with New Edition group and scintillating 1988 LP **Don't Be Cruel**, which included mega-selling **My Prerogative** hit single.

JACK BRUCE – Former Cream bassist/vocalist whose career began promisingly with **Songs For A Tailor** LP. Unfortunately later work was less successful.

FELICE AND BOUDLEAUX BRYANT – Nashville-based composers who wrote **Bye Bye Love**, **Wake Up Little Suzie**, **Bird Dog** and other hits for Everly Brothers. Also wrote **Raining In My Heart** for Buddy Holly and **Let's Think About Living** for Bob Luman. Recorded own albums in the 60s.

TIM BUCKLEY – One of rock's great 'might have beens' this Washington folkie turned rocker scored heavily with 1972 LP **Greetings From LA**. Died from drug overdose in 1975.

BUCKS FIZZ – 1981 Eurovision winners with **Making Your Mind Up**. Highly produced pop in Abba mould did well with hits such as **The Land Of Make Believe** and **My Camera Never Lies** (both No. 1s).

BUFFALO SPRINGFIELD – Pioneer San Franciscan band from 60s featuring Stephen Stills, Neil Young, Richie Furay and later Jim Messina. Melodic style enjoyed one US hit **For What It's Worth** (1967).

DORSEY BURNETTE – Bass player in brother Johnny's famed rock 'n' roll trio. Had own hits with big ballads **Tall Oak Tree** and **Big Rock Candy Mountain**. Also wrote hits for Jerry Lee Lewis and Ricky Nelson.

JOHNNY BURNETTE – US rocker whose **Dreamin'** and **You're Sixteen** have stood the test of time. Died in a boating accident in 1964.

JAMES BURTON – Sought after guitar sessioneer who came to public attention as Presley sideman in 70s and as a member of Emmylou Harris's Hot Band. Also worked with Ricky Nelson Group in 50s and 60s.

Below: Hairway To Steven, The Butthole Surfers. Courtesy Touch And Go Records.

PRINCE BUSTER – King of bluebeat, who influenced generation of British bands like UB40 and The Specials.

PAUL BUTTERFIELD – With the Blues Band, became major concert attraction in 60s and 70s before HM scene overwhelmed him. This talented vocalist and harmonica player surrounded himself with ace musicians, such as Mike Bloomfield, Elvin Bishop and David Sanbourne. Died of drug-related causes in 1987.

BUTTHOLE SURFERS – New generation punk band who stole show on Lollapalooza tour (with Siouxsie And Banshees and Ice-T among others) in US during 1991. Rude and irreverent, as witnessed by LP **Piouhgd** (Rough Trade), 1991.

JERRY BYRNE – White New Orleans rock 'n' roller. Cut 1958 pounding classic **Lights Out** with producer Harold Battiste.

C

C&C MUSIC FACTORY – Recipients of 1992 Dance Grammy, the Factory made big noises with Columbia debut LP **Gonna Make You Sweat** in 1991.

J.J. CALE – Enigmatic modern country performer who threatened to turn the world on its ear in early 70s with barrage of tastefully laid back material, of which **After Midnight** is now a classic.

JOHN CALE – Founder of Velvet Undergound, later rock/theatrical experimentalist.

GLEN CAMPBELL – Former session guitarist whose smooth vocals enhanced Jim Webb's classic work **By The Time I Get To Phoenix** and **Wichita Lineman**. Became cabaret favourite and television performer.

CANNED HEAT – Pioneering US blues band who scored in US/UK singles charts with **On The Road Again** (1968). Founder members Al Wilson and Bob Hite both died of heart attacks.

Above: Naturally, J.J. Cale. Courtesy Shelter Records.

FREDDIE CANNON – Boston native brought to fame via Philadelphia-based Swan Records and *American Bandstand* TV show. 18 hits in a row – notably hard-rocking **Tallahassie Lassie** and **Way Down Yonder In New Orleans**. **Palisades Park** made him major star of tail-end of rock 'n' roll's golden 50s.

CARAVAN – Long-established Canterbury-based outfit formed around guitarist Pye Hastings and keyboard-player Dave Sinclair. Popular concert act during 70s, who never made impact on charts despite excellent albums, particularly **If I Could Do It All Over Again I'd Do It All Over You**.

ERIC CARMEN – Former Raspberry who hit US No. 2 with **All By Myself** in 1976.

CARLENE CARTER – Talented country rock singer, daughter of country star June Carter and wife of Nick Lowe. Paul Carrack played keyboards in her excellent backing band.

JOHNNY CASH – The 'man in black' whose straight-down-the-line approach to country music has endeared him to audiences since the mid-50s.

DAVID CASSIDY – Star of popular 70s TV series *The Partridge Family*. Became massive hero of teeny-bopper audiences before being ousted by Donny Osmond and Michael Jackson.

CATE BROS – Ernie (keyboards) and Earl (guitar) Cate received acclaim in late 70s as powerful live act. Record sales proved sporadic, despite excellent Steve Cropper-produced albums.

NICK CAVE – Ghoulish Australian singer/songwriter and most recently novelist, who has featured in notorious bands Birthday Party and Bad Seeds. Also exceedingly scrawny.

THE CHAMPS – Highly rated US instrumental combo who topped charts with debut hit **Tequila** (1958). Their raunchy singles are now prized collectors' items. Latter-day members Jimmy Seals and Dash Crofts went on to further success as Seals And Crofts duo.

BRUCE CHANNEL – R&B-flavoured rocker. **Hey Baby** made US No. 1 in 1962. Went on to tour UK with Beatles in same year. Fluid harmonica playing set Channel apart from dozens of contemporaries.

CHEAP TRICK – Innovative American quartet led by guitarist Rick Nielsen who had solitary US chart hit with **I Want You To Want Me** in 1979, and consistent run of LPs.

NENEH CHERRY – Daughter of jazz/R&B trumpeter Don Cherry, Neneh's obdurate attitude in choice of material has, to date, precluded superstardom, although **Buffalo Stance** made UK charts in 1988.

CHIC – Archetypal late 1970s disco outfit formed by Nile Rodgers and Bernard Edwards whose **Le Freak** and **Good Times** both made US No 1. Rumoured to re-form in early 1992.

THE CHIPMUNKS – Studio creation (sounding like a 33 RPM record on 45 speed) of David Seville. The perky **Chipmunk Song** sold three and a half million copies, proving that either poor taste was alive and well in 1958 or that a lot of children talked parents into buying it.

JIMMY CLANTON – White New Orleans kid who scored initially with black-sounding R&B ballad **Just A Dream**; then promoted as all-American boy-next-door with million-selling **Venus In Blue Jeans** (1962).

STANLEY CLARKE – Dextrous American bass player who ventured into heavy funk after establishing himself in jazz field. Work best personified by collaboration with keyboard player George Duke as Clarke/Duke project.

CLASSICS IV – Backing band on hits for Billy Joe Royal and The Tams, they scored in 1967 with ballady **Spooky**. Guitarist James Cobb and group's arranger/producer Buddy Buie went on to join the Atlanta Rhythm Section.

JIMMY CLIFF – Ace Jamaican reggae star who peaked with **The Harder They Come** and movie album in 1972. Also well-known for **You Can Get It If You Really Want**. Maintains a high profile in West Indies and occasionally supports major acts.

BILLY COBHAM – Prolific jazz-rock drummer who has worked with everyone from Miles Davis to James Brown. Stream of competent albums kept Cobham in the forefront of instrumentalists, and his reputation ensured 'sell-out' notices for his drum clinics.

THE COCTEAU TWINS – Scottish trio comprising Elisabeth Fraser, Robin Guthrie and Simon Raymonde. Stubborn resolve to remain as indie output precluded national chart success until **Treasure** LP in 1984, and subsequent albums also consolidated success.

LEONARD COHEN – Purveyor of lugubrious bedsit ballads but nonetheless a great influence on many 70s singers and songwriters. Best remembered for **Suzanne** and **Hey, That's No Way To Say Goodbye**, although more recent songs, such as **First We Take Manhatten**, were covered successfully by other artists.

JUDY COLLINS – Highly respected folkie who established huge following in the 60s with melodic albums for Elektra Records. Best known for version of **Amazing Grace**, a 1970 Top 20 hit on both sides of the Atlantic.

PERRY COMO – 'King of the crooners' with 50s hits like **Tina Marie**, **Magic Moments** and **Catch A Falling Star**. His top-rated TV show provided admirable showcase for many emergent R&B and rock acts as well as influencing teen fashion trends.

HARRY CONNICK, JR – Relaxed New Orleans crooner who can turn his hand to a myriad of vocal styles. Also adept pianist and promising actor; appeared in *Memphis Belle* and *Little Man Tate*.

RITA COOLIDGE – Vocalist from Tennessee who was discovered while working with Delaney And Bonnie. Laid-back vocal style was fashionable in late 70s when she enjoyed her greatest single success. Once married to Kris Kristofferson.

JULIAN COPE – Perennial fringe rocker who has tried everything from punk to psychedelia; front-man for Teardrop Explodes (1978-84). Scored UK Top 20 with **World Shut Your Mouth** 45 in 1987, but enjoyed greatest critical success upon release of **Peggy Suicide** double album in 1991.

COWBOY JUNKIES – Low-key country-styled Canadian quartet led by pleasing vocalist Margo Timmins. Signed to RCA records in 1989, for which company they've cut a quartet of albums, latterly the excellent **Black-Eyed Boy** (1992).

THE COWSILLS – Pop-harmony family group earned gold discs for **The Rain, The Park And Other Things** (1967), and **Hair** (1969).

FLOYD CRAMER – Top session pianist at RCA's Nashville Studios. Backed hits by Elvis Presley, Chet Atkins, Jim Reeves and others, and enjoyed million-seller in own right with atmospheric **Last Date** (1960).

CRAMPS – Dated, turgid, but also occasionally and maniacally funny post-apocalyptic purveyors of rockabilly signed to Big Beat, for whom 1991 set **Look Mom No Head** was typical amalgam of nausea and divine joy.

BEVERLEY CRAVEN – UK singer/songwriter/pianist whose plaintive warbling re-introduced 60s-styled love ballads to the charts in 1990.

CRAZY HORSE – Former Neil Young back-up band, whose heyday was before death of guitarist/vocalist Danny Whitton in 1974. Re-formed units met less success despite quality work.

THE CREATION – UK mod/pop group in Who mould; Shel Talmy produced their minor hits in 1966. Now mostly of interest to 60s collectors of music of the genre.

MARSHALL CRENSHAW – Solid American vocalist/guitarist whose contract with Warner Bros has produced decent albums, particularly self-titled debut offering from 1982.

Below: Crusaders' reed man (and bass player), Wilton Felder.

THE CRICKETS – With guitarist/singer Sonny Curtis and drummer Jerry Allison (the constant core of a changing line-up), The Crickets started out as Buddy Holly's backing group, splitting from him shortly before his death. In 1962 they toured and recorded with Bobby Vee, enjoying two UK hits. After break-up, Curtis and Allison played on Eric Clapton's 1970s solo albums, following which Crickets were re-formed.

JIM CROCE – Croce was killed in an air crash in 1973 at the height of his career, and this laid-back singer/songwriter was surely destined to add to his collection of chart albums and singles, of which **Time In A Bottle** is a classic.

Above: Sonic Temple, The Cult. Courtesy Beggar's Banquet Records.

CHRISTOPHER CROSS – Rotund US vocalist/guitarist who exploded onto the rock scene with his sensational self-titled debut album in 1980. Has threatened to re-affirm this success, but the effort has not yet been forthcoming.

CRUSADERS – Crack jazz/funk aggregation featuring Wilton Felder and Joe Sample, which has, at various stages of line-up, included Wayne Henderson, Larry Carlton and long-time drummer Stix Hooper. Scored with guest singers on singles **Street Life** (Randy Crawford) and **Soul Shadows** (Bill Withers).

THE CULT – British hard-rockers formed in early 1980s. Sporadic output has stifled success, but they enjoy critical acclaim and loyal following. 1989 set **Sonic Temple** is band's tour-de-force to date.

CURLY LEADS AND SWITCHES – Legendary R&B outfit who produced classic **Plug Me In** album in early 60s. Curly (real name Maximillian De Frost) was grandson of French Ambassador to US who joined with local black musicians after moving to Louisiana. Now noted chef in French quarter of New Orleans, but still playing part-time.

KING CURTIS – Wonderful R&B tenor sax player who fronted own band, as well as playing for Buddy Holly, Coasters, Donny Hathaway, and Aretha Franklin. 1971 classic album **Live At The Fillmore West** proved testament to career that was cut tragically short when he was stabbed to death in New York the same year.

D

CHARLIE DANIELS BAND – Hard working country-rock unit led by wily vocalist/violinist/guitarist Daniels. Had major chart success in 1979 with **The Devil Went Down To Georgia**.

DANNY AND THE JUNIORS – Group of Italian Americans from Philadelphia whose **At The Hop** (1957) remains one of the all-time great rock 'n' roll waxings.

BOBBY DARIN – Influential 50s rocker cum crooner whose divided loyalties restricted success. Nonetheless left legacy of classic material including **Mack The Knife**, **Things**, **Splish Splash** and **Multiplication** following death from heart attack in 1973.

JAMES DARREN – Philadelphia contemporary of Frankie Avalon, Steve Alaimo and Fabian. His corny but catchy **Goodbye Cruel World** made him a star in 1961.

DARTS – London-based doo-wop revivalists who charted a dozen times in UK between 1977 and 1980, including a trio of No. 2s: **Come Back My Love**, **Boy From New York City** and **It's Raining**, in 1978.

BILLIE DAVIS – Teamed with Mike Sarne for novelty item **Will I What?**, then charted as solo in 1963 with **Tell Him** before linking up with ex-Shadows' bass player Jet Harris for long and traumatic relationship. In 1967 cut classic soulful version of **Angel Of The Morning**.

SPENCER DAVIS GROUP – Popular UK outfit best remembered as Stevie Winwood's first band. Had single success on both sides of the Atlantic, with **Gimme Some Lovin'** making both US and UK Top 10.

DE LA SOUL – New York funk/rap trio signed to East Coast-based Tommy Boy Records. First two LPs **3 Feet High And Rising** and **De La Soul Is Dead** enjoyed cross-over success.

JACKIE DE SHANNON – Enormously talented and underrated Californian singer/songwriter prolifically recorded by Liberty. **Needles And Pins** was major hit for British group The Searchers.

DEAD KENNEDYS – Bad taste US quartet formed in late 70s. Founded Alternative Tentacles label to avoid compromise over controversial lyrics. After period of inactivity, band resurfaced in late 80s, but with little distillation of demented attitude.

JOEY DEE AND THE STARLIGHTERS – Resident band at the Peppermint Lounge in New York, their **Peppermint Twist** rode the dance craze wave in 1961. Felix Cavaliere, Eddie Brigati and Gene Cornish were in group in 1963 before moving on to form Young Rascals.

KIKI DEE – Powerful English vocalist who has never attained deserved recognition. Biggest chart record **Don't Go Breaking My Heart** (1976) cut with Elton John, but **Amoreuse** remains her classic track. Once signed to Motown.

DESMOND DEKKER – Pioneering reggae performer from Kingston, Jamaica, who introduced British audiences to joy of this indigenous West Indian music. Topped UK charts in 1969 with **The Israelites** following earlier success of **007 (Shanty Town)**.

DELANEY AND BONNIE – Soul duo whose superlative bands feaured, at various times, Eric Clapton, Leon Russell, Rita Coolidge, Duane Allman, Jim Keltner and Bobby Whitlock, and made waves in early 70s.

CATHY DENNIS – Red-haired, green-eyed English dance vocalist who enjoyed surprising US chart success with collection of singles from **Move To This** LP in 1991, after stint with Norwich-based D-Mob. Nominated for 1992 BRIT Newcomer award.

JOHN DENVER – Twee but sincere American balladeer whose country-tinged opuses dominated US charts during 1970s. **Annie's Song** (1974) made No. 1 in both US and UK.

AL DI MEOLA – Outrageously talented guitarist who has flirted with a variety of music. His jazz-rock work is best personified by his association with Paco De Lucia and John McLaughlin.

DINOSAUR JR – Cult US indie band formed in 1985 whose 1991 deal with Sire records spawned **Green Mind**, an errant collection of adolescent warbling penned by guitarist/vocalist J. Mascis.

WILLIE DIXON – Long-time producer and composer at Chess Studios where he nurtured major talent. A workman-like double bass player, he has released many quality blues albums. Best known composing credits include **I'm A Man**, **Hootchie Kootchie Man** and **Wang Dang Doodle**.

DR FEELGOOD – Underrated English rock band who have soldiered on entertaining audiences for nearly 20 years with their brand of homegrown R&B. Made UK Top 10 in 1979 with **Milk And Alcohol**.

DR JOHN – The good doctor (Mac Rebennack) is a stalwart of the New Orleans music scene and in-demand session pianist. Enjoyed short tenure in early 70s as headliner in own right.

THOMAS DOLBY – UK vocalist electro-pop wizard with mad-scientist looks to match. First UK hit was **Windpower**. Actually broke in the US first with **She Blinded Me With Science** (1982) accompanied by fantastic video featuring Magnus Pyke.

DOLLAR – UK duo with several hits from 1978-1982, most notably **Love's Got A Hold On Me**, **Mirror Mirror** and **Give Me Back My Heart**.

Below: Malpractice, Dr Feelgood. Courtesy United Artists Records.

JASON DONOVAN – Aussie actor/popstar and teen idol 'discovered' on *Neighbours* TV soap. Starred in London production of *Joseph And His Amazing Technicolor Dreamcoat* in 1991.

THE DOVELLS – Blue-eyed soul group from Philadelphia with penchant for dance craze discs, which earned them eight hits in four years. Lead singer Len Barry went on to solo fame.

LES DUDEK – Talented US guitarist/producer who has been involved with various projects throughout 70s and 80s. Has cut several solo albums, as well as recording with Allman Bros, Steve Miller. Had own Dudek, Finnegan, Krueger Band before joining Cher for **Black Rose** LP and group of same name.

SLY DUNBAR AND ROBBIE SHAKESPEARE – Leading Jamaican reggae sidemen (drums and bass respectively) who have featured on a host of hit singles as well as cutting own albums.

JOHNNY DUNCAN – Tennessee-born country singer/guitarist. Settled in UK on discharge from army. Replaced Lonnie Donnegan as resident skiffle singer in Chris Barber's band, then formed own Blue Grass Boys making UK No. 2 with **Last Train To San Fernando** single (1957).

E

STEVE EARLE – Hard-edged country performer born in Virginia who found success with MCA records after lacklustre stint with Epic. Live 1991 set **Shake Up And Die Like An Aviator** threatened to break artist (and band, The Dukes) in pop charts.

THE EASYBEATS – Formed in Australia where they had four chart-toppers in quick succession. Went to Britain in 1966 and cut worldwide hit **Friday On My Mind**. After lesser hits, group broke up in 1969.

ECHO AND THE BUNNYMEN – Liverpool-based pop unit who have hovered on fringes of international stardom since 1982.

RANDY EDELMAN – US singer/songwriter, and excellent piano player, particularly popular in UK. Charted in UK during 1976 with re-make of **Concrete And Clay** and **Uptown Uptempo Woman**.

ELECTRIC FLAG – Rock/soul supergroup bringing together guitar wizard Mike Bloomfield, Nick 'The Greek' Gravenites and black drummer Buddy Miles, plus brass. Hard-hitting sound wowed audience at 1967 Monterey Pop Festival but albums disappointed.

RAMBLING JACK ELLIOTT – Itinerant American folk singer/songwriter. Companion to Woody Guthrie while in teens and major influence on Bob Dylan.

EMF – English baggy outfit (in mould of Stone Roses and Inspiral Carpets) from West Country whose debut single **Unbelievable** for EMI made UK No. 3, and later topped US charts. Latterly, quartet consolidated US success with major tour in 1992.

BRIAN ENO – Former Roxy Music alumnus who has built reputation as synth innovator and experimental video artist.

THE EQUALS – UK pop-soul band. Topped chart with **Baby Come Back** (1968); had further hits with **Viva Bobby Joe** and **Black Skin Blue-Eyed Boys**.

F

FABIAN – Glamour boy from the 50s who stuck around in TV movies and revival shows. Real name Fabiano Forte.

FABULOUS THUNDERBIRDS – Old-fashioned R&B belters led by guitarist Jimmy Vaughan, brother of late blues player Stevie Ray. Made US Top 10 in 1987 with **Hot Number** set, but have since suffered from personnel moves (including loss of Vaughan).

MARIANNE FAITHFULL – Ex-convent schoolgirl most remembered for notorious liaison with Mick Jagger. The Jagger-Richard song **As Tears Go By** was her best and biggest record.

GEORGIE FAME – Sprang to prominence with his band Blue Flames during UK 'blues boom' of the 60s. Later switched to lightweight pop material, which established career longevity. Career highs for this talented vocalist/keyboard player were concert performances with Count Basie and Harry South big bands.

CHARLIE FEATHERS – Influential Mississippi rockabilly singer/guitarist. Never a hitmaker but a cult figure during 70s.

JOSE FELICIANO – Multi-talented performer whose brilliant re-working of Doors **Light My Fire** should have

Above: Schubert Dip, EMF. Courtesy Parlophone Records.

meant eternal superstardom. However, all-encompassing musical outlook has limited chart success.

FISHBONE – Yes! With Living Colour, the positive future of American rock 'n' roll. **The Reality Of My Surroundings** LP (1991) is an amalgam of rap, zap and snap, with a spadeful of high-powered R&B thrown in for good measure.

THE FIXX – UK group who got exposure in the US with melancholy hit **Stand Or Fall** (1982).

ROBERTA FLACK – US vocalist/pianist whose career was established by classic ballad **The First Time Ever I Saw Your Face**. Also enjoyed chart success with Donnie Hathaway.

FLAMIN' GROOVIES – San Franciscan favourites of Continental audiences having built cult following for their purist approach to rock 'n' roll in 50s/Beatles' mould.

FLASH AND THE PAN – Australian group formed from remnants of Easybeats. Unusual sound is readily identifiable by nasal vocals that sound as if singer is locked in a box. Re-entered US/UK chart scene with **Waiting For A Train** (1983).

FLOCK OF SEAGULLS – Melodic Liverpool band who flirted with charts in early 80s, and also saw gold album success in USA with **Listen** (1983).

FLYING BURRITO BROS – Seminal outfit who introduced country music to the 'drop-out' generation. Members included the late Graham Parsons, Chris Hillman, Sneaky Pete Kleinow, Bernie Leadon and Michael Clark.

FOCUS – First Dutch band to become rock superstars thanks to distinctive blend of rock, modern jazz and the classics. **Sylvia** and **Hocus Pocus** both scored in 1973. Thijs van Leer (keyboards, flute) and Jan Akkerman (guitar) had some solo success.

DAN FOGELBERG – American singer/songwriter on the fringes of the first division who became a US chart regular following **Same Old Lang Syne** in 1981.

FOGHAT – US/UK aggregation formed by ex-patriot Brits, Tony Stevens, Dave Peverett and Roger Earl (all ex-Savoy Brown), in 1972. Group enjoyed album/concert success in US during 70s while being totally ignored in Britain.

WAYNE FONTANA – Leader of Mindbenders. Hit UK No. 2 with cover of Major Lance's **Um Um Um Um Um Um**, then went to No. 1 in US and No. 2 in UK with **Game Of Love** (1965). Had solo success after group broke up in 1966.

TENNESSEE ERNIE FORD – Seminal rockabilly performer, who dominated C&W charts during 50s and 60s, as well as scoring pop success, most notably with **Sixteen Tons** in 1955.

THE FORTUNES – Birmingham, England group that cut Coca Cola's familiar theme **It's The Real Thing**, as well as the pirate radio theme **Caroline**. Scored big US/UK hits with **You've Got Your Troubles**, **Here It Comes Again** and **This Golden Ring**, thanks to their classy harmonies.

THE FOUR PREPS – Barber-shop harmonies won them late 50s hits and made them major influence on nascent Beach Boys.

FOURMOST – Early 60s UK pop/Mersey group, produced by Brian Epstein, who scored with hits **Hello Little Girl** and **A Little Loving**.

KIM FOWLEY – Important figure of Los Angeles 'garage rock' scene. Wrote and produced for Jayhawks, B. Bumble And The Stingers, Hollywood Argyles, Rivingtons, and Paul Revere And The Raiders. Worked in England throughout 1965, producing Rockin' Berries, P.J. Proby, Cat Stevens, Soft Machine and others. Worked Stateside on first Mothers Of Invention album. Cut run of solo albums besides writing hit songs for Byrds, Emerson, Lake And Palmer, Helen Reddy, and many more.

CONNIE FRANCIS – American pop singer of the late 50s and early 60s who enjoyed five year run of Top 20 action in US and UK. In 1960 achieved three double-sided million sellers: **Mama/Teddy**, **Everybody's Somebody's Fool/Jealous Of You** and **My Heart Has A Heart Of It's Own/Many Tears Ago**. Career more or less halted by rape at knife-point in 1974 and subsequent psychological problems.

FREDDIE AND THE DREAMERS – Lightweight British pop act of 60s. Freddie Garrity's on-stage leapings inspired Chubby Checker record **Do The Freddie**, which group then recorded as their seventh and final hit. Became active on cabaret circuit.

BOBBY FULLER FOUR – Recorded 1966 hits **I Fought The Law** and **Love's Made A Fool Of You**, but Fuller was shot dead within months.

JERRY FULLER – Managed minor hits of his own but famous for writing biggies for Ricky Nelson (including **It's A Young World**) and Gary Puckett And The Union Gap (**Young Girl**).

FUN BOY THREE – London trio formed by ex-members of The Specials; UK chart regulars from 1981 (also teamed with Bananarama) before splitting in 1983.

BILLY FURY – British teen icon who had slew of hit singles in 60s, most notably **Halfway To Paradise** and **Jealousy**. Died of heart attack in 1983.

G

GALLAGHER AND LYLE – Scottish duo whose A&M output included hit singles **I Want To Stay With You** and **Heart On My Sleeve**. Graham Lyle has subsequently provided material for Tina Turner and Art Garfunkel.

GANG OF FOUR – Aggressive English group who were on the verge of national success for some time. Personnel changes and lack of musical direction have certainly stunted growth despite decent LP product.

J. GEILS BAND – Under stewardship of charismatic vocalist Peter Wolf (who later married Faye Dunaway), this Boston outfit (with guitarist J. Geils and harmonica-player Magic Dick) had handful of hits from 1974-82, including **Centerfold** and **Freeze Frame**. Wolf's firing in 1983 led to rapid downfall, although singer has enjoyed modicum of solo success.

DEBBIE GIBSON – US teen sensation who wowed bobbysoxers with stream of innocuous pop fodder in late 80s/early 90s.

DON GIBSON – Legendary country performer/writer who penned **I Can't Stop Loving You**, **Oh Lonesome Me**, **Sweet Dreams**, **Legend In My Time**, etc. Made pop charts in US/UK with **Sea of Heartbreak** in 1961.

MICKEY GILLEY – Cousin of Jerry Lee Lewis and regular entrant in lower reaches of country charts; enjoys cult status thanks to 50s rockabilly cuts.

GIPSY KINGS – French acoustic flamenco band who became darlings of Yuppie set upon release of eponymous debut album in 1988. Led by powerful baritone of Nicolas Reyes, Gipsy Kings quickly attained arena status in early 90s.

GIRLSCHOOL – Female HM quartet who cut handful of LPs for Bronze label in 1980s, most notably **Screaming Blue Murder** (1982). Although toured extensively with Motorhead, group failed to hit big-time.

GO WEST – Talented duo (Peter Cox and Richard Drummie) whose debut single **We Close Our Eyes** (1985) promised the earth. Despite Cox's gutsy vocals on solid material, outfit later meandered into movie work. A waste of talent.

GOLDEN EARRING – Dutch band who've been around for a while, mostly in the background except for big transatlantic hit **Radar Love** (1973 and 1977). Had some US success via MTV with **Twilight Zone** (1982).

GONG – Adventurous French/Australian/English band that included Bill Bruford (ex-Yes) and guitarists Steve Hillage and Allan Holdsworth among its members. Officially split in 1977, but then group re-formed temporarily until 1979.

GRANDMASTER FLASH AND THE FURIOUS FIVE – Pioneering rap sextet led by innovative DJ Flash. **The Message** single 1982 was vanguard for subsequent rap explosion.

AMY GRANT – Canadian-born soulster who enjoyed US chart hit singles with **Baby, Baby** and **That's What Love Is For** in 1991.

DOBIE GRAY – Former soul star (**The In Crowd**) who moved to the country-rock field with varying degrees of success. Cut classic **Drift Away** album (title track made US Top 10) in 1973.

RICK GRECH – French-born bass guitarist; emerged from Family to join short-lived Blind Faith with Eric Clapton. Progressed to Ginger Baker's Airforce, Traffic and Crickets before working with Eric Clapton again in 1973.

THE GROUNDHOGS – Earthy British R&B band (taking name from John Lee Hooker song) led by wizard guitarist Tony McPhee. Produced admirable albums for United Artists.

JAMES GUERICO – Chicago catalyst. Produced **Kind Of A Drag** hit for Buckinghams in 1966. Joined Mothers Of Invention on guitar in 1968. Produced second and biggest-selling Blood, Sweat And Tears album. Masterminded Chicago Transit Authority (Chicago). Set up Caribou studios in Colorado (where Elton John and others recorded). Produced, directed and scored *Elektra Glide In Blue* movie. Became Beach Boys' manager in 1975 and appeared on stage with them.

GUESS WHO – Canadian rockers who spawned Bachman-Turner Overdrive after successful career which included several US singles.

ARLO GUTHRIE – Son of legendary Woody Guthrie and spokesman for the Woodstock generation of the late 60s. Best known work is **Alice's Restaurant**.

WOODY GUTHRIE – The original rambling man who left a legacy of classic songs, such as **This Land Is Your Land**.

Below: Champion fiddler Byron Berlin on stage with country music outfit The Flying Burrito Brothers.

H

MERLE HAGGARD – Staunch right-wing country artist whose compelling **Okie From Muskogee** outraged anti-Vietnam faction in 1970. Has been mainstay of US C&W charts for two decades.

TOM T. HALL – Influential country performer and songwriter with string of superb albums. Wrote Jeannie C. Riley hit, **Harper Valley PTA**.

JOHNNY HALLYDAY – France's answer to Elvis Presley – with a lot of Gene Vincent influence thrown in. Cut countless major American and British hit songs in French and managed to stay at top during two decades, but found little recognition beyond Continent, where he enjoyed superstar status.

JAN HAMMER – Super-talented techno keyboardist from Prague, whose collaborations with Jeff Beck provided outstanding work during 1980s. Scored *Miami Vice* theme which picked up Grammy award in 1986.

ALBERT HAMMOND – London-born, Gibraltar-raised US West Coast stalwart. Hit big in 1972 with **It Never Rains In Southern California**.

JOHN HAMMOND JR – Son of Columbia/CBS's venerated A&R man. Among best – and most esoteric – of white blues singers to emerge in 60s. String of superior albums, including **Triumvirate**, cut in 1973 with Mike Bloomfield and Dr John.

HERBIE HANCOCK – Classically-trained jazz pianist who moved from the uncertain confines of the Miles Davis Group to a dazzling new career in jazz-rock. Has returned to his roots, whilst retaining international audience; composed music for impressive movie *Round Midnight* in 1986.

PAUL HARDCASTLE – Re-mix engineer who sprang to prominence with anti-war disco item **19** in 1985.

HARPERS BIZARRE – Purveyors of lightweight but classy five-part pop harmonies. Scored with Paul Simon's **59th Street Bridge Song (Feeling Groovy)** and remakes of Cole Porter's **Anything Goes** and Glenn Miller's **Chatanooga Choo Choo**. Producer Ted Templeman was outfit's drummer.

EMMYLOU HARRIS – Popular country performer from Alabama whose fixation with roots music has precluded any pop hits. However, illustrious album catalogue (including two superb LPs with Dolly Parton and Linda Ronstadt) are testimony to undoubted talent.

Below: Little Village member John Hiatt, on edge of fame in early 90s.

ALEX HARVEY – Powerful Scottish performer who came close to major international success in the 70s with The Sensational Alex Harvey Band. Died of a heart attack in 1981, a decade after his brother Les was killed onstage with his group Stone The Crows.

MOLLY HATCHET – Originally rock trio, formed by guitarist Dave Hubek, burgeoning line-up coincided with string of successful US albums.

DONNIE HATHAWAY – Cult soul performer whose inspired work was cut short by suicide in 1979. His classic album remains **Live**, although pop fans will remember his teaming with Roberta Flack on singles such as **Where Is The Love** and **The Closer I Get To You**.

LALAH HATHAWAY – Highly-talented daughter of revered soul artist Donnie, whose uncanny resemblance to her father's vocal styling was demonstrated to exquisite effect on self-titled debut LP.

RICHIE HAVENS – Black American troubadour who earned considerable reputation in early 70s for frenetic guitar style and heartfelt vocals.

DALE HAWKINS – Superior Louisiana rockabilly singer who injected heavy R&B flavour into his 1957 masterpeice **Susie Q**.

RONNIE HAWKINS– Canadian rocker whose parties would have made Nero blush. Members of his Hawks backing group later became The Band.

SCREAMING JAY HAWKINS – Theatrical American pianist/vocalist famous for classic **I Put A Spell On You** and coffin-bound stage appearances.

ISAAC HAYES – Shaven-headed soul guru who turned from songwriter to star performer for legendary Memphis-based Stax label. Best remembered for *Shaft* soundtrack.

HEATWAVE – Multi-national soul outfit led by Rod Temperton and Johnny Wilder, who cut seven hit singles from 1977, including **Boogie Nights** and classic R&B ballad **Always And Forever**. Car crash paralysed Wilder in 1979, while Temperton went onto success with Michael Jackson and his **Off The Wall** LP.

HEAVEN 17 – Stylish UK band formed from remains of original Human League (Martyn Ware, Ian Craig Marsh), now based around lead singer Glenn Gregory. Appealing disco-electronic sound and futuristic/socio-ecological lyrics have provided hits (**We Don't Need This) Fascist Groove Thing** and **Temptation**. Debut LP **Penthouse And Pavement** (1981) deserves a listen.

THE HERD – Built by songwriters Ken Howard and Alan Blakeley around teen-appeal good looks of Peter Frampton (billed as 'The Face Of 1968'). After run of hits, Frampton left to form Humble Pie with Steve Marriott, then found subsequent solo success while The Herd fell apart.

JOHN HIATT – Country-styled performer from Indianapolis, once employed in Ry Cooder's band and seemingly on edge of stardom for past decade. Formed own band The Goners in late 80s before pacting with A&M for couple of 'oh, so near' LPs. Recently joined up with Cooder again in Little Village group.

ROBYN HITCHCOCK – English singer/songwriter stuck in 60s time warp. With Egyptians, cut haunting **Perspex Island** LP in 1991, evoking Beatles and Beach Boys.

Below: Too Hot To Handle, Heatwave. Courtesy GTO Records.

HOLLAND/DOZIER/HOLLAND – Brothers Eddie and Brian Holland and Lamont Dozier – legendary Motown songwriters responsible for host of classic material before moving to Invictus/Hot Wax and later HDH labels.

HOOKFOOT – Superior British rock band formed from session men working behind Elton John and others at DJM Records.

BRUCE HORNSBY AND THE RANGE – Revered session pianist Hornsby saw stock rise even further when debut album **The Way It Is** (1987), part-produced by Huey Lewis, sold over a million copies.

JOHNNY HORTON – Country-pop singer best remembered for epic **Battle Of New Orleans**. Died in November 1960 car crash.

HOT CHOCOLATE – Errol Brown-led band who dominated UK charts in 70s and 80s with pleasing soul-tinged dance material including **So You Win Again, You Sexy Thing** and **It Started With A Kiss**.

HP LOVECRAFT – Chicago acid-rock outfit formed in 1966. Hauntingly mystic albums.

HÜSKER DÜ – Minneapolis trio that emerged in 1981 with **Land Speed Record**, an exhilarating hardcore collection. By **New Day Rising** (1985), their finest album, the songs had become more melodic, but still sizzled with emotional intensity and buzzsaw guitars. After three more albums, the Hüskers disbanded in 1987. Their work stands out as a high-water mark of American punk music.

BRIAN HYLAND – Scored at 15 with crass **Itsy Bitsy Teeny Weeny Yellow Polka Dot Bikini**. Friend and protégé of Del Shannon, he redeemed himself with **Sealed With A Kiss** (1972) and Shannon-produced version of Curtis Mayfield-penned **Gypsy Woman** (1970).

I

JANIS IAN – Precocious New Yorker wrote social diatribe **Society's Child** aged 14 and followed it with enchanting teen anthem **At Seventeen** (both US hits). Career foundered during 80s, although sights are now set on serious comeback.

ICE CUBE – LA rapper who dabbles on the edge of racism. Earned billboard Top 10 place with **Death Certificate** LP in 1991.

ICEHOUSE – Australian band formed by guitarist and vocalist Ira Davies in 1978. Enjoyed UK hit in 1983 with **Hey Little Girl**.

FRANK IFIELD – British-born, but raised in Australia. Returned to UK in 1959 to establish himself with falsetto flavour ballads and outbreaks of yodelling. Hit No. 1 with **I Remember You, I'm Confessin', Lovesick** and **Wayward Wind**.

IMPRESSIONS – US soul trio led by Curtis Mayfield, who penned group's classic cuts including **Amen, People Get Ready** and **It's Alright**.

INCREDIBLE STRING BAND – Glasgow, Scotland-based jug band. Flowered into fully fledged folk-rock outfit with well-made hippy-orientated albums.

INNER CIRCLE – Jamaican reggae outfit destined for superstardom until death of founder Jacob Miller. Recorded **Everything Is Great** UK chart hit in 1979.

IRON BUTTERFLY – American rock quintet whose **In-A-Gadda-Da-Vida** album was elephantine accompaniment to all zonked-out early 70s social occasions.

IT'S A BEAUTIFUL DAY – Superior San Franciscan post-psychedelic rock band hinged around violin sound of classically trained leader David La Flamme.

J

TERRY JACKS – Rod McKuen translated **Seasons In The Sun** from the Jacques Brel original for The Beach Boys. They recorded but never released it. Instead a version by Canadian Terry Jacks crashed the charts. Previously he had sold more than four million records in partnership with his wife Susan Pesklevits as The Poppy Family.

JOE JACKSON – Jazz, pop or what? Jackson's diverse and occasionally pretentious offerings have ranged from swing to jump jive and straight-ahead rock. A genuine musical talent who is trying to bite off more than he can choo-choo.

LATOYA JACKSON – Michael's older sister, who has had the hardest time of any member of the famous family in establishing career. Latterly in headlines after marriage to alleged mobster Jack Gordon.

JAMES – Unusually, a Manchester band deemed 'out' of the 'baggie' phase. Having tried a myriad of styles, group seemed to have settled for more mainstream rock approach which threatens superstardom. Signed to Phonogram after unsuccessful tenure with US label Sire and prominent UK indie Factory Records.

THE JAMES GANG – US group which flourished upon recruitment of guitar superstar Joe Walsh. Split in mid-70s, having seen career tumble when Walsh departed to join The Eagles.

RICK JAMES – US vocalist originally signed by Motown as writer/producer. Own career has been overshadowed by artists with whom he has collaborated, including Teena Marie and Eddie Murphy.

TOMMY JAMES AND THE SHONDELLS – Their cover of Raindrop's **Hanky Panky** on local Michigan label Snap remained obscure for two years; it was then picked up for national distribution by Roulette and rocketed to No. 1. Subsequent hits included: **Money Money, Crimson And Clover** and **Crystal Blue Persuasion**.

JANE'S ADDICTION – Post-punk band led by exquisitely tatooed vocalist Henry Rollins. Following two acclaimed albums and success on 1991 US Lollapalooza tour, outfit threatened permanent split.

JAPAN – Effete British quartet who were on fringes of mega-success before band's figurehead David Sylvian left for unsuccessful solo career.

JEAN-MICHEL JARRE – Purveyor of the 'bigger the better' school of music, Jarre's mega-laser concerts have been enjoyed from China to Texas. This French composer and keyboard player also tickled charts in 1977 with **Oxygene** 45.

JAY AND THE AMERICANS – Had 18 US chart entries between 1962 and 1977. Clean-cut all-American image was fostered by ace producer West Farrell.

WAYLON JENNINGS – Modern country all-rounder happiest when recording and touring with close pals Willie Nelson and Tompall Glaser, collectively known as 'The Outlaws'.

JESUS JONES – UK dance band in mould of Happy Mondays and Beautiful South. 1991 LP debut looked like earning international success; cut **Real Real Real** made US Top 10.

JOHNNY AND THE HURRICANES – Formed at high school in Toledo, Ohio, Johnny And The Hurricanes scored with series of rock 'n' roll instrumentals between 1959 and 1961, of which **Red River Rock** remains a favourite.

GEORGE JONES – Acknowledged as one of the finest vocalists in American music, Jones overcame severe drink problem (which cost him his marriage to Tammy Wynette) to re-establish career in country charts.

TOM JONES – Started out as Presley-styled rock 'n' roller. After years in obscurity, discovered by Gordon

Mills who took him to London, changed his name from Thomas J. Woodward and took him to No. 1 with Mills-penned **It's Not Unusual** (1965). Seven weeks at No. 1 the following year, **Green Green Grass Of Home** paved way to Las Vegas, TV spectaculars and superstardom. Although his performances were often over-the-top, at his best Tom Jones could be extremely soulful and commanded wide respect from black American R&B artists.

JUICY LUCY – Blues-based UK band fronted by vocals of former Zoot Money Big Roll Band bass player Paul Williams. Scored with 1970 version of Bo Diddley's **Who Do You Love?**.

BILL JUSTIS – Birmingham, Alabama-born Memphis rock 'n' roll session stalwart. Hooting alto-sax playing earned him 1957 million-seller with **Raunchy**.

Above: Tropical Gangsters, Kid Creole And The Coconuts. Courtesy Island Records.

K

THE KALIN TWINS – A five-week stint at No. 1 in UK with **When** (1958) led to a British tour, but despite success of follow-up **Forget Me Not**, they quickly sank into obscurity.

EDEN KANE – Richard Sarstedt took his stage name from title of Orson Wells' movie *Citizen Kane*. Run of UK hits from 1961-62 included No. 1 **Well I Ask You**. Re-emerged in 70s with brothers Clive and Peter as The Sarstedt Brothers.

KANSAS – US heavy metal outfit whose success was masterminded by Monkees and Archies mentor Don Kirshner. **Point Of No Return** LP represents their very best work.

KC AND SUNSHINE BAND – Good-time US disco outfit led by Harry Casey who were dance favourites throughout 70s. Casey secured songwriting reputation with Grammy for Betty Wright's **Where Is The Love?** in 1975. Resurfaced in 1983 with UK No. 1 **Give It Up**.

JERRY KELLER – Scored with delightful **Here Comes Summer** in 1959. Also wrote 1965 hit **Almost There** for Andy Williams.

NIK KERSHAW – Whatever happened to? Recipient of slew of successful UK singles during 1984-85, UK born pianist/vocalist/composer Kershaw seemed destined for greatness before stalling and subsequently disappearing. Resurfaced briefly as co-writer of Chesney Hawkes' **The One And Only** British hit in 1991.

KID CREOLE AND THE COCONUTS – Brainchild of Haitian-born August Darnell, this happy-go-lucky dance band enjoyed brief liaison with British charts in 1982 before joining concert and cabaret circuit, where irresistible rhythms scored solid following.

JOHNNY KIDD AND THE PIRATES – Image-laden British rockers. Kidd (Frederick Heath) co-penned their 1960 debut hit **Shakin' All Over**, arguably the most authentic rock 'n' roll original ever cut in Britain. Influenced early 60s bands. Johnny Kidd died in 1966, but Pirates continued for a time.

THE KINGSMEN – Place in rock history assured by superlative 1964 re-make of Richard Berry's R&B number **Louie Louie**.

THE KINGSTON TRIO – Folksy pop harmony group. Made No. 1 in 1958 with Civil War movie theme-song **Tom Dooley**.

EARL KLUGH – American virtuoso guitar player, who specializes in smooth jazz-rock on his unique collection of classical guitars.

KNACK– Short-lived LA pop band that never lived up to critics' expectations after 1979 hit **My Sharona**.

BUDDY KNOX – Texan country singer turned rock 'n' roller. Cut his 1957 **Party Doll** and **Hula Love** hits at Norman Petty's studio in Clovis, New Mexico.

AL KOOPER – Seminal US rock producer/musician usually associated with Blood, Sweat And Tears (he featured on and produced their debut LP **Child Is The Father Of Man**). Later worked with Mike Bloomfield and Stephen Stills on classic Super Session LPs.

ALEXIS KORNER – Father figure of British R&B explosion of 60s. Later sang lead with successful studio band CCS. Fronted excellent R&B/blues programme on BBC radio until death in 1984.

LEO KOTTKE – Superb US acoustic guitarist with roots in folk. Giddying release of albums since debut set **Circle Around The Sun** in 1970.

KRAFTWERK – German synthesizer duo who surprisingly made charts on both sides of the Atlantic with **Autobahn** in 1975.

BILLY J. KRAMER AND THE DAKOTAS – Members of Brian Epstein's Merseybeat stable. Six British Top 20 records in two years, included Lennon/McCartney songs **Do You Want To Know A Secret**, **Bad To Me**, **I'll Keep You Satisfied** and **From A Window**.

KRIS KRISTOFFERSON – Texan-born singer and songwriter responsible for monumental youth opus **Me And Bobby McGee** and oft-covered **Help Me Make It Through The Night**. Later reverted to movies with fluctuating success.

KROKUS – Swiss HM outfit led by vocalist Marc Storace and guitarist Fernando Von Arb who competed successfully in the international head-bangers market.

L

THE LA'S – Liverpudlian quartet very much in Beatles' mould. Purveyors of straight-ahead pop music who debuted in 1991 with self-titled album, and then headed for America, with promise of fame and fortune.

RONNIE LANE – Originally half of Small Faces song writing duo with Steve Marriott. Went on to Faces, then quit to work with own back-up band Slim Chance. Scored in 1974 with **How Come** and **The Poacher**. In 1977 recorded mellow **Rough Mix** LP with Pete Townshend.

ALBERT LEE – Highly respected London guitarist who emerged from Chris Farlowe's Thunderbirds and was later member of Poet And The One Man Band and Head Hands And Feet before stint with The Crickets, and role with Emmylou Harris band.

GARY LEWIS AND THE PLAYBOYS – Son of Hollywood comedian Jerry Lewis, Gary and his group had seven breezy US pop hits in just two years in mid-60s.

GORDON LIGHTFOOT – Canadian vocalist/guitarist/pianist/composer whose pleasant interpretation of own material has earned valuable niche in recording industry. International success highlighted by **If You Could Read My Mind** single in 1970, and as part of Bob Dylan's Rolling Thunder Review a year later.

LISA LISA AND CULT JAM – US hip-hopper of Hispanic parentage whose trio is now well established in rap mainstream after quartet of successful albums for CBS. First charted in 1985 with **I Wonder If I Should Take You Home Tonight**, and then topped US lists with **Head To Toe** and **Lost In Emotion** (1987).

LITTLE RIVER BAND – Antipodean sextet whose ear for a melody won hearts of American audiences and permanent place in charts from 1977-82. **The Night Owls** (1981) may yet become a classic.

LL COOL J – 90s rap/hip-hop superstar. MTV regular who picked up fourth platinum album for 1991 set **Mama Said Knock You Out**.

LOGGINS AND MESSINA – American soft-rock duo who enjoyed major success in early 70s. Since split in 1976, Loggins has gone on to score movies as well as notch up several hit singles (**Whenever I Call You Friend**, **I'm Alright**, **Footloose**). Loggins also co-wrote Doobies' classic **What A Fool Believes** with Michael McDonald.

TRINI LOPEZ – A folksy sing-along style with a Latin flavour was the format which took Trini Lopez to success with **If I Had A Hammer**, **La Bamba** and **Lemon Tree** in early to mid-60s.

LOS LOBOS – Mexican-American quintet who began as Top 40 copy band before switching to traditional Tex-Mex sounds. Enjoyed US and UK No. 1 single in 1987 with their rendition of **La Bamba**, featured in biopic (of same title) of pioneering Mexican-American rocker Richie Valens.

Right: Tex-Mex group Los Lobos is best known for its 1987 chart-topper single La Bamba.

LOVERBOY – Canadian rock band formed in late 70s signed to CBS Records, for whom they have cut slew of solid HM material.

LULU – Astute management has kept this bouncy Scottish songstress at the top of the showbiz tree for two decades. Re-issued **Shout** was hit again in 1987, although singer has not depended on chart success since move into theatrical career.

FRANKIE LYMON AND THE TEENAGERS – Young lead singer Frankie Lymon sadly died from heroin overdose after period as child star with 50s group The Teenagers. **Why Do Fools Fall In Love** (1956), **I'm Not A Juvenile Delinquent**, and **Baby Baby** (both 1957) are now classics.

M

CHARLIE McCOY – Superb country-rock harmonica player who has appeared on many of Bob Dylan's records, as well as being member of Nashville sessioneers' group Area Code 615.

THE McCOYS – Covered The Vibrations' **My Girl Sloopy** as **Hang On Sloopy** for 1965 gold disc. Later became back-up band for Johnny Winter. Guitarist Rick Derringer went on to work with Edgar Winter and cut solo album **All American Boy**.

SCOTT McKENZIE – The man who sang the 1967 hippy flower-power love and peace anthem **San Francisco (Be Sure To Wear Some Flowers In Your Hair)**.

JOHN McLAUGHLIN – The guitarist's guitarist, McLaughlin flourished in rock idiom with Mahavishnu Orchestra during 1970s before reverting to mainstream jazz. With fellow finger-flashers Al Di Meola and Paco De Lucia, cut masterful live **Friday Night At San Francisco** in 1981.

RALPH McTELL – Long-established UK folk purveyor whose loyalty to that music has prevented consistent national attention. Made UK charts in 1974 with **Streets Of London**.

HARVEY MANDEL – White Detroit blues-rock guitarist who has recorded prolifically under own name and as member of Canned Heat and John Mayall's Bluesbreakers. Also did session work with Love, The Ventures, Charlie Musselwhite and others.

MANIC STREET PREACHERS – Welsh post-modern power quartet led by ultra-camp guitarist Richey Edwards and singer James Dean Bradfield. Scored indie success with single **Repeat/Love's Sweet Exile** before 'proper' Top 40 entry **Stay Beautiful**, both 1991.

MARKY MARK AND THE FUNKY BUNCH – East Coast rapper, and brother of New Kids On The Block's Donnie Wahlberg. Topped US chart with **Good Vibrations** (from LP **Music For The People**) in 1991.

JOHN MARTYN – British singer/songwriter whose soulful left-field approach kept him at arm's length from major success, despite string of well-crafted albums.

MAZE – Smooth American soul combo led by super-cool vocalist and keyboard player Frank Beverley, whose delivery of classic **Joy And Pain** was pantheon of 80s R&B releases.

MC5 – Tough, uncompromising American band formed in late 60s who were forerunners to the punk movement a decade later.

MEAT PUPPETS – US hard-core roots band whose musical excursion through American musical styles is well-chronicled on series of multi-faceted albums, the latest (1991) being London-released set **Forbidden Places**.

MEKONS – UK garage punk band who seem to have found a home on indie Blast Fire label, for whom **The Curse Of The Mekons** (1991) was debut.

MELANIE – Diminutive but powerful voiced vocalist who enjoyed best moments with magnificent **Lay Down** (with Edwin Hawkins Singers) and **Ruby Tuesday** singles. Ahmet Ertegun-produced **Photograph** album in 1975 for Atlantic signalled end of creative period.

THE MEMBERS – UK white reggae band formed around lead singer Nick Tesco. Enjoyed some US success with lighthearted single and popular MTV video **Working Girl**, until Tesco left in 1983.

Above: Business As Usual, Men At Work. Courtesy Epic Records.

MEN AT WORK – Australian soft-rockers who scored two successive US No. 1 singles with **Who Can It Be Now?** and **Down Under** (also a UK No. 1) in 1982.

THE MERSEYBEATS – Liverpool band who scored with cover of Dionne Warwick hit **Wishin' And Hopin'** and **I Think Of You** in 1964. After brief break-up, re-emerged as Merseys duo to score with **Sorrow**.

METERS – Classic New Orleans R&B/funk band who were sought-after backing unit for wide variety of artists, including Fats Domino, Lee Dorsey, Irma Thomas, Robert Palmer and Paul McCartney. Founder Art Neville now appears with brother Aaron as The Neville Brothers.

BETTE MIDLER – Buxom chanteuse whose ribald stage persona has successfully translated into movie medium, with especially notable star appearance in *The Rose*. Now more widely known for acting roles in such films as *Ruthless People*, *Outrageous Fortune* and *Beaches*.

JOHN MILES – UK guitarist/vocalist from Jarrow who scored with ambitious **Music** in 1975, and disco-oriented **Slowdown** a year later. Miles has subsequently remained in second division of rock performers despite undoubted talent.

RONNIE MILSAP – Blind (since birth) American country vocalist/pianist whose soulful performances have earned a host of Grammy awards. A regular in the C&W and pop charts in the US.

THE MINDBENDERS – Originally led by Wayne Fontana, they split from him and found success in 1965 with **Groovy Kind Of Love**. Guitarist Eric Stewart later became member of 10cc.

KYLIE MINOGUE – The Aussie soap *Neighbours* has a lot more to answer for! Female equivalent of Jason Donovan, another performer featured in the Antipodean drama. Minogues' efforts to 'grow up' in early 90s resulted in criticisms of mimicking Madonna.

MISSING PERSONS – Formed by Bozzio Bros in 1980, this American band should have made major impact, having learnt the ropes with artists such as Frank Zappa, and with producer Ken Scott at the helm.

GUY MITCHELL – Tin Pan Alley-styled pop singer who dabbled in rock 'n' roll, notably with **Singing The Blues** (1956), covered in UK by Tommy Steele.

WILLIE MITCHELL – Legendary Memphis producer and multi-instrumentalist who had been a cornerstone of the Tennessee R&B sound for over thirty years. Most widely known for work with Al Green.

MOBY GRAPE – The heaviest of all 60s East Coast bands, led with gusto by vocalist and bassist Bob Mosely. Career floundered in early 70s, despite outstanding eponymous debut LP. Regular efforts to re-form came to little of significance.

MODERN ROMANCE – Up-tempo 80s combo with brass-heavy, Latin-tinged party approach, evident on UK hits **Everybody Salsa**, **Ay Ay Ay Ay Moosey** and **Best Years Of Our Lives**. Also quite popular in foreign regions, such as South America.

ZOOT MONEY – With his powerful Big Roll Band, was a mainstay of British R&B/soul club scene and cut some fine records, of which only **Big Time Operator** made chart impact. From his band, Paul Williams went on to front Juicy Lucy while Andy Somers (Summers) ended up in the Police.

BILL MONROE – Founder of bluegrass music, who, with his group Blue Grass Boys, influenced generations of country and rock performers.

MONSOON – Unique blend of traditional East Indian music and pop, with inspired vocals from young Indian beauty Sheila Chandra. 1982 singles **Ever So Lonely** and **Shakti** definitely worth a listen.

MONTROSE – San Franciscan rock unit who reformed as Gamma in 1982 following collection of albums for Warner Brothers and Pacific in early 70s.

MOTHER EARTH – Rock/blues/country showcase for superbly soulful voice of Tracy Nelson. Recorded admirable late 60s albums on Mercury.

MOTORS – UK band formed from remnants of Ducks De Luxe. Charted in UK during 1978 with **Airport** and **Forget About You**. Strong material supplied by bassist Andy McMaster and guitarist Nick Garvey.

MOUNTAIN – Archetypal melodic HM outfit led by the gigantic Leslie West on guitar, whose first album **Nantucket Sleighride** was a feast of tasty guitar licks, sharp vocals, and topflight songs.

MUD – Basic British beat group used as vehicle for the songs of Nicky Chinn and Mike Chapman, before going into self-production and achieving run of Top 20 singles. Mud's two No. 1 singles in the UK were **Tiger Feet** (1974) and **Oh Boy** (1975).

Below: Nantucket Sleighride, Mountain. Courtesy Windfall Records.

MUNGO JERRY – Up-dated jug band with skiffle flavour made Mungo Jerry rave success of 1970 open-air concerts: led to million selling smash **In The Summertime**. Further hits established big following on Continent, which band's leader Ray Dorset has exploited skilfully through to 80s.

ANNE MURRAY – Nova Scotia-born easy-listening country singer with enormous following. From first big hit **Snowbird** in 1970, material has crossed over into pop charts.

MY BLOODY VALENTINE – Quartet formed in Dublin in 1984, who have metamorphosed into cross between Jesus And Mary Chain and Clannad. Group reaped critical success with 1988 LP **Isn't Anything** and 1991 collection **Loveless**.

N

JOHNNY NASH – US soul singer whose smooth style earned him several hit singles in the late 60s and early 70s, most notably **Hold Me Tight** and **I Can See Clearly Now**.

NAZARETH – Scottish heavy metal group led by rough-house vocalist Dan McCafferty who charted in the early 70s with some regurgitated and predictable rock 'n' roll 45s.

FRED NEIL – Influential component of Greenwich Village folk scene. From his debut album **Bleeker And McDougal**, **Candy Man** was later covered by Roy Orbison and **The Other Side Of Life** by Lovin' Spoonful. Most successful song was **Everybody's Talkin'**, recorded by Harry Nilsson for soundtrack of *Midnight Cowboy*.

SANDY NELSON – American session drummer who scored a couple of instrumental hits pre-Beatles, notably the percussion anthem **Let There Be Drums**.

WILLIE NELSON – Top-flight American country star, whose bedraggled appearance belies a smooth writing and vocal style personified by the lilting **Always On My Mind**. An important contributor to Farm Aid concert in the US.

MICHAEL NESMITH– Left the super-successful Monkees pop outfit to find solo recognition for his polished brand of country rock and his First National Band. Best known solo hits are **Joanne** and **Rio**. Moved into film and video production.

THE NEW BEATS – Perky falsetto sound made **Bread And Butter**, **Everything's Alright** and **Run Baby Run** into hits for this Nashville-based trio.

NEW MODEL ARMY – From Bradford, Yorkshire, this dramatic and powerful trio with strong political message have enjoyed success throughout Europe without seriously testing US market. Split from label EMI in 1991 after five albums.

NEW YORK DOLLS – Innovative glam band from East Coast, who revelled in pioneering punk era. Became passé in mid-80s, and broke up following **Red Patent Leather** album.

MICKEY NEWBURY – Superior country writer who adapted **American Trilogy** single covered by Elvis. His own material has been recorded by Andy Williams, Kenny Rogers, Jerry Lee Lewis and Ray Charles, among others. His finest work can be found on Elektra Records.

OLIVIA NEWTON-JOHN – British-born, Aussie-raised vocalist inextricably linked with John Travolta following their outing in *Grease* movie. Almost permanent fixture in UK and US charts from 1971-80 with total of 16 Top 10 entries, of which **You're The One That I Want** (with Travolta) topped listings on both sides of the Atlantic.

THE NICE – Formed as backing band for P.P. Arnold, The Nice made showy rock albums. Caused controversy by burning the American Flag during their stage renditions of **America**. Keyboard virtuoso Keith Emerson went on to found Emerson, Lake And Palmer.

NIGHT RANGER – Yet another band caught in a 70s time warp. **Don't Tell Me You Love Me** video showcased them as one of the most unbearable bunch of poseurs on MTV.

NINE INCH NAILS – Hardcore rockers from US led by Trent Reznor whose development was stunted by legal wranglings with TVT label following success of **Pretty Hate Machine** LP in 1991.

NIRVANA – Wailing US guitar blasters from Washington State who blitzed US charts in 1991 with **Nevermind** LP and **Smells Like Teen Spirit** single. Originally signed to local indie label Sub Pop.

NITTY GRITTY DIRT BAND – Innovative folk/bluegrass band who maintained a regular album output from beginning of 1970. In 1977 became first US band to tour USSR.

NWA – Lock up the population! Outlandish US rap aggregation who have offended everyone, and seem on the permanent edge of incarceration. Musically, check out 1991 set **Efil4Zaggin**, which came under scrutiny of UK's Obscene Publications Bureau.

LAURA NYRO – New York singer who cut masterpiece **Eli And The Thirteenth Coming**, since when she recorded only sporadically. Wrote pop classics **Stoned Soul Picnic**, **Wedding Bell Blues**, **And When I Die** and **Stoney End**.

O

OAK RIDGE BOYS – Former gospel stars, this vocal quartet have been permanent fixtures in the country, and, more recently, pop charts in US. Recipients of a host of country music awards.

PHIL OCHS – American folk singer with sincere, but heavy-handed, lyrical approach, who struggled to survive against quality opposition including Dylan and Baez. Satirical pop/folk mix of album **Greatest Hits** (1970) was his one flirtation with commerical success before suicide in 1976.

O'JAYS – Leading soul vocal group, who have charted regularly since their 1972 classic **Backstabbers**. Lead vocalist Eddie Levert can now proudly watch over his two sons who are featured in R&B outfit Levert.

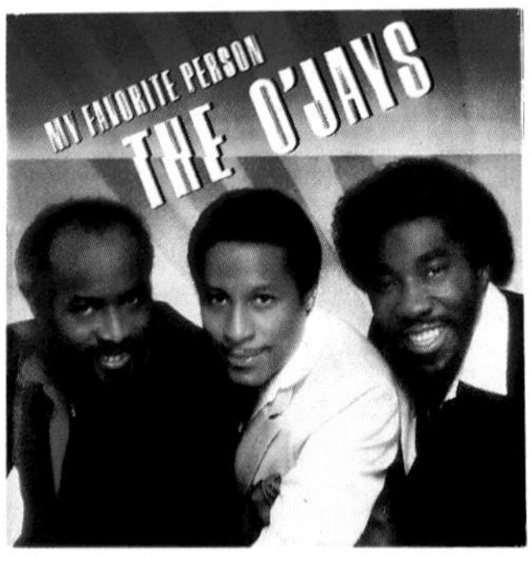

Above: My Favorite Person, The O'Jays. Courtesy Philly International Records.

YOKO ONO – Esoteric talent who took commercial advantage of her marriage to John Lennon in pop field. Better testimony can be found in her avante-garde films and art.

TONY ORLANDO – Worked for Don Kirshner cutting demos before being launched as artist in own right in 1961 with **Halfway To Paradise**. Following solo hits in 60s he was re-launched as lead singer of Dawn in 70s for further triumphs. Biggest US/UK Dawn hits were **Knock Three Times** and **Tie A Yellow Ribbon Round The Old Oak Tree**. Also had US TV variety show.

Above: Nirvana blasted their way from cult to mainstream fame in 1991 with award-winning Nevermind LP.

ORLEANS – Melodic East Coast band who charted briefly in the USA with outstanding singles **Dance With Me** (1975) and **Still The One** (1976).

OSIBISA – Introduced African rock music to British audiences and commanded large following from 1970 to 1976 when **Sunshine Day** gave them their first chart hit single.

GILBERT O'SULLIVAN – Managed to get break with Gordon Mills management outfit by squatting in MAM office reception. Given short-trousers and cloth cap working-class image he scored with thoughtful and melodious songs, hitting pinnacle with transatlantic hit **Alone Again (Naturally)** (1972). Enjoyed total of 12 UK Top 20 records between 1970-1974, including No. 1's **Clair** and **Get Down**.

OUTLAWS – Leading exponents of Southern US rock, along with the Allman Brothers Band and Lynyrd Skynyrd. Voracious appetite for gigs maintained group's high profile in USA.

OZARK MOUNTAIN DAREDEVILS – Country-rock exponents who enjoyed major success in mid-70s. Charted, however, with pure pop **Jackie Blue** in 1975.

P

PABLO CRUISE – American band led by bassist Bud Cockrell (ex-It's A Beautiful Day) and keyboard/vocalist Cory Lerois (ex-Stoneground) who scored a series of US hit singles from 1977 without really establishing first division credentials.

GRAHAM PARKER – Decent British R&B vocalist who led riotous brass-based band Rumour through a succession of exciting but predictable albums from mid-70s.

LES PAUL – Frontrunner of electric pop, who enjoyed hit status in 50s with wife Mary Ford. Along with Leo Fender's 'Stratocaster', Paul's eponymous guitar is the axe that rockers swear by.

PAVLOV'S DOG – Adventurous US band from New York featuring dual keyboards and falsetto vocalizing of David Surkamp. Band split after two eccentric albums recorded in mid-70s.

TOM PAXTON – Self-effacing folk performer who packed concert halls throughout the 70s with his dry humour, and 'spoken' style.

PEARLS BEFORE SWINE – US cult band led by Tom Rapp which enjoyed underground success in late 60s and early 70s. After couple of solo albums, Rapp moved to Europe and quit recording scene.

TEDDY PENDERGRASS – Former lead vocalist with Harold Melvin and Bluenotes, Pendergrass quickly established himself as a premier live performer before catastrophic car crash halted career.

PENTANGLE — Revered pop/folk unit from the 70s who attracted cult following from British concert audiences.

PERE UBU — US underground band formed in 70s who cut four albums for Chrysalis before splitting in 1982. Group revived in 1990 by vocalist David Thomas.

PETER AND GORDON — Peter Asher's actress sister Jane was Paul McCartney's girlfriend, which explains how duo got to record fresh Lennon/McCartney material, bringing them hits with **World Without Love** and **Nobody I Know**. Peter Asher went on to manage James Taylor and Linda Ronstadt.

BOBBY 'BORIS' PICKETT — Pickett's imitation of Boris Karloff's spooky voice took **Monster Mash** to the top in 1961.

PIXIES — Primal sci-fi guitar-based indie four-piece from Boston signed to high-flying 4AD label. Earned plaudits in 1991 for **Trompe Le Monde** set.

PLASMATICS — Lightweight punk group whose success was based on appearance rather than musical ability, and they will be remembered for nothing more than vocalist Wendy O. Williams' erotic stage behaviour.

POCO — American country/rock pioneers formed from ashes of Buffalo Springfield (Richie Furay and Jim Messina), who maintained high profile for fifteen years despite countless personnel changes.

POISON — Second generation US powerglam outfit. Low budget debut LP **Look What The Cat Dragged In** (1986) went platinum and band later enjoyed US No. 1 single **Every Rose Has It's Thorn**.

POLECATS — Modern-day rockabilly band from London, who were perhaps too innovative for then punk audience. Split in 1983 after two good albums.

PREFAB SPROUT — Modern pop quartet from UK and no baggy in sight! Ably led by Paddy McAloon, band's sporadic output (no sign of a thing since **Jordon: The Comeback**, 1990) has limited success to indie charts.

BILLY PRESTON — Highly rated keyboard performer who has worked with Little Richard, Sam Cooke and The Stones. Scored notable single success with Syreeta and **With You I'm Born Again** (1979).

JOHNNY PRESTON — Recorded solo in 1959, scoring internationally with **Running Bear**, on which vocal chant effects were contributed by the Big Bopper.

THE PRETTY THINGS — Anarchic UK R&B/rock band who tried to be even more outrageous than The Rolling Stones. Made some interesting but usually excessively noisy singles, plus competent **S.F. Sorrow** and **Parachute** albums.

ALAN PRICE — Former Animal and founder of Alan Price Set who has pursued varied solo career. Hit singles included **Simon Smith And His Amazing Dancing Bear** and **The House That Jack Built**. Went on to concentrate on writing and performing music for television, film and theatre.

Above: Travellin' Man, Alan Price. Courtesy Trojan Records.

MAXI PRIEST — Appealing laid-back reggae singer who has made regular sorties into UK charts with 45s such as **Close To You**, **Wild World** and **House Call**.

PRIMAL SCREAM — Archetypal 90s English dance band, whose move from indie status was completed upon release of eponymous debut album for Alan McGee's Creation Records.

P.J. PROBY — US vocalist probably more famous for his then outrageous hairstyles and splitting trousers than his hits **Hold Me**, **Together**, **Somewhere** (all 1964) and **Maria** (1965).

PSYCHEDELIC FURS — UK new wave band who enjoyed US success courtesy of MTV and single **Love My Way** in 1982.

GARY PUCKETT AND THE UNION GAP — Civil War-inspired stage uniforms and breezy Jerry Fuller-produced pop songs gave this San Diego group their moments of glory, notably with 1968 chart-topper **Young Girl**.

PURE PRAIRIE LEAGUE — Country-rock exponents who cut US Top 10 single **Let Me Love You Tonight** in 1980.

Q

QUARTERFLASH — Portland, Oregon-based sextet fronted by brother and sister pairing of Mark and Rindy Ross. Geffen record deal prompted trio of hit singles during early 80s.

QUEEN LATIFAH — Hip-hop queen of early 90s, who demonstrates excellent vocal qualities as well as pertinent street vibes. Equally at home with rap and reggae, as demonstrated by first two albums **All Hail The Queen** and **Nature Of A Sista**.

QUESTION MARK AND THE MYSTERIANS — Basic garage-rock sounds of **96 Tears** (1966) gave this Flint, Michigan-based Tex-Mex group their lone smash hit.

QUICKSILVER MESSENGER SERVICE — Archetypal West Coast group formed in 1965 who cut handful of excellent rock albums during 60s. Another band who didn't survive the decade of love.

QUINTESSENCE — Eastern-flavoured jazz-rock outfit formed via *Melody Maker* magazine adverts in 1969. Series of Island albums were aimed at underground hippy audiences.

R

EDDIE RABBIT — Country artist who has made regular inroads into US pop charts. Best known for **Every Which Way But Loose** movie theme, which enjoyed Top 50 status in both US/UK in 1979.

RARE EARTH — Bringing heavy rock flavour to essentially soul material, this band launched Motown's Rare Earth label (named after them). Under ace black producer Norman Whitfield, cut classic long versions of such Motown classics as **Get Ready**, **(I Know) I'm Losing You** and **Ma** in early 70s.

THE RASCALS — Pioneer blue-eyed soul band on Atlantic, formed in 1966 as Young Rascals. Topped charts year later with **Good Lovin'; Groovin'** was 1967 classic. Sheer musicanship made them delightful live attraction. Organist Felix Cavaliere, singer Eddie Brigati and guitarist Gene Cornish had all previously been with Joe Dee And The Starlighters.

RED HOT CHILI PEPPERS — American funk/soul/rock aggregation whose manic presentation threatens superstardom. Surprisingly, Rick Rubin-produced 1991 Warner Bros set **BloodSugarSexMagik** was inadequate testimony to bands multi-faceted talent.

RENAISSANCE — Formed by ex-Yardbirds Keith Relf and Jim McCarty, group was major UK concert attraction through 70s, and scored Top 10 single **Northern Lights** in 1978. Relf, who left band in 1972, died in 1976.

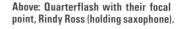

THE REPLACEMENTS — An uneven Minneapolis rock unit, which, nevertheless, is renowned for brilliant songwriting and a raucous live act. Long independent label favourites of critics and hardcore fans, their fourth album **Let It Be** (1984) won a contract with Sire Records. Their handful of LPs (particularly **All Shook Down**) have shown promise but lack of discipline.

PAUL REVERE AND THE RAIDERS — US Band who, thanks to their colourful American Revolutionary War garb (including long hair in ponytails) and strong musicianship, made immediate impact when they appeared in 18th-century costumes on Dick Clark's *Where The Action Is* TV show. Recorded string of pop classics in long career, including American No. 1 **Indian Reservation** in 1971. Band saw many personnel changes, but lead singer Mark Lindsay remained constant factor. Lindsay enjoyed some solo success, including own US TV show in early 70s.

CHARLIE RICH — Former rockabilly singer whose country ballads saw plenty of chart action in the early 70s, with **The Most Beautiful Girl** topping US listings (No. 2 in UK) in 1973.

JOHNNY RIVERS — Personable vocalist/guitarist who became US teen idol in mid-60s with clever re-makes of R&B hits, including **Memphis**, **Baby I Need Your Lovin'**, **Maybellene** and **Rockin' Pneumonia-Boogie Woogie Flu**.

TOM ROBINSON — Gay activist and radical, who has dented the UK charts on three occasions, most notably with **2-4-6-8-Motorway** in 1977.

TOMMY ROE — Buddy Holly soundalike from Atlanta, Georgia, who scored a couple of US No. 1s with his own compositions in the 60s, **Sheila** (1962) and **Dizzy** (1969). Went on to work on US club circuit, playing with own trio.

KENNY ROGERS — Country-pop vocalist who has been a chart regular on both sides of the Atlantic since 1968, when his group the First Edition made US No. 5 with **Just Dropped In**.

Above: Quarterflash with their focal point, Rindy Ross (holding saxophone).

TIM ROSE — A member of the Big Three folk group with Mama Cass, Rose composed classic **Morning Dew** for his debut/solo album. Also included brilliant **Hey Joe**, which Jimi Hendrix covered successfully. Rose later settled in Britain, setting up band there.

DAVID LEE ROTH — Former front-man for Van Halen who went solo to hit charts with 1985 singles **California Girls** and **Just A Gigolo**.

RUN-D.M.C. — Trio of New York rappers who were from Hollis, Queens, and were first group to attract white listeners to rap in large numbers. Jason Mizzell, Joe Simmons and Darryl McDaniels formed unit who crossed-over successfully with **Walk This Way** collaboration with HM unit Aerosmith in 1986.

BOBBY RYDELL — The original Robert Lewis Ridarelli had sensational period in US charts from 1959-64, scoring 22 Top 60 hits, including teen classics **Wild One**, **Volare** and **Cha-Cha-Cha**. Became active on supper-club circuit.

Above: Facades, Sad Cafe's 1979 album. Courtesy RCA Records.

S

SAD CAFE — Manchester rock group who looked on horizon of big future after UK Top 10 single **Every Day Hurts** in 1979, but who, subsequently, virtually disappeared without trace.

SALT 'N' PEPA — Limited female vocal trio whose commercial rap style disguises paucity of talent. Hit singles **Push It** and **Let's Talk About Sex** signalled peak of creative powers.

SAM AND DAVE — US soul duo whose heyday was in 60s, when they belted out a dozen R&B anthems on the Stax label, including **Hold On I'm Coming**, **Soul Man** and **I Thank You**.

SAVOY BROWN — English blues band who had approaching two thousand members since formation in 1966, the most notable of which were founder member guitarist Kim Simmonds, and former Chicken Shack axeman Stan Webb.

Left: David Lee Roth became a successful solo act in 1985, after a decade fronting Van Halen.

SAXON — English metal band formed in 1977 who were unlikely guests in 1980-81 with four UK Top 20 singles, of which **And The Bands Played On** threatened Top 10.

LEO SAYER — Astutely managed by one-time teen idol Adam Faith, Sayer's flexible image kept fans on their toes during ten-year chart tenure from debut hit. **The Show Must Go On** (1972).

SCREAMING LORD SUTCH — An anachronism throughout his long career and master of the publicity stunt. His **Jack The Ripper** parody kept him in work for two decades, although he enjoyed US success with Atlantic album **Lord Sutch And Heavy Friends**, which included his ex-band members Jimmy Page, Nicky Hopkins and Ritchie Blackmore. Now prospective UK parliamentary candidate and founder of Monster Raving Loony Party.

SCRITTI POLITTI — Brainchild of Welsh-born Green Gartside, SP (Italian for 'political writing') began as shambolic punksters before evolving into techno-gods. Enjoyed slew of UK hits during 80s, of which **Oh Patti** made Top 20.

SEAL — Leather-clad lead singer of Adamski whose subsequent solo outing provided **Crazy** hit single from excellent eponymous debut album (1991).

SEALS AND CROFTS — Lightweight US pop duo who dented US charts in 70s. Jim Seals was former member of The Champs.

PETE SEEGER — The grandaddy of the US 60s folk movement, whose left-wing politics appealed to the college and university set while leaving two generations of middle-class Americans cold.

SHA NA NA — American rock revivalists who starred in Woodstock movie and soundtrack; own recording career was a pale imitation of their live shows.

SHAKIN' STEVENS — UK rocker (born in Wales) who enjoyed unbroken run of pop/rockabilly hits during 80s. Initially attracted attention with starring role in long-running London musical *Elvis*.

SHALAMAR — Funky US soul trio led by Howard Hewitt who enjoyed single success with collection of inspired electro-disco soul. Founder members Jody Watley and Jeffrey Daniels have since found solo success.

SHAM 69 — Creation of vocalist Jimmy Pursey whose lyrical content decried social conditions of British working class. Biggest hits were **If The Kids Are United** and **Hurry Up Harry** in 1978. Pursey subsequently pursued solo career with negligible success.

HELEN SHAPIRO — Husky-voiced singer who charted with melodic teen material in early 60s. Topped UK charts with **You Don't Know** and **Walkin' Back To Happiness** in 1961. Became active on cabaret/supper-club circuit.

PETE SHELLEY — Formerly with The Buzzcocks with several hits such as **Ever Fallen In Love (With Someone That You Shouldn't Have)** and **Promises**. Notable solo single was **Homosapien**.

BOBBY SHERMAN — Launched via *Shindig* TV series, Sherman was archetypal American teen idol and his records were predictably unadventurous though they gave him a 1969-70 chart run.

MICHELLE SHOCKED — Honorary member of rock's 'club-circuit', Michelle has dabbled on fringes of stardom for near-decade. Signed to Cooking Vinyl label for whom **Short Sharp Shocked** is current highlight.

SHOWADDYWADDY — UK's answer to Sha Na Na, this collection of MOR rockers were mainstays of UK pop listings for five years from 1974, scoring 10 Top 10 singles.

Below: Styx, monsters in America in the 70s, but almost unknown in Britain.

Above: Ex-Adamski vocalist Seal became UK hit sensation almost overnight in 1991 due to Crazy single and help of producer Trevor Horn.

SISTERS OF MERCY — UK gothic-rockers perennially on verge of major breakthrough. Morbid **First And Last And Always** debut album (1984) was never bettered, although 1989 set **This Corrosion** came close.

PETER SKELLERN — UK singer/songwriter/pianist from Lancaster, UK with a penchant for wistful 30s-flavoured material. Won UK/US success with debut single **You're A Lady**. Has cut run of highly entertaining albums, often using softly muted brass band to add to the Northern England feel.

SKY — Brainchild of classical guitarist John Williams, group were popular concert attraction, particularly in UK, with uneasy amalgam of rock and classics.

SLAUGHTER — Derivative riff runts from USA who saw **Stick It To Ya** opener for Chrysalis strike paydirt. Lead vocalist Mark Slaughter is currently exploring vocal range beyond top C.

PATTI SMITH — Chicago-born poet turned rocker, best known for hit interpretation of Bruce Springsteen's **Because The Night** (1978). Reappeared on music scene during 90s after prolonged absence.

SOFT MACHINE — Seminal UK jazz-rock band, whose members have included Robert Wyatt, Kevin Ayers, Mike Ratledge and Hugh Hopper. Broke up in 1979.

SONIC YOUTH — Nuclear-powered dual-sex guitar crew who are everything you want (or not) a space-age rock band to be. Try **Sex Is Confusion** LP for starters.

JOE SOUTH — Influential session guitarist/writer/producer; worked with The Tams, Joe Smith, Simon And Garfunkel, Aretha Franklin, Bob Dylan and many more. Scored own solo success in 1969 with classic **Games People Play**.

J.D. SOUTHER — Guitarist founder of ill-fated Souther (John David), Hillman (Chris), Furay (Richie) band which did not live up to enormous potential during two-album 18-month tenure. Has enjoyed modicum of solo success

while recording with Linda Ronstadt (for whom he wrote superb **Heart Like A Wheel**), Warren Zevon, Joe Walsh and Christopher Cross.

SOUTHSIDE JOHNNY AND THE ASBURY JUKES — Goodtime rock band who were precursor for Bruce Springsteen and E Street Band. Outstanding live act who never enjoyed international chart success. After prolonged break, band returned in 1991 with outstanding **Better Days** set, produced by Steve Van Zandt.

SPARKS — Novelty American pop group formed by Mael Bros in 1974. Unusual presentation eventually lost support, despite run of UK chart singles from 1974.

CHRIS SPEDDING — Anonymous guitar hero of countless recording sessions, Spedding had taste of solo glory with **Motorbiking** hit on Mickie Most's Rak label in 1975.

SPINNERS — Superb US black vocal group known as Detroit Spinners in the UK; formed in the 50s. Enjoyed most chart success between 1961 and 1978 with US/UK hits like **It's A Shame**, **Could It Be I'm Falling In Love**, **Ghetto Child**, **Rubberband Man** and US No. 1 **Then Came You**. Group's best work featured lead vocalist Phillipe Wynne.

SPOOKY TOOTH — Major band on late 60s progressive rock scene in Britain; had only moderate success with albums. Dogged by personnel changes, including loss of American-born founder Gary Wright.

RICK SPRINGFIELD — US singer/guitarist and soap-star who never quite made the big time, but who hung in there for over a decade with such hits as **Speak To The Sky** (1972), and more recently **Jessie's Girl** (a No. 1 in 1981), **I've Done Everything For You** (1981), **Don't Talk To Strangers** (No. 2 in 1982), and **Affair Of The Heart** (1983).

BILLY SQUIER — Annoying poseur who relies mostly on good looks for appeal. Nevertheless has come up with some good hooks on US hits like **Everybody Wants You** (1982).

STAPLE SINGERS — Gospel family who found favour in singles charts in early 70s. Lead singer Mavis later went on to successful solo career.

ALVIN STARDUST — A 60s star as Shane Fenton, he burst into charts with new name and black leather image. Topped charts with **Jealous Mind**.

AL STEWART — Lightweight singer/songwriter from Glasgow who enjoyed major hit in 1977 with **Year Of The Cat**. Dippy vocalizing precluded serious attention from audiences, although he retains his cult following.

STIFF LITTLE FINGERS — Irish high-energy quartet who saw a promising career disappear when founder member Jake Burns called it a day. Made UK Top 20 in 1980 with **At The Edge**.

STEVE STRANGE — Poseur extraordinaire who landed recording contract. Charted (as Visage, with Midge Ure of Ultravox) in UK with **Fade To Gray** (1980), **Mind Of A Toy** (1981), **Damned Don't Cry** (1982) and **Night Train** (1982).

STRAWBS — Formerly The Strawberry Hill Boys, folk trio from London suburbs led by Dave Cousins, group evolved into popular rock quartet (featuring Rick Wakeman) before splitting in late 70s. Cousins went on to run radio station in West Country.

STRAY CATS — New York rockabilly trio who had decent chart run in early 80s (**Rock This Town** made both UK and US Top 10) before splitting in 1984.

BARBRA STREISAND — US vocalist and actress who hit charts with, among others: **The Way We Were**, **Evergreen**, **My Heart Belongs To Me** and **Woman In Love**. From roles in *Funny Girl* and *A Star Is Born* through self-produced *Yentl* to *The Prince Of Tides*, Streisand has become one of the foremost female show-biz stars in the US.

ANDREW STRONG — Teenage lead vocalist from Alan Parker's *The Commitments* movie about Dublin soul band. Strong's powerful presence led to contract with MCA in 1991. Authentic and emotional, and innocent enough to strut out any number of R&B cliches like 'Get yer hands together' and 'Good God, y'all'. Tell him someone!

STYLISTICS — Excellent US black vocal group who've managed several US/UK pop singles from 1972-76, including hits **I'm Stone In Love With You**, **Break Up To Make Up**, **Rock 'N' Roll Baby**, **You Make Me Feel Brand New**, **Let's Put It All Together**, **Sing Baby Sing**, **Can't Give You Anything (But My Love)**, and more.

STYX — US AOR band formed in 1970 with succession of hit singles in US from 1975. 1979 No. 1 single **Babe** is typical of their pleasant but unremarkable style.

DONNA SUMMER — US-born disco-queen who established career after moving to Germany under aegis of Giorgio Moroder. Topped American charts with **MacArthur Park**, **Hot Stuff**, **Bad Girls** and **No More Tears**, the latter with Barbra Streisand. Relaunched career in 1991.

SURVIVOR — American 70s-styled AOR band whose theme from Rocky III **Eye Of The Tiger** was major 1982 smash. Have maintained success with similarly crafted material, including US Football theme **American Heartbeat**.

BILLY SWAN — Bill Black Combo and Clyde McPhatter both scored with Swan's composition **Lover Please**. After stint as roadie for country stars, became Monument Records' staff producer, working on Tony Joe White's **Polk Salad Annie** hit. As an artist he adopted soft-rocking style to achieve No. 1 hit single with **I Can Help** (1974).

SWEET — Unpretentious pop band who secured regular UK chart placings from 1971 to 1978. Brainchild of Nicky Chinn, Michael Chapman songwriting/production partnership, who wrote **Blockbuster** No. 1 for group in 1973.

SWINGING BLUE JEANS — Liverpool band led by vocalist/guitarist Ray Ennis who had string of UK hits. **Hippy Hippy Shake**, **You're No Good**, etc. (and a couple of minor US chart entries) in mid-60s.

T

TANGERINE DREAM — German synthesizer outfit popular in Europe since formation in 1967. Members Edgar Froese, Christoph Frank and Johannes Schmoelling were also active on solo projects. Recorded soundtrack for James Caan movie *Thief* (*Violent Streets* in UK) in 1981.

Above: Natalie Merchant of 10,000 Maniacs, who have yet to hit bigtime.

TEARDROP EXPLODES — UK outfit formed in 1978 who achieved two UK Top 10 singles, **Reward** and **Treason**, in 1981. Image maker and guiding light Julian Cope split band in 1982.

TEENAGE FANCLUB — Beatlesque quartet from Glasgow, Scotland, complete with John Lennon-lookalike Norman Blake on vocals and Rickenbacker guitar. Signed to Creation Records, band debuted in 1990 with **A Catholic Education**.

TELEVISION — Clever pre-punk outfit from New York featuring talents of Richard Hell and Tom Verlaine. Influential and under-valued, band reformed in 1992 after prolonged absence.

NINO TEMPO AND APRIL STEVENS — Tempo played sax on Bobby Darin records before signing to Atco as duo with his sister and notching No. 1 with **Deep Purple**. In late 70s, Tempo came back to prominence as an instrumentalist, riding disco boom with his Fifth Avenue Sax band.

10,000 MANIACS — American former new wave quartet (originally six-piece founded by John Lombardo, who quit in 1986), whose current musical influences range from country to rock with pointed political message. Produced by British AOR specialist Peter Asher. Fronted by high-profile vocalist Natalie Merchant.

TENPOLE TUDOR — Tartan punk from Eddie Tenpole and his look-alike band, who specialized in raucous, singalong pub-style tunes, anachronistic clothes and Scottish nationalism. 1981 hits **Swords Of A Thousand Men** and **Wunderbar** typical of sound. Founder Eddie Tudor-Pole has returned to acting since demise of band, appearing in *Absolute Beginners* and *Sid And Nancy*.

TEXAS — Enterprising Scottish band fronted with gusto by singer/guitarist Sharleen Spiteri. And no, not from

Below: They Might Be Giants duo, cult favourites of the US college circuit.

Austin, TX, but Glasgow, Scotland, although you could never tell from Spiteri's authentic down-home vocals.

THEY MIGHT BE GIANTS — Idiosyncratic duo (accordinist John Linnell and percussionist John Flansburgh) from Boston wowing US college circuit (as of 1992). Signed to Elektra Records, for which label they've cut four albums.

3RD BASS — Unlikely (white, Jewish) but authentic New York hardcore rappers Pete Nice and MC Serch deliver potent message on material like **Portrait Of The Artist As Hood** and **Words Of Wisdom**. Enjoyed critical thumbs-up for **Derelicts Of Dialect** LP in 1991.

THIRD WORLD — Jamaican soul/reggae outfit who should have achieved superstardom after magnificent **Now That We've Found Love** single in 1978.

.38 SPECIAL — Formed by Donnie Van Zant (younger brother of Lynyrd Skynyrd's Ronnie), rocking five-piece never quite achieved mega-success despite promising output with A&M Records.

B.J. THOMAS — One of pop's anomalies, a soulful singer who has contented himself with lifeless MOR material. His anthem is wimpish **Raindrops Keep Fallin' On My Head**, but also enjoyed seven other US Top 20 entries from 1969-75.

KENNY THOMAS — Outstanding UK soul crooner, whose tough upbringing in London's East End has given him authentic edge. Enjoyed trio of hits in 1991 from debut album **Voices**.

RICHARD AND LINDA THOMPSON — Folk duo who enjoyed solo and group success (Richard with Fairport Convention) before teaming up. *Rolling Stone* magazine nominated their 1982 collection **Shoot Out The Lights** as Album Of The Year. Subsequent break-up of marriage, however, resulted in separate 1985 albums, but pair later toured together again. Richard is reckoned one of the best guitarists in rock, but has preferred to maintain a low profile.

THOMPSON TWINS — UK trio led by flimsy vocalists Tom Bailey and Alannah Currie. **Hold Me Now** 45 (1983) was career high spot, although decent material could prompt a comeback.

GEORGE THOROGOOD AND THE DESTROYERS — R&B blasters from Delaware who have been around for as long as George Burns. Opened for Rolling Stones on 1981 US tour, and seem destined for 'also starring...' musical role.

THUNDERCLAP NEWMAN — Andy Newman met The Who's Pete Townshend at art college. Formed Thunderclap Newman with Jimmy McCullough and Speedy Keene. Townshend produced, through the Who's Track label; group scored in 1969 with **Something In The Air** but success was not sustained. McCullough went onto play with Stone The Crows, then Wings.

TANITA TIKARAM — English vocalist/guitarist (latter-day Janis Ian?) born to Fijian father and Malaysian mother. Enjoyed greatest success with **Good Tradition** single, which heralded popularity throughout Europe.

JOHNNY TILLOTSON — Melodic **Poetry In Motion** (1958) made star of this former country singer. Eight-year run found him consistently on the American charts, his other biggie being **It Keeps Right On A-Hurting**.

TINY TIM — Long-time Greenwich Village weirdo. Appeared in 1968 *You Are What You Eat* movie and *Laugh-In* TV series before bizarre re-make of **Tiptoe Through The Tulips** single and **God Bless Tiny Tim** album shot him to temporary international prominence.

Below: Twisted Sister, HM band who reached audiences via MTV in the 80s.

THE TOKENS — Originally purely a studio outfit, with such luminaries as Neil Diamond, Neil Sedaka and Carole King playing on records. Eventually working band of Hank Medress, Jay Seigel, Phil Margo and Mitch Margo was formed. Folksy style gave them American No. 1 with **The Lion Sleeps Tonight**.

THE TORNADOS — Put together as London-based session band by producer Joe Meek; became The Tornados when they started to work as Billy Fury's backing outfit. 1962 brought enormous organ-dominated space-flavoured instrumental hit **Telstar**. Guitarist Heinz left for solo career with material based on his fascination with Eddie Cochran, scoring with single **Just Like Eddie** (1963).

Above: Ancient Heart, Tanita Tikaram. Courtesy WEA Records.

TOWER OF POWER — San Francisco-based R&B rock outfit at forefront of brass-laced bands of early 70s. Original vocalist Lenny Williams has enjoyed chart status with enterprising soul material.

JOHN TRAVOLTA — One-time king of disco, Travolta became a superstar following starring role in *Saturday Night Fever* movie, and later scored with trio of forgettable pop ditties and duets with Olivia Newton-John, co-stars in *Grease* teenage movie flick.

THE TREMELOES — As backing group to Brian Poole they had UK No. 1 with cover of Contours' US soul hit **Do You Love Me?**. Poole quit in 1965 for solo stardom but soon sank — returning to job as a butcher — while his erstwhile support went on to run of seven Top 10 hits from 1967-1970, including chart-topping cover of Four Seasons' oldie **Silence Is Golden**.

TWISTED SISTER — New York glam metal band in mould of New York Dolls who split in 1989 after departure of vocalist Dee Snider. Enjoyed minor notoriety with series of Atlantic albums in mid-80s.

CONWAY TWITTY — Country star who topped US and UK charts with rock anthem **It's Only Make Believe** in 1958. Now oversees Twitty City theme park founded in Nashville during late 70s, as well as making regular concert appearances.

BONNIE TYLER — Gifted Welsh vocalist who saw renewed chart action in the 80s with Jim Steinman-penned **Total Eclipse Of The Heart** (1983), and then powerful **Holding Out For A Hero** (1985).

U

THE UNITED STATES OF AMERICA — Lone eponymous album (1968) for Columbia was superbly innovative slice of progressive rock, parodying everything from **Sergeant Pepper** to Jefferson Airplane.

PHIL UPCHURCH — Noted US session guitarist (who worked with artists such as Cat Stevens, Howlin' Wolf, George Benson, Quincy Jones, etc) who charted in 1962 with million-selling dance opus **You Can't Sit Down**. Has released sporadic solo albums.

V

LUTHER VANDROSS — Smooth soul stylist and former lead singer of Change. Signed to Epic in 1981, artist has enjoyed run of platinum albums and string of hit singles including classic **Never Too Much** His finely-crafted albums showcase his wide emotive range.

VANGELIS — Pioneering synthesizer maestro from Greece, whose movie themes for such films as *Chariots Of Fire*, *Blade Runner*, and *Mask* have provided pomp in the right circumstances.

VANILLA FUDGE — US East Coast band whose claim to fame was turgid version of **You Keep Me Hangin' On**. Drummer Carmine Appice and bassist Tim Bogert went on to bigger things.

STEVIE RAY VAUGHAN — Powerhouse blues guitarist who was enjoying burgeoning career before tragic death in plane crash in 1990. **Live Alive** LP is excellent testimony to his talent, although posthumous **Sky Is Crying** made US Top 10 in winter of 1991. Latterly paired with brother Jimmy (from Fabulous Thunderbirds) as Vaughan Brothers.

VENTURES — US instrumental group who inspired generation of 'beat bands' in early 60s. Their **Walk Don't Run** (1960) is now rock classic.

Above: Tom Verlaine's eponymous album. Courtesy Elektra Records.

TOM VERLAINE — Founder of Television, this talented New Jersey guitarist/vocalist is sure to achieve international success when the rough edges have worn down.

BOBBY VINTON — Major US pop artist in early 60s with decidedly MOR ballad material like **Roses Are Red**, **Blue Velvet**, **Blue On Blue** and **I Love How You Love Me**. Makes maximum use of Polish heritage in well-worked, but corny, cabaret show.

VIOLENT FEMMES — Noisy acoustic band from USA, who resurfaced with **Why Do Birds Sing?** LP in 1991 after persistent rumours of demise. If you're into lust and anger, VF are your thing.

Below: Mari Wilson possesses one of the finest 60s-styled voices heard today.

Above: Wishbone Ash unit was another of the UK's long-lived 70s groups.

VOICE OF THE BEEHIVE — Talented US group whose brand of heathly pop is topped by distinguished harmonizing and sophisticated studio technique. Admirable **Honey Lingers** album was released in 1991.

W

WALKER BROS — American trio who achieved teen success in UK in mid-60s with succession of powerful pop ballads. Re-formed in 1976 for one-off hit single **No Regrets**.

JUNIOR WALKER — Motown stalwart whose screaming sax and vocals generated a dozen hit singles for the label in the 60s and 70s, most notably **Shotgun** and **Roadrunner**.

WALL OF VOODOO — Mexican-American LA band with unique blend of cultures evident in off-the-wall music. Hit with single **Mexican Radio** (1982).

CLIFFORD T. WARD — Singer/songwriter from English Midlands who went Top 10 with melodious debut single **Gaye** in 1973; scored again in 1975 with **Jigsaw Girl**.

JIMMY WEBB — Wrote songs for Johnny Rivers and Fifth Dimension, who recorded for Rivers' Soul City label, to establish self as major LA-based writer. Fifth Dimension's **Up Up And Away**, Glen Campbell's **By The Time I Get To Phoenix** and Richard Harris's **MacArthur Park** were among his formidable triumphs. In 1970 Webb started touring and signed own contract with Reprise, the following year leading to albums for variety of labels.

BERT WEEDON — Veteran British session guitarist who charted with cover of Virtues' **Guitar Boogie Shuffle** in 1959 to make him one of longest-toothed rock 'n' rollers. Has wielded considerable influence over younger musicians thanks to his highly proficient technique.

WET WET WET — Scottish quartet who take themselves too seriously. Have enjoyed handful of UK hits, of which **With A Little Help From My Friends** re-make topped UK charts in 1988 and **Goodnight Girl** reached No. 1 in early 1992.

IAN WHITCOMB — Active on UK R&B scene, Whitcombe went to US West Coast on holiday, recording version of **Sporting Life** to notch minor hit. Jerry Dennon flew to Dublin, where Whitcomb was studying, to record **You Turn Me On**. A US Top 10 hit in 1965, single missed in UK. Whitcomb subsequently stayed in US and turned author.

MARTY WILDE — Member of the Larry Parnes school of British rock 'n' rollers. Resident on TV's *Oh Boy!* and *Boy Meets Girl* shows, he had string of British hits at tail-end of 50s, starting with **Endless Sleep** in 1957. Tried to launch son Ricky as British teeny-bopper idol, without success; did better with daughter Kim Wilde who ranks as major artist in own right.

DON WILLIAMS — Low-key C&W performer who sent middle-aged ladies crazy with his old-fashioned, but well-crafted ditties. **I Recall A Gypsy Woman** made UK Top 20 in 1973.

HANK WILLIAMS — Arguably the king of country music, he penned classic songs **Cold Cold Heart**, **Your Cheating Heart**, **Hey Good Lookin**, **Jambalaya** and **Take These Chains From My Heart** before death from heart attack caused by usual rock excesses in 1953.

PAUL WILLIAMS — Diminutive US writer who wrote hits for Carpenters and Barbra Streisand among others. Went on to carve out successful career as singer/writer/actor in movies and on television, as well as a soundtrack composer.

MARI WILSON AND WILSATIONS — 60s-styled vocalist with back-up group. Biggest hit was 1982's **Just What I Always Wanted**.

THE WINANS — Multi-faceted Detroit family whose consummate command of soul and gospel music placed them on fringe of superstardom in early 90s. Signed to Quincy Jones' Qwest Label.

PETE WINGFIELD — Keyboard player with British R&B band Jellybread, diverted into sessions for Freddie King, Van Morrison, Colin Blunstone and others before own 1975 transatlantic hit **Eighteen With A Bullet**. Later a member of the Olympic Runners soul band. Toured with Van Morrison in the 70s.

EDGAR WINTER — Sax-blowing, keyboard-playing brother of Johnny (and also an albino), the younger Winter's hard-driving brand of R&B placed him in singles charts with **Frankenstein** in 1972.

WISHBONE ASH — Pillars of 'twin lead guitar' syndrome, these UK rockers had fifteen year career before calling it a day in 1982.

THE WONDER STUFF — UK quintet who broke through in 1991 with **Never Loved Elvis** album and collaborations with British comic Vic Reeves on silly **Dizzy** single and Kirsty MacColl on **Welcome To The Cheap Seats**.

LINK WRAY — Legendary swamp-rock guitarist of Shawnee Indian extraction. Big hit with **Rumble** instrumental in 1958 followed by long spell in obscurity before re-emergence with hypnotic if at times strangely metered albums.

ROBERT WYATT — Soft Machine drummer turned British progressive rock guru. Scored in 1974 with

Below: The Best Of Tammy Wynette. Courtesy Epic Records.

surprise Cockney version of **I'm A Believer**. Re-emerged in 1983 with Elvis Costello-penned Falklands War comment **Shipbuilding**.

TAMMY WYNETTE — Country legend and champion of the down-trodden housewife, Wynette's working class anthems **D.I.V.O.R.C.E.** and **Stand By Your Man** have been the backbone of a long career. Recently re-emerged to have UK hit with KLF, **Justified And Ancient**.

Y

THE YOUNGBLOODS — Formed by talented New York singers Jesse Colin Young and Jerry Corbitt, who shared lead vocal role. Expanded group became resident at Café Au Go Go in 1966 with strong jug-band/folk-rock flavour. After cutting Dino Valenti's **Get Together** in 1957 (a Top 10 in 1959 on re-release), they moved to West Coast, cutting much acclaimed **Elephant Mountain** and other fine albums before folding in 1973, leaving Young to continue as respected solo artist.

TIMI YURO — Diminutive white girl singer with amazingly soulful voice, reminiscent of black star Esther Phillips. At her finest on R&B ballads, she benefited from lush yet totally sympathetic Nashville string arrangements. Scored with **Hurt** (1961) and superb albums, before moving into MOR and disappearing from scene due to marital problems.

Above: Odessey And Oracle, The Zombies. Courtesy CBS Records.

Z

ZAGER AND EVANS — Fashionably futuristic lyrics of **In The Year 2525** made this duo from Omaha, Nebraska, 1969's most successful one-hit wonder.

WARREN ZEVON — Well-established but usually hitless (sorry, forgot **Werewolves Of London**) cult mod-rocker who has flitted from label to label for approaching a dozen albums. Tetchy but succinct, and certainly adult.

ZOMBIES — Intelligent UK pop group from 1960s who charted with **She's Not There** in 1964. Founder Rod Argent (keyboards) and Colin Blunstone (vocals) later enjoyed solo successes.